Apple Pro Training Series

macOS Support Essentials 10.14

Arek Dreyer and Adam Karneboge

Apple
Certified

macOS Support Essentials 10.14 – Apple Pro Training Series
Arek Dreyer and Adam Karneboge
Copyright © 2019 by Peachpit Press

All Rights Reserved.
Peachpit Press
www.peachpit.com
Peachpit Press is an imprint of Pearson Education, Inc.
To report errors, please send a note to errata@peachpit.com

Apple Series Editor: Laura Norman
Development Editor: Victor Gavenda
Senior Production Editor: Tracey Croom
Production Coordinator: Maureen Forys, Happenstance Type-O-Rama
Technical Editor: Steve Leebove
Apple Instructional Designer: Susan Najour
Apple Project Manager: Debbie Otterstetter
Copy Editor: Elizabeth Welch
Proofreader: Scout Festa
Compositor: Cody Gates, Happenstance Type-O-Rama
Indexer: Valerie Perry
Cover Illustration: Paul Mavrides
Cover Production: Cody Gates, Happenstance Type-O-Rama

ISBN 13: 978-0-13-539058-0
ISBN 10: 0-13-539058-3
1 18

Thanks to Heather Jagman for her love, support, and encouragement.

—*Arek Dreyer*

*This book is dedicated to my children, Daniel and Elijah,
who are the best thing to ever happen to me.*

—*Adam Karneboge*

Acknowledgments Thank you, dear reader, for staying on top of what's new, while keeping your users' needs as the root of what you do.

Thanks to Tim Cook and everyone at Apple for always innovating. Thank you to Susan Najour and the Enterprise and Technical Training group for help and direction.

Thank you to Steve Leebove for insightful technical editing.

Thanks to Craig Cohen for technical assistance.

Thank you to the amazingly capable Laura Norman and Victor Gavenda for gently making sure these materials made it into your hands, and to Liz Welch, Scout Festa, and Maureen Forys and her team at Happenstance Type-O-Rama for working their editorial and production magic.

Thanks to the people who generously provided feedback and assistance, including:

Gino Bough	Leann Gavelan	Vernon Rooze
Tom Bridge	Richard Goon	Alby Rose
Armin Briegel	Claudia Ingram	Joe Schuepach
Jason Bruder	Andre LaBranche	Kamil Steglinski
Chad Calease	Ben Levy	Michael Sweet
Jon Clough	Nicholas McDonald	Jon Synowiec
Chris Dawe	Keith Mitnick	Walter Urbina
Weldon Dodd	Thomas Montgomery	Sam Valencia
Sam Coniglio	Tim O'Boyle	Steven Vogt
Charles Edge	Joshua Paseka	Eric Wales
Steve Hayman	Timothy Perfitt	Simon Wheatley
Christopher Holmes	Mehdi Rahman	Kevin White
Adrienne Gaskins	Schoun Regan	Josh Wisenbaker

Contents at a Glance

Apps and Processes

Network Configuration

Network Services

System Management

Table of Contents

User Accounts

Network Configuration

Network Services

System Management

About This Guide

The *macOS Support Essentials 10.14* guide in the Apple Pro Training Series prepares you for the macOS Support Essentials 10.14 exam. To prepare for the exam, use the guide alone or use the guide in the macOS Support Essentials 10.14 course. Either way, if you pass the exam, you're eligible for the Apple Certified Support Professional (ACSP) 10.14 certification.

Audience

Whether you're an experienced system administrator or you just want to dig deeper into macOS, you'll learn what ACSPs do to update, upgrade, reinstall, configure, maintain, diagnose, and troubleshoot macOS Mojave.

You should be comfortable using a Mac before you read this guide or take the course. If you're not sure about basic Mac use, visit "Meet your Mac" at support.apple.com/explore/new-to-mac.

How to Use the Guide

Use the reference sections to get familiar with macOS Mojave. Then, use the exercises to practice what you've learned. After you've completed the guide, you should be able to:

► Explain how macOS Mojave works
► Explain the best practices for updating, upgrading, reinstalling, configuring, and using macOS Mojave
► Explain macOS Mojave troubleshooting and repair procedures
► Use appropriate tools and techniques in macOS Mojave to diagnose and resolve issues

Accessing the Web Edition and Exercise Files

Unless otherwise specified, references to macOS in this guide refer to macOS Mojave 10.14.0. As Apple updates macOS Mojave, this guide might also be updated. Updates are delivered to you through the Web Edition, which contains the complete guide, including updates. When you purchase this guide from Peachpit (in any format), you automatically get access to its Web Edition.

If you bought an eBook from peachpit.com, your Web Edition will appear under the Digital Purchases tab on your Account page. If you bought an eBook from a different vendor or you bought a print book, you must register your purchase on peachpit.com to access the online content:

1   Go to www.peachpit.com/register.

2   Sign in or create a new account.

3   Enter ISBN: 9780135390580.

4   Answer the questions as proof of purchase.

    The Web Edition appears under the Digital Purchases tab on your Account page.

5   Click the Launch link to access the Web Edition.

6   Get supporting exercise files under the Registered Products tab on your Account page:

    Click the Access Bonus Content link below the title of your product to go to the download page, then click the lesson file links to download the supporting exercise files.

Exercises

For the most part, the exercises in this guide work in the classroom or for those learning independently. If you're learning independently, you must use a dedicated Mac. If you use a Mac that is used for daily productivity, the exercises will not work as expected and they might disrupt your Mac. To complete the exercises, ensure you have the following:

▶   A Mac that meets the requirements to install macOS Mojave

▶   macOS Mojave (see Exercise 2.3, "Erase a Mac and Install macOS Mojave")

- A high-speed Internet connection
- Exercise files (see "Accessing the Web Edition and Exercise Files," above)
- An Apple ID dedicated to your independent learning (you don't need to provide credit card information to get free apps from the App Store)

You don't have to have these items, but they can be helpful:

- An iCloud account associated with the Apple ID you use for your independent learning
- An erasable external storage disk with a capacity of at least 12 GB for Exercise 5.2, "Create a macOS Install Disk"
- A classroom environment that is running on an isolated test network set up using the specifications outlined in the Classroom Setup Guide
- At least two Wi-Fi networks (one should be visible)
- The required Thunderbolt, USB-C, or FireWire cable to connect two Mac computers in target disk mode
- A Mac with all-flash storage

Additional Materials

Apple Support
The Apple Support website (support.apple.com) includes the latest free online Apple Support articles.

Apple Course
Participants use this guide in the macOS Support Essentials 10.14 course. Apple Certified Trainers teach each course and give presentations and demonstrations. Participants practice macOS support with hands-on exercises. The course prepares you for the macOS Support Essentials 10.14 exam.

ACSP 10.14 Certification
An ACSP 10.14 certification verifies that you understand macOS core functionality and can configure key services, troubleshoot, and support users. If you pass the

macOS Support Essentials 10.14 exam, you are eligible for an ACSP 10.14 certification. Apple macOS certifications are for IT professionals who:

▶ Want to know how to add a Mac to a Windows or other standards-based network

▶ Support macOS users

▶ Manage networks of Mac computers; for example, a system administrator at a large organization, a technology specialist who manages computer labs, or a teacher who manages classroom networks

▶ Manage complex, multiplatform networks that include Mac computers

Apple certification exams are delivered at Apple Authorized Training Provider locations. Visit locate.apple.com to find a location. To learn more about Apple certifications and to find the *macOS Support Essentials 10.14 Exam Preparation Guide*, visit training.apple.com/us/en/courses/macos/macos_support_essentials_10_14. To prepare for the macOS Support Essentials 10.14 exam, do the following:

▶ Read the reference sections of this guide.

▶ Complete the exercises in this guide.

▶ Complete the macOS Support Essentials 10.14 course.

▶ Gain experience on a Mac running macOS Mojave.

▶ Study the *macOS Support Essentials 10.14 Exam Preparation Guide*.

Installation and Configuration

Lesson 1

Introduction to macOS

Since its introduction in 2001, macOS (formerly known as Mac OS or OS X) comes preinstalled on Mac computers. It offers the ease of use that the iPhone, iPad, and Apple Watch are famous for. macOS also provides an exceptional software development platform, with the result that a large selection of high-quality third-party software is available for macOS.

GOALS

▶ Describe macOS

▶ Describe new macOS Mojave 10.14 features

Reference 1.1
macOS Mojave 10.14

macOS Mojave 10.14 is the latest version of macOS. macOS is the only operating system that combines a powerful open source UNIX foundation with a state-of-the-art user interface.

Integration Through Standards

Much of the success of macOS can be attributed to Apple embracing industry-standard formats and open source software. Adoption of common standards saves engineering time and allows for much smoother integration with other platforms. When Apple developers engineer a technology for a new feature, Apple often releases the technical specifications to the developer community. This fosters a new standard. An example of this is Bonjour network discovery, which Apple pioneered and has maintained as an industry-standard protocol commonly known as Multicast DNS (mDNS) for others to develop and use.

Another example is the Swift programming language. After Apple unveiled the Swift programming language, it quickly became one of the fastest-growing languages in history. Swift makes it easy to write software that is incredibly fast and safe by design.

Here are some examples of common standards supported by macOS:

▶ Connectivity standards—Universal Serial Bus (USB), IEEE 1394 (FireWire), Thunderbolt, Bluetooth wireless, and the IEEE 802 family of Ethernet and Wi-Fi standards

▶ File-system standards—A file system determines how information, usually in the form of a file, is stored on and retrieved from storage media such as a disk. macOS supports file-system standards including File Allocation Table (FAT), New Technology File System (NTFS), ISO 9660 optical disc standard, Universal Disk Format (UDF), and the Xsan file system based on the StorNext file system

▶ Network standards—Dynamic Host Configuration Protocol (DHCP), Domain Name System (DNS), Hypertext Transfer Protocol (HTTP), Internet Message Access Protocol (IMAP), Simple Mail Transfer Protocol (SMTP), File Transfer Protocol (FTP), Web Distributed Access and Versioning (WebDAV), and Server Message Block/Common Internet File System (SMB/CIFS) including SMB3

▶ App and development standards—Single UNIX Specification v3 (SUSv3), Portable Operating System Interface (POSIX), C and C++, Objective C, Ruby, Python, Perl, and Swift

▶ Document standards—ZIP file archives, Rich Text Format (RTF), Portable Document Format (PDF), Tagged Image File Format (TIFF), Joint Photographic Expert Group (JPEG), Portable Network Graphics (PNG), Advanced Audio Coding (AAC), the Moving Picture Experts Group (MPEG) family of media standards, High Efficiency Video Coding (HEVC, also known as H.265), and High Efficiency Image Format (HEIF, based on HEVC)

Reference 1.2
What's New in macOS Mojave

In addition to the features you can find in previous versions of macOS, macOS Mojave includes hundreds of small improvements and a few significant new features. macOS Mojave is the 14th major version of the Mac operating system since its initial release in 2001. Each release of the Mac operating system has a version number (10.14) and associated name (Mojave). In this book, older Mac operating system versions are called out with the version name and number, such as macOS High Sierra 10.13. For more details about changes with macOS Mojave, read Apple Support article HT209208, "Prepare your institution for iOS 12 and macOS Mojave."

In macOS Mojave, Apple File System (APFS) is the default file system for all Mac computers. APFS features include the following:

► Cloning

► Space sharing

► Snapshots

► Fast directory sizing

► Atomic safe-save

► Sparse files

If you upgrade to macOS Mojave, your startup disk is automatically converted to APFS.

Dark Mode is a new look with macOS Mojave that helps you focus on your work. Go to the macOS Mojave webpage (www.apple.com/macos/mojave/) to see what Dark Mode looks like for several apps, like Keynote, Safari (the web browser that comes with macOS), Calendar, Messages, and Xcode (an app you can use to develop apps). The macOS Mojave webpage includes a window divided between the familiar light appearance and Dark Mode. When you move the divider, the figure is interactively updated on the webpage.

macOS Mojave introduces two new time-shifting desktop backgrounds. Visit
the macOS Mojave webpage to use an interactive slider to see how the Dynamic Desktop
changes throughout the day.

macOS Mojave includes improvements for the Finder, the first thing that you see when
your Mac finishes starting up. The Finder opens automatically and stays open as you use
other apps. The Finder displays the menu bar at the top of the screen and the desktop
below that. It's called the Finder because it helps you to find and organize your files and
documents. You can use Stacks, a new feature of the Finder for macOS Mojave, to keep
your desktop free of clutter. When you Control-click the desktop and choose Use Stacks,
macOS organizes your desktop by creating stacks of similar kinds of files. Control-click
again and change how the stacks are grouped. Click a stack to see the contents of the
stack. To scrub through the contents of a stack, place your pointer over a stack, then use
two fingers on a trackpad or one finger on a Multi-Touch mouse. To open a file, click
to expand the stack. The macOS Mojave webpage includes an animation of how Stacks
works.

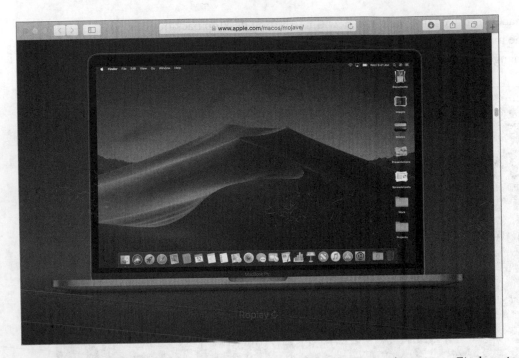

You can use the Finder to view your files as icons, as a list, or as columns in a Finder window. In macOS Mojave you can also view them in Gallery View. With Gallery View, the Finder window displays thumbnails of your files that you can scroll through.

When you select a file, the Finder window displays a large preview of the file along with all its metadata, or information about a file. Basic metadata includes a file's name, type, size, creation date, and modification date. Different kinds of files can have different kinds of metadata, such as aperture exposure for an image file, sample rate for an audio file, and color profile for a video file. In macOS Mojave you can now control what kinds of metadata the Finder window's Preview pane displays for your files.

Also new with macOS Mojave, you can use Quick Actions to perform actions on a file, such as rotating an image or trimming an audio or video clip, without opening the file.

With Quick Look you can preview the contents of many common file types, even without having the apps installed. This includes Pages, Keynote, Numbers, and Microsoft Office documents. And now in macOS Mojave you can use Quick Look to take actions on documents, such as marking up a PDF, trimming a video or audio clip, or even sharing a file, while previewing the file.

Use the new Screenshot utility in macOS Mojave to capture the screenshot you need. Just press Shift-Command-5. The pointer turns into a camera icon; then you can move your pointer to highlight different windows. Click to capture the highlighted window. Or use the Screenshot menu to change what's captured, to capture video, to change where you save the file, to set a timer, or to change several other options. A preview of your screenshot or video is displayed in the corner of the screen. Drag the preview into a document, or click the preview and mark it up, or just leave it and it will automatically get saved. Go to the macOS Mojave webpage to see an animation of the new Screenshot utility in action.

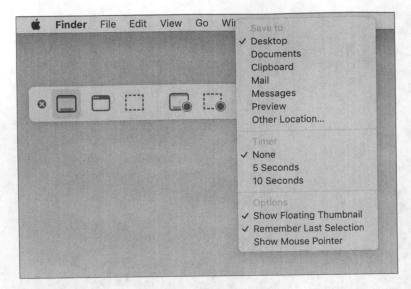

You can use Continuity Camera to import photos and scans from your iOS device to your Mac. Take a photo of something or scan a document with your iOS device and insert it into a document on your Mac, if your Mac is using macOS Mojave, your iOS device is using iOS 12, and you are signed in to your iCloud account on your devices. iCloud is a powerful service from Apple that securely stores your content, like photos, videos, music, and documents; keeps that content on your devices updated across all your devices; and lets you easily share content with friends and family. Continuity Camera works in the Finder, Mail, Messages, Notes, TextEdit, Keynote 8.2 or newer, Pages 7.2 or newer, and Numbers 5.2 or newer.

macOS Mojave brings four great iOS apps to the Mac:

▶ News—Start reading on one device, then pick it up later on another.

▶ Stocks—Track the market and read about what's driving it.

▶ Home—Securely configure and control your accessories that work with HomeKit, such as lights, thermostats, cameras, doorbells, and locks.

▶ Voice Memos—Capture and revisit audio from your Mac or your iPhone.

The App Store in macOS Mojave has a new look and updated editorial content. See Reference 18.1, "The App Store," for more information.

macOS Mojave includes privacy and security enhancements. An app must get your consent before it can access the camera or microphone on your Mac or access sensitive data like your location, your Messages history, and your Mail database. Safari limits advertisers' ability to track you by reducing the amount of information that sites can learn about your browser and device. Intelligent Tracking Prevention keeps embedded content like social media buttons and content from tracking you without your permission. Safari can help you use unique and strong passwords by offering to create and store passwords, then auto-fill the right password when you visit a website. You can use Safari preferences to update passwords that you've used across more than one website so that you can ensure you have unique and robust passwords for every website that requires one.

Siri enables you to use your voice to request actions. This virtual assistant performs tasks or finds things locally on your Mac and on the Internet. Siri uses a microphone to listen to your requests. You can now do more with Siri and macOS Mojave. Use Siri to control your HomeKit-enabled devices; find your saved passwords; discover more information about food, celebrities, and motorsports; and even find your devices that are associated with your iCloud account and have Find My iPhone, Find My iPad, or Find My Mac turned on. Read Reference 9.5, "Manage System-wide Security," for more information about Find My Mac.

macOS Mojave adds improved maps for China and additional language and input options.

Go to the macOS Mojave webpage (www.apple.com/macos/mojave/) for more information and to experience interactive demonstrations of the new features of macOS Mojave. Read Apple Support article HT209028, "Prepare your institution for iOS 12 or macOS Mojave," and the macOS Mojave support page at https://support.apple.com/macos/mojave to prepare your organization for macOS Mojave.

After you set up your Mac, as described in Reference 3.1, "Configure a Mac with a New Installation of macOS Mojave," go to the menu bar, click the Help menu, and choose one of the three commands to discover more about macOS Mojave and the features of your Mac.

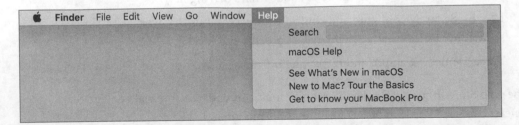

Each of the three commands opens a webpage in Safari, the default web browser:

▶   See What's New in macOS

▶ New to Mac? Tour the Basics

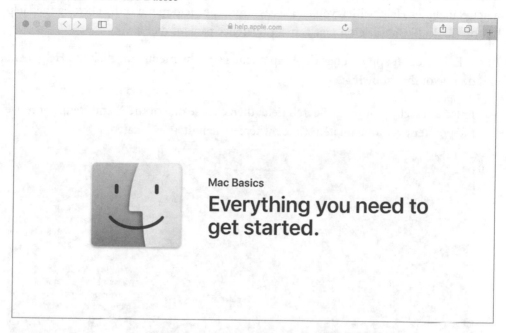

▶ Get to know your *Mac model* (this command varies depending on your Mac model)

Using macOS Help

macOS includes Help, which you can access from the Help menu or by clicking the Help button (looks like a question mark) in a preference pane or dialog.

In the Finder or an app that has the Help menu, go to the menu bar, click the Help menu, and do one of the following:

▶ Enter a search term in the Search field, then choose one of the Menu Items, or move the pointer over a menu item to see where a menu item is located.

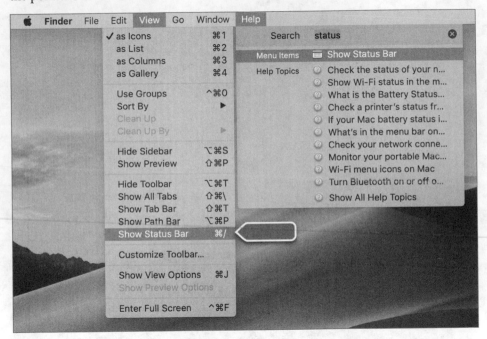

▶ Enter a search term in the Search field, then choose one of the Help Topics in the results.

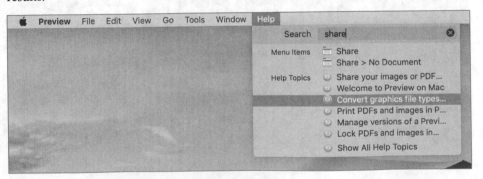

▶ Enter a search term in the Search field, then choose Show All Help Topics.

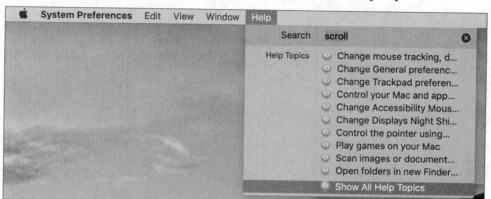

▶ Leave the Search field blank and choose "*app* Help," where *app* is the name of the app in the foreground, to open the User Guide for that app. If the Finder is the app in the foreground, choose "macOS Help" to open the macOS User Guide.

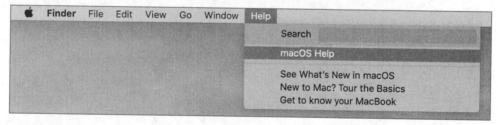

When you use the macOS User Guide or the User Guide for an app, the window stays visible on top of your desktop and all your other apps, so you can always see its contents. The following includes some things you can do while using the macOS User Guide or the User Guide for an app:

▶ Drag the toolbar to move the entire window.

▶ Click and drag an edge or corner of the window to resize the window.

▶ Enter a search term in the Search field.

▶ Show the Previous (<) topic or Next (>) topic.

▶ Click and hold the Previous button to see a list of previously viewed topics.

▶ Click the Table of Contents button next to the Next button to show or hide more topics.

► Click the Share button (looks like a box with an arrow pointing up) to open the topic in Safari, Print the topic, or choose other options.

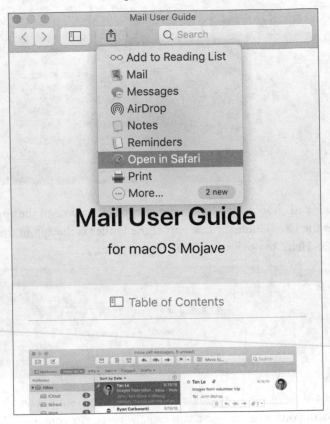

► Press Command-Plus (+) or make the text bigger or press Command-Minus (-) to make the text smaller.

► Press Command-F then enter the text you want to find in the current topic.

Most of the app user guides are available at a URL that has the pattern of support.apple.com/guide/*app*, where *app* is the name of the app.

You can read more about using the built-in help on your Mac by visiting "Use built-in help on your Mac" at support.apple.com/guide/mac-help/use-the-built-in-help-hlpvw003 with any modern web browser.

Reference 1.3
macOS History

The following table shows Mac operating system versions since OS X 10.8, which is the earliest Mac operating system that you can directly upgrade to macOS Mojave. Read Apple Support article HT201260, "Find out which macOS your Mac is using," for more information.

Name and version	Release date	Latest version	Latest date
OS X Mountain Lion 10.8	July 25, 2012	10.8.5	October 3, 2013
OS X Mavericks 10.9	October 22, 2013	10.9.5	September 17, 2014
OS X Yosemite 10.10	October 16, 2014	10.10.5	August 13, 2015
OS X El Capitan 10.11	September 30, 2015	10.11.6	July 18, 2016
macOS Sierra 10.12	September 20, 2016	10.12.6	July 19, 2017
macOS High Sierra 10.13	September 25, 2017	10.13.6	August 28, 2018
macOS Mojave 10.14	September 24, 2018	10.14.2	December 5, 2018

Lesson 2

Update, Upgrade, or Reinstall macOS

Every new Mac comes with the latest Mac operating system. And, to get the latest features and security updates, you will eventually need the latest macOS. If you have a qualifying Mac, you can upgrade at no cost.

NOTE ▶ Some exercises in this lesson involve significant changes to your Mac setup. Some of the steps are difficult or impossible to reverse. If you perform the exercises in this lesson, do so on a spare Mac or an external disk that doesn't contain critical data.

Reference 2.1
macOS Installation Methods

To understand the difference between an upgrade and an update, it helps to identify the parts of a Mac operating system name. A Mac operating system has a version name and a version number, such as macOS High Sierra 10.13.

When Apple releases an update of the Mac operating system:

▶ The version name stays the same.

▶ A dot followed by an incremental number is added after the version number (for example, 10.13 is the version number, and .1 is added, to make 10.13.1).

Completing the update example, macOS High Sierra 10.13.1 is a version update to macOS Sierra 10.13.

GOALS

▶ Describe the differences between a macOS update, upgrade, and reinstallation

▶ Describe the macOS Installer

▶ Verify system information

▶ Update macOS

▶ Upgrade macOS

▶ Reinstall macOS

▶ Troubleshoot an upgrade or reinstallation

When Apple releases a major version upgrade of the Mac operating system:

▶ There is a new version name (for example, Mojave instead of High Sierra).

▶ The number after "10." increments (for example, 10.13 increments to 10.14).

Completing the upgrade example, the next major version upgrade from macOS High Sierra 10.13 is macOS Mojave 10.14.

This list summarizes the differences between updating, upgrading, reinstalling, and installing a Mac operating system:

▶ Update: Installs an incremental update of the Mac operating system but doesn't upgrade it to the next major version (if one exists).

▶ Upgrade: Installs a next major standalone version of the Mac operating system.

▶ Reinstall: Installs the same major version of macOS on a disk that already has macOS. This overwrites existing system files but leaves apps, user home folders, and other files in place.

▶ Install: Installs macOS on a disk that doesn't have macOS—for instance, a disk you erased.

Lesson 6, "Update macOS," describes updating macOS and keeping macOS automatically updated in more detail.

Upgrading, Reinstalling, or Installing macOS Mojave requires Internet access.

Erase Your Startup Disk

If you want to get a fresh start with macOS, and you don't need the existing content on your Mac, erase the startup disk before you install macOS. The macOS Installer (an app named Install macOS Mojave) doesn't erase disks, but you can use Disk Utility to erase a disk before you run the macOS Installer:

▶ If you want to erase the system disk your Mac is currently running from, you can erase it if you start up from macOS Recovery, as covered in Lesson 5, "Use macOS Recovery."

▶ If the destination is another disk, such as an external storage device, erase and install from your Mac, as covered in Lesson 11, "Manage File Systems and Storage."

Reference 2.2
Prepare to Upgrade or Reinstall macOS

Follow these steps to start a macOS upgrade:

1   Verify installation requirements.

2   Plug notebook computers into power.

3   Verify app compatibility.

4   Back up important content.

5   Document network settings.

6   Open Software Update or the App Store.

Verify Installation Requirements

Verify that the Mac and Mac operating system that you have meet the requirements for an upgrade to macOS Mojave.

Upgrading to macOS Mojave has the following requirements:

▶   OS X Mountain Lion 10.8 or later

▶   2 GB of memory

▶   12.5 GB of available storage for a new installation (or up to 18.5 GB of available storage to upgrade from OS X Yosemite 10.10 or earlier)

▶   Compatible Internet service provider

▶   Apple ID (for some features)

Most Mac models introduced in 2012 or later are compatible with macOS Mojave. macOS Mojave supports the following Mac models:

▶   MacBook (Early 2015 or later)

▶   MacBook Air (Mid 2012 or later)

▶   MacBook Pro (Mid 2012 or later)

▶   Mac mini (Late 2012 or later)

▶   iMac (Late 2012 or later)

▶   iMac Pro

▶   Mac Pro (Late 2013, plus Mid 2010 or Mid 2012 models with a recommended graphics card capable of using Metal, an Apple technology that lets the system and apps efficiently tap into the capabilities of today's graphics processors (GPUs))

There are additional requirements for installing macOS Mojave on Mac Pro (Mid 2010) or Mac Pro (Mid 2012). The graphics cards offered by Apple in Mac Pro (Mid 2010) and Mac Pro (Mid 2012) lack a GPU that supports Metal, so these systems require upgraded graphics cards in order to install macOS Mojave. Many third-party graphics cards won't show anything on the display when macOS Mojave is starting up, including the Apple logo and startup progress bar. As a result, you can't do the following with a Mac that has macOS Mojave installed with a third-party graphics card that lacks the proper GPU:

▶   Log in to a system that uses FileVault full disk encryption, covered in Lesson 12, "Manage FileVault"

▶   Choose a different startup disk before your Mac boots into macOS

▶   Perform some hardware diagnostics

So you'll need to turn off FileVault before you install macOS Mojave on your Mac Pro (Mid 2010) and Mac Pro (Mid 2012). If your Mac has more than one volume with macOS installed, you need to use the Startup Disk pane in System Preferences (covered later in this section) to switch between operating systems; holding down Option while restarting doesn't allow you to choose an operating system on these Mac Pro models.

Read Apple Support article HT208898, "Install macOS 10.14 Mojave on Mac Pro (Mid 2010) and Mac Pro (Mid 2012)," for more information.

Read Apple Support article SP777, "macOS Mojave – Technical Specifications," for more information about requirements for specific features. Some features of macOS Mojave require specific Mac and iOS device models, such as the following features:

▶   Continuity Camera—Use your iPhone, iPad, or iPod touch with iOS 12 installed to scan documents or take a picture of something nearby and it appears instantly on your Mac. Continuity Camera is supported in many apps, including Mail, Messages, the Finder, and more. Read Apple Support article HT209037, "Use Continuity Camera on your Mac," for more information.

▶   Handoff—With Handoff, you can start work on one device, then switch to another nearby device and pick up where you left off. Use Handoff with any Mac, iPhone, iPad, iPod touch, or Apple Watch that meets the Continuity system requirements. Read Apple Support article HT204689, "System requirements for Continuity on Mac, iPhone, iPad, iPod touch, and Apple Watch," for more information.

▶ Instant Hotspot—With Instant Hotspot, the Personal Hotspot on your iPhone or iPad (Wi-Fi + Cellular) can provide Internet access to a Mac, iPhone, iPad, or iPod touch without requiring you to enter the password on those devices. Use Instant Hotspot with any Mac, iPhone, iPad, or iPod touch that meets the Continuity system requirements.

▶ Universal Clipboard—With Universal Clipboard, you can copy content such as text, images, photos, and videos on one Apple device, then paste the content on another Apple device. Use Universal Clipboard with any Mac, iPhone, iPad, or iPod touch that meets the Continuity system requirements.

Verify System Information

You need to know your Mac computer's specifications when you install new software, upgrade installed software, perform maintenance, or troubleshoot a problem. In this section you learn how to find essential system information with About This Mac and System Information.

You can open the Apple menu and choose About This Mac to gather most of the information necessary to confirm that your Mac supports macOS Mojave. The initial view in About This Mac shows you the macOS software version, Mac model name, processor type and speed, total system memory, graphics card information, and Mac serial number. Click the system version number to see the system build number.

NOTE ▶ Mac computers that have improperly replaced logic boards may not display the correct serial number in About This Mac.

The Mac in the preceding figure has 16 GB of RAM and meets the memory requirements to run macOS Mojave.

A few items are vital to identify your macOS version and Mac model:

▶ The system version number represents the system software version currently installed.

▶ The system build number appears when you click the system version number. It shows the system software version. Apple engineers create versions of each macOS release as they refine it. The build number identifies each version. The macOS version that comes with a new Mac may differ from standard installation versions.

▶ The Mac computer model name is derived from the product marketing name for the Mac, followed by a relative release date. For example, the previous screenshot was taken on a "MacBook Pro (15-inch, 2017)."

▶ The Mac serial number is located on the Mac case. The serial number is a unique number used to identify a Mac for maintenance and service.

Click the Storage button to review how much disk space is available.

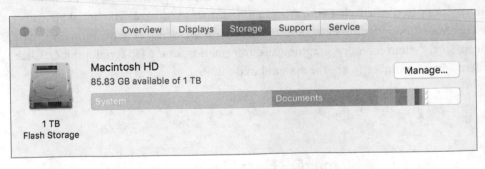

The Mac in this figure meets the available-storage requirements to upgrade to macOS Mojave.

The Support and Service buttons link directly to specific areas of the Apple Support website. The contents of the links are generated dynamically to show the most up-to-date support information about macOS and your Mac. For example, the Specifications link opens a webpage with the full specifications for your Mac.

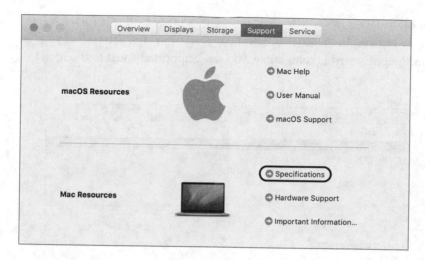

The information in the About This Mac window is a subset of what you can find with System Information. From the Overview window in the About This Mac window, click the System Report button to open System Information. Or you can press and hold the Option key and then choose Apple menu > System Information. Or you can use Spotlight: click the Spotlight icon (which looks like a magnifying glass) in the menu bar in the upper-right corner of your screen, enter **System Information** in the search field, and then press Return.

If you have a version of the Mac operating system that shipped with the name OS X, it includes System Profiler instead of System Information.

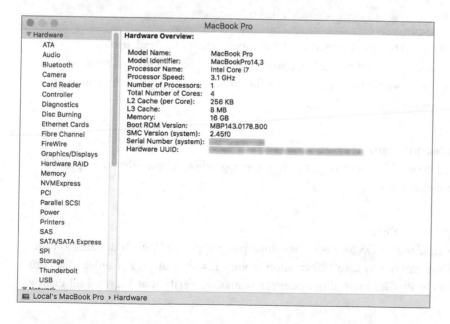

You can use System Information to confirm that your graphics card supports Metal, a requirement of macOS Mojave. In the sidebar, select Graphics/Displays, then select your graphics card. If your graphics card is compatible, you see "Supported" next to the Metal entry.

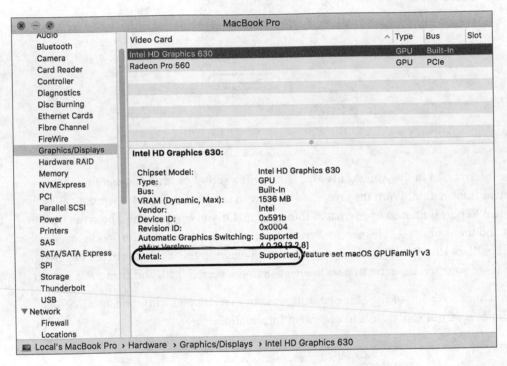

When you need to create a file to document the current state of a Mac, use System Information. Go to the menu bar, and choose File > Save. This creates a System Information–specific file (with the .spx filename extension) that you can open from other Mac computers.

Plug Mac Notebooks into Power

Plug your Mac into an AC power outlet during the upgrade to ensure that the upgrade completes successfully.

Verify App Compatibility

When you upgrade to macOS Mojave, your third-party apps might need updates to function properly. You can use System Information to view installed apps. For older Mac computers with System Profiler instead of System Information, verify that View > Full Profile is selected to reveal the Applications section in the Contents list. Selecting Applications from the Contents list prompts macOS to scan common locations on the local disk for available apps.

You don't have to worry about the apps that came with your Mac. They are replaced when you install macOS Mojave. You might have to visit third-party vendor websites to see if your third-party apps require updates.

If the Install macOS Mojave app detects incompatible software during an upgrade, it usually moves that software to an Incompatible Software folder at the top level of your startup disk. In some cases, the incompatible software isn't moved, but macOS prevents you from opening it and displays a warning dialog stating that the software is incompatible. Find out more about this feature in Apple Support article HT201861, "About incompatible software on your Mac."

Back Up Important Files and Folders

It's always crucial to keep backups of your important files and folders. Having a current backup is even more critical when you make significant changes to a Mac, such as installing a major version upgrade to the Mac operating system. If a new installation or upgrade is done improperly, it could result in complete data loss.

You can't uninstall or revert an update or upgrade. If it turns out that an app you need is not compatible with macOS Mojave, the only way to install an earlier version of macOS is to erase and restore from backup.

You can use Time Machine to create a backup before you start your installation. Using Time Machine is covered in Lesson 17, "Manage Time Machine."

Document Network Settings

The macOS Installer helps ensure that you don't lose previous settings when you upgrade to macOS Mojave. But some settings are so vital to your Mac that you should document them in case something goes wrong.

Specifically, if you have any special network configuration, such as a static IPv4 address, or a specific Domain Name Service (DNS) server to use, document your network settings before you upgrade. Open System Preferences and click the Network icon to see your current network settings. Avoid missing settings by navigating through all the available network interface and configurations.

You can quickly document your settings by using the screen capture keyboard shortcut Shift-Command-3 to capture each network configuration. Each screen capture figure will be saved to your desktop with a filename of "Screen Shot" followed by the date and time of the capture.

Open Software Update or App Store

Ensure that your Mac has the latest Apple apps and firmware.

If your Mac is connected to the Internet, choose Software Update or App Store from the Apple menu. In the App Store, click Updates, and then install available updates (but not the macOS Mojave installer yet).

Read more about keeping your Mac updated in Lesson 6, "Update macOS."

Reference 2.3
Upgrade or Install macOS

You must be connected to the Internet when you upgrade your macOS. After your Mac confirms your connection, the installer uses your Mac model number to locate and download a firmware update specific to it.

Only the macOS Installer can download and install a firmware update. Firmware updates can't be done on external devices, such as those connected with target disk mode, Thunderbolt, USB, or FireWire.

You can use these supported tools and methods to upgrade or install macOS:

▶ macOS Installer.

▶ Bootable installer, then the macOS Installer. Read Exercise 5.2, "Create a macOS Install Disk."

▶ Start up from macOS Recovery and install macOS. Read Lesson 5, "Use macOS Recovery."

   NOTE ▶ Installing macOS Mojave on a Mac that is connected by target disk mode isn't a supported installation method.

Use the Install macOS Mojave app to install on your startup disk. For details about using macOS Recovery to upgrade, reinstall, or install macOS Mojave, read Lesson 5.

Get the macOS Installer

macOS Mojave is free and available from the App Store.

If you're using OS X El Capitan v10.11.5 or later, macOS Mojave downloads in the background, making it easier to upgrade your Mac. When the download finishes, you receive a notification indicating that macOS Mojave is ready to be installed. Click Install in the notification to get started.

Downloading macOS Mojave is as simple as buying a free app from the App Store. Details about the App Store are covered in Lesson 18, "Install Apps."

1   From the Apple menu, choose App Store.

2   Search the App Store for macOS Mojave, or go directly to the macOS Mojave page at https://itunes.apple.com/app/macos-mojave/.

3   Click Download on the macOS Mojave page. The Install macOS Mojave app downloads to your Applications folder. If you already have the app, you'll see an Install button instead of a Download button.

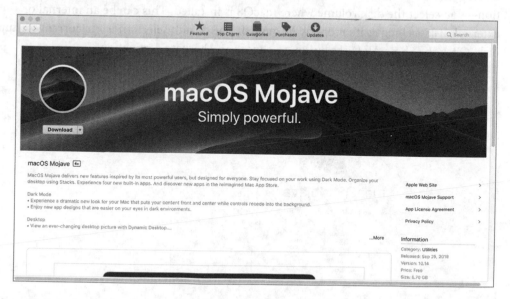

After the download is complete, the installer opens. Otherwise, click Continue and follow the instructions.

If macOS Mojave is installed on your Mac, the App Store notes that it's installed or down-loaded. In this case, the Install macOS Mojave app may still be in the Applications folder. If not, complete the steps covered in Lesson 5.

Install macOS Mojave

At the beginning of the installation, you're asked to make some choices before macOS installs. During normal installation, the Mac restarts at least once, and possibly multiple times. If a power loss or disk disconnection occurs, restart the installation.

The macOS Installer never deletes nonsystem data on the selected destination. The macOS Installer ensures that user data and compatible third-party apps remain functional after an installation. The macOS Installer upgrades your current Mac operating system or installs macOS to a disk (except a disk connected by target disk mode) that's attached to your Mac.

Select the Installation Destination

During macOS Mojave installation, the only choice you make is the installation destina-tion—you select the disk volume where macOS is installed. This can be an internal or external disk, as long as it's properly formatted. The default selection is the current startup disk. Click the Show All Disks button to choose an alternate destination.

You may need to provide administrator credentials to install a helper tool.

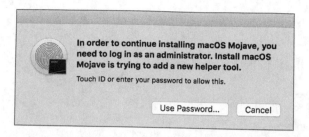

The installer may not enable you to select certain disks or partitions. This happens when the installer determines that your Mac can't start from those disks or partitions. Possible reasons include the following:

▶ The disk is in target disk mode.

▶ The disk doesn't have the proper partition scheme for your Mac. Intel Mac computers use the GPT scheme. Use Disk Utility to repartition the disk.

▶ The partition isn't formatted properly. macOS requires a partition formatted as Mac OS Extended (Journaled) or Apple File System (APFS). Use Disk Utility to erase an improperly formatted partition.

▶ The macOS Installer doesn't support installing to a volume that's part of a RAID (Redundant Array of Independent Disks) set.

▶ The macOS Installer doesn't support installing to a disk containing Time Machine backups. For more information, see Apple Support article HT203322, "If you can't install macOS on a Time Machine backup disk."

▶ The target disk isn't from Apple and isn't compatible with macOS Mojave.

To verify eligibility to install macOS, your Mac serial number is sent to Apple, and you might be asked for your Apple ID.

If you aren't connected to the Internet, the installation can't continue.

Your Apple ID is the name for your personal account. You use it to access Apple services like the App Store, iTunes Store, iCloud, iMessage, the Apple Online Store, FaceTime, and more. It includes the information you use to sign in, and all the contact, payment, and security details that you'll use across Apple services. For more information about Apple ID go to https://appleid.apple.com.

You might need to click Restart to continue the macOS Mojave installation.

During installation, your Mac might restart several times. It performs some initial setup tasks in the background.

> **NOTE ►** Read Apple Support article HT201065, "What to do before you sell, give away, or trade in your Mac," for suggestions on what to do if you sell or give away your Mac. This article includes details about how to ensure that information is cleared from the Secure Enclave in the Touch Bar.

Reference 2.4
Troubleshoot Installation Issues

The macOS Installer can back out of an installation and restore the previous system if an installation goes wrong. Verify that your Mac meets the requirements for macOS Mojave and complete the installation preparation steps as outlined in this lesson to avoid installation problems.

macOS Installer Troubleshooting

Beyond failing to prepare for an installation, the most common installation failures come from Internet access and destination disk problems. For example:

▶ The installer has filtered or no access to the Internet.

▶ The installer might be unable to verify the selected disk or partition. This indicates serious disk problems. Refer to the troubleshooting steps in Lesson 11 to resolve this issue.

For more information, see Apple Support article HT204904, "How to reinstall macOS from macOS Recovery."

Installer Log

You can use the log file to troubleshoot macOS. Nearly every process writes entries in a log file, including the installer. The Installer log contains progress and error entries for nearly every installation step, including steps not shown in the standard interface.

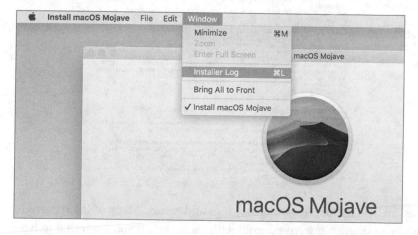

During the initial installation phases, choose Installer Log from the Window menu to access the log. The Installer log helps you pinpoint problems or verify installation.

After the preliminary installation phases, the installer enters the main installation phase and locks the Mac screen. You can only watch the installation progress bar. If the installation fails, the system restarts to the previous version.

After the Mac resumes normal operation, you can access the full installer log with Console.

When you use macOS, error dialogs appear only if an issue is something you can resolve or requires immediate attention. Otherwise, running processes and apps leave detailed information in log files throughout macOS.

Console collects log messages and reports that are generated from your Mac and connected devices. Use Console to collect diagnostic information so that you can troubleshoot problems. You can open Console in two ways:

▶ Search with Spotlight.

▶ Navigate to /Applications/Utilities/ and double-click Console.

After Console is open, select the /var/log folder in the far-left column, and select install.log in the second column.

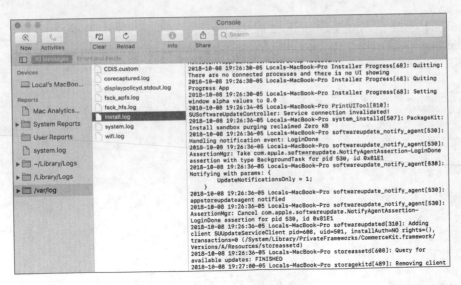

Even during a successful installation, there are warnings and errors. Many of the reported issues are benign, and you should concern yourself with them only if you are trying to isolate a problem that prevents a successful upgrade to macOS Mojave.

Exercise 2.1
Prepare a Mac for Upgrade

NOTE ▶ This exercise is for independent study only. You don't perform this exercise in a classroom environment. Complete this exercise only if you are upgrading your Mac from an earlier version of macOS.

> ► **Prerequisites**
>
> ► Your Mac must be running OS X Mountain Lion 10.8 or later.
>
> ► If your Mac is running OS X El Capitan 10.11.5 or later, it must have 2 GB of memory and 12.5 GB of available storage space.
>
> ► If your Mac is running OS X Yosemite 10.10 or earlier, it must have 18.5 GB of storage space.

In this exercise, you verify that your Mac hardware and firmware support macOS Mojave. You also check for old software and record important settings.

NOTE ► This exercise can't be used to prepare an independent study Mac for the rest of the course. Independent learners must complete Exercise 2.3, "Erase a Mac and Install macOS Mojave," to continue to Exercise 3.1, "Configure a Mac for Exercises."

Check Hardware and App Compatibility

1 Log in to your existing administrator account.

2 In the Finder, navigate to the /Applications/Utilities folder.

You can also use the Finder keyboard shortcut Shift-Command-U.

3 Open System Information.

4   Select the Hardware category in the sidebar.

5   Verify that there is at least 2 GB of memory.

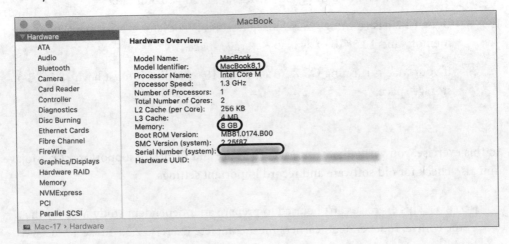

6   Record the Model Identifier and Serial Number entries:

Model Identifier:

Serial Number:

7   Select the Storage category in the Hardware section of the sidebar. If there is no Storage entry, select the entry for the bus your Mac startup disk is attached to. For most models, this is the Serial-ATA, SATA/SATA Express, or NVMExpress bus.

8   Select your startup disk in the top-right list.

9   Find your startup volume in the list on the right, and verify that it has at least 12.5 GB of available space. Ideally, a lot more than 12.5 GB should be available, but 12.5 GB is the minimum requirement for installing macOS Mojave from OS X El Capitan 10.11.5 or later.

NOTE ▶ If you are upgrading from OS X Yosemite 10.10 or earlier, you need at least 18.5 GB of available space.

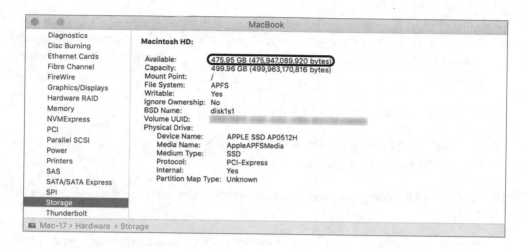

10 In the sidebar, under Software, select Applications, and wait for macOS to gather information on installed apps.

11 Click the heading for the Last Modified column on the right. If the arrow at the top of the column is pointing down, click again so that it points up.

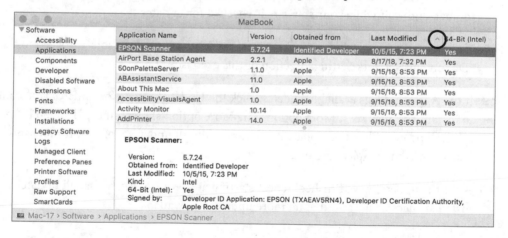

The oldest apps are listed at the top. In general, older apps are more likely to be incompatible with newer versions of macOS. Research older apps to see if they are compatible with macOS Mojave or if updates are available. Often, a developer website has information about compatibility and updates.

12 If there is a Kind column, click the heading for that column, and scroll through the list to see whether you have any PowerPC or Classic apps. These apps aren't supported by macOS Mojave. Some apps may have a blank in this column. This doesn't indicate a problem.

13 Quit System Information.

14 Open Safari, and navigate to the Apple Tech Specs website (https://checkcoverage.apple.com).

15 Enter your Mac computer's serial number (recorded in step 6) in the field, and press Return.

Your Mac computer's model name, along with information about your warranty coverage and links to set up a repair, appears. Verify that the model name is on the list of supported models in Reference 2.2, "Prepare to Upgrade or Reinstall macOS."

16 If you want, click the link to view your Mac computer's detailed specifications.

17 From the Apple menu, choose App Store. If necessary, click the Updates icon in the toolbar, and wait while your software is checked for updates.

18 If a message appears telling you that there are "No Updates Available," proceed to the "Document Network Settings" section of this exercise.

19 If the App Store lists available updates, click the Update buttons for updates you want to install. You may see a More option. The More option shows a more detailed list of system updates. Click the Update All button to install updates. Follow prompts and instructions to complete the updates.

20 After the updates have finished, repeat starting at step 17 to verify that all updates installed successfully and that no more updates are available.

Document Network Settings

1 From the Apple menu, choose System Preferences.

2   In System Preferences, click Network.

3   Select each of the network services (listed on the left of the preference pane), and record settings assigned to them. Click the Advanced button for each service to see the full settings. An easy way to do this is to take screenshots with the shortcut Shift-Command-3 to give you a record to work from.

4   If your Mac has more than one location defined, repeat this process for each location.

Back Up Your Data

You should always have a current backup copy of the content on your Mac. Third-party backup solutions are available, and macOS includes a backup utility, Time Machine, which is documented in Lesson 17, "Manage Time Machine." Whichever solution you choose, after you complete a backup, try restoring files to ensure that it works.

Exercise 2.2
Upgrade to macOS Mojave

NOTE ► This exercise is for independent study only. You don't perform this exercise in a classroom environment. Perform this exercise only if you want to upgrade your Mac from an earlier version of macOS. This exercise can't be used to prepare an independent study Mac for the rest of the course. Independent learners must complete Exercise 2.3, "Erase a Mac and Install macOS Mojave," to continue to Exercise 3.1, "Configure a Mac for Exercises."

> **Prerequisite**
>
> ► You must have performed Exercise 2.1, "Prepare a Mac for Upgrade," before you begin this exercise.

In this exercise, you download macOS Mojave from the App Store and install it, as an upgrade, on your Mac.

Use the App Store to Download the Installer

1 Log in to your existing administrator account on your Mac.

2 From the Apple menu, choose App Store.

3 In the search field of the App Store window, enter **Mojave**, and press Return.

4 Find macOS Mojave in the search results, and click the button under its name (it is labeled either "Download" or "Get").

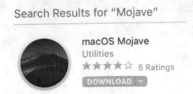

5 If a dialog appears asking you to sign in, sign in to an Apple ID account or create a new Apple ID to download macOS Mojave. See Reference 18.1, "The App Store," and Exercise 18.1, "Install an App from the App Store," for more information about using Apple IDs with the App Store.

6 If the App Store requests additional information, enter it.

7 Wait for the Install macOS Mojave app to download.

When the download is complete, the app opens automatically.

NOTE ► The installation deletes the Installer app. If you want to upgrade several Mac computers or create a macOS Mojave install disk, quit the installer and make a copy of it before you proceed. Find the process for creating an install disk in Exercise 5.2, "Create a macOS Install Disk."

Upgrade Your Mac to macOS Mojave

1   Open the Install macOS Mojave app.

Install macOS
Mojave

2   At the first screen, click Continue.

3   Read the license agreement, and if its terms are acceptable to you, click Agree.

4   In the confirmation dialog that appears, click Agree.

5   Select the installation destination. The default selection is the current startup volume. If other volumes are available, click the Show All Disks button to select a different destination.

6   Click Install to start the installation. If you're warned about not being connected to a power source, connect your power adapter before you continue.

7   Enter the password of your administrator account to authorize the installation.

To see installation details, follow the instructions in Exercise 2.4, "Verify That macOS Is Installed Correctly," after the installation starts.

The installation restarts several times and normally completes automatically.

The first time you log in to your account after you upgrade, you may be prompted to sign in with your Apple ID. Select "Don't sign in" to skip this step. You explore Apple ID and iCloud features in later exercises.

You may also be prompted to enable Siri. You can enable Siri, but you won't need to for the exercises.

Now that your Mac is running macOS Mojave, follow the instructions in Exercise 3.1, "Configure a Mac for Exercises," to set up your Mac for the rest of the exercises.

Exercise 2.3
Erase a Mac and Install macOS Mojave

NOTE ▶ This exercise is for independent study only. You don't perform this exercise in a classroom environment. Complete this exercise only if you must erase the contents of your Mac before you install macOS Mojave, as covered in Reference 2.1, "macOS Installation Methods."

▶ **Prerequisite**

▶ You need macOS Recovery with macOS Mojave or a macOS Mojave install disk (see Lesson 5, "Use macOS Recovery," for details).

NOTE ▶ This exercise erases all of your Mac content. If you want to keep the content, back it up to an external storage device before you start.

Start Up from Recovery or an Install Disk

1 Before you proceed with this exercise, back up your content to an external storage device.

2 If your Mac is running, shut it down.

3 If you are using macOS Recovery to replace your current installation of macOS Mojave:

   a Press the power button on your Mac to turn it on.

   b Immediately press and hold the Command and R keys until you see the Apple icon appear in the middle of the screen.

   c After you see the Apple icon, release the keys and skip ahead to the next section, "Erase Your Disk Drive."

4 If you are using an external macOS Mojave install disk, connect the disk to your Mac.

5 Press the power button on your Mac to turn it on, and then immediately press and hold the Option key until you see a row of icons appear on the screen.

6   Click the install disk icon (usually labeled "Install macOS Mojave").

7   Click the arrow that appears under the icon.

Your Mac starts up into the installer/recovery environment. Lesson 5 has more information about using these startup modes.

Erase Your Disk Drive

1   If a language selection screen appears, select your preferred language, and click the right-arrow button to continue.

2   Open Disk Utility.

▶   If the macOS Utilities window appears, select Disk Utility, and click Continue.

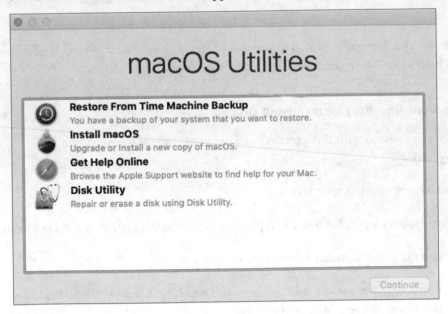

▶   If an installer screen appears, from the menu bar choose Utilities > Disk Utility.

Disk Utility opens. Lesson 11, "Manage File Systems and Storage," has more information about using Disk Utility.

3   From the sidebar, select the disk or volume that you will erase to install macOS Mojave.

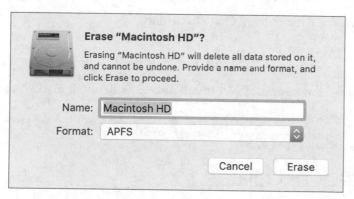

4   Click the Erase button near the top of the Disk Utility window.

5   Enter a new name for your disk. The rest of this guide assumes that it is named Macintosh HD.

6   From the Format pop-up menu, choose APFS if it is not already selected.

Many volumes may be formatted as Mac OS Extended (Journaled), which is still an option in some cases. If your volume is formatted as Mac OS Extended, the macOS Installer converts your volume to APFS automatically during installation.

7   If there is a Scheme pop-up menu, choose GUID Partition Map.

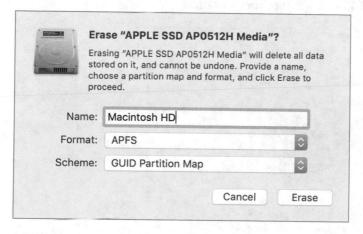

8   Click Erase.

9 When the process finishes, click Done.

10 From the menu bar, choose Disk Utility > Quit Disk Utility.

Install macOS Mojave

1 If the macOS Utilities window appears, select Install macOS or Reinstall macOS, and click Continue.

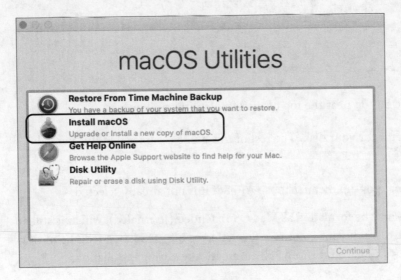

2 In the Install macOS Mojave window, click Continue.

3 If you are notified that your Mac computer's eligibility will be verified with Apple, click Continue.

4 Read the license agreement, and if its terms are acceptable to you, click Agree.

5 In the confirmation dialog that appears, click Agree.

6 Select your volume, and click Install.

7 If your volume is not listed, click Show All Disks, select your volume, and click Install.

8   If you are prompted, enter your Apple ID to sign in to the App Store. See Reference 18.1, "The App Store," and Exercise 18.1, "Install an App from the App Store," for more information about using Apple IDs with the App Store.

To see the details of the installation, follow the instructions in Exercise 2.4, "Verify That macOS Is Installed Correctly," after the installation begins.

The installation restarts several times and completes automatically.

After restart, you see Setup Assistant, as covered in Lesson 3, "Set Up and Configure macOS." Follow the instructions in Exercise 3.1, "Configure a Mac for Exercises," to set up your Mac for the rest of the exercises.

Exercise 2.4
Verify That macOS Is Installed Correctly

NOTE ▸ This exercise is for independent study only. You don't perform this exercise in a classroom environment.

▶ **Prerequisite**

▸   You must have started installing macOS Mojave using the instructions in Exercise 2.2, "Upgrade to macOS Mojave," or Exercise 2.3, "Erase a Mac and Install macOS Mojave."

In this exercise, you use the Installer log to view the installation process.

View the Installer Log
During installation, you can bring up the Installer log by following these steps:

1   If the installer is running in full-screen mode, you can't see the menu bar. Move your mouse to the top of the screen and leave it there for a few seconds to reveal the menu bar.

2   From the menu bar, choose Window > Installer Log (or press Command-L).

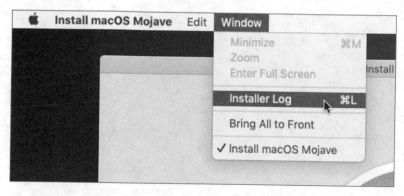

3   Choose Show All Logs from the Detail Level pop-up menu to view the entire contents of the Installer log.

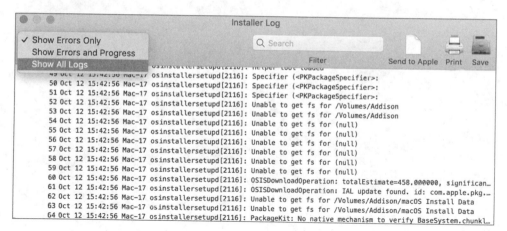

4   Use the Spotlight search field in the toolbar to view entries in the Installer log.

5   To save the Installer log, click the Save button in the toolbar.

The installer restarts the Mac partway through installation. When the Mac restarts for the second phase, the log window doesn't automatically reopen. It isn't available during this part of the installation.

Lesson 3

Set Up and Configure macOS

This lesson covers initial setup and ongoing macOS configuration. You use Setup Assistant to set up a new Mac. After that, you use System Preferences and configuration profiles.

Reference 3.1
Configure a Mac with a New Installation of macOS Mojave

If you're using a new Mac for the first time or you have just completed an upgrade to macOS Mojave, you'll see Setup Assistant. For new Mac computers or installations of macOS on a previously blank disk, Setup Assistant guides you through the preliminary configuration.

If you just upgraded an existing Mac with a previous version of a Mac operating system, you'll still see Setup Assistant, but you'll be presented with fewer configuration steps. Most importantly, you will be prompted to enter your Apple ID and password to complete the iCloud setup. Apple ID and iCloud are covered later in this lesson.

Even if you previously set up iCloud on an existing Mac, when Setup Assistant is running you need to reenter your authentication information to complete the upgrade to macOS Mojave.

iCloud is optional and free of charge. Many macOS features require iCloud.

After you turn on a new Mac, Setup Assistant starts automatically. It guides you through setting up your Mac by providing step-by-step screens. The screens you will see vary based on the features of your Mac and the choices you make while using Setup Assistant. Each screen varies in what you're required to do:

▶ Take action or make a selection

▶ Read, then click Continue

▶ Click the option to set up a feature later

These are the screens that require you to agree to something or make a selection or configuration:

▶ Region selection

▶ Keyboard setup

▶ Apple terms and conditions acceptance

▶ First account creation

You can use System Preferences to change most of the settings you selected in Setup Assistant.

Device Enrollment is a feature of Apple Business Manager and Apple School Manager. If your organization uses Apple Business Manager or Apple School Manager, you can use Device Enrollment to automate mobile device management (MDM) enrollment and simplify initial Mac setup. You can use your MDM solution to prevent some Setup Assistant screens from appearing. Unless otherwise indicated, this book describes the Setup Assistant process for a Mac that's not automatically enrolled using Device Enrollment. For more information about Device Enrollment, read Apple Support article HT204142, "Use Device Enrollment," and "Mobile device management settings for IT," at https://help.apple.com/deployment/mdm/.

Language

If you see the Language screen, select your language, then click the right arrow to continue. You can change your system language settings later from Language & Region preferences.

Welcome

The Setup Assistant screen requires that you select your region. This information is used to set regional language and keyboard options and to set the appropriate Apple online stores. You can change your Region settings later from Language & Region preferences.

During the initial stages of Setup Assistant, you can choose to enable VoiceOver to interact with macOS using only audio cues. At the Welcome screen, you can press the Esc (Escape) key to learn how to use VoiceOver. At any point you can use a keyboard shortcut to switch between turning VoiceOver on or off:

▶ Press Command-F5 (you might need to press the Fn [Function] key to access the F5 key).

▶ If your Mac has Touch ID, press and hold the Command key and then quickly press Touch ID three times at the right end of the Touch Bar.

Find out more about assistive technologies from Apple's accessibility website, www.apple.com/accessibility.

Keyboard

You must select the primary keyboard layout. You can change your keyboard layout settings later from Keyboard preferences.

Network Settings

Setup Assistant attempts to establish a connection to the Internet by automatically configuring Mac network settings. It attempts to automatically configure with the Dynamic Host Configuration Protocol (DHCP) on an Ethernet network or open Wi-Fi network. If a connection is made this way, you won't be prompted to set up networking.

Setup Assistant tries to figure out which type of network connection you need to set up and presents you with the appropriate configuration screen. If your Mac isn't connected to Ethernet with an Ethernet cable, you'll see the Wi-Fi network setup screen, where you can select a wireless network and authenticate to it. You can postpone setting up networking at this point and do it later from Network preferences. Lesson 21, "Manage Basic Network Settings," covers this topic in detail.

Remote Management

If your organization uses Apple Business Manager or Apple School Manager, and your Mac is assigned to use an MDM solution, then you will see the Remote Management screen. Click Continue to enroll your Mac with the MDM solution. If your MDM solution allows your Mac to skip enrollment, the Remote Management screen displays a Skip button.

Data & Privacy

The Data & Privacy screen displays the icon that appears when an Apple feature asks to use your personal information. Click the Learn More link to read more about privacy at Apple, or visit www.apple.com/privacy. Lesson 9, "Manage Security and Privacy," covers security and privacy in macOS in detail.

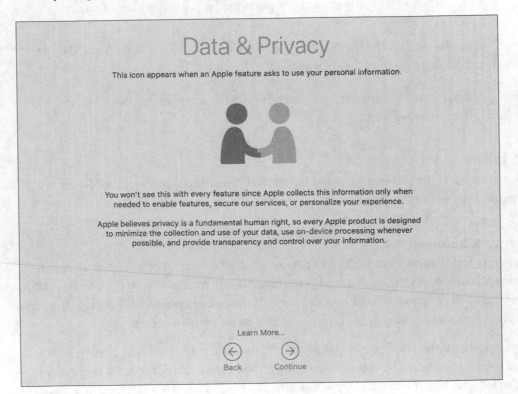

Transfer Information

When you use the optional Transfer Information utility (also called Migration Assistant), you can transfer computer and user information from another computer or from an external backup device to your Mac. If you use Transfer Information, you can skip most of the remaining Setup Assistant screens because the configuration is gathered from the previous computer or external storage device. Lesson 8, "Manage User Home Folders," covers transferring information with Migration Assistant in detail.

If you don't have a computer or external storage device to migrate settings and data from, leave the default choice, and click Continue to proceed with the Setup Assistant process.

Sign In with Your Apple ID

New Mac computers and Mac computers that are upgraded to macOS Mojave might prompt you to enter your Apple ID authentication. At the "Sign In with Your Apple ID" screen, you can enter an existing Apple ID, recover a lost Apple ID or password, create a new Apple ID, or click Set Up Later to go to the next to step.

Apple ID

You can set up an Apple ID at no cost. It provides login access for Apple online stores and services. If you've made online purchases from Apple, you already have an Apple ID.

After you enter or create an Apple ID during Setup Assistant, the account is configured for several services, including Messages, FaceTime, and iCloud. Additionally, if you ever used the Apple ID to buy anything, it's already configured in the App Store and Apple Books Store. But you still must enter your Apple ID password to buy items. In later Setup Assistant screens, this Apple ID is pre-entered for you.

If you use one Apple ID for iCloud, and a different Apple ID for store purchases, then you can click "Use different Apple IDs for iTunes and iCloud?" You'll first see the "Sign In to iCloud" screen, which prompts you to enter your Apple ID for iCloud. Then you'll see the "Sign In to iTunes and the App Store" screen, which prompts you to enter your Apple ID for store purchases.

For more information about Apple ID, see the Apple ID Support website, support.apple.com/apple-id.

Two-Factor Authentication

To improve your Apple ID security, you should enable two-factor authentication. Two-factor authentication is available for Apple IDs with iCloud enabled and at least one device that's using iOS 9 or OS X El Capitan 10.11 or later.

When you enter or create an Apple ID in Setup Assistant, you might encounter the following:

▶   If you enter an Apple ID that has two-factor authentication enabled, you are prompted to verify your Apple ID with additional steps.

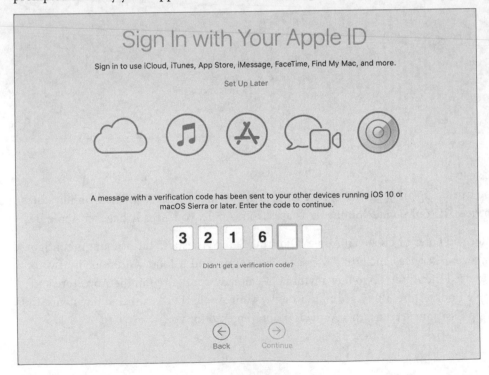

- ► If your Apple ID has two-step verification enabled, you might be informed that your Apple ID was updated to use two-factor authentication.

- ► If you're creating a new Apple ID, you are prompted to enter your birthday, then provide your name and an existing email address to use for your Apple ID, or you can click "Get a free iCloud email address." After you provide and verify a password for your new Apple ID, you're prompted to enter a phone number that can be used with a text message or phone call to verify your identity. After you verify your identity with a text message or phone call, your Mac turns on two-factor authentication for your Apple ID, and it configures your Apple ID to consider your Mac a trusted device for two-factor authentication.

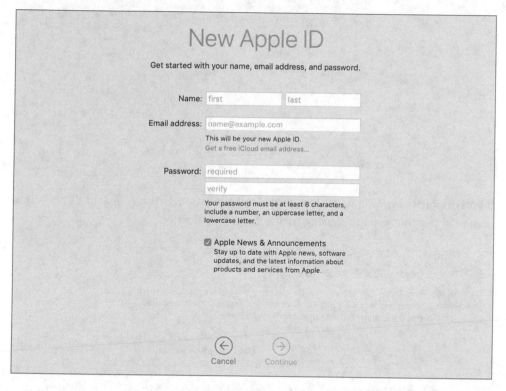

- ► If you're entering an Apple ID that hasn't been used in a while and doesn't have additional security features enabled, you are prompted to update your security settings, including optionally enabling two-factor authentication.

If you disable the option to use two-factor authentication, Setup Assistant displays information about the benefits of using two-factor authentication.

Once your Apple ID is enabled for two-factor authentication, two-factor authentication is permanently enabled for your Apple ID. For more information about two-factor authentication, see Apple Support article HT204915, "Two-factor authentication for Apple ID," article HT205075, "Availability of two-factor authentication for Apple ID," and article HT207198, "Switch from two-step verification to two-factor authentication."

iCloud

iCloud is a free cloud-storage and communication service that you can set up on current Apple devices. Though not required for completing Setup Assistant, iCloud is the easiest way to share information between macOS, iOS, and even non-Apple devices.

Only Apple IDs that are signed in to iCloud on an Apple device have access to iCloud services. If an existing Apple ID was never used for iCloud, entering this account during Setup Assistant upgrades the Apple ID to include iCloud services. Setup Assistant configures your Mac to use iCloud for most services.

The following iCloud services are enabled by default in most cases: iCloud Drive, Photos, Contacts, Calendars, Reminders, Safari, Siri, Notes, and Find My Mac. If the Apple ID you entered has two-factor authentication turned on, iCloud Keychain will be enabled. If the Apple ID you enter belongs to the @mac.com, @me.com, or @icloud.com domain, Mail is also configured.

If you enter an Apple ID that belongs to someone under the age of 13 (made possible with Apple School Manager or Family Sharing), no iCloud services are enabled by default.

After setup, you can verify and modify iCloud service settings from iCloud preferences. iCloud is covered throughout this guide, including Lesson 9, "Manage Security and Privacy," Lesson 18, "Install Apps," Lesson 19, "Manage Documents," and Lesson 24, "Manage Network Services."

For more information about iCloud, see the iCloud Support website, support.apple.com/icloud.

Terms and Conditions

You must accept the Apple terms and conditions to complete Setup Assistant. The content of the Terms and Conditions page varies depending on whether you entered an Apple ID in the previous step. When you accept the terms and conditions, you don't send personal or technical information to Apple. In fact, you can accept Terms and Conditions even if your Mac is offline and never accesses the Internet.

For more information about Apple terms and conditions, visit the Apple Legal website, www.apple.com/legal/.

Create a Computer Account

In the "Create a Computer Account" screen, you must create the initial administrator user account for the Mac. At first, this account is the only administrator user account allowed to modify system settings, including the creation of additional user accounts. Until you create additional administrator user accounts, you must remember the authentication information for this account.

Apple ID Provided During Setup

If you previously entered an Apple ID, that information is used to configure services for a new local administrator account. Setup Assistant automatically populates the full name based on your full name associated with your Apple ID. Then Setup Assistant uses the full name to prepopulate the account name, which is used to create the user's home folder. You can change the full name or account name here.

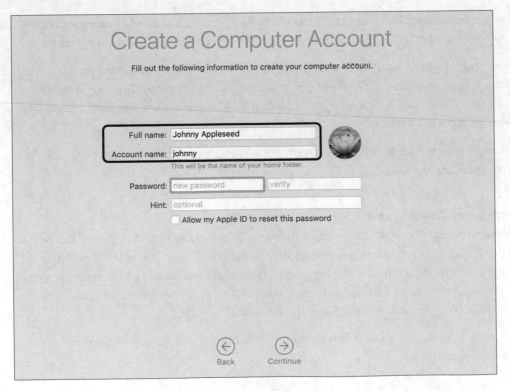

You must provide a new password for the local administrator account. The password you define for this account cannot match the Apple ID password.

You can define a password hint, which is a clue intended to help you if you forget this account's password. Although you can define more than one word for the password hint, you can't set the password hint to the same text as the password.

Apple ID Not Provided During Setup

If you didn't enter an Apple ID during Setup Assistant, the name fields won't be prepopulated. After setup, you can modify local user accounts from Users & Groups preferences, and adjust iCloud settings from iCloud preferences. Additional user account creation and management are detailed in Lesson 7, "Manage User Accounts."

iCloud Keychain

After you create the local administrator account, you might see the iCloud Keychain screen. If you provided an Apple ID that doesn't have two-factor authentication, the iCloud Keychain screen appears with two choices: "Set up iCloud Keychain" and "Set up later." This feature securely saves your private information, like service user names and passwords, to your iCloud account. This enables access from multiple devices.

If you don't set up iCloud Keychain now, you can do it later from iCloud preferences. Lesson 10, "Manage Password Changes," covers this topic in greater detail.

Express Set Up

The Express Set Up screen enables you to quickly configure several options at once.

If you click Customize Settings, you see these screens in Setup Assistant:

▶ Enable Location Services

▶ Analytics

▶ Siri (for Mac computers that have a built-in microphone)

If you click Continue, the screens are skipped. It's the same as if you click Customize Settings and then enable each option for each of the three screens.

Enable Location Services

If you enable Location Services, you allow macOS and apps to locate your Mac using a Wi-Fi–based geolocation technology. You need Location Services for Find My Mac, which you can enable later during Setup Assistant. You can further adjust Location Services in Security & Privacy preferences. Lesson 9, "Manage Security and Privacy," covers Location Services in greater detail.

Time Zone

If you enable Location Services, macOS sets the time zone based on the Mac location. This requires an Internet connection and Location Services to be enabled.

If you don't enable Location Services, you see the Select Your Time Zone screen. In this screen, if you enable the option to "Set time zone automatically using current location," you'll be prompted to turn on Location Services. Otherwise, select a city in your time zone.

After setup, you can verify and modify settings from Date & Time preferences. Regardless of your Location Services choice, macOS sets the date and time using Apple time servers.

Analytics or iCloud Analytics

macOS can send diagnostic and usage information to Apple and third-party developers. If you decide to share this information, you enable developers to improve system and app performance. If providing this kind of feedback is a privacy concern for you, you can disable this option. If you click Continue at the Express Set Up screen, this option is enabled. After setup, you can verify and modify these settings from Security & Privacy preferences, as covered in Lesson 9.

Siri

If you click Continue at the Express Set Up screen and your Mac has a built-in microphone, then Siri is enabled. If you don't want to use Siri, leave it disabled during Setup Assistant. After setup, you can verify and modify Siri settings from Siri preferences, as covered in Lesson 9.

Set Up "Hey Siri"

Some newer Mac computers support Hey Siri, a feature that enables you to say, "Hey Siri," and then make your request. If you enable Siri and your Mac supports Hey Siri, then Setup Assistant will ask you to speak various phrases to set up Hey Siri. Or you can click

Set Up "Hey Siri" Later. For more information, read Apple Support article HT209014, "Devices that support 'Hey Siri.'"

iCloud Drive

If you previously entered an Apple ID that wasn't upgraded to support iCloud Drive, you are prompted to upgrade your stored iCloud documents. You must do this once if you want to access content that you stored in iCloud on OS X Yosemite 10.10 and later or iOS 8 and later devices. If you are setting up a new Apple ID with iCloud, or if you are using iCloud Drive, you don't need to upgrade your account.

All Your Files in iCloud

Users signed in with an Apple ID that supports iCloud Drive see the option to store files from their Documents and Desktop folders in iCloud Drive.

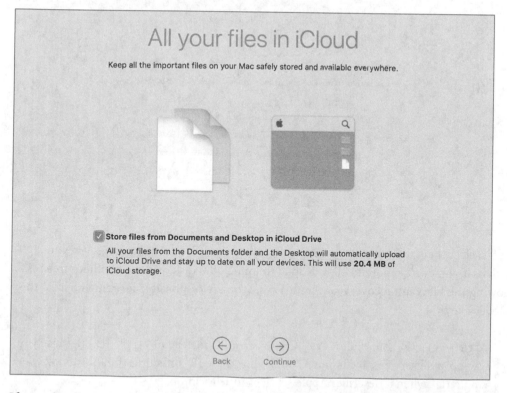

If you choose not to upgrade to iCloud Drive or move the Documents and Desktop folders to iCloud Drive, you can do so later from iCloud preferences. Lesson 19, "Manage Files," covers this topic.

FileVault Disk Encryption

You can use FileVault to protect your startup disk. If you complete Setup Assistant on a late-model portable Mac that doesn't have FileVault enabled, you might be prompted to enable FileVault. You see this screen in new Mac computers and Mac computers you upgrade to macOS Mojave only if the Mac has a single local user account and that account is signed in to iCloud.

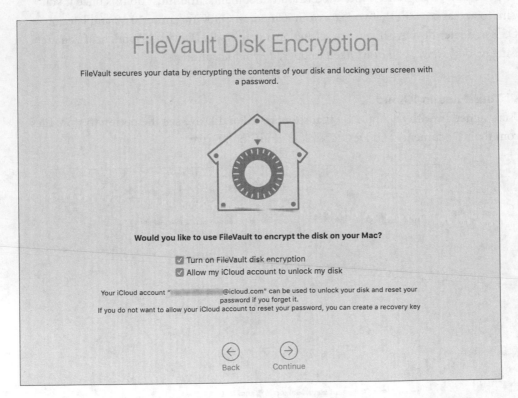

If you select the option to turn on FileVault, you can save a FileVault recovery key to iCloud. If you don't choose to allow iCloud to unlock the disk, you see another screen showing the FileVault recovery key. In this case, you are responsible for remembering the recovery key.

NOTE ▶ macOS sometimes says "iCloud account" instead of "Apple ID." Because you access Apple services, including iCloud, with Apple ID authentication, this book uses "Apple ID" when it describes Apple service authentication.

Mac computers with the Apple T2 Security Chip integrate security into software and hardware to provide encrypted-storage capabilities. The startup disk in Mac computers with the T2 chip is encrypted. Even so, you should turn on FileVault so that your Mac requires a password to decrypt your data. Read Apple Support article HT208344, "About encrypted storage on your new Mac," for more information.

If your Mac doesn't have the T2 chip and you turn on FileVault, macOS begins to encrypt the system volume contents. Encryption finishes in the background while your Mac is connected to power.

After you turn on FileVault, you need your account password to unlock the encrypted startup disk after you restart your Mac. If you create additional user accounts, the additional users can also unlock the encrypted start disk at startup. If you lose all your user account passwords, your startup disk remains locked unless you reset an account password with your iCloud account or with a FileVault recovery key.

If you don't enable FileVault, you can do so later from Security & Privacy preferences. Lesson 12, "Manage FileVault," covers this topic in greater detail.

Touch ID

MacBook Pro computers featuring Touch ID present additional setup screens. If you don't set up Touch ID, you can set it up later in Touch ID preferences. Read Apple Support article HT207054, "Use Touch ID on your Mac" for more information.

Apple Pay

If you enabled Touch ID and provided your Apple ID, you see the Apple Pay screen. If you don't set up Apple Pay, you can set it up later in Wallet & Apple Pay preferences.

Choose Your Look

Dark Mode is a new look in macOS Mojave that helps you focus on your work. Select a light or dark appearance and see how the Dock, menus, buttons, and windows adjust. You can use System Preferences to change the look later.

True Tone Display

MacBook Pro models introduced in 2018 feature a technology called True Tone that makes images on your display and Touch Bar appear more natural. True Tone technology uses multichannel sensors to adjust the color and intensity of your display and Touch Bar to match the ambient light. Click and hold the See Without True Tone Display button to see what your display looks like no matter what time of day it is.

You can turn True Tone on or off in the System Preferences Displays pane. Read Apple Support article HT208909, "Use True Tone on your MacBook Pro," for more information.

Reference 3.2
Manage System Settings

After you complete Setup Assistant, you can modify macOS and user settings with System Preferences and configuration profiles.

Open System Preferences

There are at least five ways to open System Preferences.

▶ You can open System Preferences from the Apple menu.

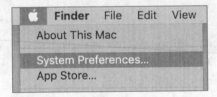

▶ You can open System Preferences from the /Applications folder.

▶ You can open System Preferences from the Dock. The Dock is a convenient place to keep items you use frequently. It's at the bottom of your screen after the first time you log in. If you see a red badge on the System Preferences icon in the Dock, you need to take one or more actions. For example, if you didn't fully set up iCloud, the badge appears on the icon in the Dock. When you click the icon, iCloud preferences opens and you can complete setup. Click and hold System Preferences in the Dock to see the preferences you can configure. With a default installation of macOS, System Preferences is in the Dock, but you can remove it.

▶ Open System Preferences from Launchpad. It's an easy way to find and open apps. Click Launchpad in the Dock, or pinch-close your thumb and three fingers on your trackpad, then click System Preferences.

▶ Open System Preferences from Spotlight.

Use System Preferences

System Preferences organizes options for your Mac into preferences. For example, use Dock preferences to set options for your Dock. System Preferences displays preferences icons in four or five unlabeled rows. The first four rows show personal, hardware, Internet, and system settings preferences that are built into macOS. A fifth row appears if you install additional preferences.

In System Preferences, the View menu gives you quick access to preferences. You can organize preferences alphabetically or by category. You can hide some preferences when you choose View > Customize.

If you're not sure which preferences you need, enter a search term in the Search field in the upper-right corner of System Preferences. System Preferences lists the options that match your search term and highlights the preference panes where they're located.

Click a preferences icon to access its settings. Most System Preferences changes are instantaneous and don't require you to click an Apply or OK button. Click the Show All button (a grid of squares) from any of the preference panes to return to the System Preferences pane.

Some preferences have a lock button in the lower-left corner. These preferences can be accessed only by an administrator user account.

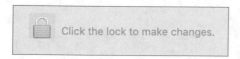

If you are logged in as a non-administrator user, more preferences are locked than if you are logged in as an administrator user. For example, if you are logged in as an administrator user, Time Machine preferences won't show the lock button. If you're logged in as a non-administrator user, Time Machine preferences is locked.

The lock button also appears outside System Preferences. The lock icon is an indication that access to an item requires administrator authentication, often when the item represents a change that affects all users.

Most System Preferences panes include a Help button (question mark) in the lower-right corner for more information about the options.

Configure Appearance, Accent, and Highlight Color

Setup Assistant asks you to select Light Mode or Dark Mode. You can always use System Preferences to change your selection. In System Preferences, open General preferences:

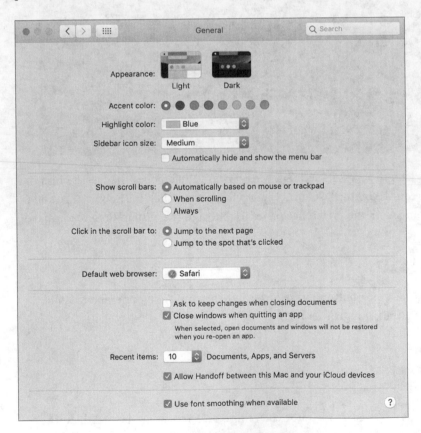

For Appearance, select Light or Dark. When you update the Accent color, the Highlight color changes, and you can further adjust the Highlight color. The changes you make happen immediately, and System Preferences updates the look of the graphics in the Appearance preview.

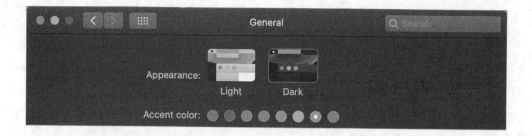

Configure Dynamic Desktop

By default, your desktop picture changes throughout the day, based on your location and time zone. You can configure this in the Desktop & Screen Saver preferences. In the following figure there are two built-in Dynamic Desktop themes you can use.

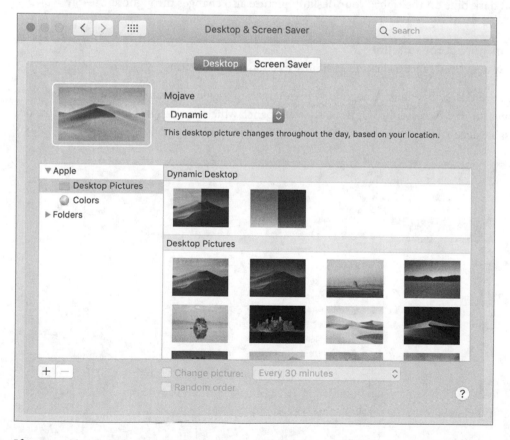

If you use the default Mojave Dynamic Desktop, you can click the menu and choose a desktop that is still.

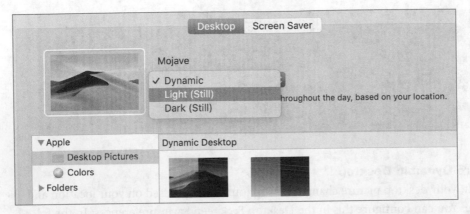

If you select the other option in Dynamic Desktop, Solar Gradients (light blue on the left and dark blue on the right), your desktop picture also changes throughout the day.

Configure Accessibility

In System Preferences, click Accessibility to configure the settings.

Use the General pane in Accessibility preferences to toggle accessibility shortcuts that appear in the Accessibility Options shortcut panel, which you can use to quickly enable or disable accessibility options.

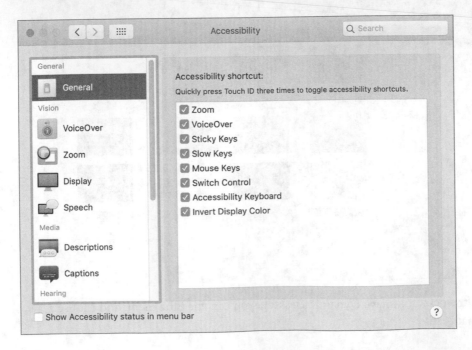

At any point when you are logged in, you can use a keyboard shortcut to open the Accessibility Options shortcut panel:

► Press Option-Command-F5.

► If your Mac has Touch ID, quickly press Touch ID three times.

In the Accessibility Options shortcut panel, select accessibility options to turn them on. Or use the Tab key to navigate, and press the Space bar to select an option. Press Return or click Done to close the Accessibility Options shortcut panel.

As another example of Accessibility preferences, you can use the Zoom pane to configure how to make the entire screen larger, or enlarge just the portion of the screen where you move the pointer.

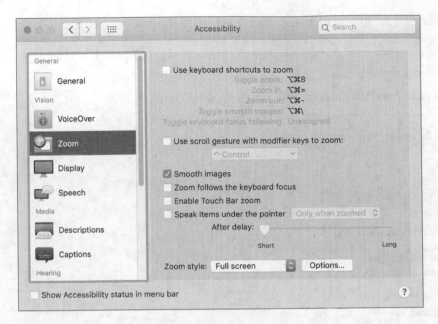

Use the Speech pane of Accessibility preferences to customize the voice that your Mac uses. You can turn on announcements when alerts are displayed or apps need your attention. You can turn on the option for your Mac to speak the selected text when you press a keyboard shortcut.

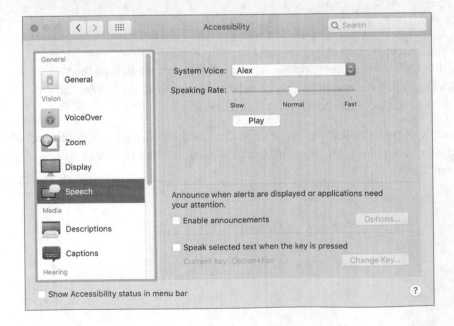

Open the Keyboard pane of Accessibility preferences to turn on Sticky Keys and Slow Keys. Sticky Keys enables you to use modifier keys (like Shift, Fn [Function], Control, Option, and Command) in keyboard shortcuts without holding down modifier keys. When Sticky Keys is turned on, each time you press a modifier key, its symbol appears in the upper-right corner until you use it in a keyboard shortcut.

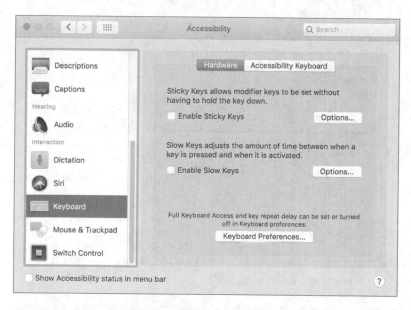

At an alternative to using the hardware keyboard, you can use the onscreen Accessibility Keyboard to type and interact with macOS.

Turn on the Accessibility Keyboard in the Accessibility Keyboard pane.

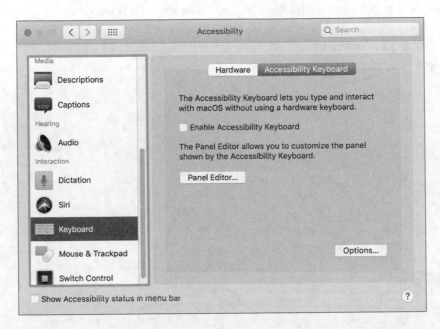

The Switch Control pane enables you to use one or more adaptive devices to enter text, interact with items on your screen, and control your Mac.

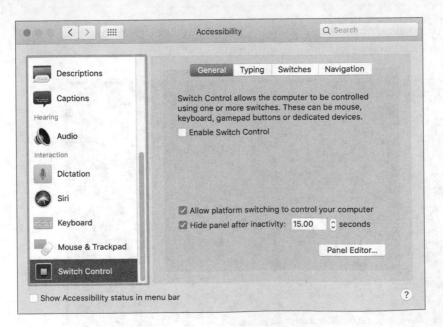

When you turn on Switch Control, the Switch Control Home panel appears.

You can use the Panel Editor to add custom panels to the Switch Control or Accessibility Keyboard panel collection.

In Accessibility preferences, select an item in the left column and click the Help button (question mark) to read more about that topic. For example, with Switch Control selected in the Accessibility pane of System Preferences, click Switches, then click Help to read "Change Switch Control Switches preferences on Mac."

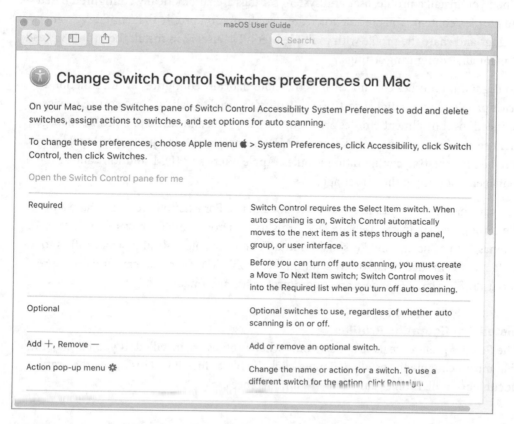

Configuration Profiles

Configuration profiles, trust profiles, and enrollment profiles enable you to configure and manage Apple devices.

A profile is a document that includes instructions for settings. For example, configuration profiles might contain settings for Internet accounts or Network preferences. Profile documents have the .mobileconfig filename extension and an icon that looks like a gear.

Wi-Fi for
PretendCo

When you install a profile, user and system settings are automatically configured based on the profile's content. You are able to create a configuration profile that contains a variety of settings and share the profile with multiple users. The users can install the profile instead of manually configuring settings.

Configuration profiles contain settings that automatically configure certain functions. Trust profiles contain digital certificates, which are used to validate and secure service connections. Enrollment profiles are used to establish a connection to a profile management service, more commonly known as MDM. Apple and third-party developers provide software for creating configuration profiles. Apple offers an MDM solution called Profile Manager, a service of the Server app.

You can share profiles just like you share documents. For example, you can share a profile through email, from a website link, or using AirDrop (which is covered in Lesson 25, "Manage Host Sharing and Personal Firewall.") You can automatically push profiles to a Mac that's enrolled in an MDM solution like Profile Manager. You can find out more about Profile Manager at help.apple.com/profilemanager/mac/.

Install Configuration Profiles

The Profiles preference pane appears only when profiles are installed. If you have a profile that must be manually installed, double-click the file to install it. This opens the profile document in the Profiles pane of System Preferences.

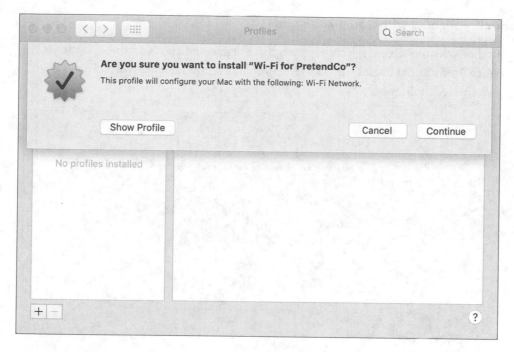

From Profiles, any user can install, verify, or remove a profile.

You might have to provide administrator authentication to install or remove some profiles. For example, a profile that enrolls your Mac in your organization's MDM solution requires that you authenticate as an administrator.

Exercise 3.1
Configure a Mac for Exercises

▶ **Prerequisite**

  ▸ Your Mac must have a new installation of macOS Mojave 10.14 and must not have been configured.

In this exercise you learn how your initial configuration settings affect macOS. You configure a clean macOS installation on a Mac as if you just took it out of the box. You use Setup Assistant to answer some questions and create the initial administrator user account.

Configure macOS with Setup Assistant

1   In the Welcome screen, select the appropriate region and click Continue. If the VoiceOver tutorial begins, you can either listen or move forward. VoiceOver is an assistive technology.

2   At the Select Your Keyboard screen, select the appropriate keyboard layout, and click Continue.

Setup Assistant evaluates your network environment and tries to determine whether you are connected to the Internet. This can take a few moments.

3   If you are asked to select your Wi-Fi network or how you connect to the Internet, respond for your Internet connection type.

Ask your facilitator how you should configure your Mac. Your Wi-Fi network might be named PretendCo and require the password **Apple321!**.

If you aren't asked about your Internet connection, your Mac network settings are already configured via DHCP, and you may move to step 4. After your network connection is configured, click Continue.

4   At the Data & Privacy screen, read Apple's privacy policy, and then click Continue.

5   In the "Transfer Information to This Mac" screen, select "Don't transfer any information now," and click Continue.

   If you were replacing a Mac, other options would assist you in migrating user data and system information from the old Mac to the new one.

6   If the "Sign in with Your Apple ID" screen appears, select "Set Up Later," and then click Skip in the confirmation dialog that appears.

   You set up an Apple ID account in a later exercise.

7   At the "Terms and Conditions" screen, read the macOS Software License Agreement. When you are done, click Agree.

8   In the confirmation dialog that appears, click Agree.

9   At the "Create a Computer Account" screen, enter the following information and then click Continue:

   NOTE ▸ Create this account as specified here. If you don't, future exercises might not work as written. This book uses **bold text** to indicate text you should enter exactly as shown.

   Full name: **Local Administrator**

   Account name: **ladmin**

   Password: **Apple321!**

   Don't provide a password hint.

   You may optionally change the account picture.

   NOTE ▸ On the Mac you use for your daily work, never use a password such as Apple321!. It's easy to guess, so it's not secure.

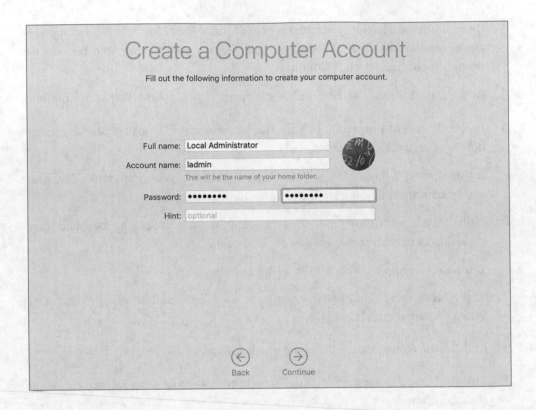

10 At the Express Set Up screen, click Continue. Your Mac enables Location Services, Analytics, and Siri, which share diagnostics and usage data with Apple and, by proxy, third-party developers.

11 If you are prompted to set up Touch ID, click Continue; click Set Up Touch ID Later, and then click Continue in the confirmation dialog. These exercises don't require Touch ID.

12 If you are prompted with the Siri screen, deselect Enable Ask Siri, and click Continue.

13 At the Choose Your Look screen, choose your preferred appearance, and then click Continue.

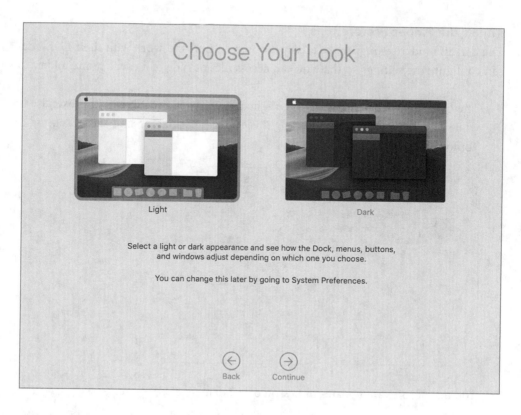

14 If the True Tone Display screen appears, click Continue.

Your Mac is now set up and ready for use.

Exercise 3.2
Configure System Preferences

> **Prerequisite**
>
> ▸ You must have created the Local Administrator account (Exercise 3.1, "Configure a Mac for Exercises").

In this exercise, you configure preference settings to ease navigation and provide a consistent classroom experience. You also configure app and system preferences. In a production environment, you can change preferences for yourself and your users.

Adjust the Finder Preferences

The default Finder settings make it easy for users to find and work with their files. You can configure the settings so that you can access files outside of a user's home folder.

1 The Updates Available notification might appear at any time during this exercise or while you're using your Mac. During this exercise, click Later, and select Remind Me Tomorrow from the pop-up menu.

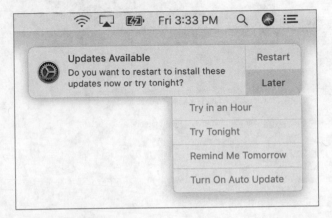

You install software updates in Lesson 6, "Update macOS," exercises.

2 If dialogs open with a "Do you want to use *some volume* to back up with Time Machine?" prompt, click Don't Use in each dialog.

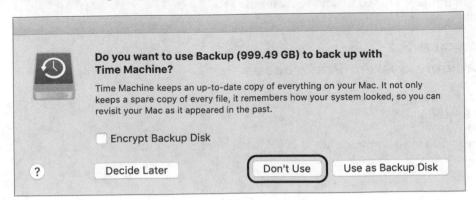

3   From the menu bar, choose Finder > Preferences. If you prefer, you can use the keyboard shortcut Command-Comma.

4   If necessary, click General in the toolbar, then select "Hard disks" and "Connected servers" to have macOS display them on your desktop.

5   From the "New Finder windows show" menu, choose your startup volume (named Macintosh HD on a fresh installation of macOS).

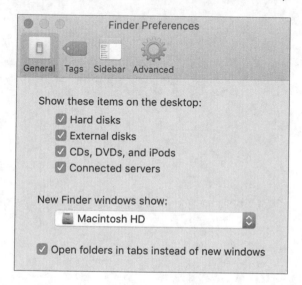

6   In the toolbar of the Finder Preferences window, click the Sidebar button.

7   Select "ladmin" in the Favorites section of the sidebar and "Hard disks" in the Locations section. "Hard disks" should be fully selected (a checkmark in the checkbox), not just partially selected (a dash in the checkbox).

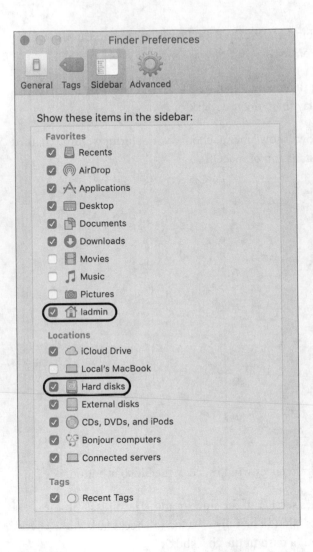

8   Close the Finder Preferences window. You can use the Command-W shortcut if
    you wish.

Set the Computer Name

When performing the exercises in a classroom setting, your Mac has the same name as the
other participants' Mac computers. To avoid confusion, give your Mac a unique name.

1   From the Apple menu, choose System Preferences.

2   In System Preferences, click the icon for Sharing preferences.

If you aren't sure where to find something in System Preferences, use Spotlight in the top right of the window. It searches for matching or related settings and highlights the preference panes where they are located.

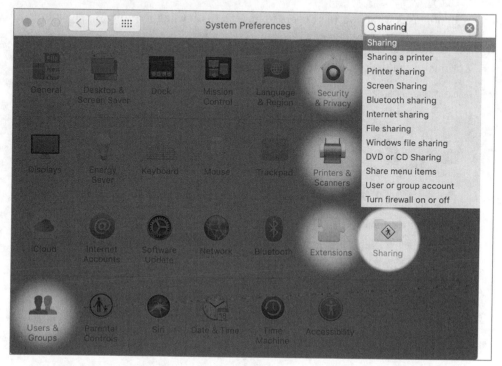

3   Enter a unique name for your Mac in the Computer Name field. If you are performing these exercises in a class, enter **Mac-NN**, where *NN* is your participant number.

4   Press Return.

Your local host name (.local name) displayed under your computer name updates to match your new computer name.

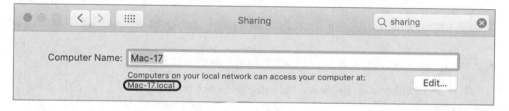

5   From the left sidebar, select the Remote Management checkbox.

Remote Management allows your facilitator to control the keyboard and mouse, gather information, and update your Mac throughout the course, enabling him or her to assist you with steps if necessary.

A dialog asks what you want users to be able to do using Remote Management.

6   Press and hold the Option key while clicking one of the checkboxes to select all options in the dialog.

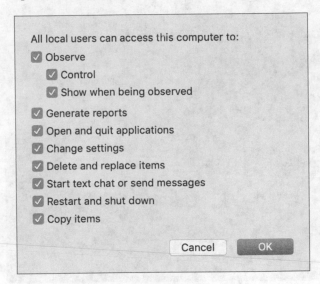

7   Click OK.

Adjust Your Trackpad and Mouse Preferences

In macOS you can customize the user interface. For example, depending on what you are used to, you might want to change the default scrolling behavior. Also, you can control how macOS recognizes primary and secondary mouse clicks (analogous to left- and right-clicks in other operating systems).

Since Control-click works as a secondary click, these exercises describe it as Control-click.

1   Click the Show All (grid icon) button in the toolbar.

The Show All button shows all System Preference pane icons and can aide your navigation.

2   If you are using a trackpad, select the Trackpad pane.

▶   Adjust the "Tap to click" and "Secondary click" options to your liking. A secondary click opens shortcut menus, equivalent to clicking the right mouse button or Control-clicking.

▶   Click Scroll & Zoom, and use the "Scroll direction: Natural" option to adjust which direction it works. The default is that if you move two fingers up you move the window contents up.

▶   Check the other options under Scroll & Zoom and More Gestures and make appropriate changes.

3   If you are using a mouse, select the Mouse pane.

▶   If your mouse has a scroll wheel or equivalent, use the "Scroll direction: Natural" option to adjust in which direction it works. The default is that if you push the wheel up you move the window contents up.

▶   If your mouse has multiple buttons, use the menu on the left side of the mouse image to control which button is the primary button. You use this button to select. It's usually the left button. Use the menu on the right side of the mouse image to control which button is the secondary button. You use this button to open shortcut menus. It's usually the right button, or Control-click.

Enable FileVault

NOTE ▶ If you lose the passwords and the recovery key for a FileVault-encrypted volume, you won't have access to the content stored in it. If you are performing this exercise on your own Mac and have files you don't want to risk losing, back up your Mac before starting this exercise.

In this exercise, you turn on FileVault to encrypt your startup volume. Enabling encryption on your startup volume is a best practice and can be done at any time. You will able to continue to work on your Mac while the startup volume is being encrypted.

1   Open the Security & Privacy pane in System Preferences.

2   Click FileVault.

3   Unlock the preference pane, and authenticate as Local Administrator (password: **Apple321!**).

4 Click Turn On FileVault.

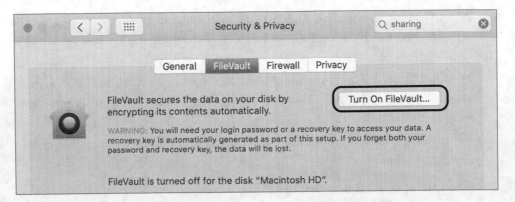

If a dialog appears saying "A recovery key has been set by your company, school, or institution," it means your Mac was preloaded with an institutional recovery key (described in Apple Support article HT202385, "Set a FileVault recovery key for Mac computers in your institution"). In this case, click Continue and skip to step 9. You will also not be able to perform Exercise 12.2, "Use a FileVault Recovery Key."

If an institutional key wasn't set, a dialog appears giving you the choice between allowing your iCloud account to unlock the disk or creating a recovery key. The dialog will be slightly different if you haven't linked the Local Administrator account to an Apple ID.

6 Select "Create a recovery key and do not use my iCloud account" and click Continue.

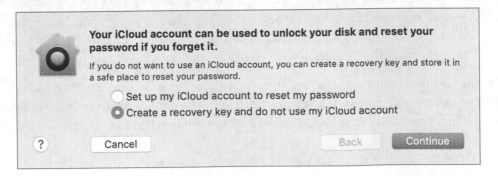

7   Record your recovery key. Your recovery key will be different than the key in this example.

Recovery key: _____

You should store the recorded recovery key in a physically secure location. You could take a screenshot of the recovery key window, but you would need to copy it to some-place else to make it available if you get locked out of your Mac.

8   Click Continue to begin the encryption process.

Encrypting the entire volume might take a while depending on the speed of your Mac, the type of hard disk, and the amount of data. You can use your Mac normally during the encryption process.

9   Quit System Preferences.

Because System Preferences is a single-window app, you can either click the close but-ton or use the System Preferences menu and select Quit System Preferences.

Exercise 3.3
Download Participant Materials

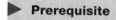 **Prerequisite**

▸   You must have completed Exercise 3.2, "Configure System Preferences."

In this exercise, you download the participant materials (called ParticipantMaterials) required for the rest of the exercises.

Connect to the Classroom Server

Connect to the file server (called server) to download the participant materials.

1   If necessary, open a new Finder window. Choose File > New Finder Window or press Command-N.

Look for the server named server in the Locations section of the sidebar. If server isn't shown, click Network to view the shared items.

2   Select server. If you had to click Network in the previous step, you have to double-click the server icon.

3   Open the Public folder.

Copy the ParticipantMaterials Folder to Your Mac

1   In the Public folder, select (single-click) the ParticipantMaterials folder.

2   Copy the folder by choosing Edit > Copy "ParticipantMaterials" from the menu bar, by pressing Command-C, or by Control-clicking the folder and choosing Copy "ParticipantMaterials" from the shortcut menu.

3   Open Macintosh HD (either from your desktop or from the Finder window sidebar).

4   Open the Users folder.

5   Open the Shared folder.

6   Paste the ParticipantMaterials folder into the Shared folder by choosing Edit > Paste Item from the menu bar, by pressing Command-V, or by Control-clicking in the Shared folder and choosing Paste Item from the shortcut menu.

This creates a copy of the participant materials on your Mac. If your facilitator included software updates in the participant materials, it may take several minutes to download them. You don't need to wait for the download to finish.

7   Put your copy of the ParticipantMaterials folder in a place where you can find it.

▶ Drag the ParticipantMaterials folder into the right section of the Dock. The Dock is divided into up to three sections. The left side holds apps, and the right side holds folders, documents, and other items. The Dock can also display a middle section that holds up to three apps that you've recently opened and aren't otherwise in the Dock. Place the ParticipantMaterials folder in the right section of the Dock, next to other entries—so it is added to the Dock—rather than over another entry, which would move it into that folder.

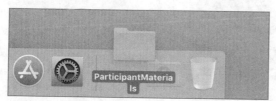

▶ Optionally, drag the ParticipantMaterials folder to the Finder sidebar in the Favorites section. Place it between other entries.

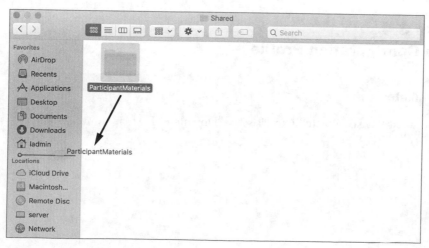

8   Choose Go > Applications or use the shortcut Shift-Command-A.

9   Drag the TextEdit app into the left side of the dividing line in your Dock so that you have an easy way to open it.

10   Wait for the ParticipantMaterials folder to finish downloading.

11   Unmount the Public folder by dragging its icon from the desktop onto the eject icon at the right side of the Dock. The Eject icon replaces the Trash icon when you select something that's ejectable.

Exercise 3.4
Install a Configuration Profile

▶ **Prerequisite**

▶   You must have completed Exercise 3.3, "Download Participant Materials."

You can manually configure settings in macOS for one Mac. You can also configure one or many Mac computers at one time with configuration profiles.

In this exercise, you manage Dock settings with a configuration profile.

Change Your Dock Settings with a Configuration Profile

1   Locate the Dock at the bottom of your screen and note its configuration. It may differ slightly from the example shown here.

2   Open the ParticipantMaterials folder. Remember that you placed a shortcut to it in your Dock.

3   Open the Lesson3 folder.

4   Double-click Dock.mobileconfig to install the profile.

The profile automatically opens in the Profiles pane of System Preferences.

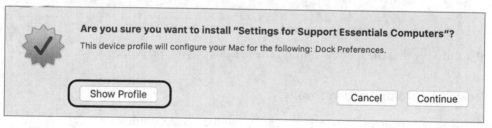

5   Click Show Profile to display the details of the profile and its payload (the settings it contains). You need to scroll down to see its full contents.

Observe that the Dock orientation has a value of left.

6   Click Continue.

7   Click Install.

8 Enter the Local Administrator account password (**Apple321!**) when prompted.

The Profiles pane lists the configuration profile as installed.

9 Observe that the Dock is now on the left side of your screen.

Remove a Configuration Profile

1 If necessary, open System Preferences, and then click Profiles.

2 With Settings for Support Essentials Computers selected, click Remove (–).

3 In the confirmation dialog that appears, click Remove.

4 If necessary, enter the Local Administrator account password (**Apple321!**) when prompted.

Observe that the profile is removed, and the Dock returns to the bottom of the screen.

5 Quit System Preferences.

Exercise 3.5
Examine System Information

▶ Prerequisite

- ▶ You must have created the Local Administrator account (Exercise 3.1, "Configure a Mac for Exercises").

System Information is the primary tool you use to gather macOS configuration information. System Information displays information and options for repair and warranty coverage of your Mac. In this exercise, you explore its features.

Use About This Mac and System Information

1   From the Apple menu, choose About This Mac.

A dialog appears showing basic information about your Mac.

2   Highlight your serial number, and copy using Command-C.

3 Click the macOS version number (below the large "macOS Mojave"). The build number (a more specific identifier for the version of macOS you are using) is displayed.

4 Click through the Displays, Storage, and (if it is shown) Memory buttons in the About This Mac window toolbar to view more information about your hardware configuration.

5 Click Service.

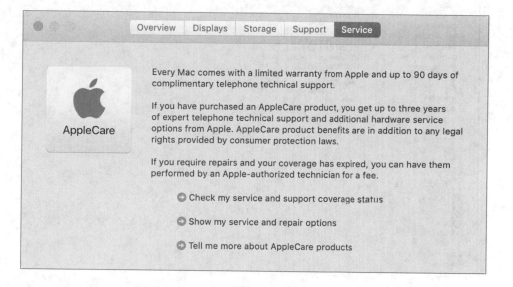

6 Click "Check my service and support coverage status."

7 In the confirmation dialog that appears, click Allow.

Safari opens and displays a coverage check page at apple.com

8 Paste your serial number, enter the CAPTCHA challenge code, and click Continue.

The coverage page shows your Mac model name and warranty status.

9 Quit Safari.

10 In the About This Mac window, click Overview in the toolbar.

11 Click the System Report button.

System Information opens and displays a more detailed report about your Mac hardware, network, and software configuration. You can also find System Information in the /Applications/Utilities/ folder or in the Other section of Launchpad. You can directly access System Information from the Apple menu by holding the Option key. This changes the About This Mac menu choice to System Information.

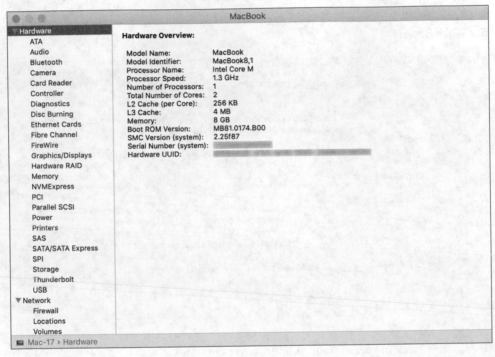

12 Click information categories in the report sidebar to explore the system. Some categories might take a while to load.

13 From the menu bar, choose File > Save, enter a name for your report, and click Save.

When you save reports like this, choose a naming convention that includes the Mac name (or other identifier) and the date.

System Information finishes gathering information about your Mac and saves it in a report that documents your Mac computer's current status.

14 Quit System Information.

Lesson 4

Use the Command-Line Interface

Use the command-line interface (CLI) to access additional administrative functionality.

Reference 4.1
CLI Basics

The CLI includes these advantages:

- Additional administrative and troubleshooting options are available from the CLI. For example, the following apps have CLI equivalents that include additional options: System Information (system_profiler), Installer (installer), Software Update (softwareupdate), Disk Utility (diskutil), and Spotlight (mdfind). These are just a few instances, as nearly every administrative function has both a graphical and a command-line tool.

- From the CLI you have more access to the file system. For example, the Finder hides many files and folders that are visible in the CLI. Also, there are many file-system permissions settings that the Finder doesn't display.

- You can remotely log in to a Mac computer's CLI using the Secure Shell (SSH) protocol. This remote access allows administrators to make changes at the command line without alerting the user to their work.

- By using the sudo command, any administrator can run commands as the System Administrator user, also known as root. This enables great administrative flexibility in the CLI. Read Reference 7.1, "User Accounts," for more information about the root account.

GOALS

- Describe when the command-line interface is useful

- Use man (manual) pages to find more information about commands

- Manipulate files in the command-line interface

▶ If you are comfortable with the CLI syntax, you can apply it to a command-line script. This enables you to automate repetitive tasks.

▶ If you combine CLI instructions with Apple Remote Desktop (ARD), you can remotely administer multiple, even thousands, of Mac computers simultaneously. ARD enables you to remotely send the same command to many Mac computers with one click. For more information about Apple Remote Desktop, go to www.apple.com/remotedesktop.

Access the CLI

A shell is the first command that runs when you access the CLI. It displays the CLI. You can access the CLI in several ways:

▶ You can use Terminal. It's in /Applications/Utilities/Terminal. Terminal has a customizable interface. It includes a tabbed interface for multiple command-line sessions, multiple split panes for viewing history, support for full-screen mode, and Touch Bar shortcuts.

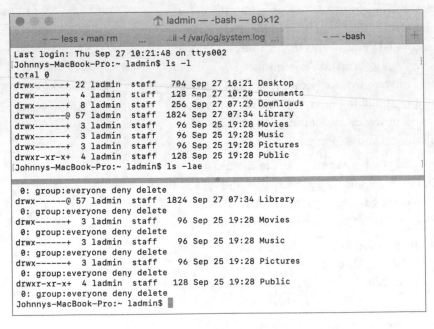

▶ At startup, press and hold Command-S to start a Mac that does not have the Apple T2 Security Chip in single-user mode. This mode starts the minimum system required to provide you with a command-line prompt so that you can enter commands to repair a Mac that can't fully start up. Read more about single-user mode in Lesson 28, "Troubleshoot Startup and System Issues."

▶ SSH remote login enables you to securely log in from a remote computer to access your Mac computer's command line. SSH is a common standard, so you can use any operating system that supports SSH to remotely log in to your Mac.

Work in the Command Line

The first thing you'll see at the command line is the prompt. The prompt indicates that you can enter a command. By default, the prompt shows you the name of the Mac you're using, followed by where you are in the file system, followed by your current user account name, and ending with a $. The $ at the end of the prompt indicates that you're using the standard Bash shell. Where you are in the computer's file system is called the working directory, and it changes as you navigate through the file system.

At the prompt you enter your command string, often more than one word, and press Return to initiate or execute the command. An executing command will take over the Terminal window with a text interface, show the results of the command and return to the prompt, or perform some work and return to the prompt when complete. Many commands display results only if a problem occurs. Read what the command returns to make sure it doesn't indicate a problem.

Some commands take time to execute and may not give a progress indication. If you don't see a new prompt, generally assume your last command is still running.

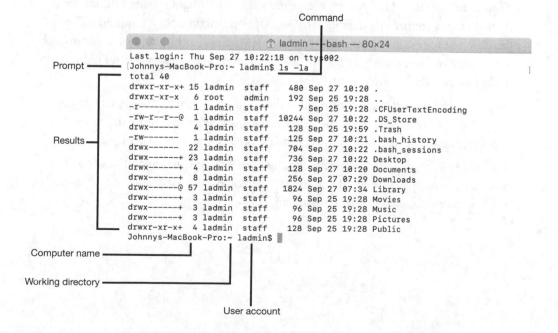

Command String

The command string includes a few parts:

1—Command Name	In this example the "ls" command displays a list of a folder's contents.
2—Command Options	Options add conditions, limits, or other modifiers to the command.
3—Arguments	This is the recipient of the action, often specified as a file or folder path.
4—Extras	Redirected output, or other commands, as needed. In this example a text file is created from the list output.

▶ **Command name (1)**—Some commands just need you to enter their name to execute.

▶ **Command options (2)**—After a command name, you might specify options (or flags) that change a command's default behavior. Options might not be required and can be different for every command. Options start with one or two dashes to distinguish them from arguments. Many commands can include several single-letter options after a single dash. For example, ls -lA is the same as ls -l -A.

▶ **Arguments (3)**—After the command and its options, you typically specify an argument (or parameter), which is the item or items you want the command to modify. An argument is needed only if the command requires an item to act upon.

▶ **Extras (4)**—Extras aren't necessary, but they can enhance the capabilities of a command. For example, you could add items that redirect the command output, include other commands, or generate a document.

Command-Line Example

Here is an example in which the user Joan works on a Mac called MyMac and her working directory is Documents. She deletes an app called Junk inside the /Applications folder. Joan presses Return after she enters her command.

> MyMac:Documents **joan$ rm -R /Applications/Junk.app**
>
> MyMac:Documents joan$

In this example the command was entered and executed properly, and macOS returns to a new prompt. This is an example of a command that returns information only if it didn't execute properly. The Mac will usually let you know if you entered something incorrectly by returning an error message or help text. macOS won't prevent or warn you from entering a destructive command, such as accidentally deleting your home folder. Always double-check your typing.

Use Manual (man) Pages

When you want to learn more about a command, you enter **man** followed by the name of the command. Manual (man) pages include detailed information about commands and references to other commands. After you open a man page, use navigation shortcuts to move through it:

- ► Use the Up Arrow and Down Arrow keys to scroll.
- ► Use the Space bar to move down one screen at a time.
- ► Enter a slash (/) and a keyword to search through a man page.
- ► Exit the man page by typing **q**.

If you don't know the name of the command you're looking for, enter **man -k** and a keyword to search the database. For example, you enter **man -k owner** to return a short list of commands used for changing file and folder ownership, including the command chown.

Enter the **apropos** command and a search term like **network**, and commands that are related to network are displayed.

Reference 4.2
CLI Navigation

The command line is case-sensitive and requires that you use full filenames with filename extensions. For example, the CLI won't locate the "itunes" app, but it will locate the "iTunes.app" app.

A path represents a file or folder's location in the file system. For instance, Disk Utility's file system path is /Applications/Utilities/Disk Utility.app. In the CLI, you use the path-name to navigate through the file system and to identify the location of items.

There are two types of file-system pathnames:

▶ **Absolute** pathnames are full descriptions of an item location, starting from the root (or beginning) of the system (startup) volume. An absolute path begins with a forward slash (/) to indicate the beginning of the file system. An example of the absolute path to the user Joan's drop box folder is /Users/joan/Public/Drop Box, which means: Start from the startup volume; go to the Users folder, then to the joan subfolder, and then to the Public subfolder; and select the item named Drop Box.

▶ **Relative** paths are partial descriptions of an item location. They're based on where you're currently working in the file system. When you first open Terminal, your session starts at your home folder. The relative path from your home folder to your drop box is Public/Drop Box. This means: From where you are now, go into the Public subfolder, and select the item named Drop Box.

Navigate with Commands

You use three commands to navigate the file system: pwd, ls, and cd. Short for "print working directory," pwd reports the absolute path of your current working location:

```
MyMac:~ joan$ pwd
/Users/joan
```

Short for "list," ls lists the folder contents of your current working location. Enter a pathname following the ls command to list the contents of the specified item. The ls command has additional options for listing file and folder information that are covered throughout this lesson.

Short for "change directory," cd is the command you use to navigate. Enter a pathname following the cd command to change your current working location to the specified folder. Entering cd without specifying a path returns you to your home folder.

Use Special Characters

You can use special characters at the prompt or in pathnames to save time and to be able to use special characters in filenames and pathnames.

Enter a space between command items to separate the items. If you don't want the space character to separate items, use the backslash (\) before a space character.

> MyMac:~ joan$ **cd Public/Drop\ Box**
>
> MyMac:Drop Box joan$ **pwd**
>
> /Users/joan/Public/Drop Box

Another way to enter filenames and paths with spaces is to surround filenames and paths with quotation marks:

> MyMac:~ joan$ **cd "Public/Drop Box"**
>
> MyMac:Drop Box joan$ **pwd**
>
> /Users/joan/Public/Drop Box

You can drag and drop items from the Finder to Terminal. When you do this, Terminal enters an item's absolute path with the appropriate backslash characters before spaces in names. Use the Tab key completion feature that's built into the command line to automatically complete filenames and pathnames.

Other special characters include !, $, &, *, ;, |, \, parentheses, quotes, and brackets. The Finder drag-and-drop and Tab key completion parse these characters. In the CLI you can enter a backslash before any special character to treat that special character as regular text rather than as a special character.

Use double periods (..) to indicate a parent folder. For example, if you are in your home folder at /Users/*username*, enter **cd ..** to navigate to the /Users folder.

Use the tilde (~) to indicate the current user home folder in a pathname. For example, say the current user's drop box is in ~/Public/. Use the tilde to specify another user's home folder. For example, **~jill/Public** specifies Jill's Public folder.

Use Tab Key Completion

Use Tab key completion to automatically complete filenames, pathnames, and command names. Tab key completion prevents you from making typos and verifies that the item you're entering exists.

Here's an example of Tab key completion. Start from your home folder by entering **cd**, then **P**, and then press the Tab key. The Terminal window will flash quickly and you may hear an audible alert, letting you know there is more than one choice for items that begin with "P" in your home folder. Press the Tab key again, and the Mac will display your two choices, Pictures and Public. Now, enter **u** after the initial P, and then press the Tab key again, and the Mac will automatically finish Public/ for you. Finally, enter **D** and press the Tab key one last time, and the computer will finish the path with Public/Drop\ Box/.

When completing a folder name, Tab key completion puts a forward slash (/) at the end. It assumes that you want to continue the path. Most commands ignore the trailing slash, but a few behave differently if it's there. You should delete the / at the end of a path.

Tab key completion reads only into folders you have permission to access. You might run into issues trying to use this feature for items that are readable only by a root user.

View Invisible Items

The CLI and the Finder hide many files and folders from view. The hidden items are often macOS support items. In the Finder, these items are set with a hidden file flag. The CLI ignores the hidden file flag and shows most hidden items. If you enter the **ls** command, you won't see filenames that begin with a period. To see hidden items in long format at the command line, add the **-a** option to the **-l** option when you enter the **ls** command:

```
MyMac:~ joan$ ls -la
total 16
drwxr-xr-x+ 14 joan staff  448 Oct 26 01:06 .
drwxr-xr-x  5 root  admin  160 Oct 26 00:54 ..
-r--------  1 joan staff    7 Oct 26 00:54 .CFUserTextEncoding
drwx------  5 joan staff  160 Oct 26 01:06 .Trash
-rw-------  1 joan staff  139 Oct 26 01:06 .bash_history
drwx------  6 joan staff  192 Oct 26 11:29 .bash_sessions
drwx------+ 4 joan staff  128 Oct 26 01:06 Desktop
drwx------+ 3 joan staff   96 Oct 26 00:54 Documents
drwx------+ 3 joan staff   96 Oct 26 00:54 Downloads
drwx------@ 54 joan staff 1728 Oct 26 09:17 Library
drwx------+ 3 joan staff   96 Oct 26 00:54 Movies
```

```
drwx------+ 3 joan staff  96 Oct 26 00:54 Music

drwx------+ 3 joan staff  96 Oct 26 00:54 Pictures

drwxr-xr-x+ 4 joan staff  128 Oct 26 00:54 Public
```

Any item with a period at the beginning of its name is hidden by default in the CLI and the Finder. These items are created and used by macOS. Leave them alone.

Navigate to Other Volumes

In the CLI, the system volume is also known as the root volume, and it's identified by a lone forward slash. Other nonroot volumes appear as part of the main file system in the Volumes folder.

Use Marks and Bookmarks

Add marks and bookmarks as you work; then use them to quickly navigate through lengthy Terminal output.

Select a line in Terminal, then choose Edit > Marks > Mark to add a mark. By default, Mark > Automatically Mark Prompt Lines is selected, so each prompt line sets a mark. Then you can choose Edit > Select Between Marks, or choose Edit > Navigate > Jump to Previous Mark, or just press Command-Up Arrow.

Choose Edit > Marks > Mark as Bookmark to add a bookmark. Then choose Edit > Bookmarks to see a list of bookmarks. Choose a bookmark to jump to that bookmark.

Reference 4.3
Manipulate Files in the CLI

When you manage and edit files in the CLI, you have more options—and more chances to make mistakes.

File Examination Commands

Use the cat, less, file, and find commands to locate and examine files. Read the man pages for these commands to find out more about them.

Short for concatenate, the cat command displays a file sequentially to Terminal. The syntax is cat, followed by the path to the item you want to view. Use the cat command to append to text files using the >> redirect operator. In the following example, Joan uses the cat command to view the content of two text files in her Desktop folder, TextDocOne.txt and TextDocTwo.txt. Then she uses the cat command with the >> redirect operator to append the second text file to the end of the first text file.

MyMac:~ joan$ **cat Desktop/TextDocOne.txt**

This is the content of the first plain text document.

MyMac:~ joan$ **cat Desktop/TextDocTwo.txt**

This is the content of the second plain text document.

MyMac:~ joan$ **cat Desktop/TextDocTwo.txt >> Desktop/TextDocOne.txt**

MyMac:~ joan$ **cat Desktop/TextDocOne.txt**

This is the content of the first plain text document.

This is the content of the second plain text document.

Use the less command to view long text files. It enables you to browse and search the text. Enter **less**, followed by the path to the item you want to view. The less interface is the same interface you use to view man pages, so the navigation shortcuts are the same.

The file command determines a file type based on its content. This is useful for identifying files that don't have a filename extension. The syntax is file, followed by the path to the file you're trying to identify. In the following example, Joan uses the file command to locate the file type of two documents in her Desktop folder: PictureDocument and TextDocument:

MyMac:~ joan$ **ls Desktop/**

PictureDocument.tiff TextDocument.txt

MyMac:~ joan$ **file Desktop/PictureDocument**

Desktop/PictureDocument.tiff: TIFF image data, big-endian

MyMac:~ joan$ **file Desktop/TextDocument**

Desktop/TextDocument.txt: ASCII English text

Use the find command to locate items based on search criteria. The find command doesn't use Spotlight, but it does enable you to set search criteria and use filename wildcards. (Filename wildcards are covered in the next section.) The syntax is find, followed by the beginning path of the search, then an option defining your search criteria, and then the search criteria within quotation marks. In the following example, Joan uses the find command to locate picture files with a .tiff filename extension in her home folder by searching only for files with names that end in .tiff:

MyMac:~ joan$ **find /Users/joan -name "*.tiff"**

/Users/joan/Pictures/FamilyPict.tiff

/Users/joan/Pictures/MyPhoto.tiff

When you use the find command to start a search at the root of the system drive, you should also use the -x option to avoid searching the /Volumes folder.

To use Spotlight from the command line, enter the mdfind command. The syntax is mdfind followed by your search criteria.

Use Wildcard Characters

You can use wildcard characters to define pathname and search criteria. Here are three of the most common wildcards:

▶ Use the asterisk (*) wildcard to match any string of characters. For instance, entering * matches all files, and entering ***.tiff** matches all files that end in .tiff.

▶ Use the question mark (?) wildcard to match a single character. For example, entering **b?ok** matches book but not brook.

▶ Use square brackets ([ ]) to define a range of characters. For example, **[Dd]ocument** locates items named Document or document, and **doc[1-9]** matches files named doc#, where # is a number between 1 and 9.

You can combine filename wildcards. Consider a collection of five files with the names ReadMe.rtf, ReadMe.txt, read.rtf, read.txt, and It's All About Me.rtf. Using wildcards to specify these files:

▶ ***.rtf** matches ReadMe.rtf, read.rtf, and It's All About Me.rtf

▶ **????.*** matches read.rtf and read.txt

▶ **[Rr]*.rtf** matches ReadMe.rtf and read.rtf

▶ **[A-Z].*** matches ReadMe.rtf, ReadMe.txt, and It's All About Me.rtf

Use Recursive Commands

When you direct a command to execute a task on an item, it touches only the item you specify. If the item you specify is a folder, the command won't navigate inside the folder to execute the command on the enclosed items. If you want a command to execute on a folder and its contents, you must tell the command to run recursively. Recursive means "Execute the task on every item inside every folder starting from the path I specify." Many commands accept -r or -R as the option to indicate that you want the command to run recursively.

Modify Files and Folders

The mkdir, touch, cp, mv, rm, rmdir, vi, and nano commands enable you to modify files and folders.

Short for "make directory," mkdir is used to create folders. The syntax is mkdir, followed by the paths of the folders you want to create. The –p option tells mkdir to create intermediate folders if they don't already exist in the paths you specify. In the following example, Joan uses the mkdir command with the -p option to create a folder called Private with two folders inside it called Stocks and Bonds:

MyMac:~ joan$ **mkdir -p Private/Stocks Private/Bonds**

Use the touch command to update the modification date of a specified item. The touch command creates an empty file if it doesn't exist.

Use the cp (copy) command to copy items from one place to another. The syntax is cp, followed by the path to the original item, ending with the destination path for the copy. If you specify a destination folder but no filename, cp makes a copy of the file with the same name as the original. If you specify a destination filename but not a destination folder, cp makes a copy in your current working folder. Unlike the Finder, the cp command won't warn you if your copy replaces an existing file. It deletes the existing file and replaces it with the copy you told it to create.

Use the mv (move) command to move items from one place to another. The syntax is mv, followed by the path to the original item, ending with the new destination path for the item. The mv command uses the same destination rules as the cp command.

Use the rm (remove) command to permanently delete items. There is no Trash in the CLI. The rm command removes items forever. The syntax is rm, followed by the paths of the items you wish to delete.

Use rmdir (remove directory) to permanently delete folders. The rmdir command removes folders forever. The syntax is rmdir, followed by the paths of the folders you want to delete. The rmdir command can remove a folder only if it's empty. You can use the rm command with the recursive option, -R, to remove a folder and all its contents.

Use the vi (visual) command to edit files in the CLI. vi is one of several built-in text editors in the CLI. Enter **vi** and the pathname to a file to edit it. macOS redirects vi to a newer version, vim. For basic functions you probably won't notice the difference. Like the less command, vi takes over the Terminal window with the contents of the text file. When you first open vi, it's in command mode and you must type predefined characters to tell vi which operation you want to complete. Use the arrow keys to browse a file in command mode. Enter the letter **a** to begin editing the text. In command mode, vi inserts new text wherever the cursor is. Use the arrow keys to move the cursor keys. Press the Esc (Escape) key to reenter vi command mode. After you're in command mode, enter **zz** to save changes and quit vi.

The text editor nano features a list of commonly used keyboard shortcut commands at the bottom of the screen.

Reference 4.4
Manage macOS from the CLI

In this section, you look at commands that enable you to access items normally restricted by file-system permissions.

Use the su (substitute user identity or super user) command to switch to another user account. Enter **su** followed by the short name of the user you want to switch to and enter the account password. The password won't display. The command prompt changes, indicating that you have the access privileges of a different user. Enter **who –m** to verify your currently logged-in identity. You remain logged in as the substitute user until you quit Terminal or enter the exit command. In the following example, Joan uses the su command to change her shell to Johnny's account, and then she will exit back to her account:

```
MyMac:~ joan$ who -m
joan ttys001 Aug 20 14:06
MyMac:~ joan$ su johnny
Password:
bash-3.2$ who -m
johnny ttys001 Aug 20 14:06
bash-3.2$ exit
exit
MyMac:~ joan$ who -m
joan ttys001 Aug 20 14:06
```

Use sudo

Precede a command with sudo (substitute user do) to tell macOS to run the command using root account access. You must have an administrator user account to use sudo. sudo works even when the root user account is disabled in the graphical interface. Be careful with sudo and limit access to it.

System Integrity Protection (SIP) prevents changes to parts of macOS, even for the root user. Read Reference 15.2, "System Integrity Protection," for more information about the specific resources that are protected.

If, as an administrator user, you need to execute more than one command with root account access, you can temporarily switch the entire command-line shell to have root level access. Enter **sudo -i** and your password to switch the shell to root access. You remain logged in as the root user until you quit Terminal or enter the **exit** command.

Reference 4.5
Command-Line Tips and Tricks

Here are some command-line tips that help you customize your experience and save time:

► Control-click a command and choose Open man Page to read more about that command.

► If your Mac has a Touch Bar, type a command and press the button for that command in the Touch Bar to view the man page. The figure shows the Touch Bar displaying a button for the **defaults** command man page.

► Use Tab key completion when you enter file paths.

► Drag and drop files and folders from the Finder to Terminal to automatically enter their locations at the command line.

► Type **open .** ("open" followed by a space, followed by a period) at the prompt to open your current command-line location in the Finder.

► Explore Terminal preferences (from the menu bar, choose Terminal > Preferences or press Command-Comma) to customize the look and feel of your command line.

▶ To cancel a command or clear your current command entry, use Control-C.

▶ You can edit commands before submitting. The Left and Right Arrow keys and the Delete key work as you would expect.

▶ At the command prompt, use the Up Arrow and Down Arrow keys to view and reuse your command history. This includes editing old commands before rerunning them. Enter the history command to see your recent command history.

▶ To clear the Terminal screen, enter the **clear** command or press Control-L.

▶ To move the cursor to the beginning of the current line, press Control-A.

▶ To move the cursor to the end of the current line, press Control-E.

▶ To move the cursor forward one word, press Esc-F.

▶ To move the cursor back one word of the line, press Esc-B.

▶ To move the cursor to a location in a command string, Option-click where you'd like the cursor to be.

▶ Use the inspector to view and manage running processes, and edit window titles and background colors. To open the inspector, press Command-I. To send a command to a process, select it, click the action pop-up menu, then choose a command from the Signal Process Group.

For more information about Terminal, read Terminal Help at support.apple.com/guide/terminal/welcome.

Exercise 4.1
Command-Line Navigation

▶ **Prerequisite**

▶ You must have created the Local Administrator account (Exercise 3.1, "Configure a Mac for Exercises").

In this exercise, you use commands to navigate the file system, to view items that aren't visible from the Finder, and to access the manual (man) pages that tell you about commands.

View Your Home Folder

1   If necessary, log in as Local Administrator.

2   Click Launchpad in the Dock.

3   In the Search field at the top of the screen, enter Terminal.

4   Click Terminal.

A new Terminal window opens.

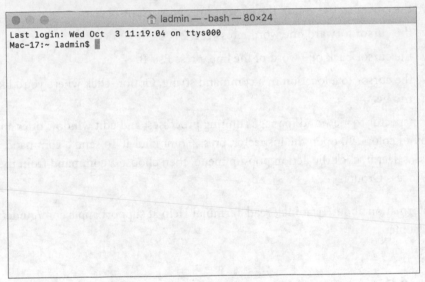

The second line you see includes your computer and user name followed by a prompt—for example:

`Mac-17:~ ladmin$`

In this example, Mac-17 is the name of the Mac you logged in to. The colon separates the computer name from the path to your current working directory. The path is ~ (the tilde [~] is shorthand for your home folder). After the space, you see the name of the logged-in user. The $ is the prompt.

5   At the prompt, type **ls** and press Return.

You will see output that looks something like this, followed by another prompt:

Desktop	Downloads	Movies	Pictures
Documents	Library	Music	Public

6   Switch to the Finder. If you don't see a Finder window that's open, go to File > New Finder Window or press Command-N.

7   Select ladmin's home folder in the Finder sidebar and compare the contents of the home folder in the Finder and Terminal.

With the exception of the Library folder, what you see in Terminal is the same as in the Finder. (User Library folders are hidden in the Finder by default; see Reference 14.1, "Examine Hidden Items.")

8   Switch back to Terminal and type **ls -A** (lowercase LS followed by space, a hyphen, and an uppercase A) at the prompt.

In general, the command-line environment is case-sensitive. For example, **ls –a** isn't the same as **ls -A**.

You will see some extra files in the list that begin with a period. Files beginning with a period are hidden in directory listings unless you ask for them by entering **ls -A**. The Finder doesn't show files beginning with a period (sometimes called dot-files).

Examine and Change Your Current Working Directory

Think of your current working directory as the place you are in the file system. When you open a new Terminal window, your default working directory is your home folder. Use the cd command to change your current working directory.

1   At the prompt, type **pwd**.

The period (.) ends the sentence and isn't part of the command, so don't type it. This book tells you if a trailing "." is part of the command. Also, press Return at the end of each step, unless otherwise instructed.

You will see:

/Users/ladmin

This is where Local Administrator's home folder exists in the file system. It's the folder you're "in" in this Terminal window.

2   At the prompt, type **cd Library**.

This changes your current working directory to the Library folder inside your home folder.

This command uses a relative path. A relative path means "Start in my current working directory."

Your prompt changes to something like this:

Mac-17:Library ladmin$

The path component of the prompt indicates the folder you are in, not the entire path.

The cd command changed your working directory without providing feedback. A command that completes and doesn't need to provide feedback will exit silently. If you get an error message, you should investigate its cause before continuing.

3   At the prompt, type **pwd**. Terminal displays:

/Users/ladmin/Library

You changed to the Library folder that was inside your previous working directory.

4   Type **ls** to view what files and folders are in this Library folder.

5   At the prompt, type **cd /Library**. Note the / that precedes Library this time.

6   At the prompt, type **pwd**. You will see output like this:

/Library

This is a different folder.

A path that starts with a leading / is an absolute path. It means "Start at the root folder and navigate from there." A path that doesn't start with a leading / is a relative path. It means "Start in your current working directory and navigate from there." For more information on file system structure, see Reference 15.1, "macOS File Resources.")

7   Enter **ls** to view the files and folders that are in this Library folder.

There is some overlap in the item names in this Library and the one in ladmin's home folder, but the names aren't entirely the same.

8   At the prompt, type **cd** and a space character. Don't press the Return key.

Terminal enables you to drag and drop items from the Finder to Terminal and have the path to the items appear in the command line.

In this part of the exercise, you use the Finder to locate a folder you want to use as your working directory in Terminal.

9   Switch to the Finder.

When you don't know exactly what you are looking for, it's sometimes faster and easier to find a file or folder in the Finder.

10 Open a new Finder window if necessary.

11 Click Macintosh HD in the sidebar.

12 Open the Users folder.

13 Drag and drop the Shared folder to Terminal.

Terminal fills in the path (/Users/Shared). Macintosh HD doesn't appear in the path that Terminal fills in.

The Finder shows you volume names to make locating a particular volume easier. Terminal doesn't show volume names in the same way.

14 Switch to Terminal and press Return.

15 Type **pwd** at the prompt.

You are in the Shared folder.

Read About ls in the Man Pages

In Terminal, you can read the details about commands using the man command.

1 Open Terminal.

2 At the prompt, type **man ls**.

This opens the man page for the ls command.

Each man page is divided into various parts. The number in parentheses on the top line indicates in which section of the manual this command is documented. In this case, ls is documented in section 1, which is for general-use commands. Next you see the name of the command and a terse summary of what the command does: "list directory contents." The synopsis is supposed to be a formal representation of how to use the command. Anything contained in square brackets is optional. The synopsis isn't always completely accurate. For example, a few options for ls are mutually exclusive of each other, but this synopsis does not indicate that. Options or switches (which change the behavior of a command) immediately follow the command, and arguments (which tell the command what to operate on) follow options or switches. The description, which describes the various uses of the command, follows the synopsis.

3 Type **q** to quit viewing the man page for ls.

4 At the prompt, enter **man man**.

5   Read about the man command.

You can also Control-click, or on a MacBook Pro with Touch Bar, tap the icon for a man page to open it.

6   When you are done, type **q** to exit.

Exercise 4.2
Manage Files and Folders with Commands

▶ **Prerequisite**

▶   You must have created the Local Administrator account (Exercise 3.1, "Configure a Mac for Exercises").

In this exercise, you learn to copy, move, rename, and delete files and folders with commands.

Create Files

1   If you aren't logged in as Local Administrator, log in now.

2   Open TextEdit.

TextEdit is in your Dock if you performed Exercise 3.3, "Download Participant Materials." If it isn't in your Dock, you can find it in /Applications.

3   In the TextEdit menu bar, choose Format > Make Plain Text, or press Command-Shift-T.

4   Add the following names to the yet Untitled (default) TextEdit document:

MacBook

MacBook Air

MacBook Pro

iMac

iMac Pro

Mac Pro

Mac mini

iPhone

iPad

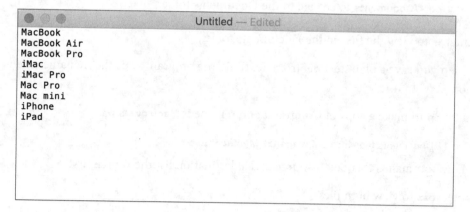

5 From the TextEdit menu bar, choose File > Save and name the document **Comps**.

Leave the document in the Documents folder.

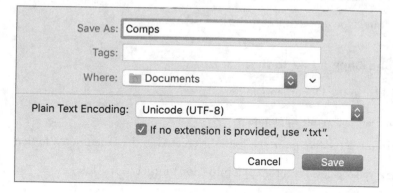

6 Close the Comps.txt document window.

7 Open a new document in TextEdit and change the format to Plain Text.

8 Save and name the new document **Empty**. Leave the document in the Documents folder.

9 Quit TextEdit.

Copy and Move Files and Create a Folder

1   Switch to or open Terminal.

2   Enter **cd ~/Documents** to change to the Documents folder.

3   Enter **ls** to view the files in the Documents folder.

When you save a plain text file from TextEdit, the program adds the filename extension ".txt" to it.

4   Enter **cp** to make a copy of Comps.txt and rename it **MacModels.txt**.

Mac-17:Documents ladmin$ **cp Comps.txt MacModels.txt**

Many commands that take a source and a destination list the source first.

5   Enter **less** to view both files.

MacModels.txt is an exact copy of Comps.txt.

Mac-17:Documents ladmin$ **less MacModels.txt**

Mac-17:Documents ladmin$ **less Comps.txt**

6   When you are done, type **q** to exit.

Create a Folder and Copy a File to It

1   Create a new folder in the Documents folder:

Mac-17:Documents ladmin$ **mkdir AppleInfo**

Because AppleInfo is a relative path, the folder is created in the Documents folder.

2   Enter **cp** to copy MacModels.txt into AppleInfo (don't forget to try Tab key completion):

Mac-17:Documents ladmin$ **cp MacModels.txt AppleInfo**

3   Enter **ls** to view the contents of AppleInfo:

Mac-17:Documents ladmin$ **ls AppleInfo**

Fix a Naming Error

The text list in MacModels.txt includes a couple of items that are not technically Mac computers. Let's rename the file and clean up the extra copies.

1   Remove the Comps.txt file from the Documents folder and the MacModels.txt file from the AppleInfo folder:

▶   Mac-17:Documents ladmin$ **rm Comps.txt AppleInfo/MacModels.txt**

You entered the command once to delete both files. The command line doesn't have an undo function. Any change you make is permanent.

2   Move the MacModels.txt file into the AppleInfo folder using the **mv** command:

▶   Mac-17:Documents ladmin$ **mv MacModels.txt AppleInfo**

3   Enter **cd** to change your working directory to AppleInfo.

4   Enter **mv** to rename the MacModels.txt file to AppleHardware.txt.

Mac-17:AppleInfo ladmin$ **mv MacModels.txt AppleHardware.txt**

You can also move and rename a file in one command:

$ mv MacModels.txt AppleInfo/AppleHardware.txt

Remove a Folder

1   Change your working directory back to the Documents folder. You can do so in one of three ways:

▶   Use the absolute path /Users/ladmin/Documents.

▶   Use the home folder shortcut ~/Documents.

▶   Use the relative path (..).

The .. notation refers to the parent directory of the current directory. Because your current working directory is /Users/ladmin/Documents/AppleInfo, .. refers to /Users/ladmin/Documents.

Occasionally, you see the .. notation in the middle of a path instead of at the beginning—for example, /Users/ladmin/Documents/../Desktop. It still has the same meaning, so in this example, it refers to Local Administrator's Desktop folder.

Similarly, a single . refers to the current directory or location in the path.

Each directory contains a reference to both itself and its parent. These are visible if you use ls -a (note the lowercase a instead of the uppercase A you used previously).

2   Move the AppleHardware.txt file to Documents and rename it **AppleHardwareInfo.txt**.

Don't press the Return key until you enter AppleHardwareInfo.txt.

Mac-17:Documents ladmin$ **mv AppleInfo/AppleHardware.txt AppleHardwareInfo.txt**

The path AppleHardwareInfo.txt is relative to your current working directory, so this step moves AppleInfo/AppleHardware.txt to the current working directory (Documents) and renames it AppleHardwareInfo.txt.

3 Enter **rmdir** to remove the AppleInfo directory:

Mac-17:Documents ladmin$ **rmdir AppleInfo**

rmdir succeeds because AppleInfo is empty. rmdir removes only folders that are empty. Enter **rm –r** to remove a folder that contains files:

Mac-17:Documents ladmin$ **rm -r AppleInfo**

Create and Edit a Text File

macOS includes several command-line text editors. In this exercise, you use the nano editor to create and edit a file.

1 Enter **nano** to create a new file named fruit.txt:

Mac-17:Documents ladmin$ **nano fruit.txt**

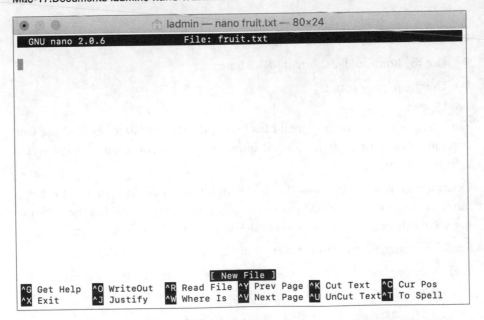

2 Enter the following words in the file on separate lines. Press Return at the end of each line.

     apple

     pineapple

     grapefruit

     pear

     banana

     blueberry

     strawberry

3 Press and hold the Control key and press and release X (Control-X) to quit nano.

You'll see "Save modified buffer (ANSWERING 'No' WILL DESTROY CHANGES)?"

4 Enter **Y**.

You'll see "File Name to Write: fruit.txt."

5 Press Return.

nano saves your file in the Documents folder inside your home folder, or ~/Documents, and exits, returning you to the prompt.

6 Quit Terminal.

Lesson 5

Use macOS Recovery

One of the most useful macOS features for troubleshooting is macOS Recovery. You can use macOS Recovery to reinstall macOS and also access administration and troubleshooting utilities. macOS Recovery is on the primary system disk. This gives you easy access to recovery utilities without the need for additional media.

In this lesson, you learn how to access macOS Recovery. You also explore the utilities available from macOS Recovery. Finally, you learn how to create an external macOS install disk that you can use when local macOS Recovery isn't available.

GOALS

▶ Access macOS Recovery utilities

▶ Reinstall macOS from macOS Recovery

▶ Create an external macOS Recovery disk

Reference 5.1
Start Up from macOS Recovery

Mac computers running macOS Mojave include a hidden macOS Recovery system on the local system disk. This built-in recovery system doesn't appear in Disk Utility or in the Finder when a Mac is running macOS.

Start macOS Recovery from the Built-In Recovery System

To start up from macOS Recovery, restart or turn on your Mac, and then immediately press and hold Command-R. Release the keys when you see the Apple logo, a spinning globe, or a prompt for a firmware password. When you see the macOS Utilities window, you've started up from macOS Recovery.

After macOS Recovery fully starts, the macOS Utilities window appears. From there you can install, reinstall, or upgrade macOS and choose from a variety of maintenance apps.

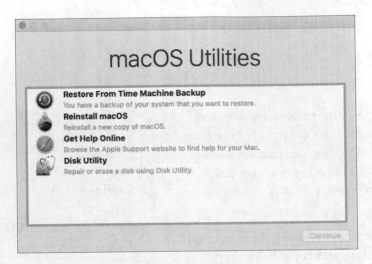

If macOS Recovery doesn't start or isn't installed on the local system disk, you have some alternatives for accessing it.

Start macOS Recovery over the Internet

If the local built-in recovery system is missing, some Mac computers automatically attempt to access macOS Recovery over the Internet. This applies to Mac computers released in mid-2010 or later with available firmware updates installed.

macOS Recovery installs different versions of macOS depending on the key combination you use while starting up. Turn on or restart your Mac, and then immediately press and hold one of these combinations:

▶ Command-R—Install the latest macOS that was installed on your Mac, without upgrading to a later version.

▶ Option-Command-R—Upgrade to the latest macOS that is compatible with your Mac. If you haven't already updated to macOS Sierra 10.12.4 or later, Option-Command-R installs the macOS that came with your Mac, or the version closest to it that is still available.

▶ Option-Shift-Command-R—Install the macOS that came with your Mac, or the version closest to it that is still available. If you haven't already updated to macOS Sierra 10.12.4 or later, Option-Shift-Command-R is not available.

If successful, this process re-creates the local built-in recovery system. Read Apple Support article HT204904, "How to reinstall macOS from macOS Recovery," for more information about the differences in the key combinations.

Read Apple Support article HT201314, "About macOS Recovery," for more details about macOS Recovery.

Start macOS Recovery from a Time Machine Disk

Time Machine backup service automatically creates a hidden recovery system on external storage devices used for Time Machine backup disks. To access macOS Recovery, connect the Time Machine external storage device to your Mac, and then start up or restart while you press and hold the Option key. This opens the Mac computer's Startup Manager, where you can use the arrow and Return keys or the mouse or trackpad to select the Time Machine external storage device. Lesson 17, "Manage Time Machine," covers this topic in greater detail.

Start macOS Recovery from an external disk

If your Mac cannot connect to the Internet to use macOS Recovery over the Internet, you can use another Mac to create an installer on an external disk. Read Reference 5.3, "Create a macOS Recovery Disk," for more information.

Reference 5.2
macOS Recovery Utilities

When you start up from macOS Recovery, you can access several administration and maintenance utilities.

When you start up from macOS Recovery, you can use Ethernet and Wi-Fi networks if they provide Dynamic Host Configuration Protocol (DHCP) services to automatically configure network settings. macOS automatically enables Ethernet if you connect your Mac to the network with an Ethernet cable. If you don't connect your Mac to the network with an Ethernet cable, macOS should automatically connect to a Wi-Fi network. If it doesn't, select one from the Wi-Fi menu.

From the macOS Utilities window in macOS Recovery, you can access the following functions:

► Restore From Time Machine Backup—Use this option to restore a full Mac Time Machine backup from either a network or a locally connected external storage device. Read Lesson 17 for more information.

- Install macOS or Reinstall macOS—Use this option to open the macOS Installer.

- Get Help Online—This option opens Safari, which takes you to the Apple Support website.

- Disk Utility—Use Disk Utility to manage disks, add, and manage volumes, and manage Redundant Array of Independent Disks (RAID) sets. It's useful when you start up a Mac from macOS Recovery because you can use it to manage a system disk that you can't manage when you use it as a startup disk. You can also use Disk Utility to prepare a disk for a new macOS installation or attempt to repair a disk that fails installation. Read Lesson 11, "Manage File Systems and Storage," for more information.

- Choose Startup Disk (by clicking the close button, quitting, or choosing Startup Disk from the Apple menu)—If you attempt to quit the macOS Utilities window, you see a prompt to click Choose Startup Disk. Use Choose Startup Disk to select the default macOS startup disk. You can override the default startup using the startup modes discussed in Lesson 28, "Troubleshoot Startup and System Issues."

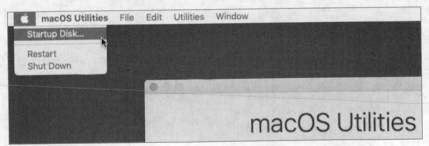

macOS Recovery has a few extra features in the Utilities menu at the top of the screen:

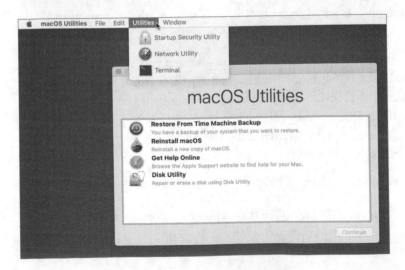

▶ Startup Security Utility—This utility enables you to secure a Mac computer's startup process by disabling alternate startup modes without a password. You can disable or enable this feature and define the required password. If your Mac has an Apple T2 Security Chip, Startup Security Utility offers two additional options. Learn more about firmware passwords in Lesson 10, "Manage Password Changes."

▶ Network Utility—This is the main network and Internet troubleshooting utility in macOS. Use it in macOS Recovery to troubleshoot network issues that could prevent the download of macOS installation assets. Network Utility is further discussed in Lesson 23, "Troubleshoot Network Issues."

▶ Terminal—This is your primary interface to the command-line interface (CLI) of macOS. The most useful command you can enter from here is resetpassword, followed by pressing the Return key. Read Lesson 4, "Use the Command-line Interface," for more information about the CLI.

The resetpassword command enables you to reset the password of any local user account on a selected system disk. This includes standard users, administrator users, and the root user. You can run resetpassword only from macOS Recovery. Find out more about the Reset Password assistant in Lesson 10.

NOTE ▶ macOS Recovery utilities can be used to compromise Mac security. Any Mac with a default startup disk that can be overridden by an unauthorized user during startup isn't secure. Use the Startup Security Utility to help protect your Mac computers. Read Lesson 10 for more information.

Reference 5.3
Create a macOS Recovery Disk

Sometimes a Mac doesn't have a local built-in recovery system. For example, if you replace the internal disk with a new blank disk, nothing is on the new disk. Also, Mac computers on RAID sets and disks with nonstandard Boot Camp partitioning won't have a local built-in recovery system.

macOS Mojave includes a command-line tool, named createinstallmedia, in the macOS Installer (Install macOS Mojave) that converts a standard disk into a macOS Recovery disk. This tool copies a macOS Recovery system and the macOS installation assets to an external storage device. To use createinstallmedia, you must have an external storage device with at least 12 GB available, and it must be formatted as Mac OS Extended. The macOS Installer includes the option—downloadassets to download on-demand assets that may be required for installation. If you don't have a copy of Install macOS Mojave, you can get it from the App Store. When you download macOS Mojave, you download the latest version of Install macOS Mojave that's available. Exercise 5.2, "Create a macOS Install Disk," outlines the steps to create this disk type.

Exercise 5.1
Use macOS Recovery

▶ **Prerequisite**

▶ Your Mac must have a hidden macOS Recovery volume. This volume is created and updated by the macOS Mojave upgrade or installation process.

In this exercise, you start up your Mac in macOS Recovery. You also review the included utilities and how macOS Recovery can reinstall macOS.

NOTE ▶ You won't perform an installation, but you'll get an opportunity to look at the steps leading up to the installation.

Start Up Using macOS Recovery

To access the installer and other utilities in macOS Recovery, start up from macOS Recovery.

1   If your Mac is on, shut it down by choosing Shut Down from the Apple menu.

2   Press the power button on your Mac, press and hold Command-R until the Apple logo appears on the screen, and then release the keys.

   When you press and hold Command-R during startup, the Mac attempts to start up using a recovery partition on the hard disk.

   If macOS Recovery isn't available on your Mac, Mac computers with newer firmware can start up from an Apple server over the Internet and get access to macOS Recovery.

If your Mac doesn't start up to macOS Recovery, you may not have held Command-R long enough. If this happens, click the Shut Down button (at the Login Window) or press Command-Q (at the Setup Assistant) and try again.

3 If a language selection screen appears, select your preferred language and click the right-arrow button.

4 After macOS Recovery starts up, you see macOS Utilities. This window is the primary interface for macOS Recovery.

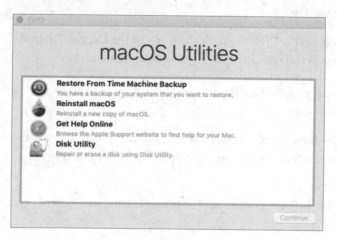

Examine the macOS Recovery Utilities

While using macOS Recovery, you have access to utilities for recovering, repairing, and reinstalling macOS. In this part of the exercise, you get to know some of these utilities.

View macOS Recovery Help

Use Safari to view the built-in instructions for macOS Recovery and to browse the web.

1 Select Get Help Online, and then click Continue.

Safari opens and displays a document with information about how to use macOS Recovery.

2 Read the document.

This document is stored in macOS Recovery, but as long as you have an Internet connection, use Safari to view online documentation such as Apple Support articles.

3 If a dialog indicates that Safari wants to use the login keychain, leave the Password field blank and click OK.

4 Click in the "Search or enter website name" field, enter **apple.com**, and press Return.

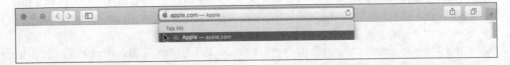

Safari displays the Apple website.

5 If Safari displays a message saying "You are not connected to the Internet," join a wireless network using the Wi-Fi icon near the right side of the menu bar.

6 Near the top right of the page, click the Support link (https://www.apple.com/support).

You are taken to the Apple Support site. If you were experiencing a problem with your Mac, look for solutions and information. You use Apple Support resources later in this book.

7 From the menu bar, choose Safari > Quit Safari (or press Command-Q) to return to the macOS Utilities screen.

When you close a window in Safari, you don't quit Safari. To quit a Mac app, choose Quit *App Name* from the app menu (the menu next to the Apple menu, named for the current app). Or you can use Command-Q.

Examine Disk Utility
Disk Utility enables you to repair, image, reformat, or repartition your Mac disk.

1 Select Disk Utility, and then click Continue.

In the device list on the left, you see your startup disk and a Base System disk image. Because your startup disk is encrypted, it is dimmed. If you are in the Show All Devices view, you see the primary entry for each disk device and an indented list of volumes on each device.

2   Select the entry for your startup volume. Typically, it is named Macintosh HD.

3   Click Mount in the Disk Utility toolbar, and enter your Local Administrator password (**Apple321!**) to unlock your startup volume.

View the other buttons in the Disk Utility toolbar. These buttons represent functions that are discussed in detail in Lesson 11, "Manage File Systems and Storage."

With Disk Utility you can use First Aid to verify or repair the startup volume file structure or erase the volume before you reinstall macOS Mojave.

4   From the menu bar, choose Disk Utility > Quit Disk Utility or press Command-Q.

You are returned to the macOS Utilities window.

Examine Time Machine Restoration

If you backed up your Mac with Time Machine, macOS Recovery can do a full system restoration from that backup. Reference 17.2, "Configure Time Machine," covers setting up Time Machine.

1 Select Restore From Time Machine Backup, and click Continue.

The Restore from Time Machine screen appears, with notes on the restoration. This restoration interface erases current content and replaces it from the backup.

2 Click Continue.

The Select a Backup Source screen appears. If you configured a Time Machine backup target, it would be available here as a source for restoring macOS.

3 Click Go Back to return to the Restore from Time Machine screen.

4 Click Go Back again to return to the macOS Utilities screen.

Examine the macOS Installer

Here you examine reinstallation, but you don't perform a reinstall. When you complete these steps, you experience the reinstallation, but you don't have to wait while macOS is copied to your Mac.

1 Select Reinstall macOS, and click Continue.

The Installer app opens.

2 Click Continue.

3 Read the license agreement, and click Agree.

4 In the license confirmation dialog, click Agree to indicate you have read and agree to the terms of the software license agreement.

The installer displays a list of volumes where you could install or reinstall macOS.

NOTE ▶ Don't click the Install button. If you do, the installer reinstalls macOS.

5 Quit the installer.

Verify Your Startup Disk and Restart

The Choose Startup Disk utility enables you to select the volume to start up from. If you encounter problems with your internal disk during startup, connect a second disk, with macOS installed, and use Startup Disk to configure your Mac to start up from the new disk.

1 From the Apple menu, choose Startup Disk.

Startup Disk lists all available startup volumes. The options might include Network Startup or one or more NetBoot images, depending on what Startup Disk finds on your network.

2 Verify that your normal startup volume (typically named Macintosh HD) is selected. If necessary, select it.

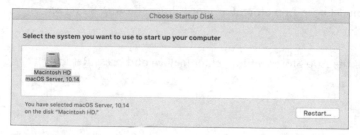

3 Click Restart.

4 In the confirmation dialog, click Restart.

You could also restart without using the Startup Disk utility by choosing Restart from the Apple menu.

Exercise 5.2
Create a macOS Install Disk

▶ **Prerequisites**

▸ You need an erasable external disk with a capacity of at least 12 GB.

▸ You must have created the Local Administrator account (Exercise 3.1, "Configure a Mac for Exercises").

In this exercise, you create a macOS install disk, which includes the macOS Recovery environment, tools, and installation assets. When you create a macOS install disk this way, you can reinstall macOS without downloading the installer app from the App Store. Record the version of the macOS installer that you use. If you need to, you can get an updated installer from the store.

Get a Copy of the Install macOS Mojave App

In class, the facilitator probably gave you a copy in the ParticipantMaterials/Lesson5 folder. Otherwise, you can download the installer using the following steps:

1   Log in as Local Administrator (password: **Apple321!**).

2   From the Apple menu, choose App Store. For more about the App Store, see Lesson 18, "Install Apps."

3   In the search field of the App Store window, enter **Mojave** and press Return.

4   Find macOS Mojave in the search results, and click the View button next to its name.

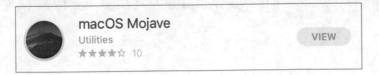

5   Click the Get button. Software Update preferences opens, and finds the update.

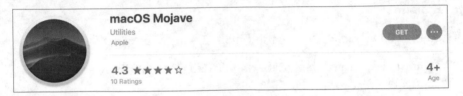

6   When you are asked if you are sure you want to download macOS Mojave 10.14, click Download.

When the installer app finishes downloading, it opens.

7   Quit both Install macOS Mojave and the App Store.

Reformat the External Disk

Most new external disks come preformatted with the Master Boot Record (MBR) partition scheme. To allow a Mac to start up from MBR, reformat the disk with the GUID partition map (GPT) scheme. For more information about disk formats, see Lesson 11, "Manage File Systems and Storage."

> **NOTE ▶** This operation erases all content on the external disk. Don't perform this exercise with a disk that contains important content.

1   Open Disk Utility. It's in /Applications/Utilities.

2   Connect the external disk to your Mac.

3   If you are prompted for a password to unlock the disk, click Cancel.

You don't need to unlock the disk to erase it.

4   In the toolbar, choose View > Show All Devices.

5   Select the external disk device entry in the Disk Utility sidebar. Select the device entry, not the volume entry indented beneath it.

6 Check the partition map listed at the bottom of the window.

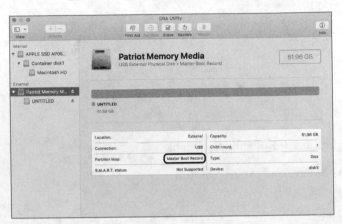

7 You might not know the partition scheme that's currently on the disk, or the disk could include the GUID scheme. In either case, erase the disk.

You can partition the disk and use part of it for the installer volume. See Reference 11.4, "Manage File Systems," for more information about partitioning.

8 Click the Erase button in the toolbar.

9 Give the disk a descriptive name, choose Mac OS Extended (Journaled) from the Format pop-up menu, and choose GUID Partition Map from the Scheme pop-up menu.

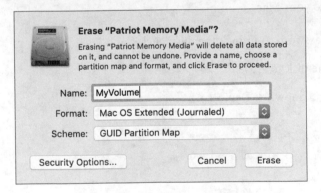

10 Click the Erase button.

11 When the process finishes, click Done to dismiss the erase dialog.

12 Verify that the Partition Map entry is GUID Partition Map.

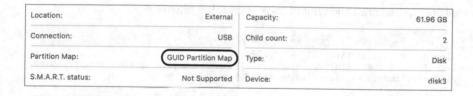

13 Quit Disk Utility.

Create a macOS Install Disk

1 Open Terminal.

2 Switch to the Finder, and navigate to the Install macOS Mojave app and do one of the following:

▶ If your facilitator provides a copy of the installer apps, open the Lesson5 folder in ParticipantMaterials.

▶ If you downloaded the installer app from the App Store, open the Applications folder.

3 Control-click the Install macOS Mojave app, and choose Show Package Contents from the shortcut menu that appears.

Read Reference 14.2, "Examine Packages," for more information.

4 In the installer package, open the Contents folder, and open the Resources folder.

5 Drag the createinstallmedia file from the Finder into Terminal.

This inserts the full path to createinstallmedia in Terminal.

6 Switch back to Terminal, and press Return.

This executes the createinstallmedia tool as a command-line program. It prints a usage summary and explains how to use the tool.

7 Enter **sudo** followed by a space to start another command, but don't press Return until step 11.

8 Drag createinstallmedia from the Finder to Terminal again.

9 In Terminal, enter **--volume** (enter two hyphens before volume) followed by a space.

10 Drag the MyVolume (or whatever you named it) volume icon from the desktop to Terminal.

At this point, the command should look something like this:

```
                        ⌂ ladmin — -bash — 80×24
Last login: Sun Sep 16 13:46:05 on ttys000
[Mac-17:~ ladmin$ sudo /Applications/Install\ macOS\ Mojave.app/Contents/Resource]
s/createinstallmedia --volume /Volumes/MyVolume █
```

11 Switch to Terminal, and press Return.

This operation requires admin access.

12 Enter the Local Administrator account password (**Apple321!**), and press Return.

This operation erases the disk, so you are prompted to confirm the operation.

13 Verify that the volume name (listed after /Volumes/) is the one you intend to use, enter **Y**, and press Return.

14 Wait while the install disk is prepared. This may take several minutes, depending on the type and speed of the external disk you use.

When the process finishes, Terminal displays several lines, ending with Install media now available at "/Volumes/Install macOS Mojave."

15 Quit Terminal.

Test the macOS Mojave Install Disk

Test the installer disk, but don't reinstall macOS.

1 Go to the Apple menu and choose Restart; then click Restart in the confirmation dialog to restart your Mac.

2 Press and hold the Option key until you see a row of icons.

3 Click the install disk icon.

4 Click the arrow that appears under the icon.

The Mac starts up in the installer environment, which is like the recovery environment. Explore it, but don't reinstall macOS.

5 When you finish exploring the installer environment, go to the Apple menu and choose Restart to restart your Mac.

Lesson 6

Update macOS

In this lesson, you configure and use macOS and App Store software update technologies, which are automatic ways to keep your Apple-sourced software up to date. You also explore an alternative to automatic software updates: manually downloading and installing software update packages.

Reference 6.1
Automatic Software Updates

You should keep your Mac software up to date. macOS updates improve the stability, performance, and security of your Mac. They include updates for Safari, iTunes, and other apps that are part of macOS.

macOS includes two software update methods that automatically check Apple servers, through the Internet, to ensure that you're running the latest Apple-sourced software.

You need an Internet connection to download update installers for both automatic and manual software updates. The automatic software update methods check only for updates of currently installed Apple-sourced software:

▶ Updates and upgrades to macOS and software bundled with macOS

▶ Updates to software you bought from the App Store

You need an administrator account to change Software Update preferences and the preferences in the App Store app.

App Store software updates require appropriate Apple ID authentication, except for apps that were assigned directly to your Mac by Apple Business Manager or Apple School Manager. You can use Apple Business Manager or Apple School Manager and your MDM solution to buy apps and books in volume, assign them to users or devices, install them on your Mac computers, and update them when updates are available. You can use Apple Business Manager or Apple School Manager and your MDM solution to assign, install, and update apps even if the App Store is disabled or if those Mac computers don't have a user with an Apple ID signed in to the App Store. Read Apple Support article HT207305, "Availability of Apple programs for education and business," to find out which Apple programs for education and business are available in your country or region. Read http://help.apple.com/businessmanager/ or http://help.apple.com/schoolmanager/ for more information.

NOTE ► The focus of this guide is the behavior of apps that weren't assigned directly to your Mac by your organization.

If there is a Mac that provides the Content Caching service on your network, your Mac will automatically use the Content Caching service to speed up updates for macOS updates and App Store updates. Read Reference 25.1, "Enable Host-Sharing Services," for more information about the Content Caching service.

Automatic Software Update Behavior

macOS Mojave uses Notification Center to tell you as soon as new updates are available.

By default, important macOS updates (for example, security updates) are automatically downloaded and installed. By default, other macOS updates are automatically downloaded in the background but not installed. When macOS updates are ready to be installed, macOS displays an Updates Available notification in an alert (a banner goes away automatically, and an alert stays on screen until you dismiss it) with a Software Update icon. Notification Center shows your alerts in the upper-right of your screen, without interrupting what you're doing. You can show and hide Notification Center by clicking its icon in the menu bar (the Notification Center icon looks like three lines, each with a dot).

From the alert you can click Restart (if an update requires a restart), Install, or Later. If you click Restart or Install, macOS immediately installs the available updates and restarts the Mac if necessary. If you click Later, you can choose an option to update the software at a more convenient time. This is useful because some system updates prevent you from using the Mac while the installation completes, and they might require a restart. The last item in the alert, Turn On Auto Update, turns on automatic macOS updates.

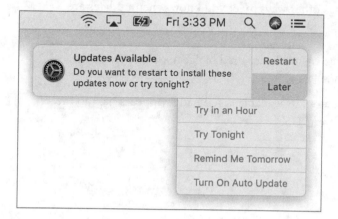

As soon as you reply to this alert, even if you're not logged in with an administrator account, macOS automatically turns on automatic updates. Then macOS displays an alert that enables you to turn off automatic updates. Apple recommends that you keep automatic updates turned on.

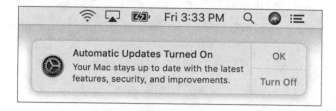

If you click Turn Off, when you are ready to manually check for new macOS updates, you can use any of the following methods:

- ▶ Open System Preferences, then open Software Update preferences.
- ▶ In the About This Mac window, click the Software Update button.

macOS Mojave treats macOS updates separately from App Store updates. When an update is available for an app from the App Store that is installed on your Mac, you receive an alert with an App Store icon.

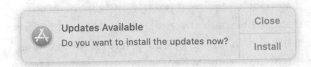

Click Install to install any available app updates, or click Close to dismiss the alert.

In addition to the alerts, macOS has other ways to let you know when updates are available:

▶ When macOS software updates are available, a red badge appears next to the System Preferences icon in your Dock.

▶ When App Store software updates are available, a red badge appears next to the App Store preferences icon in your Dock.

▶ When macOS software updates are available, a red badge appears next to the Software Update preferences in System Preferences.

▶ When macOS software updates are available, the number of updates appears in the Apple menu next to System Preferences.

▶ When App Store updates are available, the number of updates appears in the Apple menu next to App Store.

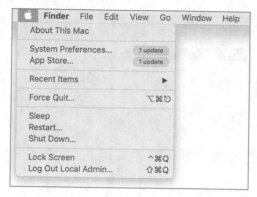

macOS Software Update Preferences Behavior

When you open Software Update preferences, it checks for available macOS updates.

Then Software Update preferences lists any available macOS updates. Otherwise, Software Update preferences displays "Your Mac is up to date," followed by your macOS version.

Click Update Now to install all the available macOS updates. Click "More info" to see a list of macOS updates that includes the update name, the version, and a description. Select an update to get more details about that update. Updates that require a restart include a notice next to the update name it its details.

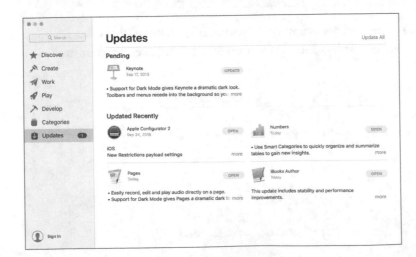

App Store Update Behavior

When you open the App Store, then click Updates in the sidebar, App Store displays the apps that have an update available. The Pending section displays each App Store app that has an update available. The Updated Recently section displays apps that were updated recently.

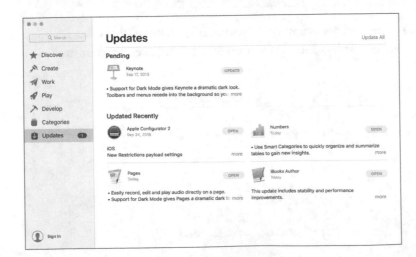

You can refresh available updates by pressing Command-R. Click More for an app to read more about its updates.

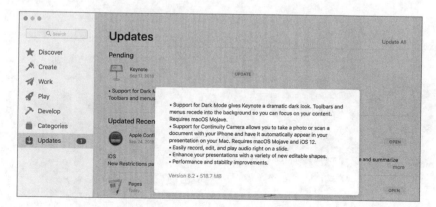

To install a single update, click the corresponding Update button, or click the Update All button to install available updates.

If you aren't signed in to the App Store, macOS prompts you to sign in with your Apple ID before you can install updates. If you want to update an App Store item that was installed with a different Apple ID, you must authenticate with the Apple ID used to buy the original item.

Software Update Preferences for Automatic Updates

You can choose to "Automatically keep my Mac up to date" from Software Update preferences. Changes you make in Software Update preferences apply to all users.

From the Advanced pane in Software Update preferences, you can enable or disable the following options:

▶ **Check for updates**—This option is enabled by default. When it is enabled, macOS checks for updates once a day. macOS needs only a small amount of Internet bandwidth to determine whether you need updates.

▶ **Download new updates when available**—This option is enabled by default. macOS might need a lot of bandwidth to download macOS system updates.

▶ **Install macOS updates**—You can enable this option. After you enable it, macOS tells you when macOS updates are automatically installed, as long as they don't require a restart. macOS updates that require a restart notify you and enable you to restart immediately or wait until later.

▶ **Install app updates from the App Store**—You can enable this option. After you enable it, the App Store automatically installs updates to App Store apps. If you enable this option, the option Automatic Updates is enabled in App Store preferences. Likewise, if you disable Automatic Updates in App Store preferences, the option "Install app updates from the App Store" is disabled in Software Update preferences.

▶ **Install system data files and security updates**—This option is enabled by default. The best practice is to leave it enabled. That way, your Mac checks daily for required security updates and tells you when one is available. If the update doesn't require you to restart your Mac, it's installed automatically. Otherwise, the update is installed the next time you restart your Mac.

NOTE ▶ To receive the latest updates automatically, it's recommended that you select "Check for updates," "Download new updates when available," and "Install system data files and security updates."

In the main Software Update preferences window, selecting the option "Automatically keep my Mac up to date" turns on all the options that are available in the Advanced pane.

You must have administrator credentials to select or deselect "Automatically keep my Mac up to date" and to select or deselect any of the options in the Advanced pane.

App Store Preferences for Automatic Updates

Reference 18.1, "The App Store," has more information about using the App Store app to install apps. This section focuses on using the App Store to automatically keep your App Store apps updated.

When you open the App Store and then open App Store preferences, the following options are available for keeping your App Store apps up to date:

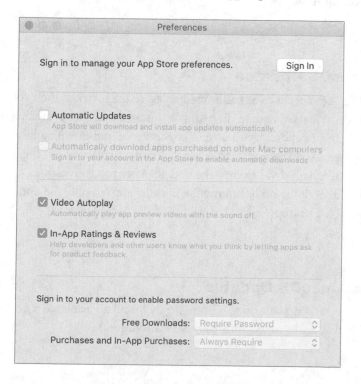

▶ **Automatic Updates**—You can enable this option if you have administrator credentials. Also, if you turn on automatic macOS updates in an Updates Available alert or
in Software Update preferences, this option is enabled. When you enable this option,
the App Store downloads and installs app updates automatically.

▶ **Automatically download apps purchased on other Mac computers**—You can enable
this option if you are signed in to the App Store. When you sign in to the App Store
with the same Apple ID on more than one Mac and you buy an app on a different
Mac, that app is installed on any Mac with this option enabled.

▶ **Password Settings**—These settings apply only if a user is signed in to the App Store
with an Apple ID. When you edit these settings, you can reduce how many times you
have to provide your password when you buy and download items or download free
items.

You can block standard users' access to the App Store with parental controls. Find out
more about parental controls in Lesson 7, "Manage User Accounts," and more about the
App Store in Lesson 18, "Install Apps."

Reference 6.2
Manually Install macOS Updates

If you support a Mac that isn't connected to or has limited access to the Internet, then you
might want to manually install a macOS update. To manually install a macOS update instead
of using automatic macOS software updates, visit http://support.apple.com/downloads/ and
manually download the update. Copy the update to other Mac computers that need the
update installed. You could use a flash drive to copy the update. After you copy a macOS
update to another Mac, double-click the update to use the Installer app to apply the update.
Or you could use Apple Remote Desktop.

Reference 6.3
Use MDM to Install macOS Updates

You might be able to use your MDM solution to automatically install all available macOS
updates on Mac computers that are enrolled with your MDM solution.

To use MDM to install available macOS updates:

▶ Your Mac must be enrolled in your MDM solution.

▶ Your MDM solution must support the "Install OS update" MDM command.

For more information about using your MDM solution to install macOS updates, visit http://help.apple.com/deployment/mdm/.

Reference 6.4
Examine Installation History

The update screen in the App Store shows only recently installed updates. Software Update preferences displays only recently installed updates. System Information lists most Apple and third-party installed software, whether it was installed manually or automatically. To view the System Information list, open System Information and select Installations in the left column. You'll see the software name, version, software source, and installation date.

Exercise 6.1
Manually Install Software Updates

▶ **Prerequisite**

▶ You must have created the Local Administrator account (Exercise 3.1, "Configure a Mac for Exercises").

If you want to keep a copy of an update or want to install additional software (such as printer drivers) available for download from the Apple Support site, this exercise shows you how to download and install updates manually.

Download an Update from the Internet

1   Open Safari.

2   Navigate to https://support.apple.com/downloads/.

This page shows the featured updates Apple makes available for download. If you don't see the update you want, you can either click one of the categories under Browse Downloads by Product or use the Search Downloads field to find the update you need.

The following screenshots use the Savin Printer Drivers package as an example, but you can choose any update for which your Mac is eligible.

3   When you find the update you want to install, click its Download button.

4   Wait for the download to complete.

A progress indicator in the Safari Downloads button, near the top right of the window, shows the download status.

5   Click the Downloads (down-arrow icon) button near the top right of the window.

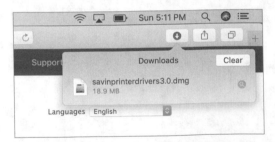

6   Click the View (magnifying glass icon) button next to the update you downloaded.

Your Downloads folder opens in the Finder, and the disk image containing the update is selected.

Install the Update

1   Open the disk image file.

The disk image mounts, and you see the installer package it contains.

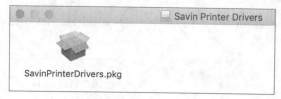

2   Open the installer package.

The installer opens and guides you through the installation process.

3   Continue through the installer prompts and agree to the license agreement if required.

4   When prompted, authenticate as Local Administrator (password: **Apple321!**).

Manual software updates usually require administrator privileges to install.

5   After the update installs, click Close or Restart as appropriate.

6   If you are prompted to move the installer to the trash and if you don't want to reuse the package on another Mac, click "Move to trash."

7   If you didn't restart, eject the disk image before proceeding.

Exercise 6.2
Use Automatic Software Update

▶ **Prerequisite**

▶   You must have created the Local Administrator account (Exercise 3.1, "Configure a Mac for Exercises").

In this exercise, you use the automatic update feature of the Software Update preferences to check for, download, and install updates for macOS. You also see how to view installed software and updates.

Check Your Software Update Preferences

1 From the Apple menu, choose System Preferences.

2 Click Software Update.

Software Update automatically checks for any available updates and indicates whether your Mac is up to date.

3 Click Advanced.

By default, macOS automatically downloads new updates in the background and notifies you when they are ready.

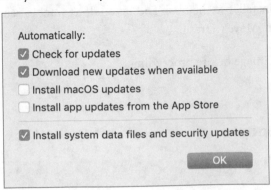

You have the option to enable Software Update to automatically Install macOS updates and app updates from the App Store. You can select other preferences if you don't want automatic downloads or updates.

4 Click OK.

5 Click "Automatically keep my Mac up to date."

6 When prompted, authenticate as Local Administrator.

7 Click Advanced.

   All options are enabled and your Mac will update automatically.

8 Quit System Preferences.

Update Your Software

1 From the Apple menu, choose System Preferences. Click Software Update and wait while your Mac checks for new software.

2 If you see the message "Your Mac is up to date," skip the rest of this section and proceed to "Check Installed Updates."

   If updates are available, an Update Now button appears, and available updates are listed.

3 Click More Info to get information about the updates

4 If any of the updates are subject to license agreements, read the agreements, and if they are acceptable to you, continue with this exercise.

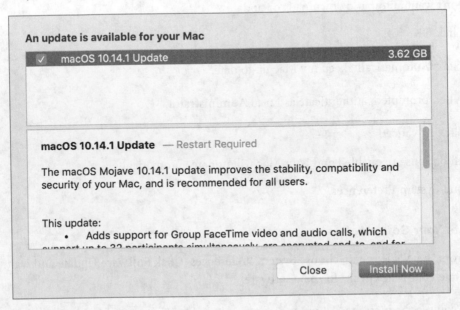

5 If more than one update is available, decide which updates you want to install.

6 Click Install Now for individual updates, or click Update All if you want all updates.

7 If you are prompted to restart your Mac, click Restart or Download & Restart.

8 If the update restarted your Mac, log back in to the Local Administrator account. If you are prompted to sign in with your Apple ID, select "Don't sign in," click Continue, and click Skip in the confirmation dialog.

9 Reopen Software Update and check for additional updates. Some updates must be installed in sequence, so you might have to repeat the update process several times.

10 When all updates are installed, quit System Preferences.

Check Installed Updates

1 Press and hold the Option key while you choose System Information from the Apple menu. The System Information menu appears in place of About This Mac only when you hold down Option.

System Information opens and displays its report.

2 In the Software section of the sidebar, select Installations.

A list of installed software and updates appears, including the updates you just installed. You can select specific updates from the list to get more information about them.

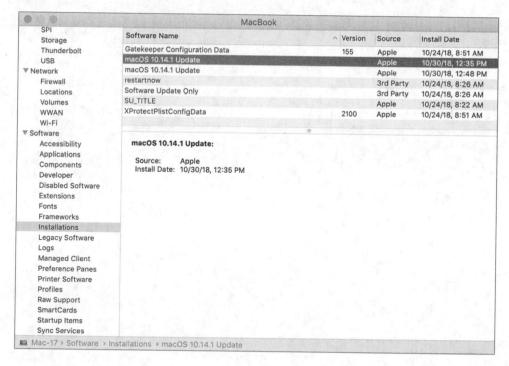

3 Quit System Information.

User Accounts

Lesson 7

Manage User Accounts

With the exception of macOS Recovery or single-user mode, you must log in with a user account to perform any task on a Mac. Even when a Mac starts up and displays the login window (the screen where you log in)—and you haven't yet authenticated—macOS is using system user accounts to maintain background services. Every file and folder on a Mac disk, and every item and process, belong to a user account. This lesson focuses on local user accounts that are available on a single Mac.

Reference 7.1
User Accounts

When you configure your Mac for the first time, Setup Assistant creates your first administrator account. This administrator account is a local user account, because macOS stores information about that user in the local user database on your Mac. This lesson focuses on local user accounts, but macOS can use other types of user accounts as well, including:

▶ Network user accounts—A network user account is available to multiple Mac computers and is stored on a shared directory server such as Active Directory that centralizes identification, authentication, and authorization information. The home folder for a network user account is usually stored on a network file server. A Mac must be able to contact both the shared directory server and the home folder server in order to use a network user account. For more information, open the Directory

GOALS

▶ Recognize various user account types and user attributes

▶ Create and manage user accounts

▶ Adjust login and fast user switching settings

Utility User Guide at http://support.apple.com/guide/directory-utility, select Active Directory, and then select "Set up home folders for user accounts."

► Mobile user accounts—A mobile user account is a network user account that has been synced with the local user database so that you can use a mobile user account even when your Mac can't contact the shared directory server. The home folder for a mobile user account is usually stored on the startup disk. This is often used with Active Directory and is outside the scope of this guide. For more information about mobile accounts, open the Directory Utility User Guide at http://support.apple.com/guide/directory-utility, select Active Directory, select "Configure domain access," and then select "Set up mobile user accounts."

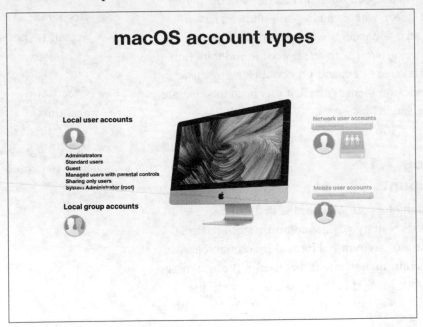

Local User Account Types

If your Mac has multiple users, set up a local account for each person so users can configure their own settings and options without affecting other users. macOS offers several different local account types to provide greater flexibility for managing user access. Because each account type allows different levels of access, be aware of each account type's potential security risk.

There are seven local account types on a Mac (six user account types and the group account type):

▶ Administrator

▶ Standard

▶ Managed with parental controls

▶ Guest

▶ Sharing only

▶ System Administrator (root)

▶ Group

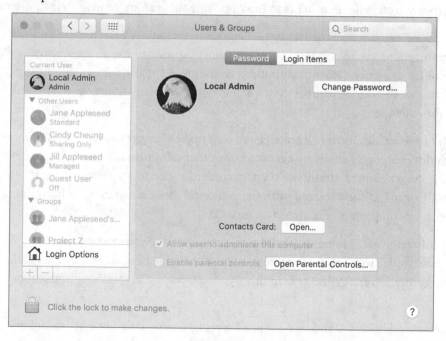

Administrator Accounts

You can use your administrator user account (also called an administrator account) to add and manage other users, install apps, and change settings that affect all users of a Mac. The first new user account you create when you first set up your Mac is an administrator account.

Your Mac can have multiple administrators. You can create new administrators and convert standard users to administrators. Administrator accounts are part of a group called admin.

Don't set up automatic login for an administrator. If you do, someone could restart your Mac and gain access with administrator privileges. To keep your Mac secure, don't share administrator names and passwords.

By default, administrator account users don't have access to other users' items except for shared items like the Public folders. Despite this, administrator account users can bypass many restrictions in the graphical environment and use Terminal if needed.

Because an administrator account is the initial account type created when you configure your Mac for the first time using Setup Assistant, many use the administrator account as their primary account type. This enables you to change almost anything on your Mac (something that administrators need to do). Also, this enables you to make changes or install software from sources other than the App Store that can make macOS insecure or unstable.

Some organizations assign a Mac to a user and allow the user to use an administrator account for daily use. Other organizations configure each Mac with an administrator account that the IT department uses. Then they provide each user with a standard account for daily use.

When you have an administrator account, you can make changes to many parts of macOS. This includes deleting or changing passwords for other administrator user accounts. You can disable current administrators or change standard users into administrators. If you open poorly or maliciously written software, you could cause harm to other users' home folder items or compromise the security of macOS.

Any administrator user can enable the root account or change an existing root account password. Two tools that enable you to make these changes are Terminal and Directory Utility. Directory Utility is in the /System/Library/CoreServices/Applications folder.

You can create additional standard accounts for more secure daily use, but managing macOS requires access to at least one administrator account.

If you need to assist a user, but don't want that user to see your user account when they log in, read Apple Support article HT203998, "Hide a user account in macOS," to learn how to hide a user account on the macOS login window.

System Integrity Protection (SIP) prevents all user account types from modifying core macOS files, even administrator accounts. Find out more about SIP in Lesson 15, "Manage System Resources."

A mobile device management (MDM) solution can modify Setup Assistant to configure an account called a managed administrator user account, or a managed administrator, on a Mac. This is possible only for Mac computers that are enrolled in Apple Business Manager or Apple School Manager and required to enroll in your organization's MDM solution. You can use your MDM solution to hide the managed administrator, and to change the password for the managed administrator. The following figure illustrates that you can use Apple's MDM solution, Profile Manager, to create a managed administrator during Setup Assistant.

NOTE ▶ You can find out more about Apple management technologies by reading http://help.apple.com/deployment/macos/ and http://help.apple.com/profilemanager/.

Standard Accounts

Standard user accounts are secure if an appropriate password is set. They have read access to most items, preferences, and apps. Users with standard accounts also have full control over their own home folder, which allows them to install apps in their home folder.

Standard account users are allowed to take advantage of nearly all the resources and features of a Mac, but they generally can't change anything that might affect other users on it. Exceptions include:

▶ Standard account users can install apps and app updates from the App Store.

▶ Standard account users can choose when to update software when they receive a notification that macOS software updates are available.

Even though standard account users are allowed full access to the App Store, they aren't allowed to manually modify the /Applications folder or use other installation methods that might modify shared parts of macOS. This means that standard account users aren't allowed to install many items that are distributed outside the App Store. Apple maintains tight control over App Store distribution. This control means content remains safe for standard account users to install.

MORE INFO ▶ If your organization needs to restrict users from installing apps, system updates, or App Store items, you can create managed accounts, or use an MDM solution to configure Mac computers. For example, you can use MDM to configure a Mac to restrict the App Store to display only apps installed by MDM and software updates. For more information visit https://help.apple.com/deployment/mdm/, click "MDM restrictions," then click "macOS restrictions."

A managed account is a standard account with parental controls enabled, as covered in Reference 7.3, "Restrict Local User Access."

Guest Account

There is a special account called the guest user, or the guest account. In Users & Groups preferences, select Guest User to configure it. The guest account is disabled by default in macOS. Select "Allow guests to log in to this computer" to enable the guest account. If you turn on Find My Mac, then macOS enables the guest account. When the guest account is enabled, it is similar to a standard user, but it doesn't require a password. Anyone with physical access to the Mac can use the guest account to log in.

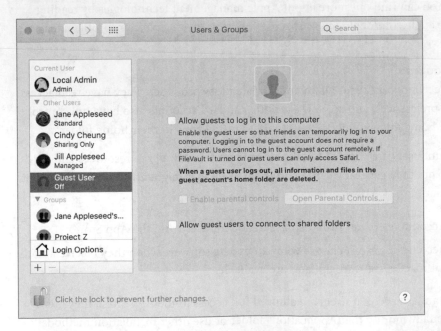

When the guest user logs out, the guest account home folder is deleted, including any home folder items that would normally be saved, like preference files or web browser history. The next time someone logs in as a guest, a new home folder is created for that user.

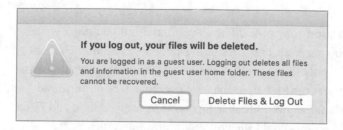

FileVault affects how a guest account operates. If you've enabled FileVault and someone logs in to your Mac with the guest account, your Mac restarts. Safari is the only app the guest user can use. A guest account doesn't have access to the startup disk.

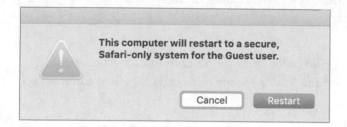

When the user with the guest account quits Safari or restarts the Mac, the guest account home folder is deleted, and the Mac restarts.

If you don't enable FileVault, the guest user has access to the /Users/Shared folder and other users' Public folders. Unlike the guest user's home folder, the contents of these other folders remain after the guest logs out. This means that a guest user could run malicious apps or fill the disk with unwanted files. Guest users can restart or shut down a Mac, potentially allowing them to attempt to compromise macOS during startup.

There are some steps you can take to further limit the guest user's access to files on your Mac. You can use parental controls, which enable you to restrict a guest user from running unapproved apps or restarting a Mac. Giving the guest user limited access, as covered in Reference 7.3, is a safe way to provide temporary user access. Additionally, you can change the access permissions on shared folders so that a guest user isn't allowed to copy items to the disk. Changing file and folder permissions is covered in Lesson 13, "Manage Permissions and Sharing."

The "Allow guest users to connect to shared folders" option allows another person to connect to your Mac computer's shared folders if you turn on your Mac computer's file sharing service, which is covered in Reference 25.1, "Enable Host-Sharing Services," without a password.

Sharing-Only Accounts

When you want to share files with someone on a different computer but you don't want that person to be able to log in to your Mac, create a sharing-only user account. Users of sharing-only accounts have access only to shared files and folders. Sharing-only accounts have no home folder, and those users can't log in to the Mac user interface or Terminal. Sharing-only accounts are, by default, allowed file sharing access to users' Public and Drop Box folders. Like a guest user, these users could fill a disk with unwanted files.

You can configure a sharing account to require a password, and you can set file and folder permissions in the account.

Sharing-only accounts are safer than guest user accounts for file sharing.

Root User Account

You can use the root user account (also called the System Administrator account, the root account, or just root) to perform tasks that require more privileges than administrator user accounts have.

Since many macOS processes run as the root account, the root account must exist. macOS wouldn't be able to start up without processes run with root privileges.

The root account can:

▶   Access most files in other users' home folders

▶   Read, write, and delete many nonsystem files

▶   Modify many system settings

▶   Install software

The root account can't change items that are protected by SIP. And now in macOS Mojave, the root account can't access additional files, including:

▶   /Library/Application Support/com.apple.TCC

▶   Many files in users' home folders

The root account is unlike an administrator account. An administrator account doesn't have access to files in another user's home folder (except Public and Drop Box folders and files stored at the top level of the other user's home folder).

The default macOS configuration doesn't have a password set for the root account. So you must set a password for the root account before you can log in with the root account or authenticate as the root account. Any administrator can use their own password to use the sudo command to run a command with root privileges in the CLI.

Any administrator user can choose to set a password for the root account or change an existing root account password using Directory Utility. Anyone with access to macOS Recovery can reset the password for any local account, including the root account. If security is a concern in your environment, you should enable FileVault, set a firmware password to restrict macOS Recovery access to your startup disk, or both. Enabling FileVault is covered in Lesson 12, "Manage FileVault." Setting a firmware password is covered in Lesson 10, "Manage Password Changes."

Local Group Accounts

A group account is a list of user accounts. Groups give you greater control over file and folder access. macOS has several built-in groups to facilitate secure processes and sharing. For instance, all user accounts are members of the staff group. Administrator user accounts are also members of the admin group. The root account has its own group (called wheel). Using groups to manage sharing is discussed in Lesson 13, "Manage Permissions and Sharing."

Standard accounts are members of the staff group. Administrator accounts are members of both the staff group and the admin group.

Reference 7.2
Configure User Accounts

In this section, you examine different ways to manage local user accounts.

Users & Groups Preferences

From Users & Groups preferences, local users can manage basic settings for their accounts.

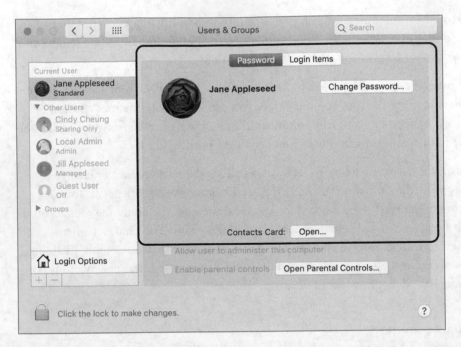

Any administrator account user can unlock Users & Groups preferences and manage attributes for local accounts.

Create and Edit New User Accounts

From Users & Groups preferences, after authenticating as an administrator, you can manage any account by selecting it from the list and modifying items to the right. Click Add (+) at the bottom of the Users & Groups list to create a new account. A dialog appears where you can define the basic attributes for a new user account.

The New Account menu at the top of the user creation pane enables you to define the type of local user account being created: Administrator, Standard, Managed with Parental Controls, or Sharing Only.

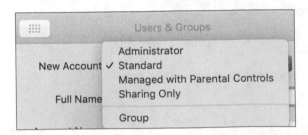

When you create a new local user account, enter a full name. macOS automatically enters an account name based on the full name, but you can change that account name. Enter an initial password for the user. You can also enter an optional password hint, but the text can't match the user's password.

Setup Assistant for Additional Users

After you've completed Setup Assistant for the first time on your Mac, the first time you log in to your Mac with an additional user account, you see an abbreviated version of Setup Assistant for that user. Setup Assistant is described in Reference 3.1, "Configure a Mac with a New Installation of macOS Mojave."

Just as in the full Setup Assistant process, at some screens you need to take action or make a selection; at other screens, you only need to read and then click Continue; and at other screens, you can click the option to set up a feature later. Here is the abbreviated Setup Assistant process:

1 You see the Data & Privacy screen.

2 You see the "Sign In with Your Apple ID" screen, where you are asked to enter an Apple ID. You can click Set Up Later, or you can provide your Apple ID. There are more details about providing your Apple ID during Setup Assistant in Lesson 3, "Set Up and Configure macOS."

3   If you provided an Apple ID, then you'll see the iCloud Keychain screen.

4   If your Mac has a microphone, then you're prompted to enable Ask Siri.

5   If you enabled Ask Siri and your Mac supports Hey Siri, then you're prompted to speak phrases to set up Hey Siri.

6   If you provided an Apple ID, then you might see the iCloud Drive screen or the "All your files in iCloud" screen, depending on the state of your Apple ID.

7   If your Mac supports Touch ID, then you're prompted to set up Touch ID. You can click Set Up Touch ID Later, or click Continue to set up Touch ID.

8   If you set up Touch ID, then you'll see the Apple Pay screen.

9   You see the Choose Your Look screen.

10 If your Mac supports True Tone Display, then you see the True Tone Display screen.

Mac computers that are enrolled in an MDM solution might show different Setup Assistant options than the defaults shown here. In certain managed situations, some of the default screens might be skipped.

User Account Attributes

On a Mac, Open Directory maintains local user account information. Open Directory stores this information in a series of XML-encoded text files in a protected location inside the /var/db/dslocal/nodes/ folder. The text files contain lists of user account attributes and their associated settings. Only the root user account can read these files, and only if System Integrity Protection (SIP) is turned off.

You can also access many user attributes from Users & Groups preferences after you unlock Users & Groups preferences. Control-click a user account to display the Advanced Options dialog and view the attributes.

Advanced Options

User: "Jane Appleseed"

WARNING: Changing these settings might damage this account and prevent the user from logging in. You must restart the computer for the changes to these settings to take effect.

User ID: `502`

Group: `staff`

Account name: `jane`

Full name: `Jane Appleseed`

Login shell: `/bin/bash`

Home directory: `/Users/jane`   Choose...

UUID: E66B47DD-E04A-4851-AF82-12E375ACAF95

Apple ID: Set...

Aliases:

`+` `−`

Cancel   OK

You can edit user account settings. For example, you can modify the location of a user's home folder by editing the Home Directory setting in the Home Directory field.

User account settings include:

▶ User ID—A number that identifies an account with file and folder ownership. This number is usually unique to each account on a single Mac, though overlaps are possible. User accounts start at 501, whereas most macOS system accounts are below 400. The user ID is unique from other users' IDs on a local Mac. Other Mac computers use similar ID numbers between Mac computers. For example, the first local user you create on a Mac will have the ID number 501. When you delete a user account, the user's ID becomes available, and the next user you create gets the lowest available ID.

▶ Group—The user's primary group. The default primary group for local users, even administrator accounts, is the staff group. An administrator account is also a member of the admin group.

▶ Account name—Also called the "short name." This is the name you use to uniquely identify an account and, by default, to name a user's home folder. A user can use either the full name or the account name, interchangeably, to authenticate. Other accounts in macOS must have a unique name, and the name can't contain special characters or spaces. Special characters not allowed include commas, slashes, colons, semicolons, brackets, quotes, and symbols. Allowed characters include dashes, underscores, and periods.

▶ Full name—The full name of the user. It can be long and contain nearly any character. Other accounts in macOS must have a unique full name. You can change the full name later.

▶ Login shell—This file path defines the default command-line shell in Terminal by the account. Any user who is allowed to use the command line in Terminal has the path set to /bin/bash by default. Both administrator and standard users are given this access.

▶ Home directory—This file path defines the location of the user's home folder. All users except for sharing-only account users, who don't have home folders, have this set to /Users/*name*, where *name* is the account name.

▶ Universally Unique ID (UUID)—Sometimes referred to as Generated UID (GUID), this alphanumeric attribute is generated by a Mac during account creation and is unique across space and time. After the attribute is created, no system will create an account with the same UUID. It is used to refer to the user's password and for group membership and file permissions. UUIDs created on one Mac are unique to that Mac.

▶ Apple ID—Used to associate the local Mac user account with an Apple ID that can be used to reset the local account password. This is optionally configured if the user enters an Apple ID during Setup Assistant or signs in to iCloud. Setting or changing an Apple ID from the Advanced Options pane in Users & Groups doesn't affect the user's iCloud service configuration.

▶ Aliases—Used to associate a local Mac user account with other service accounts. For example, a user's Apple ID can be associated with a local account. This attribute is optional for macOS, but it is required for integration with Apple Internet services like iCloud.

Local user account passwords are stored as an encrypted attribute to enhance security. Password management is covered in detail in Lesson 10.

Reference 7.3
Restrict Local User Access

macOS includes parental controls preferences that enable you to restrict what users can do on a particular Mac. You can't apply parental controls to an administrator user. Parental controls are part of MDM, too, so you can apply them to multiple Mac computers if you need to.

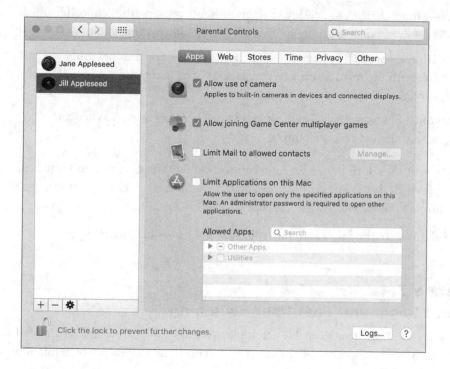

TIP Use the Action menu (gear icon) at the bottom of the parental controls user list to copy and paste complex settings from one user to another. From this menu, you can enable parental controls to be remotely managed from another Mac.

Parental controls management options include the following:

▶ Apps—Disallows camera and Game Center use, limits contacts in Mail, and limits app access.

▶ Web—Enables you to automate Safari website content filtering or manually manage a list of permitted websites, or use a combination of both automatically and manually permitted websites.

▶ Stores—Disables iTunes, iTunes U, and Apple Books stores; restricts music and books with explicit and sexual content; and sets age ratings for movies, TV shows, and apps.

For more information about iTunes U, which enables instructors to bring a classroom together on iPad, read Apple Support article HT207420, "About iTunes U."

▶ Time—Sets weekday and weekend use time limits, and prevents access during defined bedtime hours on school nights and weekends.

▶ Privacy—Limits changes to privacy settings, preventing users from choosing which apps and services can access potentially private user information.

▶ Other—Disables Siri and system dictation, limits printer and scanner edits, prevents optical disc burning, restricts explicit language in Dictionary, and prevents Dock modifications.

▶ Logs button—Maintains Safari and app use logs. The logs record allowed and attempted-but-denied access attempts.

Many third-party apps don't honor parental controls content filters or account limit settings. Examples include the Firefox browser and the Outlook email client. You can use parental controls to restrict access to these apps.

Read more about restricting access to the App Store in Lesson 18, "Install Apps."

Reference 7.4
Configure Login and Fast User Switching

With fast user switching, macOS enables multiple users to be logged in on a single Mac at the same time. Multiple users can access some resources simultaneously, which might be a security concern for your organization.

You can also manage login window behavior on multiple Mac computers with an MDM solution.

Manage User Login Items

You can adjust items that automatically open during login from the Login Items pane of Users & Groups preferences. The list of items to open applies only to the currently logged-in user.

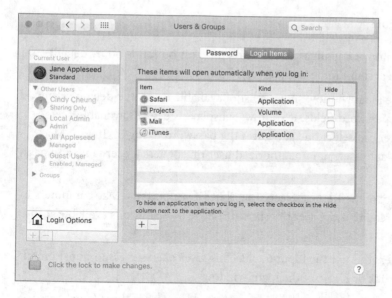

Drag items to the Login Items list or click the Add (+) button and browse for an item to add them. Select an item from the list and click the Remove (–) button to remove it. Select a Hide checkbox to make an app open but hide it from view.

Manage System Login Window Options

Authenticate as an administrator user and click Login Options at the bottom of the user accounts list to adjust the systemwide behavior of the login window.

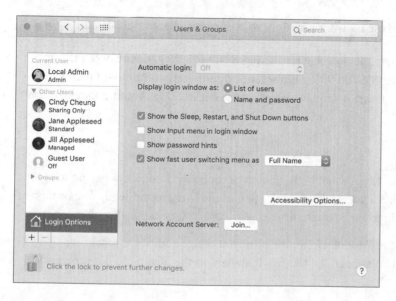

With login window options, you can:

▶ Enable or disable automatic login as a Mac starts up. This option is off by default. You can define only one account for automatic login.

▶ Choose whether the login window shows a list of available users, the default setting, or blank name and password fields. If your Mac displays the list of available users, an unauthorized user can select one and guess the password to log in. If your Mac doesn't display available users, an unauthorized user must guess a username and password to log in.

▶ Select the availability of the Restart, Sleep, and Shut Down buttons. Mac computers in environments that require more security shouldn't have these buttons available at the login window.

▶ Specify whether users can use the input menu. This gives users access to non-Roman characters, like Cyrillic or Kanji, at the login window.

▶ Determine whether the login window shows password hints after three failed password attempts.

▶ Disable the fast user switching menu or adjust the look of the menu items. The fast user switching menu can appear as the user's full name, the account name, or the generic user icon.

▶ Enable users to use accessibility items at the login window, including VoiceOver audible assistant technology, Zoom, Accessibility Keyboard, Sticky Keys, Slow Keys, and Mouse Keys.

▶ Configure a Mac to use network accounts hosted from a shared network directory.

You can configure a three-line message for the login window from Security & Privacy preferences, as covered in Lesson 9. If your organization requires a full login banner, configure it with the instructions in Apple Support article HT202277, "About policy banners in OS X."

Fast User Switching

Fast user switching lets a Mac switch between user accounts without users having to log out or quit apps. This enables a user to keep work open in the background while one or more other users are logged in to the Mac. Returning users can resume tasks after they log in.

The fast user switching menu doesn't appear until you create additional local user accounts. This menu item appears on the far right, next to the Siri menu item (or next to the Spotlight menu item if Siri is not enabled). By default, the fast user switching menu appears as the user account full name of the currently logged-in user. If you don't see this menu item, you can turn it on from the Login Options pane of Users & Groups preferences. When another user is logged in, select that user's name from the fast user switching menu and have the user enter his or her user name to switch to that user.

Fast User Switching Contention

macOS apps by Apple are fast user switching savvy. As an example, when you switch between accounts, iTunes automatically mutes or unmutes your music and Mail continues to check for new messages in the background. In rare circumstances, resource contention may occur when more than one user attempts to access an item.

Examples of fast user switching resource contention include:

▶ App contention—Some apps are designed for one user at a time use. If other users try to open these apps, they see an error dialog or the app won't open.

▶ Document contention—Sometimes one user has a document open and remains logged in with fast user switching. This can prevent other users from fully accessing the document. As an example, Microsoft Office apps such as Word and Excel allow other users to open a document as read-only and display an error dialog if the user tries to save changes. Other apps don't allow different users to open the document at all. In the worst-case scenario, an app allows two people to edit a file simultaneously but saves only changes made by the user who saved last—and it doesn't give an error message.

▶ Peripheral contention—Some peripherals can be accessed by only one user at a time. Peripheral contention can happen if a user leaves an app that's communicating with a peripheral running. The peripheral won't become available to other apps until the user quits the original app.

Fast User Switching Storage Issues

When one user attaches an external storage device to a Mac, it is available to other users, even if they weren't logged in when the device was attached.

Mounted disk images behave differently. Only the user who mounted the disk image has full read/write access to it. Other users may have read access to the mounted disk image.

Shared network volumes remain secure with fast user switching. By default, only the user who originally connected to the network volume can access it. Even if multiple users attempt to access the same network volume, macOS automatically generates multiple mount points with different access for each user. The exception to this is the network home folder shares used by network accounts. While one network user can successfully log in, additional network users from the same server won't be able to access their network home folders. For this reason, fast user switching doesn't support network accounts.

Resolving Fast User Switching Issues

Because resources and apps act differently, fast user switching issues aren't always consistently reported or readily apparent. If you are experiencing access errors for files, apps, or peripherals, see if other users are logged in. If so, have them log out and try to access the items again.

You can't change a password or manage a user account for a logged-in user. Logged-in user accounts are dimmed, as Jane's is in the following figure.

If you can't log out the other users, you can force the other users' suspect apps to quit or to force the other users to log out by restarting the Mac. Forcing an app with open files to quit might result in data loss. You can force an open app to quit, using techniques covered in Lesson 20, "Manage and Troubleshoot Apps."

If you restart a Mac, you might encounter other issues. If other users are logged in, you have to force their open apps to quit before you restart. macOS provides an authenticated restart dialog to enable you to force-quit apps, but you might lose data from open apps.

Exercise 7.1
Create a Standard User Account

> **Prerequisite**
>
> ▸ You must have created the Local Administrator account (Exercise 3.1, "Configure a Mac for Exercises").
>
> ▸ This exercise is required for most of the remaining exercises.

You created an administrator account when you first configured your Mac. In this exercise, you create an additional account (a standard user account) so that you understand the user experience.

You can also link the new account to an Apple ID so that you can access Apple iCloud services with it. Doing this enables you to complete subsequent exercises that use iCloud.

Create a Standard User Account

1 If necessary, log in as Local Administrator (password: **Apple321!**).

2 Open System Preferences, and click Users & Groups.

3 Click the lock button and authenticate as the Local Administrator user to access Users & Groups preferences.

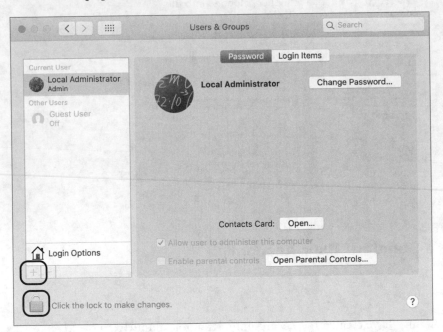

4 Click the Add (+) button beneath the account list, and enter the following information:

New Account: Standard

Full Name: **Johnny Appleseed**

Account Name: **johnny**

Password: **Apple321!**

Remember the password, as you need to reenter it periodically as you use this Mac. You can provide a hint to help you remember the password.

5   Click Create User.

Because FileVault is enabled, Johnny's account is enabled too and is able to unlock the startup volume at the next startup.

Because you authenticated as an administrator, you can configure other account properties here, including changing Johnny's user icon, granting Johnny admin rights, or using Parental Controls preferences to limit the account.

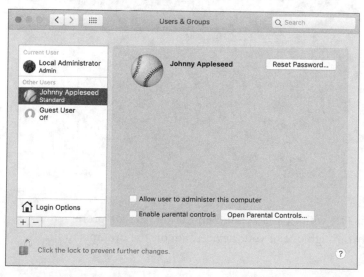

Log In to the New User Account

In these steps you log in to Johnny's user account to verify that you created it correctly. Ensure that you're connected to the Internet before you attempt this exercise

1   From the Apple menu, choose Log Out Local Administrator.

2   In the dialog that asks if you are sure, click Log Out.

3   At the login window, select Johnny Appleseed and enter the password.

4   At the Data & Privacy screen, read Apple's privacy policy, and then click Continue

You are now logged in as Johnny Appleseed. Because this account isn't associated with an Apple ID, you'll use an Apple ID, provided by your facilitator, to connect Johnny's account with the Apple ID.

1   At the "Sign In with Your Apple ID" pane, enter your Apple ID.

    You use this ID to set up iCloud on your Mac.

2   If you have an Apple ID with two-factor authentication, you are prompted to verify your identity through one of your devices. Follow the prompts to finish authenticating.

3   If the facilitator-provided Apple ID isn't two-factor enabled, and you see the Apple ID Security screen that says "Use two-factor authentication"; please deselect the option and click Continue.

4   At the "Don't upgrade" Apple ID security dialog, click Don't Upgrade.

5   If a "Terms and Conditions" screen appears, read through the terms, and if they are acceptable, click Agree. Click Agree in the confirmation dialog.

6   At the iCloud Keychain screen, select "Set up later," and click Continue.

7   At the Siri screen, deselect Enable Ask Siri, and click Continue.

8   At the "All your files in iCloud" screen, deselect "Store files from Documents and Desktop in iCloud Drive," and click Continue.

You can experiment with this feature, but if you turn it on for the Johnny Appleseed account, it may interfere with subsequent exercises.

9   If you are prompted to set up Touch ID, click Continue; click Set Up Touch ID Later and then click Continue in the confirmation dialog.

These exercises don't require Touch ID.

10   If you see the Apple Pay screen, click Set Up Later.

11   At the Choose Your Look screen, choose your preferred appearance, and click Continue.

12   If you see True Tone Display, click Continue.

Adjust Johnny Appleseed's Preferences

Just as you did with the Local Administrator account, you can adjust Johnny Appleseed's preferences to enable alternative access to content.

1   In the Finder menu bar, choose Finder > Preferences.

2   Select General to see the "Show these items on the desktop" list.

3   From the "New Finder windows show" menu, choose your system volume (typically Macintosh HD).

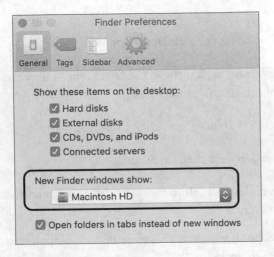

4   Click the Sidebar button at the top of the Finder Preferences window.

5   Select "johnny" in the Favorites section of the sidebar and "Hard disks" in the Locations section.

6   Close the Finder Preferences window.

7   Navigate to the /Applications folder (choose Go > Applications or press Shift-Command-A).

8   Just as you did in the Local Administrator account, drag the TextEdit app to the left side of the dividing line in Johnny's Dock.

9   Navigate to /Users/Shared. Since Johnny's Finder preferences are set to show the hard disks on the desktop, you can open Macintosh HD from the desktop, open Users, and open Shared.

10   Drag the ParticipantMaterials folder to the right side of the dividing line in Johnny's Dock.

11 Open System Preferences, and click Desktop & Screen Saver preferences.

12 Select a different desktop picture.

13 Adjust Mouse and Trackpad preferences, like you did for the Local Administrator account.

Examine Johnny Appleseed's Account

1 If necessary, open System Preferences, and then open Users & Groups preferences.

You have different options than you had when you logged in as Local Administrator. For instance, you can't allow yourself to administer the Mac or turn on parental controls for yourself. You can configure a Contacts card or add login items (which will open every time you log in). Also, you can't select any account other than your own.

2 In the lower-left corner, click the Lock icon, and authenticate as Local Administrator (either the full name Local Administrator or the account name **ladmin**). This unlocks Users & Groups preferences and enables you to make changes to other user and group accounts while you remain logged in as Johnny.

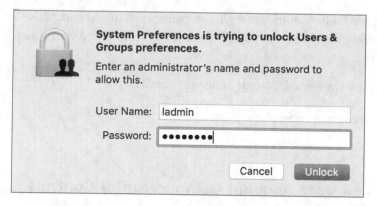

3 Control-click Johnny's account in the account list, and choose Advanced Options from the shortcut menu.

The Advanced Options dialog appears and displays the hidden attributes of the Johnny Appleseed account.

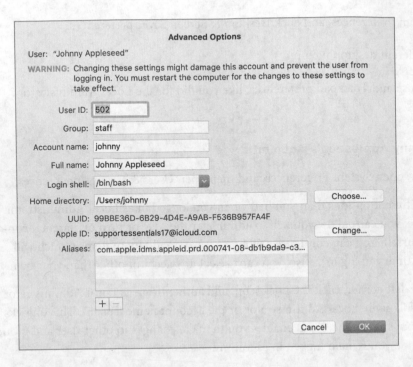

Your attributes list might have entries that relate to your Apple ID. This depends on whether you linked the account to iCloud and how you configured your iCloud account.

4   Click Cancel (or press Command-Period) to dismiss the dialog.

5   Leave System Preferences open for the next exercise.

Exercise 7.2
Create a Managed User Account Using Parental Controls

> **Prerequisite**
>
> ▶   You must have created the Local Administrator account (Exercise 3.1, "Configure a Mac for Exercises").

In this exercise, you create a managed account (one with parental controls applied) and view its restrictions.

Create an Account with Parental Controls

1   If necessary, log in as Johnny Appleseed, open Users & Groups preferences, and authenticate as Local Administrator. You can use the account name **ladmin** instead of the full name Local Administrator.

2   Click the Add (+) button under the account list, and enter the following information:

New Account: Managed with Parental Controls

Age: 4+

Full Name: **Mary Appleseed**

Account Name: **mary**

Password: **Apple321!**

Remember this password. You will need it periodically as you complete these exercises. You can provide a hint in the "Password hint" field to help you remember it.

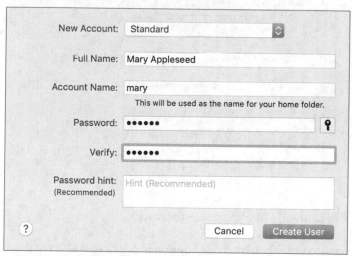

3   Click Create User.

4   Verify that Mary Appleseed's account is selected in the account list.

Since you created the account as managed, the "Enable parental controls" checkbox is selected.

5   Click Open Parental Controls.

This takes you to Parental Controls preferences.

6   If you are prompted to authenticate, enter the Local Administrator's account name and password.

7   Under the Apps pane, ensure that "Limit Applications on this Mac" is selected.

8   Click the Other Apps disclosure triangle to see what apps are allowed by default.

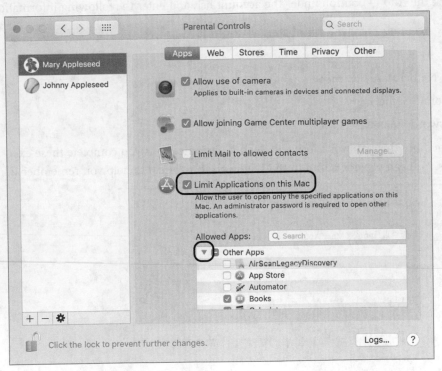

9   Click the Web button to configure Mary's web restrictions.

10   Ensure the "Allow access to only these websites" option is selected, and leave the default site list.

11   Click through the Stores, Time, Privacy, and Other buttons of Parental Controls to see other restrictions.

12   In the Other button, select "Prevent the Dock from being modified." Leave other settings at their default settings.

13   Quit System Preferences, and log out of the Johnny Appleseed account.

Test the Managed User Account

Log in to Mary Appleseed's user account to see the effects of Parental Controls.

1   At the login screen, select Mary Appleseed, enter the password (**Apple321!**), and press Return.

2   At the Data & Privacy screen, read Apple's privacy policy, and then click Continue.

3   At the "Sign In with Your Apple ID" screen, select Set Up Later, and click Skip in the confirmation dialog.

4   If you are prompted to enable Siri, deselect that option and click Continue.

5   If you are prompted to set up Touch ID, click Continue; click Set Up Touch ID Later, and then click Continue in the confirmation dialog.

    These exercises don't require Touch ID.

6   At the Choose Your Look screen, choose your preferred appearance, and click Continue.

7   If you see the True Tone Display screen, click Continue.

    Because you restricted Mary's ability to modify the Dock, the interface looks different.

8   In the Finder, choose Go > Applications.

9   Open Automator. At the dialog that says "The application Automator can't be opened," click OK.

10 At the prompt that reads "You don't have permission to use the application Automator," click OK.

Because Automator is not in the allowed Applications list, Mary is restricted from opening the app. In order for her to use Automator, a user with administrative permissions would need to allow use of the app.

11 Open Safari. If Safari is not shown on the first screen of apps, click the right arrow to show more apps.

12 Use the Safari address bar to navigate to www.wikipedia.org.

13 Since Wikipedia isn't on the list of allowed sites, an error message appears.

14 Click Add Website, and authenticate as Local Administrator.

15 If necessary, reload the page by going to the menu bar and choosing View > Reload Page, or by pressing Command-R.

This time, the Wikipedia front page loads.

16 Quit Safari and log out as Mary Appleseed.

Lesson 8

Manage User Home Folders

When you log in to your Mac, you can securely store documents in your home folder. You can store and access documents in other locations, but this lesson focuses on your home folder.

Reference 8.1
User Home Folders

The default location for a locally stored home folder is /Users/*name*, where *name* is the user account name. In the following example, johnny and jane are user account names.

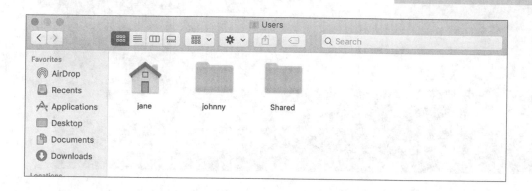

When you create a new user account, macOS generates a home folder for that account. The home folder contains these default home folders: Desktop, Documents, Downloads, Movies, Music, Pictures, and Public.

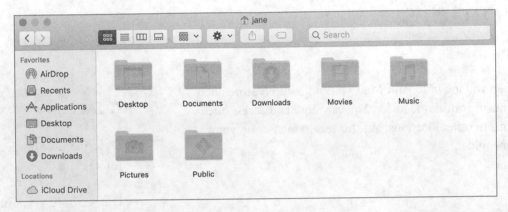

Files you save to your desktop appear on your desktop and in the Desktop folder.

New in macOS Mojave is Stacks. You can use stacks on the desktop to keep files neatly organized in groups. Whenever you save a file to the desktop, it's automatically added to the appropriate stack. This helps you keep your desktop tidy.

To turn on Stacks, click the desktop to make the Finder the active app; then from the View menu, choose Use Stacks. Or at any point you can Control-click the desktop and choose Use Stacks.

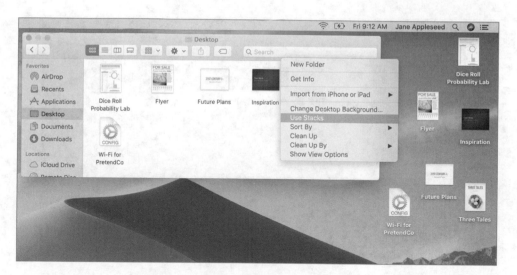

In the following figure, the Stacks feature is enabled. Only four items are displayed on the desktop: Documents (a stack of similar files), Presentations (another stack of similar files), and two other unique kinds of documents. At the same time, you can see that there are six files in the Desktop folder.

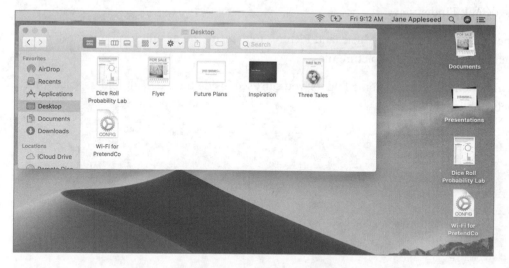

Click a stack to view the files in that stack. For more information about stacks, read Apple Support article HT209101, "How to use Stacks on your Mac."

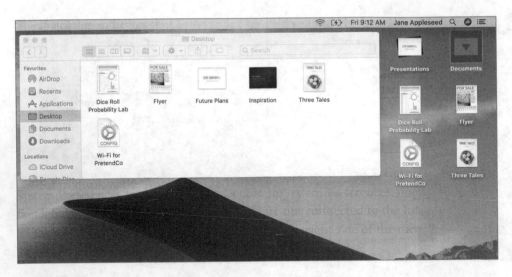

When you download content from the Internet, it goes into the Downloads folder by default.

The Library folder includes user-specific preference files, fonts, contacts, keychains, mailboxes, favorites, screen savers, and other app resources. The Library folder is hidden in the default Finder view.

The Documents, Movies, Music, and Pictures folders are the default locations for document, movie, music, and picture files.

If you open other users' home folders, you can't see inside their default folders, except for their Public folders.

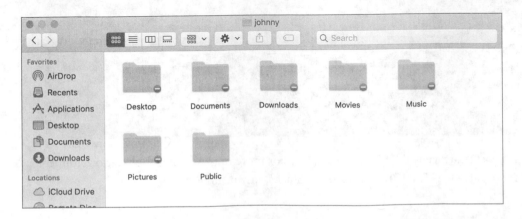

You can put items to share with other users in your Public folder.

Other users can view the contents of your Public folder, and you can view the contents of any other user's Public folder.

If you want to give a copy of a file to another user, you can use the other user's Drop Box folder. The Drop Box folder is a special folder. Every user has a folder named Drop Box that's inside that user's Public folder. You can put files into another user's Drop Box folder, but you can't remove the files once you put them there. And you can't see what's inside another user's Drop Box folder.

Except for putting items in the Drop Box, other users can't add items or make changes to files in your Public folder.

In the file system, the root folder (/) is the top folder. It contains folders—such as the Users folder that includes your home folder—and files. Other users can see what's in your root folder.

```
● ● ●                          Macintosh HD — -bash — 80×14
Johnnys-MacBook-Pro:~ jane$ cd /
Johnnys-MacBook-Pro:/ jane$ pwd
/
Johnnys-MacBook-Pro:/ jane$ ls
Applications                 etc
Library                      home
Network                      installer.failurerequests
System                       net
Users                        private
Volumes                      sbin
bin                          tmp
cores                        usr
dev                          var
Johnnys-MacBook-Pro:/ jane$
```

This figure illustrates that the Users folder is located in the root (/) folder, and it contains three folders.

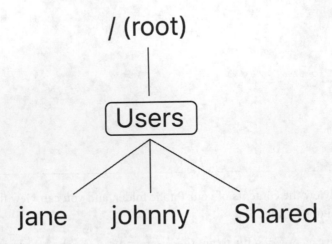

You can change folder permissions as described in Lesson 13, "Manage Permissions and Sharing."

You might see an Applications folder in your home folder. When you install some apps, they automatically create an Applications folder in your home folder. For other apps, you can choose to place them there. Only you have access to the contents of your Applications folder (though someone with access to the System Administrator account can access your Applications folder). See Reference 18.3, "Install Apps Using Software Packages and Drag-and-Drop," for more information.

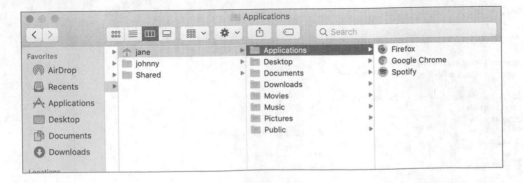

Reference 8.2
Delete User Accounts and Preserve Their Home Folder Contents

You might need to delete a user account. If you do, you must decide what to do with the user's home folder contents.

To delete a user:

1 Select the user from the list of users in Users & Groups preferences.

2 Click the Remove (–) button at the bottom of the list.

3 Select an option for the user's home folder contents.

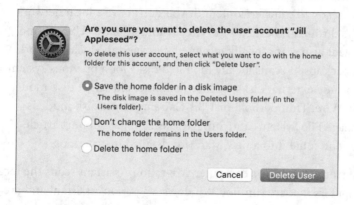

▶ Select "Save the home folder in a disk image" to save a user's home folder as a disk image file. macOS saves the disk image file in the /Users/Deleted Users folder and gives it the user account name. You can copy it to other Mac computers or into another user's home folder. You must have enough local disk space to duplicate the home folder. The process might take several hours. As this guide went to press, this option wasn't available.

▶ Select "Don't change the home folder" to leave a user home folder unchanged. macOS appends "(Deleted)" to the home folder name to signify that the user no longer exists. The deleted user home folder keeps the same access restrictions as a normal user home folder. If you want to access the deleted home folder contents, you must change folder and file ownership and permissions. Read Lesson 13 to find out more.

▶ Select "Delete the home folder" to delete home folder contents. The content won't be stored in the Trash, so you can't easily restore it.

Reference 8.3
Migrate and Restore Home Folders

Migration Assistant enables you to transfer settings, user accounts, and content from a Mac or Windows computer to your new Mac.

You can move content over Wi-Fi or Ethernet. If you have a lot of content, the move could take several hours. Be sure to plug both computers into a power source before you start.

You can use a Time Machine backup to move your content. If you don't have a Time Machine backup of the original Mac content, create one. Connect the external storage device that contains the Time Machine backup to your new Mac.

When you migrate content from another Mac, a Time Machine backup, or a startup disk, Migration Assistant scans the local network for Mac computers that are running Migration Assistant and are ready to transfer content. If you don't have a local network, connect two Mac computers through Ethernet, FireWire, Thunderbolt, or USB-C, and create one. Migration Assistant also scans locally mounted disks and the local network looking for Time Machine backups. It scans locally mounted disks for a previous system as well. Previous systems include external disks, or Mac computers in target disk mode, that are connected with FireWire, Thunderbolt, or USB-C. Using target disk mode is detailed in Lesson 11, "Manage File Systems and Storage." Read Apple Support article HT204350, "How to move your content to a new Mac," for detailed instructions.

When you migrate content from a Windows computer, Migration Assistant scans the local network for Windows computers that are running Windows Migration Assistant and are ready to transfer content. This enables you to migrate content from Windows 7 or later if the Windows computers are running Windows Migration Assistant. You can download Windows Migration Assistant from the Apple Support website. Read Apple Support article HT204087, "Move your data from a Windows PC to a Mac," for detailed instructions.

Migration Assistant runs as part of macOS Setup Assistant on new or newly reinstalled Mac computers. You can use Migration Assistant anytime. It's in /Applications/Utilities. Look for it with Spotlight or Launchpad.

1   Before you use Migration Assistant, check for Apple software updates on the source and destination computers.

This ensures that you're using the latest copy of Migration Assistant.

2   Open Migration Assistant.

3 Click Continue to start Migration Assistant.

4 Authenticate as an administrator user.

Migration Assistant quits running apps and logs out users.

5 Select how you want to transfer information:

▶ From a Mac, Time Machine backup, or startup disk

▶ From a Windows PC

▶ To another Mac

If you select "From a Mac, Time Machine backup, or startup disk" or "From a Windows PC," Migration Assistant scans attached disks and the local network for migration sources. If you select "To another Mac," open Migration Assistant on the destination Mac too.

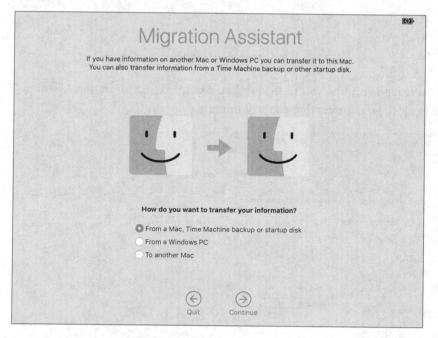

6 After you select a source, Migration Assistant scans the contents and presents you with a list of items you can migrate. If multiple disks are available, you can choose to migrate those contents too. Migration doesn't create new volumes or partitions on the destination Mac. It creates folders that include the contents of the migrated disks.

Select the information to transfer. This includes user accounts.

7   After you make selections, record the random password that Migration Assistant assigns to all standard users that you will migrate.

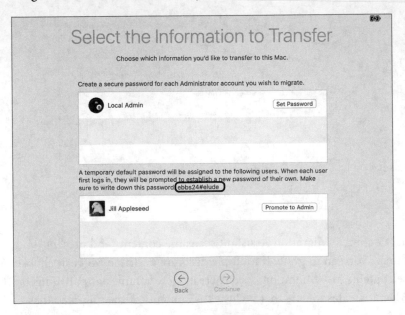

8   Create a secure password for each administrator user account you want to migrate.

9 Click Set Password for an administrator user account.

10 Enter and verify a password for the administrator account that you're migrating, then click Set Password.

11 Repeat steps 8 through 10 for any additional administrator accounts.

12 If you want to promote a standard user to an administrator user, click "Promote to Admin" next to the user, and then set and verify a new password for that user.

13 Click Continue.

14 If a user account already exists on your Mac, Migration Assistant displays a prompt. You can replace the account, optionally keeping its home folder, or keep both user accounts by entering a new name and account name.

15 To add new users to your Mac, Migration Assistant must collect a password from an existing administrator user who is authorized to create new users. Next to an administrator user, click Authorize.

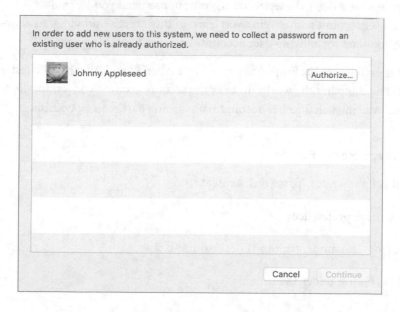

16 Enter the password for the user you selected, then click OK.

17 Click Continue to begin the transfer. The more content you transfer, the longer it takes.

Manually Restore a User Home Folder

See Exercise 8.1, "Restore a Deleted User Account," for information about how to restore a user's home folder after you delete that user.

Exercise 8.1
Restore a Deleted User Account

▶ **Prerequisite**

▶ You must have created the Local Administrator account (Exercise 3.1, "Configure a Mac for Exercises").

In this exercise, you create a user account and populate the home folder for the user. Then, you delete the account, preserving the contents of the home folder. You also create a new account, ensuring that the new user gets the old user's home folder contents. Besides showing you how to restore a deleted user account, you can use what you learn in this exercise to change a user account name. What you learn in this exercise provides an alternative to Migration Assistant for moving user accounts between Mac computers.

The scenario for this exercise is that Emily Parker recently married and now has the last name of Davidson. The company she works for uses the account naming convention *first initial, last name*. So, you must change her account name from eparker to edavidson.

Create Emily Parker's Home Folder

1   Log in as Local Administrator (password: **Apple321!**).

2   Open Users & Groups preferences.

3   Click the Lock icon, and authenticate as Local Administrator.

4   Click the Add (+) button under the user list.

5   Enter the account information for Emily Parker:

New Account: Standard

Full Name: **Emily Parker**

Account Name: **eparker**

Password: **Apple321!**

Verify: **Apple321!**

Don't provide a password hint.

You can optionally change the account picture.

6   Click Create User.

7   Control-click Emily Parker's account, and choose Advanced Options from the short-cut menu.

Take a screenshot of the System Preferences window to record Emily Parker's account attributes for later reference.

8   Press Shift-Command-4, followed by the Space bar.

Your pointer changes to a camera icon, and the region of the screen it is over is high-lighted in blue. If you see a crosshair, press the Space bar again.

9   Move the camera pointer over the System Preferences window, and click to record its contents.

This is one of several ways of taking screenshots in macOS. Shift-Command-3 records the entire screen, Shift-Command-4 (without the Space bar) enables you to select a rectangular region to record, and Shift-Command-4 with the Space bar enables you to select a single window.

The image is saved to your desktop and named "Screen Shot," followed by the date and time you took it.

10   In the Advanced Options dialog, click Cancel, or press Command-Period, which is a way to select Cancel in most macOS dialogs.

11   Log out as Local Administrator.

12 Log in as Emily Parker (password: **Apple321!**).

13 At the Data & Privacy screen, read Apple's privacy policy and click Continue.

14 At the "Sign In with Your Apple ID" screen, select Set Up Later, and click Skip in the confirmation dialog.

15 At the Siri screen, deselect Enable Ask Siri, and click Continue.

16 If you are prompted to set up Touch ID, click Continue, click Set Up Touch ID Later, and then click Continue in the confirmation dialog.

17 At the Choose Your Look screen, choose your preferred appearance, and click Continue.

18 If you see True Tone Display, click Continue

19 In the Dock, click the Launchpad icon.

Launchpad gives you an easy way to open apps that aren't in your Dock. You don't have to navigate to the Applications folder in the Finder.

20 In Launchpad, begin typing **Text.**

TextEdit should become available.

21 Click the TextEdit icon to open TextEdit.

22 In the Untitled document, enter the text **This is Emily Parker's project document.**

23 From the menu bar, choose File > Save (or press Command-S) to save the file.

24 Name the file **Project**, and save it to Emily Parker's desktop. You can use the shortcut Command-D to select the desktop.

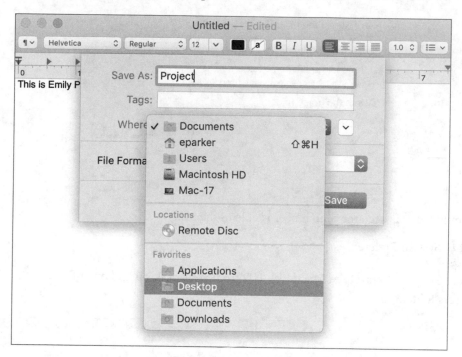

25 Quit TextEdit, and log out of the Emily Parker account.

Delete Emily Parker's Account

Now, you delete Emily Parker's account without removing the files in her home folder.

1 Log in as Local Administrator.

2 Open Users & Groups preferences and unlock the pane.

3 Select Emily Parker's account name and click the Remove (–) button to remove her account.

4   In the dialog that appears, make sure "Don't change the home folder" is selected.

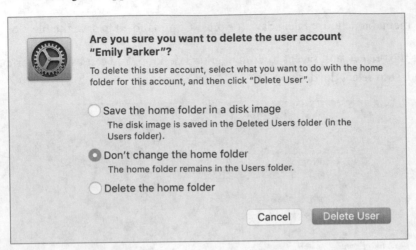

5   Click Delete User.

Emily Parker's account is no longer visible in the list.

6   Quit System Preferences.

7   Navigate to /Users. Open Macintosh HD from your desktop and open the Users folder.

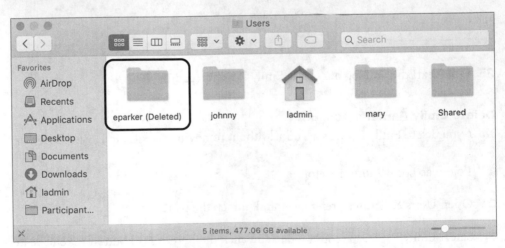

Emily Parker's home folder still exists, and (Deleted) is appended to the end of the name.

Restore Emily Parker's Account for Emily Davidson

Emily Parker's files (soon to be Emily Davidson's files) still exist in the Users folder. Now you rename the home folder so that when you create the new account, she gets her old (Emily Parker account) files.

1   Navigate to the folder /Users.

2   Control-click the eparker (Deleted) folder, choose Rename, and change the folder name to **edavidson**.

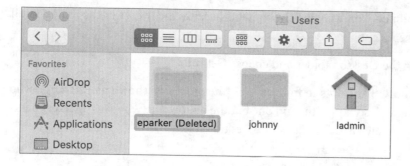

3   Press Return.

The file permissions in the /Users folder don't enable you to modify items within it. The Finder asks you to authenticate as an administrator to override the permissions.

4   Enter the Administrator password and click OK.

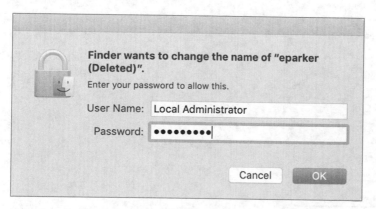

5   Open the edavidson folder, and then attempt to open the Desktop folder.

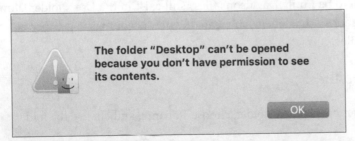

You are prohibited from viewing the contents because the owner of the folder is still the old eparker account.

6   Control-click the Desktop folder and choose Get Info.

Notice that macOS attempts to find eparker (the process is shown as Fetching), who no longer exists. Also notice that no one but the old owner (who was eparker) has permissions to view anything inside the Desktop folder.

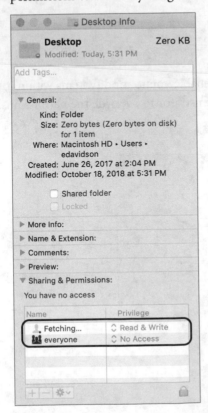

7 Click the lock and authenticate as Local Administrator.

8 Click Add (+).

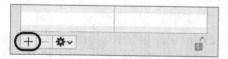

9 Choose Local Administrator, and click Select.

Notice that you are granted Read Only permissions by default. You could change this to Read & Write, or become the owner of the folder, but for the purposes of this exercise, Read Only is sufficient.

Also notice that the prohibitory badge is no longer displayed on the Desktop folder.

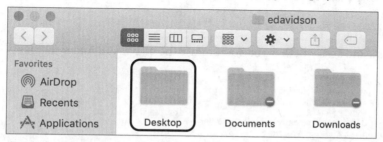

10 Open the Desktop folder.

You see Emily Parker's Project document. After you create Emily Davidson's account, she retains this document, along with all the other settings pertaining to her account.

Now you will remove Local Administrator's permissions to see the Desktop folder.

11 If necessary, right-click the Desktop folder and select Get Info.

12 Authenticate as Local Administrator, and remove ladmin (Me).

It's no longer necessary for the Local Administrator user to have permissions to view the Desktop folder and its contents. If you leave Local Administrator's permissions to see Emily's Desktop folder, the Local Administrator will be able to see files that are not intended for the Local Administrator to view.

Create and Verify Emily Davidson's Account

Now you create the Emily Davidson user account using the renamed home folder as her new account home folder.

1 Open Users & Groups preferences.

2 Click the Lock button, and authenticate as Local Administrator.

3 Click the Add (+) button to create another account:

New Account: **Standard**

Full Name: **Emily Davidson**

Account Name: **edavidson**

Password: **Apple321!**

Don't provide a password hint.

You may optionally change the account picture.

4 Click Create User.

A dialog appears and asks whether you want to use the edavidson folder for this account.

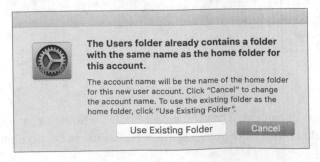

The Users folder already contains a folder with the same name as the home folder for this account.

The account name will be the name of the home folder for this new user account. Click "Cancel" to change the account name. To use the existing folder as the home folder, click "Use Existing Folder".

Use Existing Folder   Cancel

5 Click Use Existing Folder.

6 Control-click Emily Davidson's account, and choose Advanced Options from the shortcut menu.

7 Open the Screen Shot file on your desktop, and compare the account attributes of Emily Davidson's new account with her original account (Emily Parker).

You could have used the user ID of the old account for the new account, but the UUID would be different. macOS assigns each account a new UUID when you create it.

8 Quit Preview.

9 In the Advanced Options dialog, click Cancel, and then quit System Preferences.

10 Try to reopen the Desktop folder in Emily Davidson's home folder. If your Finder window is still displaying the Desktop folder, click the Back button, and then double-click the Desktop folder. You no longer have permission to see the files because they are owned by Emily Davidson's new account.

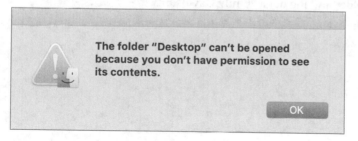

11 Close the Finder window.

Verify Emily Davidson's Home Folder

To make sure Emily Davidson's files are available, explore her renamed home folder.

1 Log out as Local Administrator, and log in as Emily Davidson.

2 Verify that the Project file is on the desktop.

3 In the Finder, open Emily Davidson's home folder by choosing Go > Home (or by pressing Shift-Command-H).

4   Make sure you see the default subfolders: Desktop, Documents, Downloads, Movies, Music, Pictures, and Public.

5   Open the Desktop folder, and verify that you see the Project document.

6   Navigate back to the home folder, and then open the Public folder, where you see a Drop Box folder. For more information about these folders, read Lesson 13, "Manage Permissions and Sharing."

In addition to the visible folders in Emily Davidson's home folder, it should contain an invisible Library folder.

7   Press and hold the Option key, and from the menu bar, choose Go > Library.

The Library choice is hidden except when you hold the Option key.

Emily Davidson's Library folder contains many subfolders. For more information about this folder and its contents, read Reference 14.1, "Examine Hidden Items," and Lesson 15, "Manage System Resources."

8   Close the Library folder and log out as Emily Davidson.

Lesson 9

Manage Security and Privacy

This lesson covers built-in macOS security features and how to manage and troubleshoot them.

Reference 9.1
Password Security

There are several ways to authenticate, or to verify your identity. In macOS, you can provide your user name and password to authenticate. If your Mac has a Touch Bar and you set up Touch ID, you can use your fingerprint instead of typing when you're asked for your password as long as you're logged in. Read Apple Support article HT207054, "Use Touch ID on your Mac" for more information.

Passwords You Use in macOS

You use several passwords to secure your Mac. You set an account password, and you can set a firmware password and resource and keychain passwords.

Users might use several password types:

▶ Each local user account has attributes that define the account. Users enter their local account password (an account attribute) to log in to their Mac. For security reasons, a user's local-account password is encrypted and stored in the user account record.

GOALS

▶ Describe password types and use

▶ Manage secrets in Keychain

▶ Manage Startup Security Utility

▶ Enable and manage iCloud Keychain

▶ Obtain User-Approved MDM enrollment

▶ Manage systemwide security and user privacy

▶ Approve Kernel Extension Loading

▶ Users might have an Apple ID and password. They use these to authorize Apple services, including iCloud, iTunes, and the App Store.

▶ With the exception of a user account password, macOS protects authentication assets in encrypted keychain files. Each keychain file is encrypted with a keychain password. macOS keeps keychain passwords synchronized with a user's local account password. You can maintain unique keychain passwords separate from an account password too. Maintaining synchronization between a user's keychain password and account password is covered in Lesson 10, "Manage Password Changes."

▶ Resource passwords are required by most macOS services (for example, email, websites, file servers, apps, and encrypted disk images). Many resource passwords are saved for you by Keychain Access.

▶ A firmware password prevents you from starting up a Mac from any disk other than your designated startup disk. As a result, it also blocks you from using most startup key combinations. For example, if you set a firmware password, an unauthorized user can't hold down the Option key during startup to select an alternate operating system, bypassing your secure startup disk. Setting a firmware password is covered in Lesson 10.

Keychain

macOS keeps your resource passwords, certificates, keys, website forms, and secure notes in encrypted storage called keychains. When you allow macOS to remember a password or other sensitive items, it saves them to a keychain. Your login password is not saved to a keychain.

macOS encrypts keychain files. They are impenetrable unless you know the keychain password. If you forget a keychain password, you lose the file contents forever.

You can use Keychain Access to view and modify most keychain items. You can use Launchpad or Spotlight to open Keychain Access, and it's in /Applications/Utilities. You can also create and delete keychain files, and change keychain settings and passwords. You can manage web-specific keychain items from Safari preferences.

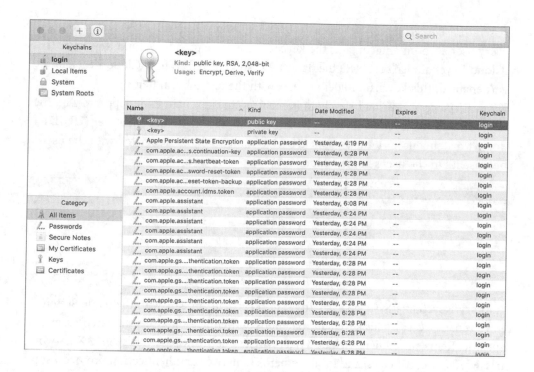

Local Keychain Files

Keychain files are stored throughout macOS for different users and resources. Here are some examples:

▶ /Users/*username*/Library/Keychains/login.keychain—When you use Keychain Access, this keychain name is "login." macOS creates every standard or administrator user with a single login keychain. As a default, the password for this keychain matches the user's account password, so this keychain is automatically unlocked and available when the user logs in. If the user's account password doesn't match the keychain password when the user logs in, macOS renames the keychain with a filename that begins with "login_renamed_" followed by a number. For example, the first time the password mismatch happens, the new filename is login_renamed_1.keychain-db. macOS then creates a new login keychain with a password that matches the user's password.

▶ /Users/*username*/Library/Keychains/*others*.keychain—You can create more keychains if you want to segregate your authentication assets. For example, you can keep your default login keychain for items that require less security and create a more secure keychain that doesn't automatically unlock for items that require a lot of security.

▶ /Users/*username*/Library/Keychains/*UUID*/—This keychain folder is created for every user account and contains the keychain database used by iCloud Keychain. If iCloud Keychain isn't enabled, the database is still created. When iCloud Keychain isn't enabled, this keychain folder appears with the name Local Items in Keychain Access. If iCloud Keychain is enabled, this keychain folder appears with the name iCloud in Keychain Access. The folder's universally unique identifier (UUID) doesn't match a user's local account UUID, but the folder is associated with the user because it's in the user's home folder.

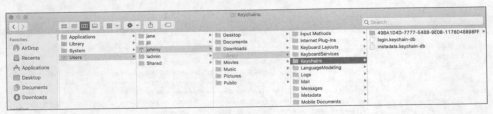

▶ /Library/Keychains/System.keychain—This keychain appears with the name System in Keychain Access. This keychain maintains authentication assets that aren't user specific. Items stored here include Wi-Fi wireless network passwords, 802.1X network passwords or certificates, and local Kerberos (a network authentication protocol) support items. Although all users benefit from this keychain, only administrator users can make changes to it.

▶ /System/Library/Keychains/—Most of the items in this folder don't appear in Keychain Access by default. The one item you will see in Keychain Access from this folder is System Roots. This keychain stores root certificates that are used to identify trusted network services. You can't modify these items.

Apple and third-party developers might create additional keychains for securely storing data. You can find keychain files with seemingly random names throughout macOS. Leave these files alone unless you're instructed by a trusted source to remove or modify them to resolve an issue.

Reference 9.2
Manage Secrets in Keychain

To manage keychain items, including saved passwords, open Keychain Access. The default selection shows a user's login keychain contents. Select another keychain from the list to view its contents.

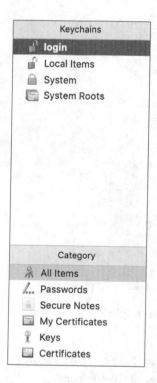

Double-click a keychain item to view its attributes. If the item is a password, select "Show password" to see the saved password. You're often prompted to provide a keychain password.

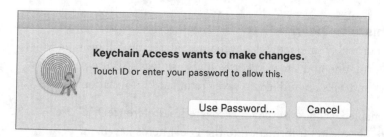

This ensures that only a keychain owner can make changes. After you authenticate, you can change attributes in the keychain item dialog. Click the Access Control button to adjust app access for a selected item.

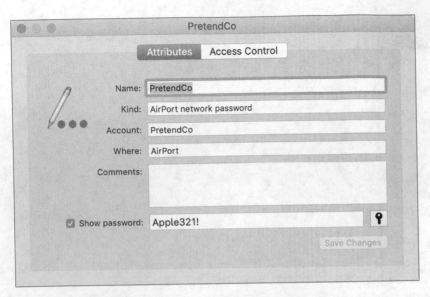

iCloud authentication mechanisms create keychain items that you might not recognize. Many of these are certificates or keys, which you shouldn't modify.

To search through keychain items in Keychain Access, select a keychain category on the left, or search for an item with Spotlight in the upper-right corner of the toolbar.

You can store secret text in keychains. In Keychain Access, choose File > New Secure Note Item to create a new secure note.

Manage Keychain Items with Safari

When you use Safari, you probably interact with keychains. Safari AutoFill prompts you to start saving web-form information and site passwords. It also suggests secure passwords for you to use for websites and asks if you'd like to save credit card information.

If iCloud Keychain isn't enabled (iCloud Keychain is covered in Reference 9.3, "Use iCloud Keychain"), Safari saves secret information to the Local Items keychain.

If iCloud Keychain is enabled, Safari saves secret information to iCloud Keychain.

When you revisit a site or navigate to a new site with similar form information, Safari AutoFill automatically fills in information for you, as long as the keychain file is unlocked. If allowed, Safari also pulls information from your contact information.

To manage Safari AutoFill settings, choose Safari > Preferences, and click the AutoFill button. The settings enable you to set which items are automatically saved and filled. Edit buttons enable you to manage items such as website passwords and saved credit cards.

With the exception of your contact information, which is stored in Contacts, Safari AutoFill data is securely stored in your iCloud or your Local Items keychain. Click the Help button (question mark) in the AutoFill pane of Safari preferences to read more about AutoFill items. You can view and manage AutoFill items from Keychain Access.

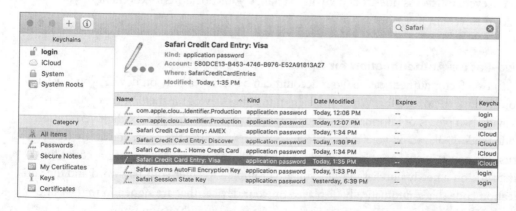

Some websites remember your authentication inside a cookie, so you might not see an entry in a keychain file for every website that automatically remembers your account. Open Safari preferences and click the Privacy button to view and delete cookies.

Reference 9.3
Use iCloud Keychain

iCloud Keychain shares your commonly used secrets between your Apple devices through iCloud. iCloud includes strong personal security technology, as detailed in Apple Support article HT202303, "iCloud security overview."

When you need to create a new password for a website, Safari suggests a unique, hard-to-guess password and saves it in your iCloud Keychain. Safari fills it in automatically the next time you need to sign in, so you don't have to remember it or enter it on any of your devices. Use iCloud Keychain to keep information safe. Read Apple Support article HT203783, "Get help with iCloud Keychain," for more information.

If you enable iCloud Keychain, the Local Items keychain is renamed iCloud. Contents in your iCloud Keychain are also stored on the Apple iCloud servers and pushed to your other configured Apple devices. iCloud Keychain provides a secure way to access your secrets from any of your Apple devices that are connected to the Internet.

If you disable it, your iCloud Keychain is renamed Local Items, and you can choose to keep secret items locally.

Use your login keychain password to access your Local Items keychain or your iCloud Keychain. When you change your login keychain password, macOS applies the change to your Local Items keychain or your iCloud Keychain. For this reason, Keychain Access doesn't allow you to change your Local Items keychain or your iCloud Keychain password.

Two-Factor Authentication for Apple ID

With two-factor authentication, your account can be accessed only on devices you trust, like your iPhone, iPad, or Mac. When you sign in to a new device for the first time, you must provide two pieces of information—your Apple ID password and the six-digit verification code that's displayed on your trusted devices. When you enter the code, you verify that you trust the new device. For example, if you have an iPhone and sign in to your account for the first time on a newly purchased Mac, you are prompted to enter your password and the verification code that's automatically displayed on your devices that are signed in to the same Apple ID. You can have the verification code sent to trusted phone numbers as well.

Because your password alone is no longer enough to access your account, two-factor authentication dramatically improves the security of your Apple ID and all the personal information you store with Apple.

After you sign in, you won't be asked for a verification code on that device again unless you sign out completely, erase the device, or need to change your password for security reasons. When you sign in on the web at www.icloud.com, you can choose to trust your browser so that you won't be asked for a verification code the next time you sign in from that Mac.

For more information about two-factor authentication, see Apple Support articles HT204915, "Two-factor authentication for Apple ID," HT205075, "Availability of two-factor authentication for Apple ID," and HT207198, "Switch from two-step verification to two-factor authentication."

iCloud Security Code

iCloud Keychain is enabled by default only when you use an Apple ID that has two-factor authentication turned on. Alternatively, when you first enable iCloud Keychain using an Apple ID without two-factor authentication, macOS prompts you to enter your iCloud Security Code. Or if you don't have one yet, macOS prompts you to create an iCloud Security Code that is used to further protect your secrets.

The iCloud Security Code is a separate security technology. When you enable iCloud Keychain with an Apple ID that doesn't have two-factor authentication, macOS prompts you to select one of the following iCloud Security Code options:

► Code plus verification is the default iCloud Security Code. It's a simple code paired with Short Message Service (SMS) text message verification. You must select a six-digit numeric code and provide a phone number that can receive SMS text messages for further verification.

► You can create a code up to 32 characters long, but you must keep track of this code.

► You can choose to have a random complex (32-character) iCloud Security Code generated and paired with an SMS text message verification. You must keep track of the code. You provide a phone number that can receive SMS text messages for verification.

► You can opt to not create a security code. If you don't create a security code, setting up iCloud Keychain on a new device will require your approval from a different device.

NOTE ▶ If you enter the wrong iCloud Security Code too many times when using iCloud Keychain, your iCloud Keychain is disabled on that device, and your keychain in iCloud is deleted. Read Apple Support article HT202755, "If you enter your iCloud Security Code incorrectly too many times" for more information.

If you sign in to another Apple device using an Apple ID with two-factor authentication, iCloud Keychain is automatically enabled. For Apple IDs without two-factor authentication, you can grant access for additional devices with a device authorization mechanism. Any device configured with the iCloud Keychain service is a trusted device. Any trusted device can be used to verify additional devices for iCloud Keychain.

For example, after you set up iCloud Keychain on your Mac and try to enable it on a different Mac, macOS will ask if you want to allow this.

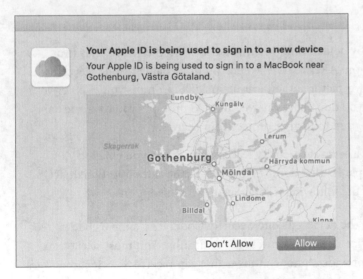

After you click Allow you'll see a randomly generated six-digit code. Continuing the example, enter this verification code on your second Mac and then click Done.

If you don't have two-factor authentication enabled, and you set up an iCloud Security Code instead, you can use the iCloud Security Code for verification instead of device-based authorization.

Reference 9.4
User-Approved MDM

"User-Approved MDM" enrollment was introduced in macOS High Sierra 10.13.2. This enrollment type is required only if you want to manage certain security-sensitive settings that include:

▶ Kernel extension loading policy

▶ Autonomous single-app mode (often used in education for testing apps, and for kiosk apps)

▶ User consent for data access

You can already manage security-sensitive settings on devices whose MDM enrollment is done through automatic device enrollment such as with Apple Business Manager or Apple School Manager, so User-Approved MDM is unnecessary for these devices.

You can still manage settings that aren't security sensitive for devices that are enrolled in MDM without the User-Approved option.

Here are ways a Mac gets enrolled with User-Approved MDM:

▶ If you use Apple Business Manager or Apple School Manager to automatically enroll your Mac in an MDM solution, its enrollment is equivalent to User-Approved.

▶ If a Mac was enrolled in non-User-Approved MDM before it was updated to macOS 10.13.4 or newer, its enrollment is converted to User-Approved when installing macOS 10.13.4 or newer.

▶ If you download or email yourself an enrollment profile, then double-click the enrollment profile, you must follow the prompts in System Preferences to enroll in MDM.

▶ If you use a screen sharing solution to enroll a Mac in MDM, synthetic input detection prevents User-Approved enrollment.

▶ If you use automation to enroll a Mac in MDM, it won't result in User-Approved enrollment.

If your Mac was enrolled in MDM without user consent in macOS 10.13.4 or later, its enrollment will not be User-Approved.

To manage security-sensitive settings, you can approve your enrollment and attain User-Approved enrollment with the following steps:

1   Choose Apple menu > System Preferences, and then click Profiles.

2   Select your enrollment profile. It has a yellow badge:

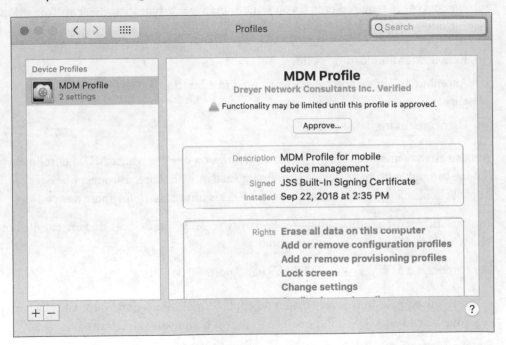

3   Click the Approve button on the right, and then follow the onscreen instructions.

The badge is removed in Profiles preferences, and you have User-Approved MDM enrollment.

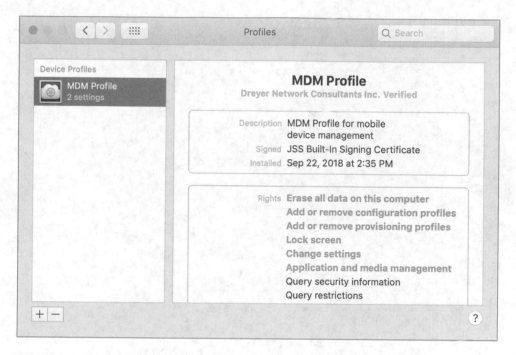

For more information about User-Approved enrollment, read HT208019, "Prepare for changes to kernel extensions in macOS High Sierra."

Reference 9.5
Manage System-wide Security

In addition to account passwords and keychain items, there are macOS-wide security preferences that affect all users on a Mac. Several of these preferences are disabled by default.

Security & Privacy: General Settings

Security & Privacy preferences is a combination of systemwide settings and personal settings that enable you manage macOS security features. You must be an administrator user to make changes to settings that might affect systemwide security or other users. In Security & Privacy preferences, systemwide security settings are dimmed when the lock is locked. The lock indicates that administrator user authentication is required. Personal security settings are always available.

In addition to using Users & Groups preferences, users can change their passwords in the General settings pane.

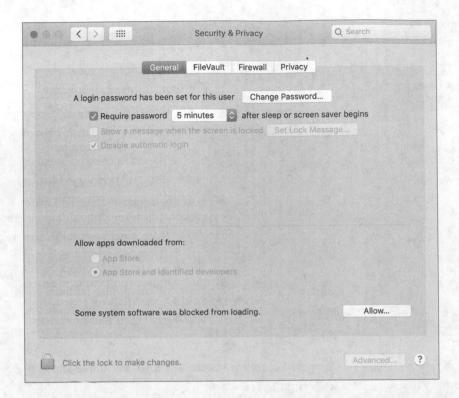

You can choose to require a password to wake a Mac from sleep or screen saver mode and to define a delay before this requirement sets in. Both standard and administrator users can set this for their accounts. If you want to set this for every account from Security & Privacy preferences, consider using a configuration profile.

Administrators can also configure a custom message to show at the login window or when the screen is locked. When setting the message, you can press Option-Return to force a new line. You can have up to three lines of text.

Administrators can disable automatic login for all accounts. This setting is required on Mac computers with FileVault enabled.

If you're logged in with your iCloud account, and it's associated with an Apple Watch, this option is displayed: "Allow your Apple Watch to unlock your Mac." For more information. see support article HT206995, "How to unlock your Mac with your Apple Watch."

macOS enables you to restrict untrusted apps that are downloaded from the Internet from being opened. Near the bottom of the General pane you can configure the sources of apps that macOS allows you to run. Lesson 18, "Install Apps," covers this topic in greater detail.

Security & Privacy: Advanced Settings

Advanced security settings show after you unlock Security & Privacy preferences and click the Advanced button in the lower-right corner of the pane.

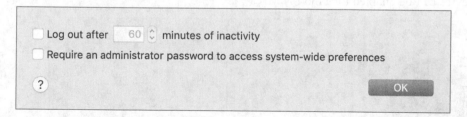

You can choose to require users to automatically log out of accounts after a certain amount of inactivity, and to require an administrator password to access systemwide preferences.

Security & Privacy: FileVault Settings

This pane is where you enable and configure FileVault. Lesson 12, "Manage FileVault," covers FileVault in greater detail.

Security & Privacy: Firewall Settings

This pane is where you enable and configure personal network firewall settings. Lesson 25, "Manage Host Sharing and Personal Firewall," covers this topic in greater detail.

Use Find My Mac

Find My Mac helps you locate a lost Mac by enabling you to remotely access the Mac computer's Location Services. In addition to locating a lost Mac, Find My Mac enables you to remotely lock, erase, and display a message on a Mac.

You can use iCloud to locate a lost iPhone, iPod touch, or iPad. This service is collectively known as Find My iPhone, which is also the name of a free iOS app that you can use to find Mac computers and iOS devices.

Find My Mac prerequisites:

▶   The Mac must have an active Internet connection.

▶   The Mac must have Location Services enabled. If you don't enable Location Services during Setup Assistant or from Security & Privacy preferences, you're prompted to when you turn on Find My Mac.

► You must configure the Mac to use iCloud, with Find My Mac enabled. You can configure or disable Find My Mac any time from iCloud preferences. Although multiple users can sign in to most iCloud services on a single Mac, only one iCloud account per device can be enabled for Find My Mac.

After you configure Find My Mac, access iCloud at www.icloud.com to look for a lost device from another Mac or PC. Log in with the appropriate iCloud account, and select Find iPhone on the iCloud homepage.

If Find My iPhone is successful, iCloud displays a map with the relative location of all the devices configured with the iCloud account. When you select a located device on the map, you can play a sound on, lock, or erase the device. You can also see the power status in the upper-right corner of the device view.

When you issue a remote lock or erase, you first see a prompt to confirm that you want to lock or erase.

▶ For a remote lock, the prompt is "Lock this Mac? Are you sure you want to lock this Mac? A locked Mac cannot be erased." This is because a locked Mac won't receive a remote erase command until the Mac is unlocked again. Before you take action, decide whether you want to send a remote lock command or a remote erase command.

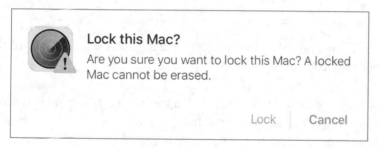

▶ For a remote erase, the prompt is "Erase this Mac? All your content and settings will be erased. Erasing a Mac may take up to a day to complete." After you click Erase, to continue with the remote erase you must provide your Apple ID credentials and then use two-step or two-factor authentication to prove your identity.

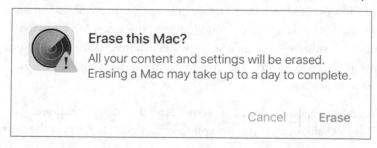

To continue with the remote lock or erase, you must provide a six-digit passcode (also referred to as a PIN), and then verify the passcode.

Cancel	**Lock**

Lock this Mac by entering a passcode.

— — — — — —

1	2 ABC	3 DEF
4 GHI	5 JKL	6 MNO
7 PQRS	8 TUV	9 WXYZ
Clear	0	⌫

After you enter and verify the passcode, you can enter a message that will be displayed on the Mac after it has been locked or erased.

> **NOTE ▸** MDM solutions provide remote lock and erase (also called wipe) operations similar to the remote lock and erase operations that Find My iPhone provides, but MDM solutions do not require Location Services to be enabled.

Once a Mac receives a command for a remote lock or a remote erase, the Mac immediately restarts. Upon restart the Mac prompts you for the passcode with the message, "Enter your system lock PIN code to unlock this Mac." The passcode protects the contents of the Mac from unauthorized users. Without the correct passcode, an unauthorized user can't access any internal disk on the Mac. Also, without the correct passcode, an unauthorized user can't start the Mac in target disk mode (covered in Lesson 11, "Manage File Systems and Storage") or otherwise modify how the Mac starts up. The remote lock function works even while the Mac is using a firmware password, which is covered in Reference 10.4, "Secure Mac Startup."

For the remote erase operation, upon restart a Mac removes all user data. Additionally, a Mac that's protected with FileVault deletes the encryption keys needed to decrypt the startup disk. This is called an instant wipe, and it makes the data on your startup disk completely inaccessible. See Lesson 12, "Manage FileVault," for more information about FileVault.

When you enable Find My Mac, macOS automatically enables the guest account for local login. It's a trap for unauthorized users. The intent is to help a stolen Mac become locked when found. The unauthorized user can choose Guest User as a login option at startup or wakeup, which allows limited access to macOS. If the Mac has the default settings, the unauthorized user is allowed only to select a Wi-Fi network and use Safari. This enables the lost Mac to get back online so that the owner can use Find My Mac to locate it.

Disabling Find My Mac doesn't automatically disable the guest account. If you disable Find My Mac and you don't want the guest user account to be enabled, you have to disable it manually in Users & Groups preferences.

> **NOTE ▶** If you set a firmware password on your Mac before it was lost, then erase it and later find it, you may need to take your Mac to an authorized repair center to unlock it before you can use it again.

Reference 9.6
Manage User Privacy

macOS includes privacy settings that are enabled by default for every user. These settings might prevent functionality that a user would like. You can edit these settings to allow access to private information. macOS Mojave introduces a privacy database, which stores decisions a user makes about whether apps may access personal data. Read the following section to find out more about how you edit settings to allow access to private information.

Find out more about Apple's deep commitment to personal privacy at www.apple.com/privacy/.

More information on managing privacy for Siri and Spotlight is in Lesson 16, "Use Metadata, Spotlight, and Siri."

Security & Privacy: Privacy Settings

Administrator and standard users can manage service access to personal information in the Privacy pane.

When an administrator specifies a privacy selection (enabled or disabled), standard users can't change it. For example, if an administrator disables the ability for Weather to access Location Services, it remains disabled for all standard users.

When a new app requests information to certain classes of data, macOS asks you for permission. For example, when you make a new event and specify a location for the event, Calendar asks you to allow access to Location Services to provide you with improved location searches and travel time estimates.

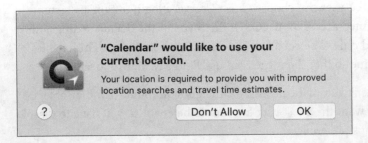

If you click OK, the app or service is added to your privacy database for the appropriate class of data. If you click Don't Allow, the app or service won't have permission to the class of data, and it won't ask for permission again unless you reset the privacy database. For more information about resetting the privacy database, see the man page for tccutil.

You can use your MDM solution to apply a Privacy Preferences Policy Control payload with a configuration profile if each of the following conditions are met:

▶   Your Mac has macOS Mojave or newer.

▶   Your Mac has User-Approved MDM.

▶   Your MDM solution supports the Privacy Preferences Policy Control payload.

If your MDM solution installs a Privacy Preferences Policy Control payload on a Mac with macOS High Sierra, you might have to reinstall the configuration profile after you upgrade the Mac to macOS Mojave for the settings to take effect. For more information about using this payload, see Apple Support article HT209028, "Prepare your institution for iOS 12 or macOS Mojave" and the Configuration Profile Reference at https://developer.apple.com/enterprise/documentation/Configuration-Profile-Reference.pdf.

From the Privacy pane, you can view apps or services that have asked for information and choose to allow or disallow further attempts by them to collect information. The left column in the Privacy pane displays a list of classes of data related to information that apps and services might request.

Each class of data on the left has a list on the right of apps and services that can access that class of data. Some settings in the Privacy pane apply to all users on your Mac. Other settings—for example, Contacts, Calendars, Reminders, and Photos settings—are limited to the currently logged-in user.

Select a class of data on the left, and then deselect an app or service on the right to prevent it from accessing the class of data. For some categories such as Accessibility and Full Disk Access, you can click Add (+) and add an app to the list of apps that can access the category.

▶ Location Services—Location Services allows apps and websites to gather and use information based on the current location of your Mac. Your approximate location is determined using information from local Wi-Fi networks, and is collected by Location Services in a way that doesn't personally identify you. Location Services lets apps, such as web browsers, gather and use information based on your location. You can turn off Location Services completely, or you can select which apps can see information about your location. Click About Location Services & Privacy for detailed information. Click Details next to System Services to see or edit the list of services that can determine your location. While Location Services is selected, next to System Services you can click Details to configure the system services that are allowed to access Location Services. You can modify these settings only if

Security & Privacy preferences is unlocked. There's also an option to display a location icon in menu bar when System Services requests your location. The menu item appears as a northeast compass arrow.

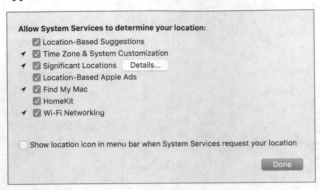

► Contacts, Calendars, Reminders, and Photos—Shows apps that may gather and use information from your contacts, photos, calendar, or reminders.

► Camera and Microphone—Shows apps that have access to the microphone or camera on your Mac.

► Accessibility—Shows apps that run scripts and system commands to control your Mac. After you enable them, assistive apps grant access to control macOS input and modify interface behavior.

▶ Full Disk Access—Shows apps that can access your entire disk. macOS Mojave introduces Full Disk Access as a new pane in the Privacy pane of Security & Privacy preferences. If an app requires full disk access, the first time you open that app in macOS Mojave, it might prompt you to manually add one or more apps to the Full Disk Access pane. If you've upgraded your Mac to macOS Mojave, then you might need to manually add apps and even helper apps that require full disk access to the Full Disk Access pane in order for those apps to continue to work correctly in macOS Mojave.

▶ Automation—Shows apps that can access and control other apps on your Mac. macOS Mojave introduces Automation as a new pane in the Privacy pane of Security & Privacy preferences. This list can include apps that are created with Automator or Script Editor, which are built in with macOS. Automator enables you to automate much of what you do on your Mac. It creates workflows with hundreds of actions that are available in the Automator Library. Script Editor enables you to create scripts, tools, and apps that perform repetitive tasks, automate complex workflows, manipulate apps, or even control your Mac. You can use various scripting languages, including AppleScript, JavaScript for Automation, shell scripts, and some third-party scripting languages. For more information about automation, open Automator and choose Help > Automator Help, or go to http://macosxautomation.com.

▶ Analytics—To help Apple and other developers serve customers better and improve the quality of their products, you can choose to automatically send analytics information to Apple and app developers. If you agree to send Mac Analytics to Apple, you include the following: details about app or macOS crashes, freezes, or kernel panics; information about events on your Mac (for example, whether a function such as waking your Mac was successful); and usage information (for example, data about how you use Apple and third-party software, hardware, and services). This information helps Apple and app developers resolve recurring issues. All analytics information is sent to Apple anonymously.

▶ Advertising—macOS Mojave introduces Advertising as a new pane in the Privacy pane of Security & Privacy preferences. Sometimes you'll receive ads in Apple apps and on your macOS devices that are targeted to your interests. To limit these ads, select the Limit Ad Tracking option. You may still receive ads, but they won't be sent based on data captured by ad tracking. To view what information about your device is used to deliver ads to you in Apple News, Stocks, and the App Store, click View Ad Information. To review Apple's Advertising and Privacy policy, click About Advertising and Privacy.

Dictation Privacy

Enable and manage the Dictation feature in the Dictation pane of Keyboard preferences. Dictation supports many languages, including multiple regional dialects.

To use a different language or to help Dictation automatically enter the correct spoken text, click the Language menu, choose Add Language, and then select the languages and dialects that the users of your Mac speak. Dictation supports basic text-related spoken commands for formatting and punctuation.

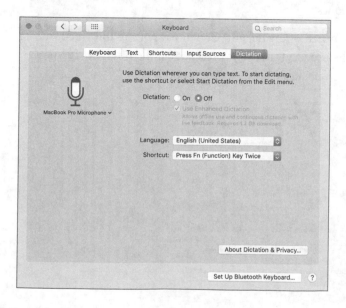

Dictation is off by default. After you turn Dictation on, the Enhanced Dictation option is enabled by default, and your Mac attempts to download additional dictation assets. When you use Enhanced Dictation, your Mac converts what you say into text without sending your dictated speech to Apple.

If you turn Enhanced Dictation off, when you dictate text what you say is sent to Apple to be converted to text. To help your Mac recognize what you're saying, other information is sent, too, such as your Contacts names.

If you turn Enhanced Dictation back on, user data and recent voice input data are removed from Apple servers. Click About Dictation & Privacy for more details.

Read Apple Support article HT202584, "Use your voice to enter text on your Mac."

Safari Privacy

Safari can try to block the hidden methods used to gather information about your web use. Find additional privacy settings in the Safari preferences window.

The "Prevent cross-site tracking" option is turned on by default. Some websites use third-party content providers, which can track you across websites to advertise to you. With this option turned on, tracking data is periodically deleted unless you visit the third-party content provider.

The "Ask websites not to track me" option is turned off by default. With this option turned on, each time you get content from a website, you add a request not to track you, but it's up to the website to honor this request.

The "Block all cookies" option is turned off by default. Cookies are bits of information about your web history that can be used to track your presence on the Internet. Turning on this option might prevent some websites from working properly.

Click Manage Website Data to see which websites store cookies and other information on your Mac. You can remove cookies and website data for individual websites or for all of them.

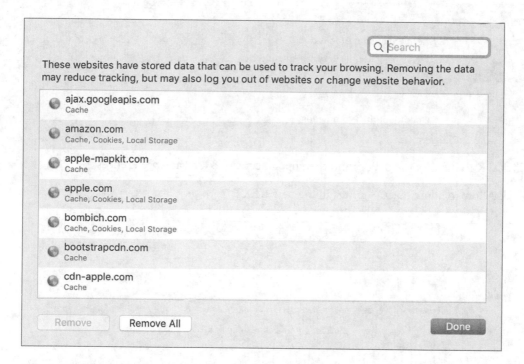

Reference 9.7
Approve Kernel Extensions

macOS High Sierra introduced a feature that requires user approval before loading new third-party kernel extensions (KEXTs). A KEXT is a dynamically loaded bundle of executable code that runs in kernel space to perform low-level tasks that cannot be performed in user space. KEXTs typically belong to one of three categories:

▶ Low-level device drivers

▶ Network filters

▶ File system

macOS requires user consent to load KEXTs with or after the installation of macOS High Sierra or macOS Mojave. This is known as User Approved Kernel Extension Loading. Any user can approve a kernel extension, even without administrator privileges.

When you install software that attempts to install a KEXT, macOS displays a dialog that states that it blocked installing the KEXT.

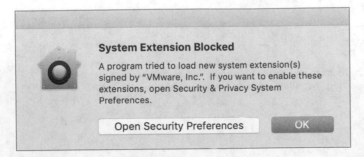

Click OK to dismiss the dialog, and then open Security & Privacy preferences.

Click Allow to allow macOS to install the new KEXT.

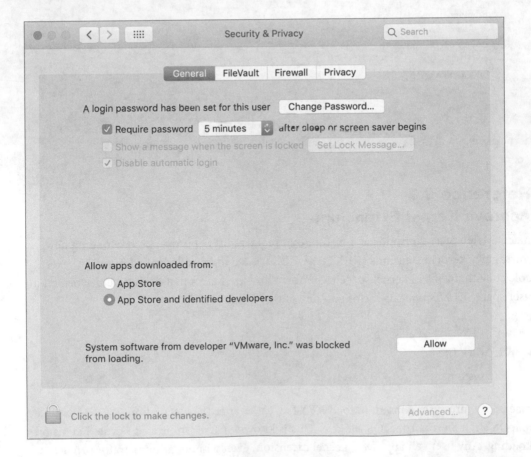

If macOS blocked more than one KEXT, click Allow to view the list of items that were blocked from loading.

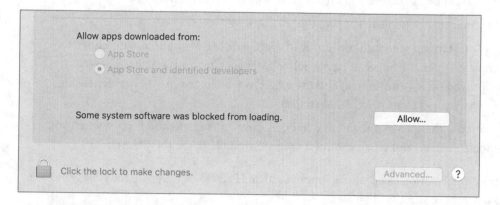

Select the checkbox for each KEXT you want to allow to load, and then click OK.

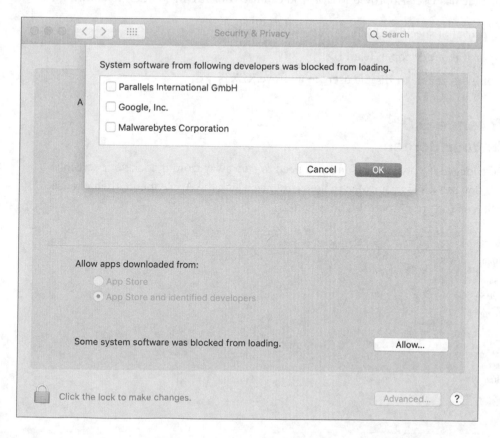

Kernel extensions don't require authorization if they:

▶ Were on the Mac before you upgraded to macOS High Sierra.

▶ Are replacing previously approved extensions.

▶ If your Mac was automatically enrolled with your MDM solution with either Apple Business Manager or Apple School Manager, or your Mac has User-Approved MDM enrollment, and the KEXT is whitelisted in a Kernel Extension Policy payload from your MDM solution.

▶ If you use the spctl command in macOS Recovery. This method is reset when you update macOS, and when you reset your nonvolatile RAM (NVRAM).

For more information, read Apple Support article HT208019, "Prepare for changes to kernel extensions in macOS High Sierra."

If your Mac has User-Approved MDM, you can use your MDM solution to allow:

▶ Approval of specific KEXTs

▶ Approval of developer Team IDs

▶ Ability to enable or disable users to approve KEXTs

Reference 9.8
Lock Your Screen

If you're logged in to your Mac and you need to step away from it, lock your screen so that no one can access your Mac in your absence. Click the Apple menu, then choose Lock Screen (or press Control-Command-Q).

macOS locks your screen immediately, and you'll see a login window with your user picture, your full name, and the password field. No one can use your Mac without first authenticating as you.

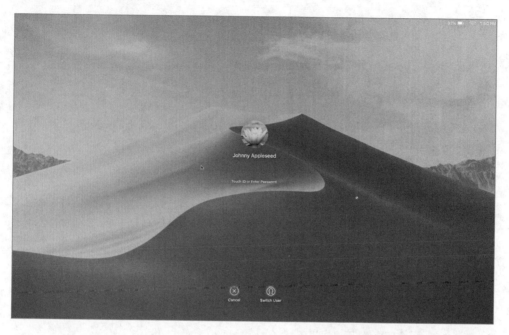

If your organization requires a Mac to display a lock screen message, read Apple Support article HT203580, "How to set a lock message on the login window of your Mac."

Exercise 9.1
Manage Keychains

> **Prerequisites**
>
> ▶ You must have created the Johnny Appleseed account (Exercise 7.1, "Create a Standard User Account").
>
> ▶ You must have performed Exercise 8.1, "Restore a Deleted User Account").

By default, when you log in to your account, your keychain is automatically unlocked and remains unlocked until you log out. If you want more security, you can configure the keychain to lock after a period of inactivity or when your Mac goes to sleep.

In this exercise, you explore keychain management techniques.

Configure the Keychain to Lock Automatically

1   Log in as Johnny Appleseed (password: **Apple321!**).

2   In the Finder, open the Utilities folder choosing Go > Utilities or by pressing Shift-Command-U.

3   In the Utilities folder, open Keychain Access.

    In the upper-left corner, you will notice that the open padlock icon next to the login keychain indicates that it is unlocked.

4   From the menu bar, choose Edit > Change Settings for Keychain "login."

5   Select "Lock after 5 minutes of inactivity" and "Lock when sleeping."

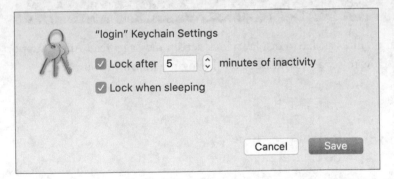

6   Click Save.

7   Open System Preferences, and select Security & Privacy preferences.

8   If necessary, click General and deselect the "Require password" option.

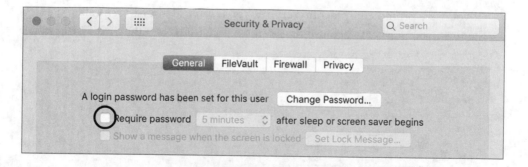

9   If you are prompted to enter Johnny Appleseed's password (**Apple321!**), do so and click OK.

This is a per-user preference setting, so administrator authorization isn't required.

10 If a confirmation dialog appears, click Turn Off Screen Lock.

11 Close System Preferences.

12 If you are presented with a "Do you want to turn off iCloud Keychain?" dialog, click Turn Off Keychain.

13 Choose Apple menu > Sleep.

14 Press any key to wake the Mac.

15 If you are prompted to enter your keychain password for the accountsd or identityservicesd process, click Cancel. Don't enter Johnny's password.

16 If necessary, open Keychain Access.

The lock icon next to the login keychain appears locked (not open), indicating that the keychain is locked.

If you were prompted by identityservicesd or accountsd, they weren't able to access items in your keychain because the keychain was locked and they were inaccessible.

17 In Keychain Access, Control-click the login keychain and select Unlock Keychain "login."

18 Enter Johnny's password and click OK.

The lock opens and your keychain unlocks.

Configure the Login Session to Lock

Instead of locking only the keychain, you can configure the entire login session to lock on sleep or after a period of inactivity.

1 Open Security & Privacy preferences and click General.

2 Select "Require password," and choose "immediately" from the menu.

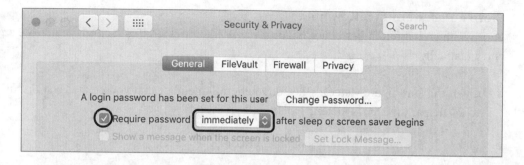

3 If you are prompted, enter Johnny Appleseed's password (**Apple321!**)

4 Choose Apple menu > Sleep.

There are many ways to activate this lock. You could use Desktop & Screen Saver preferences to configure a hot corner to activate the screen saver, or if your keyboard has a media eject key or power button, press Control-Shift-(media eject or power) to put your Mac to sleep.

5 Press any key to wake the Mac.

You see an unlock screen similar to the login screen, but with only Johnny's account shown.

6 Enter Johnny's password and press Return.

Your session unlocks. When you entered the password, the keychain unlocked along with the login session.

To simplify the rest of the exercises, you can relax these security measures.

7 Deselect the "Require password" option in Security & Privacy preferences. If necessary, click Turn Off Screen Lock in the confirmation dialog.

8 Quit System Preferences.

9 In Keychain Access, from the menu bar, choose Edit > Change Settings for Keychain "login."

10 If you are prompted, enter Johnny's password to unlock the keychain.

11 Deselect both "Lock after 5 minutes of inactivity" and "Lock when sleeping."

12 Click Save.

Store a Password in a Keychain

Your keychain has a number of automatically created entries. In this section, you create an entry manually.

1   Open the ParticipantMaterials/Lesson9 folder. Remember that you created a shortcut to ParticipantMaterials in your Dock.

2   Open the file named "Johnny's private files.dmg."

This disk image is encrypted, so the system prompts you for the password to open it.

3   Select "Remember password in my keychain."

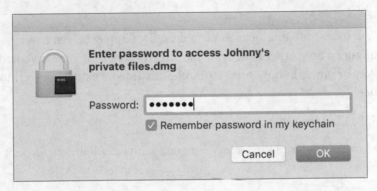

4   Enter the password **private**.

5   Click OK.

6   If you are prompted to enter the keychain password, enter Johnny's account password.

7   Select the disk image on your desktop, and press Command-E to eject it.

8   Open the disk image again.

Since the password is now stored in your keychain and the keychain is unlocked, the image opens without asking you for the password.

9   Eject the disk image.

Retrieve a Password in a Keychain

Even though passwords are stored to make them available for apps, there may be times when a user needs to retrieve a stored password. For example, a user who wants to use webmail on a different Mac may want to retrieve his or her email password to do so. In this section, you use the keychain to retrieve a forgotten password.

1   If necessary, open Keychain Access from the Utilities folder. Remember that you can reach this folder in the Finder by choosing Go > Utilities or by pressing Shift-Command-U.

2   Double-click the password entry named "Johnny's private files.dmg." Scroll down or use the search filter at the upper-right corner of Keychain Access if you need to.

A window opens, displaying information about this password entry.

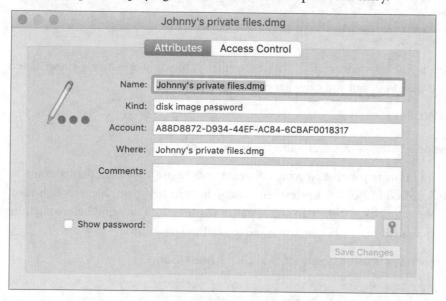

3   Click Access Control.

The Access Control pane displays information about what apps or system components are allowed access to the keychain entry. In this case, the diskimages-helper app can automatically access the password, but if any other app requests access, macOS asks the user for confirmation first.

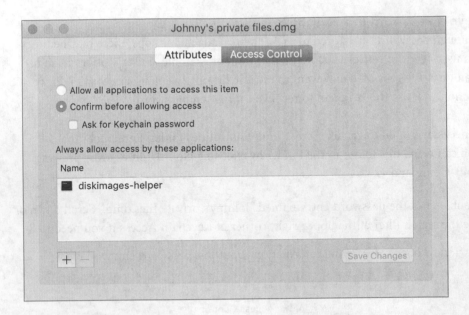

Normally, the app that created a keychain entry is the only one that is allowed automatic access to it, but you can change this policy.

4 Click Attributes.

5 In the Attributes pane, select Show Password.

A dialog informs you that Keychain Access wants to use your confidential information, stored in "Johnny's private files.dmg," in your keychain. Even though your keychain is unlocked, this item access policy requires confirmation before anything other than diskimages-helper is allowed to read the password.

6 Enter Johnny's account password, and click Always Allow.

The disk image password becomes visible.

7   Click Access Control.

Keychain Access is added to the "Always allow access" list for this item. If you had clicked Allow, Keychain Access would have been allowed access to the password but would not have been added to this access control list. Since it is added to the list, Keychain Access can display the password without asking for confirmation.

8   If Keychain Access doesn't appear in the Access Control tab, quit Keychain Access and select the Access Control tab for "Johnny's private files.dmg" again.

9   Close the "Johnny's private files.dmg" window.

Move a Password to the System Keychain

Normally, resource passwords are stored in a user keychain and are accessible only by that user. You can move resource passwords to the System keychain, making them accessible to all users.

1   Find the "Johnny's private files.dmg" keychain item, and drag it to the System keychain in the Keychains section of the sidebar.

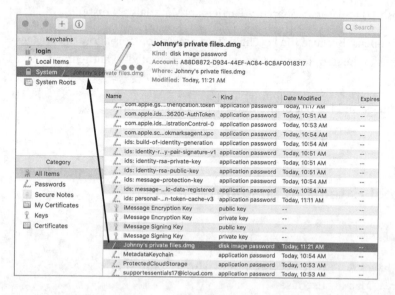

2   Authenticate as Local Administrator (password: **Apple321!**).

3 When you're prompted to allow kcproxy to use the confidential information in "Johnny's private files.dmg," click Allow, and if necessary, authenticate as Johnny.

kcproxy is a tool that Keychain Access uses to move entries into the System keychain. "Johnny's private files.dmg" disappears from your login keychain.

4 Click the System keychain.

"Johnny's private files.dmg" is now listed here, along with several automatically created items, and any Wi-Fi passwords stored on your Mac are listed.

5 Quit Keychain Access and log out of the Johnny Appleseed account.

6 Log in as Emily Davidson (password: **Apple321!**).

7 Use the next two steps to open /Users/Shared/ParticipantMaterials/Lesson9/Johnny's private files.dmg.

Emily's Finder preferences aren't customized to allow easy access outside her home folder.

8 Choose Go > Computer (Shift-Command-C).

9 Open Macintosh HD > Users > Shared > ParticipantMaterials > Lesson9.

The disk image opens. Because the keychain item access controls allow diskimages-helper full access to the item for all users, you aren't prompted to authenticate or allow access.

10 Eject the disk image and log out of the Emily Davidson account.

Exercise 9.2
Approve Kernel Extension Loading

> **Prerequisite**
>
> ▸ You must have created the Local Administrator account (Exercise 3.1, "Configure a Mac for Exercises")

macOS Mojave requires user approval before loading new third-party kernel extensions (KEXTs). This required user approval is called User Approved Kernel Extension Loading. Normally macOS loads and unloads kernel extensions as needed. The kernel extension for this exercise was created as an example, so for the purposes of this exercise, you install a kernel extension manually and approve its loading.

Install a Kernel Extension

1   Log in as Local Administrator (password: **Apple321!**).

2   Open the ParticipantMaterials/Lesson9 folder.

There is a shortcut to ParticipantMaterials in the Finder sidebar and in your Dock.

3   Open the file named DemoExtension.dmg.

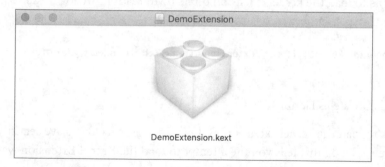

The disk image mounts and displays a kernel extension. Often, a kernel extension is part of an installer or app. In this example, you install it manually by copying the kernel extension to the /Library/Extensions folder. You will learn more about installing apps in Lesson 18, "Install Apps."

4   Click Launchpad in the Dock and open Terminal.

You could also use Spotlight, or from the menu bar choose Go > Utilities, then open Terminal from the Utilities folder.

5   In Terminal, type **sudo cp -r /Volumes/DemoExtension/DemoExtension.kext /Library/ Extensions** and press Return.

```
                   ☖ ladmin — -bash — 80×24
Last login: Tue Nov 13 12:08:19 on ttys000
[Mac-17:~ ladmin$ sudo cp -r /Volumes/DemoExtension/DemoExtension.kext /Library/E]
xtensions
```

Because you are using the sudo command, you must authenticate as Local Administrator (either the full name Local Administrator or the account name ladmin). to elevate your permissions.

6   Type your password.

7   Press Return.

The command should return no output. This indicates that copying the kernel extension to /Library/Extensions succeeded.

This command copies the kernel extension to the appropriate third-party location, and the extension is ready to be loaded.

Load and Approve a Kernel Extension

1   If macOS attempts to load the kernel extension on its own, read the dialog in step 3 and continue with step 4. Otherwise, proceed with step 2.

2   In Terminal, type **sudo kextutil /Library/Extensions/DemoExtension.kext**, and press Return.

3   If necessary, authenticate as ladmin.

macOS attempts to load the kernel extension. But, because of macOS Mojave security measures, you see a dialog that tells you the attempt to load the Kernel Extension was blocked.

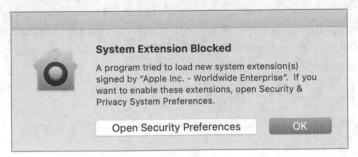

System Extension Blocked

A program tried to load new system extension(s) signed by "Apple Inc. - Worldwide Enterprise". If you want to enable these extensions, open Security & Privacy System Preferences.

Open Security Preferences   OK

4   Read the dialog, and then click OK.

5 Open Security & Privacy preferences.

In the General pane of Security & Privacy preferences, you see a button that enables a user to allow this kernel extension to load.

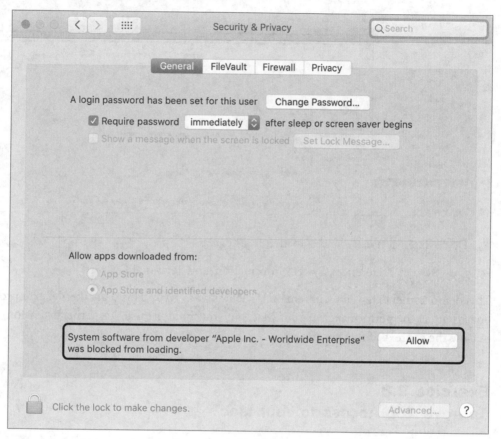

6 Click Allow.

The message disappears, and the kernel extension is loaded. Users do not need to authenticate or be in the admin group to allow a kernel extension to load.

7 Open System Information. Press and hold the Option key and choose
Apple > System Information.

8 Locate Software in the sidebar, and click Extensions.

DemoExtension exists and is loaded.

9 Quit System Preferences, System Information, and Terminal.

This demo kernel extension will remain loaded on your Mac. This demo kernel extension doesn't affect the performance of your Mac, but you shouldn't use this kernel extension outside the context of these exercises.

Exercise 9.3
Approve App Access to Your Mac

> **Prerequisite**
>
> ▸ You must have created the Johnny Appleseed account (Exercise 7.1, "Create a Standard User Account").

macOS Mojave requires user approval before it allows cross-app data requests. You manage this in Security & Privacy preferences. In this exercise, you install an app that requests access to your contacts.

Install an App

1   Log in as Johnny Appleseed (password: **Apple321!**).

2   Open the ParticipantMaterials/Lesson9 folder.

There is a shortcut to ParticipantMaterials in the Finder sidebar and in your Dock.

3   Open the file named Directory.dmg.

Directory is an app that must be installed in the Applications folder.

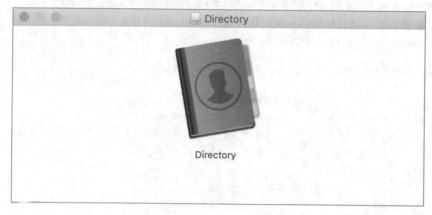

4   From the menu bar, choose Go > Applications (Shift-Command-A).

5   Drag and drop the Directory app from the disk image to your Applications folder.

6   At the "Modifying 'Applications' requires an administrator name and password" prompt, select Authenticate, and authenticate as Local Administrator.

The Directory app is installed in your Applications folder.

Approve an App

1 Open Directory.

Directory

In Directory, you see a Request Contacts Access button. Many apps have different mechanisms for app approval, but if an app in macOS Mojave wants data from another source, it must first obtain user consent.

2 Select the Request Contacts Access button in Directory.

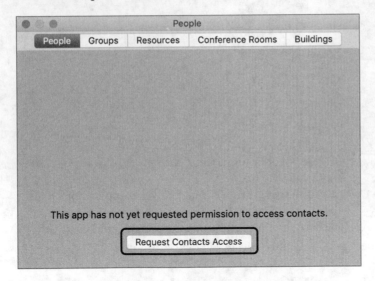

3 At the "Directory would like to access your contacts" prompt, click OK.

You approved the cross-app data request.

In Directory, it says that Contacts access is authorized.

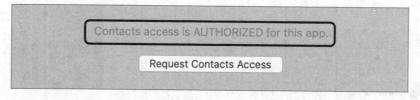

4   Quit Directory, and open Security and Privacy preferences.

5   Click Privacy.

Note the different categories in the left sidebar.

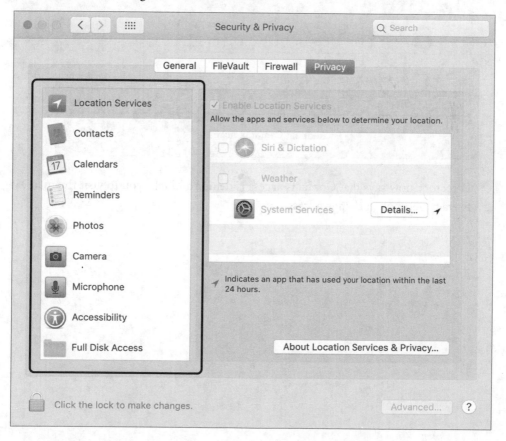

6   Select Contacts.

There is a checkbox next to Directory. This tells you that Directory is approved for access to Contacts.

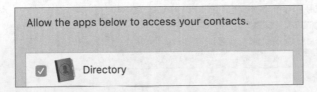

7   Deselect the checkbox next to Directory, and then reopen Directory.

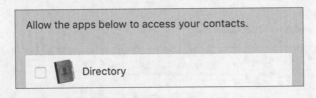

Directory now says that Contacts access is denied and tells you to visit the macOS Privacy Settings to change access.

Manage Password Changes

A password change is different from a password reset. You can change a password if you know it, but if you don't know it, you might be able to reset it. Changing and resetting passwords both result in a new password, but you should reset a password only if a user doesn't know his or her password.

In this lesson, you learn how to change and reset passwords and how to set a firmware password. You also learn about the ramifications of modifying passwords.

In addition, you learn how to configure the Secure Boot and external boot options features that help secure your Mac with the Apple T2 Security Chip against unauthorized access.

GOALS

▶ Change known passwords

▶ Reset lost user passwords

▶ Set a firmware password to secure macOS startup

▶ Manage Secure Boot and external boot options for Mac computers that have the Apple T2 Security Chip

Reference 10.1
Change Known Passwords

If you know your local computer account password but want to change it, you can do so from the General pane of Security & Privacy preferences or you can select your user account in Users & Groups preferences. In either case, you click Change Password.

265

You must enter your old password once, followed by the new password twice. You enter the new password twice to avoid typos. Because you are using a local account password, the new password has to conform to the requirement of being three characters or longer for macOS Mojave (unless a profile has been installed that configures a password policy).

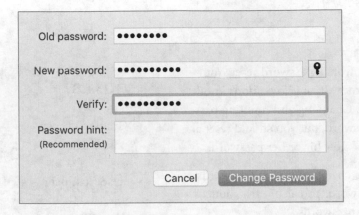

Use Password Assistant

To pick a strong password, use Password Assistant, which gauges the strength of your passwords or creates strong passwords for you. Anytime you create or modify a local password that grants access to a substantial resource, like an account or keychain password, you can use Password Assistant. It's available whenever you see the small key icon next to a password field, as you can see in the previous screenshot showing the local account password change dialog.

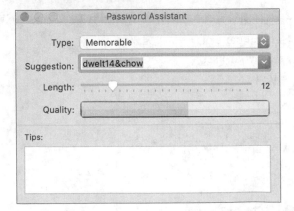

Reference 10.2
Reset Lost Passwords

There are multiple ways to reset a local user account password.

Reset the Password of Another User

If you have access to an administrator account on a Mac, you can reset other user account passwords from Users & Groups preferences. Authenticate as an administrator, select the user account for the password you want to change, and click Reset Password.

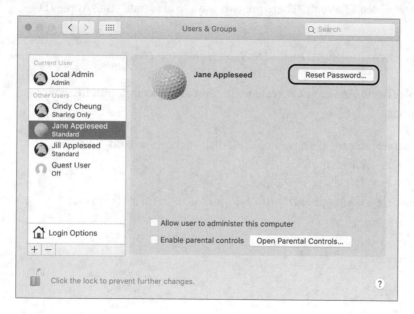

Enter and verify the new password. Optionally enter a password hint, and then click Change Password.

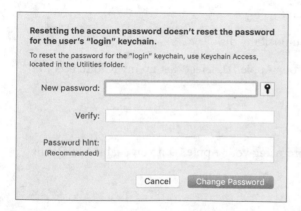

When you log in to your Mac, if your login password doesn't match your login keychain password, macOS creates new empty keychain items for you and sets their new passwords to match your login password. See Exercise 10.3, "Observe Automatic Login Keychain Creation," for details.

Reset Your Login Password Using Your Apple ID

You can reset your login password using your Apple ID if you turn on FileVault and select the option "Allow my iCloud account to unlock my disk." Read Lesson 12, "Manage FileVault," for more details on FileVault. There are two ways to associate your Apple ID with FileVault.

The first way to associate your Apple ID with FileVault is in Setup Assistant:

1   When you first use Setup Assistant to create your computer account, provide your Apple ID credentials.

2   In the FileVault screen, select "Turn on FileVault disk encryption" and "Allow my iCloud account to unlock my disk."

The second way to associate your Apple ID with FileVault is in Security & Privacy preferences:

1   Open System Preferences.

2   Open Security & Privacy preferences.

3   Click Turn On FileVault.

   If FileVault is already on, you can turn off FileVault, wait for decryption to complete if necessary, then click Turn On FileVault.

4   Select "Allow my iCloud account to unlock my disk."

   If you aren't already logged in with your Apple ID, select "Set up my iCloud account to reset my password."

5   Click Continue.

There are two ways to reset your password using your Apple ID if you enabled FileVault and associated it with your Apple ID.

The first way:

1   Start or restart your Mac.

2   Select your user account.

3   If a question mark doesn't appear in the password field, enter a wrong password for your user account three times.

4   Click the question mark in the password field.

5   Next to "reset it using your Apple ID," click the arrow.

6   Confirm that your Mac has a wired Ethernet connection, or if you're using Wi-Fi, use the Wi-Fi menu item to confirm that you're connected to an active Wi-Fi network.

7   Enter your Apple ID, then click Next.

8   Enter your Apple ID password, then click Next.

9   If prompted, enter the verification code that was sent to your other devices, and then click Next.

10 In the Reset Password screen, select a user to reset the password for and then click Next.

11 Enter and verify a new password. You can enter a password hint if you like.

12 Click Next.

13 In the Reset Password Completed screen, click Restart.

The second way:

1   Start or restart your Mac.

2   Wait up to 60 seconds until a message similar to this appears: "If you're having a problem entering your password, press and hold the power button on your Mac to shut it down. Then press it again to start up in Recovery OS."

3   Press and hold the power button on your Mac to shut it down, wait a moment after your Mac shuts down, then press the power button again to start up in macOS Recovery.

This screen should appear:

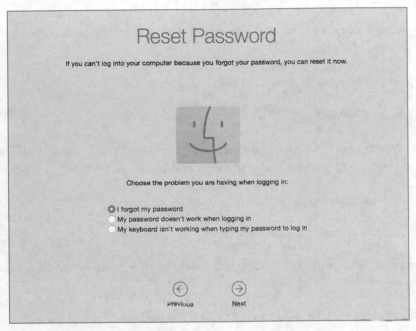

4   Select "I forgot my password" and then click Next.

5   Confirm that your Mac has a wired Ethernet connection, or if you're using Wi-Fi, use the Wi-Fi menu item to confirm that you're connected to an active Wi-Fi network.

6   Enter your Apple ID, then click Next.

7   Enter your Apple ID password, then click Next.

8   If prompted, enter the verification code that was sent to your other devices, and click Next.

9   In the Reset Password screen, select a user to reset the password for and then click Next.

10 Enter and verify a new password. You can enter a password hint if you like.

11 Click Next.

12 In the Reset Password Completed screen, click Restart.

Reset Your Login Password Using a Recovery Key

When you turn on FileVault, if you select "Create a recovery key and do not use my iCloud account," you can use the recovery key to reset your login password.

There are two ways to reset your password using your recovery key if you enabled FileVault and created a recovery key.

The first way:

1 Turn on or restart your Mac.

2 Select your user account.

3 Click the question mark in the password field.

4 Click the arrow next to "reset it using your Recovery Key."

5 Enter the recovery key, and then click the right arrow.

6 Follow the onscreen instructions to reset your login password.

The second way:

1 Start or restart your Mac.

2 Wait up to 60 seconds until a message similar to this appears: "If you're having a problem entering your password, press and hold the power button on your Mac to shut it down. Then press it again to start up in Recovery OS."

3 Press and hold the power button on your Mac to shut it down, wait a moment after your Mac shuts down, then press the power button again to start up in macOS Recovery.

4 Select "I forgot my password" and then click Next.

5 Enter your recovery key, then click Next.

6 In the Reset Password screen, select a user to reset the password for and then click Next.

7 Enter and verify a new password. You can enter a password hint if you like.

8 Click Next.

9 In the Reset Password Completed screen, click Restart.

Reset Passwords Using macOS Recovery

The Reset Password assistant is available only from macOS Recovery. After you start up from macOS Recovery, choose Utilities > Terminal, type **resetpassword**, and press Return. The Reset Password assistant opens and provides methods to reset the local user's account.

The Reset Password assistant presents screens that vary based on the Mac computer's storage and configuration:

▶ Storage volume selection—If a Mac has more than one attached external storage device, you must select the system volume containing the account password that you wish to reset.

▶ FileVault enabled volume—If the selected volume is protected with FileVault and you stored the recovery key with your iCloud account, enter the password for that iCloud account. If you did not store the recovery key with your iCloud account, you must restart and then use your recovery key to unlock the volume in the login window.

▶ Local user selection—If there is more than one local account user on the selected system volume, you must select the account you want to reset the password for.

▶ Local user with associated Apple ID—If the selected local account is associated with an Apple ID, then you may be able to reset the local account password by entering the password for the associated Apple ID.

▶ Local user without an associated Apple ID—If the selected local account isn't associated with an Apple ID, you can enter a new password for the local account.

See Exercise 10.1, "Reset Account Passwords in macOS Recovery," for more details.

Anyone with access to macOS Recovery can use the Reset Password assistant to reset local account passwords. Consider requiring authentication to access the Mac disk from macOS Recovery by either turning on FileVault or using a firmware password, or both. Read Lesson 12, "Manage FileVault," for more details on FileVault and Reference 10.4, "Secure Mac Startup," for more details on using a firmware password.

Read Apple Support article HT202860, "Change or reset the password of a macOS user account," for more details about changing or resetting a password.

Reference 10.3
Manage User Keychains

When a user's account password is reset (as opposed to changed), the user's existing login and Local Items/iCloud keychain items are moved aside. A new login keychain and a new Local Items keychain are created with the same password as the user's login password. The user isn't notified.

Manage Keychain Files

Choose File > New Keychain, and enter a six-, or longer, character password for the keychain to create a new local keychain file. The default location for new keychains is the Keychains folder inside your home folder.

Select a keychain from the sidebar. Then choose Edit > Change Settings for Keychain to adjust keychain settings. A dialog appears where you can change automatic keychain locking settings for a selected keychain file.

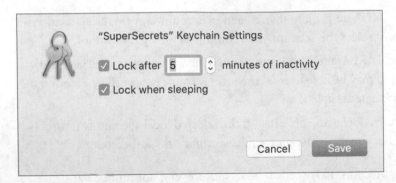

To change a keychain's password, select it from the list, and then go choose Edit > Change Password for Keychain. You must enter the keychain's current password, followed by a new password and verification.

To delete a keychain, select it from the sidebar and choose File > Delete Keychain. When the Delete Keychain dialog appears, click Delete References to ignore the keychain, or click Delete References & Files to erase the keychain file.

Avoid deleting the original login keychain file manually in the Finder. Don't delete the Login keychain unless another keychain is available to take its place. A user should have access to at least one local keychain.

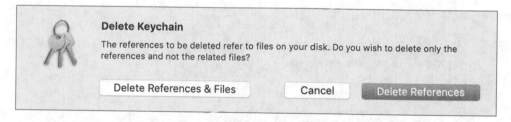

Move keychain items between keychains by dragging and dropping an item from one keychain to another. The exception to this is the Local Items/iCloud keychain, for which macOS manages the addition and removal of items.

Reset Keychain Files

If macOS is unable to open a keychain file or retrieve secrets from it, the keychain file may be corrupted. If so, you must replace or reset your keychain.

If you have a Time Machine backup, as covered in Lesson 17, "Manage Time Machine," you can manually replace a user's Keychains folder with earlier versions of the files. After you replace the keychain files, restart the Mac and log in as the user. Open Keychain Access to verify the presence of the recovered keychain files.

If the user's keychain files are corrupted, and the user doesn't have a backup, you must reset the keychain items. In this case, reset the user's password, or delete the contents of the user's Keychains folder and restart the Mac. Log in as the user, and macOS creates new empty keychain items for the user.

Keychain Access allows any user to reset their own keychains. Open Keychain Access > Preferences, and then click Reset My Default Keychains.

After you click Reset My Default Keychains, macOS asks for a password.

Enter a new password, and then click OK. If the password you enter isn't the same as your login password, the next time you log in, macOS creates new empty keychain items for you that match your login keychain. See Exercise 10.3 for details.

Reset iCloud Keychain

The iCloud Security Code gives you an additional way to add new devices, and it provides a last resort to recover your iCloud keychain if you lose all your devices. If you don't create an iCloud Security Code and you have disabled iCloud Keychain or your devices are lost, your iCloud keychain contents aren't accessible and you must reset your iCloud keychain.

If your login keychain password is lost, so is your access to the local instance of the iCloud keychain. If you create a new login keychain, as recommended in the keychain update dialog, the local iCloud keychain is reset. This results in a new empty Local Items keychain and the contents of iCloud Keychain remain in the cloud.

You can reenable iCloud Keychain to access your secrets, but iCloud Keychain will treat your Mac as if it were new. You are prompted to authenticate with an Apple ID and to use either the iCloud Security Code or two-factor authentication to regain access to the iCloud Keychain.

Read more about iCloud Keychain in Apple Support article HT204085, "Set up iCloud Keychain."

Reference 10.4
Secure Mac Startup

Use Startup Security Utility to configure the features that help secure your Mac against unauthorized access. Startup Security Utility offers additional features for Mac computers that have the T2 chip.

To open Startup Security Utility, start your Mac in macOS Recovery, as covered in Lesson 5, "Use macOS Recovery." Then from the Utilities menu choose Startup Security Utility.

If your Mac doesn't have the T2 chip, you can use Startup Security Utility only to turn on or off a firmware password, which is covered in the next section.

If your Mac has the T2 chip, Startup Security Utility offers two additional features to help secure your Mac against unauthorized access: Secure Boot and External Boot. These additional features are explained after the following firmware password section.

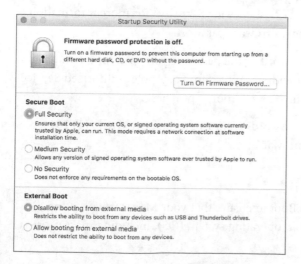

Turn On a Firmware Password

A firmware password prevents users who don't have the password from starting up from any disk other than your designated startup disk. It also blocks use of most startup key combinations.

Even if you don't set a firmware password, you can enable FileVault to prevent unauthorized access to the startup disk. Lesson 12, "Manage FileVault," covers FileVault in greater detail.

For example, on a Mac with a firmware password enabled, if you start up while you press and hold the Option key, an authentication window appears and prompts you to enter the firmware password. If you enter the correct firmware password, you can select a different startup disk from Startup Manager. This enables you to start up from another Mac but prevents other users from changing the standard macOS startup process. Startup keyboard shortcuts are covered in Lesson 28, "Troubleshoot Startup and System Issues."

If you want the most security for your Mac, you must set a firmware password. For a Mac without the T2 chip, any user with access to macOS Recovery can set the password if it isn't already set. For a Mac with the T2 chip, you must provide an administrator password before you can set a firmware password. You set a firmware password with Startup Security Utility. If the firmware password isn't set, click Turn On Firmware Password and enter the password. Remember this password, and store it somewhere safe.

If a firmware password is set, you can change or disable it, but you must know the current firmware password to do so.

You can also use Find My Mac to remotely lock your Mac with a firmware passcode for one-time use. Read Reference 9.5, "Manage System-wide Security," for more information. Lost Mode works even while you're using a firmware password.

If you can't remember your firmware password or the passcode you used for a remote lock or erase, schedule a service appointment with an Apple Store or Apple Authorized Service Provider. Bring your original receipt or invoice as proof of purchase.

You can find out more about firmware passwords from Apple Support article HT204455, "How to set a firmware password on your Mac."

Secure Boot

If your Mac has the T2 chip, use Secure Boot to ensure that your Mac starts up using only a legitimate and trusted version of an operating system (OS), including macOS or Microsoft Windows.

There are three Secure Boot settings:

▶ Full Security

▶ Medium Security

▶ No Security

Configure Secure Boot for Full Security

Full Security is the default Secure Boot setting. Full Security is the highest level of security.

If you select the Full Security setting, during startup your Mac verifies that the OS on your startup disk is trusted by Apple. If the OS is unknown or can't be verified as legitimate, your Mac uses the Internet to download updated integrity information from Apple. The integrity information is unique to your Mac. If FileVault is turned on while your Mac attempts to download updated integrity information, you must first unlock your disk.

If your Mac can't verify that the OS being used during startup is legitimate even after downloading updated integrity information, then the next steps vary depending on the OS:

▶ macOS: An alert informs you that a software update is required to use this startup disk. Click Update, then reinstall macOS on the startup disk. Or click Startup Disk to use a different startup disk (which your Mac must verify).

▶ Windows: An alert informs you that you need to install Windows with Boot Camp Assistant. For more information about Boot Camp Assistant, read Apple Support article HT201468, "Install Windows on your Mac with Boot Camp."

If your Mac can't verify the OS on your startup disk, and your Mac can't connect to the Internet, then you'll see an alert that an Internet connection is required. In this case, if you're using Wi-Fi, use the Wi-Fi status menu item to make sure you're using an active Wi-Fi network.

If your Mac doesn't have an Internet connection and your Mac can't verify the integrity of the OS on your startup disk, then you can click Startup Disk and choose another startup disk, or use Startup Security Utility to change the security level to Medium Security.

Configure Secure Boot for Medium Security

When Medium Security is turned on, your Mac verifies only the signature of the OS on your startup disk. Apple signs macOS, and Microsoft signs Windows. The

Medium Security setting doesn't require an Internet connection, and it doesn't use updated integrity information from Apple, so your Mac can still start up from an OS even if Apple or Microsoft no longer trusts the OS.

If the OS doesn't pass verification, an alert appears for macOS or Windows just like it does when High Security is turned on.

Configure Secure Boot for No Security

When you select No Security in the Secure Boot section, your Mac doesn't enforce any of the security requirements that High Security or Medium Security enforce for your startup disk.

For more information about Secure Boot, read Apple Support article HT208330, "About Secure Boot."

Configure External Boot Options

Use External Boot to control whether your Mac with the T2 chip can start up from an external hard drive, thumb drive, or other external media. Apple doesn't support Mac computers that have the T2 chip starting up from network volumes.

The default and most secure setting is "Disallow booting from external media." When this setting is selected, your Mac can't be made to start up from any external media. If you attempt to start up from external media, the following happens:

▶ Startup Disk preferences displays a message that your security settings don't allow this Mac to use an external startup disk.

▶ Startup Manager enables you to select an external startup disk, but doing so causes your Mac to restart to a message that your security settings don't allow this Mac to use an external startup disk. You'll have the option to restart from your current startup disk or select another startup disk.

If you select the option "Allow booting from external media," then your Mac can start up from an external volume, such as an external hard drive, thumb drive, or other external media.

For more information about the Apple T2 chip, read the Apple T2 Security Chip Security Overview at www.apple.com/mac/docs/Apple_T2_Security_Chip_Overview.pdf.

Exercise 10.1
Reset Account Passwords in macOS Recovery

▶ **Prerequisites**

▶ You must have created the Local Administrator (Exercise 3.1, "Configure a Mac for Exercises") and Johnny Appleseed (Exercise 7.1, "Create a Standard User Account") accounts.

▶ You must have turned on FileVault (Exercise 3.2, "Configure System Preferences").

▶ Your Mac must have a local hidden macOS Recovery volume. This volume is normally created when you install macOS.

macOS provides several ways to reset lost account passwords. In this exercise, you use macOS Recovery to reset Johnny Appleseed's password.

Reset a User Password in macOS Recovery

1   Restart your Mac, and press and hold Command-R until the Apple logo appears.

2   If a language selection screen appears, select your preferred language, and click the right-arrow button to continue.

3   From the menu bar, choose Utilities > Terminal.

4   If you are prompted to provide an administrator name and password because macOS Recovery is trying to change system settings, select Local Administrator, enter the password (**Apple321!**), and click OK.

5   Type the command **resetpassword**, and press Return.

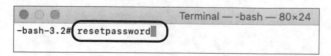

The Reset Password utility opens.

6   At the Reset Password screen, select "I forgot my password."

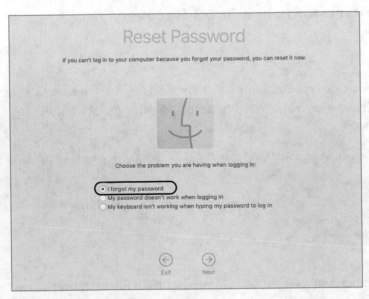

7   Enter the recovery key you recorded when you enabled FileVault in Exercise 3.2, "Configure System Preferences."

Because your startup volume is locked, you can't select a user to reset until the volume is unlocked.

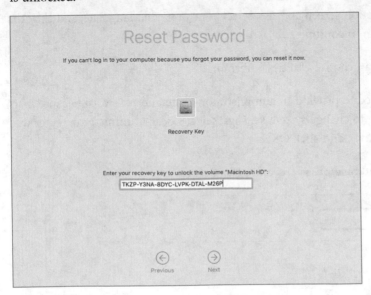

8 Once your volume is unlocked, select the Johnny Appleseed user account (displayed as "johnny"), and click Next.

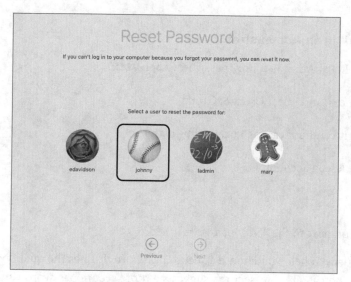

9 Enter **password1** in both password fields. Leave the hint field blank.

10 Click Next.

11 When you are notified that your user account password is reset, click Restart.

NOTE ▶ Johnny Appleseed's login keychain is no longer synchronized with his login password. You may perform Exercise 10.2, "Reset Account Passwords," next, followed by Exercise 10.3, "Observe Automatic Login Keychain Creation," or you may skip directly to Exercise 10.3. In any case, reset Johnny's keychain by performing Exercise 10.3 before going on to any other lesson.

Exercise 10.2
Reset Account Passwords

▶ **Prerequisites**

▶ You must have created the Local Administrator (Exercise 3.1, "Configure a Mac for Exercises") and Johnny Appleseed (Exercise 7.1, "Create a Standard User Account") accounts.

macOS provides several ways to reset lost account passwords. In this exercise, you reset Johnny Appleseed's password as an administrator.

Reset a User Password as an Administrator

1   If necessary, log in as Local Administrator (password: **Apple321!**).

2   Open System Preferences, and select Users & Groups.

3   Click the Lock icon, and authenticate as Local Administrator.

4   Select the Johnny Appleseed account.

5   Click Reset Password.

6   Click the small key icon next to the "New password" field.

Password Assistant opens to help you choose a secure password. It rates the quality of the password (red, to indicate it's non-secure), suggests a more secure password (in the Suggestion field), and lists tips on how to avoid non-secure passwords.

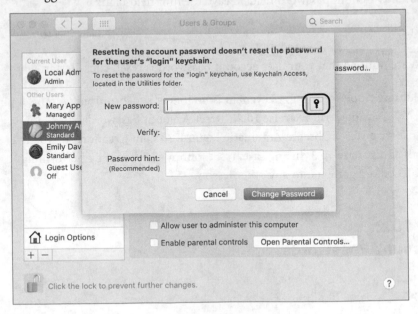

7   Click the triangle next to the Suggestion field to show more suggested passwords.

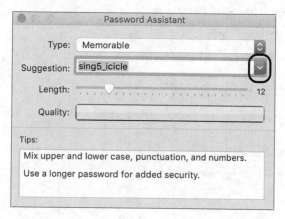

8   Click one of the suggested passwords. The selected password is copied into the "New password," Verify, and Suggestion fields, and the Quality bar expands and turns green to indicate a more secure password.

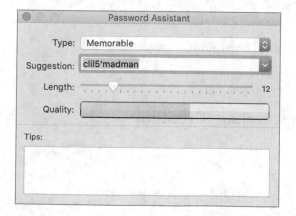

You don't need to memorize or record this password. You choose another password in the next step.

9   Close Password Assistant.

10 In the reset password dialog, enter **password2** in the "New password" and "Verify" fields to replace the chosen Password Assistant password.

11 Click Change Password.

12 Quit System Preferences, and log out as Local Administrator.

Exercise 10.3
Observe Automatic Login Keychain Creation

> **Prerequisites**
>
> ▸ You must have created the Local Administrator account (Exercise 3.1, "Configure a Mac for Exercises").
>
> ▸ You must have created the Johnny Appleseed account (Exercise 7.1, "Create a Standard User Account").
>
> ▸ You must have completed Exercise 10.2, "Reset Account Passwords."

After Johnny's (or anyone's) account password is reset, without notification, macOS creates a new login keychain to keep the account password and login keychain password in sync. The login keychain that existed prior to the password reset is archived and is still encrypted with the old account password.

If Johnny remembers his old password, he can manually import the archived login keychain and move the items he needs to the new login keychain. If his password is reset, he won't be able to recover the old keychain contents.

In this exercise, assume that Johnny's account password was reset because he forgot his old password. He needs to abandon the old keychain after macOS automatically creates a new one.

Observe the Effects of a New Login Keychain

1   Log in as Johnny Appleseed (after the previous exercise, his password is **password2**).

Johnny's account password was changed, and a new login keychain was created for him.

2   If a dialog appears indicating that your Mac can't connect to iCloud, click iCloud Preferences.

Since Johnny's keychain was reset automatically, his iCloud credentials are lost and you need to reenter them.

3   Enter the password for the Apple ID Johnny's account is linked to, and click Next.

4   If the Apple ID has two-factor authentication enabled, follow the prompts to finish authenticating.

5   Quit System Preferences.

Verify the New Login Keychain Creation

1 Open Keychain Access.

Keychain Access displays the status and contents of your login keychain. The keychain is unlocked, which means that macOS created a new login keychain with the correct password.

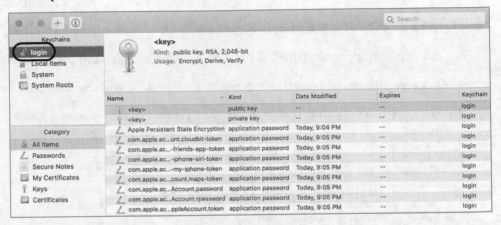

The new keychain normally contains several entries, but it consists only of items that are automatically created in a new keychain plus those items relating to the Apple ID Johnny's account is linked to. The items that were in the old keychain are no longer available.

2 Control-click the login keychain and select Lock Keychain "login" to lock the keychain.

3 Control-click the login keychain and select Unlock Keychain "login" to unlock it.

You are prompted for the keychain password.

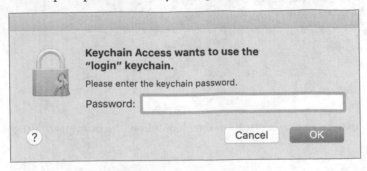

4 Enter Johnny's current account password (**password2**), and click OK.

Since this is the new keychain password, it unlocks.

5 Quit Keychain Access.

Inspect and Import the Archived Login Keychain

1 In the Finder, navigate to ~/Library/Keychains. Choose Go > Go To Folder, and enter the path.

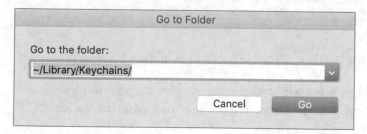

2 Find the item named login_renamed_1.keychain-db, and double-click it.

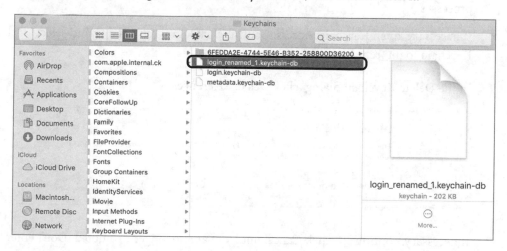

3 Keychain Access opens, and the archived keychain appears in the Keychains sidebar. Select login_renamed_1 and inspect its contents.

If Johnny remembered the password for this keychain, he could unlock it and drag items such as passwords and certificates that he needs into his new login keychain. Because we are assuming that Johnny doesn't know his old login keychain password, don't perform these actions.

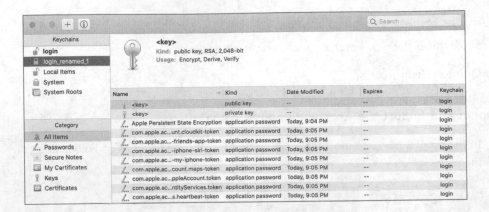

4   Log out as Johnny Appleseed, and then log back in as Johnny Appleseed.

5   If you are prompted to enter your keychain password for the accountsd or identityservicesd process, click Cancel. You can also use Command-period repeatedly until the prompts go away.

The processes accountsd and identityservicesd are daemons, or background processes.

6   If necessary, open Keychain Access. Control-click login_renamed_1 and select "Delete Keychain login_renamed_1."

7   In the Delete Keychain dialog, click Delete References.

8   If necessary, continue to click Cancel until you are no longer prompted. Don't enter Johnny's password.

Deleting references leaves login_renamed_1.keychain.db inside the ~/Library/ Keychains folder. It remains there in case you need it again. If you remove the archived keychain from the keychains list, you prevent macOS from prompting you to unlock it if macOS finds a secret it wants to use in the login_renamed_1 keychain.

9   Quit Keychain Access and log out as Johnny Appleseed.

Change Johnny's Password

When you reset Johnny's account password, macOS created a new keychain. If a user with a standard account changes a password, macOS doesn't create a new keychain. To test this, change Johnny's password.

1 Log in as Johnny Appleseed.

2 If you are prompted to enter your keychain password for the accountsd or identityservicesd process, click Cancel. You can also use Command-period repeatedly until the prompts go away.

3 Open the Users & Groups pane in System Preferences and make sure the Johnny Appleseed account is selected.

4 Click Change Password.

Unlike the Reset Password option you used earlier, this option has a field for the old password. macOS uses this old password to decrypt the login keychain and then re-encrypt it with the new password.

5 Enter the following:

Old password: **password2**

"New password" and Verify: **Apple321!** (or whatever you chose when you originally created his account)

Enter a password hint if you want.

6 Click Change Password.

7 Quit System Preferences.

Verify Synchronization

1 Reopen the Keychain Access utility.

2 Lock and unlock the login keychain.

3 Enter Johnny's current account password (**Apple321!**) in the Password field, and click OK.

As before, the account password unlocks the keychain.

4 Quit Keychain Access.

5 Log out as Johnny Appleseed.

Exercise 10.4
Set a Firmware Password

> ▶ **Prerequisites**
>
> ▶ Your Mac must have a local hidden macOS Recovery volume. This volume is normally created when you install macOS.

In this exercise, you set a firmware password to control your Mac computer's startup process.

NOTE ▶ If you forget your firmware password, you might have to take your Mac to an Apple Authorized Service Provider and provide proof that you own the Mac before the Apple Authorized Service Provider will help you. If you aren't certain that you'll remember your firmware password, skip to the next lesson.

Set a Firmware Password

1   Restart your Mac, and press and hold Command-R until the Apple logo appears.

2   If a language selection screen appears, select your preferred language, and click the right-arrow button.

3   From the menu bar, choose Utilities > Startup Security Utility.

4   If you are prompted to enter your admin password, click Enter macOS Password.

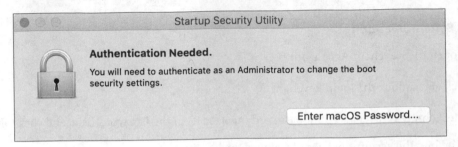

5   Click Turn On Firmware Password.

6 Enter the password **apple** in both the "New password" and Verify fields.

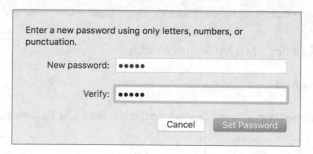

7 Click Set Password.

The Startup Security Utility indicates that password protection is enabled.

8 Click Quit Startup Security Utility.

Test the Firmware Password

1 From the Apple menu, choose Restart.

Your Mac restarts normally. The firmware password doesn't interfere with normal startup.

2 At the login screen, click Restart, and press and hold Command-R until a Lock icon appears.

Alternate startup modes, including macOS Recovery, aren't available if you don't enter a firmware password.

3   Enter the password (**apple**), and press Return.

Remove the Firmware Password

If you are performing these exercises on your own and want to leave the firmware password enabled, restart your Mac and skip these steps.

If you are performing these exercises in a classroom environment or you don't want to leave the firmware password set on your Mac, follow these steps to remove the password:

1   From the menu bar, choose Utilities > Startup Security Utility.

2   Click Turn Off Firmware Password.

3   When prompted, enter the firmware password (**apple**), and click Turn Off Password.

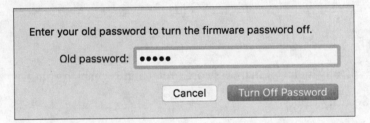

NOTE ▶ There is no simple way to remove or reset a forgotten firmware password. You might have to take your Mac to an Apple Authorized Service Provider to unlock it.

The Startup Security Utility shows that password protection is disabled.

4   From the Apple menu, choose Restart.

Your Mac restarts normally.

File Systems

Manage File Systems and Storage

macOS High Sierra introduced APFS (Apple File System) to Mac computers. APFS is the default file system for Mac computers with macOS Mojave.

In this lesson, you examine the storage technology used by macOS. You learn about storage hardware, such as flash disks, and logical storage concepts like partitions, containers, and volumes. You learn how to manage and troubleshoot these storage assets. Also, this lesson shows you how to verify and potentially repair file-system elements.

Reference 11.1
File Systems

Before you manage storage in macOS, you need to understand the distinction between storage, volumes, partitions, and containers.

Storage

Computer storage is the technology made up of components that store data. Formatting is the process of applying logic to storage in the form of volumes, partitions, and containers (for APFS).

Volumes

A volume is a single storage area with a single file system. It typically resides on a single partition of a single disk, but in special cases it may span multiple disks, like a Redundant Array of Independent Disks (RAID) set or an Xsan volume. For more information about Xsan, read the Xsan 5 Guide. You can download it using the Books app on your Mac or iOS device. For more information about RAID, choose Help in Disk Utility and search for RAID.

Volumes define how the files and folders are stored on the hardware. It's the volume that you see represented as a usable storage icon in the Finder.

Partitions

When you partition a disk, you divide it into individual partitions, which are listed as separate volumes below the Devices section in the Finder sidebar. You can partition a disk if you want to install multiple kinds of operating systems or if you need to change the disk's format. How you partition a disk depends on the file format it uses.

If you're partitioning your internal physical disk because you want to install Windows, use Boot Camp Assistant. Read Boot Camp Assistant Help at https://support.apple.com/guide/bootcamp-assistant/ for more information.

Partition Schemes

Mac supports three types of partition schemes:

▶ GUID Partition Map (GPT)—This is the default partition scheme used by Mac computers. It is also the only partition scheme supported for Mac computers to use for a disk to start up from.

▶ Apple Partition Map (APM)—This is the default partition scheme used by previous PowerPC-based Mac computers.

▶ Master Boot Record (MBR)—This is the default partition scheme used by most non-Mac computers, including Windows-compatible PCs. This partition scheme is commonly used by peripherals that use flash memory for storage.

Volume Formats

The volume format defines how the files and folders are saved to a disk. To maintain compatibility with other operating systems and provide advanced features for later model Mac computers, macOS supports a variety of storage volume formats.

Volume formats supported as read/write in macOS include:

- APFS—When you upgrade to or install macOS Mojave on your Mac startup volume, it is automatically converted to APFS. APFS supports advanced features required by macOS, including Unicode filenames, rich metadata, POSIX (Portable Operating System Interface) permissions, access control lists, UNIX-style links, and aliases.

- Encrypted APFS—This APFS format option adds full disk encryption. This technology supports FileVault system volume encryption. Lesson 12, "Manage FileVault," covers this topic in greater detail.

- Case-sensitive APFS—This APFS format option adds case sensitivity to APFS. In its default state, APFS is case-preserving but case-insensitive. For example, case-insensitive APFS won't recognize "Makefile" and "makefile" as different filenames. Case sensitivity is generally an issue only for volumes that need to support traditional UNIX clients, like those shared with the File Sharing service in Sharing preferences.

- Case-sensitive and encrypted APFS—This APFS format option adds case sensitivity and encryption to APFS.

- Mac OS Extended—The file system that comes with macOS Sierra and earlier (also referred to as HFS Plus).

- Case-sensitive Mac OS Extended—This option adds case sensitivity to Mac OS Extended.

- Journaled or case-sensitive journaled Mac OS Extended—File-system journaling helps preserve volume structure integrity for Mac OS Extended volumes. The journal records what file operations (creation, expansion, deletion, and so on) are in progress at any given moment. If macOS crashes or loses power, the journal can be "replayed" to make sure operations that were previously in process are completed rather than left in a half-completed, inconsistent state. This helps avoid the possibility of file corruption and greatly reduces the amount of time it takes to complete the check-and-repair process on the volume after a crash.

- Journaled and encrypted or case-sensitive, journaled, and encrypted Mac OS—This Mac OS Extended format option adds full disk, XTS-AES 128 encryption.

- File Allocation Table (FAT)—FAT is the legacy volume format used by Windows PCs and by many peripherals. Apple Boot Camp supports running Windows 7 or newer from a FAT32 volume, but macOS can't start up from it.

▶ Extended File Allocation Table (ExFAT)—Created specifically for large flash storage disks, ExFAT extends the legacy FAT architecture to support disks larger than 32 GB. Many flash-based digital camcorders use ExFAT to support the large storage volumes required for high-definition video.

At least one volume format is supported as read-only in macOS:

▶ New Technology File System (NTFS)—Recent versions of Windows use this as their default native volume format. Boot Camp supports running Windows from an NTFS volume, but macOS can't write to or start up from it. Disk Utility doesn't support the creation of NTFS volumes.

APFS

APFS features enhanced data performance, security, and reliability and provides a foundation for future storage innovations. An advanced architecture optimized for today's massive storage technologies, APFS makes common operations such as copying files and folders instantaneous, helps protect data from power outages and system crashes, and keeps files safe and secure with native encryption. macOS Mojave also maintains complete read-and-write compatibility with previously formatted HFS Plus drives and data and is designed to accommodate future advancements in storage technology.

APFS is a system of virtual volumes, in which an APFS container holds one or more APFS volumes. APFS volumes share storage space within their container. When you create an APFS volume, you can specify a reserve size, which ensures that an amount of storage remains available for that volume. You can also specify a quota size, which limits how much storage the volume can use. For most purposes, you don't need to create multiple APFS volumes per container. If you are a member of the Apple Beta Software Program or the Software Customer Seeding program, you can create a new volume to test a prerelease version of macOS. Read Apple Support article HT208891, "How to install the macOS Mojave public beta on a separate APFS volume," for more information.

For a Mac startup disk, an APFS container has at least three volumes, and only the System volume is visible:

▶ System volume—This volume contains macOS Mojave and the Users folder.
▶ Preboot volume—This hidden volume contains data needed for booting each of the system volumes in the container. Only one Preboot volume per APFS container is allowed. The Preboot volume contains one folder per System volume in the container.

▶ Recovery volume—This hidden volume contains macOS Recovery. Only one Recovery volume per APFS container is allowed. The Recovery volume contains one folder per System volume in the container.

▶ VM volume—The virtual memory (VM) volume is created for the first time after a Mac with macOS Mojave starts up.

When you install or upgrade to macOS Mojave, macOS automatically creates the Preboot and Recovery volumes if they don't already exist. During the install or upgrade, macOS also updates information about the System volume in the Preboot and Recovery volumes.

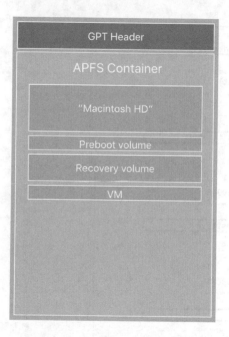

In this lesson, you'll use About This Mac, System Information, and Disk Utility to inspect, manage, and troubleshoot file-system components. These tools don't display information about hidden APFS volumes, because you won't ever need to edit those volumes.

To learn more about APFS containers and volumes, open Terminal and enter the **diskutil apfs list** command.

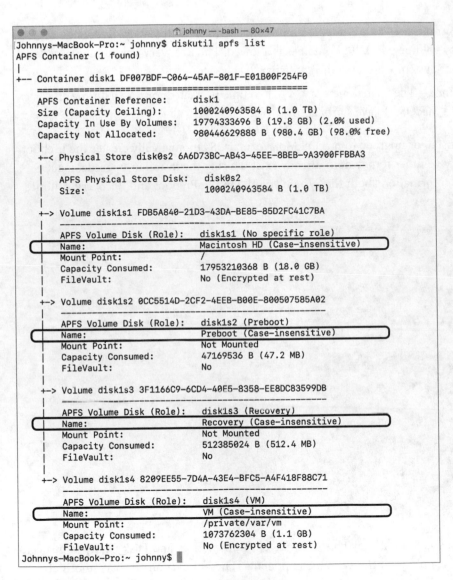

```
                         ⬆ johnny — -bash — 80×47
Johnnys-MacBook-Pro:~ johnny$ diskutil apfs list
APFS Container (1 found)
|
+-- Container disk1 DF007BDF-C064-45AF-801F-E01B00F254F0
    =================================================
    APFS Container Reference:     disk1
    Size (Capacity Ceiling):      1000240963584 B (1.0 TB)
    Capacity In Use By Volumes:   19794333696 B (19.8 GB) (2.0% used)
    Capacity Not Allocated:       980446629888 B (980.4 GB) (98.0% free)
    |
    +-< Physical Store disk0s2 6A6D73BC-AB43-45EE-8BEB-9A3900FFBBA3
    |   ---------------------------------------------------------
    |   APFS Physical Store Disk:   disk0s2
    |   Size:                       1000240963584 B (1.0 TB)
    |
    +-> Volume disk1s1 FDB5A840-21D3-43DA-BE85-85D2FC41C7BA
    |   ---------------------------------------------------------
    |   APFS Volume Disk (Role):    disk1s1 (No specific role)
    |   Name:                       Macintosh HD (Case-insensitive)
    |   Mount Point:                /
    |   Capacity Consumed:          17953210368 B (18.0 GB)
    |   FileVault:                  No (Encrypted at rest)
    |
    +-> Volume disk1s2 0CC5514D-2CF2-4EEB-B00E-800507585A02
    |   ---------------------------------------------------------
    |   APFS Volume Disk (Role):    disk1s2 (Preboot)
    |   Name:                       Preboot (Case-insensitive)
    |   Mount Point:                Not Mounted
    |   Capacity Consumed:          47169536 B (47.2 MB)
    |   FileVault:                  No
    |
    +-> Volume disk1s3 3F1166C9-6CD4-40F5-8358-EE8DC83599DB
    |   ---------------------------------------------------------
    |   APFS Volume Disk (Role):    disk1s3 (Recovery)
    |   Name:                       Recovery (Case-insensitive)
    |   Mount Point:                Not Mounted
    |   Capacity Consumed:          512385024 B (512.4 MB)
    |   FileVault:                  No
    |
    +-> Volume disk1s4 8209EE55-7D4A-43E4-BFC5-A4F418F88C71
    |   ---------------------------------------------------------
    |   APFS Volume Disk (Role):    disk1s4 (VM)
    |   Name:                       VM (Case-insensitive)
    |   Mount Point:                /private/var/vm
    |   Capacity Consumed:          1073762304 B (1.1 GB)
    |   FileVault:                  No (Encrypted at rest)
Johnnys-MacBook-Pro:~ johnny$ █
```

You can find out more about APFS in the Apple Developer article "About Apple File System," available at https://developer.apple.com/documentation/foundation/file_system/about_apple_file_system.

APFS Compatibility

Devices formatted as Mac OS Extended can be read from and written to by devices formatted as APFS.

Devices formatted as APFS can be read from and written to by:

▶ Other devices formatted as APFS

▶ Devices formatted as Mac OS Extended, if using macOS High Sierra or newer

APFS and Boot Camp

Boot Camp doesn't read from or write to APFS-formatted volumes, but it is compatible with macOS Mojave.

APFS and File Sharing

Volumes formatted as APFS can't offer share points over the network using Apple Filing Protocol (AFP).

APFS supports Server Message Block (SMB) and Network File System (NFS), with the option to enforce only SMB-encrypted share points.

APFS and Time Machine

You don't need to change any Time Machine settings to back up APFS-formatted disks.

Any Time Machine share points must be shared over SMB instead of AFP.

Fusion Drive

Fusion Drive combines the performance of flash storage with the capacity of a hard drive.

Presented as a single volume on your Mac, Fusion Drive moves files that you use frequently to flash storage so that you can access them faster. Fusion Drive moves files that you don't use a lot to a high-capacity hard disk. As a result, you enjoy shorter startup times and—as the system learns how you work—you can open apps and files faster.

Reference 11.2
Mount, Unmount, and Eject Disks

When you mount a volume, your Mac establishes a logical connection to that volume. Users don't normally need to think about this because a Mac automatically mounts any connected volume. When you plug in a disk, the disk's volumes automatically appear in the Finder and Disk Utility. You will need to enter a password to unlock encrypted volumes.

Ensuring that users properly unmount and eject volumes is critical to maintaining data integrity. The term *unmount* refers to the process of having the Mac cleanly disconnect from a disk's volumes, whereas the term *eject* refers to the process of having the Mac additionally disconnect electronically from the hardware disk or media. When you choose to eject a disk from the Finder, the Mac unmounts the volumes first and then ejects the disk.

Eject Disks

There are seven ways to unmount and eject a disk from the Finder:

▶ In the Finder, select the disk you want to unmount and eject, and choose File > Eject.

▶ In the Finder, drag the disk icon to the Trash icon in the Dock. The Trash icon changes to an Eject icon, indicating the appropriate action.

▶ In the Finder sidebar, click the small Eject button next to the volume you want to unmount and eject.

▶ In the Finder, select the volume you want to unmount and eject, and then choose File > Eject *diskname*.

▶ In the Finder, select the volume you want to unmount and eject, and then use the Command-E keyboard shortcut.

▶ In the Finder, select the volume you want to unmount and eject, and then Control-click to reveal a menu enabling you to select Eject *diskname*.

▶ In a Finder window, select the disk you want to unmount and eject, click the Action button in the Finder window toolbar (it looks like a gear), and then choose Eject *diskname*.

When you use the Finder to unmount and eject a single volume that is part of a disk with several mounted volumes, you see a warning dialog giving you the choice to unmount and eject all the volumes on the disk or just the one you originally selected. To eject all volumes of a disk, select one of the volumes in the Finder, and then press the keyboard shortcut Option-Command-E, or press and hold the Option key, then choose File > Eject *number of volumes* Volumes. You shouldn't experience problems with a disk if some volumes are mounted and others remain unmounted.

Remount Volumes

If you're using the Finder to remount a volume on a connected disk, you must first unmount and eject remaining volumes and then physically disconnect and reconnect the disk. Alternatively, you can open Disk Utility to manually mount and unmount volumes without physically disconnecting and reconnecting the disk.

In the following screenshot of Disk Utility, several volumes are shown. The startup disk is selected in the left column. The Secrets volume appears in dimmed text because it's physically connected to the Mac but isn't mounted. The External Data volume is mounted, so macOS displays an Eject button near its name.

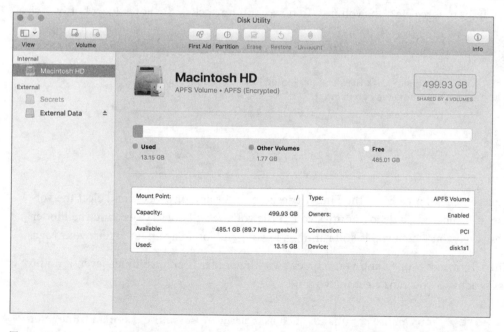

To mount an unmounted volume on a connected disk, select the volume's dimmed name and then click the Mount button in the toolbar. The volume immediately mounts and appears in the Finder, and its name is undimmed in Disk Utility.

Eject In-Use Volumes

If you remove a volume that contains a file that's still in use, then you might corrupt data if an app or process tries to write to the file. The Finder won't allow you to eject a volume with in-use files, but it might try to help you eject the volume. If the app or process using the volume belongs to your account, the Finder displays the following dialog.

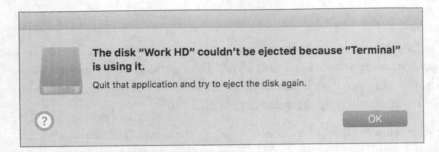

If you see this dialog, quit the app and try to eject the volume again.

If you don't own the app or process that is using the volume, the Finder asks if you want to attempt to force eject the volume. To do so, you must click the Force Eject button twice.

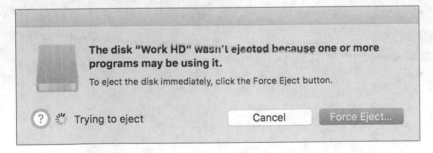

After you click Force Eject, the Finder tries to quit the app or process and eject the volume. If it succeeds, a dialog notifies you. If the volume still doesn't eject and the Finder doesn't tell you which app is still running, log out and log in again, or restart your Mac.

When Terminal is open and your current working folder is on a volume—even if no process is active—you can't eject the volume.

NOTE ▶ You can use commands such as **fs_usage** or **lsof** in the command-line interface (CLI) to discover which process is using the volume. See the man page for those commands for more information.

Reference 11.3
Inspect File-System Components

If you plan to manage or troubleshoot the Mac file system, become familiar with its current configuration. You can access a graphical overview of the Mac storage from the Storage pane of the About This Mac window, which you can open from the Apple menu.

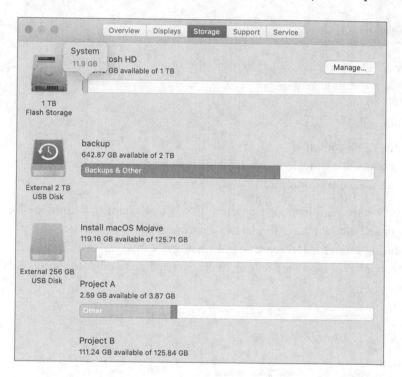

You can find out more about Purgeable items and storage optimization features (accessed with the Manage button in the About This Mac dialog) in Lesson 19, "Manage Documents."

For a more detailed examination of the storage systems, use Disk Utility and System Information. These tools enable you to inspect the availability and status of storage hardware.

Examine Storage with Disk Utility

Use Disk Utility as your primary storage management tool in macOS. When you open Disk Utility, it scans the file system for attached devices and volumes.

By default, Disk Utility displays volumes. To view information about the physical disk, click View in the upper-left corner, then choose Show All Devices.

When you select Show All Devices, macOS lists items in this order:

1. Storage hardware (disk)

2. APFS containers in the disk

3. APFS volumes in the APFS container

When you select any item in Disk Utility, you see information about the item, including its utilization, formatting, and connection information.

Select a disk name to view information about a physical disk. A disk's name is a combination of the manufacturer and model name. To identify a hardware failure, view a disk's S.M.A.R.T. (self-monitoring, analysis, and reporting technology) status. S.M.A.R.T. can determine if a disk has an internal hardware failure. Many external disks don't support S.M.A.R.T.

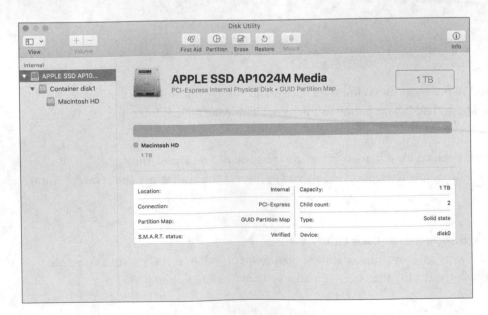

Select an APFS container to view information about that container, including information about its APFS volumes. The container name is automatically generated.

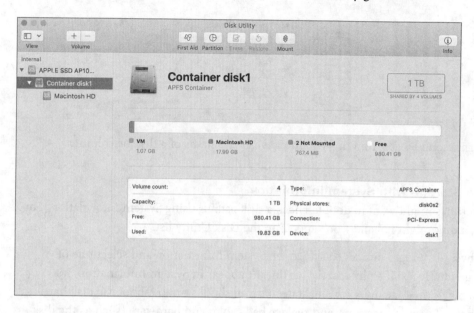

Select an APFS volume to view information about that volume. Volume names are set when the volume is formatted, but you can change them.

To gather detailed information about a disk or volume in Disk Utility, select the item from the column on the left and click the Info button in the toolbar.

The information you get from this window reveals the status of a disk or volume.

Examine Storage with System Information

You sometimes might want to double-check a disk's status using System Information. For example, a disk might fail and won't appear in the Disk Utility list.

To see physical storages devices (disks), open System Information and select one of the storage interfaces. If a physical device doesn't appear in System Information, it's not available to the Mac in its current state and you should troubleshoot the disk hardware. Tighten loose connections, and replace bad cables and hardware (such as the disk enclosure).

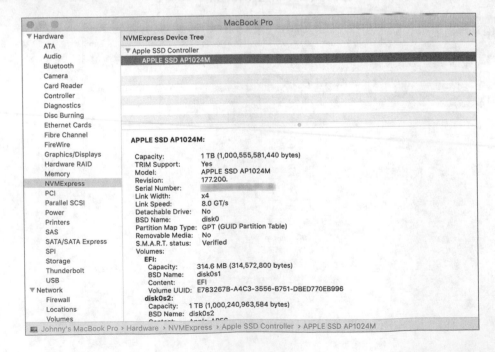

The Storage section shows currently mounted volumes.

Reference 11.4
Manage File Systems

In the Finder, you can rename any volume without having to reformat or erase its content. Select the volume, press Return, edit the name, and then press Return to stop editing the name. Or, from the Finder sidebar, Control-click to rename it.

In this section, you explore how you can use Disk Utility to modify disks and volumes.

Format Unreadable Disks

Many new storage devices are formatted for Windows. For the most part, you can use Windows-formatted disks on the Mac without reformatting. If you want to install macOS on a disk, or you have a new disk that is completely blank, you have to erase and format (or initialize) the disk.

If you attach an unformatted or unreadable disk, macOS prompts you to Initialize, Ignore, or Eject. If you click Initialize, Disk Utility opens.

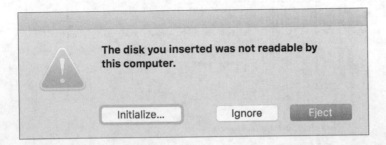

Erase a Disk or Volume

When you erase a disk or volume in Disk Utility, the storage is formatted (initialized). When Show All Devices is selected, select the disk or volume you want to erase, and click Erase in the toolbar.

When you erase a disk, Disk Utility creates a new volume format and partition scheme. Disk Utility defaults to the Mac OS Extended (Journaled) format and the GUID Partition Map scheme, even if the disk has an APFS container. To select a different format or scheme, select it from the appropriate menu.

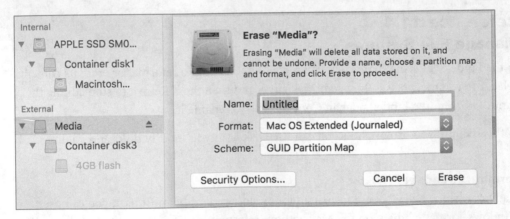

When you erase a volume (as opposed to a disk), Disk Utility creates a new volume format. If the volume you erase is an APFS volume, the Format menu offers APFS-related formats.

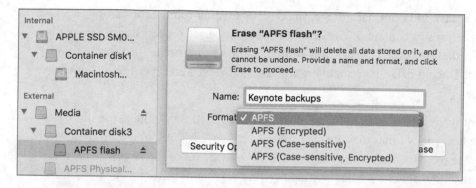

If the volume you erase has a Mac OS Extended format, you have options for the new volume format.

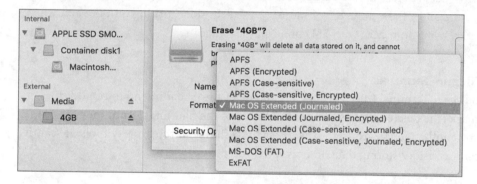

When you erase a selected volume, no other volumes on the disk are affected. Further, you can't change the disk partition scheme—that would affect all volumes on the disk.

If you select an encrypted volume format, a dialog appears that enables you to set the encrypted volume's password. If you lose the password, you won't be able to recover data from the encrypted volume.

When you erase and reformat storage, you destroy existing volume formatting (a reformatted disk loses its contents). The default Disk Utility erase process doesn't erase files from the disk. Disk Utility creates new empty volumes by replacing the file and folder structures. The old data files remain on the disk, and you can recover them using third-party tools.

To prevent the erased files from being recovered, click Security Options, use the slider to choose how many times to write over the erased data, click OK, and then click Erase. Writing over the data three times meets the U.S. Department of Energy standard for securely erasing magnetic media. Writing over the data seven times meets the U.S. Department of Defense 5220-22-M standard.

> **NOTE ▶** Secure erase options are available in Disk Utility only for HDD (hard disk drive) and some flash storage. For more security, consider turning on FileVault when you start using your Mac with SSD or all-flash storage.

Erase Files in Terminal

When you open Terminal (the macOS CLI) and enter the rm command to remove files, macOS marks the deleted files as free space and leaves the files intact until they are written over by another action. You can still access these files with third-party tools. If security is a concern, consider storing data on encrypted volumes.

Encrypt an External Disk

You can convert an existing disk to an encrypted disk using the Finder. It's best to encrypt a flash-based disk before saving any sensitive data to it. To encrypt the macOS system volume, enable FileVault. Lesson 12, "Manage FileVault," covers FileVault in greater detail.

To encrypt a disk in the Finder, Control-click the disk you want to encrypt, and from the shortcut menu choose Encrypt *diskname*, where *diskname* is the name of the disk you selected.

The Finder prompts you to set a password and a password hint for the encrypted disk. You must set a password hint.

You can continue to use a disk while macOS encrypts its contents in the background. When you attempt to connect an encrypted disk, you're prompted for the disk password, unless you store the password in your keychain. Using keychains is covered in Lesson 9, "Manage Security and Privacy."

In the Finder, Control-click the disk to see if the encryption finished. In the shortcut menu, a fully encrypted disk shows a Decrypt *diskname* option, where *diskname* is the name of the disk you selected.

From the Disk Utility File menu, you can change the password or decrypt an encrypted disk.

Reference 11.5
Troubleshoot File Systems

Bad hardware and media cause most file-system failures.

First Steps

If you have a storage device (disk) with a problem, try these steps:

1   Find out if the hardware connection is good from the external storage device to the internal disk.

2 If a nonsystem disk has a problem, see Reference 11.3, "Inspect File-System Components," and follow the instructions there to resolve the problem.

3 If the problem involves the system disk, try to start up from macOS Recovery.

▶ Press and hold Command-R at startup.

▶ From macOS Recovery, open Disk Utility to see and possibly repair the system disk.

▶ If the default macOS Recovery system doesn't work, use the methods detailed in Lesson 5, "Use macOS Recovery."

4 If you think that a catastrophic hardware failure is the problem, there isn't anything you can do from a software perspective to repair the Mac. A commercial data recovery service might be able to recover your data.

5 If you're experiencing file-system issues but the storage hardware seems to function, you might be experiencing partial hardware failure or file-system corruption. In these cases, you can use the built-in utilities in macOS to repair the volumes or recover data.

Disk Utility First Aid

To access data on a disk, the file system must read the partition scheme and volume directory structure to find the appropriate bits that make up the requested item or items. The file system uses the partition scheme to define the space where volumes exist. It uses the volume directory structure to catalog where files and folders exist. Damage to the partition scheme or volume directory structure might cause serious problems, including data loss.

Before a disk is mounted, a Mac performs a quick consistency check to verify the disk's partition scheme and volume directory structure. A Mac also quickly scans the startup disk during startup. If a Mac is unable to mount a disk or its volumes, or you have problems accessing a disk's content, use Disk Utility First Aid to verify and repair the partition scheme or volume directory structures.

To use the First Aid feature in Disk Utility, verify that the disk you want to repair is attached to the Mac, and then open Disk Utility. Select the disk or volume you want to inspect or repair from the column on the left, and then click the First Aid button in the toolbar.

When you select a disk, you indicate that you want to repair its partition scheme. When you select a volume, you indicate that you want to repair its directory structure. Start with a disk's partition scheme, then move to its volumes to resolve problems.

First Aid verify and repair might take a few minutes to complete because it runs until it finds no problems. During this time, Disk Utility shows a progress indicator and log entries in the history area. Click the Show Details disclosure triangle to view more detail in the history log.

If First Aid doesn't find any problems, you see a green checkmark. If First Aid finds problems, it describes them in bright red text in the log and attempts to repair them.

Target Disk Mode

Target disk mode enables you to share files between two Mac computers that are connected through their ports that are compatible with target disk mode.

You can use the following ports for target disk mode:

▶ Thunderbolt 3 (USB-C) ⚡—Available on iMac Pro, iMac models from 2017, Mac mini (2018), MacBook Pro models from 2016 or later, and MacBook Air (Retina, 13-inch, 2018)

▶ USB-C ⎓—Available on MacBook models from 2015 or later

▶ Thunderbolt 2 ⚡

▶ FireWire ⚞

With target disk mode, one Mac appears as an external disk on the other Mac, enabling you to browse and copy files. Use target disk mode when you need high transfer speeds or if the display on one of your Mac computers isn't working and you need to get files from it.

MacBook (12-inch, Retina, Early 2015) and newer support USB target disk mode using the following USB-C cables to transfer data:

▶ USB 3.0 or USB 3.1 USB-C Cable (USB-C to USB-C)—Use this cable to share files between a Mac with a USB-C port and a MacBook with a USB-C port.

▶ USB 3.0 or USB 3.1 USB-A to USB-C Cable—Use this cable to share files between a Mac with USB-A port(s) and a MacBook with a USB-C port, for example, the Belkin USB-A to USB-C Cable (USB 3.1).

You can use target disk mode to transfer data between Mac computers with Thunderbolt 3 and other Mac computers:

▶   To use target disk mode between a Mac with Thunderbolt 3 (USB-C) and another Mac computer's Thunderbolt 3 (USB-C) port, connect the two Mac computers with a Thunderbolt 3 (USB-C) cable such as the Apple Thunderbolt 3 (USB-C) Cable.

▶   To use target disk mode between a Mac with Thunderbolt 3 and another Mac with Thunderbolt 2, connect a Thunderbolt 3 (USB-C) to Thunderbolt 2 Adapter to your Mac and then use a Thunderbolt 2 cable to connect the adapter to the other Mac.

Target disk mode doesn't support the following cables:

▶   Apple USB-C Charge Cable

▶   USB-A to USB-A cable

▶   Mini DisplayPort cable |▢|

For more information, read Apple Support article HT207443, "Adapters for the Thunderbolt 3 (USB-C) or USB-C port on your Mac or iPad Pro," and Apple Support article HT201462, "How to use target disk mode to move files to another computer."

Because target disk mode is built into Mac hardware, you can use it even if the installed macOS volume is corrupted. An administrator user can enable target disk mode on a running Mac by clicking the lock, authenticating with administrator credentials, then clicking the Target Disk Mode button in Startup Disk preferences if it's available. Alternatively, assuming macOS doesn't have a firmware password, any user can engage target disk mode during Mac startup by pressing and holding the T key while turning on the Mac.

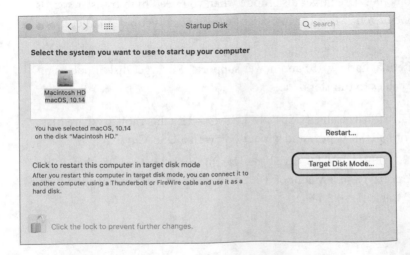

After target disk mode is engaged, FireWire, Thunderbolt, or USB symbols appear on the screen. Plug the targeted Mac into another Mac using a FireWire, Thunderbolt, or appropriate USB-C cable.

The targeted Mac computer's internal volumes mount normally on the other Mac, as if you had plugged in a normal external disk. At this point, you can do almost anything to the targeted Mac computer's internal disk that you could do to any local disk, including installations, repairs, and data migration.

As useful as target disk mode is, be aware of these caveats:

▸ Older USB-A ports on Mac computers don't support target disk mode. Older Mac computers with USB-A ports can mount disks of newer Mac computers in target disk mode through USB-C with an appropriate USB-C to USB-A adapter.

▸ Target disk mode isn't supported on disks that use third-party storage interfaces, like those found on PCI Express expansion cards.

▸ The Install macOS Mojave app won't allow you to upgrade or install on a destination that is in target disk mode.

▸ If you set a firmware password on your Mac, covered in Reference 10.4, "Secure Mac Startup," then you can't start your Mac in target disk mode without first providing the firmware password.

▸ Secure Boot and External Boot settings (covered in Reference 10.4 and available for Mac computers with the Apple T2 Security Chip) do not prevent you from starting your Mac in target disk mode.

▸ Some hardware failures prevent a Mac from entering target disk mode. If you suspect this is the case, try using Apple Hardware Test. It's covered in Lesson 28, "Troubleshoot Startup and System Issues."

Recover Data from a Nonstarting System

If your Mac won't start up from its internal system disk, you can still recover data from the disk if it functions with target disk mode. Use it to access the internal system disk and transfer your data to another working Mac.

First, turn on or restart the problematic Mac while pressing and holding the T key to engage target disk mode. Then connect the Mac to another, fully functioning Mac using an appropriate cable. If the problem Mac computer's volume appears in the Finder, try to repair the disk and volumes with Disk Utility First Aid, as detailed earlier in this lesson.

If your Mac doesn't support, or can't engage, target disk mode, visit an Apple Authorized Service Provider.

You could also try to remove the disk from the troubled Mac and attach it to a fully functional Mac.

After you complete repairs, try one of these options to recover your data:

▶ Use the Finder to copy data from the problem Mac to an external storage device that is attached to the functioning Mac.

▶ Use Disk Utility on the functioning Mac to create a disk image archive of the problem Mac computer's system volume. Creating disk images is covered in Lesson 14, "Use Hidden Items, Shortcuts, and File Archives."

▶ Use Migration Assistant to transfer data to the functioning Mac as detailed in Lesson 8, "Manage User Home Folders."

▶ After you transfer the data, use Disk Utility to reformat macOS. Lesson 2, "Update, Upgrade, or Reinstall macOS," covers this topic in greater detail.

Depending on the amount of corruption to the problem system disk, you might not be able to use Disk Utility or Migration Assistant. If so, try to manually copy the data.

For more information, read Disk Utility Help at https://support.apple.com/guide/disk-utility.

Exercise 11.1
View Disk and Volume Information

> **Prerequisite**
>
> ▶ You must have created the Local Administrator account (Exercise 3.1, "Configure a Mac for Exercises").

In this exercise, you view information that pertains to your Mac computer's internal disk. You'll see multiple ways to view information about the storage in your Mac. You'll also see the internal disk device and the volume that the disk contains.

View Storage Information with About This Mac

1   Log in as Local Administrator.

2   Choose Apple menu > About This Mac.

3   Click Storage.

This pane shows the volumes that are mounted on your Mac. Usually Macintosh HD is the only volume. This pane also shows how much disk space is in use. Hover your pointer over the colored sections of the bar to see what kind of content is using disk space.

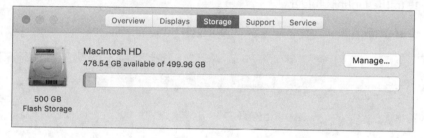

4   Click Manage.

System Information opens and shows options for reducing disk use. Read Reference 19.5, "Optimize Local Storage," for more information.

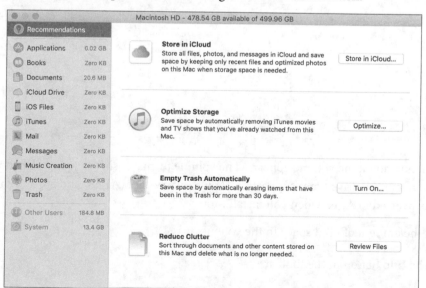

5 Click through the other items in the sidebar.

These items show details about different content. You're unable to view the details of Other Users and System.

6 Quit System Information.

View Disk Information with Disk Utility

1 Open Disk Utility.

Disk Utility is in the Utilities folder. Choose Go > Utilities or press Shift-Command-U to navigate to the Utilities folder.

2 Select your startup volume (generally Macintosh HD) in the sidebar.

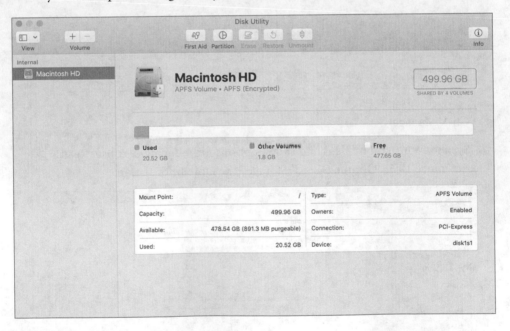

Information about the volume appears. The volume format is shown just under the volume name. All drive types support the Apple File System (APFS) and are automatically converted to APFS when you install Mojave.

3 Check the amount of used space in the volume.

4 Click the Info button in the toolbar.

A window opens showing additional details about the volume. You might need to scroll down to see all of the window contents.

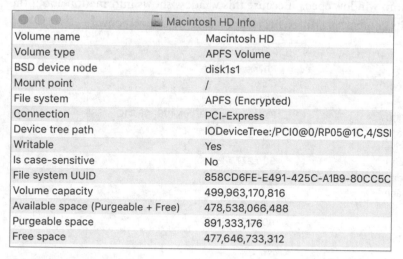

Macintosh HD Info	
Volume name	Macintosh HD
Volume type	APFS Volume
BSD device node	disk1s1
Mount point	/
File system	APFS (Encrypted)
Connection	PCI-Express
Device tree path	IODeviceTree:/PCI0@0/RP05@1C,4/SSI
Writable	Yes
Is case-sensitive	No
File system UUID	858CD6FE-E491-425C-A1B9-80CC5C
Volume capacity	499,963,170,816
Available space (Purgeable + Free)	478,538,066,488
Purgeable space	891,333,176
Free space	477,646,733,312

5   Close the Info window.

6   In the toolbar, choose View > Show All Devices.

7   Select the entry for your internal disk (generally the top item) in the sidebar.

Information about the disk (including its total capacity and partition map type) appears near the bottom of the window.

8 Click the Info button in the toolbar.

The Media Info window opens. Because this window shows information about the entire disk, its contents are different from the volume Info window.

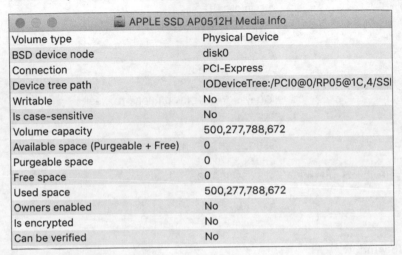

Volume type	Physical Device
BSD device node	disk0
Connection	PCI-Express
Device tree path	IODeviceTree:/PCI0@0/RP05@1C,4/SSI
Writable	No
Is case-sensitive	No
Volume capacity	500,277,788,672
Available space (Purgeable + Free)	0
Purgeable space	0
Free space	0
Used space	500,277,788,672
Owners enabled	No
Is encrypted	No
Can be verified	No

9 Close the Info window.

Exercise 11.2
Erase a Disk

> **Prerequisites**
>
> ▶ You must have created the Local Administrator account (Exercise 3.1, "Configure a Mac for Exercises").
>
> ▶ You must have an erasable external disk, such as a flash disk, which your facilitator will provide.

In this exercise, you use Disk Utility to erase an external disk using a new partition scheme. You use this disk again later in classroom environment exercises.

Use Disk Utility to Erase and Reformat a Disk

Many external storage devices (for example, USB flash drives and USB hard disks) are pre-formatted for Windows, using the Master Boot Record (MBR) partition scheme and the FAT32 volume format. For the best compatibility with macOS, reformat external storage devices to use the GUID partition table (GPT) scheme and Mac OS Extended (Journaled) or the APFS volume format. Use the format that best meets your macOS backward compatibility needs. Additionally, services like Time Machine require a Mac OS Extended volume.

1   If necessary, log in as Local Administrator.

2   Plug in the external disk that your facilitator provided.

> **MORE INFO** ► This exercise erases all information on the external disk. Don't perform this exercise with a disk that contains content you want to keep.

3   Open Disk Utility from the Utilities folder.

The Disk Utility sidebar divides internal and external storage devices.

4   In the sidebar, select the external storage device. Be sure to select the device, not the volume or volumes it contains.

5   Click Erase in the toolbar.

6   View the options in the Format and Scheme menus, and choose Mac OS Extended (Journaled) and GUID Partition Map.

7   Name the disk **Backup**.

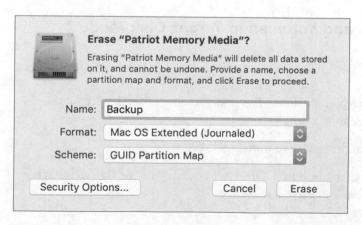

8   Click Erase.

9   Click the Show Details disclosure triangle to view the details.

When the details pane is open, the disclosure triangle's label changes to Hide Details.

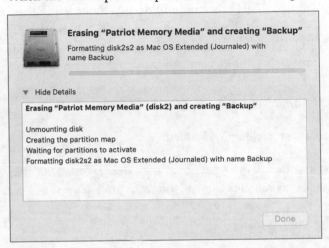

10   When the reformatting is finished, click Done.

11   Click the Eject button next to the new volume in the Disk Utility sidebar.

When the volume (in this case named Backup) ejects, it's removed from the desktop. It remains in the Disk Utility sidebar.

12   Unplug the external storage device from your Mac.

Exercise 11.3
Repair Partitions and Volumes in Target Disk Mode

▶ **Prerequisites**

▶   You must have created the Emily Davidson account (Exercise 8.1, "Restore a Deleted User Account").

▶   You must have another Mac running macOS Mojave.

▶   Both Mac computers must have FireWire, Thunderbolt, or USB-C interfaces and an appropriate cable to connect them.

In this exercise, you start your Mac in target disk mode and use the other Mac to check its file structure and to examine its content in the Finder. You can use these methods to repair or recover content from a Mac that can't start up normally because of file-system damage.

Start Your Target Mac in Target Disk Mode

Choose one of your Mac computers to act as a host (the Mac that runs the disk repair tools) and one to act as a target (the Mac that gets its disk repaired). The target Mac should be the Mac that you configured in Exercise 8.1, "Remove Home Folders."

1   Shut down the target Mac.

2   Press and hold the T key on the target Mac while you press the power button. Keep holding the T key until you see a FireWire, Thunderbolt, or USB logo.

3   When you see the FireWire, Thunderbolt, or USB logo on the screen of the target Mac, release the T key.

4   Log in to the host Mac.

5   Connect the two Mac computers with a FireWire, Thunderbolt, or USB-C data cable.

6   If a dialog appears asking if you want to use this disk as a Time Machine device, click Don't Use.

7   If the target Mac startup disk is encrypted with FileVault, you are prompted for a password to unlock the disk. Enter the password of any FileVault-enabled account.

Repair the Partition Table and Volume

1   On the host Mac, open Disk Utility.

2   In the toolbar, choose View > Show All Devices.

3   In the External section of the Disk Utility sidebar, select the target Mac computer's disk device.

The connection is listed as FireWire, Thunderbolt, or USB.

4   Click the First Aid button in the toolbar.

5   In the confirmation dialog, click Run.

6   Click the Show Details disclosure triangle.

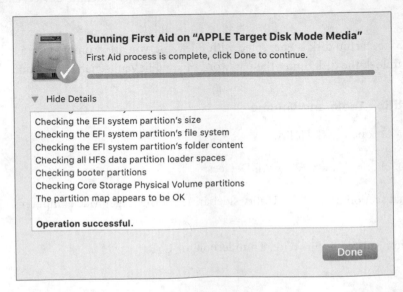

Disk Utility checks and, if necessary, repairs the partition table and hidden disk contents.

Disk Utility shouldn't find any problems. If it does, use First Aid to ensure that the problems are repaired.

7 When the process finishes, click Done.

8 Select the entry for the target Mac Macintosh HD volume, and click First Aid again.

9 Click Run, and click the Show Details disclosure triangle.

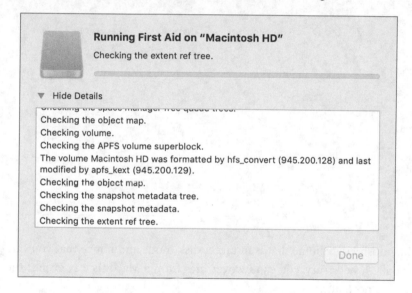

Disk Utility checks and, if necessary, repairs the file structure within the Macintosh HD volume. Since the volume includes a large number of files, this process might take a few minutes.

10 Disk Utility shouldn't find problems. If it does, use First Aid to ensure that problems are repaired. You can also repair the Backup volume.

11 When the process finishes, click Done.

12 Quit Disk Utility.

Examine Files Manually in Target Disk Mode

1   In the Finder of the host Mac, press Shift-Command-C to open the target Mac.

Both Mac computers' volumes appear. Generally, you can distinguish between them because the icons of the volumes of a Mac in target disk mode are orange.

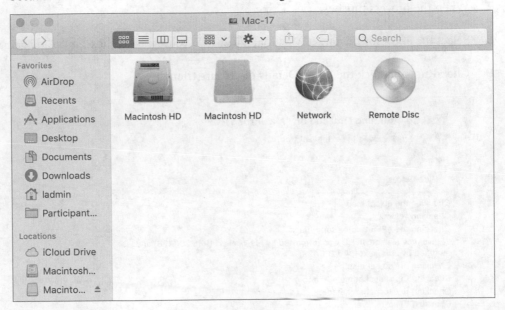

2   Open the Macintosh HD volume that is in target disk mode and notice that you can access all the data. If necessary, you can recover files from a Mac this way even if the Mac can't start up normally.

3   After you have finished browsing the data, go to the Finder sidebar and Option-click the Eject button next to one of the target Mac volumes.

If you hold Option while you click Eject, you tell the Finder to eject all volumes on that disk, not just the one for which you clicked the Eject button.

4   Wait for the target Mac volumes to disappear from the sidebar and desktop.

5   Press and hold the power button to shut down the target Mac, and unplug the cable after you turn off the Mac.

6   If you aren't going to perform the next exercise, restart the target Mac normally.

Exercise 11.4
Repair Partitions and Volumes in Recovery Mode

▶ **Prerequisites**

  ▶ You must have created the Johnny Appleseed account (Exercise 7.1, "Create a
     Standard User Account").

  ▶ Your Mac must have a local hidden Recovery partition.

In this exercise, you start your Mac in macOS Recovery and check its file structure and
home folder permissions. Use these techniques to repair a Mac that won't start up normally because of file-system damage.

Repair the Partition Table and Volume

1   Restart your Mac, and press and hold Command-R until the Apple logo appears.

2   In the macOS Utilities screen, select Disk Utility and click Continue.

3   In the toolbar, choose View > Show All Devices.

    If your startup volume is encrypted with FileVault, it appears dimmed in the disks
    and volumes list.

4   Select your startup volume and click the Mount button in the toolbar. Enter the pass-
    word of any FileVault-enabled account.

5   Select your Mac computer's internal disk device (generally the top entry in the
    sidebar).

6   Click the First Aid button in the toolbar.

7   In the confirmation dialog, click Run.

8   Click the Show Details disclosure triangle.

    Disk Utility checks the partition table and hidden disk contents. It attempts to repair
    problems.

9   When the process finishes, click Done.

10   Select the entry for the Macintosh HD volume, and click First Aid.

11   Click Run, and click the Show Details disclosure triangle.

Disk Utility checks the file structure in the Macintosh HD volume and repairs it if necessary.

12   When the process finishes, click Done.

13   Repair the Backup volume if you want.

14   Quit Disk Utility.

Lesson 12

Manage FileVault

In this lesson, you learn how FileVault protects a system volume and how to enable it. You also learn how to recover a Mac protected with FileVault when all local users' passwords are lost.

Reference 12.1
FileVault Introduction

FileVault encrypts the startup volume to protect macOS. If you use more than one volume, you should encrypt them too. Read more about encrypting additional volumes in Lesson 11, "Manage File Systems and Storage."

Full-System Encryption for Mac Computers with the Apple T2 Security Chip

The T2 chip is a custom chip for Mac that integrates the functionality of several controllers that other Mac computers use. The T2 chip integrates the System Management Controller (SMC), image signal processor, audio controller, and SSD controller. The T2 chip also has a secure enclave coprocessor that enables a Mac to provide new encrypted storage and secure boot features.

The T2 chip uses its built-in hardware-accelerated Advanced Encryption Standard (AES) engine to encrypt data on the built-in SSD. The T2 chip encrypts data by using 256-bit encryption keys that are tied to the chip's unique identifier. You'll need that specific T2 chip to decrypt data stored on the SSD, and if the portion of the chip containing your encryption keys becomes damaged, you might need to

GOALS

▶ Describe how FileVault helps protect data

▶ Enable FileVault protection

▶ Describe how to regain access to a FileVault-protected Mac when all local user account passwords are lost

restore the content of your SSD from a backup. This content includes system files, apps, accounts, preferences, music, photos, movies, and documents.

Always back up your content to a secure backup location so that you can restore it, if necessary. Read Lesson 17, "Manage Time Machine," for more information on backing up your Mac.

The encrypted SSD in your Mac that has the T2 chip automatically mounts and decrypts when connected to your Mac. You should turn on FileVault so that your Mac requires a password to decrypt your data.

These Mac computers have the T2 chip:

- MacBook Air models from 2018
- Mac mini models from 2018
- iMac Pro
- MacBook Pro models from 2018

You can also use System Information to learn whether your Mac has this chip:

1   Open System Information.

2   In the sidebar, select either Controller or iBridge, depending on the version of macOS in use.

3   If you see "Apple T2 chip" on the right, your Mac has the Apple T2 Security Chip.

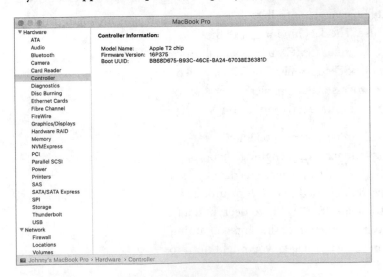

For more information, read Apple Support article HT208862, "Mac computers that have the Apple T2 Security Chip," and Apple Support article HT208344, "About encrypted storage on your new Mac."

Full-System Encryption for Mac Computers Without the T2 Chip

For Mac computers without the T2 chip, FileVault full-disk encryption uses XTS-AES-128 encryption with a 256-bit key to help prevent unauthorized access to the information on your startup disk. FileVault performs the encryption at the file system driver level of macOS. Most processes and apps run normally when the startup volume is encrypted.

Login Window Behavior on a Mac with FileVault Enabled

When a Mac starts up from an encrypted startup disk, it presents a login window. macOS is not yet running, because the system disk is still locked. At the login window, you enter your account password, which your Mac uses to unlock the protected system volume. After your Mac accesses the system volume, startup continues normally. And because you already authenticated to unlock encryption, you're logged directly into your account.

Reference 12.2
Enable FileVault

As covered in Lesson 3, "Set Up and Configure macOS," if you provide your Apple ID during Setup Assistant, you are asked, "Would you like to use FileVault to encrypt the disk on your Mac?"

If you didn't turn on FileVault when prompted by Setup Assistant, you can turn on FileVault at any time from Security & Privacy preferences. Click the lock button and authenticate as an administrator user, and then click Turn On FileVault.

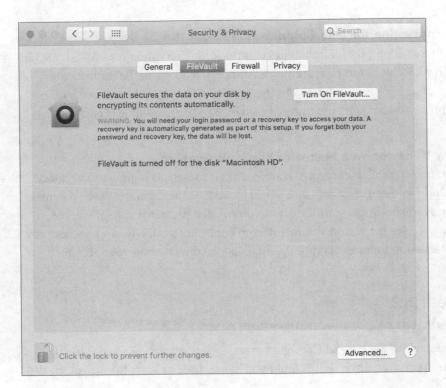

Configure FileVault Recovery

During FileVault setup, a dialog appears and offers you two ways to recover if FileVault-enabled user passwords are lost.

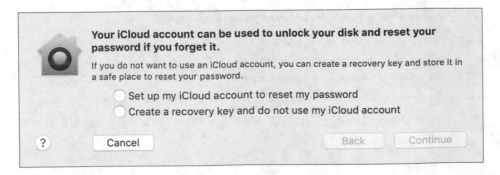

The first way to recover is to use your Apple ID to unlock the FileVault volume and reset your password. This generates a random FileVault recovery key and saves it to your iCloud account on Apple servers. Although you can't see the recovery key, your Mac can retrieve the key from iCloud after you authenticate your Apple ID.

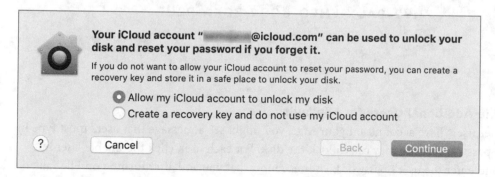

You must have Internet access and sign in using an Apple ID for this to work.

You can configure only one user Apple ID for FileVault recovery. You can enable other users to log in to the FileVault-protected Mac, but they won't have access to the recovery key stored in iCloud.

The second way is to record the key that FileVault randomly generates. You must keep the key letters and numbers somewhere safe and not on your encrypted startup disk.

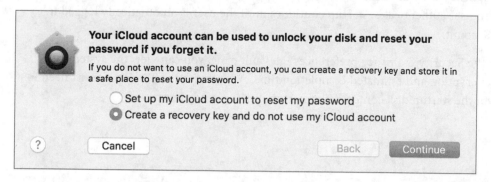

Use the key to unlock the FileVault-protected volume and reset a lost user password.

NOTE ▶ Make a copy of your recovery key and store it in a safe place. If you forget your password and lose your recovery key, you won't be able to access your startup disk. Apple can help you reset your password with your recovery key, but it can't provide your recovery key if you lose it.

The recovery key is a code which can be used to unlock the disk if you forget your password.

Make a copy of this code and store it in a safe place. If you forget your password and lose the recovery key, all the data on your disk will be lost.

ZHY2-9AQX-5HFO-6QB4-ZCXA-P2UZ

?   Cancel   Back   Continue

Enable Additional Users for FileVault

If other users have accounts on your Mac, you might see a message that users must type in their password before they can unlock the disk. For each user, click the Enable User button and enter the user's password. User accounts that you add after turning on FileVault are automatically enabled.

For more information about using Terminal to list, add, or remove enabled FileVault users, and to obtain status about the current state of FileVault, see the fdesetup man page.

Confirm FileVault Is On

After you turn on FileVault, the next time you restart your Mac, the login window appears more quickly. Only FileVault-enabled users appear in the login window. After a FileVault-enabled user authenticates, startup continues until the user is automatically logged in to their account.

From the Security & Privacy preferences FileVault pane, you can view the system volume encryption and estimated completion time. A Mac with the T2 chip doesn't need to encrypt the startup disk contents; the startup disk is already encrypted.

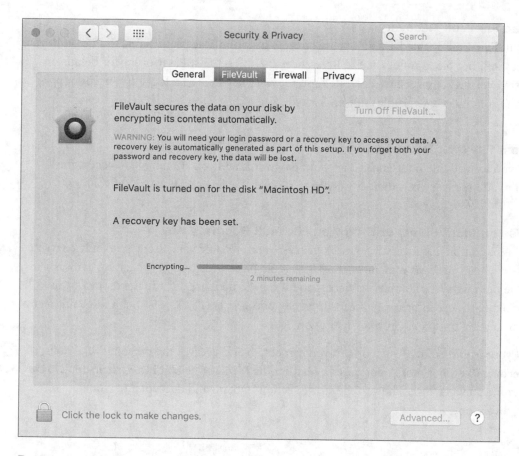

During encryption, you can close Security & Privacy preferences and use your Mac normally. No notification appears after encryption finishes.

To conserve battery power, portable Mac computers that don't have the T2 chip might pause encryption when they aren't plugged in. Encryption continues after you connect the Mac to a power source.

You can turn off FileVault from Security & Privacy preferences. FileVault shows you the decryption progress. If you have a Mac with the T2 chip, then your startup disk contents aren't decrypted when you turn FileVault off.

Use FileVault Recovery

If all FileVault-enabled account passwords are lost for a Mac protected with FileVault, you may still be able to unlock it. See Reference 10.2, "Reset Lost Passwords," for details on using your iCloud account or a FileVault recovery key to reset a local user account password and unlock your FileVault-encrypted system disk.

Lost FileVault Recovery Key

If you lose all FileVault-enabled account passwords and you are unable to access the FileVault recovery key, there is no way to recover the data on your startup volume.

Use an Institutional or Escrowed FileVault Recovery Key

An institutional recovery key (IRK) enables you to recover your users' FileVault-encrypted data when they can't remember their Mac login password. Your organization can set a FileVault recovery key, but the details about how to do it are outside the scope of this book. For more information, read Apple Support article HT202385, "Set a FileVault recovery key for computers in your institution."

If your MDM solution supports it, you can obtain and decrypt the personal FileVault recovery key. For more information, read Profile Manager help at https://help.apple.com/profilemanager/mac/ and search for the section "Obtain and decrypt a personal recovery key."

Exercise 12.1
Restart a FileVault-Protected Mac

> **Prerequisites**
>
> ► You must have created the Local Administrator (Exercise 3.1, "Configure a Mac for Exercises") and Johnny Appleseed (Exercise 7.1, "Create a Standard User Account") accounts.
>
> ► You must have enabled FileVault (Exercise 3.2, "Configure System Preferences").

In Exercise 3.2, you enabled FileVault. In this exercise, you see how FileVault modifies the macOS startup process by requiring a user password.

Your Mac restarts and displays a FileVault access screen. This screen looks identical to the login screen, but macOS hasn't started yet. You must unlock the disk before your Mac can read system files.

If Find My Mac is turned on, you see a Guest account in the access screen. If you select Guest, you start the Mac in a Safari-only mode with no access to the startup volume. The ability to log in as a guest from a lost Mac exists primarily to tempt unauthorized Mac users to connect the Mac to the Internet. This enables you, through Find My Mac, to remotely locate, lock, or wipe the Mac.

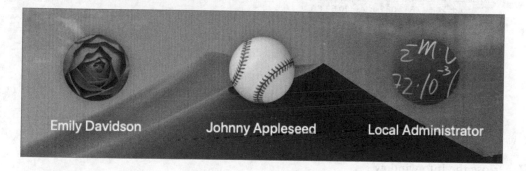

1   Restart your Mac.

2   On the FileVault access screen, click Johnny Appleseed.

3   Enter Johnny's password, and press Return.

   As you have noticed throughout the course, after restart you are presented with a FileVault access screen. After authentication, the macOS startup proceeds, and you are logged in as Johnny Appleseed. Since you authenticated as Johnny Appleseed at the FileVault access screen, macOS facilitates an automatic login for you.

4   Select your startup volume from the desktop.

5   In the Finder menu bar, choose File > Get Info (Command-I).

6   If necessary, click the triangle to expand the General section of the Info window.

The format of the volume is APFS (Encrypted).

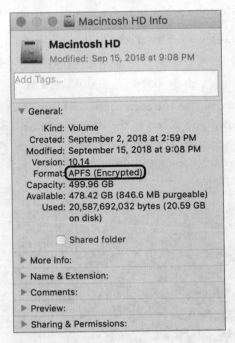

7   Close the Info window.

Exercise 12.2
Use a FileVault Recovery Key

> **Prerequisites**
>
> ▸   You must have created the Local Administrator (Exercise 3.1, "Configure a Mac
>   for Exercises") and Johnny Appleseed (Exercise 7.1, "Create a Standard User
>   Account") accounts.
>
> ▸   You must have enabled FileVault (Exercise 3.2, "Configure
>   System Preferences").

You can use the FileVault recovery key to reset user passwords at startup. In this exercise,
you use the recovery key to reset Johnny Appleseed's password.

Reset Johnny Appleseed's Password

1   Restart your Mac.

2   At the FileVault access screen, click Johnny Appleseed.

3   Click the Help (?) button at the right of the Password field, or intentionally fail to authenticate with the correct password three times.

You see an option that enables you to reset the password with the recovery key.

4   Click the arrow to start the reset process.

A Recovery Key field replaces the Password field.

5   Enter the recovery key you recorded earlier, and press Return.

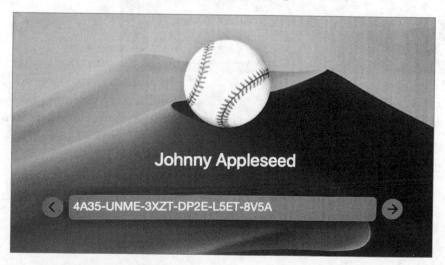

Note: If the Recovery Key field shakes and resets, reenter your recovery key.

The Recovery Key field will continue to shake and reset until you enter your recovery key correctly. If you are unable to enter your recovery key correctly, you can't perform the password reset portion of this exercise. In that case, click the left-arrow button, log in normally to an enabled account, and skip the rest of this exercise.

The Mac starts up. After the startup process finishes, a Reset Password dialog appears under the Johnny Appleseed account icon.

6   In the Reset Password dialog, enter **vaultpw** in the "New password" and "Verify password" fields, and click Reset Password.

You are logged in to Johnny's account. Since his password was reset, Johnny's keychain was again archived, so saved items would have to follow the recovery method outlined in Lesson 10, "Manage Password Changes."

7   If you are prompted to reenter the iCloud password, click iCloud Preferences and enter the password for your facilitator-provided Apple ID.

Restore Johnny Appleseed's Original Password

To prepare for the remaining exercises, change the Johnny Appleseed password back.

1   Open the Users & Groups pane in System Preferences.

2   Click Change Password.

3   Enter **vaultpw** as the old password, and enter the Johnny Appleseed account's original password (**Apple321!**) in the "New password" and Verify fields.

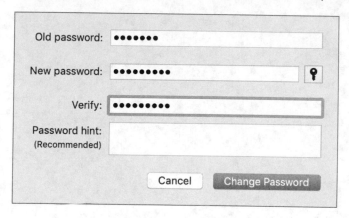

4   Click Change Password.

Johnny's account password is now in sync with his keychain password.

5   Log out as Johnny Appleseed.

Lesson 13

Manage Permissions and Sharing

You use file-system permissions to control macOS file and folder authorization. Used with user account identification and authorization, file-system permissions provide the Mac with a secure multiuser environment.

In this lesson, you learn how file-system ownership and permissions enable controlled access to local files and folders. You also explore macOS default permission settings that provide secure access to shared files. You then use the Finder to make ownership and permissions changes.

Reference 13.1
File-System Permissions

macOS applies permission rules to every item on the system volume. The rules define file and folder access for standard, administrator, guest, and sharing users. Only users and processes with root account access can ignore file-system permission rules.

View File-System Permissions

Any user can view file and folder permissions using the Finder Info window. There are several ways you can open the Finder Info window:

▶ Press Command-I.

▶ From the menu bar, choose File > Get Info.

▶ Control-click the selected item and choose Get Info from the shortcut menu.

▶ In a Finder window toolbar, click the Action menu (gear icon), and choose Get Info.

You can select multiple items to open multiple Info windows.

After you open an Info window, click the Sharing & Permissions disclosure triangle to view the item permissions. The permissions list is in two columns. The left column is a list of users or groups with access to this item. The right column is the associated privilege assigned by user or group. Modifying these settings is covered in Reference 13.3, "Manage Permissions."

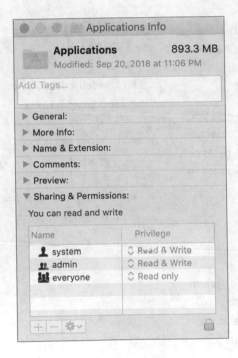

Permission Ownership

Every file and folder has owner, group, and "everyone" permission settings:

▶ Owner—By default, an item owner is the user who created the item or copied it to the Mac. Users usually own most of the items in their home folder. The root user usually owns system software items, including system resources and apps. In macOS, an administrator user can change item ownership and permissions regardless of who owns an item.

▶ Group—By default, the group permissions for an item are inherited from the folder it was created in. Most items belong to the staff (the primary group for local users), wheel (the primary group for the root system account), or admin groups. Group ownership enables users other than the owner access to an item. For instance, even though root owns the Applications folder, the group is set to admin so administrator users can add and remove apps in this folder.

▸ Everyone—Use the Everyone permission settings to define access for anyone who isn't the owner and isn't part of the item's group. This means everyone else, including local, sharing, and guest users.

The items in the Sharing & Permissions pane of a file's Info window appear in the following order:

1. Owner—displayed with a single silhouette and the owner's name
2. Group—displayed with two silhouettes and the group's name
3. Everyone—displayed with the word "everyone"

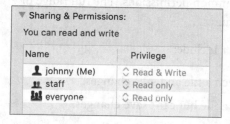

If the group permissions are set to "No Access" (see the next section), macOS omits the group listing.

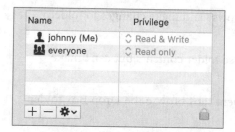

If a user or group doesn't exist, for example, because it was removed, then macOS lists a shadowed silhouette with a dot and the word "Fetching" for that user or group.

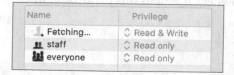

NOTE ▸ The order isn't always user then group then everyone, because you can click a column to sort the list alphabetically. When you close a file's Info window and open it again, the Info window returns to its default listing of owner, then group, then everyone.

Standard Permissions

The standard file-system permissions structure of macOS is based on standard UNIX-style permissions. This system is also referred to as POSIX-style permissions. You can use POSIX-style permissions to define privilege rules separately at each ownership tier. The owner, the group, and everyone else have individually specified access to each file or folder. Because of the inherent hierarchy built into the file system, where folders can reside inside other folders, you can create a complex file structure that allows varying levels of sharing and security.

Apple streamlined the Finder to enable the most common permissions. The full range of UNIX privilege combinations is available with Terminal.

File-level permissions options available in the Finder include:

▸ Read & Write—User or group members can open a file and save changes.

▸ Read Only—User or group members can open a file but can't save changes.

▸ No Access—User or group members have no access to a file.

Folder-level permissions options available in the Finder include:

▸ Read & Write—User or group members can browse and make changes to folder contents.

▸ Read Only—User or group members can browse folder contents but can't make changes.

▸ Write Only (Drop Box)—User or group members can't browse the Drop Box folder but can copy or move items to it.

▸ No Access—User or group members have no access to folder contents.

Although the Finder doesn't show or allow changes to the UNIX execute permission (which allows you to run a process or move into a folder), it assigns this permission when read access is granted for folders.

Access Control Lists

Access control lists (ACLs) expand the standard UNIX permissions architecture to allow more file and folder access control. macOS adopted a style of ACLs similar to that available on Windows-based NTFS file systems and UNIX systems that support Network File System v4 (NFSv4). The ACL implementation is flexible but increases complexity by adding more than a dozen unique privilege and inheritance attribute types.

The macOS implementation of ACLs supports an essentially unlimited number of access control entries (ACEs). An ACE is a set of permissions defined for a specific user or group. An ACL consists of one or more ACEs.

If an ACL rule applies to a user or group, this rule trumps standard UNIX permissions. Any users or groups that don't apply to a specific ACL are still bound by the standard permissions currently in place.

In the following figure, the folder has an ACL with one ACE that adds "Read only" permissions for the group "marketing," and another ACE that adds "Read & Write" permissions for the user jane.

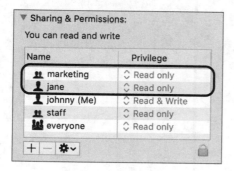

Permissions in a Hierarchical Context

Permissions don't exist in isolation. They're applied in a folder hierarchy. Your access to an item is based on an item's permissions in combination with the permissions of the folder in which it resides. Think of permissions as defining access to an item's content, not to the item itself. Remember the word "content" as you consider the following three examples.

Read & Write

Read & Write

Can edit the file content
Can view or copy the file
Can move or delete the file
Can rename the file

Read Only

Can't edit file content*
Can view or copy the file
Can move or delete the file
Can rename the file

Example 1: You have both read and write permissions to the folder. You have full access to the first file, because your permissions here are read-and-write. You can view and copy the second file, but you can't make changes to the file content because your permissions are read-only. You can still move, delete, or rename the second file because you have read-and-write access to the folder contents. In this example, the second file isn't secure because you can make a copy of the original file, change the copied file's content, delete the original file, and replace it with the modified copy. This is how many apps save document changes, to allow files to be edited.

NOTE ▶ The asterisk (*) in these examples indicates that editing behavior varies based on app design. For some apps, you might need read-and-write access to the file and the folder it's inside to save changes.

Read Only

Read & Write

Can edit the file content*
Can view or copy the file
Can't move or delete the file
Can't rename the file

Read Only

Can't edit the file content
Can view or copy the file
Can't move or delete the file
Can't rename the file

Example 2: You have read-only permission to the folder. You can edit the content of the first file because you have read-and-write access to it, but you can't move, delete, or rename it because you have read-only access to the folder contents. You can delete the file by erasing its contents. The second file is the only truly secure file, because you're only allowed to view or copy it. You make changes to the contents of a copied file, but you can't replace the original.

Read & Write

Read & Write
Locked File

Only owner can edit the file*
Can copy, but copies **locked**
Only owner can move, delete
Only owner can rename

Example 3: Your permissions are identical to the first document in the first example, with one significant change. The owner of this file enabled the locked attribute, perhaps through the Versions document control feature. Even though you have read-and-write access to the example folder and file, the locked attribute prevents users who aren't the file owner from modifying, moving, deleting, or renaming it. In most apps, only the owner can change the file content or delete it. The owner can disable the locked attribute to return the file to normal permissions. You can make a copy of a locked file, but the copy is locked. You own the copy, so you can disable the locked attribute on the copy, but you can't delete the original locked file unless you're the owner.

Managing the Versions feature and the locked file attribute is detailed in Lesson 19, "Manage Documents."

Reference 13.2
Examine Permissions for Sharing

Explore how the local file system is set up by default to provide a secure environment that enables users to share files.

If you don't have fast user switching enabled, as outlined in Lesson 7, "Manage User Accounts," enable it to make it easy to test file-system permissions as different users. Use the Finder Inspector window. This single floating window, which refreshes as you select items in the Finder, enables you to explore default permissions settings without opening multiple Finder Info windows.

Open the Inspector from the Finder by pressing Option-Command-I, and then click the disclosure triangle to reveal the Sharing & Permissions section.

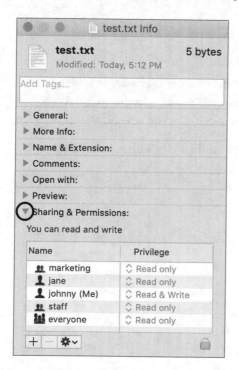

Home Folder Permissions

Default home folder permissions protect user files and enable them to be shared. Users have read-and-write access to their home folder. The staff group and everyone else are allowed only read access.

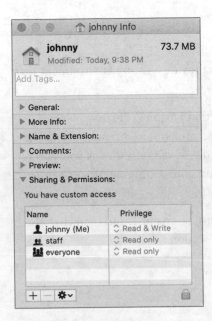

Every local and guest user can view the first level of every other user's home folder. Guest users are allowed access to your Mac without a password. You can disable guest access in Users & Groups preferences.

Most user data is stored inside a subfolder in a user's home folder. Other users aren't allowed to access most of those subfolders.

Some subfolders in a user home folder are designed for sharing. The Public folder is readable by "everyone." A user can share files—without configuring permissions—by moving files into their Public folder. Other users are able to read the files, but they can't make changes to them.

By default, user-created files and folders at the root of a home folder have permissions similar to a Public folder. To secure new items at the root of a home folder, change the permissions, as outlined in Reference 13.3, "Manage Permissions."

The Drop Box folder is in the Public folder. Drop Box folder permissions enable other users to copy files into it. But users can't see others' files in Drop Box. This enables users to discreetly transfer files to a specific user.

When items are created or copied, they are owned by the user who created or copied them. Because a Drop Box folder has a custom ACE, which ensures that the owner of a Drop Box folder has full access to all items in that drop box, normal ownership rules don't apply.

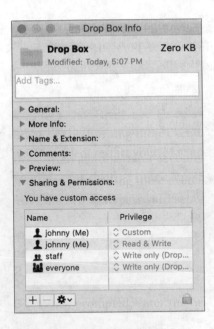

The Shared Folder

The /Users/Shared folder enables local users to read items in it and write items to it. This folder has a permissions setting (called a sticky bit) that prevents other users from deleting items they don't own. You can manage sticky bits in Terminal.

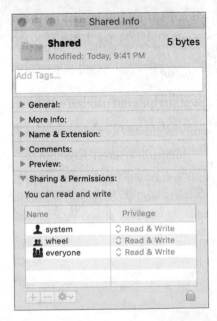

Secure New Items

New items are created with unrestricted read access. For example, when users create a new file or folder at the root of their home folder, by default other users can view the item contents. The same is true for new items created by administrators in local areas, such as the root of the system volume and the local Library and Applications folders.

To store items in a public area so that they are accessible only to the owner, change the item's permissions using the Finder or Terminal, as outlined later in this lesson.

In the Finder's Sharing & Permissions section of the Info window, remove other users and group accounts from the permissions list. Configure the Everyone setting to No Access. After you change the permissions, only the owner has access to the item.

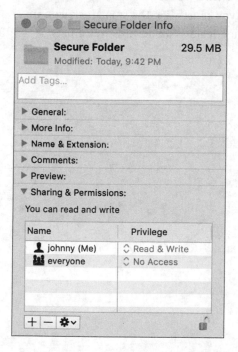

The Finder hides an item's group permission if no access is granted. Click the Remove (–) button to "remove" an item's group permission. This sets the permissions for the group to No Access, but it doesn't remove the group assignment.

Reference 13.3
Manage Permissions

The Finder hides full UNIX and ACL permission complexity by showing a simple view of item permissions. For most common permission settings, the Finder permissions interface provides the simplest way to manage permissions.

This section explores the permissions changes you make to get full access to a deleted user's home folder.

Manage Permissions with the Finder

You can use the Sharing & Permissions section of the Info window to manage permissions. To do so, if you aren't the owner of the item, you must click the small lock icon in the lower-right corner of the Info window and authenticate as an administrator user.

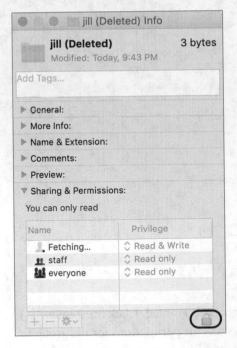

macOS immediately applies the changes you make using the Info window. As long as you keep the Info window open, the Finder remembers the original permissions setting for an item. Use the Finder to test different permission configurations. You can revert to the original permissions setting before you close the Info window. To revert, click the Action menu (gear icon) at the bottom of the Info window and then choose "Revert changes."

Add a Permissions Entry

To add a new permissions entry for a user or group, click the Add (+) button in the lower-left corner of the Info window. A dialog appears that enables you to search for and select a user or group.

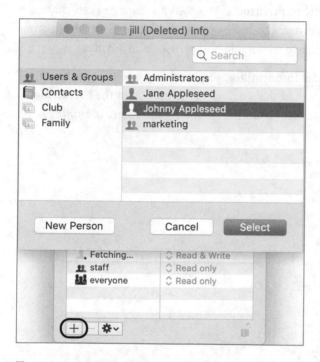

To create a new Sharing user, click the New Person button or open your Contacts and select a contact. You must enter a new password for the new Sharing user. Details about creating Sharing user accounts and how to create additional groups are covered in Lesson 7, "Manage User Accounts."

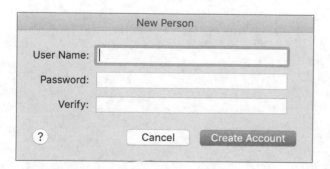

Change Ownership

Even though ACLs enable you to define multiple user permissions for an item, a file or folder can have only one owner. After you open an Info window, the bottom three entries in the permissions list are owner, group, and then everyone. You can click the Name and Privilege column labels to sort by name or privilege. If you own an item, you can change its privileges, but you can't change its ownership unless you authenticate as an administrator user. An administrator user can change ownership and privileges of any item.

To assign a new owner using the Finder Info window, you must first add the user as an additional permissions entry. After you add the user, select the user from the permissions list, and choose "Make *username* the owner" from the Action menu, where *username* is the selected user.

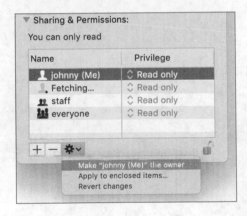

Remove a Permissions Entry

To remove a user or group permissions entry, select the account from the permissions list and click the Remove (–) button in the lower-left corner of the Info window.

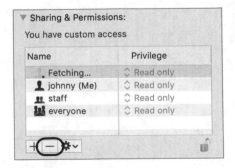

Modify a Permissions Entry

To assign different permissions to an entry, click a privilege and choose another access option for the user or group from the menu that appears.

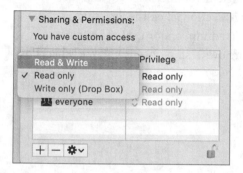

Propagate Folder Permissions

When you change permissions for a folder, you might want to propagate the same permissions to the items inside the folder. Choose "Apply to enclosed items" from the Action menu to do so.

When you apply permissions to enclosed folder items, you apply all permission settings to all enclosed items, not just the changes you recently made. Locked items inside the folder remain in their original state.

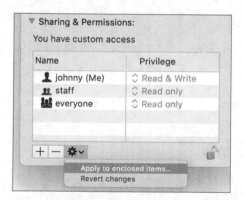

Permissions for Nonsystem Volumes

External storage devices are useful for transferring files and folders from one Mac to another. But most Mac computers don't have the same user accounts, so when you move content from one Mac to another, macOS ignores ownership for nonsystem volumes on internal and external disks. This means local users have full access to the content in non-system volumes, including other partitions of a system disk.

To force macOS to recognize ownership on a nonsystem volume, select it, and then open the Info window. In the Sharing & Permissions section, click the lock button in the lower-right corner, and authenticate as an administrator user to unlock the Sharing & Permissions section. Deselect the "Ignore ownership on this volume" checkbox.

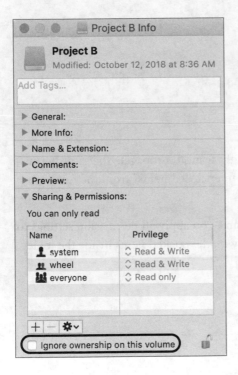

Exercise 13.1
Create Items with Default Permissions

▶ **Prerequisites**

▶ You must have created the Local Administrator (Exercise 3.1, "Configure a Mac for Exercises"), Johnny Appleseed (Exercise 7.1, "Create a Standard User Account"), and Emily Davidson (Exercise 8.1, "Restore a Deleted User Account") accounts.

In these exercises, you set permissions to control which users have access to files and folders.

Store Files and Folders in Johnny Appleseed's Home Folder

To see the effects of macOS default permissions, you create items while you're logged in as the user Johnny. You inspect the item permissions as well.

1 Log in as Johnny Appleseed.

2 Open TextEdit. There should be a shortcut to it in your Dock.

3 Click New Document (or press Command-N).

4 From the menu bar, choose File > Save (or press Command-S), name the new file **Secret Bonus List**, and save it to the desktop. Leave the File Format selection as Rich Text Document.

In a Save dialog, you can use the shortcut Command-D to select the desktop.

5 Click Save, and quit TextEdit.

6 In the Finder, choose Go > Home (or press Shift-Command-H) to navigate to your home folder.

7 Choose File > New Folder (or press Shift-Command-N) to create a new folder.

8 Name the new folder **Payroll Reports**.

9 Make sure the new Payroll Reports folder and the default user folders are in your home folder.

10 Drag the Secret Bonus List.rtf file from your desktop to the Payroll Reports folder.

As you will see, the root of your home folder isn't a good place to store confidential documents.

Examine Permissions as Another User

Now that Johnny Appleseed created a test folder and file, experiment to see what Emily Davidson can do with them.

1 Use the fast user switching menu item (near the right side of the menu bar) to switch to Emily Davidson.

2 In the Finder, navigate to Johnny Appleseed's home folder.

You haven't customized Emily's Finder preferences to show hard disks on the Desktop.

3 Choose Go > Computer (or Shift-Command-C), and open Macintosh HD > Users > johnny.

Most of the folders in Johnny's home folder have indicators showing that you aren't allowed to access them.

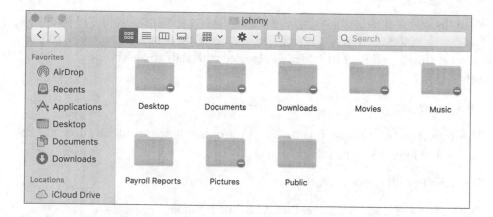

4   Press and hold the Option key while choosing File > Show Inspector (or press Option-Command-I).

The inspector follows your selection in the Finder, enabling you to inspect items quickly.

5   If necessary, click the disclosure triangle in the inspector window to expand the Sharing & Permissions section.

6   Select (single-click) the folders in Johnny's home folder, and watch what the inspector shows about permissions.

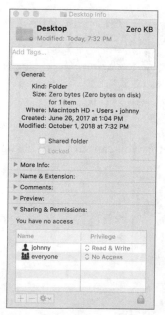
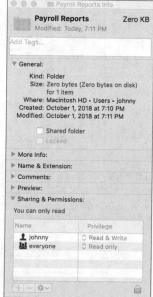
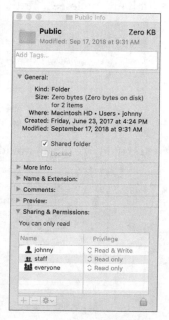

With the exception of Public, the folders that macOS creates by default in the home folder are protected from access by other users (the No Access permission). In this exercise, the Payroll Reports folder was created with staff and everyone given read-only access.

7 Click in the background of Johnny's home folder.

The inspector shows that staff and everyone are also allowed read-only access to the top level of Johnny's home folder.

8 Open the Payroll Reports folder.

The folder opens, and the Secret Bonus List file is visible.

9 Select (single-click) the Secret Bonus List file.

The inspector shows that staff and everyone have read-only access.

This result may be contrary to what is expected by users. Be sure to guide your users to store their folders in appropriate places, based on the type of access they want to allow for other users. Although others can't add or remove items stored in the Payroll Reports folder, they can open and read the contents.

10 Open the Secret Bonus List file.

Since the file is readable by everyone but writable only by its owner, Johnny Appleseed, TextEdit shows that it is locked.

11 Try to enter some text into the file.

TextEdit asks if you would like to create a duplicate so that you can save your changes.

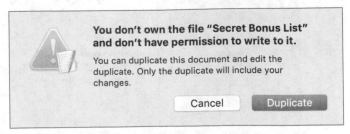

12 Click Duplicate.

A duplicate document named Untitled (Secret Bonus List copy) opens and allows you to enter text.

13 Save the duplicate document to your desktop (leave the name "Secret Bonus List copy").

14 Quit TextEdit.

15 In the Finder, navigate back to Johnny's home folder, and open Johnny's Public folder.

16 Select the Drop Box folder.

The inspector shows that staff and everyone have write-only access to this folder. Johnny has read and write access, as well as a custom access control entry (ACE). "Custom" means that the ACE grants something other than normal read, write, or read/write access. In this case, it's an inheritable ACE that grants Johnny additional access to items moved to this folder.

17 Try to open Johnny's Drop Box folder.

The write-only permission doesn't allow you to open another user's Drop Box folder.

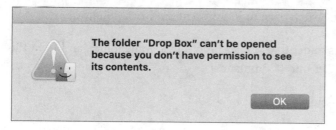

The folder "Drop Box" can't be opened because you don't have permission to see its contents.

OK

18 Try to copy the Secret Bonus List copy file from your desktop into Johnny Appleseed's Drop Box folder.

The Finder warns you that you won't be able to see the items you put into the Drop Box folder.

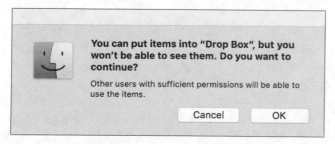

You can put items into "Drop Box", but you won't be able to see them. Do you want to continue?

Other users with sufficient permissions will be able to use the items.

Cancel   OK

19 Click OK.

In the next exercise, you see how to adjust the permissions on the Payroll Reports folder.

Exercise 13.2
Test Permissions Changes

> **Prerequisite**
>
> ▶ You must have performed Exercise 13.1, "Create Items with Default Permissions."

In this exercise, Johnny Appleseed changes the permissions on the Payroll Reports folder and tests the results from Emily Davidson's account.

Change Permissions as Johnny Appleseed

1 Use fast user switching to switch back to Johnny Appleseed's account.

2 Select the Payroll Reports folder that resides in Johnny's home folder, and from the menu bar, choose File > Get Info (Command-I).

3 Expand Sharing & Permissions.

4 Click the small lock button in the Info window, and authenticate as Local Admin.

5 Select the group (staff), and click the Remove (–) button below the permissions list.

6 Change the privilege level for everyone to No Access.

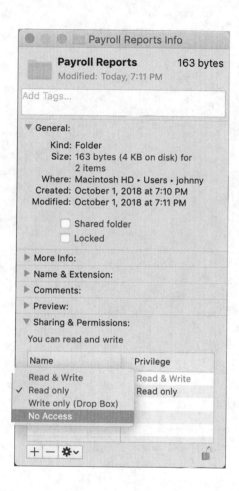

7　Close the Info window.

8　Navigate to Johnny's Drop Box folder (inside the Public folder).

9　Select the Secret Bonus List copy file that Emily placed in Johnny's Drop Box folder.

10 From the menu bar, choose File > Get Info. If necessary, expand the Sharing & Permissions section.

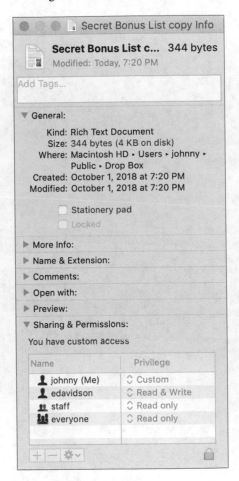

Since Emily created this file, she is its owner. When she copied it to Johnny's Drop Box folder, the inheritable custom access control entry in the Drop Box folder granted Johnny full access to it.

11 Close the Info window.

12 Open the Secret Bonus List copy file, and edit its contents.

The inherited access control allows Johnny to edit the file, and the changes are saved automatically.

13 Quit TextEdit.

Test the New Permissions as Emily Davidson

1 Use fast user switching to switch back to Emily's account.

2 Try to open the Payroll Reports folder.

This time you can't open the folder because the new permissions don't grant you read access.

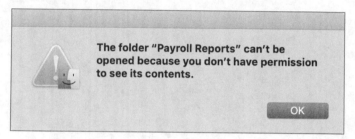

The default permissions didn't protect the Payroll Reports folder as Johnny intended, but after Johnny changed the permissions, the folder is protected from access by other users.

3 Log out of Emily's account.

4 At the login window, switch to Johnny Appleseed.

5 Navigate back to Johnny's home folder (Go > Home or Shift-Command-H), and drag the Payroll Reports folder to the Trash.

6 From the Finder menu, choose Empty Trash.

7 In the dialog that appears, click Empty Trash.

Lesson 14

Use Hidden Items, Shortcuts, and File Archives

macOS makes complex file-system structures simple. For example, the Finder displays just four folders at the root level of the system volume. Also, many items are shown in convenient locations but are stored elsewhere. And archiving technology enables you to combine multiple items into a compressed file.

In this lesson, you explore hiding, redirecting, and archiving items. You learn how to manage file-system aliases and links. You also open and create ZIP file format (.zip) archives and disk images.

Reference 14.1
Examine Hidden Items

The root level of the system volume contains resources that macOS processes require and that you probably won't ever need to see. You can identify many of these resources because they have a period (.) at the beginning of the filename.

macOS enables you to hide files and folders in two ways. You can use Terminal to add a period at the beginning of a filename or enable an item's hidden file flag. A hidden flag hides the item only in the Finder. To prevent confusion, macOS doesn't enable you to hide items using the Finder or the default apps.

GOALS

▶ Navigate to hidden files and folders

▶ Examine packages and bundles

▶ Manage aliases and links

▶ Create and open ZIP archives and disk images

Reveal Hidden Folders in the Finder

To reveal hidden items, go to the Library folder or open the Finder and select the Go menu.

The user Library folder includes important resources, but it's hidden in the Finder. Press and hold the Option key, and click the Go menu to reveal the Library menu.

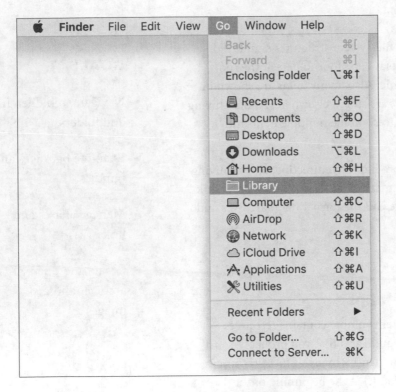

If you frequently access a user Library folder, you can make it constantly visible.

1. Go to the Finder preferences (Command-Comma).
2. Select the Sidebar button from the top of the pane.

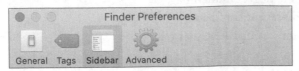

3. Select the checkbox for your home folder.

4. Close the Finder Preferences window.

5. Choose Go > Home

6. In the Finder window toolbar, click the button to show items as icons, in columns, or in a gallery.

7. Choose View > Show View Options (Command-J).

8. From the View Options window, select the Show Library Folder checkbox.

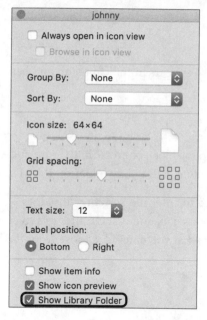

To reveal all hidden items in a folder or volume, in the Finder press Shift-Command-Period. Hidden items remain visible in the current folder or volume until you use the keyboard shortcut again to return the items to their default hidden state.

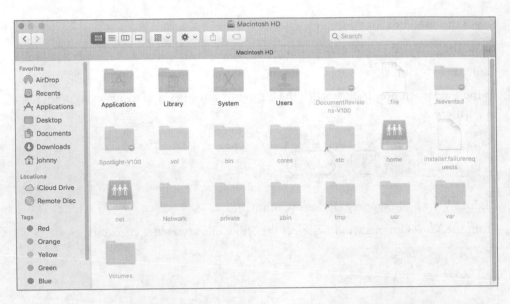

If you show a user Library folder in the Finder, it also appears in the Go menu and has a keyboard shortcut (Shift-Command-L).

Go to Folder

To reveal hidden folders in the Finder, choose Go > Go to Folder, or press Shift-Command-G. This opens a dialog that enables you to enter an absolute path to any folder on the Mac.

In the "Go to Folder" dialog, use Tab key completion to enter file-system pathnames. Enter the first few letters of a pathname, and then press Tab, and macOS attempts to complete the name. If there are multiple possibilities for what you entered, choose from the displayed list.

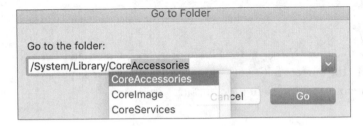

Click Go after you enter the pathname. The Finder reveals the folder in a window.

For example, to navigate to /private, enter **/p** and press Tab.

You can also navigate to past destinations from the "Go to Folder" menu. Click the down-arrow button to the right of the text field to see past destinations.

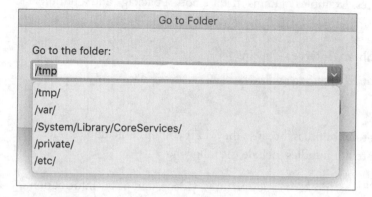

As you can see, /private, a hidden folder, contains common macOS resources.

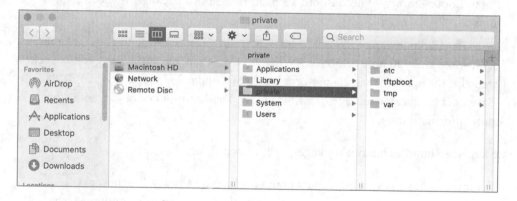

Reference 14.2
Examine Packages

Although bundles and packages are sometimes referred to interchangeably, they represent distinct concepts:

▶ A package is any folder that the Finder presents to the user as if it were a single file.

▶ A bundle is a folder with a standardized hierarchical structure that holds executable code and the resources used by that code.

An item can be both a package and a bundle. It's a package because when you double-click it, the Finder does not show you its contents. It's a bundle because it's a folder that holds executable code and resources. Examples of items that are both a package and a bundle include:

▶ Optional plug-ins in /Library/Internet Plug-Ins

▶ Screen savers in /System/Library/Screen Savers

▶ Most apps

Some items are packages but not bundles, because they don't contain executable code. Examples of packages that are not bundles include the following:

▶ Photos Library—The Photos app keeps your pictures, videos, and other information in your Photos Library package, which is in your Pictures folder.

▶ Photo Booth Library—Photo Booth keeps its data in this package in your Pictures folder.

▶ Large Pages, Numbers, or Keynote documents—If you're working in Pages, Numbers, or Keynote and you have created a file that is larger than 500 MB, saving it as a package helps the app you're using perform better. See Apple Support article HT202887, "Save documents as a package or a single file in Pages, Numbers, or Keynote," for more information.

Some items are bundles but not packages. Examples include:

▶ The frameworks in /System/Library/Frameworks and /Library/Frameworks. Frameworks contain shared resources that multiple apps can use simultaneously. macOS loads frameworks into memory as needed and shares the one copy of the resource among all apps whenever possible.

Because packages are folders, you can copy them as regular folders to another volume even if it isn't formatted as APFS or Mac OS Extended. The Finder recognizes the items as packages even when they are on a third-party volume.

View Package Content

To access a package's contents in the Finder, secondary-click (or Control-click) the item you want to view, and choose Show Package Contents from the shortcut menu. If you want to create or modify a bundle or package bundle, join the Apple Developer Program. You can find out more at https://developer.apple.com.

Installer Package Resources

An installer package contains a compressed archive of the software you want to install and a few configuration files used by Installer. Other software bundles and packages contain resources for the app or software.

Software packages often include:

- Executable code for multiple platforms
- Document description files
- Media resources such as images and sounds
- User interface description files
- Text resources
- Resources localized for specific languages
- Private software libraries and frameworks
- Plug-ins or other software to expand capability

Reference 14.3
Use File-System Shortcuts

File-system shortcuts are files that refer to other files or folders. This enables you to have an item appear in multiple locations or with multiple names without having to create multiple copies of the item. Shortcuts in the Dock or in the Finder aren't file-system shortcuts. The Dock and the Finder save references to original items as part of their configuration files. File-system shortcuts are files that you can find anywhere on a volume.

About File-System Shortcuts

macOS uses three primary file-system shortcut types: aliases, symbolic links, and hard links. To help you compare these shortcut types, this section uses a 15.7 MB Pages document file named BigReport.pages for demonstration purposes. This file is referred to using each shortcut type. You see the differences in the Finder Info window.

Aliases

You can create aliases using the Finder, but they aren't recognized by Terminal. Command-line tools can't follow alias references created in the Finder back to the original items.

Aliases are more resilient than other shortcut types. If the original item is replaced or moved, the alias almost never loses the original item.

The following screenshot shows the Finder Info window inspecting an alias pointing to BigReport.pages. The kind is reported as Alias and the file is much smaller than the 15.7 MB original. The Size field reports that the file is 992 bytes and uses 4 KB of disk space. The extra information in the alias is what allows macOS to keep track of the original item should it ever change location.

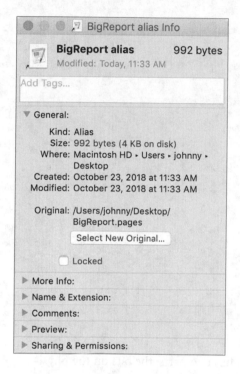

Symbolic Links

Symbolic links are pointers to the file-system path of the original item. In many cases, if you move the original item, the symbolic link is broken. You can replace the original item with a file of the same name because the path remains the same.

You can create symbolic links only in Terminal, but the Finder follows symbolic links to an original item. An example of symbolic links is the way macOS stores some folders in the /private folder but also makes those folders available at the root of the file system using symbolic links. For example, this guide refers to paths that start with /var in several places, and /var is a symbolic link to /private/var.

The following screenshot shows the Finder Info window inspecting a symbolic link pointing to BigReport.pages. The kind is also reported as Alias, but the file is only 37 bytes. This illustrates a symbolic link saving a path to the original item. There is no Select New Original button. This indicates that you can't use the Finder to repair a symbolic link.

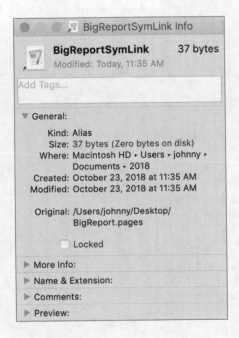

Hard Links

Hard links are references to an original item. A file has two parts: the bits on the physical disk that make up the file content and a name that points to those bits. Every file has at least one hard link. If you create an additional hard link, you create another name that points to the same bits on the physical disk.

If you remove an additional hard link, you don't delete the original item. If you delete the original item, you don't delete the data or additional hard links because the other hard links still point to the same bits on the disk, which won't be freed until there are no links left to them. With aliases and symbolic links, deleting the original item leaves the shortcut pointing at nothing.

You can create hard links only in Terminal, but the Finder can follow them. To save space, Time Machine uses hard links to refer to items that haven't changed since the previous backup. macOS uses folder hard links for Time Machine.

Create Aliases

To create an alias in the Finder, select the item you want to create an alias for and choose one of the following methods:

▶ Choose File > Make Alias.

▶ Press Command-L.

▶ In a Finder window, choose Make Alias from the Action menu (the small gear icon).

▶ In the Finder, Control-click an item, and choose Make Alias from the shortcut menu.

▶ Drag the original item while pressing and holding the Option and Command keys to drop the alias in another location. This method doesn't append the extension ".alias" to the filename of the new alias, but it updates the icon.

▶ Drag an app to the desktop. This gives you access to the app without the risk of accidentally removing it from its original installed location.

After you create an alias, you can rename it or move it. As long as the original item remains on the original volume—even if it's replaced or its name changes—the Finder can locate the alias. An alias file has a small curved arrow at the lower-left corner of the icon. Locate an alias target from the Finder by Control-clicking the alias and choosing Show Original from the shortcut menu, or by pressing Command-R.

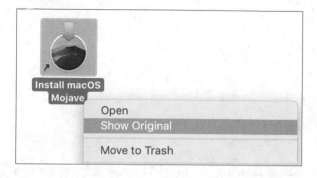

Repair Aliases

Double-click a broken alias to repair it in the Finder. The Finder tells you if it can't find the original for a broken alias. In the dialog, you can delete the broken alias, click Fix Alias to select a new original item, or click OK to dismiss the dialog.

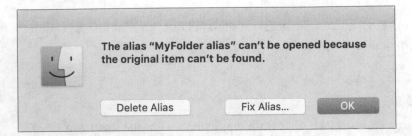

You can also redirect an existing alias. Select the alias, open its Finder Info window, and in the General area, click the Select New Original button.

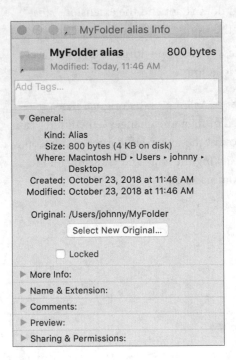

Both methods open a file browser dialog, enabling you to select a new original item for the alias.

Reference 14.4
Use File Archives

Unlike automated backup solutions, archiving is typically a manual process where you create compressed copies of data. Archive formats are efficient for storage and data transfer. In this section, you learn about ZIP archives and disk images.

File Archives

You can select files and folders to compress (or zip) into ZIP archives. This is an efficient way to archive small amounts of data. The ZIP archive format is widely compatible. Many operating systems include software to decompress ZIP archives back to their original state.

You can create disk images using Disk Utility. Disk images enable you to archive an entire file system, including files, folders, and associated metadata, into a single file. You can compress, encrypt, or make read-only any disk image. You can also give disk images read/write permissions so that you can make changes. macOS relies on disk images for macOS Recovery and network Time Machine backups.

Disk images you create with Disk Utility that use the .dmg filename extension can be accessed only by Mac computers. Other systems require third-party software to access Mac disk images.

Create ZIP Archives

By default, creating a ZIP archive in the Finder doesn't delete the original items, and expanding a ZIP archive doesn't delete the original archive.

To create a ZIP archive in the Finder, select the items you want to archive and compress in the Finder. Press and hold the Shift key to select contiguous lists of items, or press and hold the Command key to select noncontiguous items. From the Finder choose File > Compress *Items*, or Control-click the items and choose Compress *Items* from the shortcut menu, where *Items* is the name of a single item or the number of items you selected.

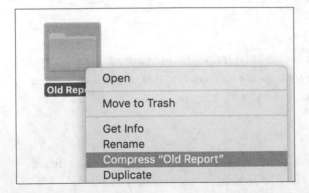

The Finder might show a progress dialog with the estimated time required to complete the compression. You can cancel the archive by clicking the small x button on the far right. When the process finishes, you are left with a ZIP archive named either Archive.zip or *Item*.zip, where *Item* is the name of the item you chose to archive and compress.

After the archiving is complete, compare the original item size with the archive size using the Info or Inspector window in the Finder. Many media formats come compressed, so your results may vary when you again compress these file types.

Expand ZIP Archives

Expand a ZIP archive in the Finder by double-clicking the archive file. The Finder cannot list or extract individual items from a ZIP archive.

If you need more control over how ZIP archives are expanded, open Archive Utility and choose Archive Utility > Preferences. These preferences enable you to adjust how ZIP archives are expanded and compressed. The preferences include options for handling original items after an archive transition.

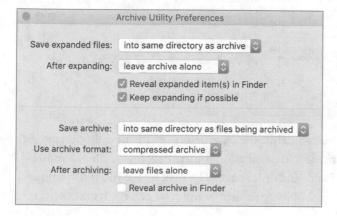

Mount Disk Images

Safari mounts downloaded disk images, but you can manually mount disk images from the Finder too. To access the contents of a disk image, double-click the disk image file in the Finder. This mounts the volume inside the disk image file as if you just connected an external storage device. Even if the disk image file is on a remote file server, you can mount it as if it were a local disk. You can treat the mounted disk image volume as you would other storage devices by navigating through its hierarchy and selecting files and folders. If the disk image is read/write, you can add to the contents of the disk image by dragging items to the volume.

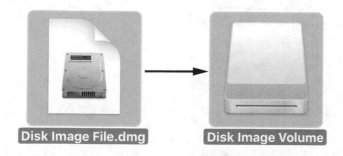

Create Empty Disk Images

To create an empty disk image, which you can fill with content over time, open Disk Utility and choose File > New Image > Blank Image.

In the New Blank Image dialog, you can define the parameters for the new disk image. At a minimum, you need to select a name and destination for the disk image file. You should also enter a name for the volume inside the disk image. The disk image file and volume names don't have to match, but they should be similar so that you can recognize their relationship.

Disk image size is limited by the storage destination capacity. You can select the "sparse disk image" image format to create an image file that's only large enough to store items that are in the disk image volume. Empty space inside a disk image volume doesn't count as storage space.

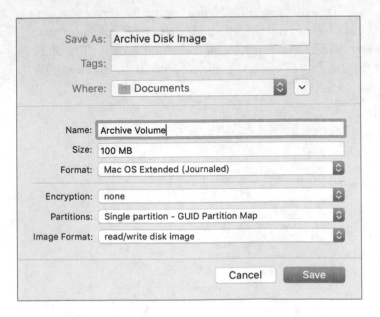

After you define your disk image options, click Save to create the disk image. After macOS creates the new blank disk image, macOS mounts it. If you chose to create a sparse disk image, you can open Info windows in the Finder for the disk image file and the disk image volume to verify that the volume size is much larger than the image size. As you copy files to the volume, the disk image file grows.

You can change the format of a disk image with Disk Utility by choosing Images > Convert. This opens a dialog where you can select the image you want to change and save a copy of the image with new options.

Create Disk Image Archives

To create a disk image that contains copies of items, open Disk Utility and choose File > New Image > Image from Folder. This opens a file browser window in which you can select the folder you want to copy into a new disk image.

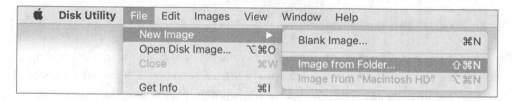

To create a disk image from the contents of an entire volume or disk, select the source from the Disk Utility window disks list and choose File > New Image > Image from *Source* (where *Source* is the name of the selected volume or disk).

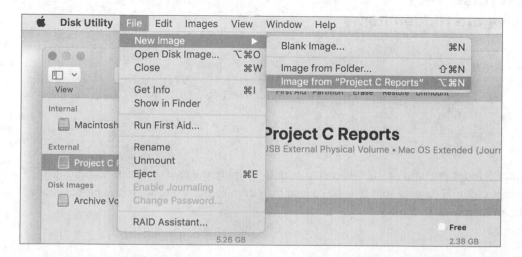

After you select the disk image source, a Save dialog appears. At a minimum, you must select a name and destination for the resulting disk image file. The name of the volume inside the disk image is set to the name of the selected source. You can compress the disk image contents to save storage space. Also, you can enable encryption for the disk image. If you do, you must set a password and hint for the resulting secure disk image. Be sure to use Keychain Access to save the password to a keychain for easy, secure access.

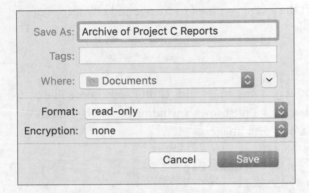

After you define your disk image options, click Save to create the disk image. Depending on the amount of data to be copied and the image format you choose, it can take seconds to hours for the disk image to copy. Disk Utility opens a progress dialog that enables you to cancel the copy.

Exercise 14.1
Navigate Hidden Items

> **Prerequisite**
>
> ► You must have created the Johnny Appleseed account (Exercise 7.1, "Create a Standard User Account").

macOS hides portions of the folder structure to simplify the user experience and to prevent accidental damage that may be caused by a user. In this exercise, you explore some of the hidden folders in macOS.

Examine Your User Library Folder

1   Log in as Johnny Appleseed.

2   In the Finder, open your home folder. You can do this by going to the menu bar and choosing Go > Home (or pressing Shift-Command-H).

   No folder named Library is visible.

3   In the Finder, open the Go menu. Don't choose anything yet.

4   Press and hold the Option key.

   As long as you hold down the Option key, a Library choice appears in the menu.

5   With the Option key held down, choose Library.

   This opens the hidden Library folder in Johnny's home folder.

6   Choose View > as Columns (or click the Column View button in the Finder toolbar).

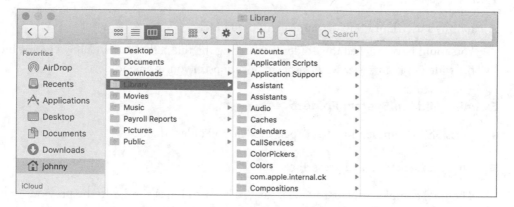

   Johnny's user Library folder is shown in Johnny's home folder. It's dimmed to indicate that it's normally invisible.

7   Explore some subfolders in Johnny's user Library folder. You can navigate into them normally.

8   Close the Finder window that shows Johnny's user Library.

9   Press Shift-Command-H to open Johnny's home folder in a new Finder window.

The Library folder isn't shown.

10   From the menu bar, choose Go > Go to Folder (Shift-Command-G).

11   In the "Go to Folder" dialog, enter **~/Li**, and press Tab.

The field completes the path to ~/Library/.

This is an example of how you navigate to a folder by its path.

12   Click Go.

Johnny's user Library folder appears in the Finder.

You could have reached this folder by entering the full path, **/Users/johnny/Library**, but the tilde (~) is an easier way to specify locations in your home folder.

Examine Hidden System Folders

1   Press Shift-Command-G to reopen the "Go to Folder" dialog.

2   This time, enter **/L**, and press Tab.

The field completes the path to /Library/. This path looks similar to the previous one, but because it doesn't start with a tilde, it specifies a different folder. When a path starts with a slash (/), it starts at the top level of the startup volume (sometimes called the root of the file system).

3   Click Go.

This time, the Finder opens the Library folder at the top of the startup volume. The next lesson discusses the various Library folders.

This Library folder isn't hidden, but you can use the same technique to reach any folder you know the path to, whether or not it is hidden.

4   Use the "Go to Folder" dialog to reach the /private/var/log/ folder. (You can type part of a name and then press Tab to complete it.)

The /private folder holds some of the macOS "private" system files. The /private/var/log folder holds some of the system log files (there are more in /Library/Logs and ~/Library/Logs). Normally, you don't need to access these files in the Finder, so they are hidden from view unless you specifically navigate to them.

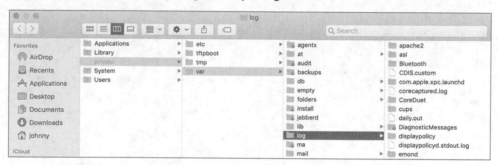

5   Use the "Go to Folder" dialog to reach the /var/log/ folder.

This takes you to /private/var/log because /var is a symbolic link to /private/var.

Data Management

Lesson 15
Manage System Resources

The macOS system files are streamlined and organized in a layout that is easy to manage and that provides strong security. This lesson focuses on the composition and organization of the files and folders that make up macOS.

Reference 15.1
macOS File Resources

If you look at the root (beginning) of the file system from the Finder, you see four default folders: Applications, Library, Users, and System. If you look at the root from Terminal, you see much more.

GOALS

- ▶ Explore and understand macOS file layout

- ▶ Discover common system files, their location, and their purpose

- ▶ Describe System Integrity Protection

- ▶ Manage font resources

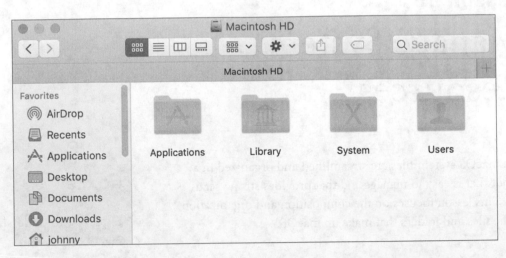

Here are descriptions of the default system root folders you see from the Finder:

▶ Applications—Often called the local Applications folder, this is the default location for apps available to local users. Only administrator users can make changes to the contents of this folder.

▶ Library—Often called the local Library folder, this is the default location for ancillary system and app resources available to users. Only administrator users can make changes to the contents of this folder.

▶ System—This folder contains resources required by macOS for primary functionality. With System Integrity Protection (SIP) enabled by default in macOS, no user or process can make changes to most of the content of the System folder. Properly created third-party macOS software, including hardware drivers, can function outside of the System folder. Details regarding SIP are covered later in this lesson.

▶ Users—This is the default location for local user home folders. Lesson 8, "Manage User Home Folders," covers this topic in greater detail.

Library Resources

macOS-specific system resources are in Library folders throughout the system volume. A system resource is a resource that is not a general-use app or a user file. The Library folder keeps user and system resources organized and separated from the items you use every day.

You should be familiar with these system resources:

▶ Application Support—This folder is in the user and local Library folders. Any ancillary data needed by an app might be in this folder. For example, it often contains help files or templates for an app.

▶ Containers and Group Containers—These folders contain resources for sandboxed apps. There is more information about these folders later in this section.

▶ Extensions—Also called kernel extensions, these items are found only in the /Library and /System/Library folders. Extensions are low-level drivers that attach themselves to the kernel, or core, of the operating system. Extensions provide driver support for hardware, networking, and peripherals. Extensions load and unload automatically. Extensions are covered in greater detail in Lesson 26, "Troubleshoot Peripherals."

▶ Fonts—Fonts are files that describe typefaces used for both screen display and printing. Font management is covered later in this lesson.

▶ Frameworks—Frameworks are repositories of shared code used among different parts of the operating system or apps. Frameworks load and unload automatically. You can view your Mac computer's currently loaded frameworks with System Information.

▶ Keychains—Keychains are used to securely store sensitive information, including passwords, certificates, keys, Safari AutoFill information, and notes. Keychain technology is covered in Lesson 9, "Manage Security and Privacy."

▶ LaunchDaemons and LaunchAgents—These define processes that start with the launchd process. macOS uses many background processes that are started by launchd. LaunchAgents are for processes that need to start up only when a user is logged in, whereas LaunchDaemons are used to start processes that always run in the background, even when no users are logged in. More about launchd can be found in Lesson 28, "Troubleshoot Startup and System Issues."

▶ Logs—Many system processes and apps archive progress or error messages to log files. You can view log files using Console.

▶ PreferencePanes—PreferencePanes are used by System Preferences to provide interfaces for system configuration. Using System Preferences is covered in Lesson 3, "Set Up and Configure macOS."

▶ Preferences—Preferences are used to store system and app configuration settings. Every time you configure a setting for any app or system function, it is saved to a preference file. Because preferences play such a critical role in system functionality, troubleshooting preference files is covered separately in Lesson 20, "Manage and Troubleshoot Apps."

Resource Hierarchy

Library folders are in separate domains: user, local, network, and system (network domains are legacy and outside the scope of this guide). Segregating resources into domains provides increased administrative flexibility, resource security, and system reliability. Resource domains allow for administrative flexibility, because you can choose to allocate certain resources to all users or just specific users. Standard users can add resources only to their own home folder and cannot access other users' resources.

The system resource domains are, in order:

▶ User—Each user has his or her own Library folder in the home folder for resources. When resources are placed here, only the user has access to them. The user's Library folder is hidden by default to prevent users from accidentally making changes that could be detrimental. Many apps and processes continue to rely on this location for resources.

▶ Local—Both /Applications and /Library are part of the local resource domain. Any resources placed in these two folders are available to all local user accounts. By default, only administrator users can make changes to local resources.

▶ System—The system domain encompasses the items necessary to provide core system functionality. This includes an app folder located at /System/Library/CoreServices. Many hidden items at the root of the system volume also make up the system resource domain, but the only one you see in the Finder is the /System/Library folder. With SIP enabled, no user or process can modify most of the /System folder.

With different domains containing resources, there may be multiple copies of similar resources available to the Mac and user. macOS handles this by searching for resources from the most specific (those in the user domain) to the least specific (those in the system domain). The following graphic represents the order in which resource contention is resolved from a user's home folder (1) to the System folder (3).

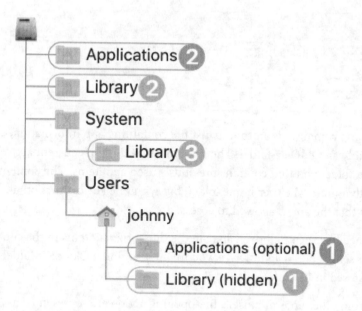

If multiple similar resources are discovered, macOS uses the resource most specific to the user. For example, if two versions of the font Times New Roman are found—one in the local Library and one in the user's Library—macOS uses the copy of the font in the user's Library.

App Sandbox Containers

App sandbox containers enhance running-app security. Sandboxed apps are allowed access only to the specific items they need to function. Most apps built into macOS and apps from the App Store are sandboxed apps.

Sandboxed apps can access special folders that are referred to as containers. macOS manages the content of these containers to ensure that an app isn't allowed access to other items in the file system. A user opening a document outside of an app container is the only way a sandboxed app is allowed access outside of its container.

App containers are in ~/Library/Containers. When a sandboxed app starts up the first time, macOS creates a container folder for the app, named with its bundle identifier. The bundle identifier identifies an app by its creator and app title. For example, the container folder for News is ~/Library/Containers/com.apple.News.

The root content of an app container is a property list file containing app information, a Data folder, and possibly an OldData folder. The Data folder is the app's current active container. Any OldData folder you find contains previously used app items. The content of the Data folder mostly mimics the user home folder, but with one key distinction: it contains only the items that the app is allowed to access.

Items created and managed by the sandboxed app are the only original items in the container Data folder. If a user enables iCloud Drive, you might also find a CloudKit folder for maintaining items stored in iCloud.

Items that originated from other apps or a user's file-opening action are represented as symbolic links that point to the original item outside of the container. macOS creates these symbolic links when the user opens an item in the sandboxed app. By representing external items this way, an original item can stay in its original location while also being accessible to a sandboxed app that can see only its own container.

App Group Containers

Although a user can allow sandboxed apps to access files beyond the app container, sandboxing prevents apps from doing this automatically. To facilitate sharing app resources automatically, developers of sandboxed apps can request that macOS create a shared app group container.

The ~/Library/Group Containers folder contains shared app containers. When a sandboxed app starts up the first time and requests access to share app resources, macOS creates a group container folder for the app, named with its bundle identifier.

Unlike app sandbox containers that simulate an entire user home folder, app group containers hold only items to be shared between apps. Using Notes as an example, in the previous screenshot you can see the NoteStore database and Notes property list file. In this instance, the Notes data is shared so that other apps can access user note entries. macOS controls access to this to ensure that only Apple-verified processes can access the user's Notes database.

Troubleshoot System Resources

You might see an error message calling out an issue with a specific item, but you might also experience a situation where the item appears to be missing. macOS ignores a system resource if it determines that the resource is corrupted or missing. Replace the suspect or missing item with a working copy.

When troubleshooting system resources, remember the resource domain hierarchy. Using fonts as an example, you might load a version of a font in the local Library folder, as required by your workflow to operate properly. In spite of this, a user might load another version of the same font in their home folder. In this case, the user might experience workflow problems even though it appears that they are using the correct font.

Logging in with another account is a quick way to determine whether the problem is in the user's home folder. You can also use System Information to list active system resources. System Information shows the file path of the loaded system resources, so you can spot resources that are loading from the user's Library.

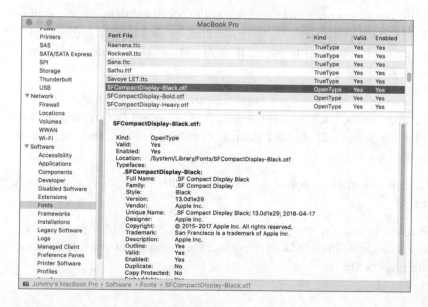

Reference 15.2
System Integrity Protection

System Integrity Protection (SIP) protects your Mac by preventing potentially malicious software from modifying protected files and folders. SIP restricts the System Administrator account (the root user account) and limits the actions that the root user can perform on protected parts of the Mac operating system.

SIP includes protection for these parts of macOS:

▶ /System

▶ /usr

▶ /bin

▶ /sbin

▶ Apps that are preinstalled with macOS

▶ /private/var/db/ConfigurationProfiles

Third-party apps and installers can continue to write to the following paths:

▶ /Applications

▶ /Library

▶ /usr/local

SIP allows only processes that are signed by Apple with special entitlements to modify parts of your Mac that are protected by SIP. For instance, Apple software updates and Apple installers are entitled to write to system files. Apps that you download from the App Store already work with SIP.

SIP also helps ensure that only a user, and not malicious software, can change a startup disk. To select a startup disk, click the Apple menu, choose System Preferences, and then click Startup Disk. Or press and hold the Option key while you restart, and then choose from the list of startup disks.

If you upgrade from an earlier version of macOS, the installer might move an item aside if it conflicts with SIP.

Older peripheral and printer driver software might be impacted by SIP. If you discover that a third-party product is impeded by SIP, contact the developer to provide a version compatible with macOS Mojave.

You can temporarily bypass SIP by starting from another, non-SIP-protected system. You could also place your Mac in target disk mode and then connect to another Mac running a previous version of macOS. These methods all enable you to modify a non-SIP-protected system volume. After you've made your changes, restart the Mac back to the macOS Mojave system and your changes should remain.

You can disable SIP by using the csrutil command when started from macOS Recovery. The setting is saved to the Mac computer's firmware, so resetting the parameter RAM enables SIP again. It's also possible that a software update will reenable SIP.

If SIP is disabled, the root user has unlimited access to any system folder or app on your Mac. Malicious software can obtain root-level access if a user enters an administrator name and password to install the software. This would allow the software to modify or overwrite any system file or app. It's best practice to keep SIP enabled at all times.

To prevent an unauthorized user from disabling SIP, you can set a computer firmware password to disallow starting from macOS Recovery, as detailed in Lesson 10, "Manage Password Changes."

For more information about SIP, read Apple Support article HT204899, "About System Integrity Protection on your Mac."

Reference 15.3
Manage Font Resources

One way to experience the system resource domain hierarchy is by managing fonts. macOS has advanced font-management technology that enables a nearly unlimited number of fonts using nearly any font type, including bitmap, TrueType, OpenType, and all PostScript fonts.

Fonts are installed in the Font folders in the Library folders throughout macOS. A user can manually install fonts by dragging them into ~/Library/Fonts. Administrators can install fonts for all users by dragging them into /Library/Fonts. This flexible font system enables administrators to better control font use. For example, a font vendor licensing model may grant only specific access for an individual user.

Install Fonts Using Font Book

macOS includes a font-management tool, Font Book, which automatically installs fonts for you. Font Book can also be used to organize fonts into more manageable collections, enable or disable fonts to simplify font lists, and resolve duplicate fonts. See Exercise 15.1, "Manage Font Resources," for detailed instructions for managing fonts.

NOTE ▶ Third-party font-management tools interrupt Font Book and take over font management for macOS.

Exercise 15.1
Manage Font Resources

▶ Prerequisite

▶ You must have created the Local Administrator (Exercise 3.1, "Configure a New Mac") and Johnny Appleseed (Exercise 7.1, "Create a Standard User Account") accounts.

In this exercise, you remove a font from /Library/Fonts, where it is available to all users, and install it in a single user's Fonts folder.

Remove a Font

Use Font Book to watch what happens when you move a font to the Trash.

1 Verify that no users have fast user switching sessions active. If users other than Johnny are logged in, log them out.

2 If necessary, log in as Johnny Appleseed.

3 Open the Font Book app, which is in the /Applications folder.

4 Locate Andale Mono in the Font column.

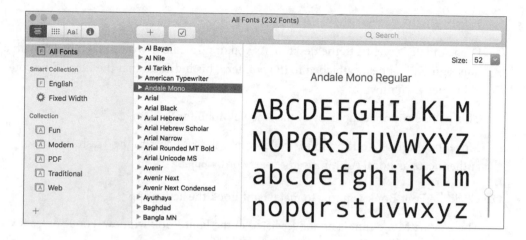

5   In the Finder, navigate to the folder /Library/Fonts.

    If Macintosh HD isn't displayed on Johnny's desktop, find it in the Computer view. Choose Go > Computer (or press Shift-Command-C), and open Macintosh HD > Library > Fonts.

6   If necessary, to verify your location, choose View > Show Path Bar.

    Make sure the path bar at the bottom of the window matches the following screenshot (although the rest may not match unless you are in the column view):

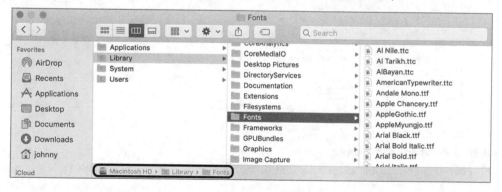

The path bar includes the volume name in the path, so the path /Library/Fonts is displayed as Macintosh HD > Library > Fonts. The fonts in this folder are available to all users.

7   Locate the file Andale Mono.ttf.

8   Drag Andale Mono.ttf to the desktop. As you drag, a cursor with a green badge with a plus sign on it appears attached to the pointer. This indicates that the file will be copied rather than moved.

This will be your backup copy of the Andale Mono font.

9   Move the original Andale Mono.ttf file from /Library/Fonts to the Trash. To do so, authenticate as Local Administrator (password: **Apple321!**).

10   Click the Font Book window to make Font Book the active app.

The Andale Mono font is no longer listed in the Font Book window. Font Book shows a real-time display of the fonts in the macOS search path.

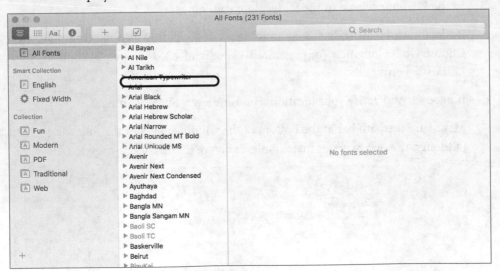

Add a Font for One User

You can use Font Book to install a font that only one user of the Mac can use.

1   In the Font Book app, choose Font Book > Preferences (Command-Comma).

2   Ensure that Default Install Location is set to User.

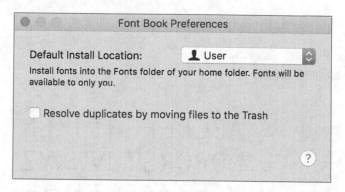

3   Close Font Book Preferences.

4   Switch to the Finder, and double-click Andale Mono.ttf on the desktop.

This opens Andale Mono.ttf in Font Book, which shows a preview of the font and gives you the option to install it.

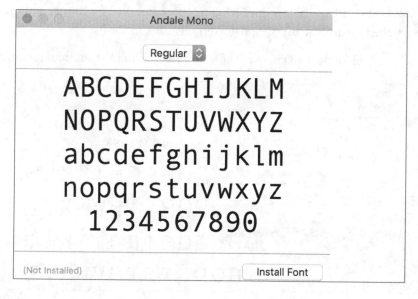

5   Click Install Font.

6   If necessary, select User from the sidebar.

Andale Mono is the only font installed in Johnny's user account.

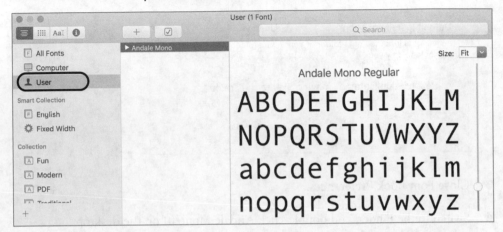

7   Select All Fonts from the sidebar.

Since this view shows all available fonts, including those installed for the current user and those installed for all Mac users, Andale Mono is back in the list.

8   Control-click Andale Mono, and choose "Show in Finder" from the shortcut menu.

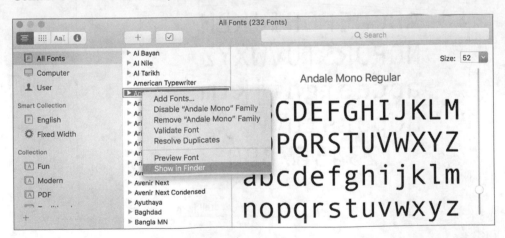

The Finder opens a window that displays the font file. Its path bar shows that the font file is in the Fonts folder in Johnny's user library, previously referred to as ~/Library/Fonts, /Users/johnny/Library/Fonts, and Macintosh HD > Users > johnny > Library > Fonts. It's the only font installed there.

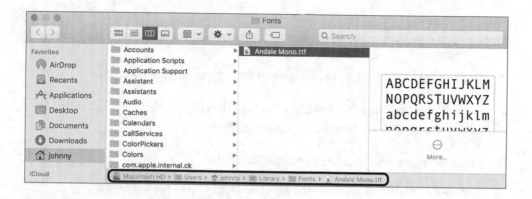

Confirm a Font Is Unavailable to Other Users

If you log in as a different user, even as an administrator, you don't have access to the fonts in Johnny's Fonts folder.

1   Use fast user switching to switch to the Local Administrator account.

2   Open the Font Book app, and look for the Andale Mono font.

Andale Mono isn't visible in Font Book for the Local Administrator account. At this time, you could add Andale Mono to this account, just as you added it to Johnny's account. You would have to copy the font file to a location that Local Administrator can access.

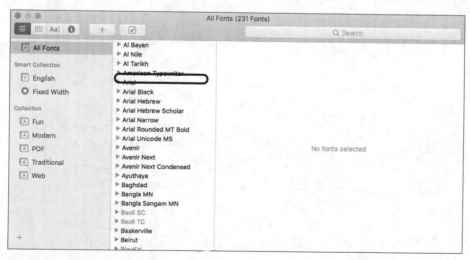

3   Quit Font Book.

Validate Fonts

Since you changed your font configuration, you use Font Book to check your new setup.

1   Use fast user switching to switch back to the Johnny Appleseed account.

2   In the Font Book window, select All Fonts in the sidebar, click any font in the Font column, and press Command-A to select all fonts.

3   From the menu bar, choose File > Validate Fonts.

Font Book reads and validates the font files, and checks for corruption.

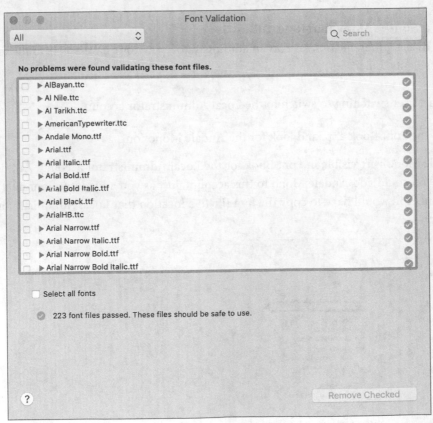

4   When the validation scan finishes, quit Font Book.

5   Log out as Johnny Appleseed.

Test System Integrity Protection

Unlike with the user and local libraries, you can't modify the system library, even if you have administrator rights.

1   Log back in as Local Administrator.

2   In the Finder, navigate to /System/Library/Fonts.

3   Find the file Apple Color Emoji.ttc, and drag it to the Trash.

If you can't find this file, make sure you're in the correct Library/Fonts folder. You need to be in the folder that's in the System folder for this part of the exercise.

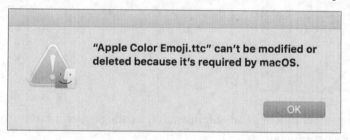

A dialog appears indicating that the file can't be modified or deleted.

4   With Apple Color Emoji.ttf selected, choose File > Get Info (Command-I).

5   If necessary, expand Sharing & Permissions.

6   Click the small lock button, and authenticate as Local Administrator.

7 Try to change the privilege level for everyone to Read & Write.

Even though you have authenticated as an administrator, a dialog appears informing you that you don't have permissions.

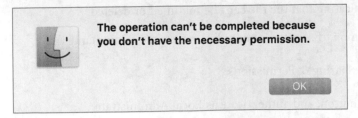

8 Dismiss the dialog, and close the Info window.

9 If you want, you can try other methods to make modifications in the /System folder, but System Integrity Protection will block your attempts. For more information, see Reference 15.2, "System Integrity Protection."

10 Log out as Local Administrator.

Lesson 16
Use Metadata, Spotlight, and Siri

Metadata is information used to describe content. The most basic forms of file and folder metadata are names, paths, modification dates, and permissions. Metadata isn't part of an item's content; rather, it describes an item in the file system.

In this lesson you learn how macOS uses file metadata and how this metadata is stored in file systems. You learn how to take advantage of metadata by using the file-system tags feature. And you learn how to use Siri and Spotlight to search.

Reference 16.1
File-System Metadata

Forked file systems, such as Apple File System and Mac OS Extended, enable data to appear as a single item in the file system. A file appears as a single item but is composed of two pieces: a data fork and a resource fork. This technology enables macOS to support file type identification in the data fork, whereas the extra information specific to macOS resides in the resource fork.

Some third-party file systems, like FAT, don't know how to store this additional data. The solution to this problem is addressed with the AppleDouble file format, covered later in this lesson.

File Flags and Extended Attributes

macOS also uses metadata in the form of file-system flags and extended attributes to implement system features. Examples of file-system flags include the hidden flag, covered in Lesson 14, "Use Hidden Items, Shortcuts, and File Archives," and the locked flag, covered in Lesson 19, "Manage Documents."

Any process or app can add an arbitrary number of custom attributes to a file or folder. This enables developers to create new forms of metadata without having to modify the existing file system.

File-System Tags

Assign file-system tags to your files, and then use those tags to search for or organize your files. File-system tags are stored as extended attributes. macOS uses extended attributes for several file features, including the Stationery Pad option, Hide Extension option, and comments. You can access these items from the Info window in the Finder. The following Info window screenshot shows a document featuring Red and Whitepaper file-system tags and a searchable text comment.

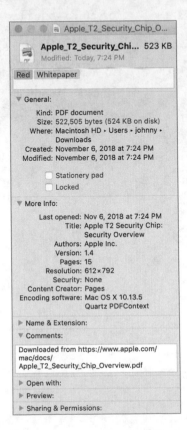

You can assign multiple tags with custom user-defined tag colors and tag names. You can modify tags for documents in any app that presents a Save dialog. When you select tags for a document, you can create a new tag by typing a new name in the Tags field.

You can customize tags in the Tags pane of the Finder preferences by choosing Finder > Preferences or by pressing Command-Comma. From the Tags pane, you can create additional tags by clicking the Add (+) button, and you can remove existing tags by clicking the Remove (–) button. To rename a tag, click the tag name, and to change the color, click the tag color. You can also define which tags are shown in the Finder sidebar by selecting the tag checkbox, and you can set the tag order by dragging tag entries in the list. Below the tags sidebar list, you can define favorite tags so that they will appear in the Finder menus.

As mentioned in Reference 1.2, "What's New in macOS Mojave," Stacks is a new feature in macOS Mojave that enables you to organize your desktop by automatically organizing your files into related groups. In the Finder, from the View menu, choose Use Stacks, or just Control-click anywhere in the Desktop and choose Use Stacks.

By default, macOS Mojave organizes stacks by kind. Here's an example of some files organized in stacks by kind.

macOS Mojave uses metadata to enable you to group your stacks by the following:

▶   Kind

▶   Date Last Opened

▶   Date Added

▶   Date Modified

▶   Tags

Here's an example of a desktop with stacks grouped by tags.

When stacks are organized by tag, files that don't have a tag get their own stack: "No Tags." A stack looks like a stack of files. You can place your pointer over a stack, then use two fingers on a trackpad or one finger on a Multi-Touch mouse to scroll through the contents. Click a stack to see its contents. You can have multiple stacks expanded at the same time. If you sort stacks by tags, each file that has multiple tags will appear in multiple stacks.

In macOS Mojave you can edit a file's tags in the Preview field when you view items in the Finder in columns or as a gallery. The following figure also illustrates that you can use quick actions for this image (Rotate Left, Markup, and More) while viewing images as a gallery.

macOS enables you to search for or organize your items by tag. In the Finder, you can find tags with Spotlight or in the sidebar. Using Spotlight is detailed later in this lesson.

AppleDouble File Format

File-system metadata compatibility with third-party file systems might be an issue. Only volumes formatted with the APFS or Mac OS Extended file system fully support resource forks, data forks, file flags, and extended attributes. Third-party software exists for Windows operating systems to enable them to access the extended metadata features of

APFS and Mac OS Extended. More often, though, users take advantage of the compatibility software built into macOS to help other file systems work with these metadata items.

For almost anything other than APFS or Mac OS Extended volumes, including FAT volumes, older Xsan volumes, and older NFS shares, macOS stores metadata from the file system in a separate hidden data file. The data retains the original name, but the metadata is saved with a period and underscore (._) before the original name. This file is sometimes referred to as a dot-underscore file. This technique is called AppleDouble.

For example, if you copy a file that contains metadata and is named My Document.docx to a FAT32 volume, macOS automatically splits the file and writes it as two discrete pieces on the FAT32 volume. The file's internal data is written with the same name as the original, but the metadata is written to a file named ._My Document.docx, which remains hidden from the Finder. This works out well for most files, because Windows apps only use the contents of the data fork. But if you use Windows to edit and save a file like this to a FAT32 volume, the resource fork will not be preserved, so if you later open the file on your Mac, information might be missing. And if users on other operating systems display hidden files, they will see the dot-underscore files if they exist.

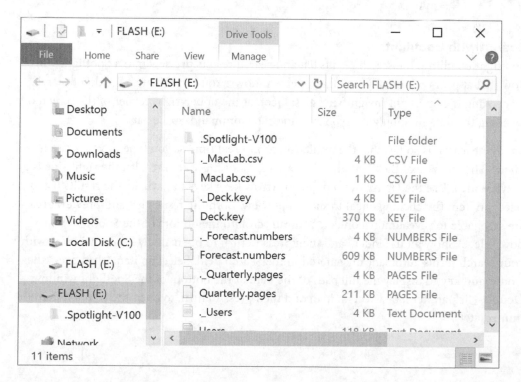

Windows systems default to automatically hiding dot-underscore files. In fact, to acquire the Windows screenshot shown here, we had to manually enable Hidden Items. macOS includes a method for handling metadata on SMB network shares from NTFS volumes that doesn't require the AppleDouble format. The native file system for current Windows-based computers, NTFS, supports something similar to file forking, known as alternative data streams. The file system writes the metadata to the alternative data stream, so the file appears as a single item on both Windows and macOS.

Reference 16.2
Spotlight and Siri

For any query, Spotlight and Siri can go beyond file-system searches and find relevant information from inside local documents, app function results, and Internet sources. The Spotlight icon is in the upper-right corner of the screen. If you enabled Siri, the Siri icon is between the Spotlight icon and the Notification Center icon.

Search with Spotlight

Spotlight combines the search results list and search results preview into a Spotlight window that appears on top of your other open windows. You can initiate a Spotlight search by clicking the Spotlight (magnifying glass) icon at the upper-right corner of the screen or by using the default Spotlight keyboard shortcut: Command-Space bar.

Spotlight search is so fast that the results change in real time as you type in your search query. The left side of the Spotlight window is a list of the search results; the right side is a preview area. Use the Up Arrow and Down Arrow keys keys to navigate the results list, or select an item (by clicking once) to show a preview. Both the results list and preview area are scrollable to reveal more content. You can scroll to the bottom of the Spotlight window, select "Show all in Finder," and then press Return to open a new Finder window with your search terms automatically entered in the Search field. Select an item, then press the Command key to display the full path of the item at the bottom of the Spotlight window. Double-click an item, or select an item and then press Return, to open the selected item immediately.

Search with Siri

With Siri you can speak plain-language requests and macOS returns the results, often both in spoken word and as a visual representation. You can initiate a Siri request by clicking the Siri icon (to the right of the Spotlight icon) at the upper-right corner of the screen or by using the default Siri keyboard shortcut: press and hold Command-Space bar until the Siri window appears.

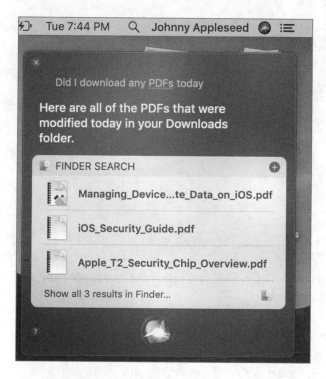

As you speak, Siri will translate your words to text and, more importantly, interpret your meaning. As you can see in the preceding screenshot, Siri interpreted "Did I download any PDFs today" to mean "PDFs that were modified today in your Downloads folder" and returned a Finder search.

When you make a request with Siri, your Mac will send the translated text to Apple servers to interpret the meaning of your words. In a local file search, Siri leverages Spotlight to provide the file list results.

Double-clicking any item in the Siri search results will open that item in an appropriate app. You can also save the results of a Siri search by clicking the Add (+) button at the top right of the Siri search results. This will create a Notification Center widget that can be accessed by clicking the Notification Center icon, which is the farthest-right icon in the menu bar.

If you ask Siri to find a password, Siri opens Safari and then opens the Passwords pane in Safari preferences.

> **MORE INFO ►** This guide primarily focuses on using Siri to search for local items, but Siri is capable of much more, like helping you find your iPhone. You can find out what else you can ask by opening Siri, not asking anything, and waiting a few moments. You can also check out Apple Support article HT206993, "How to use Siri on your Mac."

Search with Hey Siri

Hey Siri enables you to access Siri hands-free. Just say "Hey Siri," then make your request. The following Mac computers support Hey Siri:

► MacBook Pro (15-inch, 2018)

► MacBook Pro (13-inch, 2018, Four Thunderbolt 3 ports)

► MacBook Air (Retina, 13-inch, 2018)

► iMac Pro

Hey Siri can also access HomeKit and control your HomeKit-compatible devices.

For more information about devices that support Hey Siri, read Apple Support article HT209014, "Devices that support 'Hey Siri.'"

About Search Results

The following figure shows the results of a Spotlight search for "secure enclave."

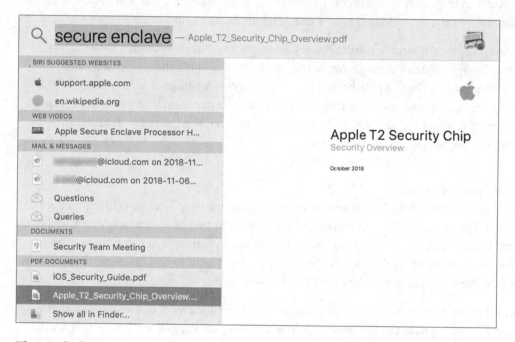

The results list contains results from Internet sources, notes from Notes, documents, and even messages from Mail and Messages. Spotlight can also search inside app data sources. In the preceding Spotlight search result, the selected item being previewed is a PDF document. Note the Preview app icon in the upper-right corner of the Spotlight search window. Neither the document's name nor the previewed cover page contains the words "secure enclave." Instead, Spotlight searched inside the text of the PDF file for the words "secure enclave."

Spotlight and Siri can also take advantage of an app's functions. For example, Spotlight and Siri can perform mathematical calculations and unit conversions (including market-based currency conversion) by integration with Calculator.

The metadata technologies covered previously in this lesson are also searchable with Spotlight and Siri, including filenames, file flags, modification dates, and file-system tags. Additionally, many files contain internal metadata used to describe the file's content. For example, many photo files contain additional camera setting information embedded as metadata inside the file. Spotlight and Siri can search through this document-specific metadata information as well.

In addition to local files, Spotlight (and by proxy Siri) can search through the contents of shared files from other Mac clients, Time Machine backups, and iCloud Drive.

Extending beyond local network services, Spotlight and Siri can search a variety of Internet sources through Apple services known as Spotlight Suggestions and Siri Suggestions. These Apple-hosted services use a combination of search history, location information, and user information to generate relevant search results from a wide variety of Internet sources. An Internet connection is required to take advantage of Spotlight Suggestions and Siri Suggestions.

Spotlight Indexing

Spotlight (and by proxy Siri) is able to perform wide and deep searches of local items and shared files quickly because it works in the background to maintain highly optimized databases of indexed metadata for each attached local volume. When you first set up macOS, it creates these databases by indexing all the available local volumes. macOS also indexes new volumes when they are first attached.

A background process automatically updates the index databases on the fly as changes are made throughout the file system. As these indexes are kept current, Spotlight needs to search only the databases to return thorough results. Spotlight preemptively searches everything for you in the background, so you don't have to wait for the results when you need them.

Spotlight directly indexes Time Machine and AirDisk volumes (disks shared with AirPort Extreme), but it doesn't index shared volumes from other computers. Spotlight can connect to indexes on shares hosted from other Mac operating systems.

You can find the Spotlight general index databases at the root level of every volume in a folder named .Spotlight-V100. A few apps maintain their own databases separate from these general index databases. One example is Mail, which maintains its own optimized email database in each user's folder at ~/Library/Mail/V6/MailData/Envelope Index.

If you are experiencing problems with local file searching, you can force Spotlight to rebuild the index databases by deleting them and restarting your Mac or by managing the Spotlight preferences, as covered later in this lesson.

Spotlight Plug-ins

Spotlight can create indexes, and search—from an ever-growing variety of local metadata—using plug-in technologies. Each Spotlight plug-in examines specific types of files or databases. Many Spotlight plug-ins are included by default, but Apple and third-party developers can create additional plug-ins to expand Spotlight search capabilities.

Included Spotlight plug-ins enable you to:

▶ Search with basic file metadata, including name, file size, creation date, and modification date

▶ Search with media-specific metadata from picture, music, and video files, including timecode, creator information, and hardware capture information

▶ Search through the contents of a variety of file types, including text files; app databases; audio and video files; Photoshop files; PDF files; Pages, Numbers, and Keynote files; and Microsoft Office files

▶ Search through personal information like the contents in Contacts and Calendar

▶ Search for correspondence information like the contents of Mail messages and Messages chat transcripts

▶ Search for relevant information like your favorites or web browser bookmarks and history

▶ Perform Internet searches using Google or Apple Spotlight Suggestions

Spotlight plug-ins are stored in various Library folders. The Apple built-in Spotlight plug-ins can be found in both /System/Library/Spotlight and /Library/Spotlight. Third-party plug-ins should always be installed in either /Library/Spotlight or ~/Library/Spotlight, depending on who needs access to them.

You can create custom metadata for Spotlight by entering Spotlight comments in the Info and Inspector windows from the Finder.

Search Security

To provide security on par with the rest of the file system, Spotlight indexes every item's permissions. Even though Spotlight indexes every item on a volume, it automatically filters search results to show only items that the current user has permissions to access. For example, you can't search the content of another user's Documents folder. All users can search through locally attached nonsystem volumes, including mounted disk images, even if another user attached the device.

Spotlight Suggestions and Siri take advantage of many Apple services and Internet sources, but they always adhere to the Apple Privacy Policy. Apple takes user privacy very seriously and always attempts to keep a user's information as safe as possible while still providing advanced services. You can disable searches that require Internet services in the Spotlight preferences and Siri preferences, as covered later in this lesson.

For more information about Apple's Privacy Policy, see www.apple.com/privacy/.

Perform an Advanced Spotlight Search

The default Spotlight search provides quick search results, but as you've learned in this lesson, Spotlight has a powerful range of search features.

You can use the Finder to perform an advanced file-system search with any of the following methods:

► At the bottom of a Spotlight search list, double-click "Show all in Finder."

► In the Finder, choose File > Find (or press Command-F).

► In a Finder window, enter a word or phrase in the Search field (in the upper-right corner).

You can select an item next to the word Search under the toolbar to limit the scope of the search.

Enter a word or phrase in the Search field in the upper-right corner. A menu appears with suggestions for search types, based on what you've entered. You can choose something from the menu or just press Return to include anything related to your search term.

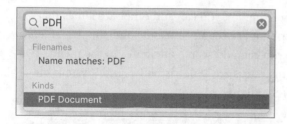

You can select an item from the search results to display the path to the selected item at the bottom of the Finder window.

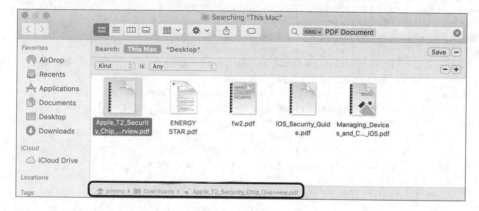

You can select an item and then press the Space bar to open a preview of the selected item.

Refine your Spotlight search from the results in a Finder window by clicking the small Add (+) button below the Search field; this allows you to add as many search attributes as you need. After you add a new search attribute, click the first word in the search attribute to choose another type from the menu.

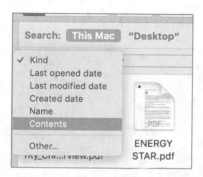

If you don't see the search attribute you're looking for, you can add other attributes that aren't enabled by default. To add search attributes, select any attribute and choose Other from the menu. In the dialog that appears, you can add search attributes to the menu. Two especially useful search attributes for administrators are "File visibility" and "System files," neither of which is shown by default in any Spotlight search.

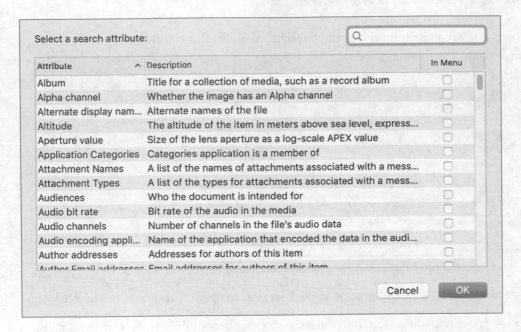

TIP ▶ Take some time to explore the additional search attributes. Search attributes include specifying audio file tags, digital camera metadata, authorship information, contact information, and many other metadata types.

You can click the Save button on the right to save your search criteria as a Smart Folder.

You can remove the suggested name for the Smart Folder, enter a descriptive name, and then click Save. By default, the option to add the Smart Folder to the Finder sidebar is enabled.

Smart Folders are like normal folders in that they can be given a unique name and placed anywhere you like, including the Finder sidebar. Smart Folders are special because their contents always match your search criteria no matter how the file system changes. The Recents and Tags items in the Finder sidebar are predefined Smart Folders.

Manage Spotlight Preferences

From Spotlight preferences, any user can choose to disable specific categories so they do not appear in Spotlight searches. For example, users can choose to disable Spotlight Suggestions if they don't want any search information sent over the Internet. You can also prevent some volumes from being indexed by specifying those volumes in the privacy list. However, by default, all new volumes are automatically indexed, so users must manually configure Spotlight to ignore a volume.

The Spotlight privacy list is a system-wide setting that remains the same across all user accounts, but users can change the privacy list.

Opening Spotlight preferences defaults to the Search Results tab, where you can disable specific categories from the search results. Deselect the checkboxes next to the categories you want to ignore. You can also drag categories to change their order in the search results. Individual users have their own separate Search Results settings.

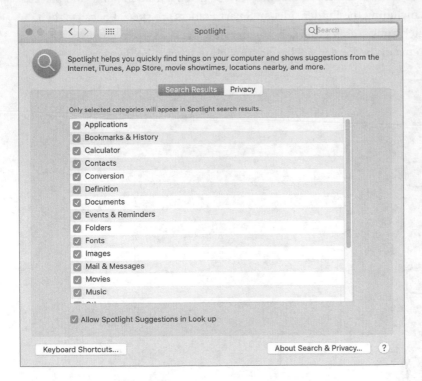

To prevent Spotlight from indexing specific local items, click the Privacy tab to reveal the list of items for Spotlight to ignore. To add new items, click the Add (+) button at the bottom of the privacy list and choose the items from a browser dialog, or drag items into the privacy list. You can remove an item from the privacy list by selecting it and then clicking the Remove (–) button at the bottom of the list.

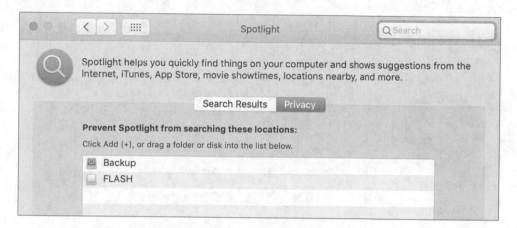

All Spotlight settings are applied immediately. If you add an entire volume to the privacy list, macOS deletes the Spotlight index database from that volume. In turn, removing a volume from the privacy list rebuilds the Spotlight index database on that volume.

Manage Siri Preferences

When you use Siri, the words you say will be recorded and sent to Apple to process your requests. Your device will also send Apple other information, such as your name and nickname; the names, nicknames, and relationships (for example, "my dad") found in your contacts; song names in your collection; the names of your photo albums; and the names of apps installed on your device (collectively, your "User Data"). All of this data is used to help Siri understand you better and recognize what you say. It is not linked to other data that Apple may have from your use of other Apple services. When you use Siri to search for your documents, the Siri request is sent to Apple, but the names and the content of your documents are not sent to Apple. The search is performed locally on the Mac.

If you have Location Services turned on, the location of your device at the time you make a request will also be sent to Apple to help Siri improve the accuracy of its response to your requests. You may choose to turn off Location Services for Siri. To do so, open System Preferences on your Mac, click Security & Privacy, click the Privacy button, click Location Services, and deselect the checkbox for Siri.

Siri requires an Internet connection to query Apple services to interpret the meaning of your requests. Siri is enabled by default, and you may not want to have an Internet connection by default.

You may choose to turn off Siri at any time. You can disable Siri with Setup Assistant during a macOS setup or upgrade, or from System Preferences > Siri preferences by deselecting Enable Ask Siri.

In addition to enabling or disabling Siri, you can adjust several features from Siri preferences, including:

▶ You can select the language that Siri will be expected to understand and respond in. Siri supports over 40 languages and dialects.

▶ You can select the voice that Siri will use to speak responses. The choices in the Siri Voice menu are based on the selected language. You can also disable the voice feedback.

▶ You can select the microphone input that Siri will use to listen for your requests. The internal microphone on Apple portable computers is optimized for Siri input and often includes noise-cancellation technology. For desktop Mac computers lacking a microphone, or if you are in a particularly noisy environment, you can use a dedicated headset-style microphone.

▶ You can select the keyboard shortcut used to start a Siri request.

▶ You can click Siri Suggestions & Privacy to modify the list of apps that Siri will learn from and use to make suggestions.

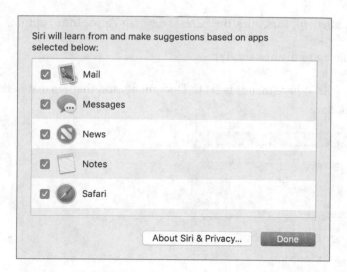

Exercise 16.1
Examine File Metadata

▶ **Prerequisite**

You must have created the Johnny Appleseed account (Exercise 7.1, "Create a Standard User Account").

In this exercise, you examine file metadata in the Finder Info window and add custom metadata.

Use Tag and Comment Metadata

1   Log in as Johnny Appleseed.

2   Open Safari, and navigate to **www.apple.com**.

3   Choose File > Save As (or press Command-S).

4   In the Tags field, enter **Apple Info**. The tag might complete automatically if a previous participant performed this exercise using the same iCloud account.

5   If necessary, in the menu that appears, click the "Create new tag 'Apple Info'" option.

6   Click elsewhere in the dialog to dismiss the Tags.

7   Ensure that the location (the Where menu) is set to Documents and that Format is set to Page Source, and click Save.

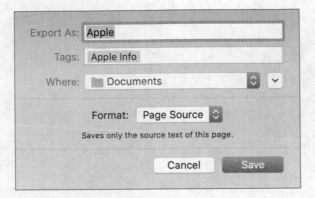

8   Quit Safari.

9   In the Finder, navigate to your Documents folder (choose Go > Documents, or press Shift-Command-O).

10   Select the web archive file, probably called "Apple," and choose File > Get Info (or press Command-I).

11   Expand the General, More Info, and Comments sections of the Info window.

The Info window in the Finder displays information about the file, for example:

▶   Basic metadata such as its size

▶   Information about where on the web it came from

▶   The tag you added when you saved it

You can also edit some metadata types in the Info window.

12   In the Comments section, type **The Apple Orchard**.

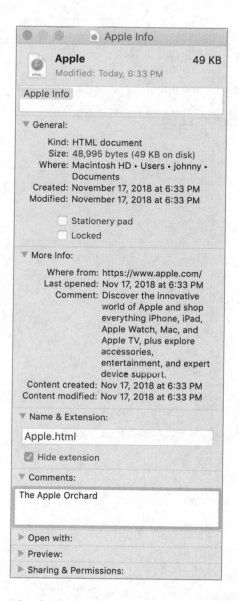

This field adds custom metadata to the file, enabling you to attach searchable comments and keywords. You see how to use this comment later, in step 2 of "Use Spotlight to Search for Documents."

13 Close the Info window.

14 If necessary, change the Finder view of the Documents folder to list view (click the List View button in the toolbar; choose View > as List; or press Command-2).

15 Choose View > Show View Options (or press Command-J).

16 In the Show Columns section, select Comments and Tags.

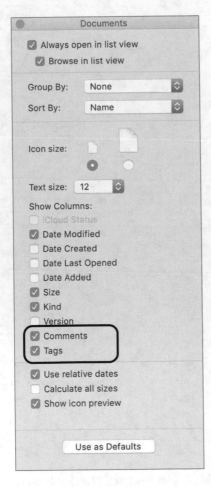

This setting applies only to this folder. If you click "Use as Defaults" you make it the default for all folders.

17 Close the View Options window, and if necessary, widen the Documents window until you see the Tags and Comments fields.

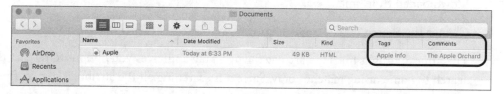

18 Close the Documents window.

Use Spotlight to Search for Documents

1 In the Finder, choose File > Find (Command-F).

2 In the Search field of the window that opens, type **orchard**.

The search finds the web archive you saved earlier because the word "orchard" appears in its Spotlight comment. You can also restrict the search to files with "orchard" in the name.

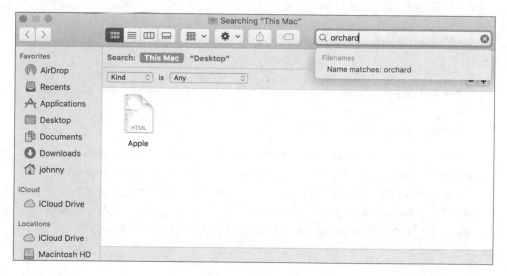

Spotlight searches file contents and all metadata. It displays all matches and then suggests ways to narrow your search (for example, it suggests only filename matches or "downloaded from" matches).

3 Change the Search field to **apple info**.

This time Spotlight finds the archive file by its tag and gives you options to restrict the search to name or tag matches only. Since it is searching all file attributes, it may find other matching files.

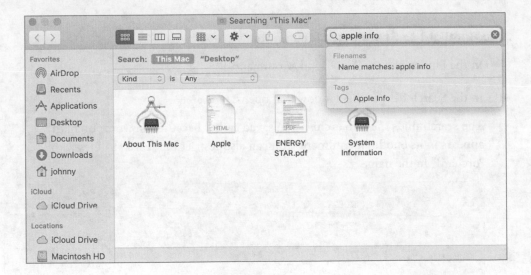

4 Change the search to **apple.com**.

The web archive is found, this time because your search matches the site it was downloaded from. It also finds the Dock.mobileconfig file in the ParticipantMaterials/Lesson3 folder, because it contains a document type descriptor that says it conforms to a format defined at www.apple.com/DTDs/PropertyList-1.0.dtd. If you had text or PDF files that mentioned www.apple.com, they would also be listed.

Lesson 17

Manage Time Machine

In this lesson, you learn how Time Machine enables you to browse the backup history of a file system. You become familiar with how to configure Time Machine. And you explore ways to recover files from Time Machine backups.

Reference 17.1
About Time Machine

Every Mac includes Time Machine. Time Machine backs up your entire Mac, including system files, apps, music, photos, email, and documents to an external storage device. If you accidentally delete or change files, you can use Time Machine to recover them.

Time Machine also performs local snapshots, which capture your content at a specific time when your external storage device for Time Machine isn't available. These backups and local snapshots enable you to use Time Machine to restore files even when your external storage device isn't available. Time Machine keeps:

- Hourly backups for the past 24 hours
- Daily backups for the past month
- Weekly backups for all previous months
- Local snapshots as space permits

To make sure that you have storage space when you need it, when your external storage device becomes full, Time Machine deletes the oldest backups. And, Time Machine stores local snapshots only on disks that have plenty of free space. When storage space gets low, Time Machine deletes the oldest snapshots. This is why the Finder, About This Mac, and Get Info don't include local snapshots in their calculations of available disk storage space.

You can turn off Time Machine and wait a few minutes for macOS to delete local snapshots. When you turn Time Machine back on, it remembers the previous external storage devices you were using.

Backups

An initial Time Machine backup copies most of the contents of your file system to your Time Machine external storage device. Your initial backup might take a long time, depending on how many files Time Machine needs to back up. But you can use your Mac while Time Machine backs it up. Time Machine backs up only files that changed since the previous backup, so your subsequent backups complete faster than your first backup. Read Apple Support article HT204412, "If a Time Machine backup takes longer than you expect," for more information.

After you set up Time Machine, it automatically makes hourly backups. Between backups, a background process, like the one Spotlight uses, tracks changes to the original file system. When the next scheduled backup occurs, Time Machine backs up only files that have changed. Time Machine then combines the new content with hard-link file-system pointers (which occupy nearly zero disk space) to the previous backup content and creates a simulated view of the entire file system at that point in time.

Time Machine ignores files that don't need to be backed up (ones that can be re-created after a restoration) to save space. Generally speaking, Time Machine ignores temporary files, Spotlight indexes, items in the Trash, and anything that can be considered a cache. Time Machine doesn't back up system log files. Software developers can also instruct Time Machine to ignore specific app data that doesn't need to be backed up. For example, apps for Internet file storage providers, like Dropbox or OneDrive, can instruct Time Machine to ignore files saved to a cloud service.

Time Machine always ignores files listed in the configuration file StdExclusions.plist, which is stored in /System/Library/CoreServices/backupd.bundle/Contents/Resources.

Some database files appear as large, single files to the file system. Using a database app, a user might edit only a few bytes in a large database file. Even so, Time Machine creates another copy of the entire file. This can fill your external storage device much more quickly than if the database was stored as many smaller files. Check with third-party database app developers, such as FileMaker, Inc., on their recommendations for backing up database files with Time Machine.

Even though Time Machine creates local snapshots, you should also periodically connect your external storage device—that's configured for Time Machine—to your Mac to back up your files to a location besides your internal disk. If anything happens to your Mac or its internal disk, you can use your external storage device to restore your entire system to another Mac or to a blank replacement disk on your Mac.

Local Snapshots

Time Machine saves local snapshots under four circumstances:

▶ When you start a Time Machine backup to an external storage device for the first time.

▶ Every hour after you turn on Time Machine.

  An hourly local snapshot is saved for 24 hours. macOS saves Time Machine local snapshots hourly, unless you deselect Back Up Automatically in Time Machine preferences.

▶ Until macOS needs to use the storage space that the local snapshots use.

  In this case, Time Machine saves a local snapshot of your last successful Time Machine backup.

▶ Before you install any macOS update, even if you don't turn on Time Machine.

For more information about local snapshots read Apple Support article HT204015, "About Time Machine local snapshots," and the **tmutil** man page.

Reference 17.2
Configure Time Machine

Get one of these types of external storage devices:

▶ One that can connect to a USB, FireWire, or Thunderbolt port on your Mac

▶ On a Mac using macOS 10.13 or later: a shared folder configured to be a Time Machine backup destination on your network

▶ An AirPort Time Capsule on your network

▶ One that can be connected to the USB port of an AirPort Extreme Base Station (802.11ac model) or AirPort Time Capsule on your network

▶ Network-attached storage (NAS) device that supports Time Machine over SMB

When you connect an external storage device directly to your Mac, you might be asked if you want to use it to back up your Mac with Time Machine.

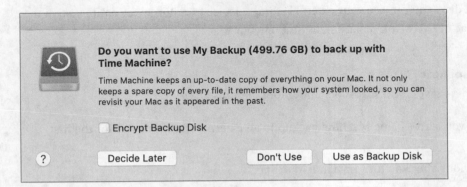

If Time Machine doesn't ask you to select an external storage device when you connect the drive to your Mac:

1   Open Time Machine preferences.

2   Click Select Backup Disk, Select Disk, or Add or Remove Backup Disk.

3   Select an external storage device from the list.

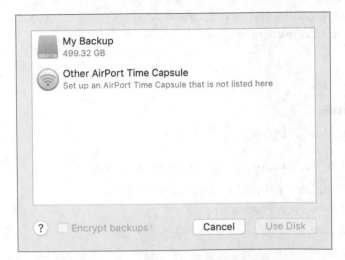

NOTE ▶ It's recommended to enable "Encrypt backups" and then enter a password to use for encryption. See the next section for more information about encryption.

4 Click Use Disk.

The most common format for a Time Machine external storage device that's connected to a USB, FireWire, or Thunderbolt port on your Mac is Mac OS Extended (Journaled) (HFS Plus Journaled). Time Machine also supports all Mac OS Extended (Journaled) formats and Xsan formats for external storage devices that are attached to a USB, FireWire, or Thunderbolt port on your Mac.

If you select an attached external storage device that doesn't use one of these supported formats to be your Time Machine backup disk, macOS offers to erase it. If you click Erase, macOS reformats the disk with the format of Mac OS Extended (Journaled).

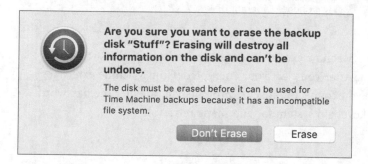

For additional backup security and convenience, you can repeat the steps from earlier in this lesson to add another external storage device. For example, you might use one external storage device for work and another for home.

Time Machine works best if you use your external storage device only for Time Machine backups. If you keep files on your external storage device, Time Machine won't back up those files, and there will be less space for Time Machine backups.

Enable Encryption

If you select the option to encrypt:

▶ You must provide a password and a password hint.

▶ Your backups will be accessible only to users with the password.

▶ macOS reformats the external storage device as Mac OS Extended (Journaled, Encrypted).

NOTE ► Reformatting erases all files on the disk, so do it only if you no longer need the files or have copied them to a different external storage device.

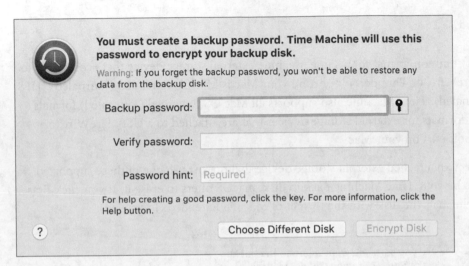

When you encrypt your Time Machine external storage device, macOS doesn't initially save the encryption password. After you eject your encrypted Time Machine external storage device, the next time you connect it, macOS prompts you to enter the password and optionally save it to the keychain system for automatic retrieval.

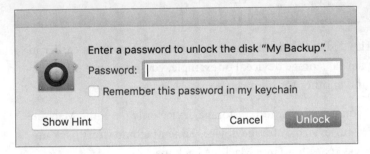

If the encryption checkbox is dimmed, hover your pointer over it to see an explanation of why. For example, the explanation might say that you must reformat or repartition the selected disk. If no explanation appears, the disk you selected doesn't support encryption.

If you connect your encrypted external storage device to another Mac, you must enter the password to access the backed-up files.

If you don't encrypt your external storage device, then the first time you make a Time Machine backup, you'll see an alert that tells you that your external storage device isn't encrypted. You can click Settings and then configure your Time Machine external storage device to be encrypted.

Configure Time Machine Preferences

You can use Time Machine preferences to do the following:

▶ Select a network backup disk.

▶ Verify the backup status.

▶ Manually configure backup settings.

▶ Configure the option to show Time Machine in the menu bar.

▶ Configure the option to back up automatically.

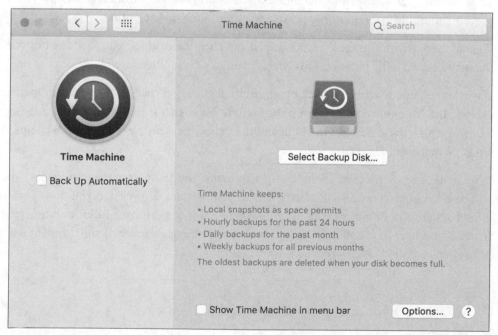

Manage Time Machine Options

Click the Options button at the bottom of Time Machine preferences to adjust backup settings.

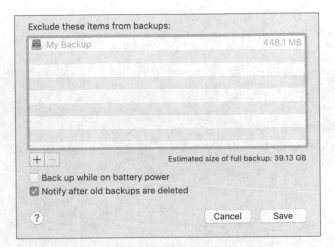

You can exclude items from a backup to reduce the backup space you'll need. Time Machine excludes Time Machine external storage devices from its backups. This prevents multiple external storage devices from backing up each other.

You can drag items into the list field, or you can click the Add (+) button at the bottom of the list to reveal a file browser. This enables you to select folders or volumes to exclude.

If you want Time Machine to back up an external storage device, remove it from the exclude list. To remove an item from the exclude list so that it will be included in the next Time Machine backup, select the item and then click the Remove (–) button. Backups won't be made until you click Save.

If you want to save space by excluding system items, add /System to the exclude list. You will be prompted to exclude all system files or just /System. However, if you don't perform a full backup of your system volume, you won't be able to perform a full restoration of it. Instead, you have to install macOS, and then restore the remainder of your content using Migration Assistant, as covered later in this lesson.

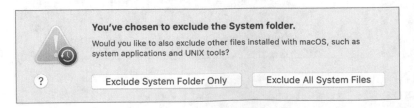

By default, the option "Notify after old backups are deleted" is enabled, so you'll be notified if your external storage device is full and Time Machine deletes old backups to make space for new Time Machine backups.

Reference 17.3
Remove Files from a Time Machine Backup

If you want to remove files from your Time Machine backup, use Time Machine instead of the Finder. You can use the following steps to remove files from your Time Machine backup:

1 Open a window for the file that you want to remove from your Time Machine backup.

2 Open Time Machine.

3 Find the file to remove from your Time Machine backup.

4 Control-click the file.

5 Choose "Delete All Backups of *filename.*"

6 Click OK at the confirmation dialog.

7 If necessary, provide administrator credentials, then click OK.

8 In Time Machine, click Cancel to exit Time Machine.

Your files are no longer available to restore from your Time Machine backup.

Reference 17.4
Restore Files

You can restore:

► Specific files with Time Machine

► User accounts and entire home folders with Migration Assistant

► An entire Mac with macOS Recovery

► Specific files with the Finder

Restore Files with Time Machine

Complete the following steps to restore files from a Time Machine backup to your Mac.

1 Open a window for the file that you want to restore. For example:

► To restore a file you deleted from your Documents folder, open the Documents folder.

► To restore an email, open Mail, then open the mailbox that the email message was in.

► If you're using an app that saves versions of documents as you work on them, you can open a document and use Time Machine to restore earlier versions of that document.

2 Connect your Time Machine external storage device to your Mac if it's available.

Otherwise, Time Machine uses your local snapshots.

If you back up to multiple external storage devices, you can switch them before you enter Time Machine. Press and hold the Option key, click the Time Machine menu item, then choose Browse Other Backup Disks. In the "Choose Time Machine Disk to Browse" window, select a disk, and then click Use Selected Disk. Time Machine opens, and you can skip to step 4.

3   Open Time Machine with any of the following actions:

▶   Open Spotlight, enter Time Machine, then press Return.

▶   Choose Enter Time Machine from the Time Machine menu.

▶   Click Time Machine if you see its icon in the Dock.

The following figure shows Time Machine for the Documents folder:

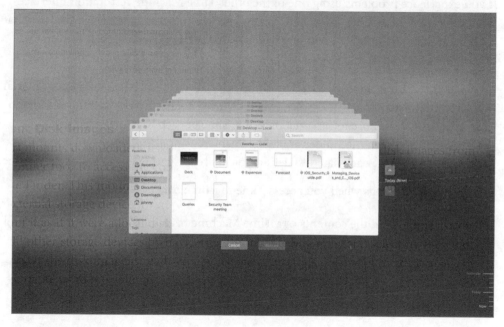

4   Find the files to restore:

▶   Use the timeline on the edge of the screen to see the files in your Time Machine backup as they were at that date and time.

▶   A bright red tick mark is a backup that can be restored now, either from a local snapshot or from your external storage device. When your external storage device isn't available, only the local snapshots are bright red.

▶   A dimmed red tick mark is a backup that can be restored from your external storage device after it becomes available. Until then, the stack of windows on the screen shows a blank window for that backup.

▶ Use the onscreen up and down arrows to jump to the last time the contents of the window changed. You can also use the Search field in a window to find a file, and then move through time while focused on changes to that file.

5   Select a file and press the Space bar to preview it and make sure it's the one you want.

6   Click Restore to restore the selected file, or Control-click the file for other options.

Restore with the Finder

If you experience problems using one of the other Time Machine restoration interfaces, you can browse the backup from the Finder. Time Machine uses file system features that are part of standard Mac OS Extended volumes, so you don't need special software to browse through backup contents.

If you access a locally attached Time Machine external storage device, the backup files are in the root of the external storage device in a database folder named Backups.backupdb. This folder contains more folders that have the name of each Mac that was backed up to the disk. Inside each Mac folder are folders named using the date and time of each backup. Finally, inside each dated folder are folders representing each backed-up volume.

Remember these things when you access Time Machine backups from the Finder:

▶ You can only read the contents of a Time Machine backup, which has access control entries (ACEs) that deny write access.

▶ If you don't have file-system permissions to the backup folders, you have to change the ownership or permissions to open the folders in the Finder. You can find out more about changing permissions in Lesson 13, "Manage Permissions and Sharing."

If you access Time Machine over a network, you must manually connect to the Time Machine share first. Connecting to shares is covered in Lesson 24, "Manage Network Services." After you're connected, you must locate the Time Machine backup disk images. They're at the root of the Time Machine share and are most commonly named Backups. Each Mac computer's backup is saved as a separate sparse disk image file named with the Mac computer's sharing name.

Restore Files with Migration Assistant

You can restore a complete user home folder or other nonsystem files from a Time Machine backup using Migration Assistant. If you want to restore an entire Mac from Time Machine, start from macOS Recovery. This process is covered in the next section of this lesson.

1   When Migration Assistant opens—either during the initial Setup Assistant or when you open it—choose to restore from a Time Machine backup.

Initial Setup Assistant is covered in Reference 3.1, "Configure a Mac with a New Installation of macOS Mojave."

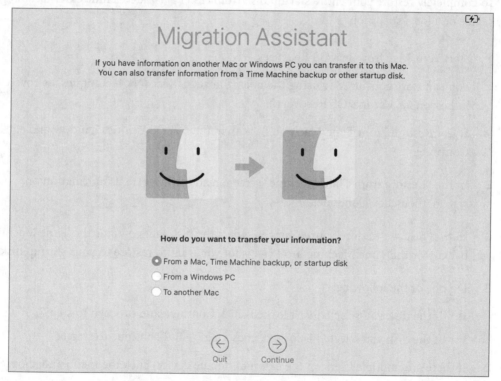

2   Select an external storage device and authenticate to access its content.

The remainder of the Migration Assistant process is like the standard migration process covered in Lesson 3, "Set Up and Configure macOS," for settings, or in Lesson 8, "Manage User Home Folders," for user-specific items.

Restore an Entire Mac with macOS Recovery

To completely restore your Mac, use the "Restore from Time Machine Backup" utility in macOS Recovery. Before you restore your Mac, keep the following in mind:

▶ Restoring erases the destination disk.

▶ If you're setting up a new Mac or a Mac with a new installation of macOS Mojave, then you should use Migration Assistant instead of restoring from Time Machine.

▶ To restore just individual files, settings, or user accounts, use Time Machine in the Finder instead of restoring your entire Mac from Time Machine backup.

To completely restore your entire startup disk from either a Time Machine external storage device or a local snapshot:

1 Start your Mac from macOS Recovery.

You can start up your Mac using the normal macOS Recovery techniques, as covered in Lesson 5, "Use macOS Recovery."

2 Select Restore From Time Machine Backup in the macOS Utilities window and click Continue.

3 In the "Restore from Time Machine" screen, read the important information on screen, then click Continue.

4 In the "Select a Restore Source" screen, select the disk that contains the Time Machine backup or the Time Machine local snapshot you want to restore to your startup disk.

5 Do one of the following:

▶ If the disk you selected isn't locked, click Continue and proceed to step 7.

▶ If the disk you selected is locked, click Unlock and continue to step 6.

6 If there are multiple users on the external storage device, click the menu and choose a user.

Enter the password for the user to unlock the external storage device, then click Unlock. Select the disk you just unlocked, and click Continue.

7 Do one of the following:

▶ If you selected a Time Machine local snapshot, then in the "Select a Local Snapshot" screen, select a local snapshot and click Continue. Proceed to step 8.

▶ If you selected a Time Machine external storage device, then in the "Select a Backup" screen, select a backup and click Continue. Proceed to Step 8.

8 In the "Select a Destination" screen, select your startup disk that will be erased and restored.

9 Click Restore.

10 At the confirmation dialog, click Erase Disk.

The disk you restore is erased before it receives macOS and the other contents of your Time Machine backup. All changes you made to your startup disk after the Time Machine backup or Time Machine local snapshot was taken are lost.

For more information, read Apple Support article HT203981, "Restore your Mac from a backup."

Exercise 17.1
Configure Time Machine

▶ **Prerequisites**

▶ You must have created the Local Administrator (Exercise 3.1, "Configure a Mac for Exercises") and Johnny Appleseed (Exercise 7.1, "Create a Standard User Account") accounts.

▶ You must have an external storage device (USB flash drive or other media) to use for backups.

In this exercise, you configure Time Machine to back up your user home folders to your external storage device.

Configure Exclusions for Time Machine

By default, Time Machine backs up the startup volume (excluding some file types). In this exercise you configure it to back up only user files. In most cases, backing up only user files works because you can always reinstall macOS and apps. If you want to do a full system restore, don't add any exclusions to Time Machine's exclusions list.

1 Log in as Johnny Appleseed.

2 Open System Preferences, and click Time Machine.

3 Click the lock button, and authenticate as Local Administrator.

4 Select the "Show Time Machine in menu bar" checkbox if it isn't selected.

5 Click the Options button to reveal a dialog that enables you to exclude folders from backups.

There might be an entry for /Users/Shared/adi in the exclude list. This is used internally by Apple Books, and you can ignore it.

6 Click the Add (+) button at the bottom of the list.

7 Navigate to your startup volume (generally Macintosh HD), and select the Applications, Library, and System folders.

You can Command-click folders to add them to the selection.

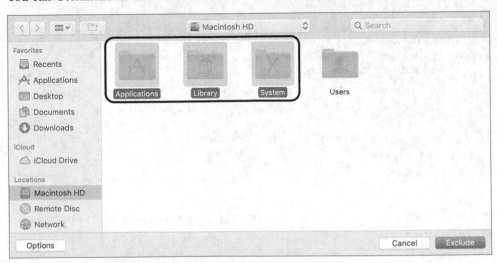

8   Click Exclude.

9   When you see the message "You've chosen to exclude the System folder," click Exclude All System Files.

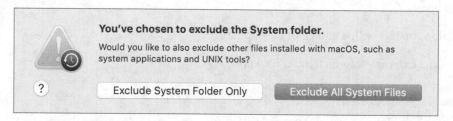

Your exclusion list now looks like the following figure (although the sizes may be different, /Users/Shared/adi might be listed, and the option to back up while on battery power appears only on laptop computers).

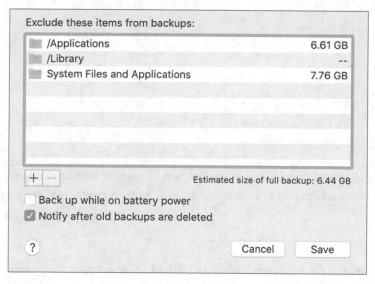

10   Click Save.

Select a Backup Volume

1   Connect your external storage device to the Mac.

2   If a dialog appears and asks if you want to use the disk to back up with Time Machine, click Decide Later so that you can configure the backup manually.

3 If your external disk isn't currently named Backup, select it, choose File > Rename, and type **Backup** to rename the disk.

4 In the Time Machine pane of System Preferences, select the Back Up Automatically checkbox.

A dialog appears with a choice of backup targets.

5 Select the external volume named Backup.

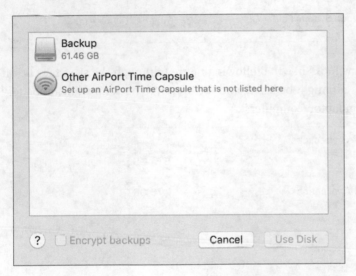

Note the "Encrypt backups" checkbox that enables you to encrypt backups. When you select this checkbox, you encrypt the backup volume the same way you would encrypt it in the Finder.

6 Click Use Disk.

If your external storage device is formatted as APFS, FAT32, or another file system, a dialog appears and asks if you are sure that you want to erase the backup disk. The dialog shows the current destination selected having an incompatible file system. Time Machine destinations must be formatted as Mac OS Extended (Journaled) or HFS Plus using the GPT partition scheme. Destinations formatted with other file system schemes—besides Mac OS Extended (Journaled)—are incompatible and are erased and formatted as HFS Plus for use with Time Machine.

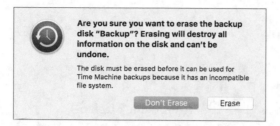

7 If you want to continue, click Erase, and authenticate as Local Administrator.

You see a "preparing disk" message. The Backup disk unmounts, formats as HFS Plus (Journaled), and reappears. Time Machine starts backing up in two minutes. You don't have to wait for it before proceeding with the exercise.

8 Open Disk Utility, and in the sidebar, select Backup.

The Backup volume is formatted as Mac OS Extended (Journaled).

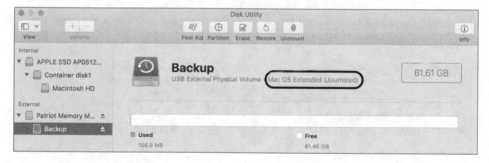

9 Quit Disk Utility.

10 Quit System Preferences.

11 After the backup begins, you might see a notification that the Backup isn't encrypted. Close this notification.

Now, perform Exercise 17.2, "Restore Using Time Machine," to test the backup.

Exercise 17.2
Restore Using Time Machine

> **Prerequisite**
>
> ▸ You must have performed Exercise 17.1, "Configure Time Machine."

In this exercise, you learn how to use Time Machine to recover lost files from the backup.

Wait for the Backup to Finish

Before testing the backup, make sure it is finished and up to date.

1 Log in as Johnny Appleseed.

2 Click the Time Machine menu bar item. If the menu indicates that the backup is still in progress, wait for it to finish.

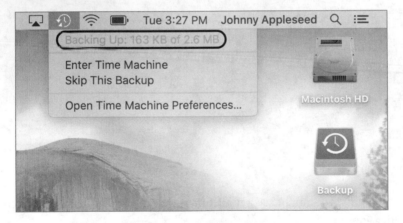

3 When you are notified that the backup is finished, click Close.

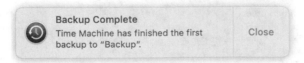

Delete Files

Here you delete files and folders from the participant materials.

1   In the Finder, open /Users/Shared/ParticipantMaterials/Lesson17.

2   Move the "Archived announcements" folder to the Trash.

This folder contains the Pretendco company's old media information.

3   If you are prompted to, authenticate as Local Administrator.

4   Choose Finder > Empty Trash. In the confirmation dialog, click Empty Trash.

Restore a File Using Time Machine

Search for an announcement about Pretendco's plans for solid-state encabulation device (SSED) development.

1   Choose Time Machine > Enter Time Machine.

Time Machine opens and shows successive snapshots of your files with more recent ones in front of older ones, which appear to recede into the past.

2   Enter **SSED plans** in the Search field at the upper right of the window.

No matching files appear, since the only match was in the folder you deleted and you are viewing files as they exist now.

3   Use the up and down arrows to navigate through time until the file SSED plans.rtf appears.

You can also navigate through time using the timeline along the right side of the screen.

4 Select SSED plans.rtf and press Command-Y or the Space bar.

A Quick Look preview opens. Quick Look is available in Time Machine so that you can verify that you have the right file before you restore it.

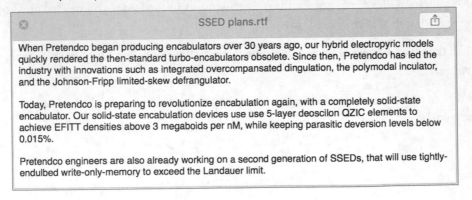

5 Press Command-Y, or the Space bar, to close Quick Look.

6 With the file selected, click Restore.

Since the folder the file was in was deleted, Time Machine gives you the option to re-create the original enclosing folder or choose a new location for the restore.

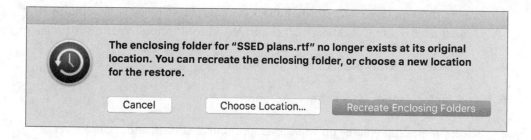

7   Click Choose Location. The Choose Folder dialog opens.

8   Navigate to your Documents folder by selecting it in the sidebar, and click Choose.

9   If you are prompted, authenticate as Local Administrator.

10 In the Finder, navigate to your Documents folder (choose Go > Documents, or press Shift-Command-O).

The restored SSED plans.rtf file is visible.

Restore Directly from Time Machine

Inspect the backup and copy files out of it to restore them.

1   In the Finder, open the volume you chose to back up to.

2   Open the Backups.backupdb folder. In this folder is a folder for your client. Open it.

The folder contains one or more snapshot folders, named with the date and time they were taken. There is an alias named Latest that points to the latest backup.

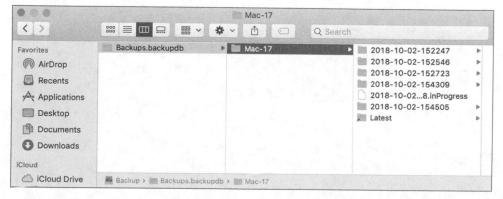

3   Browse through these folders: /Backups.backupdb/Mac-*NN*/Latest/Macintosh HD/ Users/Shared/ParticipantMaterials/Lesson17/Archived announcements/2010/04-April.

4   Drag a copy of SSED plans.rtf to your desktop.

5   If prompted, authenticate as Local Administrator.

6   Select the Backup volume on your desktop, Control-click it, and choose Eject "Backup."

7   Unplug the external storage device from your Mac.

Apps and Processes

Lesson 18
Install Apps

It's easy for Mac users to find and install apps. In this lesson you install apps using the App Store and other installation methods. You also explore app security measures used in macOS.

Reference 18.1
The App Store

To see hundreds of macOS and third-party apps, visit the App Store. To find an app, you can search for it by name or browse the store. After you find the app you want, you can buy it using your Apple ID, a download code, or a gift card.

Browse

To browse the App Store, open App Store in the Dock, select App Store in Launchpad, or choose App Store from the Apple menu.

The first time you open App Store, you see the Welcome screen and the privacy icon. The privacy icon tells you that App Store shares information with Apple. Click the "See how your data is managed" link to read more about how your information is shared, or click Continue to use App Store.

> ## GOALS
>
> ▶ Install apps from the App Store
>
> ▶ Describe app support and identify security issues
>
> ▶ Install apps using software packages and drag-and-drop

App Store initially displays the Discover tab. The Discover tab displays new and updated apps. Each week App Store editors feature new apps with in-depth stories. Check out a featured app's preview video to see how it works. The Discover tab also includes other features, such as perspectives from developers, top charts, and themed collections.

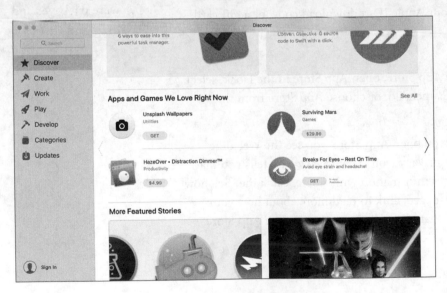

For each of the themed tabs—Create, Work, Play, and Develop—App Store editors provide expert recommendations and tutorials. Scroll to the bottom of any of the themed tabs to reach the Quick Links section.

The Categories tab includes popular categories of apps. Each category includes an editor's choice, a suggested app to try, and top charts for that category.

You can use these keyboard shortcuts:

▶ Press Command-1 for Discover

▶ Press Command-2 for Create

▶ Press Command-3 for Work

▶ Press Command-4 for Play

▶ Press Command-5 for Develop

▶ Press Command-6 for Categories

▶ Press Command-7 for Updates

Search the App Store

If you enable Siri, you can use it search for apps. Siri takes your request, opens App Store, and enters your request in the App Store Search field.

Or you can use the Search field at the top left of the App Store window. Enter part of the name of an app or developer, and the search returns a list of matching items.

Press the Return key or select an item to see a search results page. This gives you a more detailed view of the matching items.

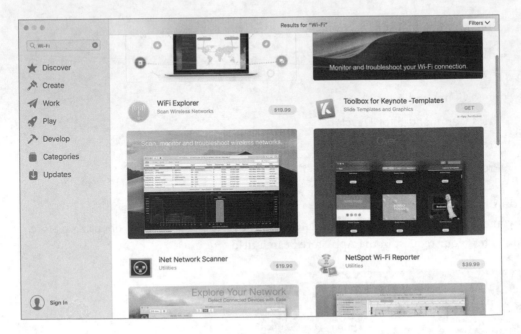

Click an app icon or name to view the details page. In the details page, you can read more about the app, view screenshots of the app, and browse or write your own customer ratings and reviews. This page displays more developer and app information, including the version, download size, and system requirements.

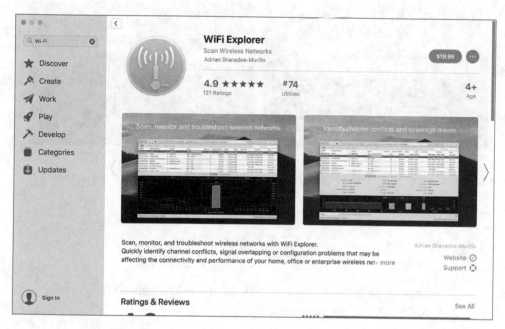

Click the ellipsis button to copy or share a link to the app.

A free item displays the word "Get." A paid app displays a button with its price. If the button next to a purchased item says "Open," the item is already installed.

The following figure shows a free app and a paid app:

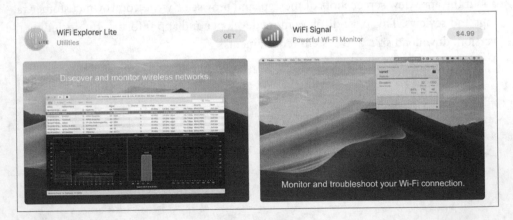

For a free item, click Get. The button changes to Install. Click Install to start installing an app.

If you see a button with the price of an item, click the price. The button changes from the price to Buy App. Click Buy App to purchase the app.

To install an app that you already bought but didn't install on your Mac, click the Redownload button. (The Redownload button looks like a cloud with an arrow pointing down.)

Get an Apple ID

You don't need serial numbers or activation codes to buy apps from the App Store. You just need your Apple ID, a verified email address, and an Internet connection for free items. You'll also need a payment method if you want to buy something. Read Apple

Support article HT202631, "Payment methods that you can use with your Apple ID" for details about that forms of payment you can use. It's helpful to have a high-speed broadband connection too. Any items you buy are associated with your Apple ID, and you can install them on any Mac you personally own or control. Using apps on multiple Mac computers is possible because Apple keeps track of the items you buy and install using your Apple ID.

If you don't have an Apple ID, you can create one in the App Store. If your primary email address is from a non-Apple source, you can use it to define an Apple ID. Alternatively, you can use a free iCloud account, which provides a free email address.

If your organization uses Apple Business Manager (https://help.apple.com/businessmanager/) or Apple School Manager (https://help.apple.com/schoolmanager/) you can acquire multiple app licenses for App Store items. The rest of this lesson focuses on buying apps outside the scope of Apple Business Manager and Apple School Manager.

You can update or reinstall any item you buy with your Apple ID. You'll receive a warning if you try to install an app from the App Store that replaces an earlier version of the same app that you bought outside the App Store.

To manage your App Store account, click the Sign In link at the bottom-left corner of App Store, or choose Store > Sign In.

The App Store authentication dialog appears. If you're already logged in to iCloud, macOS enters your Apple ID, and you just need to enter your password. Otherwise, if you have an Apple ID, enter it.

What happens next depends on the state of your Apple ID. If you click Sign In, you might proceed directly to install items, you might need to agree to updated terms and conditions, or you might need to verify or update your Apple ID information. If you don't have an Apple ID, or if you want to create a new one just for purchases, click Create Apple ID.

After you enter your name, email address, and password, you must enter a billing address. You might have to provide payment information. Read Apple Support article HT201266, "Change or remove your Apple ID payment information," for instructions about removing your payment information.

For more information about creating a new Apple ID that you can use for free items, see Apple Support articles HT204034, "Create or use an Apple ID without a payment method," and HT203905, "If you can't choose None when you edit your Apple ID payment information."

You'll receive an email from Apple asking you to verify your account. Click the link in the email to open a webpage where you can do so. After you verify your account, sign in to the App Store again to buy items.

If you need to verify or update your Apple ID information, you're prompted to review your account. You must agree to the App Store terms and conditions and verify your Apple ID security details. You might also have to verify or update your billing information to continue with purchases.

When you are signed in, the App Store displays your Account page, and your name appears in the lower-left corner.

Apps Bundled with a New Mac

Five apps come preinstalled on new Mac computers that are treated a little differently than the other preinstalled apps. These apps include creativity apps (iMovie and GarageBand) and productivity apps (Pages, Keynote, and Numbers).

Unless installed by mobile device management (MDM) with Apple Business Manager or Apple School Manager, these apps:

▶ Aren't automatically installed when you erase a disk and reinstall macOS Mojave on a blank volume

▶ Are available in the App Store for free

▶ Require someone to adopt them (enter an Apple ID to associate the app license with that Apple ID) before you can install an update to them

When you adopt the bundled apps, they are assigned to your Apple ID. macOS sends a unique hardware identifier from your Mac to Apple to verify eligibility.

After a user with an Apple ID owns a license for an app, that user can install the app on any other Mac as follows:

1   Sign in to the App Store.

2   Click their name in the lower-left corner to open their Account page.

3   Scroll to the Purchased section.

4 Click Redownload next to any purchased item.

You can also view your signed-in Apple ID and sign out of your account from the Store menu.

Visit App Store Help at support.apple.com/guide/app-store, or iTunes Support at support.apple.com/itunes, for more details.

Manage Your Apple ID

If you want to make changes to your Apple ID:

1 Open the App Store.

2 Click the Account link in the lower-left corner of the App Store sidebar.

3 Choose Store > View My Account, or press Command-0 (zero).

4 From the Account page, click View Information to manage settings, including your Apple ID, payment information, country or region setting, and your Apple nickname.

Your Apple nickname is used to hide your personal identification in reviews you post in any of Apple's online stores.

If you, or an unauthorized user, make significant changes to your Apple ID, you'll receive an automated email letting you know changes were made.

Install

You don't have to be signed in to the App Store to browse, but you do need to be signed in to buy, install, or update an app. After you click Buy App or Install, if you haven't signed in yet, you will be asked to.

If you use more than one Mac, you can enable automatic downloads of purchased apps. You can set this option in the App Store preferences for every Mac that you configured with your Apple ID.

Use the Apps pane of Parental Controls preferences to select the apps and features children can access.

Manage Family Sharing

Family Sharing makes it easy for up to six people in your family, without sharing accounts, to share iTunes, Apple Books, and App Store purchases; an Apple Music family membership; and an iCloud storage plan. When the family organizer turns on purchase sharing, you can pay for family purchases with the same credit card and approve kids' spending right from a parent's device. Family Sharing also enables you to share photos, a family calendar, and more to help keep everyone connected. You can find out more at www.apple.com/family-sharing.

Manage Purchased Apps

To install an app that you or another member of your Family Sharing group has already bought, open the App Store, sign in with your Apple ID, and then click your name in the sidebar. The Purchased section of your Account page shows all the items owned by the signed-in Apple ID, both installed and not installed on the Mac. If you're part of a Family Sharing group, you can also view another family member's purchases. To do so, click the name in "Purchased by *name*," and then choose another name in the pop-up menu.

Hover your pointer over an app to reveal an ellipsis button (...).

To temporarily hide a purchase, click the ellipsis button, then choose Hide Purchase. You can unhide purchases later from the Account Info page.

Update App Store Apps

The automatic software update mechanisms for macOS and the App Store, and notifications for available updates, are covered in detail in Reference 6.1, "Automatic Software Updates."

To install App Store updates manually, click the Updates tab in the App Store. Then you can do either of the following:

▶   Click Update next to an app that has an update available.

▶   In the upper-right corner of the Updates page, click Update All.

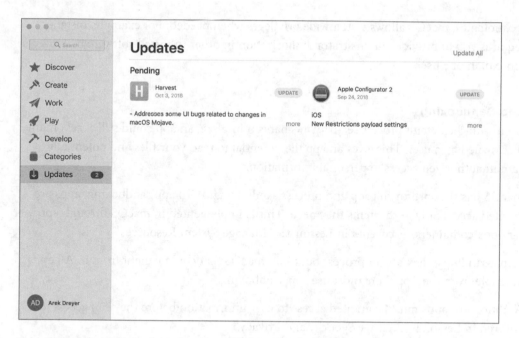

For more information about buying and downloading apps, read Apple Support article
HT204266, "Download apps and games using the App Store."

Reference 18.2
App Security

The safest place to get apps for your Mac is the App Store. Apple reviews each app in the
App Store, and if there's ever a problem with an app, Apple can quickly remove it from the
store.

The only apps in the App Store that might ask for administrator authorization are those
developed by Apple. For example, macOS Server and Xcode require administrator authorization because each installs additional system services.

About Process Security

macOS includes several app security technologies that help protect you when you install
third-party apps. For example, System Integrity Protection (SIP) is enabled by default,
and processes can't access resources unless specifically allowed. Despite these security

technologies, macOS allows systemwide privileges when needed. For example, Installer requires you to provide administrator authorization in order to install software that affects more than one user.

App Sandboxing

Even with the default process security mechanism in place, an app could still access many files owned by a user. This gives an app the potential to read your files and potentially gain unauthorized access to personal information.

macOS has support for full app and process sandboxing. With app sandboxing, apps are granted access only to the items they need. This is implemented in macOS through app sandbox containers, as covered in Lesson 15, "Manage System Resources."

Apple sandboxes any app or process built into macOS that could benefit from it. All apps available from the App Store must use app sandboxing.

Additionally, apps must be granted access to user information before they can access it, as covered in Lesson 9, "Manage Security and Privacy."

Code Signing

Code-signed apps and processes include a digital signature, which is used by macOS to verify the authenticity and integrity of the software code and resources. macOS verifies code at rest before you open it, and as it's running as well. Even if some part of the app's or process's code is inappropriately changed while it's active, macOS can automatically quit it.

In addition to identifying changes to apps, code signing provides guaranteed app identification for other parts of macOS, including the keychain, the personal app firewall, Parental Controls preferences, and app sandboxing.

macOS uses code signing to identify and trust newly installed items. All Apple software and apps from the App Store are code signed.

Software developers who choose not to use the App Store can still take advantage of code signing. Developers can code-sign their installers and apps using an Apple-granted Developer ID. This way, code-signed apps installed from any origin can be trusted by macOS.

Notarization

macOS Mojave introduces software notarization—an indication that Apple performed a security check on software that was signed with a Developer ID and that no malicious software was found in the signed software.

At some point in the future in an upcoming release of macOS, macOS will require Developer ID signed software to be notarized by Apple.

For more information about code signing and notarization read https://developer.apple.com/developer-id/.

> **NOTE ▶** See the man page for the spctl command, specifically the -a and -v options, to perform an assessment on items.

File Quarantine

macOS includes a file quarantine feature, which displays a warning (or just a dialog if the item is notarized) when you attempt to open an item downloaded from an external source such as the Internet. Quarantined items include many file types, such as documents, scripts, and disk images. This lesson focuses primarily on quarantine as it relates to downloaded apps.

Quarantine starts only when an item is marked for quarantine by the quarantine-aware app that downloaded it. All apps built into macOS are quarantine aware. But not all third-party apps that can download apps are quarantine aware. Also, if you copy items to a Mac using any other method, they aren't marked for quarantine. For example, if you use the Finder to copy an app from an external disk, you don't engage the quarantine service, so you won't see warnings about items that aren't notarized, for example.

When an item is marked for quarantine, macOS requires you to verify your intent to open the item or cancel if you have any suspicions about the safety of it. Any administrator user can permanently clear a quarantine by clicking Open. After an administrator clears the quarantine, macOS no longer shows the quarantine warning. When a standard user clicks Open on a quarantined item, the item opens but the quarantine remains. Subsequent users who try to open the item still get the quarantine warning.

You can also remove an item quarantine with the xattr command-line tool. Use this tool to remove the quarantine on multiple items at once or in cases where the Finder can't remove the quarantine. To use this tool in Terminal, enter **xattr –dr com.apple.quarantine**, followed by the path of the item.

Malware Detection

Apple further secures macOS by maintaining a list of known malicious software. If you attempt to open any software on this list, macOS presents a warning dialog suggesting that you move the item to the Trash and report the malware to Apple to protect other users. The list of malicious software is automatically updated with the macOS Software Update.

To find out more about item quarantine, read Apple Support article HT201940, "About the 'Are you sure you want to open it?' alert (File Quarantine / Known Malware Detection) in OS X."

Configure "Allow apps downloaded from" Settings

macOS uses technology that leverages both code signing and file quarantine to protect your Mac from malicious apps. It does this by giving you the choice to allow downloaded apps from only trusted app sources.

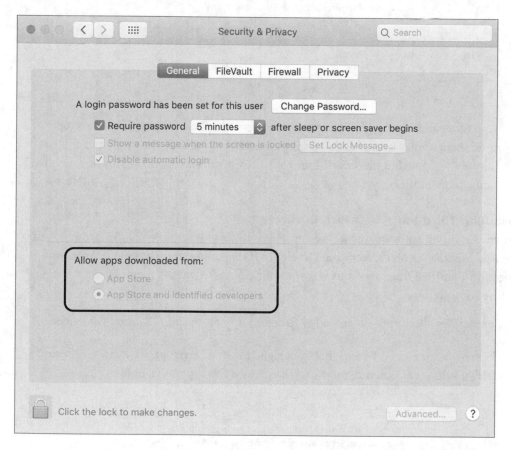

The "Allow apps downloaded from" setting has two options:

▶ App Store—Allow only apps from the App Store to open. Even when a version of the app is available from the App Store, if you download the app from somewhere else, it will still be blocked.

- App Store and identified developers—The default option for macOS. If developers used their Apple-verified code-signing certificate to identify their app, the app is allowed to open, but macOS still presents the file quarantine dialog for downloaded items if quarantine is set.

Installing Third-Party Software Securely

When you install software, including apps, plug-ins, and installer packages, from outside the App Store, your Mac checks the Developer ID signature to verify that the software is from the identified developer and wasn't modified. And it checks the notarization status for the software.

If your settings allow apps downloaded from the App Store and identified developers:

- When you first open an app that's not signed with a Developer ID, you see an alert with a yellow exclamation mark. You can't open the app at this point.

- When you first open an app that's signed with a Developer ID but isn't notarized by Apple, you see an alert with a yellow exclamation mark. You can cancel, show the source of the app, or open the app.

▶ If you have Internet access when you first open an app that is signed with a Developer ID and notarized by Apple, you see an alert that states "Apple checked it for malicious software and none was detected." You can cancel, open the app, or if the dialog offers the option, show the source of the app.

▶ If you don't have Internet access when you first open an app that is signed with a Developer ID and notarized by Apple, you see an alert that states "As of *date*, Apple checked it for malicious software and none was detected." You can cancel, open the app, or if the dialog offers the option, show the source of the app.

macOS also identifies modified or damaged apps regardless of your security settings.

To find out more about safely opening apps, read Apple Support article HT202491, "Safely open apps on your Mac."

Temporarily Bypass App Installation Settings

Even after you select an option for the "Allow apps downloaded from" setting, you can override it and allow untrusted apps with administrator credentials. In the Finder, Control-click the app file and then choose Open from the shortcut menu. A warning appears to verify your intent.

Click Open to open the app and clear the file quarantine (if you aren't logged in as an administrator, you must provide administrator credentials). However, doing this might not be enough for all unsigned apps, because some apps might automatically open other background or child apps. Examples include apps that also provide background software to facilitate hardware functionality.

These secondary apps might also trigger restrictions from running software. You won't be able to override these files from the Finder. In these cases, contact the software developer to ensure you have the latest macOS Mojave–compatible version of the software.

You can also override an item blocked by macOS in the General pane of Security & Privacy preferences. Click Open Anyway (if you aren't logged in as an administrator, you must provide administrator credentials).

Allow apps downloaded from:

○ App Store

● App Store and identified developers

"Finder Services Installer" was blocked from opening because it is not from an identified developer.

[Open Anyway]

🔒 Click the lock to make changes.

[Advanced...]   (?)

Reference 18.3
Install Apps Using Software Packages and Drag-and-Drop

In addition to using the App Store, you can install software using drag-and-drop installations or installation packages.

If a software developer creates a product that requires a folder that contains only a few items or even a single item, it's often deployed as a disk image that contains a drag-and-drop installation.

However, if a software developer creates a product that requires a set of items that must be installed in multiple specific locations throughout macOS, it's often deployed as an installation package.

Install with Drag-and-Drop

When you download software from the Internet, it is often in an archive format or a disk image format.

In macOS, Safari downloads files by default to ~/Downloads. Safari by default unarchives ZIP files. You must open (or double-click) a downloaded disk image to make its contents available to you in the Finder.

You should move the new app to another location. The default location for apps available to all users is /Applications. Only administrator users can manually make changes to /Applications. However, users can place apps anywhere inside their own home folders.

To perform a drag-and-drop installation, drag the app to the /Applications folder or an alternative location. In the following example, the developer provided an alias to your Applications folder to make dragging and dropping easy.

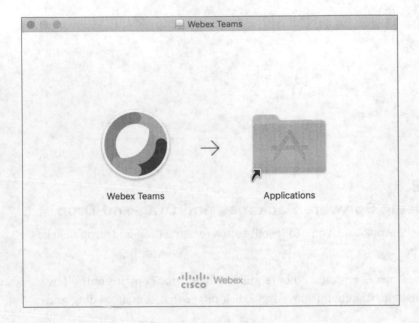

Drag-and-Drop App Security

Apps that a standard user is allowed to install and open can't interfere with other users on the Mac. However, poorly written or malicious software could potentially harm items in the user's home folder.

Installation Packages

Some developers distribute software installation packages (also called just packages) that are ready for you to install when you open the package.

When you open an installation package, Installer opens automatically. Installer walks you through a few simple screens so that you can configure and initiate the installation process. Installer is in /System/Library/CoreServices.

Many third-party apps install items that can affect other users and macOS, so their installer packages require you to provide administrator credentials before you can install the apps. This is in contrast to the App Store, which does not require administrator access to install apps.

Installer supports signed packages. Signed packages contain code used to validate the authenticity and completeness of the software during installation. This makes it nearly impossible for unauthorized parties to insert illegitimate files in trusted installation packages. You can recognize a signed installer package by the small lock button in the far right of the installer window title bar.

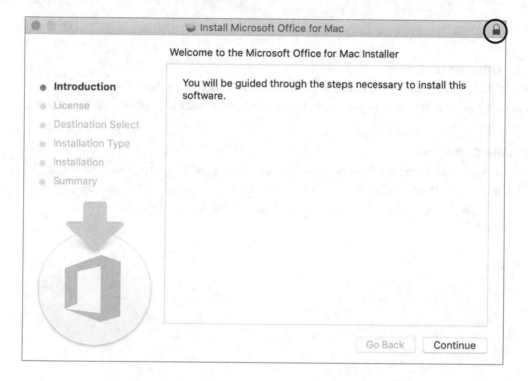

Clicking the Lock button displays details about the signed package, including its certificate status.

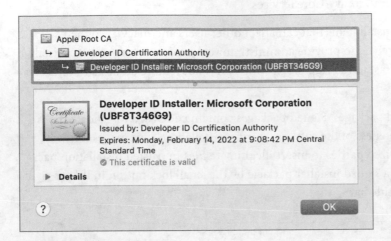

Use Other Installers

Some third-party installers use an installation method other than drag-and-drop or an installer package. If you have problems with a third-party installer, contact the developer.

Enable Software

When you install some third-party software, you might need to approve access to your Mac or approve the installation of kernel extensions. See Reference 9.6, "Manage User Privacy," and Reference 9.7, "Approve Kernel Extensions," for more details.

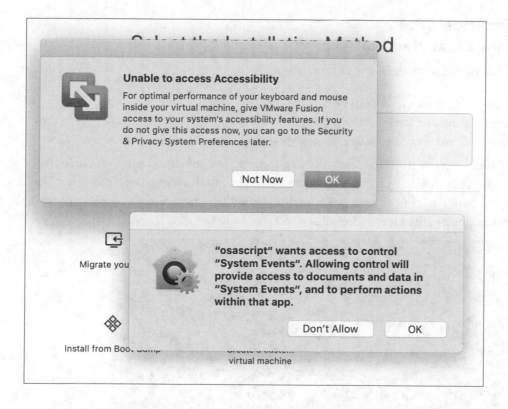

Update Installed Software

You can keep your software updated in several ways:

▶ Apple software and App Store software—Software you get from the App Store, including Apple and third-party software, is updated by the App Store. See Lesson 6, "Update macOS," for more details.

▶ Automatically update third-party software—Automatic update mechanisms for third-party software vary. There is no standard method to determine whether an app has an automatic update capability. You can start by looking in common locations, including the app menu (the menu that appears with the app's name), the app's preferences window, or the app's Help menu. If the third-party item installed a preference pane, an automatic update mechanism might be there.

▶ Manually update third-party software—In some cases, you must manually install a newer app version.

Reference 18.4
Remove Installed Software

You can remove software in one of three ways:

▶   You can drag an app to the Trash. If the software item is a type of resource, like a preference pane or a font, locate the item in one of the Library folders and drag it to the Trash. Then empty the Trash. This method might leave some residual support files.

▶   You can remove App Store apps from Launchpad. In Launchpad, press and hold the Option key. A small x button appears next to apps installed from the App Store. Click the x button to remove an app. Using this method to remove some apps (GarageBand, for example) might leave residual support files behind.

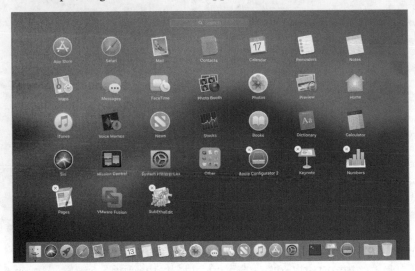

▶   Some third-party developers distribute an uninstaller app with the original app installer. Use the uninstaller app.

Exercise 18.1
Install an App from the App Store

> ▶ **Prerequisites**
>
> ▶   You must have created the Local Administrator (Exercise 3.1, "Configure a Mac for Exercises") and Johnny Appleseed (Exercise 7.1, "Create a Standard User Account") accounts.

In this exercise, you use the App Store app to buy, download, and install a free app on your Mac.

Select an Apple ID to Use with the App Store

The way you configure Johnny Appleseed's account with an Apple ID for the App Store depends on whether you want to use the same Apple ID for iCloud and App Store purchases and what the Apple ID was used for in the past. The instructions in this exercise attempt to cover most of the possibilities, but if you find that your experience doesn't match these exercises, App Store instructions can guide you.

1   Log in as Johnny Appleseed.

2   From the Apple menu, choose App Store.

3   At the Welcome to the App Store screen, read Apple's privacy policy, and click Continue.

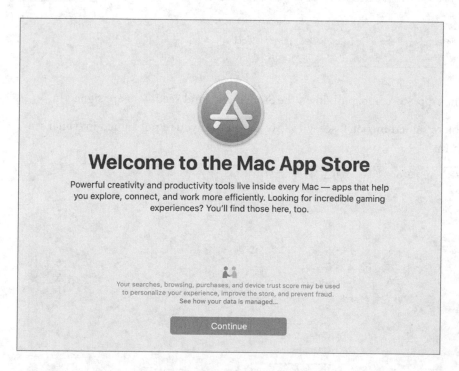

4   In the menu bar, choose App Store > Preferences.

5   If "Automatically download apps purchased on other Mac computers" is selected, deselect the checkbox.

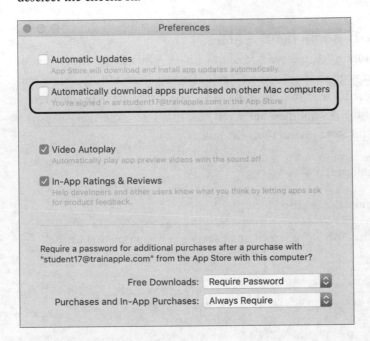

6   In the App Store app, pull down the Store menu, and see if you are signed in.

If you're signed in, you'll see View My Account. If you're not signed in, you'll see Sign In.

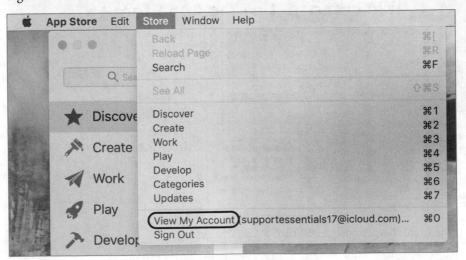

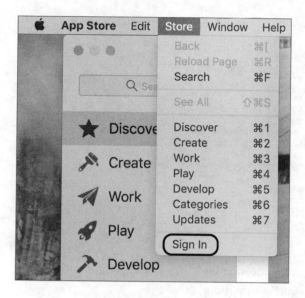

You can also look at the lower-left corner of the App Store window. If you are signed in, your name appears.

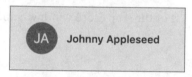

You should be signed in using the facilitator-provided Apple ID you used for iCloud. Apple recommends using the same account for both iCloud and the App Store (see Apple Support article HT204053, "Sign in with your Apple ID"). But you can use a different Apple ID for iCloud and the App Store.

7   In this course, you use the same Apple ID that your facilitator provided. If you aren't signed in using the Apple ID your facilitator provided, choose Store > Sign Out if necessary, and from the menu bar, choose Store > Sign In.

8 Enter your facilitator-provided Apple ID and password, and click Sign In.

9 If the Apple ID has two-factor authentication enabled, your facilitator will provide you with the additional verification information.

Select an App to Buy

1 Enter **the unarchiver** in the Search field (at the top left of the App Store window), and press Return.

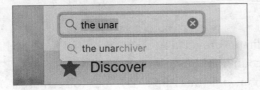

The App Store might display more than one relevant app. Find a free app named The Unarchiver. Free apps show a Get button instead of a price (although if the app was previously acquired under this Apple ID, you see a Redownload button).

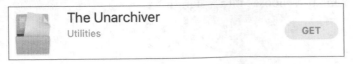

2   Click the free app's name.

The App Store displays more details about the app. You see a Get or Redownload button.

3   Perform one of the following actions:

▶   If you see a Get button, click Get, and then click Install.

▶   If you see a Redownload button, click it to redownload the app.

If additional confirmation or configuration is required, a dialog appears and asks you to sign in to download the app. Depending on your App Store preference settings, the Apple ID password might be required, even though this is a free app.

4   If you are prompted to, enter the Apple ID password, and click Get.

5   If you are prompted to choose to always require a password when making a purchase, choose the policy you prefer and click the appropriate button.

6   If the Apple ID has two-factor authentication enabled, your facilitator will provide you with the additional verification information.

7   If you are asked to verify billing information for your Apple ID, click Billing Info, and enter the information provided by your facilitator.

8   If you receive a warning that the terms and conditions have changed, click OK and read the new terms.

After agreeing to the new terms and conditions, you might need to reselect The Unarchiver.

When the app starts to download, the progress is shown in the App Store and under the Launchpad icon.

Test the App

1 Open Launchpad.

If the app hasn't finished downloading, Launchpad displays the progress. When an app finishes downloading, you see its icon. A blue dot appears next to its name, indicating that it is new.

2 Click The Unarchiver's icon to open the app.

3 At the Unarchiver Welcome screen, click the close (X) button in the upper-left corner of the window.

4 Quit the app.

Examine the App Store

1 In the App Store, go to the menu bar and choose Store > View My Account.

The App Store app lists the apps purchased with this Apple ID. If your facilitator used this Apple ID for this course before, you might see apps that previous participants bought.

If you had enabled the "Automatically download apps purchased on other Mac computers" option in App Store preferences, additional apps would be downloaded and installed. Since this option is disabled, you see Install buttons that enable you to download and install them manually.

The App Store terms and conditions limit the situations in which an app might be installed on several computers. See www.apple.com/legal/itunes/us/terms.html for the current terms and conditions.

If other apps are listed, don't install them now.

2   In the App Store sidebar, click the Updates button. If you are prompted, authenticate as Local Administrator.

App Store displays updates available for apps installed on this Mac that were purchased from the App Store.

3 Quit the App Store.

Exercise 18.2
Use an Installer Package

> **Prerequisites**
>
> ▶ You must have created the Local Administrator (Exercise 3.1, "Configure a Mac for Exercises") and Johnny Appleseed (Exercise 7.1, "Create a Standard User Account") accounts.

Install an App with an Installer Package

1 Log in as Johnny Appleseed.

2 Open the ParticipantMaterials/Lesson18 folder.

3 Open Trust Me.dmg.

The image mounts, with the Trust Me package inside it.

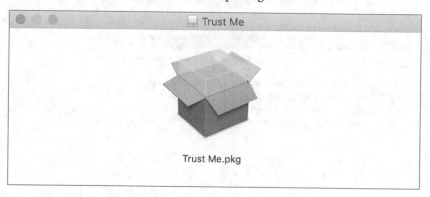

4 Open Trust Me.pkg.

The Installer opens and prepares to install the Trust Me app.

5 Click the lock button in the upper right of the Installer window.

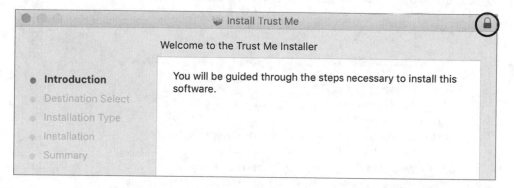

The lock button indicates that this is a signed package; clicking it displays information about the certificate it was signed with. In this case, it was signed with Apple Inc. – Worldwide Enterprise's Developer ID Installer certificate, which was signed by the Developer ID Certification Authority, which in turn was signed by the Apple Root CA. Essentially, this means that the Apple Root CA vouches for the authenticity of the Developer ID Certification Authority, which vouches for the authenticity of Apple Inc. – Worldwide Enterprise's certificate, which vouches for the authenticity of the installer package.

This is the standard format of an Apple-issued Developer ID certificate.

6   Click OK to dismiss the certificate dialog.

7   Go to the menu bar, and choose File > Show Files.

This shows what files the installer package contains. In this case, it is a folder named Trust Me containing Trust Me.app and the app package's files.

8   Close the "Files from Trust Me" window.

9   In the main Installer window, click Continue.

Some packages include additional items, such as readme information, license agreements, and choices of components to install. This is a simple package, so it proceeds to the install pane.

10   In the Standard Install pane, click Install.

11   Authenticate as Local Administrator when prompted.

The installation completes quickly, and the Installer informs you that it was successful.

12   Click Close, and the Installer exits.

13   Eject the disk image.

14   In the Finder, navigate to the Applications folder (you can go to the menu bar and choose Go > Applications or press Shift-Command-A).

The Trust Me app is installed.

15   Open Launchpad.

The new app is displayed with your other apps.

16   Open Trust Me.

Because this app was installed with a package (and the package was properly signed), Gatekeeper doesn't activate and no warning is displayed. You see what happens with an untrusted app in the next exercise.

17   Quit Trust Me.

Unlike with the App Store, there is no standard update process for package-installed apps. Some apps manage their own updates; others require you to manually download and install updates.

Exercise 18.3
Drag and Drop to Install an App

> **Prerequisites**
>
> ▸ You must have created the Local Administrator (Exercise 3.1, "Configure a Mac for Exercises") and Johnny Appleseed (Exercise 7.1, "Create a Standard User Account") accounts.

In this exercise, you drag and drop to install an app.

Obtain an App from ParticipantMaterials

1 Log in as Johnny Appleseed.

2 Open the ParticipantMaterials/Lesson18 folder.

3 Open Dead End.dmg.

This disk image contains an app that was previously downloaded from a website and is still in quarantine, so macOS treats it as coming from an untrusted source.

Copy the App to /Applications

The Dead End app comes as a disk image with instructions in the background image.

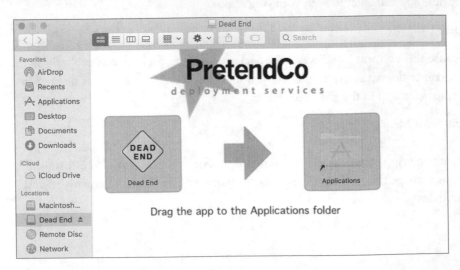

1   Drag the Dead End icon onto the Applications icon (which is an alias to /Applications).

A dialog appears telling you that modifying Applications requires an administrator name and password.

2   Click the Authenticate button, authenticate as Local Administrator, and click OK.

The Finder copies Dead End into /Applications.

macOS enables you to run apps no matter where they're stored, even if they aren't in /Applications. Running the copy of the app in the disk image you downloaded works, but it might cause odd behavior. Don't run the app in the disk image.

Don't open the Dead End app yet.

3   Eject the disk image.

Test Gatekeeper Security Settings

1   Open Security & Privacy preferences.

2   Click General.

3   If necessary, authenticate and set the "Allow apps downloaded from" option to "App Store and identified developers."

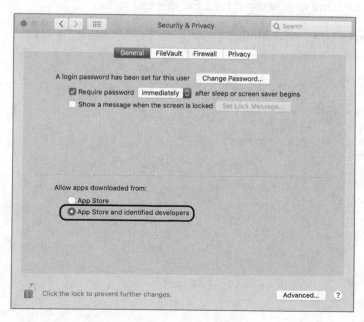

4 Quit System Preferences.

5 In the Finder, navigate to the Applications folder (Shift-Command-A).

6 Double-click Dead End.

Dead End is labeled with metadata to indicate that it's in quarantine because it was downloaded from the Internet. The first time you open it, Gatekeeper checks it against your allowed apps policy. Since the app isn't signed with a Developer ID, Gatekeeper doesn't allow it to open.

7 Click OK.

8 Control-click Dead End, and choose Open from the shortcut menu.

This time, Gatekeeper warns you about the app but gives you the option to bypass normal policy and open the app.

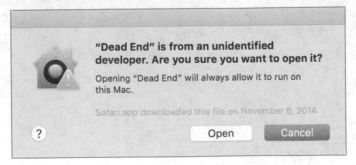

9 Click Open.

10 When you are prompted, authenticate as Local Administrator.

Because Johnny Appleseed is a standard user, he isn't allowed to open unsigned apps without an administrator's credentials.

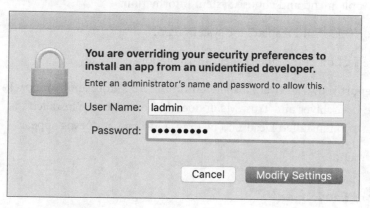

11 If necessary, click the Dead End icon in the Dock to bring it to the foreground.

Don't click "Download the Internet." If you do, see Exercise 20.1, "Force Apps to Quit," for information on forcing apps to quit. This app isn't harmful, but it doesn't do anything useful.

12 Quit Dead End (go to the menu bar and choose File > Quit Dead End or press Command-Q).

13 Double-click Dead End to reopen it.

This time it opens without the warning. Since you opened it once, your Gatekeeper policy is modified to allow it to run normally.

14 Quit Dead End again.

Exercise 18.4
Remove Apps

▶ **Prerequisites**

▶ You must have performed Exercise 18.1, "Install an App from the App Store," and Exercise 18.2, "Use an Installer Package."

View Installed Apps

1   Option-click the Apple menu and choose System Information.

System Information opens and displays the system report.

2   From the Software section of the sidebar, select Installations.

This part of the report shows software installed from the App Store and from packages. It shows The Unarchiver and Trust Me. It doesn't show software installed in other ways. Because you installed Dead End by drag-and-drop, it doesn't appear.

3   Quit System Information.

Remove an App from Launchpad

1   Open Launchpad.

2   Click and hold The Unarchiver (or the app you installed from the App Store) until an "X" appears in the top left of its icon and the other icons begin to jiggle.

In this mode, Launchpad enables you to drag app icons around to rearrange them. You can also use the delete (X) button to delete apps you bought from the App Store, like The Unarchiver.

3   Click The Unarchiver's delete (X) button.

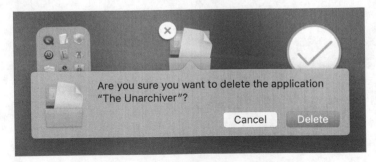

4   In the confirmation dialog that appears, click Delete.

5   If you are prompted, authenticate as Local Administrator.

The Unarchiver is uninstalled from your Mac. Your preference file or files and user data still exist, so if you decide to reinstall the app, your settings are available.

6   Click twice in the background to exit Launchpad.

Reinstall an App from the App Store

1   Open the App Store.

2   Go to the menu bar and choose Store > View My Account.

Since you bought The Unarchiver, it's listed and available to redownload. Depending on the history of the Apple ID you're using, other apps might be listed.

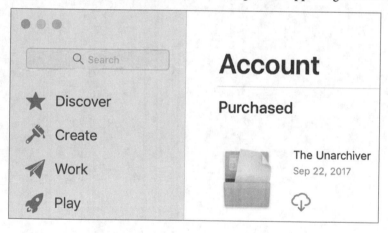

3   Click the Redownload button for The Unarchiver.

4   If you are prompted, enter your Apple ID's password to authenticate to the App Store.

The app is downloaded and reinstalled.

5   Wait for the download to finish, and quit the App Store.

Remove an App in the Finder

1 In the Finder, navigate to the Applications folder.

2 Select The Unarchiver, and drag it to the Trash.

3 When you are prompted, authenticate as Local Administrator.

4 From the menu bar, choose Finder > Empty Trash, and click Empty Trash in the confirmation dialog.

The Unarchiver is uninstalled from your Mac.

Lesson 19
Manage Files

In this lesson you learn about tools that help you manage documents, beginning with Launch Services and continuing with Quick Look for previewing most document types. Then you learn about Auto Save, Versions, and document management in iCloud. You see how macOS attempts to resume documents and apps. Finally, you learn how macOS can help you optimize storage to reclaim space on your system volume.

Reference 19.1
Open Files

In macOS, you double-click a file in the Finder or select a file in the Finder and choose File > Open to open it. When you do this, you also tell macOS to launch the appropriate app for the file. macOS uses Launch Services to do this. Launch Services uses a filename extension to know which app to open.

A filename extension is a string of characters preceded by a period (.) at the end of a filename. For example, *filename*.jpg is a file with a .jpg extension.

Joint Photographic Experts Group (JPEG) is a format for compressing many file types. Sometimes there can be more than one filename extension that indicates a file type. For example, a JPEG file can have the filename extension .jpg or .jpeg.

GOALS

▸ Use Launch Services and Quick Look to open files

▸ Describe how Launch Services uses the app database

▸ Preview files with Quick Look and the Preview pane

▸ Learn how to browse document versions and go back to an older version in apps that support Auto Save and Versions

▸ Open documents that were saved to iCloud

▸ Save documents to iCloud

▸ Optimize local storage to reclaim space on the system volume

By default, the Finder hides filename extensions. If you want to see them, select a file, choose File > Get Info, and click the disclosure triangle to display the Name & Extension information. In the following screenshot, the "Hide extension" option is deselected for the file, so its filename extension isn't hidden. The name that's displayed at the top of the Info window changes too.

You can choose Finder > Preferences, click the Advanced button, and select the checkbox next to "Show all filename extensions" to see filename extensions for all documents.

If you choose to show all filename extensions in the Finder, you override the individual file attribute that hides a filename extension.

If you leave the option "Show warning before changing an extension" selected in the Finder preferences, you'll get a warning before you try to make a filename extension change or remove a filename extension. This might prevent you from accidentally changing a file extension.

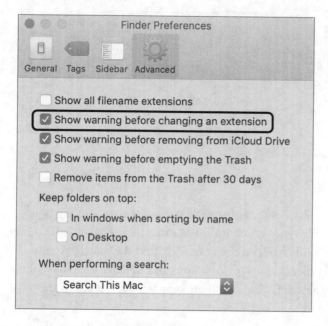

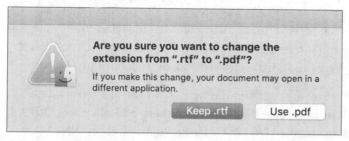

If you need to change the file type of an existing file, use an app to export the file as a different type. For example, in Pages, you can use File > Export To and choose a different file type.

App Registration

When you try to open a file, Launch Services reads from a database of apps and file types to determine the correct app for the file type. When it finds a match, it caches it. So when you try to open the file again, Launch Services can quickly find the match. After you startup or log in, a background process scans for new apps and updates the database. The Finder and Installer track new apps and add their supported file types to the database.

If macOS displays a message that there is no app to open a file, you probably don't have the correct app for the file. Launch Services maps many common file types to Preview and TextEdit if the appropriate app is missing. For example, Numbers or Microsoft Excel spreadsheets open in Preview; Pages and Microsoft Word documents open in TextEdit.

With Quick Look you can preview many common file types, even without having the appropriate apps installed. This includes Pages, Keynote, Numbers, and Microsoft Office documents. Quick Look details are covered later in this lesson in the section "Preview Documents with Quick Look."

If Preview, or other apps, can't open a file, change Launch Services settings to force the files to open in an appropriate app, as outlined in the following section. Launch Services might not have an app set to use for the file type. If you try to open a file type that isn't stored in the Launch Services database, macOS prompts you to find an app that supports the file in the App Store.

Manage Launch Services

If you prefer to open a file with an app different than that file type's default app, you can override the Launch Services default app settings for any file type. To override the default app settings for a file, use the Info or Inspector window in the Finder. Using the Info window is detailed in Lesson 13, "Manage Permissions and Sharing."

After you select the files for which you want to change Launch Services settings and open the Inspector, click the "Open with" disclosure triangle to reveal the default app selected by Launch Services. To change just the selected files' default app, select another app from the menu. This information is saved to the files' metadata and defines Launch Services settings only for the selected items.

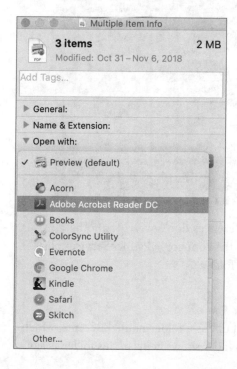

To change the default app for all files of the type of files selected, select the app you want to define as the default, and then click the Change All button.

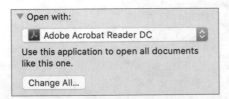

You can also modify Launch Services settings in the Finder. Control-click the selected files and then choose Open With from the shortcut menu. Press and hold the Option key to change the menu command to Always Open With.

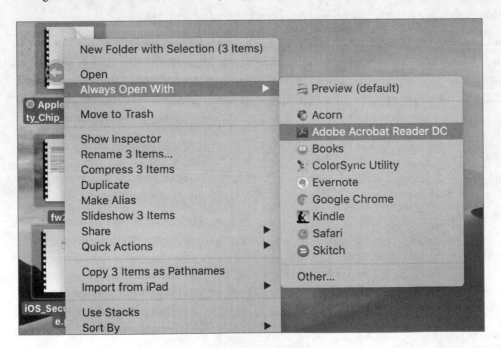

This setting is saved per user, so one user's app preferences don't override another's. A user's custom Launch Services settings are saved to the com.apple.LaunchServices.plist preference file in each user's ~/Library/Preferences folder.

Preview Documents with the Finder Preview Pane

By default, when you open a new Finder window, it opens a folder named Recents, which displays files you've recently opened. By default, the Finder shows items in this folder as icons.

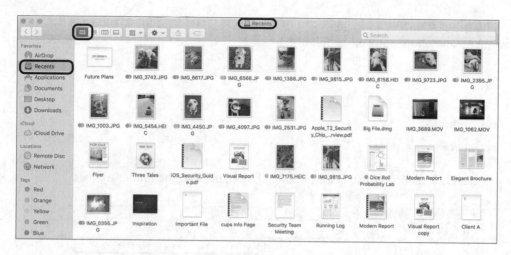

The Preview pane in the Finder is a new feature of macOS Mojave. You can use the Finder Preview pane to get a view of more information about a selected file, including:

► A preview of the contents of a document or image

► A list of the metadata for the file (metadata is covered in detail in Reference 16.1, "File-System Metadata")

► Quick Actions buttons for the selected file if available

If you don't see the Preview pane on the right side of the Finder window, choose View > Show Preview (or press Shift-Command-P). The following figure illustrates the Preview pane.

To change how the Finder displays items in the selected Finder window, you can click the View menu and choose any of the following:

▶ as Icons

▶ as List

▶ as Columns

▶ as Gallery

Or you can click the icons, list, columns, or gallery buttons in the Finder toolbar.

The Finder automatically displays the Preview pane when you show items in columns or in a gallery. But you can also show the Preview pane when viewing items in the Finder as icons or as a list. To change how the Finder displays a window, choose View > Show View Options (or press Command-J). The options vary depending on whether you're viewing as icons, in a list, in columns, or in a gallery.

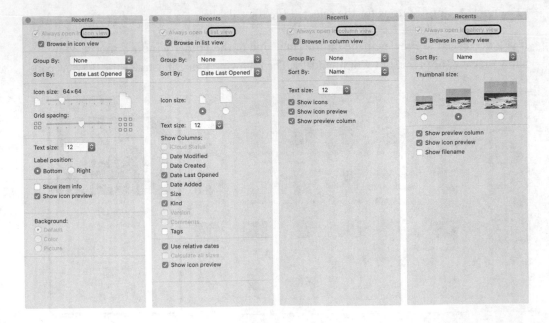

If the Finder displays the Preview pane, you can choose View > Show Preview Options to control whether the Preview pane shows Quick Actions and to select the metadata that the Preview pane shows for the type of file selected. The following figure displays a few kinds of file types.

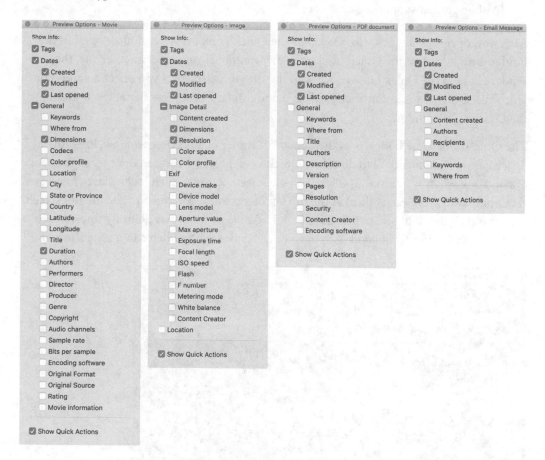

Preview Documents with Quick Look

Quick Look enables you to preview most file types without opening additional apps or when you don't have the appropriate apps installed.

You can open and close Quick Look previews by selecting a file and pressing the Space bar in the following contexts:

▸ In the Finder (you can also press Command-Y instead of the Space bar)

▸ In the Time Machine restore interface

▶ In most Open and Save browser dialogs

▶ In Mail

▶ In active printer queues

▶ In any app that supports Quick Look

After you open Quick Look, macOS keeps the Quick Look preview window open in the Finder until you close the Quick Look preview window. If you select another file, the Finder changes the Quick Look preview to the file you selected. If you select an audio or video file, Quick Look automatically plays it and displays a progress bar at the bottom of the Quick Look window.

The Quick Look close button is in the upper-left corner of a preview window. Press the Space bar (or Command-Y) to dismiss a Quick Look preview. You can drag an edge of a Quick Look window to resize it. Click the Full Screen button (which looks like twin arrows that point away from each other) at the top left of a preview window to view the full screen, then the click Exit Full Screen button (which looks like twin arrows pointing toward each other). Press Option-Command-Y to open one or more selected items in a slide show.

Quick Look provides the Finder with the previews that the Finder displays when you view files on your desktop and when you view files in a Finder window.

Quick Look Plug-ins

Quick Look previews file types using plug-ins. Each Quick Look plug-in previews specific file types. Many Quick Look plug-ins are included in macOS by default. Apple and third-party developers create additional plug-ins to expand the Quick Look preview capabilities.

Included Quick Look plug-ins enable you to:

▶ Preview audio or video file that can be decoded by QuickTime

▶ Preview graphics files, including digital camera files, PDF files, EPS files, and standard graphics files

▶ Preview productivity files, including standard text files, script files, and files you create with Pages, Numbers, Keynote, and Microsoft Office suites

▶ Preview Internet-centric files, including mailboxes, Messages transcripts, and web archives

Quick Look plug-ins are stored in Library folders. Built-in Apple Quick Look plug-ins are in /System/Library/QuickLook/ and /Library/QuickLook/. Install third-party plug-ins in /Library/QuickLook/ or ~/Library/QuickLook/ depending on who must access them.

Quick Look Window

In the right portion of the title bar of the Quick Look window, you'll find other options for previewing a selected item. The options vary depending on the type of file you've selected and the app extensions installed on your Mac. Read Reference 20.2, "Manage App Extensions," for more information on adding app extensions to the Share menu.

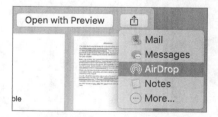

For many types of apps, the Quick Look window displays the "Open with *App*" button, where *App* is the name of the default app for the selected file. For ZIP files, instead of "Open with *App*," the button displays Uncompress. For a disk image file, the button displays Mount.

The Share button (the box with the up-pointing arrow) enables you to share a document. The list of options in the Share menu varies depending on the file type of the item you're previewing and the installed app extensions. Find out more about managing app extensions in Lesson 20, "Manage and Troubleshoot Apps."

If you've selected multiple files when you open Quick Look, use the arrow keys to navigate and preview the items adjacent to the original previewed item in the Finder. If the previewed file has multiple pages, you'll be able to scroll through the document. In some cases—Keynote presentations, for example—Quick Look shows a thumbnail preview of each slide, enabling you to scroll through the thumbnails.

If you select multiple items to preview, the Quick Look window allows some basic slideshow features with buttons at the top left of the window. To start a slide show of files in the Finder, select the files, Control-click, press the Option key, then choose Slideshow *number of selected files* Items.

For some files, the Quick Look window also displays one or more Quick Actions, like in the following figure. Quick Actions are discussed in the next section.

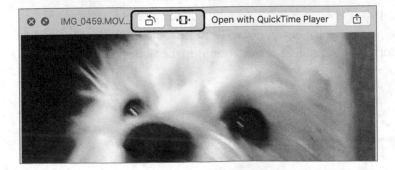

Quick Actions

The Quick Actions feature enables you to perform tasks right from the Finder without opening another app. There are three ways to use Quick Actions in the Finder:

► Click the Quick Action that appears in the Quick Look window.

► Click the Quick Action that appears in the Preview Pane.

► Control-click a file, then choose Quick Actions.

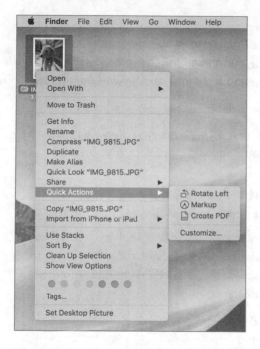

The list of actions available in Quick Actions depends on the kind of file or files you selected. The built-in Quick Actions include:

► Rotate an image or movie—Rotate Left is the default command, but you can press and hold the Option key to change it to Rotate Right.

► Mark up a document or image—After you choose Markup, the file opens in a Markup window. Read more about the Markup window in the next section.

► Trim a movie or audio file—Choose Trim, and then use the yellow handles in the trimming bar. Click Play to test your changes, then click Revert, or click Done to save your changes and close the window. After you click Done, macOS prompts you to replace your original file, cancel, or save your changes in a new clip.

- Create a PDF—macOS creates a new PDF file from one or more selected files when you choose Create PDF. Enter a filename, or you can just leave the suggested name. Press Return or click somewhere else when you're done entering the filename.

- Customize—Choose Customize to open the Extensions preferences in System Preferences. You can use Automator to create custom workflows for Quick Actions. Learn more about the Extensions preferences in Lesson 20.

Mark Up Files

Quick Look and Quick Actions enable you to mark up files without opening a separate app. If you're viewing a file in Quick Look or the Finder Preview pane, click the Markup tool (looks like the tip of a marker). If you're using Quick Actions, choose Markup. The collection of tools offered by Markup depends on the type of file you're working on. The collection can include:

- Sketch—Sketch a shape with a single stroke. macOS replaces your stroke with a shape if it recognizes your stroke as a standard shape, and you can select your original stroke.

- Draw—Draw a shape with a single stroke. This only appears if you have a Force Touch trackpad. Use a firmer press to draw a heavier, darker line.

- Shapes—Click the Shape button, select a shape, and then drag the shape where you want it. Use the blue handles to resize the shape. Use the green handles to change the shape. Select the Loupe tool to magnify an area. Select the Highlight tool, and then use the blue handles to modify the highlighted area.

- Text—Enter text, then drag the text where you want it.

- Highlight Selection—Highlight selected text.

- Sign—Create a new signature with a trackpad or your Mac computer's built-in camera, and select one of your signatures to insert it. Then you can drag and resize it.

- Shape Style—Change the thickness and type of lines in a shape, and add or remove a shadow to the lines in the shape.

- Border Color—Change the color of the lines in the shape.

- Fill Color—Change the color inside the shape.

- Text Style—Change the font, color, size, and characteristics of text.

- Rotate Right—Rotate to the right.

▶ Rotate Left—Rotate to the left.

▶ Crop —Drag the corner handles until only the area you want to keep is shown within the frame's border. You can also drag the frame to reposition it. When you're ready, click the button with the "Crop" text label.

When you're finished with your markup, click Done, or click Revert to discard your changes. Once you click Done, you can't undo your changes.

Reference 19.2
Save Documents

macOS apps save files for you, and they can also maintain a version history of your files. In this section, you learn how Auto Save and Versions work together. These two features work with Locked and Resume to maintain the current state of your work environment even if you log out or restart your Mac.

About Auto Save and Versions

For apps that support Auto Save, after you save a file the first time, the app doesn't ask you again if it should save changes. If you want to use the file in another app or share it with other users, you don't have to remember to save the latest version of the file. The file you see in the Finder is the same as the file you see in the app. The location where you first saved a file is always the latest version.

Apps that support Auto Save also support document versions. This provides an environment where macOS maintains a history of changes for any document. You can return a document to a previous state with a few clicks, or you can navigate to an earlier version of a document and copy elements to the latest version.

You can access a document version history using an interface similar to the Time Machine Restore interface. The document version histories are saved in a hidden folder named .DocumentRevisions-V100 at the root of the disk containing the original document. The most recent version of a document is always saved to its original location, and you can copy or share it with other apps or users immediately after you make a change.

For information about how restore versions of Pages, Numbers, and Keynote documents, read Apple Support article 205411, "Restore previous versions of iWork documents."

Apps that support macOS Auto Save and Versions are identified by the content of the File menu in the app. Apps that support Auto Save have the following commands in the File menu:

▶ Duplicate (instead of Save As)

▶ Rename

▶ Move To

Updated apps offer the File > Save command for saving a document the first time, but after you save a document, the behavior of this menu option changes to saving a version of the document. Most Apple-designed apps, including TextEdit, Preview, Pages, Numbers, and Keynote, support Auto Save and Versions.

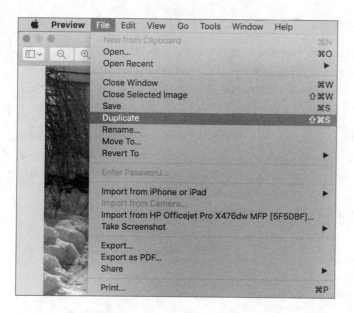

Automatically Save Document Changes

When you open an app that supports Auto Save for the first time, one of two things happens. If you are not signed in to iCloud or the app doesn't support saving to iCloud, the app opens a new document (or displays a Choose a Template dialog). If you are signed in to iCloud and the app supports saving documents to iCloud, you are prompted with an Open dialog.

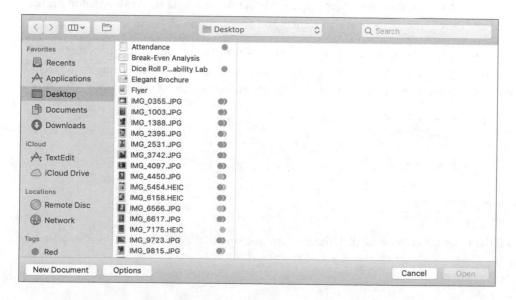

Saving documents to iCloud is covered in the next section of this lesson.

When you open a new document in an app that supports Auto Save, it's saved, even though you haven't set a location for it. Changes you make to the new document are saved, even if you have yet to manually save the document. The document is saved to the Versions history database on the system volume.

By default, if you choose to close a document window or app, macOS prompts you to save the document if you haven't saved the document yet. You can also choose File > Save, or press Command-S. The resulting Save dialog enables you to choose a name and location for the document. You can expand a minimized Save dialog to show a full file-system browser. Click the small arrow to the right of the filename.

You can also click the document name in the title bar to save it. This reveals a dialog similar to the Save dialog, except there are no Cancel and Save buttons.

When you enter a change in the dialog, it's saved after you click anywhere outside the title bar. You can return to the dialog to save changes to the document. For example, to rename a document enter a new name and then click elsewhere to dismiss the dialog.

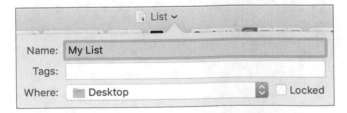

Hold the Command key and click the document name in the title bar to reveal its path in the file system.

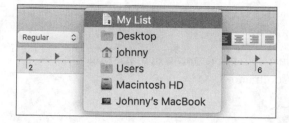

Auto-saves occur:

▶ When you make a change to a document

▶ When you close a document window

▶ When you close an app

▶ When you select the document in the Finder

▶ When you attempt to access the document from another app

▶ During pauses in your work

▶ Every five minutes as you work

As you make changes to a document, you might see "Edited" in the document title bar. This is a visual cue to let you know macOS is saving changes. You can test this by making changes to a document and immediately using Quick Look to preview the document by selecting it in the Finder and pressing the Space bar. The Quick Look preview is identical to the open document in the app.

Save Duplicate Documents

To save a copy of a document, use Duplicate. With the document open, choose File > Duplicate (Shift-Command-S). A new window appears with a copy of the document. The filename in the title bar is highlighted, indicating that you can change the name of the duplicate document.

The Move To command in the File menu moves the original document to a new location without creating a new copy. Even though the document is moved, in most cases the version history is preserved.

The document is saved in the same folder as the original document. With Auto Save you never have to manually save this document again.

If you press and hold the Option key, the File > Duplicate menu option changes to File > Save As. You can also press Option-Shift-Command-S.

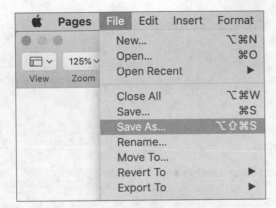

Choosing the Save As command is the same as choosing Duplicate, except that it presents the full Save dialog, enabling you to choose a different filename and location, and then it closes the original document. The new document replaces the original document in the active window. You have the option to also save the changes to the original document. This option is enabled by default, meaning that any changes made up to this point will also be saved to the original document. If you disable this option, you revert the original document to its previous state (before you made changes) and save a new document with the latest changes.

Explore Document Versions

With Versions, apps maintain a history of your changes. Whenever a document.is saved, automatically or manually, a new document version is also saved. When you manually save by choosing File > Save or by pressing Command-S, macOS saves another version of the document in the version history.

If you're editing a document and have yet to trigger a manual or automatic save, you can revert to the previously saved state by choosing File > Revert To > Last Saved or File > Revert To > Last Opened. If a deeper version history is available, macOS enables you to browse the history of a document. To open the version history browser, choose File > Revert To > Browse All Versions.

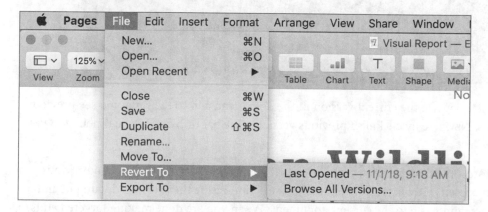

A document's version history isn't saved within the document. Instead, document history is stored on the volume where the original document is saved—specifically, in the .DocumentRevisions-V100 folder at the root of the volume. When you share the document by creating or sending a copy of the document, other users won't have access to the document version history.

Version history isn't always maintained on files being edited from a shared network volume. If you want to ensure that a version history is maintained, you must copy the shared file to a local disk.

The Versions browser interface looks similar to Time Machine. In fact, if you have Time Machine enabled, as covered in Lesson 17, "Manage Time Machine," an app's version history can go much deeper by showing you versions that are also saved in the Time Machine backup.

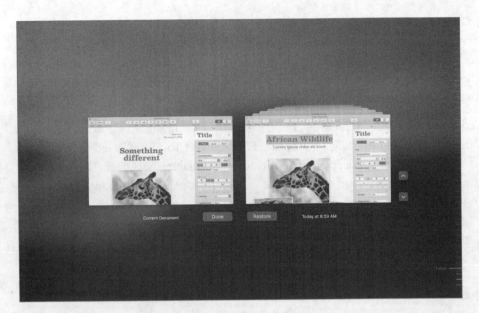

To the left you see the current version of the document, and to the right you see previous versions. Navigate by clicking a previous version's title bar or by using the timeline to the right.

To restore a previous version, click Restore. If you want a specific section of a previous version copied to the latest version, make a selection inside the previous document and then copy and paste to the current document. When you are done making targeted edits, click Done to return to the standard app interface.

In the Versions browser, you can copy and paste using the Command-C and Command-V keyboard shortcuts or by Control-clicking to reveal a shortcut menu.

To delete a previous document version, in the Versions browser select the document name in the title bar to reveal a menu enabling you to choose Delete This Version.

Locked Files

The APFS and Mac OS Extended file systems include a file and folder attribute that trumps all write privileges and administrator user access. Users can choose to lock a file or folder that they own from the Finder Info window or any app that supports Auto Save.

Locking an item renders it unchangeable by any user except the item's owner. Even administrator users are prevented from making changes to another user's locked file in the graphical interface.

Locking a document prevents users—or, more appropriately, their apps—from accidentally auto-saving changes.

Manage File Locking with the Finder

Use the Finder and the Info or Inspector window to view and change a file's lock state.
After an item is locked, no other users can modify, move, delete, or rename it in the
Finder. Using the Info window to inspect files and folders is detailed in Lesson 13,
"Manage Permissions and Sharing."

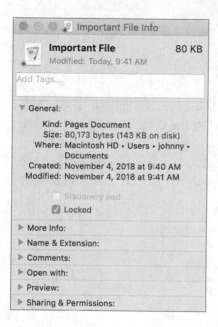

After the file is locked, the Finder prevents the owner from moving, renaming, or changing ownership and permissions for the locked item. If you as the owner try to move a
locked item, the Finder defaults to making a copy. However, unlike other users, the owner
can return the file to the normal state by disabling the locked attribute from the Info or
Inspector window.

Duplicating a locked document in the Finder results in another locked copy of the
document. In macOS, apps that support Auto Save can create an unlocked duplicate of a
locked file.

Manage File Locking with an App

Apps that support Auto Save also provide access to document locking. As long as you are the owner of a document, which is often the case if you created the document or are editing a copy of the document, you can manually lock it to prevent further changes. To manually lock a document in an app that supports Auto Save, select the document's filename in the title bar. You'll see a dialog that enables you to select the Locked checkbox.

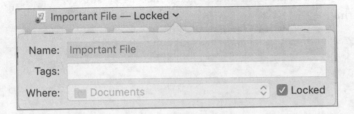

In the title bar, locked documents are labeled "Locked" and display a small lock icon. As long as you are the owner of a document, you can deselect the Locked checkbox to enable changes. You can also open a locked document that you own. You'll see a dialog that enables you to select what you want to do with the file. You can duplicate the file and keep the previous version unchanged. You can unlock the file to edit it. And, you can cancel and do neither.

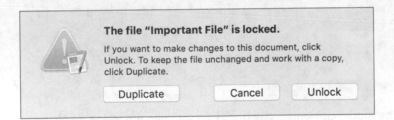

If you aren't the owner of a locked document, you aren't allowed to unlock it—which means you aren't allowed to edit it. Also, as covered in Lesson 13, if you don't have write file permissions, you aren't allowed to edit a document. In both cases, the document's title bar displays "Locked."

You can treat a locked document as a template by duplicating the document and editing the copy. If you try to edit a locked, or otherwise unwritable, document, you see a prompt that enables you to duplicate the document.

You can manually duplicate a locked document. Choose File > Duplicate or File > Revert To > Browse All Versions. After the app makes a copy, you can save the copy as you would a new document.

Reference 19.3
Manage Automatic Resume

Auto Save allows supported apps to maintain their current state even if you log out or quit the app. When an app quits, any open documents and the app state are saved.

macOS can quit apps that support Resume when resources, specifically memory, run low. macOS quits only apps that are idle (not in active use).

Manage Resuming After Logout

By default, macOS automatically resumes apps and windows after you log out. To prevent this, deselect the option "Reopen windows when logging back in" when you see the dialog that asks if you want to quit all apps and log out. Your selection remains active until you change it.

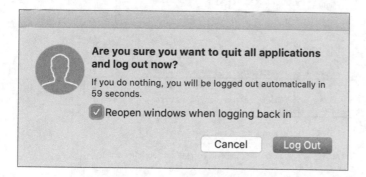

If "Reopen windows when logging back in" isn't selected, you can temporarily enable it by pressing and holding down the Option key when you log out.

Manage Resuming After Quit

By default, macOS closes associated open files and windows when you quit an app. In General preferences you can deselect "Close windows when quitting an app" to make macOS resume previously open files and windows when you open an app.

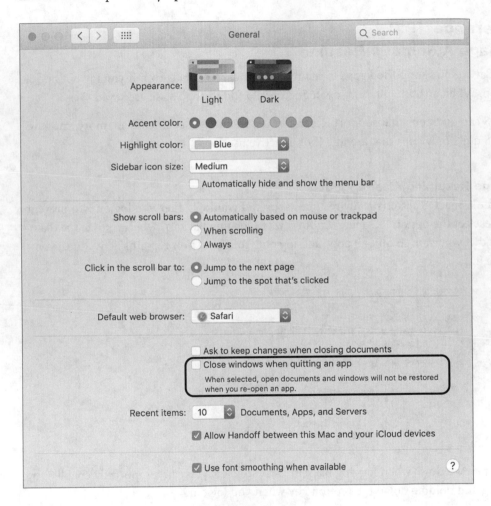

Disable Auto Save

Select "Ask to keep changes when closing documents" to disable the Auto Save feature for any app that supports it. Even if you disable the Auto Save feature, apps that support Auto Save still retain the rest of their document management behavior. For example, apps that support Auto Save offer a Duplicate menu option and automatically maintain a version history whenever you manually save documents.

Reference 19.4
Store Documents in iCloud

With iCloud Drive, you can safely store your presentations, spreadsheets, PDFs, images, and any other kind of file in iCloud. You can access them from your iPhone, iPad, iPod touch, Mac, or PC. You can also invite people to work on the same file with you—without creating copies, sending attachments, or managing versions.

Turn On iCloud Drive

When you provide your Apple ID during Setup Assistant, macOS automatically turns on the iCloud Drive service. Before Setup Assistant completes, it asks if you want to save the contents of your Desktop and Documents folders to iCloud Drive.

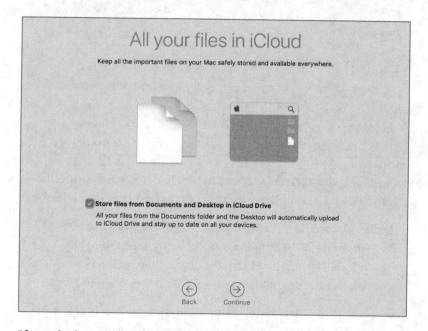

If you don't provide your Apple ID during Setup Assistant, you can turn on the iCloud Drive service in iCloud preferences. First provide your Apple ID name and password; then select "Use iCloud for your documents and data." This turns on iCloud Drive automatically, but it doesn't automatically save the contents of your Desktop and Documents folders to iCloud Drive.

You can verify that iCloud Drive is enabled from iCloud preferences.

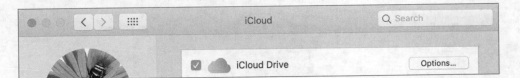

If iCloud Drive is turned on, you can click the Options button to configure app-specific iCloud Drive settings. Details about iCloud Drive options are covered later in this lesson.

If your existing Apple ID doesn't have the iCloud Drive service turned on, and you sign in to an iOS 8 or OS X Yosemite 10.10 or newer device, you're asked to upgrade your iCloud account to use iCloud Drive. iCloud Drive is compatible with iOS 8 or OS X Yosemite 10.10 or newer, and the upgrade process to iCloud Drive is one-way.

If you didn't choose to enable iCloud Drive during Setup Assistant, you can enable it in iCloud preferences. Just select iCloud Drive. You'll be asked to verify the upgrade.

You can find out more about iCloud Drive from Apple Support article HT201104, "iCloud Drive FAQ," and the iCloud Drive website at www.apple.com/icloud/icloud-drive/.

Use iCloud Drive

With iCloud Drive, iCloud storage appears as if it were an external storage device. All Finder file management features (move, copy, rename, folder creation, and more) work on files that you store in iCloud Drive.

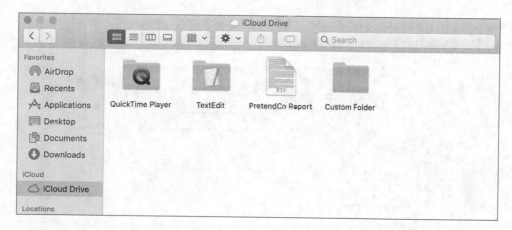

A pie chart indicator immediately to the right of iCloud Drive in the Finder sidebar gives you the status of a file copy to iCloud Drive. If you don't see a pie chart icon, the copy is complete.

iCloud Drive also appears in Open and Save dialogs for any app. In iCloud Drive, you can create custom folder hierarchies and save documents inside any folder you choose. Apps can create folders in iCloud Drive with app-specific folders to facilitate document management. For example, for some apps like Pages, Numbers, and Keynote, when you create a new document and make any change to that document, the app automatically creates an app-specific folder in iCloud Drive before you save the document.

For example, the following screenshot shows the Open dialog for TextEdit. The menu at the top of the Open dialog contains a TextEdit-specific folder. The sidebar of the

Open dialog contains an iCloud section with two items: a TextEdit-specific folder in iCloud Drive, and the top level of iCloud Drive.

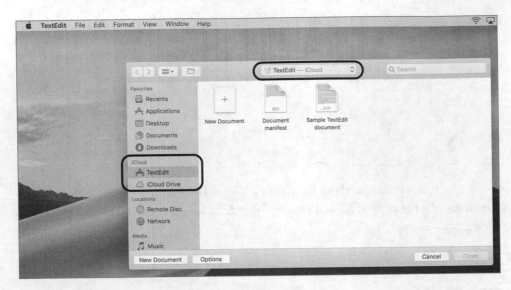

For some apps, the Save dialog offers an iCloud Library section in the menu. The following two screenshots show the iCloud Drive folder in two states.

In the first screenshot, the Finder window shows that iCloud Drive doesn't yet have a custom folder for Pages. There's a blank Pages file open.

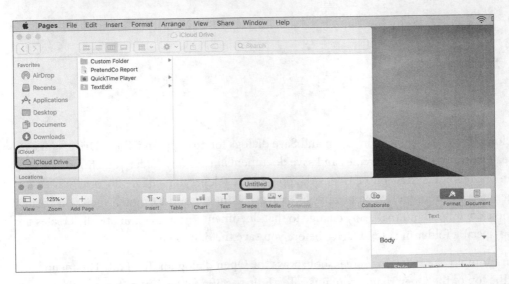

In the second screenshot, you see that immediately after text was entered into the previously blank document, macOS created a Pages-specific folder and automatically saved the Untitled document in that folder.

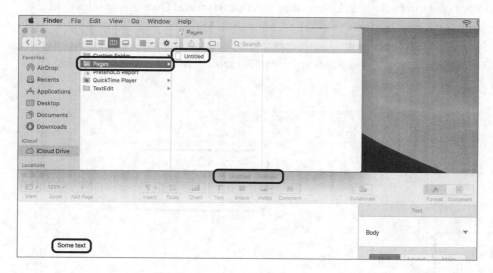

You can access custom folders and documents that were saved to iCloud Drive with the iCloud website (www.icloud.com), with the iCloud Drive app on iOS devices with iOS 10, and with the Files app on iOS devices with iOS 11 and newer. Further, you can share items in iCloud Drive with others, which enables collaborative document editing.

Store Desktop and Documents in iCloud Drive

You can save the content in your Desktop and Documents folders to iCloud Drive. Unlike upgrading to iCloud Drive, choosing to save your Desktop and Documents folders to iCloud is reversible.

You can enable and disable saving Desktop and Documents in iCloud Drive in the iCloud Drive options in iCloud preferences.

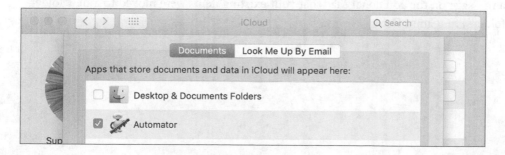

When you turn on Desktop & Documents Folders in iCloud preferences for the first time per iCloud account, the Desktop and Documents folders from your home folder on that Mac are moved to iCloud Drive. Items in your Desktop folder still appear in the Finder and on your desktop background. Accessing your Desktop and Documents folders in the Finder with the Keyboard shortcuts (Shift-Command-D to open your Desktop folder and Shift-Command-O to open your Documents folder) and the Go menu work as before. Your Desktop and Documents folders appear in iCloud Drive and in the Finder sidebar under iCloud.

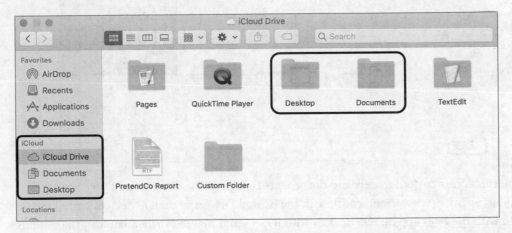

When you use Terminal, your Desktop and Documents folders appear in their normal location at the root of your home folder, but the Finder doesn't display these folders at the root of your home folder.

An iCloud account can have only one set of Desktop and Documents folders in iCloud Drive. So, the first Mac on which you enable Desktop & Documents Folders in iCloud preferences defines the base contents in iCloud Drive.

When you enable Desktop & Documents Folders in iCloud on an additional Mac, and you have items in the Desktop folder or the Documents folder on the additional Mac, you'll see a message on the additional Mac that your existing items were moved to a new folder (or folders) in iCloud Drive.

Content from additional Mac computers is represented by new subfolders.

Make sure the initial upload to iCloud Drive is fully complete (wait until there is no pie chart status icon to the right of iCloud Drive in the Finder's sidebar) before you enable Desktop & Documents Folders in iCloud Drive on another Mac. This ensures that all items are available to all Mac computers with iCloud Drive.

In the following screenshot, another Mac, named Johnny's MacBook Air, was added as a second computer with Desktop & Documents Folders in iCloud preferences enabled for the account. This move was necessary so that the items already in the Desktop and Documents folders in iCloud Drive on the original Mac that turned on Desktop & Documents Folders in iCloud (Johnny's MacBook) could replace the local Desktop and Documents folders on Johnny's MacBook Air. Now the content from the Desktop and Documents folders on the original Mac and on Johnny's MacBook Air are available on both computers.

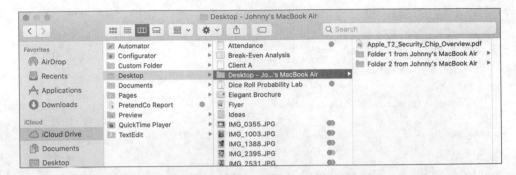

After you set up additional Mac computers, if you want to have a unified Desktop and Documents folder experience, move the items out of the computer-named subfolders to the base folders. With iCloud Drive, changes made on one Mac automatically apply to other Mac computers with the same iCloud account. Reorganization of your Desktop and Documents folders on one Mac automatically applies to your configured Mac computers. If you move all items out of the computer-named subfolders, the folders can be deleted, leaving you with the content in one set of Desktop and Documents folders available to all your Mac computers with iCloud Drive.

You can find out more about using iCloud Drive by reading Apple Support article HT206985, "Add your Desktop and Documents files to iCloud Drive."

Remove Items from iCloud Drive

To remove an item from iCloud Drive, move it out of an iCloud Drive folder to the Trash or any other local file on your Mac. Moving something from iCloud Drive to a local folder on your Mac removes the item from iCloud and other Apple devices configured for iCloud Drive.

Because iCloud Drive items appear alongside locally stored items on your Mac, you might accidentally remove an item from iCloud Drive. macOS warns you when you move something out of iCloud Drive.

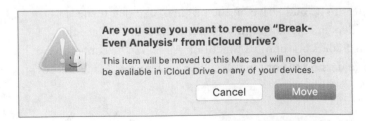

You can configure whether macOS shows this warning in the Advanced tab of the Finder preferences.

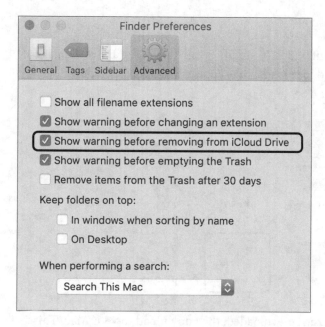

iCloud Drive Local Storage

With the exception of the Desktop and Documents folders, items saved in iCloud Drive are maintained locally in each user's ~/Library/Mobile Documents/ folder. It doesn't matter whether or not Desktop and Documents storage in iCloud Drive is enabled; those items are maintained locally in their normal locations, ~/Desktop and ~/Documents. Although you can see the Mobile Documents folder in the Finder, double-clicking this folder will redirect you to the root iCloud Drive view in the Finder.

App-specific folders, custom user folders, and all documents are visible in Terminal. Avoid using Terminal to modify content directly in the Mobile Documents folder. Any changes you make to the contents of the Mobile Documents folder are immediately saved to iCloud Drive.

Multiple devices on the same network that share an iCloud account transfer the data locally to improve performance. If you make changes to iCloud Drive while offline, macOS caches the changes and then silently pushes them the next moment an Internet connection to the iCloud servers is available.

Consider using content caching to speed up downloads from iCloud. See Reference 25.1, "Enable Host-Sharing Services," for more details.

iCloud Drive Optimized Storage

iCloud Drive keeps older files and infrequently used files only in iCloud Drive. Items in iCloud Drive that aren't downloaded locally to a Mac appear with an iCloud download icon (which looks like a cloud).

When you try to access items that aren't downloaded, they download to your Mac. This might take a few moments if the items are large or your Internet connection is slow. If you want to prevent iCloud Drive from optimizing storage, force it to save items locally too. In iCloud preferences, deselect Optimize Mac Storage at the bottom of the iCloud Drive options dialog to make the change.

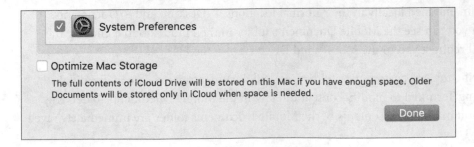

Turn Off iCloud Drive Features

By default, when you turn on iCloud Drive, compatible apps save files to iCloud. If you want to stop an app from saving content to iCloud Drive, in the iCloud preferences options dialog, deselect it.

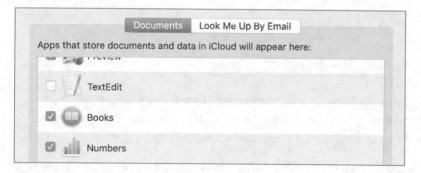

This doesn't delete existing data in iCloud. It prevents an app from accessing iCloud Drive and hides the associated folder from the Finder.

You can also deselect Desktop & Documents Folders to stop content from being saved to them. If you do this, you won't remove already stored content from iCloud Drive or from other Apple devices.

If you click Turn Off, you revert the iCloud Drive configuration for the Mac back to using local-only Desktop and Documents folders.

In this case, your home folder on the local Mac will have new, empty Desktop and Documents folders. You can still access the Desktop and Documents folders in iCloud Drive.

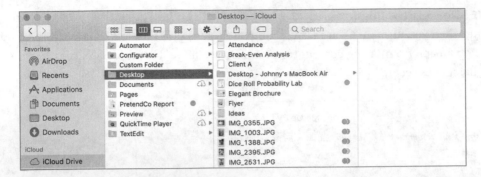

Nothing is lost, but you must move or copy items from iCloud Drive back to the local folders on your Mac. Moving something from iCloud Drive to another folder on your local Mac removes the item from iCloud Drive and configured Apple devices.

If you decide to completely turn off all iCloud Drive features, you can do so by deselecting the iCloud Drive checkbox in the iCloud preferences. Turning off iCloud Drive completely presents you with two options.

If you have Desktop & Documents Folders enabled, the dialog also notifies you that this affects your Desktop and Documents folders.

Neither option removes items from iCloud Drive or removes items from other Apple devices configured for it. Instead, selecting the "Remove from Mac" button removes iCloud Drive items only from the local Mac. Selecting the "Keep a Copy" button creates an iCloud Drive (Archive) folder in your home folder on the local Mac. If you click

"Keep a Copy" but you haven't yet finished downloading files from iCloud, you see a dialog with a progress bar and the message, "iCloud Drive needs to finish updating before being turned off. Your documents will be downloaded and copied to a folder named 'iCloud Drive (Archive)' in your home folder on this Mac."

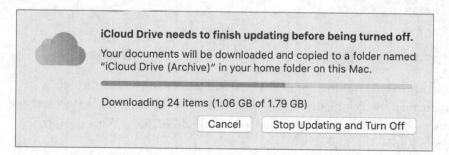

This local archive folder contains copies of items currently in your iCloud Drive.

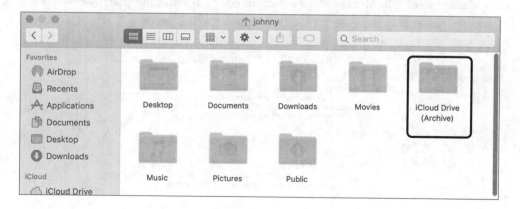

Reference 19.5
Optimize Local Storage

To see a summary of how the storage space on your Mac is being used, choose About This Mac from the Apple menu, and then click the Storage button. The Storage button shows an overview of your free space and the space used by different categories of files, including apps, documents, and photos, for each disk. Each segment of the bar is an estimate of the storage space used by a category of files. Move your pointer over each segment for more detail.

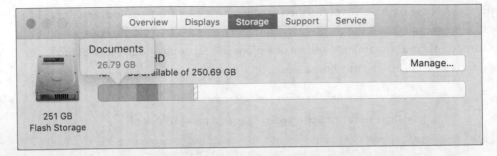

The calculations are based on storage optimization techniques that you can further inspect and implement by clicking the Manage button to open the Storage Management window. For more information, read Apple Support article HT202867, "What is 'other' and 'Purgeable' in About This Mac?"

System Information includes storage optimization features that are available in Storage Management. The Storage Management interface dynamically changes based on what features you enable. It might not look as it appears in this guide.

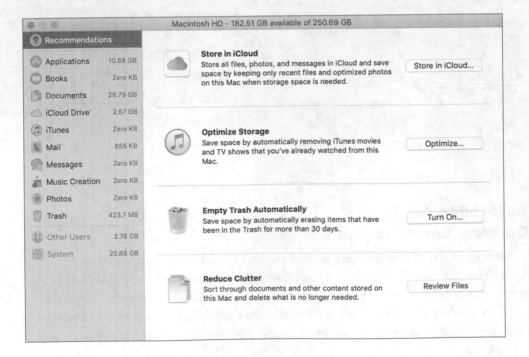

Storage Management opens with Recommendations, which offers suggestions to optimize local storage. You can also inspect and implement space-saving optimizations by selecting items from the list on the right of the Storage Management pane.

Recommendations offers various ways you can optimize storage:

► Store in iCloud—Click "Store in iCloud" to bring up a dialog that may vary based on your current iCloud Drive settings. You can choose what you would like to store in iCloud by selecting Desktop and Documents, Photo, and Messages. These selections can save considerable local space by relegating infrequently used items to iCloud storage only. You can also reach these settings from iCloud and Photos preferences.

► Optimize Storage—Click Optimize to reveal a dialog that enables you to turn on the automatic removal of watched movies and TV shows in iTunes. These settings can also be accessed from iTunes preferences.

▶ Empty Trash Automatically—Click Turn On to enable the option for the Finder to automatically empty local items from the Trash if they were there for longer than 30 days.

▶ Reduce Clutter—Click Review Files to open the Documents view of the Storage Management window. From here you can view your largest and least used documents on the local Mac. You can delete items you no longer need by selecting an item and then clicking Delete in the lower-right corner of the window.

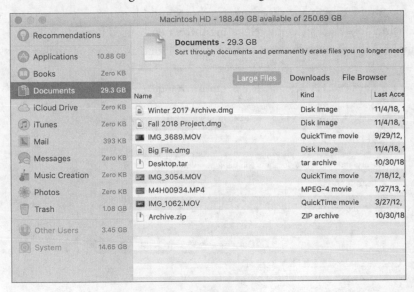

In the Storage Management window, you can select a storage category in the far-left column to inspect, and potentially remove, large files that you might not need. For example, every iOS device you sync to your Mac using iTunes creates backup and app update files that can consume a large portion of the system volume.

For more information, read Apple Support article HT206996, "How to free up storage space on your Mac."

Exercise 19.1
Use Alternate Apps

> ### ▶ Prerequisite
>
> ▸ You must have created the Johnny Appleseed account (Exercise 7.1, "Create a Standard User Account").

In this exercise, you configure which apps open files when you make a one-time choice to use a different app and when you choose to change the default app that opens a file type. You also use Quick Look to see what's in a file.

View a File with Quick Look

1   If necessary, log in as Johnny Appleseed.

2   In the Finder, open the ParticipantMaterials/Lesson19 folder.

3   Press and hold the Option key, then drag the file Pet Sitter Notes to copy it to your desktop.

The file has no visible extension, although the icon may indicate its file type.

4   Select (single-click) the Pet Sitter Notes document on your desktop.

5   Choose File > Quick Look "Pet Sitter Notes" (or press Command-Y).

Quick Look displays a preview of the document. You could click the button near the top right to open the document in TextEdit (currently the default app for this document type). You could select the document and press the Space bar to use Quick Look, or Control-click the document and choose Quick Look from the short-cut menu.

6   Press Command-Y to close the Quick Look window.

Choose an App to Open a File Once

1   Double-click Pet Sitter Notes on your desktop.

The file opens in TextEdit. TextEdit doesn't display the document headings or background image.

2   Without closing the document, on your desktop, Control-click the file.

3   In the shortcut menu, mouse over the Open With choice.

A submenu opens and shows the apps that can open this document type.

4   In the Open With submenu, choose Preview.

The file opens in Preview.

If you edit the same file in two apps at the same time, you might have unpredictable results. Here, you only view the file, so there isn't a problem.

5   Compare how the file is displayed in TextEdit and in Preview.

Preview gives a richer view of the file, showing a background image and headings that TextEdit does not show. TextEdit lets you edit its content, whereas Preview doesn't. Depending on what you want to do with the document, you might prefer either one.

6   Close the document in both apps.

7   Double-click the document again.

The document opens in TextEdit because the Open With choice you made earlier wasn't a permanent setting.

8   Close the document.

Change the Default App for a File Type

1   In the Finder, select the Pet Sitter Notes document.

2   Choose File menu > Get Info (or press Command-I).

3   If necessary, expand the General and Name & Extension sections of the Info window.

This is a Word 97 document, and it has a hidden .doc file extension.

4   Deselect "Hide extension." The extension is visible in the view of your desktop in the Finder.

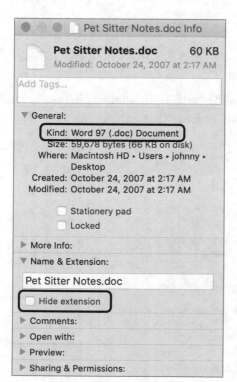

5 Expand the "Open with" section of the Info window, and choose Preview from its menu.

This menu shows the same possible apps as the Open With submenu in the Finder. If you choose an app here, you make a permanent setting but only for this file.

6 Click Change All.

7 In the confirmation dialog, click Continue.

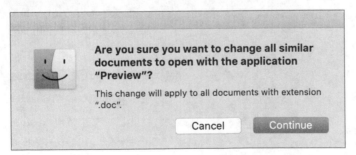

You changed the default app for opening documents with the extension .doc in Johnny Appleseed's account.

8 Close the Info window.

9 Double-click the document on your desktop.

Confirm the document opens in Preview.

10 Quit Preview.

11 Move Pet Sitter Notes.doc from your desktop to the Trash.

12 In the Finder, reopen the ParticipantMaterials/Lesson19 folder, and examine the original Pet Sitter Notes document.

The filename extension isn't shown. When you used Get Info to show the extension of the copy on your desktop, it affected only that file.

13 Double-click the original Pet Sitter Notes.

Pet Sitter Notes opens in Preview because you used Change All in the Info window to apply the setting to all Word 97 documents.

14 Quit Preview.

Exercise 19.2
Practice Auto Save and Versions

▶ **Prerequisite**

▶ You must have created the Johnny Appleseed account (Exercise 7.1, "Create a Standard User Account").

In this exercise, you edit a file in TextEdit, save several versions, and roll back to an earlier version.

Experiment with Auto Save

1 If necessary, log in as Johnny Appleseed.

2 Open System Preferences, and click General.

3 Ensure that "Ask to keep changes when closing documents" isn't selected and that "Close windows when quitting an app" is selected.

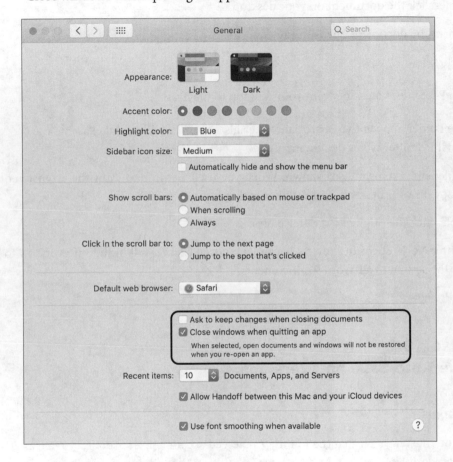

These are the default settings in macOS Mojave. If you select "Ask to keep changes when closing documents" you turn off the Auto Save feature you're about to test. If you deselect "Close windows when quitting an app," you make apps remember open documents and windows when you quit and reopen an app.

4 Quit System Preferences.

5 If necessary, navigate to ParticipantMaterials/Lesson19.

6 Copy Pretendco Report.rtfd to your desktop, and open the copy.

7 Add some text to the file.

The window title bar indicates the file status as Edited.

8 Switch to the Finder, select your copy of the Pretendco Report file, and choose File > Get Info (or press Command-I).

It was modified recently (your edits were saved automatically).

9 Close the Info window.

10 Switch to TextEdit, and add additional text to the file.

11 Select the file in the Finder, and choose File > Quick Look "Pretendco Report.rtfd" (or press Command-Y).

The Quick Look view shows the text you added to the file.

12 Close the Quick Look window.

Work with Multiple Versions

1 Switch to TextEdit, and choose File > Save (or press Command-S).

This save looks normal, but it saves a restorable version of the file.

TextEdit saves changes to a document you're editing frequently, but it saves a restorable version only when you tell it to.

2 Delete the graphic from the document.

3 Quit TextEdit.

You aren't prompted to save changes; they were saved automatically.

4 Reopen the Pretendco Report file.

5 Choose File > Revert To > Previous Save.

The graphic is restored.

6 Add more text to the document, and choose File > Save (or press Command-S).

7   Add more text, and examine the File > Revert To submenu.

It lists options to restore to the last-saved version, to restore to the last-opened version, or to browse all versions.

8   Choose File > Revert To > Browse All Versions.

TextEdit displays a full-screen version browser and shows the document state on the left and saved versions on the right. This view is similar to the Time Machine restore interface and shows versions from the Time Machine backups and restorable versions that TextEdit created.

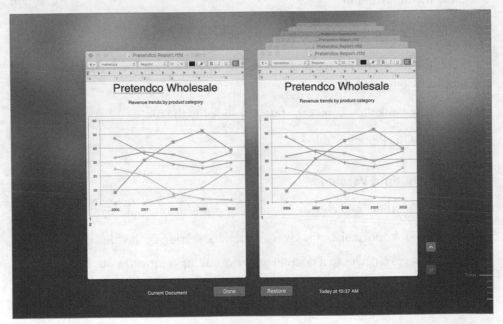

9   Experiment with the two windows. Click the arrows to the right of the stack or use the timeline on the right side of the screen to switch between saved versions. You can copy and paste content from old versions to the current document.

10   Click Done to exit the history browser.

11   Quit TextEdit.

Exercise 19.3
Manage Document Locking

▶ **Prerequisites**

▶ You must have created the Local Administrator (Exercise 3.1, "Configure a Mac for Exercises") and Johnny Appleseed (Exercise 7.1, "Create a Standard User Account") accounts.

In this exercise, you lock documents to prevent accidental changes.

Lock and Unlock a Document

1 Log in as Johnny Appleseed.

2 If you haven't completed Exercise 19.2, "Practice Auto Save and Versions," copy ParticipantMaterials/Lesson19/Pretendco Report.rtfd to your desktop.

3 Select your copy of the Pretendco Report document, and choose File > Get Info (or press Command-I).

4 In the General section of the Info window, select the Locked checkbox.

The document icon has a small lock in its corner.

5 Close the Info window.

6 Open the document.

The window title bar indicates the file is locked.

7   Attempt to add some text to the document.

A dialog appears telling you the file is locked and gives you options for the locked file.

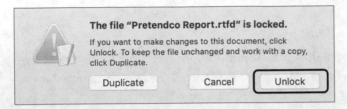

8   Click Unlock.

The lock is gone from the document icon on your desktop.

9   Add text to the document.

10   Click the document name in the title bar and select the Locked checkbox.

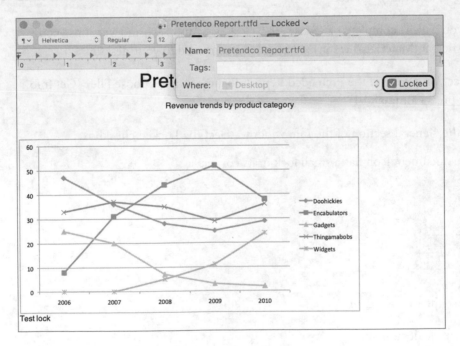

The lock reappears on the document icon on your desktop.

Since you are the owner of the document, you can lock and unlock it in the Finder or an editor that supports Auto Save.

11   Quit TextEdit.

Exercise 19.4
Store Documents in iCloud

You can save documents to the Internet with iCloud Drive and access them from Apple devices that are connected to the same iCloud account.

Enable iCloud Features

1 Log in as Johnny Appleseed.

2 Open System Preferences, and then click iCloud.

If you are already signed in to iCloud, skip to the next section, "Configure iCloud Drive."

3 If you aren't signed in to iCloud, enter your facilitator-provided Apple ID, and click Next.

4 Enter your password, and click Next.

5 If you are prompted to accept the iCloud terms and conditions, read through the new terms. If they are acceptable to you, agree and click Continue; otherwise, click Cancel and skip this exercise.

6 If the Apple ID is protected by two-factor authentication, follow the prompts to complete the authentication process.

7 If you are prompted to set up two-factor authentication, click Not Now, and click Don't Upgrade in the confirmation dialog.

8 When you are prompted to enter your Mac password to continue, type Johnny's password, and click OK.

9 When you are prompted features to set up, leave "Use iCloud for your documents and data" selected, deselect Use Find My Mac, and click Next.

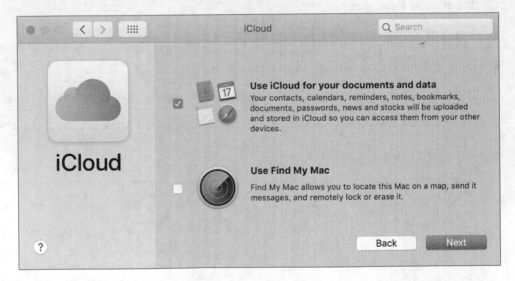

If a dialog appears and asks if you want to upgrade to iCloud Drive, it indicates that your iCloud account is being used to store documents in an older format and you must upgrade to iCloud Drive.

10 To upgrade the iCloud account to iCloud Drive, click Continue in the confirmation dialog.

11 If a dialog appears recommending requiring a password to unlock your screen, click Not Now.

12 If a dialog appears asking for your Apple ID password to set up iCloud Keychain, click Cancel.

13 Skip to step 6 of the next section.

Configure iCloud Drive

1 If iCloud preferences requires you to enter your password, click Enter Password and authenticate to iCloud. Don't enable Two-Factor Authentication.

2 If necessary, select Contacts.

3 If necessary, select iCloud Drive.

4 Click the Options button to the right of iCloud Drive.

The iCloud Drive options dialog enables you to control which apps have access to your iCloud documents and your email address.

5 In the Documents tab, make sure TextEdit is selected.

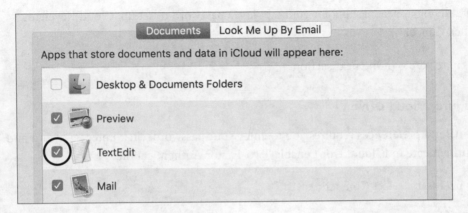

6 Click Done.

7 Quit System Preferences.

Save a Document to iCloud

1 If you haven't performed Exercise 19.2, "Practice Auto Save and Versions," copy ParticipantMaterials/Lesson19/Pretendco Report.rtfd to your desktop.

2 Open the Pretendco Report document.

3 Click the document name in the title bar.

4 If necessary, deselect Locked.

5   From the Where menu, choose iCloud Drive.

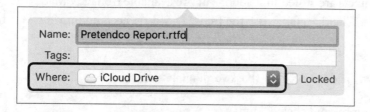

6   If a dialog appears and indicates that an item with the same name (Pretendco Report.rtf) exists in the same folder, a previous participant might have left this item in the iCloud account. Click Replace to replace the previous item with yours.

The document icon disappears from your desktop.

7   Quit TextEdit.

8   In the Finder, navigate to ParticipantMaterials/Lesson19.

9   Open the file vCards.vcf.

Contacts opens, and a dialog appears to confirm that you want to add the contacts.

If the dialog indicates that some cards are duplicates, this might be because a previous participant left them in the iCloud account.

10   Click Add or Import.

This imports eight vCards into Contacts and pushes them to your iCloud account.

11   Quit Contacts, and log out as Johnny Appleseed.

Open a Document from iCloud

Your document and contacts are stored in iCloud. They're available from any Mac account tied to the same iCloud account. Use the Emily Davidson account on your Mac to practice.

1 Log in to the Emily Davidson account (password: **Apple321!**).

2 Open System Preferences and click iCloud.

3 If iCloud isn't set up in Emily's account, enter the Apple ID and password you used with the Johnny Appleseed account, and click Next.

4 If the Apple ID is protected by two-factor authentication, follow the prompts to complete the authentication process.

5 If you are prompted to set up two-factor authentication, click Not Now, and then click Don't Upgrade in the confirmation dialog.

6 When you are prompted to enter your Mac password to continue, type Emily's password and click OK.

7 If you are prompted to enter the password you use to unlock your Mac, enter Johnny Appleseed's password and click Continue.

8 When you are prompted for features to set up, leave "Use iCloud for your documents and data" selected, deselect Use Find My Mac, and then click Next.

9 If a dialog appears recommending requiring a password to unlock your screen, click Not Now.

10 If a dialog appears asking for your Apple ID password to set up iCloud Keychain, click Cancel.

11 Make sure that iCloud Drive and Contacts are selected.

12 Quit System Preferences.

13 In the Finder, choose Go > iCloud Drive (or press Shift-Command-I).

If Pretendco Report isn't downloaded to Emily's account, it has a cloud icon indicating that it's available from iCloud.

14 Double-click Pretendco Report.

The document downloads (if necessary), and opens in TextEdit.

15 Add text to the document.

Your edits are saved to the iCloud servers and are available to other Mac computers using this iCloud account.

16 Quit TextEdit.

17 In the Finder, choose Go > Recents (or press Shift-Command-I).

Pretendco Report is listed. The Recents view shows local documents and those in iCloud Drive.

18 In the Search field, enter **pretendco report**.

Pretendco Report is shown, even though it is stored in iCloud Drive.

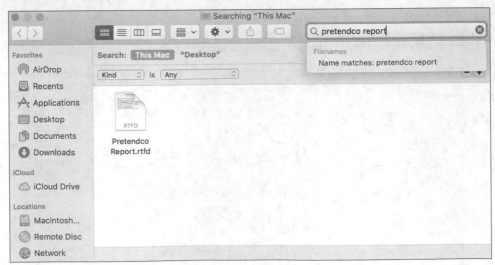

Use Contacts from iCloud

1   Open Contacts.

The contacts from the Johnny Appleseed account appear.

2   Quit Contacts, and log out as Emily Davidson.

Verify Your Changes as Johnny Appleseed

1   Log back in as Johnny Appleseed.

2   In the Finder, choose Go > iCloud Drive (or press Shift-Command-I).

3   Open Pretendco Report.

4   Verify that the edit you made as Emily appears. You might have to wait for the document to update.

5   Quit TextEdit.

Manage and Troubleshoot Apps

Your success in resolving issues with an app on your Mac depends on your experience with an app, your ability to gather relevant information about it, and your knowledge of macOS technologies. In this lesson, you learn about key elements of the macOS process architecture. You also learn to gather information about apps and processes. And you learn troubleshooting techniques that you can use for any app type.

Reference 20.1
Apps and Processes

A process is any instance of executable code that is currently activated and addressed in system memory. In other words, a process is anything that is currently running or open. macOS handles processes efficiently, so even when a process is idle and probably consuming no processor resources, it's still active, because it has dedicated address space in system memory. The four general process types are apps, commands, daemons, and agents.

Process Types

An app is a process you run in the graphical interface.

A command is a process you run in the command-line interface (CLI). An exception is when you use the open command in the CLI to open an app in the graphical interface.

GOALS

▸ Describe and support app types

▸ Manage app extensions and widgets in Notification Center

▸ Monitor and control processes and apps

▸ Explore app troubleshooting techniques

Processes that run on behalf of macOS are called background processes (or daemons) because they rarely have a user interface. Daemons usually launch during macOS startup and remain active the entire time a Mac is running. Most daemons run with root or systemwide access to all resources. Daemons are responsible for most automatic macOS features, such as detecting network changes and maintaining the Spotlight search metadata index.

An agent is a daemon that runs on behalf of a specific user. Agents are also daemons, or background processes. The primary difference is that agents run only when you're logged in. Agents are started automatically by macOS. Although apps and commands are also opened automatically, they aren't controlled by macOS the way agents are. Apps, commands, and agents are all part of the user's space because they are executed with the same access privileges the user has.

macOS Memory Management

macOS is a desirable platform for running apps and other processes because it combines a UNIX foundation with an advanced graphical user interface. Users probably recognize the interface elements right away, but it's the underlying foundation that keeps things running so smoothly.

The primary feature in macOS that keeps processes secure is protected memory. Processes are kept separate and secure in system memory. macOS manages memory allocation so that processes aren't allowed to interfere with each other's system memory space. In other words, an ill-behaved or crashed app doesn't normally affect other processes.

macOS automatically manages system memory for processes at their request. Although real system memory is limited by hardware, macOS dynamically allocates real and virtual memory when needed. So, the only memory limitations in macOS are the size of installed RAM and the amount of free space you have on your startup disk.

macOS includes software-based memory compression that increases performance and reduces energy use. Instead of swapping memory out to disk when too many processes are active, macOS compresses the content used by less active processes to free up space for more active processes. This reduces traffic between active memory and the virtual memory swap files on the startup disk.

64-Bit versus 32-Bit Mode

macOS supports 32-bit and 64-bit modes simultaneously. A process running in 64-bit mode can individually access more than 4 GB of system memory and can perform higher-precision computational functions much faster. All Mac computers compatible with macOS Mojave feature 64-bit-capable processors and can take advantage of 64-bit system features.

As noted in Apple Support article HT208436, "32-bit app compatibility with macOS High Sierra 10.13.4 and later," macOS Mojave is the last version of macOS that will run 32-bit apps. When third-party developers submit apps to the Mac App Store, those apps must support 64-bit mode, including updates to existing apps. You might still see Mac apps that support only 32-bit mode if they aren't distributed through the App Store. For more information, read "64-bit Requirement for Mac Apps" at https://developer.apple.com/news/?id=12012017a.

Although most apps that support 64-bit mode improve performance, apps that run in 64-bit mode can't take advantage of 32-bit code. This means an app that uses plug-in technology might have compatibility issues with third-party plug-ins that aren't updated to support 64-bit mode.

The "Open in Low Resolution" checkbox is on Mac computers with Retina displays. This option prevents the use of high-resolution app assets, which also might not be compatible with 32-bit app plug-ins.

System Preferences switches modes for you. When you try to open a third-party 32-bit System Preferences plug-in, a prompt to restart System Preferences appears. If you click OK (the default), System Preferences restarts in 32-bit mode and loads the selected pane.

If you open a 32-bit app, you see an alert that notifies you that the app is 32-bit. This alert appears once every 30 days when you open the app.

Reference 20.2
Manage App Extensions

App extensions allow apps to use functionality and content from other apps. In this section you explore how to use app extensions.

App Extensions

App extensions provide a standard framework that allows apps from different developers to interact with each other—so much so that with app extensions one app's features appear as if they are built in to another app.

As an example of app extensions, the Preview app includes markup features that enable you to manage pictures or PDF documents. This includes adding custom shapes, text, or your digital signature to documents. Click the Show Markup Toolbar button (pen tip icon) in the toolbar to access these features.

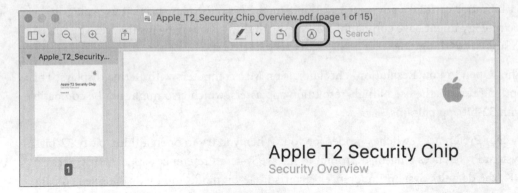

The Preview Markup toolbar appears.

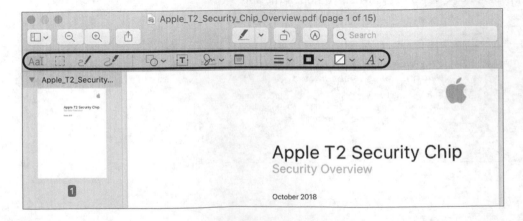

The Preview markup features are available as an app extension that can be used by other apps. In Mail, you can use markup features in an email that contains a picture or PDF document. When you send an email with an attachment, select the attachment, click Action (downward arrow icon) at the top right of the document, then choose Markup to display markup features.

Manage App Extensions

Several app extensions are included in macOS. When you install an app that provides app extensions, you don't need to do anything extra, because installing an app automatically installs any app extension resources that are part of the app.

You can view installed app extensions and enable or disable their functionality from Extensions preferences. In Extensions preferences, select the All pane to view all extensions you've installed on your Mac. The following screenshot shows some extensions from apps in the App Store (Acorn 6, CloudApp, and Evernote) and some from third-party package installers (Box Edit, Box Sync, and Dropbox).

The next several sections cover the various kinds of extensions you can configure in Extensions preferences.

Configure Actions Extensions

Actions extensions enable you to edit or view content in one app, using the features of a second app, without leaving the first app. For example, you can mark up images or PDF documents in Mail without leaving Mail. The following screenshot shows the markup action that's included with Preview. Deselect the checkbox next to an item to prevent that app extension from appearing in other apps. As an example, the checkbox next to the Skitch item is deselected (a third-party app installed from the App Store), so it doesn't appear in other apps.

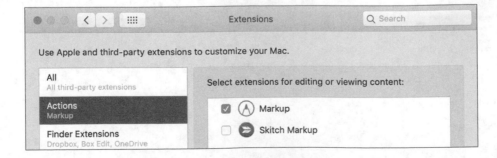

Configure Finder Extensions

Also called Finder Sync Extensions, Finder app extensions can add file-system functionality that's displayed in the Finder. As an example, the popular third-party cloud storage solution Dropbox includes an app extension that adds a menu to the Finder toolbar where you can manage Dropbox settings for files.

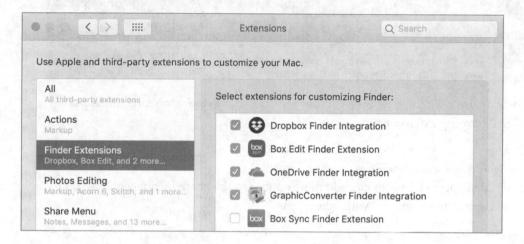

Configure Photos Editing Extensions

Photos app extensions can add photo manipulation tools to Photos.

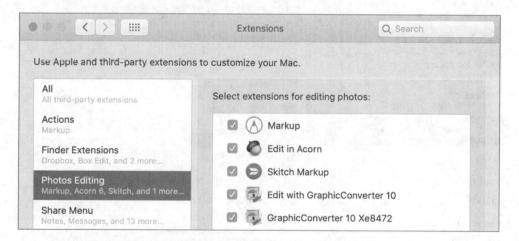

To use an app extension in Photos, open a photo in Edit mode, click the Extensions button (which looks like three dots inside a circle), and choose an app.

You can also click the Extensions button and choose App Store to search for apps that offer Photo app extensions.

Configure Share Menu Extensions

Share Menu app extensions can add more options to the Share menu, enabling you to share content from one app with other apps.

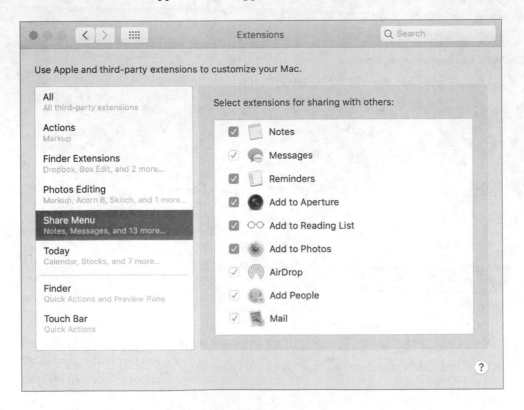

Configure Today View Extensions

These app extensions can add functionality in the form of widgets that appear in the Today view of Notification Center. The Today view in Notification Center offers information and functionality that you can customize. Click the farthest-right button in the menu bar to access Notification Center. The default view is Today.

You can change how your Today view looks by doing any of the following:

▸ Move your pointer over a widget, then click the Info (i) button that appears.

▸ Reorder your widgets by dragging a widget to another location.

Like other app extensions, widgets in the Today view are included with the app that is providing the functionality or service. For example, the Calculator extension is built into Calculator. Also, as with other app extensions, you can disable or enable widgets in the Today view from the Extensions preferences.

You can manage widgets in the Today view by clicking the button at the bottom center of Notification Center. The button at the bottom center of Notification Center often says Edit, but it can also display the number of newly added app extensions that can present widgets in the Today view.

When you're editing your Today view, you can do any of the following:

▶ Drag a widget up or down to change the order of widgets.

▶ In the left column, click Remove (the red prohibitory icon in the upper-left corner of a widget) to remove it from the Today view. After you click Remove, that widget is available in the left column if you want to add it again later.

▶ In the right column, click Add (the green plus icon to the right of the widget name) to add it to the Today view.

▶ Drag a widget from the left column to the right to remove it, or drag a widget from the right column to the left to add it.

▶ Click App Store to open the App Store to a page that features Notification Center widgets.

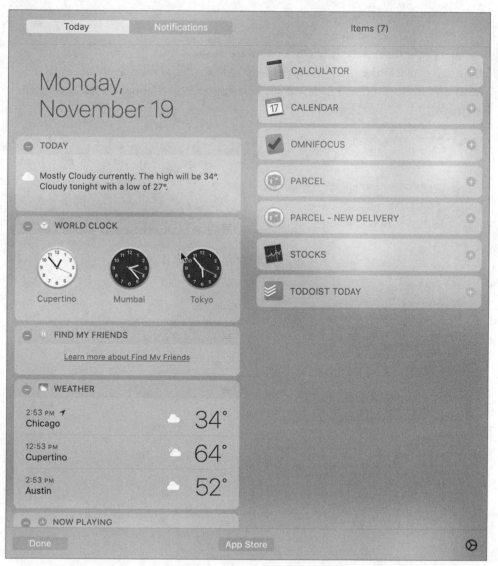

The following screenshot shows a portion of the App Store window that features Notification Center widgets.

Configure Finder Quick Actions and Preview Pane Extensions

These app extensions enable you to perform Quick Actions on documents in the Finder and in the Finder's Preview Pane. You can read more about Quick Actions in Reference 19.1, "Open Files."

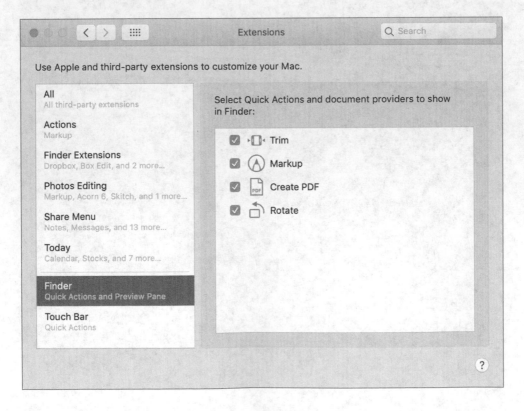

Configure Touch Bar Extensions

If your Mac has a Touch Bar, you'll see Touch Bar listed in Extensions preferences. There are no Touch Bar extensions installed with a new installation of macOS Mojave.

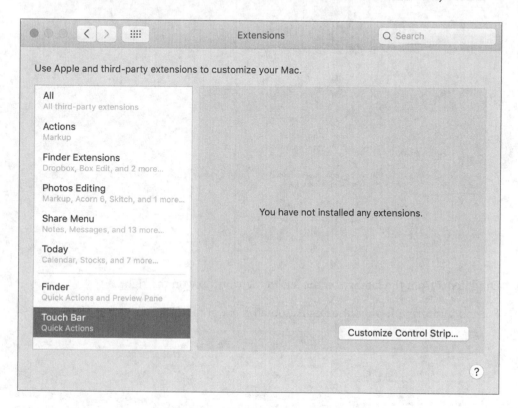

Use Automator to Create Quick Actions

You can use Automator to create workflows that you can make available in your Touch Bar and in Finder Quick Actions and in the Finder Preview Pane. To create a Quick Action with Automator, use the following steps:

1 Use Spotlight Search to open Automator.

2 In the Open dialog, click New Document (or press Command-N or choose File > New).

3 Select Quick Action, then click Choose.

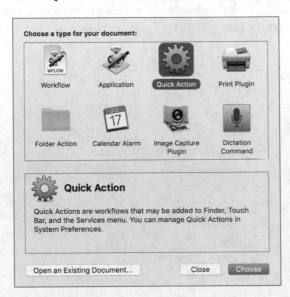

4 Drag items from the Library on the left to the workflow on the right.

For more information about using Automator, choose Help > Automator Help.

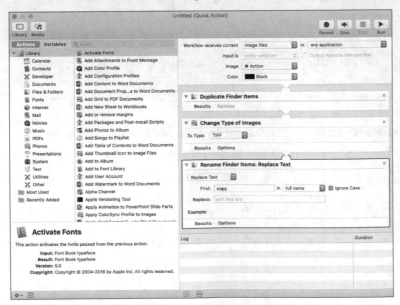

5   Choose File > Save (or press Command-S) to save the workflow.

6   Enter a name. This name will appear in Extensions preferences and in the
Quick Actions menu.

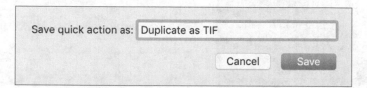

7   Click Save.

8   Open Extensions preferences.

9   Select Finder in the left column and confirm that your new Quick Action appears in
the list on the right.

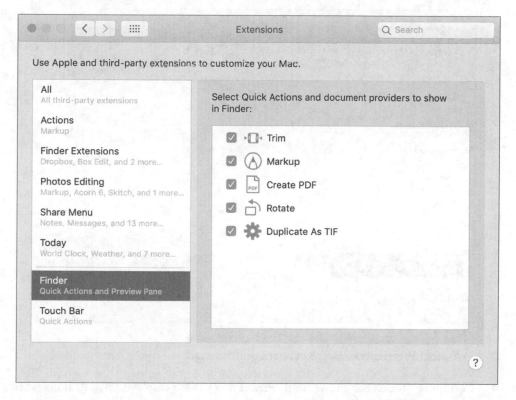

Your new Quick Action is automatically enabled and is available for applicable document types in the Finder for Quick Actions and in the Preview Pane.

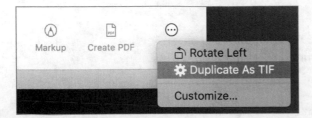

If your Mac has a Touch Bar, you can use the following steps to make your Quick Action available in the Touch Bar.

1   Open Extensions preferences, then select Touch Bar in the left column.

2   Confirm that your new Quick Action appears in the list on the right.

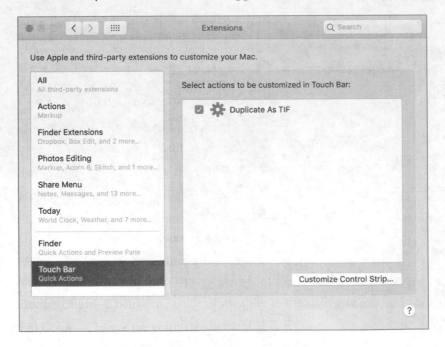

3   In System Preferences, open Keyboard preferences.

4   Configure "Touch Bar shows" and "Press Fn key to" to display Quick Actions when you want.

There are many possible configurations for these settings.

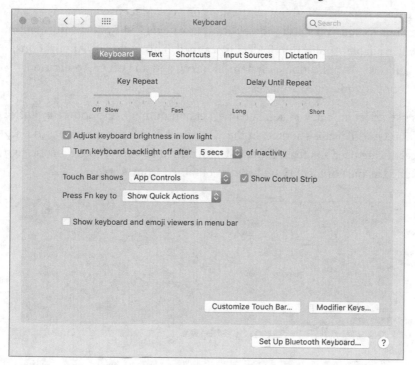

Consider the example configuration of "Touch Bar shows App Controls" and "Press Fn key to Show Quick Actions," as shown in the previous figure. When you select a file in the Finder that file that is appropriate for your Quick Action, then press the Fn (Function) key (if you configured "Press Fn key to Show Quick Action"), your Touch Bar displays your Quick Actions.

Reference 20.3
Monitor Apps and Processes

macOS provides several methods for identifying and managing apps and processes. You can use the Finder Info window to view basic app information, but you can find out a lot more about an app from System Information. To inspect an app or process as it's running on the Mac, use Activity Monitor.

Monitor Apps with System Information

If you want to gather information about all the apps on your Mac, use System Information. When you select the Applications category in System Information, the content of all available Application folders is scanned. This includes /Applications, /Applications/Utilities, ~/Applications, /System/Library/, and any other Applications folders at the root of any mounted volumes.

From the apps list, select an entry to see its name, version number, app source modification date, and app type. The app's source, in the "Obtained from" column, is based on the code-signing certificate used to create the app. Unidentified apps don't have a code signature. Apps installed as part of macOS are listed as obtained from Apple.

Monitor Processes with Activity Monitor

Activity Monitor is the primary app for monitoring running processes. If an app stops responding or is slow, check Activity Monitor. Also, check here if your Mac seems to be running slow. Activity Monitor helps you identify an app or background process that's using a significant percentage of macOS resources.

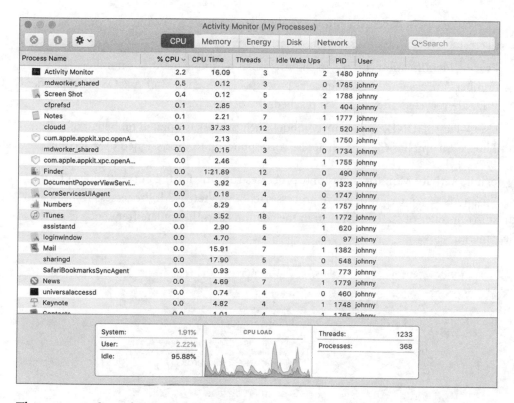

The main window of Activity Monitor presents a list of running processes and apps that belong to the current user. Below the process list you see macOS statistics. The default columns enable you to examine process statistics:

▸ Process Name—This is the name of the running process chosen by the developer who created it.

▸ % CPU—This number is the percentage of total CPU the process is consuming. The maximum percentage is 100 percent times the number of processor cores.

▸ CPU Time—This is the amount of time a process has been active since the last startup.

▸ Threads—This is the number of threads in the process. A process can be broken down into a number of thread operations. Multithreading helps increase a process's responsiveness by enabling it to perform multiple simultaneous tasks. Multithreading also increases performance, as each thread of a single process can run on a separate processor core.

▶ Idle Wake Ups—This is the number of times a process was woken up from a paused sleep state since the process was last started.

▶ Process Identification (PID)—Each process has a unique identifier number. The numbers are assigned in sequence as processes are opened after macOS startup. The PIDs are recycled after 65,535 is reached.

▶ User—Per the UNIX app security model, each process is opened on behalf of a user. Thus, each app has file-system access corresponding to the assigned user account.

By default, Activity Monitor shows only processes running for the currently logged-in user. To increase your view of active processes, choose View > All Processes. You can also adjust the number of statistics shown in the columns and the update frequency from the View menu.

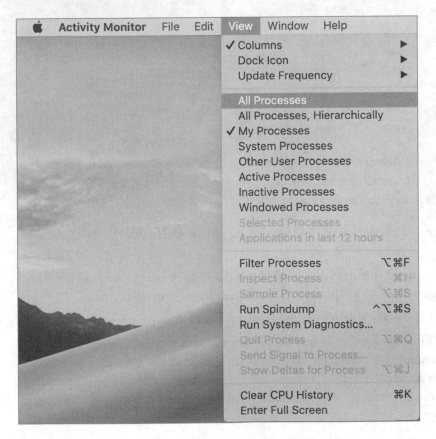

To narrow down your view, use the Search field in the upper-right corner of the Activity Monitor window.

To sort the process list by column, click any column title. Click the column title again to toggle between ascending and descending sorts. By viewing all processes and then re-sorting the list by % CPU, you can determine whether a process is using excessive resources.

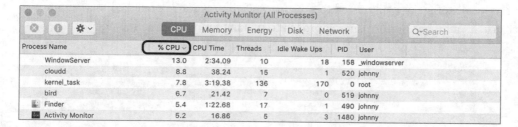

To further inspect a process, double-click its name in the Activity Monitor list. This reveals a window showing detailed process information.

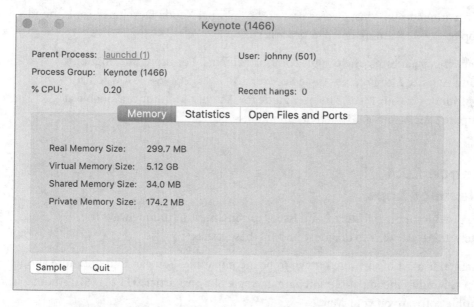

Although CPU use is generally the most important statistic for monitoring process activity, the Activity Monitor app can also monitor memory, energy, disk, and network use. Click through the buttons at the top of the Activity Monitor window to view the different categories. These monitoring features show you real-time macOS statistics.

As demonstrated in Reference 25.1, "Enable Host-Sharing Services," when you enable Content Caching in the Sharing pane of System Preferences, the Cache button appears at the top of the Activity Monitor window.

Hover your pointer over any statistic at the bottom of the Activity Monitor window to view a description of the statistic.

The Swap Used and Compressed statistics under the Memory button are a historical account, since the last macOS startup, of how much active process data was swapped out to local storage or compressed to save space. Compression is preferred to swapping because it's a higher-performance approach to making more room in memory.

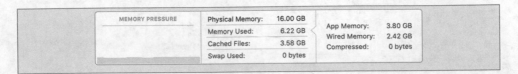

A low number of swap usage is acceptable, but a high number of swap usage indicates that macOS doesn't have enough real memory to meet the user's app demands.

Use the Instruments app—installed as part of the optional Xcode Developer Tools found in the App Store—for a more detailed process view.

Read the help page at https://help.apple.com/instruments. For more information about using Activity Monitor, see Apple Support article HT201464, "How to use Activity Monitor on your Mac." The user guide for Activity Monitor is available at https://support.apple.com/guide/activity-monitor.

Reference 20.4
Troubleshoot Apps

Each app provides unique features, and issues can manifest in unique ways too. Fortunately, there are ways to diagnose and fix these issues.

Apple maintains a list of software known to be incompatible. You can find out more about how macOS handles incompatible software in Apple Support article HT201861, "About incompatible software on your Mac."

The actions you can take in the following list are in order from the least to the most invasive and time-consuming. These actions are also presented according to the likelihood of their success in resolving an issue, from most to least likely. Generally, when you troubleshoot apps, start with one of these actions:

▶ Restart the app—Often, if you restart an app you resolve the issue, or at least you get the app to respond.

▶ Open another known working document—If the known working document opens and works, you know that the problem document is corrupted and the cause of the issue. If you discover that the problem source is a corrupted document file, usually the best solution is to restore the document from an earlier backup, as covered in Lesson 17, "Manage Time Machine."

▶ Try another app—You can open many common document types with multiple Mac apps. Try opening the problem document in another app. If this works, save a new version of the document from the other app.

▶ Try another user account—Use this method to determine whether a user-specific resource file is the cause of the problem. If the app problem doesn't occur when you use another account, search for corrupted app caches, preferences, and resource files in the suspect user's Library folder. You can create a temporary account to test, and then remove it, as covered in Lesson 7, "Manage User Accounts."

▶ Check diagnostic reports and log files—This is the last information-gathering step before you replace items. Every time an app crashes, the macOS diagnostic reporting feature saves a diagnostic report of the crash. Use Console to view diagnostic reports.

▶ Delete cache files—To increase performance, many apps create cache folders in /Library/Caches, ~/Library/Caches, and ~/Library/Saved Application State. An app cache folder often matches the app's name. Although cache folders are not likely to be the app resource causing problems, you can delete them without affecting a user's information. After you delete an app's cache folder, the app creates a new one the next time you open it. To remove the various font caches, use safe boot, which clears font caches, as covered in Lesson 28, "Troubleshoot Startup and System Issues."

▶ Replace preference files—Corrupted preference files are one of the most likely of app resources to cause problems, because they change often and are required for apps to function.

▶ Replace app resources—Although corrupted app resources can cause problems, they are the least likely source of problems, since app resources are rarely changed.

Force Quit Apps

It's easy to tell when an app becomes unresponsive—it stops reacting to your mouse clicks, and the pointer often changes to a wait cursor (spinning pinwheel) and stays that way for a while.

Because the forward-most app controls the menu bar, it may seem as if the app locked you out of the Mac. If you move the wait cursor from the frozen app to another app or the desktop, usually the pointer returns to normal and you regain control of the Mac.

You can quit apps several ways:

▶ From the Force Quit Applications dialog—Choose Apple menu > Force Quit, or press Option-Command-Escape, to open the Force Quit Applications dialog. A frozen app appears with "(not responding)" next to its name. To force quit, select an app and click Force Quit.

▶ From the Dock—Use Control-click, or press and hold the app icon in the Dock, to display the app shortcut menu. If the Dock recognizes that the app is frozen, choose Force Quit from this menu. Otherwise, press and hold the Option key to change the Quit menu command to Force Quit.

▶ From Activity Monitor—Open Activity Monitor, and select the app you want to quit from the process list. Next, click the "X" in an octagon icon on the far-left edge of the Activity Monitor toolbar, and then click the Force Quit button. Activity Monitor is the only built-in app that enables administrator users to quit or force quit other user process or background system process.

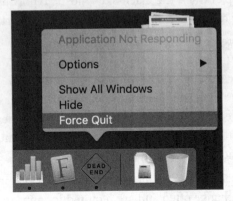

In Activity Monitor, webpages in Safari are shown as separate processes. This enables you to force quit individual pages in Safari.

Diagnostic Reports

The macOS diagnostic reporting feature displays a warning dialog that lets you know a problem occurred when an app quits unexpectedly (crashes) or stops functioning (hangs) and you have to force quit it.

Diagnostic reporting creates log files that detail an app crash or hang. Click the Report button when a warning dialog appears to see a log file.

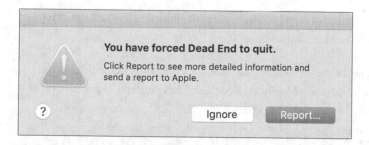

If you want, add comments to send to Apple. If you want to, configure automatic diagnostic report delivery to Apple from Security & Privacy preferences.

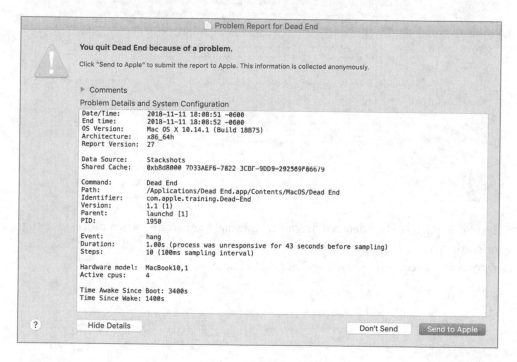

View Reports with Console

Console compiles reports that provide general diagnostic data and details about macOS and apps. User reports are from apps used by the current user. System reports are from macOS components that affect all users. If you aren't logged in as an administrator user, you can view only user reports. Some items in the Reports column are folders containing additional multiple log files. Select an item in the Reports column to reveal its contents. To share a log file with others, select the log file and then click the Share button in the toolbar.

If you're logged in as an administrator user, you can view all reports. Here are three types of logs and reports you can view with Console:

▶ Mac Analytics—Short diagnostic messages that show general use and problems are saved to /private/var/log/DiagnosticMessages. Processes can generate many diagnostic messages a day, and many of them are benign.

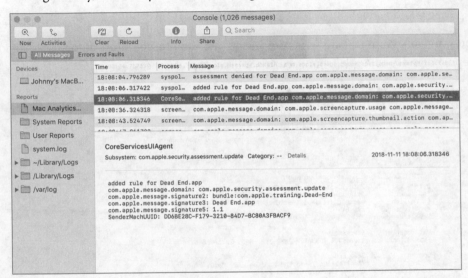

▶ System Reports—More detailed diagnostic messages are created when processes hang or crash. System reports are from macOS components that affect all users. These reports are saved to /Library/Logs/DiagnosticReports.

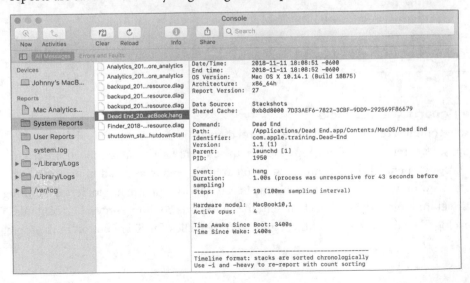

▶ User Reports— More detailed diagnostic messages are created when processes hang or crash. User reports are from apps used by the current user. If the problem report was generated by something running for the user, the log is saved to ~/Library/Logs/DiagnosticReports.

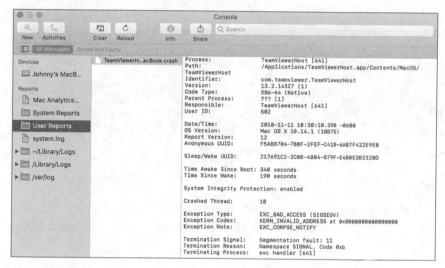

Diagnostic reports often indicate which files were being used by the app at the time. One of the reported files could be the source of the problem due to corruption.

View Activities

You can view log messages grouped by the activity they're associated with. Just click the Activities button in the toolbar. This helps you focus on specific log messages and allows for a more complete analysis.

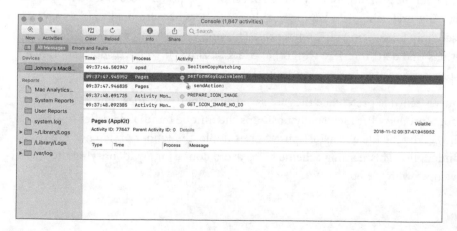

Search Logs and Activities

You can search for log messages and activities—for example, you can:

▶ Type a word or phrase to find log messages that match it

▶ Show log messages from a certain process

▶ Search for log messages that don't match certain criteria

After you complete a search, you can save it to use again

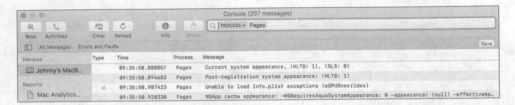

For more information about Console, including information about property shortcuts to use when searching, read the user guide for Console at support.apple.com/guide/console/.

Troubleshoot Preferences

Apps primarily access two types of often-changing files when they are in use: the documents for which the app handles viewing or editing, and the preference files that contain the app settings. From an administration perspective, preference files are often more important, because they might contain settings that are required for an app to work. For instance, an app serial number or registration information is often stored in a preference file.

You can find preferences in any Library folder, but most app preferences end up in the user's Library. App preferences are kept in user home folders because the local Library should be used only for systemwide preferences. This enables each user to have their own app settings that don't interfere with other users' settings. If you're troubleshooting a systemwide process, look for its preferences in /Library.

Most app and systemwide preference files are saved as property list files. The naming scheme for a property list file usually positions the unique bundle identifier for the app first, followed by the file extension .plist. For example, the Finder preference file is com.apple.finder.plist. This naming scheme helps avoid confusion by identifying the software developer with the app.

Some apps are still not sandboxed, so they use the default preference folder for standard apps: ~/Library/Preferences.

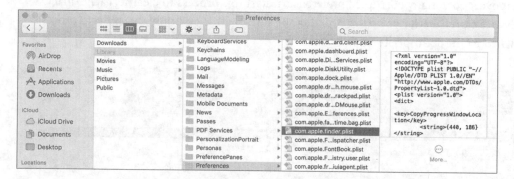

For sandboxed apps, the preference is located in the Containers or Group Containers folder. These folders are ~/Library/Containers/*BundleID*/Data/Library/Preferences and ~/Library/Group Containers/*BundleID*/Library/Preferences, where *BundleID* is the unique bundle identifier for the app.

For example, the identifier for Mail is com.apple.mail. For a user with the account name "johnny," the full path to the Mail app preference file is /Users/johnny/Library/Containers/com.apple.mail/Data/Library/Preferences/com.apple.mail.plist.

App preference files can contain both internal app configuration information and user-configured preferences. An app might frequently update information in its preference file, even if you haven't changed any preferences. It is the only file required by most apps that is regularly being rewritten, so it has the potential to become corrupted.

Many apps that use the Apple preference model, including third-party apps, recognize a corrupted preference file, ignore it, and create a new one. In contrast, some third-party apps use their own proprietary preference models that are not as resilient. In these cases, corrupted preferences typically result in an app that crashes frequently or crashes during startup.

Resolve Corrupted Preferences

To isolate a corrupted preference, rename the suspect preference file. To do this, in the Finder, add an identifier to the end of the suspect preference filename—something like .bad. To make the preference file easier to find later, put a tilde (~) at the beginning of the filename, which causes the Finder to put it at the beginning of the file listing when sorted alphabetically.

The preference architecture is maintained by a background process (cfprefsd). To improve performance, this process uses memory caching to store preference information. After you remove a potentially corrupted preference, restart this process to clear its cache. macOS restarts cfprefsd after you force it to quit. Be sure to force quit only the cfprefsd process owned by the appropriate user.

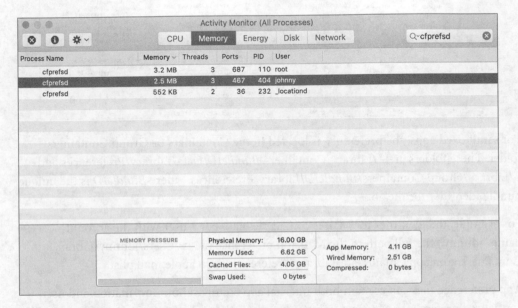

After you remove the preference file and restart the cfprefsd process, opening the app or process creates a new preference file based on the code's defaults. If this resolves the issue and doesn't remove irreplaceable settings, delete the old preference file. If it doesn't resolve the issue, move on to resource troubleshooting.

If you resolve the problem elsewhere, restore the previous settings with the following steps:

1. Delete the newer preference file.

2. Remove the temporary filename identifier you added to the original preference file.

3. Restart cfprefsd so that the app reloads its preference file.

The benefit of replacing the previous preference file is that you don't lose the settings or custom configuration saved in the file.

View and Edit Preference Files

While troubleshooting, verify settings by viewing the contents of the configuration property list file. The content of a property list file is formatted as plain-text Extensible Markup Language (XML) or binary code. Apps process binary-encoded files more efficiently than they process XML-encoded files. macOS automatically converts the format of property list files from XML to binary. You can read the binary files in two ways:

▶ In the Finder, select a property list file, and then press the Space bar. This opens Quick Look so that you can preview the file contents.

```xml
com.apple.Automator.plist                    Open with TextWrangler

<?xml version="1.0" encoding="UTF-8"?>
<!DOCTYPE plist PUBLIC "-//Apple//DTD PLIST 1.0//EN" "http://www.apple.com/DTDs/PropertyList-1.0.dtd">
<plist version="1.0">
<dict>
        <key>AMSuppressWarningForDestructiveActions</key>
        <false/>
        <key>AMSuppressWarningOnRunForAMServiceWorkflowPersonality</key>
        <false/>
        <key>NSNavLastRootDirectory</key>
        <string>~/Library/Mobile Documents/com~apple~Automator/Documents</string>
        <key>NSNavLastUserSetHideExtensionButtonState</key>
        <true/>
        <key>NSNavPanelExpandedSizeForOpenMode</key>
        <string>{712, 448}</string>
        <key>NSNavPanelExpandedSizeForSaveMode</key>
        <string>{712, 448}</string>
        <key>NSSplitView Subview Frames AMDocumentMajor</key>
        <array>
                <string>0.000000, 0.000000, 381.000000, 601.000000, NO, NO</string>
                <string>382.000000, 0.000000, 618.000000, 601.000000, NO, NO</string>
        </array>
        <key>NSSplitView Subview Frames AMDocumentMinor</key>
        <array>
                <string>0.000000, 0.000000, 618.000000, 432.000000, NO, NO</string>
                <string>0.000000, 433.000000, 618.000000, 168.000000, NO, NO</string>
        </array>
        <key>NSSplitView Subview Frames AMLibraryActionsMajor</key>
        <array>
                <string>0.000000, 0.000000, 381.000000, 439.000000, NO, NO</string>
                <string>0.000000, 440.000000, 381.000000, 136.000000, NO, NO</string>
        </array>
        <key>NSSplitView Subview Frames AMLibraryActionsMinor</key>
        <array>
                <string>0.000000, 0.000000, 163.000000, 439.000000, NO, NO</string>
                <string>164.000000, 0.000000, 217.000000, 439.000000, NO, NO</string>
        </array>
        <key>NSToolbar Configuration AMDocumentToolbarIdentifier</key>
        <dict>
                <key>TB Display Mode</key>
                <integer>1</integer>
                <key>TB Icon Size Mode</key>
                <integer>1</integer>
                <key>TB Is Shown</key>
                <integer>1</integer>
                <key>TB Size Mode</key>
                <integer>1</integer>
        </dict>
```

▶ Use Terminal to run the command **plutil -convert xml1** *myfile.plist* (where "*myfile.plist*" is the name of the property list file you've selected) to convert the property list file from binary to XML, and then use the **less** command to view its contents.

```
johnny — less ~/Library/Preferences/com.apple.Automator.plist — 80×24
<?xml version="1.0" encoding="UTF-8"?>
<!DOCTYPE plist PUBLIC "-//Apple//DTD PLIST 1.0//EN" "http://www.apple.com/DTDs/
PropertyList-1.0.dtd">
<plist version="1.0">
<dict>
        <key>AMSuppressWarningForDestructiveActions</key>
        <false/>
        <key>AMSuppressWarningOnRunForAMServiceWorkflowPersonality</key>
        <false/>
        <key>NSNavLastRootDirectory</key>
        <string>~/Library/Mobile Documents/com~apple~Automator/Documents</string
>
        <key>NSNavLastUserSetHideExtensionButtonState</key>
        <true/>
        <key>NSNavPanelExpandedSizeForOpenMode</key>
        <string>{712, 448}</string>
        <key>NSNavPanelExpandedSizeForSaveMode</key>
        <string>{712, 448}</string>
        <key>NSSplitView Subview Frames AMDocumentMajor</key>
        <array>
                <string>0.000000, 0.000000, 381.000000, 601.000000, NO, NO</stri
ng>
                <string>382.000000, 0.000000, 618.000000, 601.000000, NO, NO</st
/Users/johnny/Library/Preferences/com.apple.Automator.plist
```

The XML format is relatively easy to read. It includes normal text interspersed with text tags that define the data structure for the information. You can view the XML code of plain text–formatted property list files using any text-reading app.

If you need to edit a property list file, avoid using TextEdit, since it improperly formats any property list file that is saved as a binary. The most complete graphical app from Apple for editing property list files is Xcode. Xcode can decode binary property list files, and it enables you to view and edit any property list in an easy-to-read hierarchical format. You can get Xcode from the App Store.

Key	Type	Value	
com.apple.Automator.plist ⟩ No Selection			
▼ Root	Dictionary	(12 items)	
AMSuppressWarningForDestructiveAc...	Boolean	NO	↕
AMSuppressWarningOnRunForAMServ...	Boolean	NO	↕
NSNavLastRootDirectory	String	~/Library/Mobile Documents/com~apple~Automator/Documents	
NSNavLastUserSetHideExtensionButt...	Boolean	YES	↕
NSNavPanelExpandedSizeForOpenMo...	String	{712, 448}	
NSNavPanelExpandedSizeForSaveMode	String	{712, 448}	
▶ NSSplitView Subview Frames AMDocu...	Array	(2 items)	
▶ NSSplitView Subview Frames AMDocu...	Array	(2 items)	
▶ NSSplitView Subview Frames AMLibra...	Array	(2 items)	
▶ NSSplitView Subview Frames AMLibra...	Array	(2 items)	
▶ NSToolbar Configuration AMDocumen...	Dictionary	(4 items)	
NSWindow Frame AMDocument	String	0 154 1000 623 0 0 1280 777	

Avoid editing a property list file that is currently in use by a running app or process. The app or process might make a change to the file and save while you are editing it. If you need to edit a property list that may be in use, restart the cfprefsd process.

Troubleshoot App Resources

Rarely, corrupted app software and associated nonpreference resources cause app problems, because these file types rarely change after the initial app installation. Many apps use other resources, such as fonts, plug-ins, and keychains, from the local and user Library folders and items in the Application Support folder. After you locate the problem resource, remove or replace the corrupted resource and restart the app.

Corrupted resources in the user's home folder Library affect only that user, whereas corrupted resources in the local Library affect all users. Use this fact to narrow your search when looking for a corrupted resource. App and diagnostic report logs, covered earlier in this lesson, may tell you which resources the app was attempting to access when it crashed. Those resources should be your primary suspects.

If the app exhibits problems with only one user, try to locate the resource at the root of the problem in the user's Library folder. Start with the usual suspects. If you find a resource that you think could be causing the problem, move that resource out of the user's Library folder and restart the app. Some apps store resources in ~/Documents.

If you've determined that the app issue is persistent across all user accounts, start by reinstalling or upgrading to the latest version of the app. You will probably find that a newer version of the app is available—one that likely includes bug fixes. At the very least, by reinstalling you replace any potentially corrupted files that are part of the standard app. If you continue to experience problems after reinstalling the app, search through the local Library resources to find and remove or replace the corrupted resource.

If you discover a large number of corrupted files, this may indicate a much more serious file-system or storage hardware issue. Troubleshooting these items is covered in Lesson 11, "Manage File Systems and Storage."

Exercise 20.1
Force Apps to Quit

▶ **Prerequisites**

    ▶ You must have created the Johnny Appleseed account (Exercise 7.1, "Create a Standard User Account").

    ▶ You must have installed the Dead End app (Exercise 18.3, "Drag and Drop to Install an App").

In this exercise, you learn to assess when an app is unresponsive. You see how you can use Force Quit and Activity Monitor to force unresponsive apps to quit. You also learn how to manage background processes that stop running.

Force an App to Quit in the Dock

1   Log in as Johnny Appleseed.

2   Open the Dead End app you installed in Exercise 18.3.

    The primary purpose of Dead End is to become unresponsive. It gives you an opportunity to practice different ways to force an app to quit.

    Dead End opens a window with a "Download the Internet" button.

3   Click "Download the Internet."

    Dead End becomes unresponsive. After a few seconds you might see the wait cursor (a colored pinwheel). The wait cursor appears when you hover your mouse over the Dead End window or, if Dead End is in the foreground, the menu bar.

4   Control-click the Dead End icon in the Dock, and choose Force Quit from the short-cut menu. Or, you could click and hold the Dead End icon in the Dock and choose Force Quit from the menu.

If Force Quit doesn't appear in the menu, repeat step 4 or press and hold the Option key. When you press and hold the Option key, Quit changes to Force Quit, and you can choose it from the shortcut menu to force Dead End to quit.

Use the Force Quit Window

1   Open the Dead End app so you can try another way to force an app to quit.

     To open apps you used recently, click the Apple menu and choose Recent Items. By default, macOS remembers the last ten apps you opened.

2   Click "Download the Internet."

3   Press Option-Command-Escape to open the Force Quit Applications window.

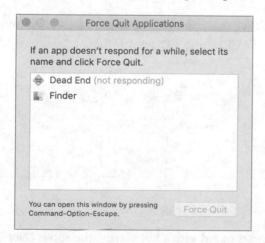

It takes about 15 seconds before Dead End is shown as "not responding."

4   Select Dead End, and click Force Quit.

5   In the confirmation dialog, click Force Quit.

6   If you are given the opportunity to send a report to Apple, click Ignore.

7   Close the Force Quit Applications window.

Practice Forcing an App to Quit with Activity Monitor

With Activity Monitor, you can force an app to quit, view running processes, gather information, and quit the processes.

1   Open Dead End.

2   Click "Download the Internet."

3   Open Activity Monitor (from the Utilities folder).

Even though the wait cursor appears in Dead End, you can make the Finder active or use Launchpad. An unresponsive app normally won't affect the rest of macOS.

Activity Monitor displays a list of running processes. When you open this window, it shows processes that you recognize as apps. It also shows processes that run in the background and that don't have a graphical user interface.

4   If necessary, click the CPU tab above the process list.

5   If the "% CPU" in the table header isn't selected, click it twice to get a top-down (most to least) list of processes in terms of their CPU usage. The arrow that appears next to "% CPU" should point down.

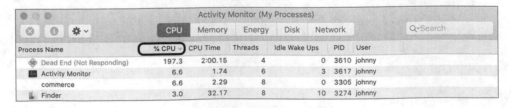

6   Look for the Dead End process by name. It should be at the top.

The name of an unresponsive app appears in red with a note saying the app is "Not Responding." As you look at the Dead End process, you see that the CPU usage is close to 200 percent. You see how an app can take over your CPU, even though the app isn't responding and seems to be doing nothing.

The % CPU statistic refers to the percentage of a CPU core being used. Current Mac computers have multiple cores and hyperthreading, so even "200%" CPU utilization isn't fully using the Mac computer's CPU power.

7 Choose Window > CPU Usage.

This opens a window that displays how many processor cores your Mac has and how busy each one is.

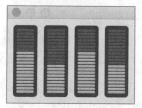

This example screenshot was taken on a Mac with two physical cores, but hyperthreading allows each of those to do two things at once, giving it four virtual cores. As you can see, 200 percent is only half what it is capable of.

8 Select Dead End in the process list and click the quit process button (its icon is an "X" in an octagon) on the toolbar.

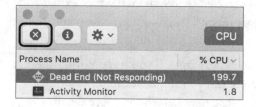

9 When asked to confirm, click Force Quit.

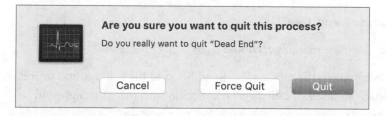

Quit is the default option in the dialog that appears. Since Dead End isn't responding, it won't respond to a normal Quit command. You must use Force Quit to stop the process.

Dead End disappears from the process list in the Activity Monitor window and from the Dock. After a few seconds, the CPU Usage window updates to show that utilization has decreased.

Unlike with the Dock and Force Quit Applications window, you can use Activity Monitor to force background processes to quit. Background processes are generally programs that start automatically. Normally, you won't have to manage them, but in a few cases forcing them to quit is useful.

10 Select SystemUIServer in the process list. You can use the Search field in the upper right of the window. The process ID (PID) number appears in a column to the right.

SystemUIServer manages the menu bar items on the right side of the menu bar. Each menu bar item runs as a plug-in inside SystemUIServer, and if one of them locks up, you might need to force SystemUIServer to quit.

11 With SystemUIServer selected, click the quit process ("X") button, and then watch the right side of the menu bar as you click Force Quit.

The right side of the menu bar goes blank, and the menu bar items reappear. Examine your process list. SystemUIServer is running but with a different process ID. The launchd process (a background process) detected that SystemUIServer exited and relaunched it. launchd starts and monitors many background processes and restarts them if necessary.

You can't force quit all processes this way. For example, if you force WindowServer (a system process) to quit, you immediately end your login session. Lesson 28, "Troubleshoot Startup and System Issues," discusses launchd in more detail.

12 Leave Activity Monitor open for the next section.

View System Processes and Use

1 From the Activity Monitor menu bar, choose View > All Processes.

You see processes appear in the process list. In addition to the background processes in your user session (sometimes called *agents*), macOS runs many background processes (sometimes called *daemons*) outside your login session.

2   At the top of the Activity Monitor window, switch through the CPU, Memory, Energy, Disk, and Network buttons, and look at the information for each process and the statistics at the bottom of the window.

3   If you are continuing to Exercise 20.2, leave Activity Monitor open.

Exercise 20.2
Troubleshoot Preferences

▶ **Prerequisite**

   ▶   You must have created the Johnny Appleseed account (Exercise 7.1, "Create a Standard User Account").

Most app preferences are created and stored for users in their personal Library folder. This helps when you troubleshoot app issues. In this exercise, you learn how to set and restore a preference and see the effect of moving a preference file out of the ~/Library folder.

Create and Locate Preview Preferences

1   Log in as Johnny Appleseed.

2   Open Preview from the Applications folder.

3   If you are prompted to open a file from iCloud, click Cancel.

4   Choose Preview > Preferences (or press Command-Comma) to open the Preview preferences window.

5   Select Images in the toolbar.

   The default setting for "When opening files" is "Open groups of files in the same window."

6   Select "Open all files in one window."

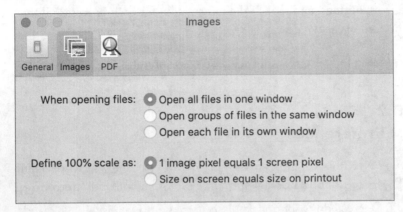

7   Close the Preferences window, and quit Preview.

8   Because the Finder normally hides the ~/Library folder, press and hold the Option key, and choose Go > Library to view the Library folder.

Preview is a sandboxed app, so its real preference file isn't in the ~/Library/ Preferences folder—it's in a sandbox container. See Reference 15.1, "macOS File Resources," for more details about sandbox containers.

9   In the ~/Library folder, open the Containers folder and then the com.apple.Preview folder.

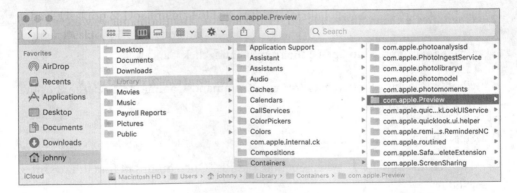

The com.apple.Preview folder contains a Data subfolder, with a structure that mirrors your home folder. Most of its contents are aliases that point to what they represent.

10 Navigate to Data/Library/Preferences, and select the com.apple.Preview.plist file.

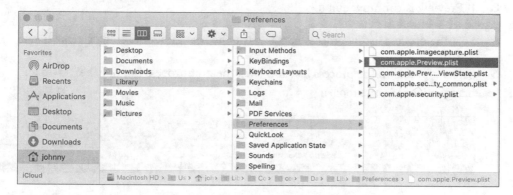

11 Use Quick Look (or press Command-Y) to view the preference file contents.

The preferences setting you made is listed in XML.

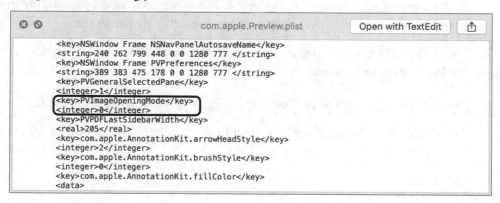

12 Close the Quick Look window.

Disable and Restore Preferences

When you move an app preferences file, you don't always reset its preferences. The preferences agent (cfprefsd) might cache old settings. To make sure the preferences reset, quit the program and the preferences agent, and move the file.

1   Open Activity Monitor.

2   From the Activity Monitor menu bar, choose View > My Processes.

3   If Preview is running, quit it.

4   Sort the process list by process name or use the Search field to find cfprefsd.

5   Select cfprefsd in the process list, and click the quit process button (the "X" in an octagon icon) in the toolbar.

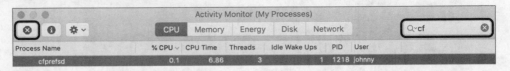

6   In the confirmation dialog, click Quit.

Since the process is responding normally, you don't have to use Force Quit.

A new cfprefsd process starts when needed. This sometimes happens so quickly that you might not see it before it disappears from the Activity Monitor list.

7   Switch to the Finder, and drag the com.apple.Preview.plist file to your desktop. Leave the Preferences folder open.

8   Open Preview, and choose Preview > Preferences (or press Command-Comma).

The setting for "When opening files" reset to its default of "Open groups of files in the same window."

9   Quit Preview.

10   Switch back to Activity Monitor, and quit cfprefsd.

11   In the Finder, move the com.apple.Preview.plist file from your desktop back to the Preferences folder.

12 If you are notified that a newer item named com.apple.Preview.plist already exists, click Replace.

13 Open Preview preferences.

This time your custom preference setting ("Open all files in one window") is restored.

14 Quit Preview.

Manage Corrupted Preferences

macOS has built-in features for dealing with corrupted preference files. In this exercise, you explore what happens when a preference file is corrupted.

1 Use Activity Monitor to quit cfprefsd.

2 In the Finder, Control-click the com.apple.Preview.plist file, and choose Open With > TextEdit from the shortcut menu.

Some plist files are stored in an XML or text format, which you can edit like other text documents. This plist file is stored in a binary format, so you see only part of the file contents.

```
com.apple.Preview.plist
bplist00fl



!"#$%&&()*+(,-._!com.apple.AnnotationKit.fillColor_*NSToolbar Configuration
CommonToolbar_v5.1_0NSSplitView Subview Frames
NSColorPanelSplitView_com.apple.AnnotationKit.font_+com.apple.AnnotationKit.userDefaultsVe
rsion_PVPDFLastSidebarWidth_!
NSNavPanelExpandedSizeForOpenMode_&com.apple.AnnotationKit.textAttributes_PVGeneralSelecte
```

3 Add some new text in the document.

4 Quit TextEdit.

Changes are saved automatically.

5 Try to view the file using Quick Look. Select the file and press Command-Y.

When you edit the file as if it were plain text, you damage its binary structure. As a result, Quick Look can't display its contents and shows a generic view.

6   Close the Quick Look window.

7   Reopen Preview, and open its preferences.

Since the preferences file is damaged, macOS reset it, and the setting for "When opening files" reset to its default "Open groups of files in the same window."

8   Quit Preview, Activity Monitor, and other apps that are open.

9   Log out as Johnny Appleseed.

Exercise 20.3
Examine App Diagnostics

> **Prerequisites**
>
> ▶   You must have created the Local Administrator (Exercise 3.1, "Configure a Mac for Exercises") and Johnny Appleseed (Exercise 7.1, "Create a Standard User Account") accounts.
>
> ▶   You must have installed and forced the Dead End app to quit (Exercise 18.3, "Drag and Drop to Install an App," and Exercise 20.1, "Force Apps to Quit").

In this exercise, you use Console to view diagnostic logs and to search the system log for app events.

View System Activity

1   If necessary, log out as Johnny Appleseed.

2   Log in as Local Administrator.

The log files you examine in this exercise are readable only by administrators.

3   Open Console.

4   Select your Mac in the Devices section of the sidebar.

5   In the toolbar, make sure that Now is selected and Activities isn't selected.

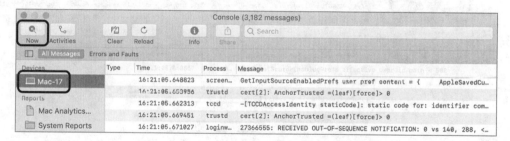

This view shows background events as they happen.

6   Select an event.

7   Select Info in the toolbar.

Details about the event are shown in the pane below the event list.

Gather Information about the Dead End App

1   In the toolbar, make sure that Now isn't selected.

2   In the Reports section of the sidebar, select "Mac Analytics Data" (the full name isn't visible).

3   In the Search field, enter **dead end** and press the Return key (the app you used in Exercise 20.1).

4   If necessary, scroll to the top of the message list.

If you performed Exercise 18.3 within the last few days, the first few messages relate to the first time you ran Dead End. The app was initially denied by Gatekeeper, but when you overrode Gatekeeper a rule was added that allows it to run.

5   If there are "assessment denied" messages, select one.

Message details include the app bundle ID (com.apple.training.Dead-End) and the reason access was denied ("no usable signature," because the app is not code-signed).

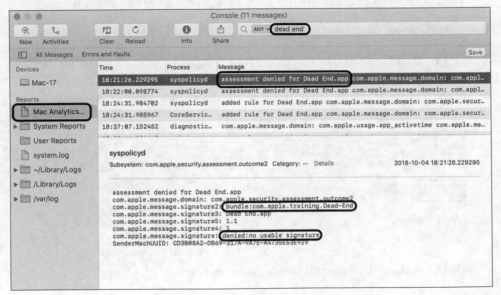

6   Click the Now button in the toolbar to show the latest messages.

The more recent messages relate to Dead End hanging or using excessive CPU time.

7   Select recent messages and examine their details.

Some of the messages from the spindump process will include the domain "com.apple.crashreporter.writereport.cpu_resource.diag," which means that spindump wrote a report with details of Dead End's status because it wasn't responding. You view these reports in this exercise.

Although you see messages relating to Dead End hanging, you don't see anything about it being force-quit. To see that, you must look in a different place.

8 In the Console sidebar, select "system.log."

9 In the Search field, enter **dead end**.

Here you also see messages relating to spindump saving reports about Dead End, but nothing about Dead End being force-quit. There are messages in this log about it being force-quit, but they don't identify the app by its name. Rather, they identify the app by its bundle ID (com.apple.training.Dead-End).

You probably have to look through multiple logs and perform multiple searches to find relevant messages for a problem or event.

10 Change the Search field to **dead-end** and press the Return key.

You see messages about the Dead End app being force-quit, and in each case showing which other process performed the force-quit.

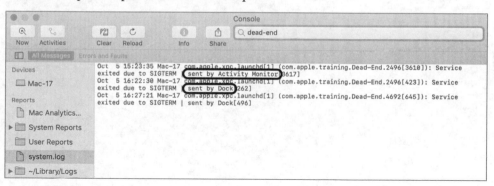

11 In the sidebar, select System Reports.

A second column opens and lists log files in this category. Unlike other logs you've seen so far, which list event sequences, each of these files contains a detailed report about a single event.

12 In the second column, select one of the log files that starts "Dead End."

13 Erase the contents of the Search field to show the file contents.

Each file shows that macOS detected a problem with Dead End (hanging, using excessive CPU resources, or both). The files give details about what was happening inside Dead End, and list related processes and what they were doing.

14 Quit Console and log out as Local Administrator.

Network Configuration

Lesson 21

Manage Basic Network Settings

In this lesson, you learn about networking concepts and configure settings for Ethernet and Wi-Fi networks.

Reference 21.1
Network Terminology

There are three basic networking elements: the network interface, network protocols, and network service.

Data flows through the network interface. Network interfaces can be physical or virtual. The most common physical network interfaces are Ethernet and 802.11 wireless (called Wi-Fi). You can use virtual network interfaces to increase the functionality of the physical interface. For example, a virtual private network (VPN) uses the existing physical network interface to provide a secure connection without the need for a dedicated physical interface.

A network protocol defines a set of standard rules used for data representation, signaling, authentication, or error detection across network interfaces. Protocols ensure that data is communicated properly. Specific protocols have a narrow focus, so often multiple protocols are combined or layered to provide a complete network solution. For example, the combined TCP/IP protocol suite provides addressing and end-to-end transport of data across the Internet.

In Network preferences, "network service" describes a configuration assigned to a network interface. For example, you might see the Wi-Fi service listed. This represents the connection settings for the Wi-Fi network interface. macOS supports multiple network services, or connections, for each physical or virtual network interface.

> **NOTE ▶** A different definition of network service is used in Lesson 24, "Manage Network Services," and Lesson 25, "Manage Host Sharing and Personal Firewall." In those lessons, a network service is information provided on the network by a server for use by clients.

MAC Addresses

A media access control (MAC) address is used to identify a physical network interface on a local network. Each physical network interface has at least one MAC address associated with it.

Because the most common network interface is Ethernet, people often refer to MAC addresses as Ethernet addresses. Nearly every other network interface type also uses some type of MAC address for unique identification. This includes, but isn't limited to, Wi-Fi, Bluetooth, and Thunderbolt.

A MAC address is usually a 48-bit number represented by six groups of two-digit hexadecimal numbers separated by colons. For example, a typical MAC address looks like this: 00:1C:B3:D7:2F:99. The first three number groups make up the organizationally unique identifier (OUI), and the last three number groups identify the network device. You can use the first three number groups of a MAC address to identify who made the network device.

IP Addresses

An Internet Protocol (IP) address identifies each computer across the Internet or a network. You need an IP address to communicate with Mac computers on local and remote networks. IP addresses, unlike MAC addresses, aren't permanently tied to a network interface. They are assigned to the network interface based on the local network they're connected to. This means that if you have a portable Mac, every new network you connect to probably requires a new IP address. You can assign multiple IP addresses to each network interface, but this approach is often only used for Mac computers that are providing network services.

IPv4 and IPv6 are the two standards for IP addresses. IPv4 is the most commonly used today. An IPv4 address is a 32-bit number represented by four groups of three-digit numbers, also known as octets, separated by periods. Each octet has a value between 0 and 255. For example, a typical IPv4 address would look something like this: 10.1.45.186. If you received an IP address that's a longer series of numbers and letters, divided by seven colons (for example, fa80:0000:0000:0123:0203:93ee:ef5b:44a0), then it's a different type of IP address, called IPv6.

Subnet Masks

A Mac uses the subnet mask to determine the IPv4 address range of the local network. Networks based on the IPv6 protocol don't require subnet masks. A subnet mask is similar to an IPv4 address in that it's a 32-bit number arranged in four groups of octets. The Mac applies the subnet mask to its own IP address to determine the local network address range. The nonzero bits in a subnet mask (typically 255) correspond to the portion of the IP address that determines which network the address is on. The zero bits correspond to the portion of the IP address that differs between hosts on the same network.

For example, assuming your Mac has an IP address of 10.1.5.3 and a commonly used subnet mask of 255.255.255.0, the local network is defined as hosts that have IP addresses ranging from 10.1.5.1 to 10.1.5.254.

Another way of writing the subnet mask is known as Classless Inter-Domain Routing (CIDR) notation. This is written as the IP address, a slash, and then the number of bits in the subnet mask. The previous subnet example would be 10.1.5.3/24.

Whenever a Mac attempts to communicate with another network device, it applies the subnet mask to the destination IP address of the other device to determine whether it's on the local network too. If so, the Mac attempts to directly access the other network device. If not, the other device is clearly on another network, and the Mac sends all communications bound for that other device to the router address.

Router Addresses

Routers manage connections between separate networks. They route network traffic between the networks they bridge. To reach a networked device beyond the local network, your Mac must be configured with the IP address of the router that connects the local network with another network or an Internet service provider. Typically, a router address is at the beginning of the local address range, and it's always in the same subnet.

TCP

The Transmission Control Protocol (TCP) facilitates end-to-end data connectivity between two IP devices. TCP is the preferred transport mechanism for many Internet services because it guarantees reliable and in-order data delivery.

Reference 21.2
Network Activity

You assign an IP address, a subnet mask, and a router address to configure a Mac to use TCP/IP-based networking on both local area networks (LANs) and WANs. Two network services are almost always involved in basic network functionality: Dynamic Host Configuration Protocol (DHCP) and the Domain Name System (DNS). These two services, combined with TCP/IP, characterize core network functionality that provides the foundation for nearly any network service.

LAN Traffic

Most LANs use some form of wired or wireless connection. After the network interface is established, you must configure TCP/IP networking, either manually or with DHCP. Then network communication can begin.

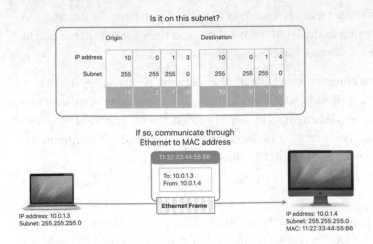

TCP/IP packets are encased inside Ethernet frames to travel across the local network. The TCP/IP packet includes the originating IP and destination IP addresses along with the data to be sent. The network device applies the subnet mask setting to determine whether the destination IP address is on the local network. If so, it consults its Address Resolution

Protocol (ARP) table to see whether it knows the MAC address corresponding to the destination IP address. Each network host maintains and continuously updates an ARP table of known MAC addresses that correspond to IP addresses on the local network. If the MAC address is not listed yet, it broadcasts an ARP request to the local network asking the destination device to reply with its MAC address and adds the reply to its ARP table for next time. Once the MAC address is determined, an outgoing Ethernet frame, encasing the TCP/IP packet, is sent using the destination MAC address.

WAN Traffic

When you send data over a WAN, it's sent through one or more network routers to reach the destination. You can use a router with Network Address Translation (NAT). This enables you to use one real-world IP address as the external interface for your router, and internally you can use private IP addresses. Private IP address ranges are 10.0.0.0–10.255.255.255, 172.16.0.0–172.31.255.255, and 192.168.0.0–192.168.255.255.

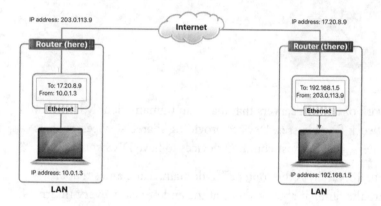

Transferring data across a WAN is similar to transferring data on a LAN. The first stop for the data destined for the WAN is at the network router on the local network. The network device prepares the packets as before by encasing the TCP/IP packets inside Ethernet frames. The subnet mask is applied to the destination IP address to determine whether the address is on the local network. In this case, the network device determines that the destination isn't on the local network, so it sends the data to the router. Because the router is on the local network, the transmission between the local network client and the router is identical to standard LAN traffic.

After the router receives the Ethernet-encased TCP/IP packets, it examines the destination IP address and uses a routing table to determine the next closest destination for this packet. This almost always involves sending the packet to another router closer to the destination. In fact, only the last router in the path sends the data to the destination network device.

In most cases, network data is transferred back and forth several times to establish a complete connection. Network routers handle thousands of data packets every second.

DNS

Even the simplest mobile phones feature a contact list so that users don't have to remember phone numbers. For TCP/IP networks, the Domain Name System (DNS) makes network addressing easier by enabling you to use a name instead of an IP address.

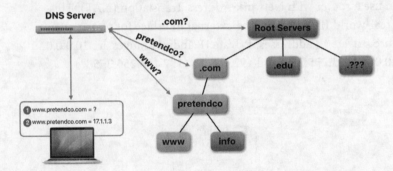

DNS is a worldwide network of domain servers that maintain human-friendly host names that are used to locate network IP addresses. Devices providing shared services, such as printers and server computers, are the most common devices to have DNS entries.

The top of the DNS naming hierarchy is the root, or " . " domain. The names that are part of the root domain are the familiar abbreviations at the end of nearly every Internet resource.

When a local network device needs to resolve a DNS name into the corresponding IP address, it sends the name query to the IP address of a DNS server. The IP address for a DNS server is usually configured along with the other TCP/IP address information for the network device. The DNS server searches its local and cached name records first. If the requested name isn't found locally, the server queries other domain servers in the DNS hierarchy.

Bonjour is a name discovery service that uses a name space similar to DNS. Bonjour is covered in Lesson 24, "Manage Network Services."

DHCP

The Dynamic Host Configuration Protocol (DHCP) is used by most network clients to automatically acquire preliminary TCP/IP configuration. DHCP assigns IPv4 addressing.

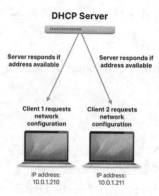

Reference 21.3
Configure Basic Network Settings

Use Network preferences to configure basic network settings. You must have an administrator user account to do so.

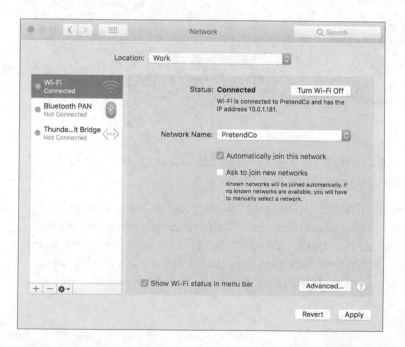

Configure Network Settings

You can configure your network address and settings in two ways:

▶ Automatically—Your Mac is assigned an address using DHCP.

▶ Manually—Your ISP or network administrator gives you an IP address, and you enter it in Network preferences.

Advanced network configuration techniques are covered in Lesson 22, "Manage Advanced Network Settings."

DHCP

When your Mac makes a DHCP request, if a DHCP server that is listening has an available IPv4 address, it sends configuration information to your Mac. This information usually includes an IPv4 address, a subnet mask, a router, which DNS servers to use, and a DHCP lease time that defines how long the client can retain the address before it's given away.

If there's no DHCP reply, your Mac generates a random self-assigned address and then checks the local network to make sure that no other network device is using that address. A self-assigned address always starts with 169.254, with a subnet mask of 255.255.0.0. The following figure shows a self-assigned IP address and the message that this Mac won't be able to connect to the Internet.

Select Wi-Fi Networks

Wireless networking, or Wi-Fi, is also known by the technical specification 802.11. It allows easy network access for portable devices.

By default, macOS remembers Wi-Fi networks it previously joined. If you start up or wake your Mac, it attempts to locate and reconnect to any previously connected Wi-Fi networks. If your Mac doesn't find an appropriate Wi-Fi network, you must choose a new one from the Wi-Fi status menu near the upper-right corner of the display. When you select this menu, macOS scans for advertised networks that are within range so you can select one.

A service set identifier (SSID) identifies a Wi-Fi network name and associated configuration information. A Wi-Fi administrator sets the network name and configuration settings. macOS uses the information in the SSID configuration to establish Wi-Fi network communications.

Aside from Wi-Fi network names, this menu displays the relative strength of a Wi-Fi network. The more black bars displayed, the greater the Wi-Fi signal strength.

Authenticate to Wi-Fi Networks

If you select an open wireless network, the Mac immediately connects to it, but if you select a secure wireless network, indicated by the lock icon, you have to enter the network password. When you select a secure network, macOS automatically negotiates the authentication type, and for many networks you need only enter a common shared Wi-Fi password.

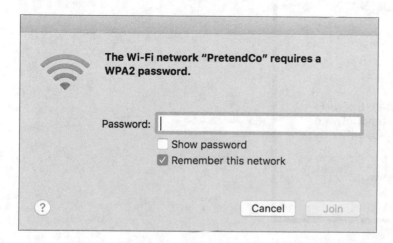

If you're logged in with your iCloud account, the dialog is slightly different. It shows that you can also access this Wi-Fi network by bringing your Mac near any iPhone, iPad, or Mac that is connected to this network and has you in its contacts.

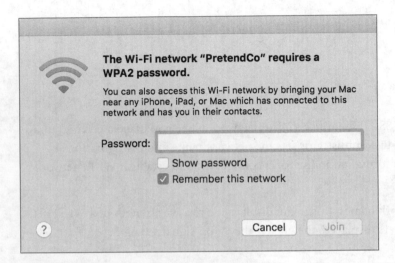

Here's an example of what your contact sees on an iPhone:

macOS supports the most common Wi-Fi authentication standards, including Wired Equivalent Privacy (WEP), Wi-Fi Protected Access (WPA), and Wi-Fi Protected Access II (WPA2). This includes support for WPA/WPA2 in both their personal and enterprise forms. Essentially, WPA/WPA2 Personal uses a common shared password for all users of the Wi-Fi network, whereas WPA/WPA2 Enterprise includes 802.1X authentication, which allows for per-user password access to the Wi-Fi network. WPA/WPA2 Enterprise authentication is covered in the next section of this lesson.

If you join a WEP or WPA/WPA2 Personal Wi-Fi network, macOS automatically saves the passwords to the System keychain. This is what allows the Mac to automatically reconnect to the Wi-Fi network immediately after startup or waking up. This enables all users to access the wireless network when they log in, without needing to reenter the network password. Details of the Keychain system are covered in Lesson 9, "Manage Security and Privacy."

Authenticate to Automatic WPA Enterprise Networks

If you join and authenticate to a wireless network that uses WPA or WPA2 Enterprise, authentication is handled with 802.1X.

When you use 802.1X, you must provide your credentials to authenticate the connection. User name and password is a common credential, but some implementations allow you to provide a digital certificate instead.

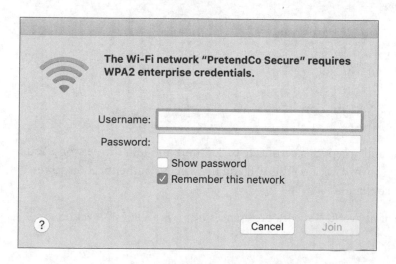

You might also be prompted with a server certificate verification dialog.

Click Show Certificate to display information about the certificate.

You must click Continue and accept this certificate to continue and join the network. You must also provide your password because this will add the wireless authentication server certificate to your login keychain.

After you join this type of network, Network preferences displays an 802.1X section for the network interface.

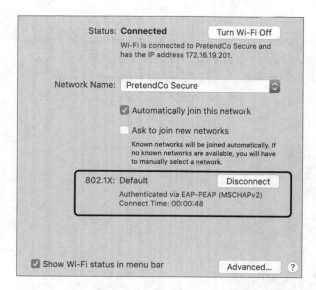

See Reference 22.5, "Configure Advanced Network Settings," for more information about configuring 802.1X settings, including using a configuration profile so that each user doesn't need to separately accept the certificate.

Join Hidden Wi-Fi Networks

In some cases, wireless networks might not advertise their availability. You can connect to these hidden wireless networks (also called closed networks) as long as you know their network name (or SSID) by choosing Join Other Network from the Wi-Fi status menu. In the dialog, you can enter all the appropriate information to join the hidden wireless network. For more information, read Apple Support article HT203211, "AirPort: Unable to join a Wi-Fi network with hidden SSID (Wi-Fi network name)."

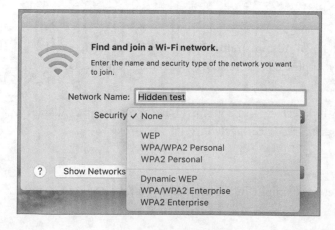

Create an Ad Hoc Wi-Fi Network

If there's no Wi-Fi network available, you can create an ad hoc wireless network to share services wirelessly with other computers. Choose Create Network from the Wi-Fi status menu and then enter the wireless network name that will be used to connect to your ad hoc network. Other devices will select this name to join your Mac computer's Wi-Fi network.

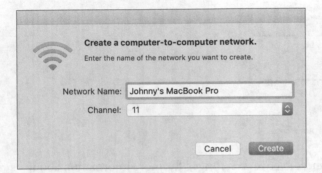

To prevent other devices from connecting to the ad hoc network, turn off the Wi-Fi hardware or choose another wireless network from the Wi-Fi status menu.

To share files with another Mac computer or iOS device, consider using the macOS AirDrop Wi-Fi sharing feature instead of creating an ad hoc Wi-Fi network. You can find out more about AirDrop in Lesson 25, "Manage Host Sharing and Personal Firewall."

Exercise 21.1
Connect to a Wi-Fi Network

▶ **Prerequisites**

    ► You must have created the Local Administrator (Exercise 3.1, "Configure a Mac for Exercises") and Johnny Appleseed (Exercise 7.1, "Create a Standard User Account") accounts.

    ► Your Mac must have a Wi-Fi interface, and you must have access to an available Wi-Fi network that you aren't already connected to.

macOS makes joining a wireless network simple. In this exercise, you find and join a wireless network.

Verify Your Network Settings

1 Log in as Johnny Appleseed.

2 Open Network Preferences.

3 Click the padlock, and authenticate as Local Administrator.

4 Select the Wi-Fi service from the sidebar.

If you don't have Wi-Fi service, you can't perform this exercise.

5 If necessary, click the Turn Wi-Fi On button.

6 If necessary, select "Show Wi-Fi status in menu."

7 Click Advanced.

8 Examine the options available on the Wi-Fi pane.

9 If you are currently connected to PretendCo, select it and click the Remove (–) button to remove it from your Preferred Networks list.

The Preferred Networks list enables you to control which networks a Mac joins automatically or manually, and it includes an option to add networks to the list as your Mac joins them. You can also control whether administrator authorization is required to change certain configuration settings.

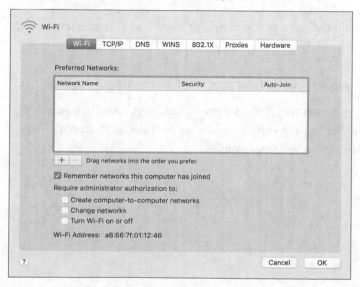

10 Click OK.

11 If you made changes, click Apply.

If you removed a Wi-Fi network, your Mac disconnects.

12 Click the Wi-Fi status menu.

A list of visible networks in your area is shown. It may take a few seconds for your Mac to discover all local networks.

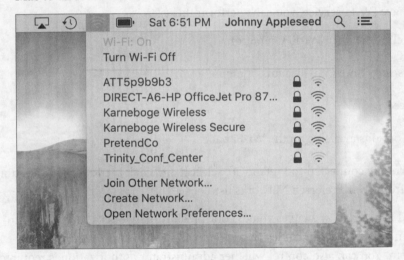

This list is also available in Network preferences, in the Network Name pop-up menu.

Your facilitator will give you the name of the network to join and, if necessary, security information for it.

1 Choose the network you want to join from the Wi-Fi status menu.

If the wireless network is encrypted, you are prompted for the network password. Selecting the "Remember this network" option allows your Mac to automatically reconnect to this network whenever it's available.

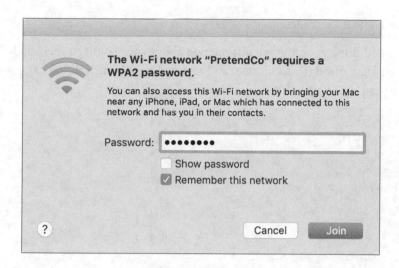

2   If you are prompted, enter the network password, and click Join.

Verify Your Connection

If macOS detects that the wireless network you joined is connected to a captive portal, it opens a window showing the portal sign-in page.

1   If a captive portal window appears, follow its instructions to get full network access. A captive portal might require you to agree to its terms of service, authenticate, watch an advertisement, or meet other requirements before it allows you full network access.

2   If you are not connected the the PretendCo Wi-Fi network, reconnect to it by choosing Wi-Fi status > PretendCo.

3   In Network preferences, look at the status indicator next to the Wi-Fi service.

The status indicator is green if your Mac is connected to a network and has address information configured. If the indicator isn't green, you didn't successfully join the network and you might have to troubleshoot the connection.

4   Click the Wi-Fi status menu.

It shows arcs to indicate the signal strength of the wireless network. If all the arcs are light gray, you aren't joined to a wireless network or are receiving a weak signal.

5 Option-click the Wi-Fi status menu.

The menu opens and displays additional information about your connection, including the current wireless speed (transmit rate) and received signal strength indicator (RSSI: –50 is a strong signal and –100 is a weak one).

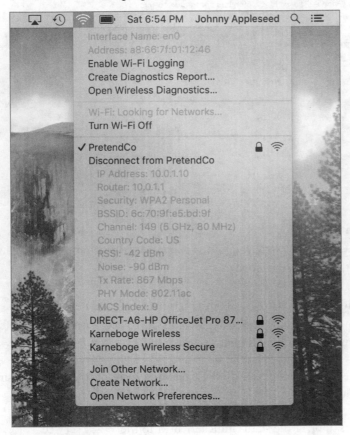

Exercise 21.2
Monitor Network Connectivity

▶ **Prerequisite**

▶ You must have created the Johnny Appleseed account (Exercise 7.1, "Create a Standard User Account").

In this exercise, you break your primary network connection and observe how Network preferences tracks the break. Network Status updates as network connectivity changes, so you can use it to troubleshoot connectivity issues.

Monitor Connectivity Using Network Preferences

The Network Status view of Network preferences shows the status of active configured network interfaces. User-initiated connections, such as VPN, are also listed. View the Network Status pane to verify active connections in order of priority.

1 Log in as Johnny Appleseed.

2 Open System Preferences, and click Network.

The status of your network connections is shown on the left side of the window. The green status indicators show which network services are active, and their order shows their priority. The service at the top of the list is your current primary service, and it's used for all Internet connectivity. Record which service is currently the primary service.

If you don't have services with green status indicators, you don't have a network connection and you can't perform this exercise.

3 Select the current primary service.

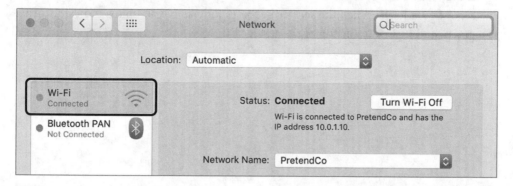

4 Watch the status indicators and service order as you disable the connection for your primary network service. How you do this depends on what type of service it is:

▶ If it is an Ethernet service, unplug the Ethernet cable from your Mac.

▶ If it is a Wi-Fi service, click the Turn Wi-Fi Off button.

When the service is disabled, its status indicator turns red or yellow, and it drops down in the service order. If you have another active service, it becomes the new primary service.

The detailed view on the right changes to indicate why the service is disabled.

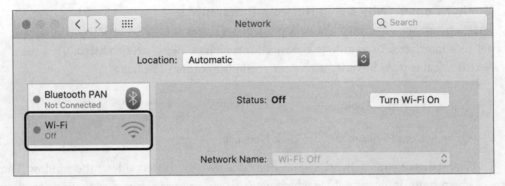

5   Watch the status indicators and service order as you reenable the connection. How you do this depends on what type of service it is:

▶   If it is an Ethernet service, plug the Ethernet cable back into your Mac.

▶   If it is a Wi-Fi service, click the Turn Wi-Fi On button, and if necessary, choose the network from the Network Name pop-up menu.

It may take a few seconds for the network connection to appear and the service to reconfigure itself. When the service becomes fully active, its status indicator turns green, and it rises to the top of the service list.

Lesson 22

Manage Advanced Network Settings

In this lesson, you learn about the macOS network configuration architecture and supported network interfaces and protocols. Then you explore advanced network configuration options.

Reference 22.1
Manage Network Locations

When you need to manually configure your network settings, you can save network settings to network locations, and then change between the locations. A network location contains network interface, service, and protocol settings. This enables you to configure unique network locations for different situations. For example, you could create one network location for home and a different one for work. Each location would contain the appropriate settings for that location's network state.

A network location can contain numerous active network service interfaces. This enables you to define a single location with multiple network connections. macOS prioritizes multiple service interfaces based on a service order that you set ("TB Bridge" stands for "Thunderbolt Bridge," discussed later in this lesson).

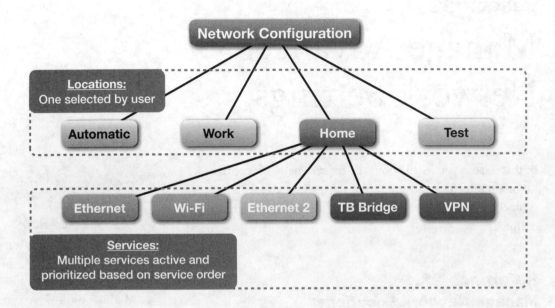

Configure Network Locations

The default network location in macOS is called Automatic.

To configure network locations:

1   Open System Preferences with Spotlight or by choosing Apple menu > System Preferences.

2   Click the Network icon.

3   You may have to click the lock icon in the lower-left corner and authenticate as an administrator user to unlock Network preferences.

4   Choose Edit Locations from the Location menu to reveal the interface for editing network locations.

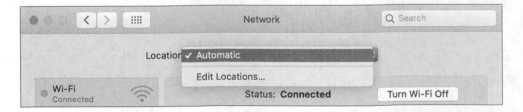

To add a new location with default settings, click the Add (+) button and then enter a new name for the location. Or you can duplicate an existing location by choosing its name from the Locations list, clicking the Action button (gear icon), and then choosing Duplicate Location from the menu. Double-click a location name to rename it.

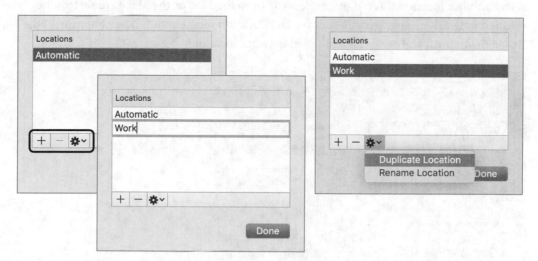

When you are done making location changes, click Done to return to Network preferences. Network preferences loads the newly created location but won't apply the location settings to macOS. To edit another location, choose it from the Location menu, and Network preferences loads it but won't apply it to macOS.

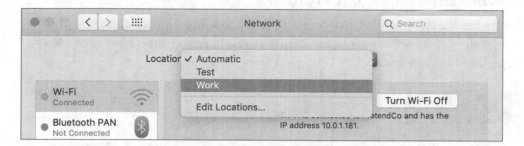

Network settings are different from other preferences in that you must click Apply to activate the new settings. This enables you to easily prepare new network locations and services without disrupting the current network configuration.

Select a Network Location

All users can change the network location by choosing Apple menu > Location > *location name*. This applies the selected network location. Changing locations might interrupt network connections. After you select a network location, it remains active until you select another location. Even if other users log in to the Mac or the Mac is restarted, the selected network location remains active. The Location menu option doesn't appear in the Apple menu until you create an additional network location.

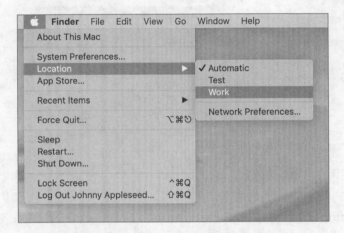

Reference 22.2
Network Interfaces and Protocols

Identify the hardware network service interfaces available to your Mac with System Information or Network Utility. Many of these interfaces appear as a network service in Network preferences.

The newest hardware interface on Mac computers is Thunderbolt 3, a high-speed connection technology. Thunderbolt is flexible, allowing for a variety of adapters, such as the Thunderbolt-to–Gigabit Ethernet adapter and a Thunderbolt-to-FireWire adapter.

NOTE ▶ You can read more about Thunderbolt 3 and USB-3, which use the same port shape and style, in Reference 26.1, "Peripheral Technologies."

macOS includes built-in support for the following hardware network interfaces:

▶ Bluetooth—This relatively low-speed wireless interface is a short-range connectivity standard. Every Mac that includes Wi-Fi support also includes Bluetooth. macOS supports Bluetooth as a network bridge to some mobile phones and hotspots, like iPhone, that can provide Internet connectivity through a cellular network.

▶ Ethernet—Ethernet is the family of IEEE 802.3 standards that define most modern wired local area networks (LANs).

▶ FireWire—FireWire is standard on many older Mac models. You can create small ad hoc networks between Mac computers that have FireWire ports by daisy-chaining them together with FireWire cables.

▶ Thunderbolt Bridge—You can create small ad hoc networks using daisy-chained Thunderbolt cables.

▶ USB—Although USB is not technically a network connectivity standard, macOS supports a variety of USB adapters for Ethernet and adapters that provide Internet access through cellular networks. Many modern phones feature a "tethering" service that provides Internet access through a USB connection to the phone.

▶ Wi-Fi—Wi-Fi is the more common name for the family of IEEE 802.11 wireless standards, which have become the default implementation for most wireless LANs. Every currently shipping Mac supports Wi-Fi.

Cellular Internet Connections

Many devices and methods are available for providing cellular Internet access. macOS supports use of cellular Internet connections with:

▶ Bluetooth personal area network (PAN)—Many current cellular devices allow for Internet connectivity by acting as a small router providing a PAN available through Bluetooth wireless. For example, an iPhone can provide Internet access through Bluetooth PAN. As with any Bluetooth device, you must first pair your Mac with the mobile device, as covered in Lesson 26, "Troubleshoot Peripherals." Once the two are paired, configuration should be automatic—the Mac should configure networking using DHCP hosted from the cellular device. You have to initiate the connection by clicking the Connect button in Network preferences or by choosing the device and clicking "Connect to Network" in the Bluetooth status menu.

▶ USB cellular network adapters—macOS supports many USB adapters and tethered phones that provide cellular Internet access. iPhone is an example, and configuration on the Mac is automatic. If tethering is available on your mobile phone data plan, first connect your iPhone to your Mac with a USB cable; then on your iPhone turn on the Personal Hotspot feature. Third-party cellular Internet devices vary, and many require the installation and configuration of third-party drivers.

▶ Wi-Fi PAN—Many cellular devices can act as a small Wi-Fi access point. On any iOS device that supports cellular connections, you can enable Personal Hotspot for Wi-Fi. Select the Wi-Fi network the iOS device is hosting and provide authentication, if necessary. You can take advantage of Handoff to automatically authenticate to an iOS device's personal hotspot service. This automatic authentication requires that Handoff is enabled and that you are signed in to iCloud on both devices.

Virtual Network Services

A virtual network service is a logical network within a hardware network interface. A virtual network service provides another network interface by carving out a section of an established network connection.

Some virtual network services are used to increase security by encrypting data before it travels across an IP network, and others are used to segregate or aggregate network traffic across LAN connections. macOS includes client software that enables you to connect to many common virtual network services and establish a virtual network service interface.

If necessary, you can define multiple separate virtual network service interfaces for each network location. Virtual network service interfaces are not always tied to a specific physical network interface; macOS attempts to seek out the most appropriate route when multiple active connections are available. Likewise, any virtual network service interface that is not destined for a LAN connection is always routed to the primary active network service interface.

Third-party virtualization tools, like Parallels Desktop and VMware Fusion, also use virtual network interfaces to provide networking for multiple simultaneous operating systems.

macOS includes built-in support for the following virtual network services:

▶ Point-to-Point Protocol over Ethernet (PPPoE)—This protocol is used by some service providers to directly connect your Mac to a modem providing a high-speed digital subscriber line (DSL) Internet connection.

▶ Virtual private network (VPN)—VPNs are primarily used to create secure virtual connections to private LANs over the Internet. Configuring VPN connections is detailed later in this lesson.

▶ Virtual local area network (VLAN)—The macOS VLAN implementation allows you to define separate independent LAN services on a single physical network interface.

▶ Link aggregate—This service enables you to define a single virtual LAN service using multiple physical network interfaces. macOS uses the standard Link Aggregation Control Protocol (LACP), also known as IEEE 802.3ad.

▶ 6to4—This service transfers IPv6 packets across an IPv4 network. There is no enhanced security when using a 6to4 connection, but your Mac will appear to be directly connected to a remote IPv6 LAN.

Network Protocols

Each network service interface provides connectivity for standard networking protocols. Network preferences show primary protocol settings whenever you select a service from the services list, but many protocol configuration options are available only when you click the Advanced button.

macOS includes built-in support for the following network protocols:

▶ TCP/IP configured with DHCP—TCP/IP (Transmission Control Protocol/Internet Protocol) is the primary network protocol for LANs and WANs, and DHCP (Dynamic Host Configuration Protocol) is a network service that configures TCP/IP clients.

▶ TCP/IP configured manually—If you do not have DHCP service on your local network, or if you want to ensure that the TCP/IP settings never change, you can manually configure TCP/IP settings.

▶ DNS—DNS (Domain Name Service) provides host names for IP network devices. DNS settings are often configured alongside TCP/IP settings either by DHCP or manual configuration. macOS supports multiple DNS servers and search domains.

▶ Wireless Ethernet (Wi-Fi) protocol options—The wireless nature of Wi-Fi often requires additional configuration to facilitate network selection and authentication.

▶ Authenticated Ethernet with 802.1X—The 802.1X protocol is used to secure Ethernet networks (both wired and Wi-Fi) by allowing only properly authenticated network clients to join the LAN.

▶ Network Basic Input/Output System (NetBIOS) and Windows Internet Naming Service (WINS)—NetBIOS and WINS are protocols used on Windows-based networks to provide network identification and service discovery.

▶ IP proxies—Proxy servers act as intermediaries between a network client and a requested service and are used to enhance performance or provide an additional layer of security and content filtering.

▶ Ethernet hardware options—macOS supports both automatic and manual Ethernet hardware configuration, as covered later in this lesson.

▶ External (analog) modem with PPP—macOS still supports this method, but since it is so rarely used in this age of broadband Internet, analog modem configuration isn't covered in this guide.

▶ Point-to-Point Protocol (PPP)—PPP is an older protocol originally intended for use with analog modems. macOS supports PPP for analog modems, but it also supports PPP for Bluetooth dial-up networking and PPPoE connectivity. PPP configuration isn't covered in this guide.

Reference 22.3
Manage Network Service Interfaces

Typically, having multiple active network service interfaces means you also have multiple active IP addresses. macOS supports IP network multihoming to handle multiple IP addresses, and it supports multiple IP addresses for each physical network interface.

Using Multiple Simultaneous Interfaces

You can have an active wired Ethernet connection and an active Wi-Fi connection at the same time.

You might have a work environment where you have one insecure network for general Internet traffic and another network for secure internal transactions. With macOS, you can be on both of these networks at the same time. However, the first fully configured active service in the list is the primary network service interface.

In most cases the primary network service interface is used for all WAN connectivity, Internet connectivity, and DNS host name resolution. The exception to this is when the primary network interface doesn't have a router configuration. In this case, macOS treats the next fully configured active service as the primary network service interface.

When multiple IP addresses are available, macOS can communicate using any of those network service interfaces, but it will attempt to pick the most appropriate route for every network connection. A network client uses the subnet mask to determine whether an outgoing transmission is on the LAN. macOS takes this a step further by examining all active LANs when determining a destination for outgoing transmission.

Any network connections that are not destined for a LAN that your Mac is connected to are sent to the router address of the primary active network service interface. Any active network service interface with a valid TCP/IP setting is considered, but the primary active network service interface is automatically selected based on the network service order. You can manually configure the network service order, as outlined later in this lesson.

Using the previous example, in which you have a Mac active on both wired Ethernet and Wi-Fi, the default network service order prioritizes wired Ethernet over Wi-Fi. In this example, even though you have two active valid network service interfaces, the primary active network service interface is the wired Ethernet connection.

macOS features automatic source routing. This means that incoming connections to your Mac over a specific network service interface are always responded to on the same interface, regardless of the service order.

View the Network Services List

When you open Network preferences, macOS identifies available network service interfaces. Even if a physical network interface isn't connected or properly configured, it creates a configuration for that interface, which shows up in the network services list. In Network preferences, each network interface is tied to one or more network services.

The network services list displays the status of all network interfaces and their configured services. Network services with a red indicator aren't connected. A yellow indicator shows services that are connected but not properly configured, as well as VPN services that are not connected. A green indicator shows connected and configured network services.

The active service at the top of this list is the primary network service interface, as defined by the network service order. This list updates dynamically as new services become active or as active services become disconnected, so it's the first thing to check when you troubleshoot a network issue.

Manage Network Services

To manage network interfaces and their configured services:

1   Open and (if necessary) unlock Network preferences.

2   Make sure the network location you want to edit is chosen in the Location menu, or create a new network location.

3   To configure a specific network service, select it from the network services list.

The configuration area to the right of the list changes to reflect options available to the selected service.

4   Click Advanced to reveal all the advanced network protocol options available to the selected network service.

To create another configurable instance of a network interface, click the Add (+) button at the bottom of the network services list. This reveals a dialog that allows you to choose a new interface instance from the Interface menu and then assign it a unique service name to identify it in the services list. Creating additional instances of a network service enables you to assign multiple IP addresses to a single network interface.

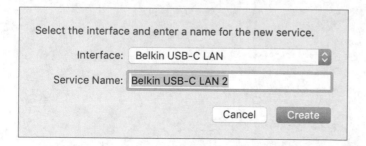

To make a service inactive, select it from the services list, click the Action button (gear icon), and then choose Make Service Inactive from the menu. A service that you make inactive doesn't activate, even if it's connected and properly configured. You can remove an existing network service by selecting its name from the services list and then clicking the Remove (–) button at the bottom of the list. To remove a network service that was added by a configuration profile, you must remove the configuration profile.

Click the Action button (gear icon) at the bottom of the network services list to reveal a menu with several management options. You can duplicate an existing network service by selecting its name from the services list and then choosing Duplicate Service from the menu. You can also rename an existing network service. You can modify the active network service interface order by choosing Set Service Order from the menu.

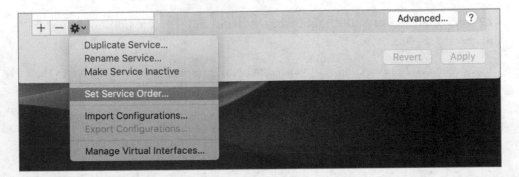

In the Service Order dialog, you can drag network services into your preferred order for selection as the primary network interface. Click OK when you finish reordering. macOS reevaluates the active network service interfaces based on the new order.

Reference 22.4
Configure VPN Settings

A VPN is an encrypted tunnel from your Mac to the network routing device providing the VPN service. After it's established, your Mac appears to have a direct connection to the LAN that the VPN device is sharing. So even if you're on a wireless Internet connection thousands of miles away from your LAN, a VPN connection provides a virtual network interface as if your Mac were directly attached to that LAN. macOS supports three common VPN protocols:

- ▶ Layer 2 Tunneling Protocol over Internet Protocol Security (L2TP over IPSec)
- ▶ Cisco IPSec
- ▶ Internet Key Exchange version 2 (IKEv2)

Some VPN services require a third-party VPN client. Third-party VPN clients usually include a custom interface for managing the connection. Although you may see the virtual network interface provided by the third-party VPN client in Network preferences, it's usually not configurable from there.

Use a VPN Configuration Profile

To manage a VPN configuration, install a configuration profile. The administrator of a VPN system or mobile device management (MDM) solution can provide a configuration profile. After you install a configuration profile that contains VPN settings, the appropriate VPN settings should be configured for you.

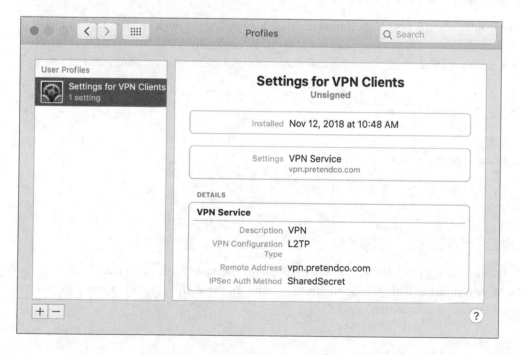

Manually Configure VPN Settings

Even with a VPN configuration profile, you might have to verify or further manage VPN connections from Network preferences. Or if the administrator of the VPN service is unable to provide a configuration profile, you must manually configure VPN services. To add a VPN interface, click the Add (+) button at the bottom of the network services list in Network preferences. This reveals a dialog where you can add a new network service interface.

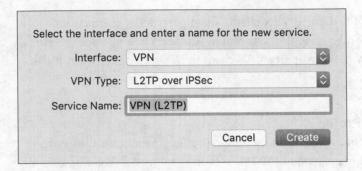

From the new network service interface dialog, you must choose the appropriate VPN protocol from the VPN Type menu.

After you create the new VPN interface, select it from the network services list, and basic VPN configuration settings appear to the right. To configure VPN settings, first enter the VPN server address and, if you use user-based authentication, an account name.

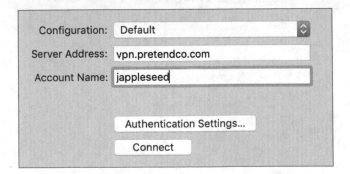

If you need to set multiple VPN configurations for the same VPN interface, choose Add Configuration from the Configuration menu. In the dialog, provide a name for the new VPN configuration and click Create.

You must also define authentication methods by clicking the Authentication Settings button and then specifying user and computer authentication settings. The VPN administrator can provide you with the appropriate authentication settings. Supplying a password here adds it to the System keychain. If you select Password in the User Authentication section and you do not enter the password, you're prompted for the password when you connect.

To configure advanced VPN settings, click the Advanced button in Network preferences. In the Advanced Settings dialog, click Options to view general VPN options. By default, active VPN connections do not move to the top of the network services list. macOS routes traffic to the VPN service only if the destination IP address is part of the LAN that the VPN service provides or if the VPN server supplies special routing information.

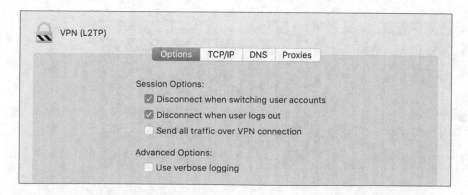

macOS also supports automatic VPN connections with certificate-based authentication and the VPN on Demand service. You can configure these VPN connections with configuration profiles.

Connect to a VPN

VPN connections aren't typically always-on connections. macOS supports automatic VPN connections with the VPN on Demand feature. You can manually connect and disconnect the VPN link from Network preferences. Click the "Show VPN status in menu bar" checkbox in Network preferences so you can connect without opening Network preferences.

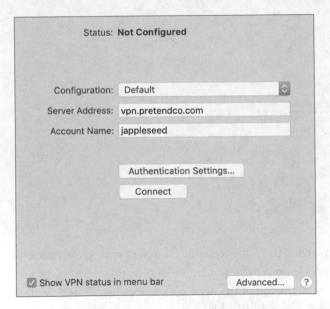

The VPN menu bar item enables you to select VPN configurations and connect, disconnect, and monitor VPN connections.

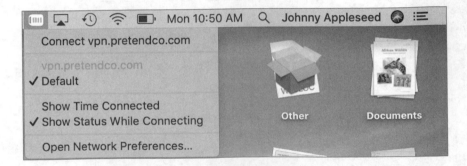

VPNs are often implemented in situations where user authentication is required, so for many, initiating a VPN connection prompts an authentication dialog. Some VPN protocols require manual authentication every time a connection is established.

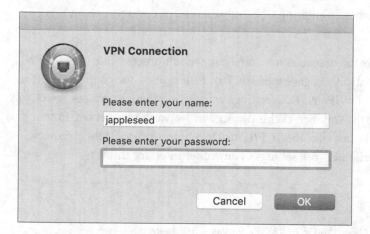

Once the connection is authenticated and established, the VPN process automatically configures TCP/IP and DNS settings using the PPP protocol. By default, VPN interfaces are set at the bottom of the network service order, so they do not automatically become the primary network interface when activated. To override this behavior, select the "Send all traffic over VPN connection" option if it's available in Network preferences. You can also manually reorder the network service order.

When you troubleshoot VPN connections, you can use Console to view the connection log information in /var/log/system.log.

Reference 22.5
Configure Advanced Network Settings

The advanced network configuration techniques covered in this section are largely optional for many configurations.

Confirm DHCP-Supplied Settings

The default configuration for all Ethernet and Wi-Fi services is to automatically engage the DHCP process as soon as the interface becomes active. To verify TCP/IP and DNS settings for hardware or virtual Ethernet services when using the DHCP service, select the service from Network preferences.

IPv6 addressing information is automatically detected, too, if available. Automatic IPv6 configuration isn't provided by standard DHCP or PPP services.

Automatically configured DNS settings show as gray text, which indicates that you can override these settings by manually entering DNS information, as covered later in this section.

Network service interfaces that may require a manual connection process, like Wi-Fi, VPN, and PPPoE interfaces, automatically engage the DHCP or PPP process to acquire TCP/IP and DNS settings. To verify TCP/IP and DNS settings when using these interfaces, select the service from the services list and then click Advanced in Network preferences. In the Advanced Settings dialog, you can click the TCP/IP or DNS buttons to view their respective settings. You can also verify network settings of any other interface this way.

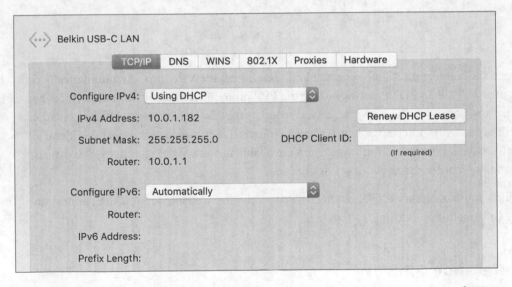

In some DHCP configurations, you must set a DHCP client ID. You can access this setting by clicking Advanced and then clicking the TCP/IP button.

Manually Configure TCP/IP

If you want to keep using DHCP but manually assign just the IP address, choose "Using DHCP with manual address" from the Configure IPv4 menu. You have to manually enter an IPv4 address for the Mac, but the rest of the TCP/IP settings remain configured by DHCP.

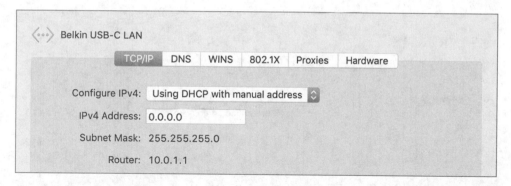

If you want to manually enter all TCP/IP settings, choose Manually from the Configure IPv4 menu. Enter the IPv4 address, the subnet mask, and the router address. The user interface caches the TCP/IP settings from the DHCP service, so you may only have to enter a new IPv4 address.

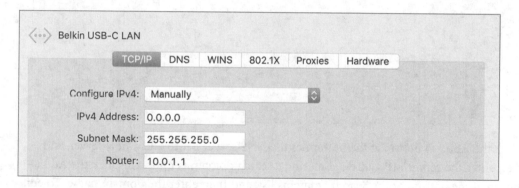

If you have to manually set up IPv6 settings as well, choose Manually from the Configure IPv6 menu. At a minimum you have to manually enter the IPv6 address, router address, and prefix length. The user interface caches automatic IPv6 settings, so you might only have to enter a new IPv6 address.

Whenever you choose to manually configure IPv4, you must manually configure DNS server settings. Click the DNS button to view the DNS settings. The user interface displays the DNS settings from the DHCP services, but these are no longer used when you switch from DHCP to a manual configuration.

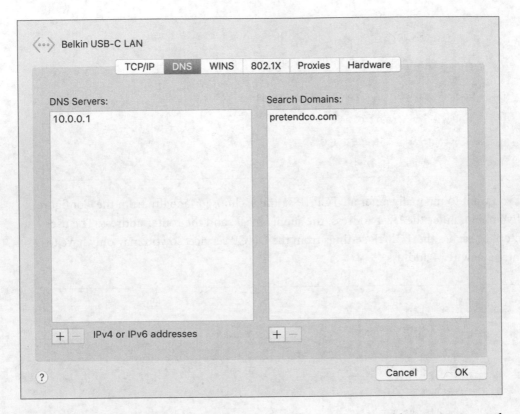

Click the Add (+) button at the bottom of the DNS server list to add a new server, and then enter the server's IP address. Entering a search domain is optional. Click the Add (+) button at the bottom of the Search Domains list, and then enter the domain name. To edit an address, double-click its entry in the list. You can remove an entry by selecting it and clicking the Remove (–) button at the bottom of the list.

Enter the appropriate IP and DNS settings, click OK to dismiss the Advanced Settings dialog, and click Apply in Network preferences to save and activate the changes.

When you manually configure TCP/IP or DNS settings, test network connectivity to verify that you properly entered all information. Using standard apps to access network and Internet resources is one basic test, but you could test more thoroughly using the included network diagnostic utilities, as covered in Lesson 23, "Troubleshoot Network Issues."

Manually Configure Wi-Fi

To manage advanced Wi-Fi options and connections:

1 Open and (if necessary) unlock Network preferences.

2 Select the Wi-Fi service from the services list.

3 Configure basic Wi-Fi settings from the Network Name menu, in much the same way that you would do it from the Wi-Fi status menu, including the ability to join or create another wireless network.

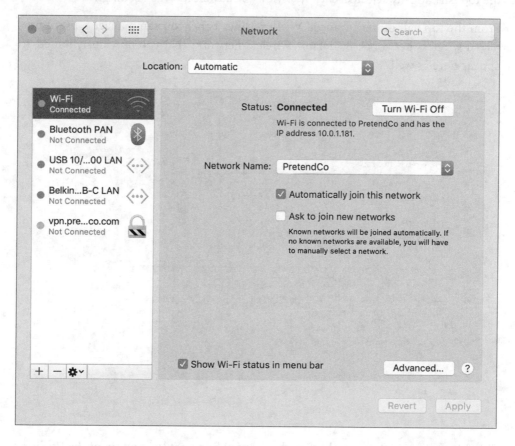

At this point you can enable non-administrator users to select Wi-Fi networks:

▶ When the "Ask to join new networks" checkbox is enabled, macOS prompts you to select another Wi-Fi network in the area when the Mac can't find a preconfigured wireless network.

▶ Enabled as a default, the "Show Wi-Fi status in menu bar" checkbox allows any user to choose a wireless network from the Wi-Fi status menu.

Click the Advanced button to reveal the Advanced Settings dialog. If the Wi-Fi button at the top isn't already selected, click it to view the advanced Wi-Fi settings.

From the top half of the advanced Wi-Fi settings pane, you can manage a list of preferred wireless networks. By default, wireless networks that you previously joined appear here as well.

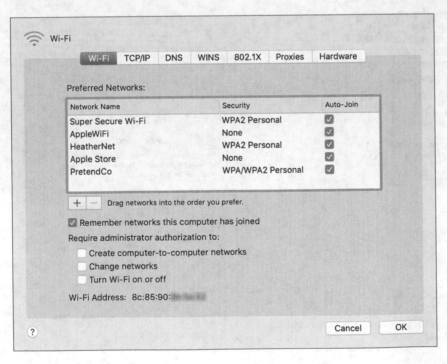

To add a new wireless network, click the Add (+) button at the bottom of the Preferred Networks list and either join a wireless network in range or manually enter the information for a hidden or not-currently-in-range network. To edit a network, double-click its entry in the list, or you can remove a network by selecting it and clicking the Remove (–) button at the bottom of the list.

The Auto-Join option is new with macOS Mojave. Deselecting the Auto-Join option for a wireless network in the Preferred Networks list enables you to temporarily configure your Mac not to auto-join a particular wireless network, while preserving the information about the network and its relative location in the Preferred Networks list. When you want to configure your Mac to automatically join a particular wireless network again, select the Auto-Join option for that network.

At the bottom of the advanced Wi-Fi settings pane, you have several settings that allow for more specific Wi-Fi administration options. You can restrict certain settings to only administrator users, including:

▶ Create computer-to-computer networks

▶ Change networks

▶ Turn Wi-Fi on or off

Configure 802.1X

The 802.1X protocol is used to secure both wired and wireless (Wi-Fi) Ethernet networks by allowing only properly authenticated network clients to join the LAN. Networks that require 802.1X don't allow traffic until the network client properly authenticates to the network.

To facilitate 802.1X authentication, macOS provides two methods for automatic configuration:

▶ User-selected Wi-Fi network with WPA Enterprise or WPA2 Enterprise authentication— As covered in the previous lesson, if you select a Wi-Fi network that uses WPA Enterprise or WPA2 Enterprise authentication, macOS automatically configures 802.1X. You can verify the 802.1X configuration by selecting Wi-Fi in Network preferences, though you cannot modify the connection details in any way.

▶ Administrator-provided 802.1X configuration profile—The 802.1X architecture often relies on shared secrets or certificates to validate client connections. In macOS, any user can join an 802.1X network on Wi-Fi, but you must use a configuration profile to set up 802.1X on Ethernet. You can install an 802.1X configuration profile by double-clicking a local copy of a profile or by using an MDM solution to install the profile.

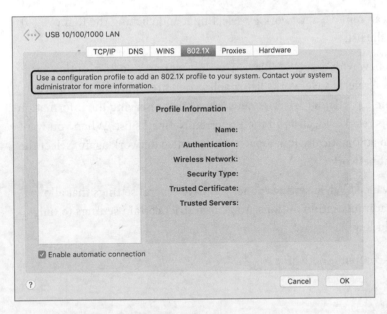

Once the configuration profile is installed, a Connect button appears in Network preferences for the appropriate network service.

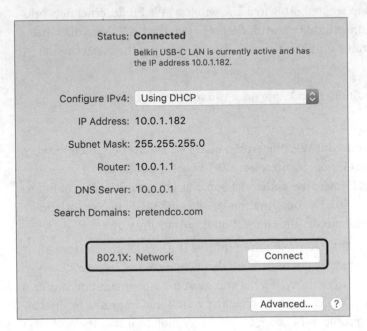

macOS Server can provide MDM services through Profile Manager. You can find out more about Profile Manager in macOS Server at www.apple.com/macos/server/.

Configure NetBIOS and WINS

Current Windows networks now use Dynamic DNS as a solution for network client discovery, but macOS still supports NetBIOS and WINS to support legacy network configurations. To manually configure NetBIOS and WINS settings:

1 Open and (if necessary) unlock Network preferences.

2 Select the network service you want to configure from the network services list.

3 Click Advanced.

4 In the Advanced Settings dialog, click the WINS button to view the NetBIOS and WINS settings.

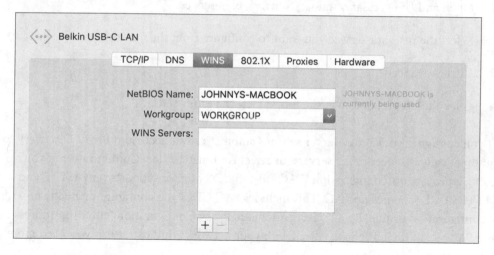

To manually configure NetBIOS, enter a unique name and choose a workgroup from the menu. It may take a while for the NetBIOS workgroup list to refresh. During this time, you won't be able to select it from the menu. If you know the name of the workgroup you want the Mac to be in, you can manually enter the workgroup name.

To enable WINS, enter at least one WINS server IP address. Click the Add (+) button at the bottom of the WINS server list to add a new server, and then enter the server's IP address. If you configure multiple WINS servers, macOS attempts to access those resources in the order in which they appear in the list. To edit a server address, double-click its entry in the list, or you can remove a server by selecting it and clicking the Remove (–) button at the bottom of the list.

Configure Network Proxies

Proxy servers act as intermediaries between a network client and a requested service. Proxy servers are often used to enhance the performance of WAN or Internet connections by caching recently requested data so that future connections appear faster to local network clients. Proxy servers are also implemented so that network administrators can limit network connections to unauthorized servers or resources, manage lists of approved resources, and configure the proxy servers to allow access to those resources only.

You might need to acquire specific proxy configuration instructions from a network administrator.

To enable and configure proxy settings:

1   Open and (if necessary) unlock Network preferences.

2   Select the network service you want to configure from the network services list.

3   Click Advanced.

4   Click the Proxies button at the top to view the proxy settings.

If you configure your proxy server settings automatically, select Auto Proxy Discovery to automatically discover proxy servers, or select Automatic Proxy Configuration if you're using a proxy auto-configuration (PAC) file. macOS Mojave supports only HTTP and HTTPS URL schemes for PAC. This includes PAC URLs you configure manually or with a configuration profile. If you select Automatic Proxy Configuration, enter the address of the PAC file in the URL field. Check with your network administrator if you need more information.

If you configure your proxy settings manually, do the following:

▶   Select a proxy server, such as FTP Proxy, and then type its address and port number in the fields on the right.

▶   Select the "Proxy server requires password" checkbox if the proxy server is protected by a password. Enter your account name and password in the Username and Password fields.

You can also choose to bypass proxy settings for specific computers on the Internet (hosts) and segments of the Internet (domains) by adding the address of the host or domain in the "Bypass proxy settings for these Hosts & Domains" field. This might be useful if you want to make sure you're receiving information directly from the host or domain and not information that's cached on the proxy server.

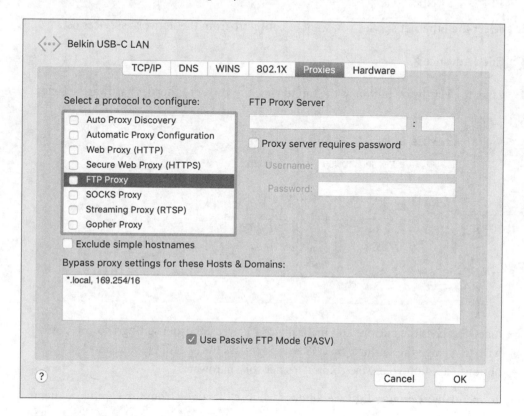

Manually Configure Ethernet

Ethernet connections establish connection settings automatically. macOS enables you to manually configure Ethernet options. You probably need to configure Ethernet options when you have Gigabit Ethernet switches and old or substandard wired infrastructure. In this case it's common for the Mac to attempt to automatically establish a gigabit connection but ultimately fail because the wired infrastructure doesn't support the high speeds. The most common symptom is that even with the Ethernet switch showing that the Mac has an active connection, Network preferences on the Mac shows Ethernet as disconnected.

To manually configure Ethernet settings:

1 Open and (if necessary) unlock Network preferences.

2 Select the Ethernet service you want to configure from the network services list.

3 Click Advanced.

4 Click the Hardware button at the top to view the current Ethernet hardware settings.

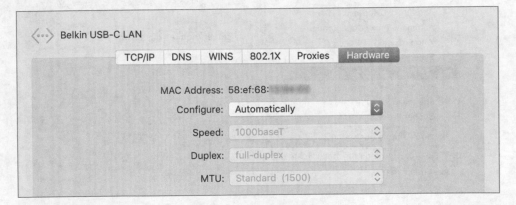

macOS caches the current automatically configured Ethernet settings, so you don't have to change the settings. macOS also populates the Speed, Duplex, and MTU options based on your Mac computer's network hardware.

5 To manually configure Ethernet options, choose Manually from the Configure menu.

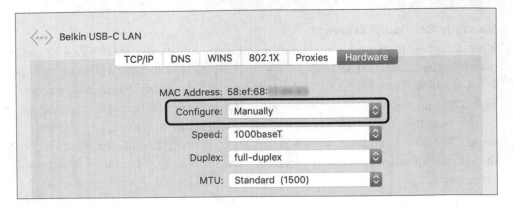

6   Make your custom selections from these menus.

7   Click OK to save the configuration changes.

After you manually configure your Ethernet settings, confirm that you have network connectivity as you expect. You can use the tools and techniques covered in Lesson 23, "Troubleshoot Network Issues."

Exercise 22.1
Configure Network Locations

> **Prerequisites**
>
> ▶   You must have created the Local Administrator (Exercise 3.1, "Configure a Mac for Exercises") and Johnny Appleseed (Exercise 7.1, "Create a Standard User Account") accounts.

Some network configurations don't have a DHCP server. Or there may be times when a DHCP server fails. In these instances, to establish and maintain network access, a Mac that's configured to obtain an IP address through DHCP self-assigns the IP address.

Examine Your DHCP-Supplied Configuration

1   Log in as Johnny Appleseed.

2   Open Network preferences.

3   Click the padlock and authenticate as Local Administrator.

4   Select the primary network service.

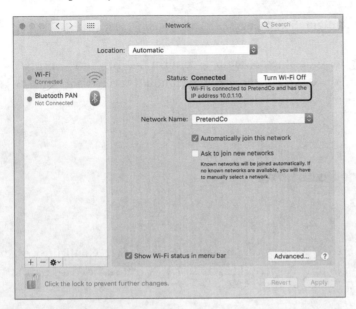

Your settings might vary from those shown in this screenshot, especially if you have different network services connected.

Create a DHCP-Based Network Location

1   From the Location menu, choose Edit Locations.

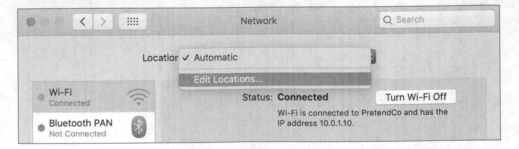

2   Click the Add (+) button under the Locations list to create a new location.

3 Enter **Dynamic** as the name of the new location.

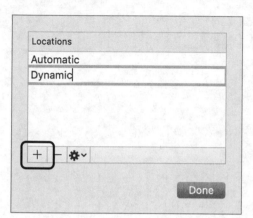

4 Click Done.

5 If necessary, choose the new Dynamic location from the Location menu.

6 Click Apply.

Network preferences is one of a few places in macOS where you must click Apply before your settings take effect.

Create a Static Network Location

Some network configurations don't have a DHCP server, or there may be times when a DHCP server fails. In these instances, to establish and maintain proper network access, you might need to configure a Mac with a static IP address.

In this exercise, you configure a new location called Static with a static IP address. The IP address you use is 10.0.1.*nn*2.

Your facilitator gave you a participant number. Use that participant number for *nn*. For example, participant #3 uses 10.0.1.032 (which macOS will shorten to .32), and participant #17 uses 10.0.1.172.

1 From the Location menu, choose Edit Locations, and select the Dynamic location.

2   From the Action (gear icon) menu, choose Duplicate Location.

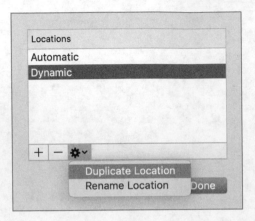

3   Name the new location **Static**, and click Done.

4   Use the Location menu to switch to the new Static location, if it's not already selected.

5   Click Apply.

6   Select the network service that's set up for these exercises from the service list on the left. It will probably be Ethernet or Wi-Fi.

7   Click Advanced.

8   If necessary, click TCP/IP.

9   From the Configure IPv4 menu, choose Manually.

10 In the IPv4 Address field, enter **10.0.1.*nn*2/24** (where *nn* is your participant number).

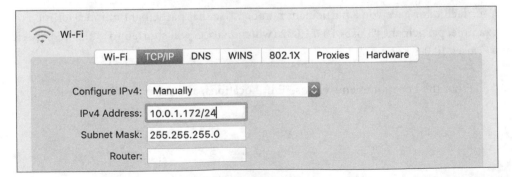

11 Press the Tab key.

The string "/24" at the end of the IP address is shorthand for the subnet mask 255.255.255.0 in CIDR (Classless Inter-Domain Routing) notation. That field is filled in when you press the Tab key. macOS also guesses that the router is at 10.0.1.1, which is correct for this network.

See https://en.wikipedia.org/wiki/Classless_Inter-Domain_Routing for more information.

12 Click DNS.

13 Click the Add (+) button under the DNS Servers list, and enter **10.0.1.2**.

14 Click the Add (+) button under the Search Domains list, and enter **pretendco.com**.

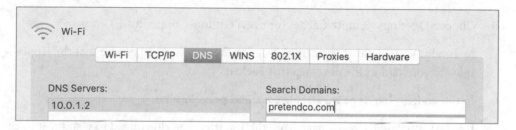

15 Click OK to dismiss the advanced settings dialog.

16 Click Apply.

The status indicator for the service changes to green to indicate that it is connected and fully configured.

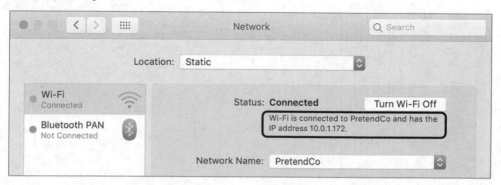

17 Quit System Preferences.

Test Internet Access

You've correctly configured your Mac to work on the network. You'll use Safari to test network access in this exercise. To make sure you're testing network connections rather than just loading pages from Safari caches, you'll empty the Safari caches first. Then you'll use Safari to verify that you can access the Apple website.

1   Open Safari.

2   Choose Safari > Preferences (or press Command-Comma).

3   Click Advanced in the preferences toolbar.

4   Select "Show Develop menu in menu bar," and close the preferences window.

5   Choose Develop > Empty Caches (or press Option-Command-E).

Normally, you wouldn't perform this action. You do here, to ensure that the Apple website you load in the next step isn't cached.

6   In the address bar, type **www.apple.com**, and press Return.

If Safari is trying to load a page from the Internet, you don't need to wait for it to finish or time out. If everything is working, the Apple website appears.

If the Apple website doesn't load, there is something wrong with your network settings or connection. Troubleshoot before you proceed. First, verify your network settings match previous instructions. If they are correct, consult Lesson 23, "Troubleshoot Network Issues."

7   Quit Safari.

Exercise 22.2
Configure Network Service Order

> ### ▶ Prerequisites
>
> - You must have created the Local Administrator (Exercise 3.1, "Configure a Mac for Exercises") and Johnny Appleseed (Exercise 7.1, "Create a Standard User Account") accounts.
>
> - You must have performed Exercise 22.1, "Configure Network Locations."
>
> - In a classroom environment, the Apple Authorized Training Provider (AATP) must have Ethernet and Wi-Fi interfaces (built-in or through an adapter) for participant Mac computers.

The network service order determines which service macOS uses to reach the Internet. Because of this, you must know how network service order is determined and what its effects are.

Create an Additional Location

1 Open Network preferences and authenticate as Local Administrator.

2 From the Location menu, choose Edit Locations.

3 Select the Static location, and choose Duplicate Location from the Action (gear icon) pop-menu below the Locations list.

4 Name the new location **Ethernet & Wi-Fi**, and click Done.

5 Switch to the Ethernet & Wi-Fi location, if necessary.

6 Click Apply.

7 Select the primary network service (the one at the top of the list on the left with an active connection and a green indicator). This service will be either Ethernet or Wi-Fi, depending on the primary connection in your classroom environment.

8 From the Action (gear icon) menu below the service list, choose Rename Service.

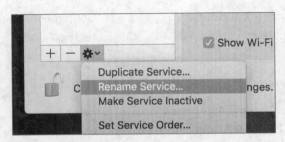

9 If your primary connection is wireless, enter **W (Without DNS)** in the New Name field, and click Rename. If your primary connection is wired (Ethernet), enter **E (Without DNS)**, and click Rename.

You will modify your DNS settings in subsequent steps.

10 Click Apply.

11 Select the secondary network service (the one second in the list on the left with an active connection and a green indicator).

This service is either Ethernet or Wi-Fi, depending on your secondary connection in your classroom.

12 From the Action (gear icon) menu below the service list, choose Rename Service.

13 If your secondary connection is a wired interface (Ethernet), enter **E (With DNS)** in the Name field, and click Rename. If your primary connection is wireless, enter **W (With DNS)**, and click Rename.

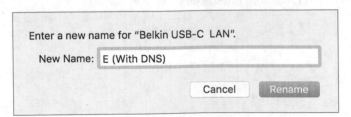

You now have two network services that are connected to the same LAN. You have two sets of network configurations (IP address, subnet mask, and so on) running on the same LAN, through different network interfaces.

Your primary interface has a static configuration, whereas your secondary interface has received its network configuration through DHCP.

14 Select the Without DNS service that you created earlier, and click Advanced.

15 Click DNS.

16 Select the entry in the DNS Servers list, and click the Remove (–) button below the list to remove it. Do not remove pretendco.com from the Search Domains list.

The DNS Servers list is empty.

17 Click OK to dismiss the advanced settings.

18 Click Apply.

The Without DNS and With DNS services have a green status indicator, and the Without DNS service is at the top of the list.

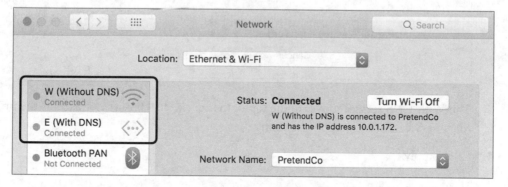

19 Open Safari, and attempt to browse to a website.

You see a page that tells you that "Safari Can't Find the Server" or "You Are Not Connected to the Internet." Safari can't find a DNS server to resolve the name of the website that you tried to visit.

The Without DNS service has priority over the With DNS service (it is higher on the Service list). Because Without DNS is a network interface configured without DNS servers, it can't look up and resolve websites by name.

Change the Service Order

1   Switch back to Network preferences.

2   From the Action menu, choose Set Service Order.

Set Service Order controls the services order. macOS reprioritizes services based on their status (active services at the top), but among active services, Set Service Order determines the primary service.

3   Drag the With DNS service to the top of the list, and click OK.

The With DNS service moves to the top of the service list, but it's not used as the primary service until you apply the change.

4   Click Apply.

5   Quit and reopen Safari.

6   Browse the web.

You can browse the web normally, because traffic is using a network interface that has proper DNS configuration.

7   From the Apple menu, choose Location > Static.

This menu enables you to switch locations without opening Network preferences. It appears in the Apple menu when more than one location exists.

8 Reload the page in Safari (it might reload automatically after a short delay).

This time you're able to load the page successfully because the Static location has DNS settings associated with its highest-priority service.

9 If you aren't performing the next exercise, quit Safari and System Preferences.

Exercise 22.3
Configure VPN Settings

▶ **Prerequisites**

▶ You must have created the Local Administrator (Exercise 3.1, "Configure a Mac for Exercises") and Johnny Appleseed (Exercise 7.1, "Create a Standard User Account") accounts.

In this exercise, you use a configuration profile to set up a VPN connection from your Mac to the classroom server private network.

Try to Connect to a Private Service

1 Log in as Johnny Appleseed.

2 Open Safari.

3 Use the address bar to access internal.pretendco.com.

Safari might try to reach the site for a while, but it fails to connect. You can only access internal.pretendco.com from the classroom server private network, but you haven't joined it yet.

4 Leave Safari open.

Configure a VPN Service

1 Open the file ParticipantsMaterials/Lesson22/VPN.mobileconfig.

The profile opens in the Profiles pane of System Preferences.

2 At the "Are you sure you want to install 'VPN (server.pretendco.com)'?" dialog, click Show Profile.

The profile contains the settings you need to connect to server.pretendco.com using the L2TP protocol. You can scroll down to see details.

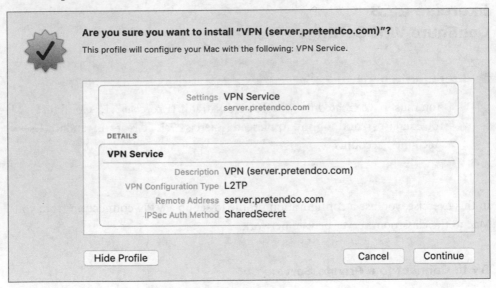

3 Click Continue, and click Continue again.

The profile doesn't specify a user name to authenticate to the VPN server, so enter the user name **participant** and click Install.

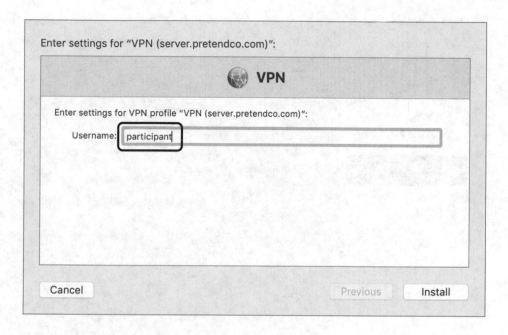

4   When you are prompted, authenticate as Local Administrator to install the profile.

Profile preferences lists the VPN profile as installed on this Mac.

5   Switch to Network preferences.

6   Select the VPN service that was added to your current location.

All the settings in the profile are applied, along with the user name (account name) you entered.

7   Select "Show VPN status in menu bar."

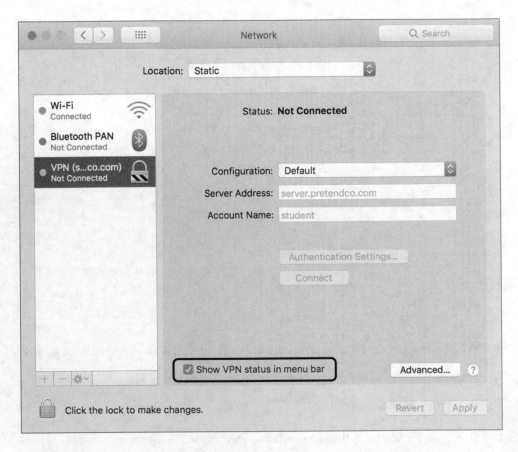

The Connect button in Network preferences might be dimmed, but you can still use the menu item to connect.

8   From the VPN menu item, choose Connect VPN (server.pretendco.com).

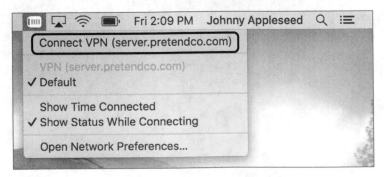

9 When you're prompted to authenticate to the VPN server, enter the password
Apple321! (the user name is already filled in) and click OK.

It may take a few seconds to connect. When it does, the VPN service status changes.

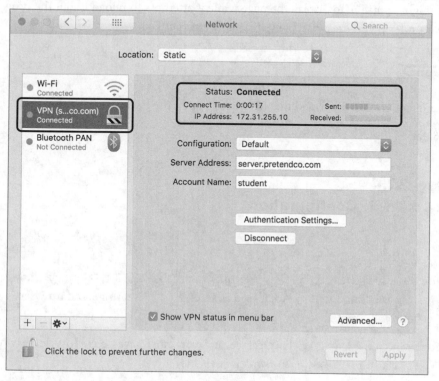

Check Your VPN Connectivity

You are connected to the classroom network through VPN. Access a network resource
that was previously unreachable.

1 Switch to Safari.

2 If the internal website didn't load, use the address bar to access internal.pretendco.com.

3 If you receive a warning that Safari can't verify the identity of the website, click
Continue.

The page loads successfully. Since you are now connected to the private network, you
have access to internal services and resources.

4 From the VPN menu item, choose Disconnect VPN (server.pretendco.com).

5 In Safari, press Command-R to reload the internal website.

Safari might continue to display the page while it attempts to reload it, but the progress bar under the address bar shows that it doesn't get far.

After a delay, you are informed that Safari can't open the page.

6 Quit Safari.

Exercise 22.4
Advanced Wi-Fi Configuration

> **Prerequisites**
>
> ▶ You must have created the Local Administrator (Exercise 3.1, "Configure a Mac for Exercises") and Johnny Appleseed (Exercise 7.1, "Create a Standard User Account") accounts.
>
> ▶ Your Mac must have a Wi-Fi interface, and you must have access to at least two Wi-Fi networks (at least one of which is visible).

In this exercise, you learn to use the Preferred Networks list to control how your Mac joins Wi-Fi networks.

Create a Wi-Fi-Only Location

1 Log in as Johnny Appleseed, open Network preferences, click the lock, and authenticate as Local Administrator.

2 Note the currently selected location so that you can return to it at the end of the exercise.

3 From the Location menu, choose Edit Locations.

4 Click the Add (+) button under the Locations list to create a new location.

5   Enter **Wi-Fi Only** as the name of the new location.

6   Click Done.

7   If necessary, choose the new Wi-Fi Only location from the Location menu.

8   Click Apply.

9   In the network service list, make the services other than Wi-Fi inactive. Select each service, and from the Action menu, choose Make Service Inactive.

When you arc done, all services except Wi-Fi are listed as Inactive.

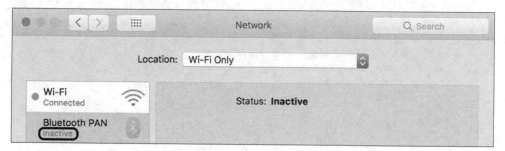

10 Click Apply.

11 Select the Wi-Fi service.

12 If necessary, click Turn Wi-Fi On.

13 If necessary, deselect "Ask to join new networks."

This prevents your Mac from suggesting networks to you when it can't find your preferred networks.

14   If necessary, select "Show Wi-Fi status in menu bar."

15   If your Mac hasn't joined a wireless network, join one by following the instructions in Exercise 21.1, "Connect to a Wi-Fi Network."

Clear the Preferred Networks List

1   Click Advanced.

2   Examine the Preferred Networks list.

This is the list of wireless networks that your Mac joins automatically when it's in range of them. If there is more than one in range, it joins the one that is highest on the list, assuming that Auto-Join is enabled.

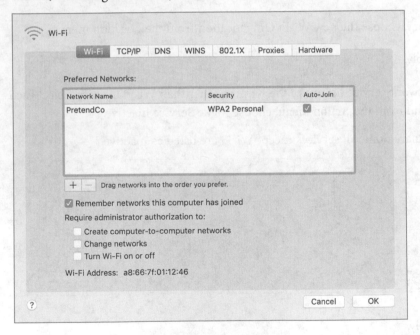

NOTE ► If you remove a wireless network from this list, you remove its password from your keychain. You must reenter the password the next time you join the wireless network. If you use iCloud Keychain, the same wireless network will be removed from other Apple devices that use the same iCloud account. If you do not know the password for the network you intend to remove, you can use Keychain Access to view its password and record it before you remove it from this list. See Reference 9.2, "Manage Secrets in Keychain," for the details of this process.

3   Select each entry and click the Remove (–) button at the bottom of the list to clear it.

4   Make sure "Remember networks this Mac has joined" is selected.

5   When the list is empty, click OK and click Apply. If prompted, authenticate as Local Administrator.

6   Click Turn Wi-Fi Off.

7   Wait ten seconds, and click Turn Wi-Fi On.

The wireless interface turns on but doesn't connect to a network.

Add a Network to the Preferred List Manually

1   Click Advanced.

2   Click the Add (+) button under the Preferred Networks list.

3   Enter the network name and security information for another network you have access to.

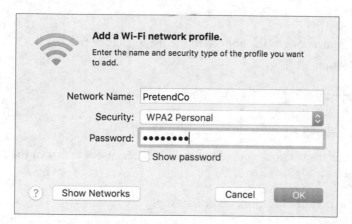

4   Click OK to add the entry.

5   Click OK to dismiss the advanced settings, and click Apply. If prompted, authenticate as Local Administrator.

Your Mac should join the wireless network. If it doesn't, there might be a problem with the manual entry, such as a typo in the name or password or an incorrect security mode. In this case, you could remove it from the list and reenter it.

Add a Network to the Preferred List by Joining It

1 From the Network Name menu, choose another of the wireless networks you have access to. Ask your facilitator which network you should join.

2 If necessary, enter the network password to join it.

3 Click Advanced.

The network you joined is added to the top of the preferred list. This is because the "Remember networks this Mac has joined" option is selected.

4 Click OK to dismiss the advanced settings dialog.

5 Click Apply.

Test the Preferred Networks Order

1 Click Turn Wi-Fi Off. Wait ten seconds, and click Turn Wi-Fi On.

After a short delay, your Mac rejoins the network you just added.

2 Click Advanced.

3 Drag the current wireless network to the bottom of the list to change the Preferred Networks order.

4 Click OK, and click Apply.

5 Click Turn Wi-Fi Off. Wait ten seconds, and click Turn Wi-Fi On.

This time, your Mac joins the network you added manually because it is first in the Preferred Networks list.

6 Switch back to the Static network location, and click Apply.

7 Quit System Preferences.

Lesson 23

Troubleshoot Network Issues

This lesson builds on the network topics covered in Lesson 21, "Manage Basic Network Settings," and Lesson 22, "Manage Advanced Network Settings." This lesson covers general network troubleshooting and common network issues. Then, you'll learn how to use the built-in macOS network troubleshooting tools, including Network Utility.

Reference 23.1
Troubleshoot General Network Issues

When you troubleshoot LAN and Internet connection network issues, consider possible points of failure. Isolate the cause of the problem before you attempt generic resolutions.

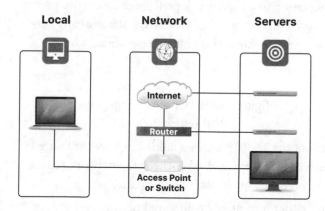

To help isolate network issues, you can categorize them into three general areas:

▶ Local issues—These are usually related to either improperly configured network settings or disconnected network connections.

▶ Network issues—Many possible points of failure could be involved. Become familiar with the physical topology of your network. Start by checking the devices that provide network access closest to your Mac. Something as simple as a bad Ethernet port on a network switch can cause problems. Start your investigation using the network diagnostic utilities included with macOS.

▶ Service issues—These issues are related to the network device or service you are trying to access. For example, the devices providing DHCP or DNS services could be temporarily down or improperly configured. You can often determine that the problem is with the service by testing other network services. If the other network services work, you're probably not dealing with network or local issues. Use diagnostic tools for testing service availability. Troubleshooting network services is also covered in Lesson 24, "Manage Network Services."

Use two main tools for diagnosing network issues in macOS: Network preferences and Network Utility.

Verify Network Preferences Status

One of the diagnostic tools you should check first is Network preferences. Network preferences features a dynamically updating list that shows you the current status of any network interface. If a network connection isn't working, you first find out about it here.

Network status indicators are:

▶ Green—The connection is active and configured with TCP/IP settings. This doesn't guarantee that the service is using the proper TCP/IP settings.

▶ Yellow—The connection is active but the TCP/IP settings aren't properly configured. If you are experiencing problems with this service, double-check the network settings. If the settings appear sound, move on to the other diagnostic utilities.

▶ Red—This status usually indicates either improperly configured network settings or disconnected network interfaces. If this is an always-on interface, check for proper physical connectivity. If this is a virtual or Point-to-Point Protocol connection, double-check the settings and attempt to reconnect.

Common Network Issues

A good starting point for resolving network issues is to check for some common causes before hunting down more complex ones. This includes verifying Ethernet connectivity, Wi-Fi connectivity, DHCP services, and DNS services.

Ethernet Connectivity Issues

If you use an Ethernet connection, verify the physical connection to the Mac, and if possible, verify the entire Ethernet run back to the switch. If that's not possible, try swapping your local Ethernet cable or use a different Ethernet port. If you use an Ethernet adapter, try a different adapter.

Verify the Ethernet status from Network preferences. Also, keep an eye out for substandard Ethernet cabling or problematic switching hardware. A symptom of these issues would be a large number of packet errors, which you can verify with Network Utility, as covered later in this lesson.

You may also find that while the Ethernet switch registers a link, Network preferences still shows the link as down. This issue may be resolved by manually setting a slower speed in the advanced hardware settings of Network preferences, as covered in Lesson 22.

> **MORE INFO** ▸ Built-in network hardware can sometimes become unresponsive and may benefit from resetting the Mac computer's NVRAM or SMC. You can find out more about resetting these items from Apple Support article HT204063, "Reset NVRAM or PRAM on your Mac," and article HT201295, "How to reset the System Management Controller (SMC) on your Mac."

Wi-Fi Connectivity Issues

If you use Wi-Fi, start by verifying that you are connected to the correct SSID from the Wi-Fi status menu or Network preferences. Often, if the Mac detects a problem the Wi-Fi status menu shows an exclamation point (!) to indicate that there is a problem with the wireless network.

The Wi-Fi status menu can also serve as a diagnostic tool if you press and hold the Option key and then click the Wi-Fi status menu. This view shows connection statistics for the currently selected Wi-Fi network. Of particular note is the Tx Rate entry, which shows the current data rate for the selected Wi-Fi network. The Wi-Fi status menu is capable of other diagnostic tasks, including helping you quickly identify network issues and opening Wireless Diagnostics.

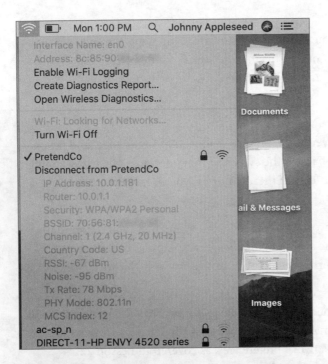

When you open Wireless Diagnostics, you see an assistant interface. Wireless Diagnostics creates and saves a diagnostic report archive about the Mac computer's wireless and network configuration. You must authenticate as an administrator user to create the report. The compressed archive is stored in /var/tmp.

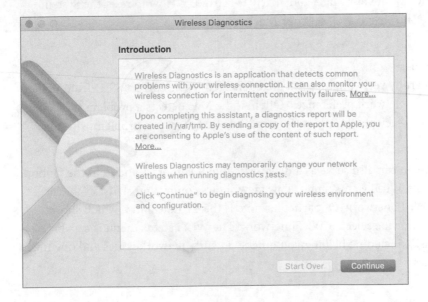

The Wireless Diagnostics archive contains relevant files that can you use to diagnose a connection issue. If the utility can't diagnose the problem, consult an experienced Wi-Fi administrator.

Open the Window menu to see additional advanced wireless network utilities in Wireless Diagnostics.

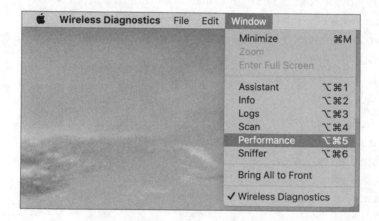

These utilities provide information that you can share with Wi-Fi vendors or support specialists to resolve Wi-Fi issues. For example, the Performance window provides a real-time view of the radio signal quality. With the Performance window open, you can physically move a Mac notebook computer around an area to identify wireless dead zones.

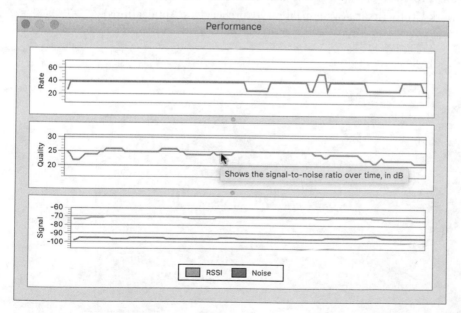

You can find out more about Apple Wireless Diagnostics from Apple Support article HT202663, "Check for Wi-Fi issues using your Mac."

DHCP Service Issues

If you configure your Mac to use DHCP, and the DHCP server runs out of available network addresses or doesn't provide configuration information to your Mac, your Mac might be able to communicate with other devices on the LAN even though it doesn't have access to WAN or Internet resources. This is covered in Lesson 21, "Manage Basic Network Settings.".

DNS Service Issues

Most network services require DNS services. If you have DNS service issues, verify the DNS server configuration in Network preferences. In most cases, the top listed network service interface is primary, and macOS uses it for DNS resolution. The exception is if the primary network service lacks a router configuration, in which case DNS resolution falls to the next fully configured network service interface.

Reference 23.2
Use Network Utility to Troubleshoot Network Issues

Network Utility provides several network identification and diagnostic tools. Use Spotlight to open Network Utility (it's in /System/Library/CoreServices/Applications).

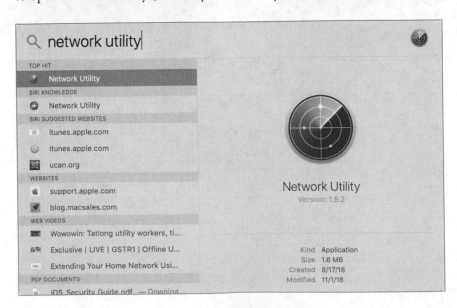

Use the following tools in Network Utility:

- ► Info—Inspect details regarding hardware network interfaces.

- ► Netstat—View routing information and network statistics.

- ► Ping—Test network connectivity and latency.

- ► Lookup—Test DNS resolution.

- ► Traceroute—Analyze how your network connections are routed to their destination.

- ► Whois—Query the whois database servers and find the owner of a DNS domain name or IP address of registered hosts.

- ► Finger—Gather information based on a user account name from a network service.

- ► Port Scan—Check whether a network device has specific services available.

You can also open Network Utility when you start your Mac from macOS Recovery (as covered in Lesson 5, "Use macOS Recovery") by choosing Utilities >Network Utility. In macOS Recovery you can access the Wi-Fi status menu to use a different Wi-Fi network.

Interface Information

When you open Network Utility, you first see the Info section. This section enables you to view the detailed status of any hardware network interface. Verify that the network interface is properly activated.

Click the menu and choose the interface you're having issues with. The selections here don't necessarily match the service names that macOS displays in Network preferences. Instead, this menu shows the interfaces using their interface type and UNIX-given names.

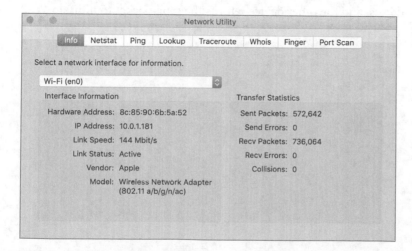

After you select an interface, view general interface information on the left and transfer statistics on the right. The more useful pieces of information here are link status, link speed, and IP address(es). Only active hardware network interfaces appear, and the link speed indicates whether the interface is establishing a proper connection. A proper IP address is required to establish a TCP/IP connection to a destination on a different subnet. You can also identify the selected interface's MAC address, which is used to identify this particular interface on the LAN.

As a final validation of the selected network interface, you can view recent transfer statistics. If you open some apps like Safari to cause some network traffic, you can verify that packets are being sent and received from this interface. If you see activity here but still experience problems, the issue is probably a network or service problem and not the network interface. Or, if this interface is experiencing transfer errors, a local network hardware connectivity issue may be the root of your problem.

To resolve hardware network interface issues, check the physical connection. With wired networks, try different network ports or cabling to rule out physical connection issues. With wireless networks, double-check the Wi-Fi settings and the configuration of any wireless base stations. If the Mac network hardware isn't working, contact an Apple Authorized Service Provider.

Ping

If your network settings are properly configured and the hardware network interface appears to be working correctly but you still experience network issues, test network connectivity using the ping tool. The ping tool determines whether your Mac can successfully send and receive data to another network device. Your Mac sends a ping data packet to the destination IP address, and the other device returns the ping packet to indicate connectivity.

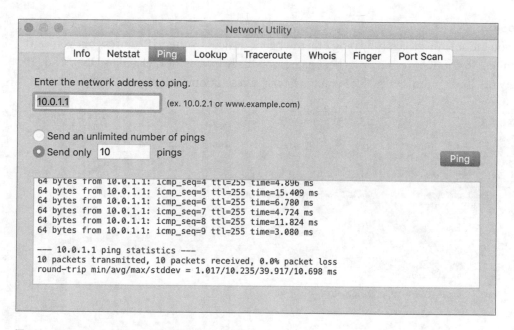

To use ping, open Network Utility and click the Ping button. Enter an IP address to a device on the LAN that should always be accessible, like the network router. Using a domain name assumes that your Mac is properly communicating with a DNS server, which might not be the case if you're troubleshooting connectivity issues.

Click the Ping button to start the ping process. If the ping is successful, it returns the amount of time it took for the ping to travel to the network device and back. This is typically within milliseconds.

Some network administrators configure their firewalls to block pings or set up their network devices not to respond to network pings.

After you establish successful pings to local devices, branch out to WAN or Internet addresses. Using ping, you may find that everything works except for the one service you were looking for that prompted you to start troubleshooting the network.

Lookup

If you are able to successfully ping other network devices by their IP address but you can't connect to another device by its host name, you likely have issues related to DNS. The network lookup process enables you to test name resolution against your DNS server.

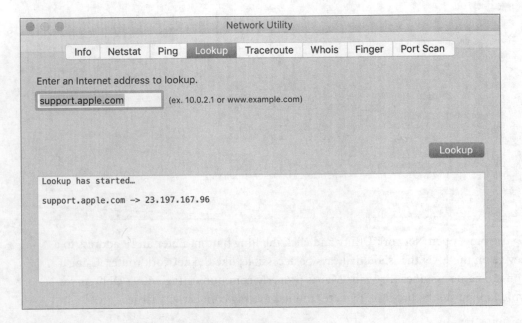

To verify DNS, enter the host name of a device or service in your local domain. If you can resolve local host names but not Internet host names, your local DNS server is resolving local names but isn't properly connecting to the worldwide DNS network. If you don't have a local domain, use any Internet host name.

Click the Lookup button to start the network lookup process. A successful forward lookup returns the IP address of the host name you entered. A successful reverse lookup returns the host name of the IP address you entered. If you are unable to successfully return lookups, your Mac isn't connecting to the DNS server. Use the ping tool to test for basic connectivity to the DNS server IP address.

Traceroute

If you are able to connect to some network resources but not others, use the network traceroute utility to determine where the connection fails. WAN and Internet connections often require the data to travel through many network routers to reach their destination.

The traceroute tool examines every network hop between routers by sending packets with low time-to-live (TTL) fields to determine where connections fail or slow down.

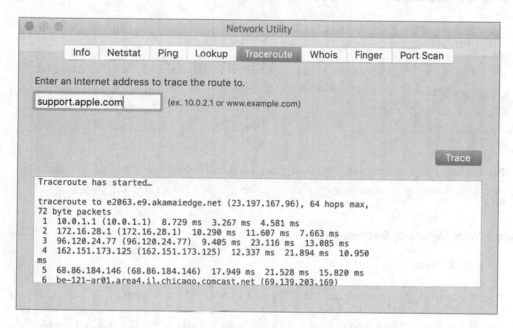

To verify a network TCP/IP route, open Network Utility and click the Traceroute button. Enter an IP address to a device on the LAN that should always be accessible, like the network router. Using a domain name assumes that your Mac is properly communicating with a DNS server, which might not be the case if you're troubleshooting connectivity issues.

Click the Trace button to initiate the traceroute process. If traceroute is successful, it returns a list of routers required to complete the connection and the amount of time it took for the test packets to travel to each network router. It sends three probes at each distance, so three times are listed for each hop. The delay is typically measured in milliseconds; experiencing delay times of any longer than a full second is unusual. If traceroute doesn't get a reply from a particular router at all, it shows an asterisk instead of listing the router address, but this could be because the network equipment is configured not to respond to network requests.

Once you've established successful routes to local devices, you can branch out to WAN or Internet addresses. Using the traceroute tool, you may find that a specific network router is the cause of the problem.

For more information about Network Utility, choose Help >Network Utility Help.

Exercise 23.1
Troubleshoot Network Connectivity

In this exercise, you intentionally misconfigure your network settings and use the macOS built-in troubleshooting tools to view symptoms and isolate the problem.

Break Your Network Settings

1 Log in as Johnny Appleseed.

2 Open Network preferences and authenticate as Local Administrator.

3 Record the currently selected location so that you can return to it at the end of the exercise.

4 From the Location menu, choose Edit Locations.

5 Select the current location, and then choose Duplicate Location from the Action (gear icon) menu below the location list.

6 Name the new location **Broken DNS**, and click Done.

7 Switch to the Broken DNS location, if necessary.

8 Click Apply.

9 Select the primary network service (the one at the top of the left sidebar), and click Advanced.

10 Click DNS.

11 If there are entries in the DNS Servers list, record them so you can reenter them, and use the Remove (–) button to remove them.

12 Click the Add (+) button under the DNS Servers list, and add the server address **127.0.0.55**.

No DNS server is available at this address. The 127.0.0 prefix (known as the local loopback addresses) is reserved for computers to talk to themselves. But macOS uses 127.0.0.1 for this purpose. As a result, 127.0.0.55 is an invalid address.

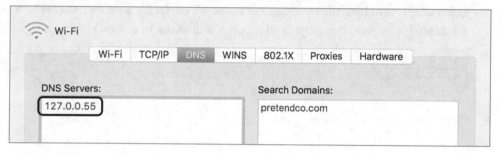

13 Click TCP/IP.

14 From the Configure IPv6 menu, choose "Link-local only."

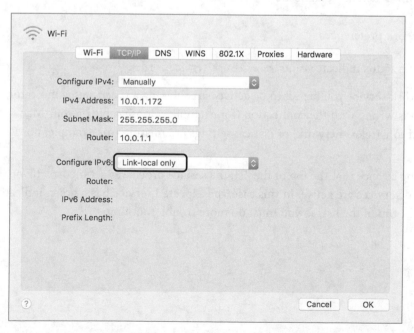

This prevents IPv6 from being an alternate Internet connection.

15 Click OK, and then click Apply.

Observe the Problem

1 Open Safari.

2 Enter **www.apple.com** in the address bar, and press Return.

Safari attempts to load the webpage, but it doesn't get far because it's not able to reach anything. If you wait, it eventually gives up and displays an error. Don't wait.

3 Quit Safari.

Check the Network Status in Network Preferences

When you have a network problem, one of the first things you should check is the network service status in Network preferences. This enables you to spot simple problems without performing detailed diagnostics.

1 Open Network preferences.

2 Examine the status indicators and the network services order.

If the network service you expect to be active isn't showing a green status indicator, something is wrong with the connection (for example, a loose cable or your Mac isn't joined to wireless network) or critical settings are missing (for example, no IP address).

If the wrong service is at the top of the list, the service order was set incorrectly or unexpected services are active. In this case, the expected service has a green indicator and is at the top of the list, so you must do more troubleshooting.

Use Ping to Test Connectivity

In this section, you use the Network Utility ping tool. You can use ping to test network connectivity and DNS resolution.

1   Press Command-Space bar to activate Spotlight.

2   Enter **network** and click Network Utility in the search results.

Network Utility might not be the first result.

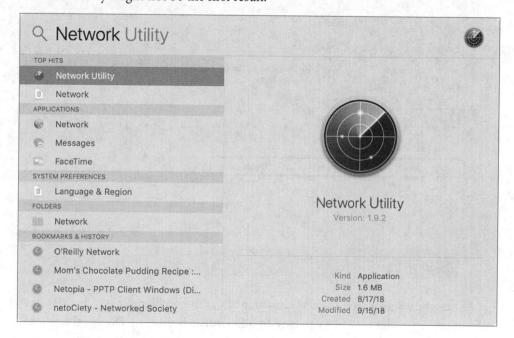

3   In Network Utility, click Ping.

4   In the "Enter the network address to ping" field, type the domain name of the server you want to reach (**www.apple.com**).

5   Enter **5** in the "Send only" field, and make sure it is selected.

6 Click the Ping button.

After about 30 seconds, you receive a message telling you that ping couldn't resolve www.apple.com. The message indicates that the ping tool wasn't able to use DNS to look up, or resolve, the name www.apple.com and match it to an IP address to send the ping to. In this case, you know that the name www.apple.com is valid because you have used it before, so this indicates that something is wrong with DNS.

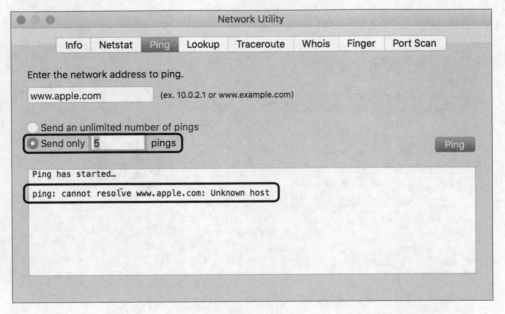

Although this gives you some information about the problem, it still doesn't tell you where the problem is. It can be hard to differentiate between a DNS problem and a complete network failure. If DNS resolution is the only thing failing, it can mimic a complete failure because almost all network access starts with (and depends on) a DNS lookup. If the network is completely disconnected, most attempts to use the network fail at the DNS step, so the only symptoms are DNS errors.

Try to reach a server by its numeric IP address to distinguish between a DNS-only problem and a complete network failure. This bypasses the usual DNS lookup and works even if DNS is broken.

7 In the "Enter the network address to ping" field, enter the numeric IP address **8.8.8.8**. This is an easy-to-remember address of a public server maintained by Google.

8 Click Ping.

This time, ping reaches its destination successfully and shows statistics for its five test pings. This tells you that your basic network connectivity is OK and probably only DNS isn't working.

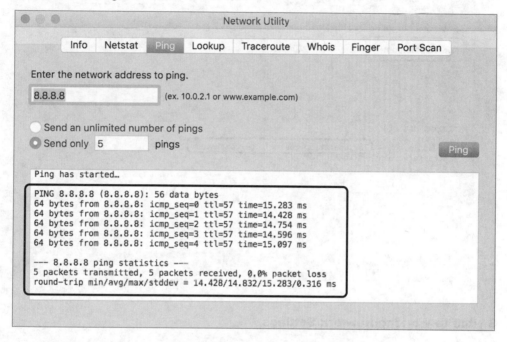

Use Lookup to Test DNS

Even though the ping error message "cannot resolve" indicates a DNS problem, try the lookup tool to see if it reveals a more specific error.

1 In Network Utility, click Lookup.

2 In the "Enter an Internet address to lookup" field, enter **www.apple.com**.

3 Click Lookup.

After about 30 seconds, you receive a message that the operation couldn't be completed. This is essentially the same result you got with the ping tool.

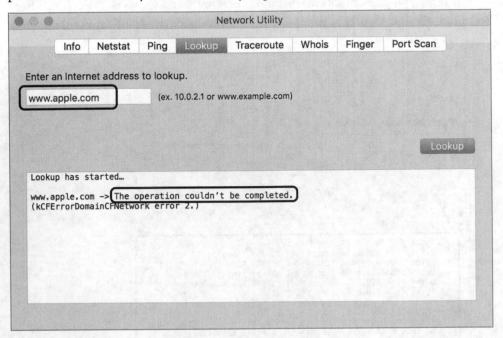

Switch to Working Network Settings

1   From the Apple menu, choose Locations and click the location you were using at the beginning of this exercise.

Unlike the Broken DNS location, this one has valid settings, so your Internet connectivity should be back to normal.

2   In Network Utility, click Lookup again.

This time the Lookup tool reaches a DNS server and finds the IP address corresponding to the domain name www.apple.com.

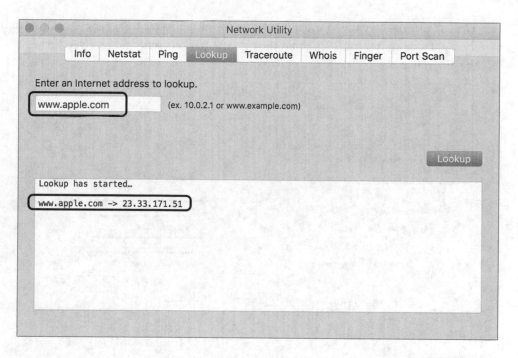

The address you see may be different from the one shown here because the Apple website is hosted by a number of servers throughout the Internet and uses DNS to direct you to a server near your network location for faster access.

If you knew the address the name should resolve to, you could verify that, but the fact that it resolved to an IP address at all is a good indication that DNS is working.

3   Open Safari, and try browsing a website.

This time, Safari is able to load webpages from the Internet.

Monitor Network Traffic

Use the Network Utility Info pane to view low-level network interface settings and to monitor network throughput for each interface.

1   Switch to Network Utility, and click Info.

2   Select your Mac computer's primary network interface from the menu.

The left side of the pane shows information about the active network connection, and the right side shows statistics about the network packets sent and received through this interface.

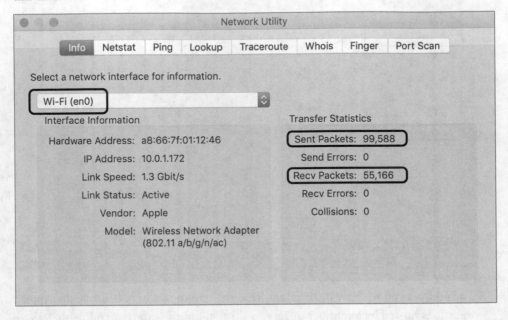

3   Arrange the Safari and Network Utility windows so that Safari is in front but not blocking the Transfer Statistics section of the Network Utility window.

4   In Safari, press Command-R to reload the current page.

The Sent Packets and Recv Packets entries increase while Safari reloads the current page.

5   In Network Utility, select another network interface from the menu.

6   Switch to Safari and reload the current page.

The packet counts for this interface might increase slightly because of network chatter, but they shouldn't respond noticeably when you refresh a page in Safari.

You can use the Info pane of Network Utility to see which network interface your connections are running through.

7   Quit Safari, Network Utility, and System Preferences.

Network Services

Manage Network Services

In this lesson, you learn about network services architecture. Then you're introduced to the key network service apps built into macOS. You learn how macOS accesses popular file-sharing services. Finally, you learn techniques for trouble-shooting network services.

Reference 24.1
Network Services

Shared network services are defined by client software (designed to access the service) and server software (designed to provide the service). The client and server software use network protocols and standards to communicate with each other.

By adhering to standards, software developers create unique yet compatible network client and server software. This enables you to choose the software tool that best fits your needs. For instance, you can use the built-in macOS Mail client created by Apple to access mail services provided by Apple, Google, Yahoo, Microsoft, and other service providers.

Network Services Software

Client software can be in the form of dedicated apps, as is the case with many Internet services, like email and web browsing. Other client software is integrated into macOS (for example, file and print services). In either case, when you establish a network service connection, settings for services are saved to preference files on the local Mac. These client preferences often include resource locations and authentication information.

Server software provides access to the shared resource. Server-side settings include configuration options, protocol settings, and account information.

When you troubleshoot a network service, you must know the port numbers or ranges that a service uses. For instance, the standard TCP port for web traffic is port 80. Apple maintains a list of commonly used network services and their associated TCP or UDP ports at Apple Support article HT202944, "TCP and UDP ports used by Apple software products."

Network Service Identification

To access a network service, you must know the service's local network or Internet location. Some network services feature dynamic service discovery, which enables you to locate a network service by browsing a list of available services. Or you must manually identify the service location with a network host address or name.

macOS can locate network services and appropriate network service resources. You can use Internet Account preferences to configure these services.

After you locate and connect to a network service, you often need to prove your identity (authenticate) to the service provider. Successful authentication to a network service is usually the last step in establishing a connection to it. After you establish a connection, security technologies are normally in place to ensure that you're allowed to access only certain resources. This process is called authorization. Both of these fundamental network service concepts, authentication and authorization, are covered in this lesson and the next, Lesson 25, "Manage Host Sharing and Personal Firewall."

Dynamic Service Discovery

macOS supports dynamic network service discovery protocols to help you find the resources you need in situations like the following:

▶   You join a new network without knowing the exact names of all its available resources.

▶   The shared resource you need is hosted from another client computer that doesn't have a DNS host name or the same IP address every time.

Dynamic network service discovery protocols enable you to browse local area and wide area network resources without knowing specific service addresses. Some devices that provide network services advertise the availability of their services on the network. As available network resources change, or as you move your client to different networks, the service discovery protocols dynamically update the list of available services.

macOS uses dynamic network service discovery. For example, dynamic network service discovery enables you to browse for available network file shares with the Finder or to locate new network printers from Printers & Scanners preferences. Other network apps built into macOS use service discovery to locate shared resources, including Image Capture, Photos, and iTunes. Third-party network apps also use dynamic network service discovery.

The discovery protocol only helps you locate available services. After it provides your Mac with a list of available services, its job is done. When you connect to a discovered service, your Mac establishes a connection to the service using the service's protocol. For example, the Bonjour service discovery protocol can provide the Finder with a list of available screen-sharing systems, but when you select another Mac from this list, your Mac establishes a screen-sharing connection to the other Mac using the Virtual Network Computing (VNC) service, which uses the Remote Frame Buffer (RFB) protocol.

Bonjour

Bonjour is the Apple implementation of Zero Configuration Networking, or Zeroconf, a collection of standards drafts that provide automatic local network configuration, naming, and service discovery. Bonjour uses a broadcast discovery protocol known as multicast DNS (mDNS) on UDP port 5353.

Bonjour is the primary set of dynamic network service discovery protocols used by macOS native services and apps. Bonjour is based on TCP/IP standards, so it integrates well with other TCP/IP-based network services. macOS also includes support for Wide-Area Bonjour, which enables you to browse WAN resources as well as LAN resources.

Local Bonjour requires no configuration. Wide-Area Bonjour requires that you configure your Mac to use a DNS server and search domain that supports the protocol.

Server Message Block

Originally designed by Microsoft, Server Message Block (SMB) is the most common network service for sharing files and printers. SMB also includes a network discovery service that runs on UDP ports 137 and 138 and TCP ports 137 and 139. Most current operating systems that provide support for SMB sharing also support dynamic discovery with SMB.

Network Host Addressing

You can reach a network host by its IP address. But you can also use other technologies that give network hosts human-friendly network names. Network host identification methods include:

▶ IP address—An IP address can always be used to establish a network connection.

▶ DNS host name—Your Mac has a host name configured by one of two methods. Your Mac attempts to resolve its host name by performing a DNS reverse lookup on its primary IP address. If your Mac can't resolve a host name from the DNS server, it uses the Bonjour name instead.

▶ Computer name—Other Apple devices use this to identify your Mac for AirDrop peer-to-peer file sharing and for Finder browsing. The computer name is part of the Apple Bonjour implementation, and you set it in Sharing preferences.

▶ Bonjour name—Bonjour is the macOS primary dynamic network discovery protocol; in addition, Bonjour provides a convenient naming system for use on a local network. The Bonjour name is usually similar to the computer name, but it conforms to DNS naming standards and ends with .local. This allows the Bonjour name to be supported by other operating systems. When you use Sharing preferences to edit the Computer Name field and then click Edit, you see the updated Bonjour name, which is displayed in the Local Hostname field.

▶ NetBIOS/WINS name—This name is used for the legacy Windows dynamic network discovery protocols as part of the SMB service. This name is automatically generated based on the name that you set in Sharing preferences, but you can update it in the Network preferences by selecting an interface, clicking Advanced, clicking the WINS button, and then updating the NetBIOS Name field.

Identifier	Example	Set by	Used by
IP address	10.1.17.2	Network preferences	Any network host
DNS hostname	client17.pretendco.com	Defined by DNS server	Any network host
Computer name	Client 17	Sharing preferences	Mac systems (Bonjour or AirDrop)
Bonjour name	Client-17.local	Sharing preferences	Bonjour hosts
SMB (NetBIOS) name	CLIENT17	Network preferences	SMB hosts

Reference 24.2
Configure Network Service Apps

Services like email can work on a local level, but these services are also communicating across separate networks and between servers. macOS includes client apps that access different network services.

Although this book focuses on the network client software built into macOS, many excellent third-party network clients are available for Mac. When you troubleshoot a network access problem, using an alternative network client is a good way to determine whether the issue is your primary client software or the service you're attempting to use.

Safari

The Hypertext Transfer Protocol (HTTP) handles web communication for Safari using TCP port 80. Secure web communication (HTTPS) encrypts HTTP over a Secure Sockets Layer (SSL) or, more recently, over a Transport Layer Security (TLS) connection that by default uses TCP port 443.

Generally, little additional network configuration is required to use web services. You must provide the web browser with the Uniform Resource Locator (URL) or web address of the resource to which you want to connect. Safari defaults to the most secure TLS communication even if you don't specify HTTPS in the URL. The only exception is if you have to configure web proxies, as described in Lesson 22, "Manage Advanced Network Settings."

Internet Accounts Preferences

Internet Accounts preferences enable you to configure network service accounts. When you enter a network service account in Internet Accounts preferences, it configures appropriate network service apps built into macOS.

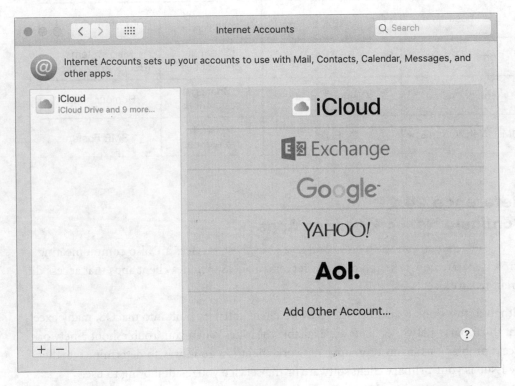

Through Internet Accounts preferences, you can configure macOS to use network service accounts for Apple iCloud, Microsoft Exchange, Google, Yahoo, and AOL. The Add Other Account option is covered later in this section.

> **NOTE ▶** For Microsoft Exchange support, macOS Mojave requires Microsoft Office 365, Exchange 2016, Exchange 2013, or Exchange Server 2010. Installing the latest service packs from Microsoft for these services is recommended. For more information read Apple Support article SP777, "macOS Mojave - Technical Specifications."

Internet Accounts preferences also includes support for services popular in countries whose primary language isn't English. These services appear when you select the appropriate Language & Region preferences.

Each service type includes support for built-in macOS apps and services. When you sign in to a service that provides multiple features, like Google or Yahoo, you configure multiple apps, such as Mail, Notes, Calendar, Reminders, Contacts, and Messages. iCloud includes support for even more features, including iCloud Drive, Photos, Safari, iCloud Keychain, Find My Mac, and FaceTime.

Configure Network Service Accounts

Use Internet Accounts preferences to configure network service accounts. Click an included service provider to sign up. You'll see a service sign-in dialog. Most services provide their own authentication dialogs.

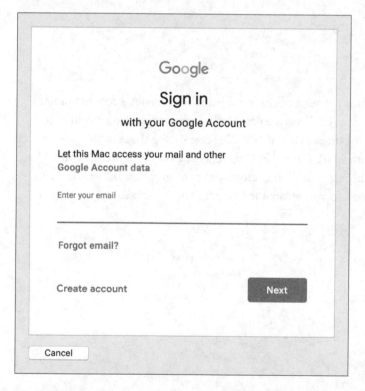

If you don't see the Internet Accounts list of services, click the small Add (+) button at the lower-left corner of the preferences pane.

If you sign in to a service that offers multiple features, after you authenticate you can enable those features. You can also return to Internet Accounts preferences to enable or disable a feature. From Internet Accounts, click the Details button to verify or reenter your account information.

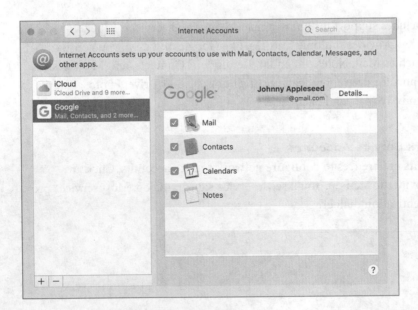

If you need to configure an Internet service that's not listed in Internet Accounts preferences, or you need to configure a local service provided by your organization, click Add Other Account at the bottom of the services list. You'll see a dialog that enables you to manually configure services for Mail, Calendar, Contacts, and Game Center. If you add a service this way, you'll probably have to define additional configuration information. This information should be provided to you by an administrator of the service.

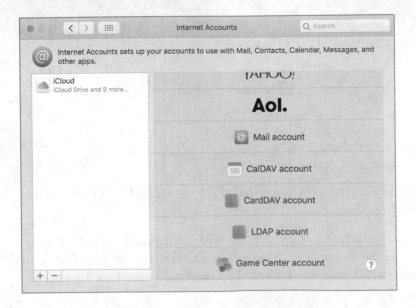

Configure Mail

Mail supports standard email protocols and their encrypted counterparts, along with a variety of authentication standards. Mail also includes support for Microsoft Exchange–based services.

Configure Mail with the Internet Accounts pane of System Preferences. In Mail, choose Mail > Accounts to open the Internet Accounts preferences. Or, you can use a configuration profile to configure Mail.

Mail also includes its own account setup assistant that walks you through configuring mail account settings. The assistant starts automatically if you open Mail but haven't yet set up an account. Choose Mail > Add Account to start it.

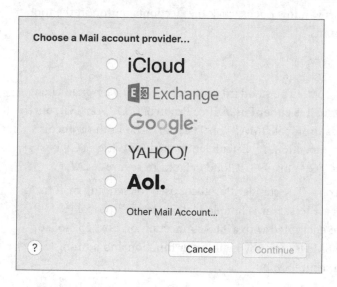

When you select one of these default mail account types, the assistant attempts to automatically determine the appropriate mail protocol, security, and authentication settings. This includes support for the Autodiscovery feature of Microsoft Exchange Server. When you set up a mail account here, macOS attempts to configure Notes, Calendar, Reminders, and Contacts too.

If you need to configure Mail for an account type not listed in the defaults, select the Other Mail Account option. After you enter basic mail account information, the assistant attempts to determine the appropriate mail settings. If your mail service uses a nonstandard configuration or is unreachable, you might have to manually enter the mail service settings here. If necessary, work with the service administrator to obtain the appropriate configuration settings.

If you need to tweak mail service settings, choose Mail > Preferences to access advanced options. When the Mail preferences window opens, click the Accounts button in the toolbar to view and manage Mail accounts.

Mail supports the following email services:

▶ Standard mailbox access protocols—The standard protocol used between mail clients and mail servers for receiving mail is either Post Office Protocol (POP) on TCP port 110 or Internet Message Access Protocol (IMAP) on TCP port 143. Both protocols can be encrypted with a TLS connection. By default, encrypted POP uses TCP port 995 and encrypted IMAP uses TCP port 993. iCloud defaults to secure IMAP.

▶ Standard mail-sending protocols—The standard protocol used for sending mail from clients to servers and from server to server is Simple Mail Transfer Protocol (SMTP) on TCP port 25. SMTP can be encrypted with a TLS connection on port 25, 465, or 587. The port used for secure SMTP varies by mail server function and administrator preference. iCloud defaults to secure SMTP.

▶ Exchange-based mail service—Mail communicates using the Exchange Web Services (EWS) protocol. EWS uses the standard ports for web traffic: TCP port 80 for standard transport and TCP port 443 for secure transport.

Configure Notes

When you add your Internet accounts to Notes, you can keep your notes with you no matter which device you're using.

If you keep notes in iCloud, you can view and edit them there. Plus you can add new notes and lock already-created ones. You can also add people so that you can collaborate with them. Within a note, you can apply paragraph styles, checklists, and most media types (such as tables, scanned documents, photos, video, freehand-drawn scribbles, and map locations).

Configure a New Notes Account

Ideally, you configure Notes with other services through iCloud or Internet Accounts preferences. In Notes, choose Notes > Accounts. macOS will redirect you to Internet Accounts preferences. Internet Accounts preferences enable you to configure Notes without configuring iCloud or Mail.

Configure Calendar and Reminders

Calendar integrates with Mail and Maps to help you plan your day. Although Calendar manages your calendar on your local Mac, it also integrates with network calendar services based on the EWS or CalDAV protocols. CalDAV, or Calendaring Extensions to WebDAV, extends WebDAV (Web Distributed Authoring and Versioning), which is an extension of HTTP.

Ideally, you configure Calendar with Mail through Internet Accounts preferences or a configuration profile. In Calendar, choose Calendar > Accounts. macOS redirects you to Internet Accounts preferences.

Calendar includes an account setup assistant, which walks you through configuring Calendar account settings. This assistant doesn't start when you open Calendar. Choose Calendar > Add Account to start it.

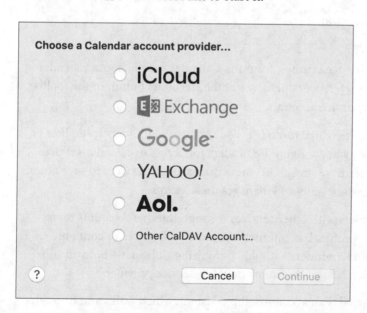

When you select one of the default calendar account types shown in the previous screenshot, the assistant attempts to determine the appropriate calendar service security and authentication settings. Calendar includes support for the Autodiscovery feature of Microsoft Exchange Server. When you set up a calendar account, macOS attempts to configure Mail, Notes, Reminders, and Contacts too.

If you must configure Calendar for an account type not listed in the defaults, select the Other CalDAV Account option. After you enter your mail address and account password, the assistant attempts to determine the appropriate CalDAV settings. If your mail service uses a nonstandard configuration or is unreachable, you might have to manually enter the CalDAV service settings here. If necessary, work with the service administrator to obtain the appropriate configuration settings.

If you need to edit Calendar service settings, from the Calendar menu choose Calendar Preferences. When Calendar preferences opens, select the Accounts button in the toolbar to view and manage calendar service accounts.

Reminders helps you to keep a personal to-do list. You can save Reminders to-do lists on all of your Apple devices when you configure Reminders for access to calendar services. This is because Reminders uses EWS or CalDAV network calendar services to save notes. Reminders creates to-do calendar events and manages these events.

Ideally, you configure Reminders with other services through Internet Accounts preferences or with a configuration profile. Use Internet Accounts preferences to configure Reminders. You can configure Reminders without configuring Calendar—but you still need an EWS or CalDAV calendar service from a network service provider.

Like Calendar, Reminders includes an account setup assistant, which walks you through configuring Reminders account settings. The assistant doesn't start when you open Reminders; you have to choose Reminders > Add Account to start it.

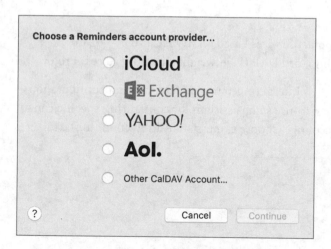

Calendar and Reminders support the following network calendar services:

▶ CalDAV collaborative calendaring—Calendar supports the CalDAV network calendar standard. This standard uses WebDAV as a transport mechanism on TCP port 8008 or 8443 for encrypted communication, but CalDAV adds the administrative processes required to facilitate calendar and scheduling collaboration. CalDAV is being developed as an open standard, so any vendor can create software that provides or connects to CalDAV services.

▶ Internet-based calendar services—Calendar and Reminders use Internet-based calendar services, including iCloud, Yahoo, and Google calendar services. These services are based on CalDAV and use the encrypted HTTPS protocol over TCP port 443.

▶ Exchange-based calendaring service—Calendar includes support for this calendar service. The macOS Exchange integration relies on EWS, which uses TCP port 80 for standard transport and TCP port 443 for secure transport.

▶ Calendar web publishing and subscription—Calendar enables you to share your calendar information by publishing iCalendar files to WebDAV-enabled web servers. Because WebDAV is an extension to the HTTP protocol, it runs over TCP port 80, or TCP port 443 if encrypted. You can subscribe to iCalendar files, identified by the filename extension .ics, hosted on WebDAV servers; just provide Calendar with the URL of the iCalendar file.

▶ Calendar email invitation—Calendar is integrated with Mail to send and receive calendar invitations as iCalendar email attachments. The transport mechanism is whatever your primary mail account is configured to use. Although this method isn't a calendar standard, most popular mail and calendar clients can use it.

Configure Contacts

Contacts integrates with network contact services based on EWS, CardDAV (Card Distributed Authoring and Versioning), or LDAP (Lightweight Directory Access Protocol).

Ideally you configure Contacts through Internet Accounts preferences or a configuration profile. Contacts also features an easy-to-use setup assistant for configuring specific contact or directory network service accounts. Choose Contacts > Add Account to start it.

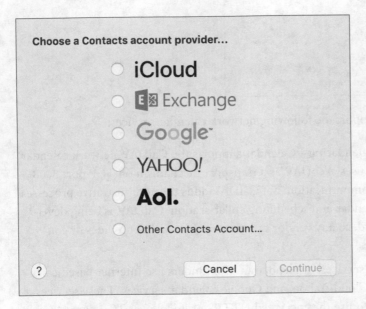

When you select one of these default contacts account types, the assistant attempts to determine the appropriate account settings. This includes support for the Autodiscovery feature of Microsoft Exchange Server. When you set up a Contacts account here, macOS attempts to configure Mail, Notes, Calendar, and Reminders too.

If you must configure Contacts for an account type not listed in the defaults, select the last option, Other Contacts Account. Contacts also supports CardDAV and LDAP account types. Select the account type from the menu, and then provide the server and authentication information. If necessary, work with the service administrator to obtain the appropriate configuration settings.

If you must make changes to contact service settings, choose Contacts > Preferences. When the Contacts preferences window opens, click the Accounts button in the toolbar to view and manage contact service accounts.

Contacts supports the following network contact services:

▶ CardDAV contacts service—Contacts supports a network contacts service standard known as CardDAV. This standard uses WebDAV as a transport mechanism on TCP port 8800 or 8843 for encrypted communication. CardDAV is being developed as an open standard, so any vendor can create software that provides or connects to CardDAV services.

▶ Internet-based contact services—Contacts can use a variety of Internet-based contact services, including iCloud, Google, and Yahoo contact services. All of these services are based on CardDAV and use the encrypted HTTPS protocol over TCP port 443.

▶ Exchange-based contact service—Contacts includes support for this contact sharing service. The macOS Exchange integration relies on EWS, which uses TCP port 80 for standard transport and TCP port 443 for secure transport.

▶ Directory service contacts—Contacts can search contact databases using LDAP, the standard for network directory services, which uses TCP port 389 for standard transport and TCP port 636 for secure transport. You can configure Contacts for LDAP services either from its account setup assistant or through integration with the macOS systemwide directory service, in Users & Groups preferences.

Configure Messages

With Messages, you can text, add images and other files, start a video or audio call, share your screen, and more. Messages requires the push-based messaging service iMessage, which also enables you to communicate with iOS devices.

Ideally Messages is configured for iMessage when you sign in to iCloud. If no account is configured when you open Messages, Messages opens its account setup assistant and walks you through configuring iMessage account settings. You can enter any valid Apple ID to configure iMessage. After you authenticate with your Apple ID, you might be prompted to choose additional iMessage identifiers that can be used to reach you, like other email accounts or mobile numbers.

Messages uses the iMessage service, which is unique to Apple. The iMessage protocol is facilitated by the Apple Push Notification service (APNs), which uses TCP port 5223, and falls back on Wi-Fi only to port 443. APNs is efficient for devices that rely on battery power and might lose network connectivity. This makes the iMessage service ideal for messaging with mobile Mac computers and iOS devices. Messages is limited to a single iMessage account per computer user account.

If you're signed in to the iMessage service using the same Apple ID on your Mac and an iPhone running iOS 8 or later, you can send and receive Short Message Service (SMS) messages with the iMessage protocol through an iPhone cellular connection. You must manually enable this feature on your iPhone in Settings > Messages before you can use SMS messaging on your Mac. For more information, see Apple Support article HT204681, "Use Continuity to connect your Mac, iPhone, iPad, iPod touch, and Apple Watch."

To edit Messages settings, choose Messages > Preferences. The General pane opens by default.

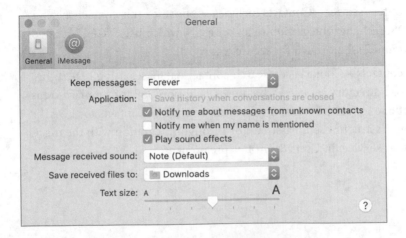

If you need to edit message service settings, click the iMessage button in the Messages preferences toolbar to edit your account settings or blocked numbers. To keep your entire message history updated and available on all your devices, select "Enable Messages in iCloud." Read Apple Support article HT208532, "Keep all your messages in iCloud," for more information.

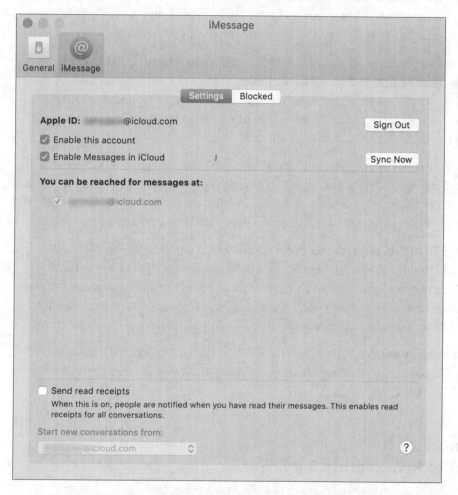

For more information about using Messages, read Apple Support article HT202549, "Use Messages with your Mac." If you're having trouble with the iMessage service, verify availability of APNs with Apple Support article HT202078, "If you use FaceTime and iMessage behind a firewall."

Configure FaceTime

FaceTime provides audio and video-conferencing abilities, including the ability to answer or call standard phone numbers with a compatible iPhone. Similar to the iMessage service, FaceTime is unique to Apple and uses APNs to start audio or video communications.

Ideally, FaceTime is automatically configured if you sign in to iCloud. Otherwise, FaceTime includes an account setup assistant that walks you through configuring FaceTime account settings. This assistant starts if no account is set when you open FaceTime.

Enter any valid Apple ID to configure FaceTime. After authentication, you might be prompted to choose additional FaceTime identifiers that can be used to reach you, like other email accounts or, if you have FaceTime on your iPhone, other mobile numbers. Unlike other network service client apps, you must sign in to use FaceTime and you can only sign in to one account per local user account.

To handle phone calls on your Mac with FaceTime, you must be signed in to FaceTime on your Mac and iPhone with iOS 8 or later. You have to sign in to FaceTime on your iPhone first to enable FaceTime cellular phone calls. Ensure that your iPhone cellular number is enabled in FaceTime preferences on your Mac. Go to FaceTime preferences to do this.

After you sign in to FaceTime, the service is ready to send and receive FaceTime calls, even when you quit FaceTime. To turn off FaceTime calls, choose FaceTime > Turn FaceTime Off or press Command-K. To start receiving FaceTime calls again, use the same keyboard shortcut or choose FaceTime > Turn FaceTime On. Sign out of your account from FaceTime preferences to permanently halt calls to your Mac.

FaceTime uses many standard and non-reserved TCP and UDP ports to facilitate calls. Verify available ports in Apple Support article HT202078, "If you use FaceTime and iMessage behind a firewall."

Reference 24.3
Connect to File-Sharing Services

The Finder provides two ways to connect to a network file system:

► Browse shared resources in the Finder Network folder.

► Enter the server address of the server that provides the file service.

File-Sharing Services

Many protocols transfer files across networks and the Internet. The most efficient are those that share file systems. Network file servers can make file systems available to your Mac across the network.

Client software built into the Finder can mount a network file service much as it would mount a locally connected storage volume. After a network file service is mounted to your Mac, you can read, write, and manipulate files and folders as if you were accessing a local file system.

Access privileges to network file services are defined by the same ownership and permissions architecture used by local file systems. Details on file systems, ownership, and permissions are covered in Lesson 13, "Manage Permissions and Sharing."

macOS provides built-in support for these network file service protocols:

► Server Message Block version 3 (SMB 3) on TCP ports 139 and 445—This is the default (and preferred) file-sharing protocol for OS X Yosemite 10.10 and later. Historically, the SMB protocol was mainly used by Windows systems, but many other platforms have adopted support for some version of this protocol. The SMB 3 implementation in macOS works with advanced SMB features such as end-to-end encryption (if enabled on the server), per-packet signatures and validation, Distributed File Service (DFS) architecture, resource compounding, large maximum transmission unit (MTU) support, and aggressive performance caching. macOS maintains backward compatibility with older SMB standards.

► Apple Filing Protocol (AFP) version 3 on TCP port 548 or encrypted over Secure Shell (SSH) on TCP port 22—This is the legacy Apple network file service. The current version of AFP is compatible with the features of the Mac OS Extended file system. Volumes formatted with Apple File System (APFS) can't be shared over AFP.

► Network File System (NFS) version 4, which may use many TCP or UDP ports—Used primarily by UNIX systems, NFS supports many advanced file-system features used by macOS.

► WebDAV on TCP port 80 (HTTP) or encrypted on TCP port 443 (HTTPS)—This protocol is an extension to the common HTTP service and provides read/write file services.

► File Transfer Protocol (FTP) on TCP ports 20 and 21 or encrypted on TCP port 989 and 990 (FTPS)—FTP is supported by nearly every computing platform. The Finder supports read capability for FTP or FTPS shares. FTPS (FTP-SSL) is different than SFTP (SSH File Transfer Protocol). FTPS uses SSL (or TLS) encryption on TCP port 990, and SFTP uses SSH encryption on TCP port 22. The Finder supports SFTP, and you can use Terminal to use FTPS and SFTP.

Browse File-Sharing Services

You can browse for dynamically discovered file services from the Network section in these two locations:

► The Finder sidebar

► The Open dialog of any app

The Finder Network folder displays a collection of dynamically discovered network file services, screen sharing services, and currently mounted file systems, including manually mounted ones. The Network folder constantly changes based on information gathered from the two dynamic network service discovery protocols compatible with macOS— Bonjour and SMB/NetBIOS/WINS. So you can browse screen-sharing services offered by other Mac computers and SMB and AFP file services.

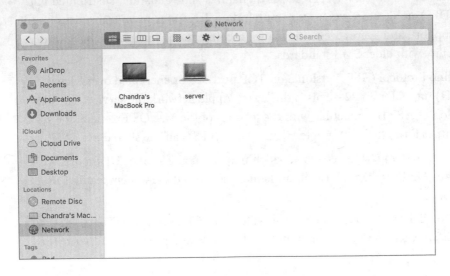

Smaller networks might have only one level of network services. If you have a larger net-work that features multiple service discovery domains, they appear as subfolders inside the Network folder. Each subfolder is named by the domain it represents. Items inside the domain subfolders represent shared resources configured for that network area.

To browse for and connect to an SMB or AFP file service, select a Mac from the Finder Network folder. You can go to the Network folder in two ways:

▶   Click Network in the Finder sidebar.

▶   Choose Go > Network (or press Shift-Command-K), and then click Browse.

If you use the Finder to select a server, and the server supports SMB and AFP, macOS defaults to SMB. It uses the most secure version of SMB that the sharing service supports.

The first time you connect to a file-sharing service, you might see a dialog that asks you to confirm that you are connecting to the server you expect. You might also see this dialog each time you connect.

Automatic File-Sharing Service Authentication

When you select a Mac that provides file-sharing services, your Mac attempts to authenti-cate using one of three methods:

▶   If you're using Kerberos single sign-on authentication, your Mac attempts to authenti-cate to the selected Mac using your Kerberos credentials.

▶   If you're using non-Kerberos authentication but you connected to the selected Mac before and chose to save the authentication information to your keychain, your Mac attempts to use the saved information.

▶   Your Mac attempts to authenticate as a guest user.

If your Mac authenticates to the selected Mac, the Finder shows you the account name it connected with and lists the shared items available to this account.

If you choose View > as List, View > As Columns, or View > As Gallery, you can choose a shared item to connect to and mount the shared item.

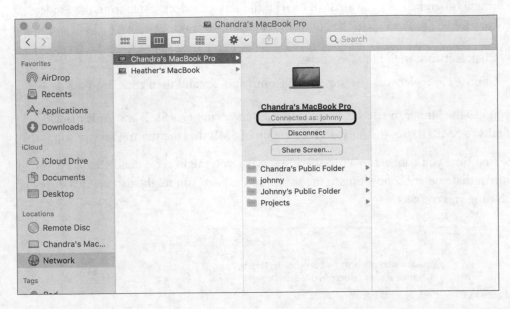

If you choose View > as Icons, double-click a shared item or select a shared item and then choose File > Open to connect to and mount the shared item.

Manual File-Sharing Service Authentication

If your Mac was unable to connect to the selected Mac, or if you need to authenticate with a different account, click the Connect As button to open an authentication dialog.

You can authenticate to a sharing service using one of three methods:

▶ If Select Guest is available, select it to connect anonymously to the file service.

▶ Select Registered User to authenticate using a local or network account known by the computer providing the shared items. Optionally, you can select the checkbox that saves this authentication information to your login keychain.

▶ If "Using an Apple ID" is available, select it to authenticate using an Apple ID. For this option to appear, your Mac and the Mac hosting the share must be running macOS (not Windows), and your local account must be associated with an Apple ID, as covered in Lesson 7, "Manage User Accounts."

Click the Connect button. Your Mac authenticates and shows you a new list of shared items that are available to the account.

Manually Connect to File-Sharing Services

Instead of browsing, you can specify a network identifier (URL) for a file service. You might also have to enter authentication information and choose or enter the name of a specific shared resource path. When you connect to an NFS, WebDAV (HTTP), or FTP service, you might have to specify the shared items or full path as part of the URL. When you connect to an SMB or AFP service, you don't have to provide the full path in the URL; you can authenticate and choose a shared item from the list of resources.

Manually Connect to SMB or AFP

To manually connect to an SMB or AFP file service from the Finder, choose Go > Connect to Server, or press Command-K, to open the Finder "Connect to Server" dialog. In the Server Address field, enter **smb://** or **afp://**, followed by the server IP address, DNS host name, computer name, or Bonjour name.

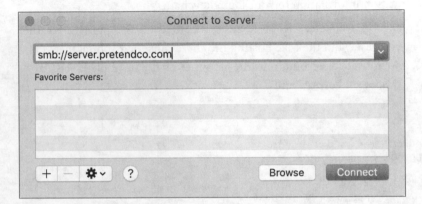

If you don't specify a protocol prefix, the "Connect to Server" dialog attempts to pick the appropriate file-sharing protocol. The default file-sharing protocol is SMB 3. Optionally, after the server address, you can enter another slash and the name of a shared item. This bypasses the dialog for selecting a file share.

If automatic file service authentication is available, you don't have to enter authentication information. Otherwise, a dialog appears requiring you to enter authentication information.

After you authenticate to a file service, if you have access to more than one shared folder, macOS displays the list of shared items that your account is allowed to access. Otherwise, the shared folder is automatically mounted.

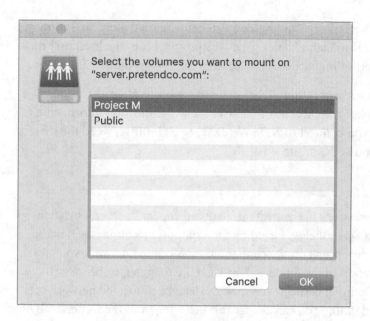

Select the shared item or items you want. Press the Command key to select multiple shared items from the list. Then click OK.

Manually Connect to NFS, WebDAV, or FTP

To manually connect to an NFS, WebDAV, or FTP file service from the Finder, choose Go > Connect to Server, or press Command-K, to open the Finder "Connect to Server" dialog.

In the Server Address field, enter one of the following:

▶ **nfs://** followed by the server address, another slash, and then the absolute file path of the shared items.

▶ **http://** for WebDAV (or **https://** for WebDAV encrypted with SSL or TLS), followed by the server address. Each WebDAV site has only one mountable share, but you can optionally enter another slash and then specify a folder inside the WebDAV share.

▶ **ftp://** (or **ftps://** for FTP encrypted with SSL or TLS), followed by the server address. FTP servers also have only one mountable root share, but you can optionally enter another slash and then specify a folder inside the FTP share.

Depending on the protocol settings, you might see an authentication dialog. NFS connections never display an authentication dialog. The NFS protocol uses the local user that you're logged in as for authorization purposes or Kerberos single sign-on authentication.

If you are presented with an authentication dialog, enter the appropriate authentication information. You can also select the checkbox that saves the authentication information to your login keychain. When you connect to NFS, WebDAV, or FTP file services, the share mounts immediately after you authenticate.

Mounted Shares

After your Mac mounts the network file share, that share can appear in several locations from the Finder or any app's Open dialog, including the Computer location, the desktop, and the sidebar Shared list, depending on the configuration. Mounted network volumes appear at the Computer location in the Finder. Choose Go > Computer, or press Shift-Command-C, to view the mounted network volumes. By default, connected network volumes don't appear on your desktop. You can change this behavior from the General tab of the Finder Preferences dialog.

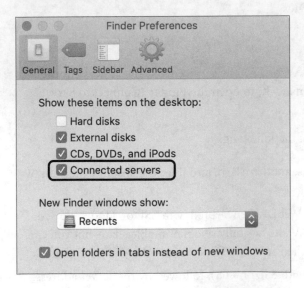

The dialog maintains a history of your past server connections. Click the menu to the right of the Server Address field to see the history. Click the Action menu (it looks like a gear) and choose Clear Recent Servers to clear the past server connections history. Select a server, then click Add (+) or Remove (–) to establish and maintain a favorite servers list.

Disconnect Mounted Shares

macOS treats mounted network volumes like locally attached volumes. So, you should unmount and eject network volumes when you're done with them. Unmount and eject mounted network volumes from the Finder using the same techniques you would use on a locally connected volume, as covered in Lesson 11, "Manage File Systems and Storage."

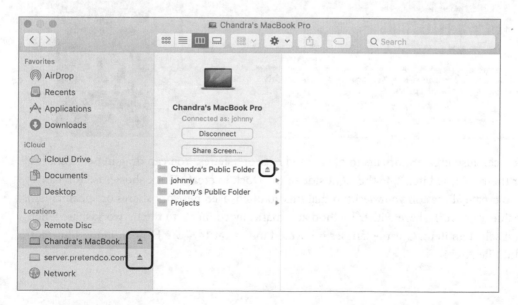

If a network change or problem disconnects your Mac from a mounted network share, your Mac tries to reconnect to the server hosting the shared items. If after several minutes your Mac can't reconnect to the server, macOS fully disconnects from the share and shows you a dialog to let you know.

Automatically Connect to File Shares

You can configure automatic connections to network shared items. You can use a configuration profile or add a network share to your login items so that it mounts automatically when you log in. You can read more about managing login items in Reference 7.4, "Configure Login and Fast User Switching."

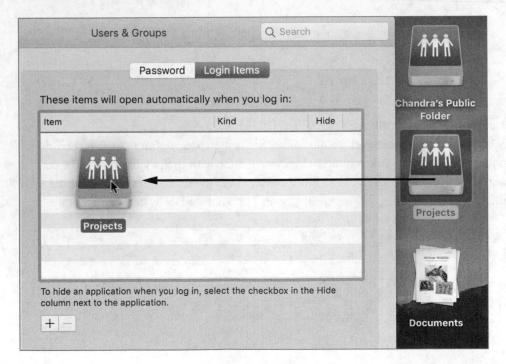

You can also create shortcuts to often-used network shares. You can drag network shares, or their enclosed items, to the right side of the Dock to create Dock shortcuts. You can also create aliases on your desktop that link to often-used network shares or specific items inside a network share. Either method automatically connects to the network share when you select an item. Creating aliases is covered in Lesson 14, "Use Hidden Items, Shortcuts, and File Archives."

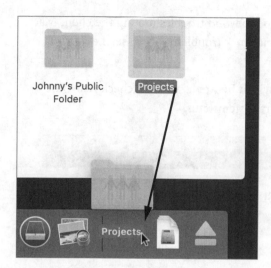

You can't drag items from the Finder sidebar to your login items or to the Dock. Instead, select the network share from the desktop or the Computer location in the Finder. From the Finder, choose Go > Computer to access the Computer location.

Reference 24.4
Troubleshoot Network Services

To troubleshoot a network issue, isolate the issue into one of three categories: local, network, or service. Most issues that involve failure to access network services probably fall under the service category. This means that you should probably focus most of your efforts on troubleshooting the service you're having issues with.

Before you troubleshoot a network service, check for general network issues. Verify that other network services work. Open Safari and navigate to local and Internet websites to test general network connectivity.

Test other network services, or test connectivity from other computers on the same network. If you experience problems connecting to a file server but you can connect to web servers, your network configuration is probably fine, and you should concentrate on the file server. If you experience problems with one service, you probably don't have local or network issues. Focus your efforts on troubleshooting just that service.

If other network clients or services aren't working, your issue is likely related to local or network issues. Use Network preferences and Network Utility to double-check local network settings to ensure proper configuration. If other computers aren't working, you might have a widespread network issue that goes beyond troubleshooting the client Mac computers. For more information on general network troubleshooting, see Lesson 23, "Troubleshoot Network Issues."

If you experience problems with a service provided by Apple, you can check real-time Apple service status at www.apple.com/support/systemstatus.

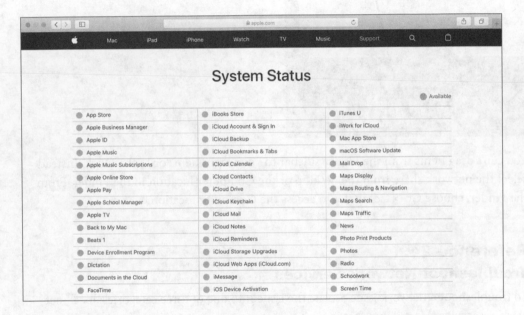

Use Network Utility: Port Scan

In Network Utility, use Port Scan to troubleshoot a network service.

Port Scan scans for open ports. If required ports aren't open, a device isn't providing the expected service or it's configured to provide the service in a nonstandard way. Either way, the issue is with the device providing the service, not with your Mac.

To troubleshoot a network service, start with ping to confirm that you can connect to the computer or device that provides the service you're trying to connect to. Ping is covered in more detail in Reference 23.2, "Use Network Utility to Troubleshoot Network Issues."

1   Open Network Utility.

2   Click Ping to view the Ping pane.

3   Enter the device network address or host name and click the Ping button.

If the ping is successful, then continue with the port scan.

To scan for a network service:

1   Open System Utility.

2   Click Port Scan.

3   Enter the network address or host name of the device that provides the service. If you're troubleshooting a specific service, limit the scan to that service's default ports by selecting the appropriate checkbox and entering a beginning and ending port range.

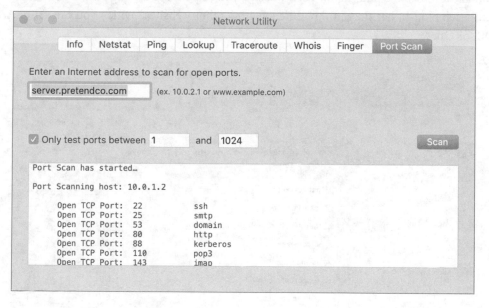

There are many TCP and UDP network ports. Scanning all of them is unnecessary and takes too much time. Even if you don't know the exact port, number, most common ports are between 0 and 1024. Further, network administrators might view repeated network pings and broad port scans as a threat. Some network devices are configured not to respond to ping requests even when they're working properly. Avoid excessive network pings and scans (a broad port range) when you test others' servers.

After you define the port range, click Scan. Depending on the range you choose, the scan might take several minutes. Network Utility lists discovered open ports with their associated network protocol. And it displays each open port with the service name that's registered by the Internet Assigned Numbers Authority (www.iana.org) for that port number, regardless of the service that uses the port.

Troubleshoot Network Apps

To troubleshoot apps, you can troubleshoot general network services. You can also double-check app-specific configuration and preference settings. Users can inadvertently cause a problem when they change a setting.

Some website designers might design a website to work with a browser other than Safari. These websites might not render properly in Safari. To provide the most secure web experience, Safari may disable third-party plug-ins. To verify the status of third-party plug-ins, choose Safari > Preferences (or press Command-Comma), click Websites, and then view the Plug-ins section in the left column. For each plug-in, you can specify which websites you allow to use the plug-in; for each website, you can choose among Ask, Off, and On. And each plug-in has the setting "When visiting other websites," which you can set to Ask, Off, or On.

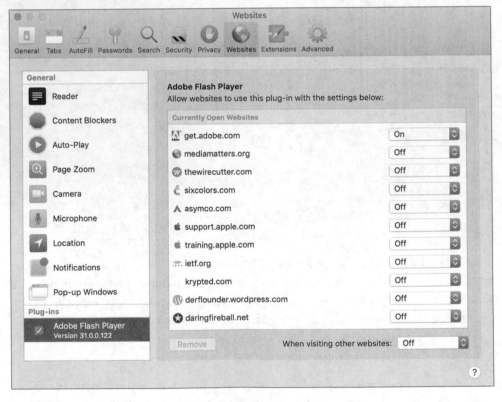

You might also try a third-party web browser.

To inspect problem webpages, open Safari preferences, click the Advanced button, and then select "Show Develop menu in menu bar."

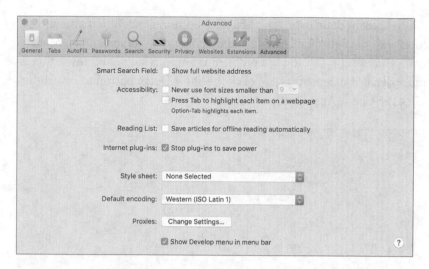

With this menu enabled, inspect the webpage details or try advanced troubleshooting, including emptying Safari caches and requesting the website with a different user agent.

Mail includes a built-in account diagnostic tool, Mail Connection Doctor, that attempts to establish a connection with configured incoming and outgoing mail servers. Open Mail, and choose Window > Connection Doctor. If a problem is found, a suggested resolution is offered, but for a more detailed diagnostic view, click the Show Detail button to reveal the progress log, and click the Check Again button to rerun the tests.

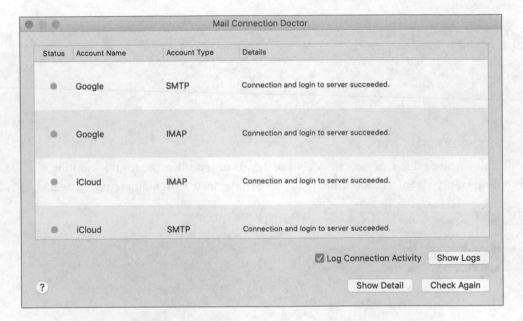

Troubleshoot File-Sharing Services

If you have problems with SMB services, try the steps in Apple Support article HT204021, "If you can't mount SMB share hosted by a Mac bound to Open Directory."

As covered in Lesson 16, "Use Metadata, Spotlight, and Siri," macOS uses separate metadata stores. The NFS and WebDAV file-sharing protocols don't support metadata of this type. So macOS splits these files into two separate files when writing to a mounted NFS or WebDAV volume. The Finder recognizes these split files and shows you only a single file. Users on other operating systems see two separate files and might have trouble accessing the appropriate one.

Exercise 24.1
Configure a Network Service Account for Mail

> ### Prerequisite
>
> ► You must have created the Johnny Appleseed account (Exercise 7.1, "Create a Standard User Account").

The built-in macOS client apps use network services and Internet Accounts preferences to make setting up Internet service accounts easy. You already set up iCloud-based services on your Mac. In this exercise, you configure your Mac to use the mail service provided by the classroom server.

View Your Existing Network Accounts

1   Log in as Johnny Appleseed.

2   Open Mail.

3   Choose Mail > Preferences (Command-Comma) to open Mail preferences.

4   Click the Accounts button to see the accounts Mail is configured to use.

If you configured iCloud services for the Johnny Appleseed account, you see the iCloud account listed here.

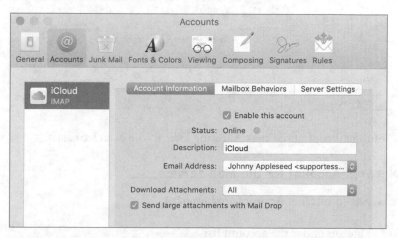

You could use this pane of the Mail preferences window to view and add a new Mail account, but more often you'll configure Mail accounts in Internet Accounts preferences.

5   Close the Mail preferences window, and quit Mail.

6   Open Internet Accounts preferences.

Your iCloud account information is listed on the left side of the window. You can manage iCloud settings here and in iCloud preferences. You might also see a Game Center account.

7   Select your iCloud account and deselect the Mail service on the right.

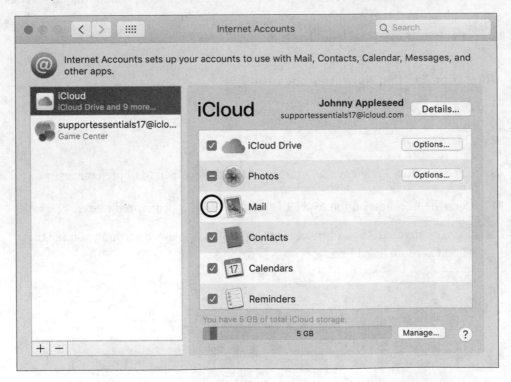

Not having iCloud mail configured makes testing later in the exercise easier.

Set Up a New Network Account for the Mail service

1   If necessary, navigate to Internet Accounts preferences.

2   Click the Add (+) button under the account list.

3   Scroll to the bottom of the list, and click Add Other Account.

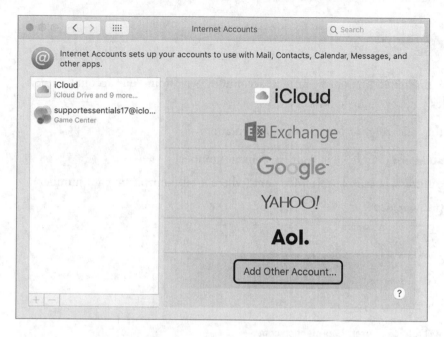

More account types appear at the bottom of the list.

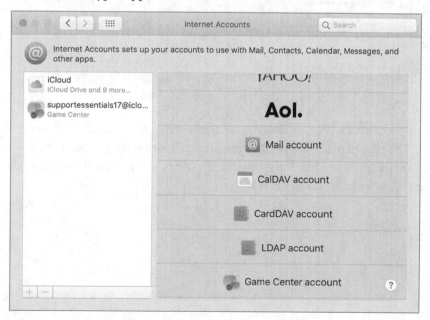

4 Click "Mail account."

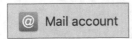

You are prompted for your basic mail account information. Your account name includes your participant number.

5 Enter the following for your account information:

Name: **User *nn*** (where *nn* is your participant number)

Email Address: **user*nn*@pretendco.com** (where *nn* is your participant number)

Password: **Apple321!**

6 Click "Sign in."

A dialog appears indicating that Internet Accounts can't verify the account name or password. The type of mail account that you are configuring doesn't have presets or auto-discovery capabilities like some other services. So, you'll enter the name of the incoming (IMAP) and outgoing (SMTP) servers.

7   In both the Incoming and Outgoing Mail server fields, enter **server.pretendco.com**.

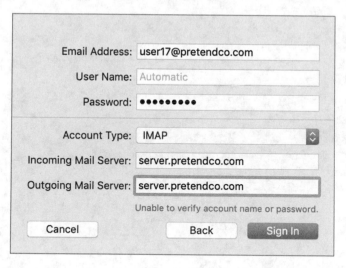

8   Click Sign In.

Now that you provided the proper Incoming and Outgoing mail servers, Internet Accounts asks you which apps you want to use with this account.

9   At the prompt, deselect Notes, and click Done.

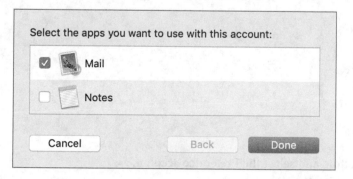

10 Notice that a new mail account was added to the Internet accounts list.

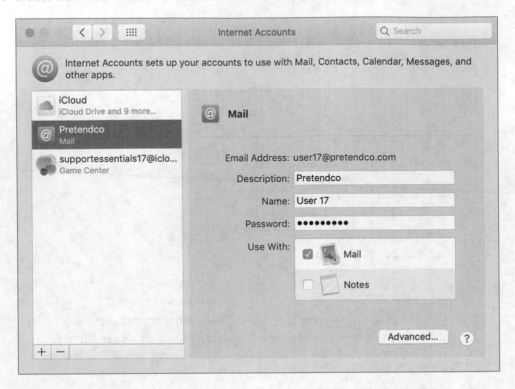

11 Quit System Preferences.

Test Your New Account

1 Open Mail.

2 Open Mail preferences.

3 Click the Accounts button, and select the Pretendco account.

In this figure, the Mail account for User 17 was automatically configured by Internet Accounts. Your participant number is on your Mac.

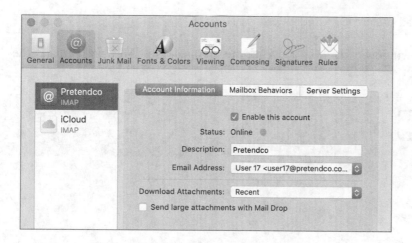

4 Click Server Settings.

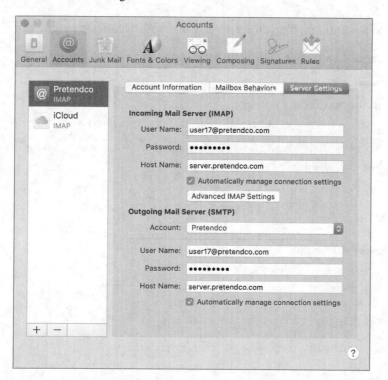

A complex setup was configured automatically by Internet Accounts.

5   Close the Mail preferences window.

6   In the main window of the Mail app, click the Compose New Message button in the toolbar.

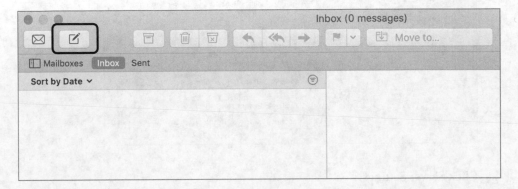

7   Send a message to a partner of your choice, or one that your facilitator assigns.

To: **user*nn*@pretendco.com** (where *nn* is your partner's participant number)

Subject: **Test Message**

Enter some text in the body of the message.

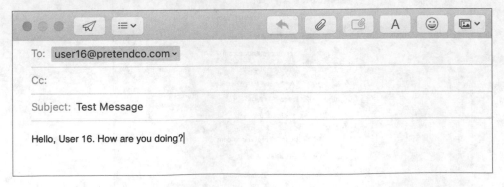

8   Ask your partner if they have received your message.

After your partner sends you a message, you receive new mail.

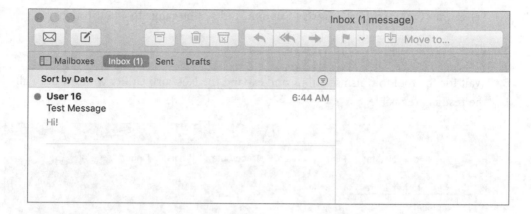

9 Read the message from your partner.

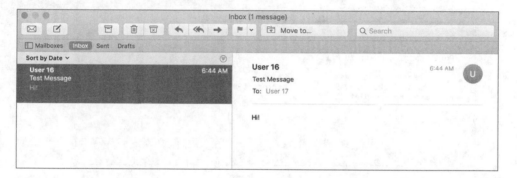

10 Quit Mail.

Scan the Server

To prepare for Exercise 24.3, "Troubleshoot Network Services," you record a baseline of what services the classroom server provides when everything is working.

1 Open Network Utility (Command-Space bar or Spotlight).

2 Click the Port Scan button.

The Port Scan tool scans a server or other IP address to see what network ports are accepting connections. This is explored in more detail in Exercise 24.3.

3 Enter the server address **server.local** in the IP address field.

4   Select the "Only test ports between" option, and set the range to **443** through **445**.

5   Click Scan.

6   Wait for the tool to finish scanning and expand the Network Utility window until all the results are visible.

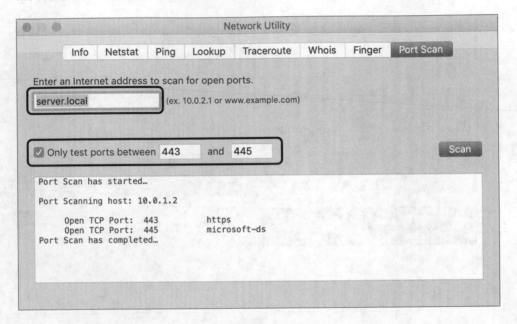

Your results might not match those shown here. Take a screenshot to record your results. For more about taking screenshots in macOS, see Exercise 8.1, "Restore a Deleted User Account."

7   Press Shift-Command-4, release the keys, and then press the Space bar.

The pointer changes to a camera icon, and the region of the screen it's over is highlighted in blue.

8   Move the pointer over the Network Utility window, and click to take the screen capture.

The image is saved to your desktop with the name "Screen Shot" followed by the date and time you took it.

9   Quit Network Utility.

Exercise 24.2
Use File-Sharing Services

> **Prerequisite**
>
> ▸ You must have created the Johnny Appleseed account (Exercise 7.1, "Create a Standard User Account").

Browse to an SMB Share

In these steps you use the Finder sidebar to mount an SMB volume on the desktop.

1 Log in as Johnny Appleseed.

2 In the Finder, select Server in the Locations section of the sidebar.

If Server isn't shown, click Network in the sidebar, and double-click Server in the network view.

Your Mac contacts Server and logs in as a guest.

3 Click the Connect As button.

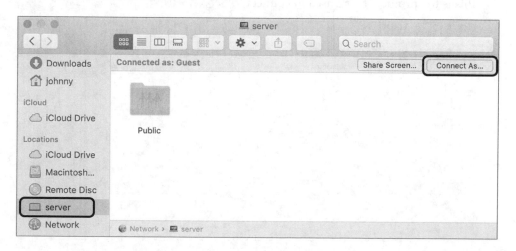

4 Click Connect at the "You are attempting to connect to the server 'server'" dialog.

5 When prompted to authenticate, select Registered User, enter the name **participant** and the password **Apple321!**, select "Remember this password in my keychain," and click Connect.

You are connected to Server with the "participant" account. The Finder shows that you have access to more shared folders than you did as a guest. The SMB Shared folder is available only over the SMB protocol, so its appearance here indicates that this is the protocol being used to connect to Server.

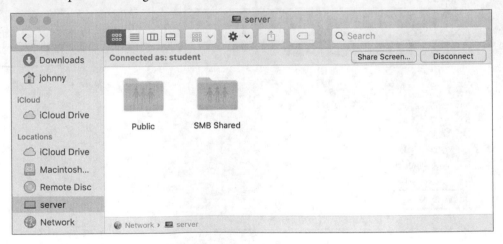

6 Open Finder preferences: choose Finder > Preferences (Command-Comma), click General, and select "Connected servers," if it isn't selected.

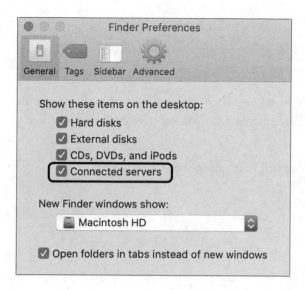

This enables mounted server volumes to be displayed on the desktop. Since you haven't mounted shared folders yet, nothing new appears on the desktop.

7   Close the Finder preferences window.

8   Open the Public shared folder.

The folder displays in the Finder, and a new network volume icon appears on the desktop.

In the Public folder you see a file (copy.rtf) and the ParticipantMaterials folder.

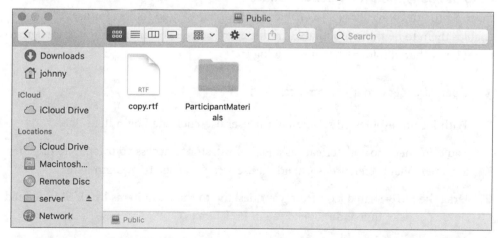

Copy Files to a Network Share

1   Drag copy.rtf to your desktop. Since you are dragging from one volume to another, this copies the file rather than moving it.

2   Rename your copy of copy.rtf to **Participant *nn*.rtf** (where *nn* is your participant number if you are in a classroom environment or 1 if you are performing these exercises on your own).

Press Return or click the filename and wait a moment to rename it.

3   Select Server in the Finder sidebar.

This returns you to the view of available shared folders.

4   Open the SMB Shared folder.

Its icon appears on your desktop.

5   Drag the renamed file from your desktop to the SMB Shared folder.

Automatically Mount a Network Share

macOS provides ways for you to enable easy access to shared folders for users. This enables them to be more productive. In this exercise, you configure your user preferences to mount a shared folder whenever you log in.

1   Open Users & Groups preferences.

2   With Johnny Appleseed selected in the user list, click the Login Items tab.

You don't need to authenticate as an administrator to access your login items. They are a personal preference, so standard users can manage their login items.

3   Drag the SMB Shared icon from your desktop to the login items list. If SMB Shared doesn't appear, quit and reopen System Preferences.

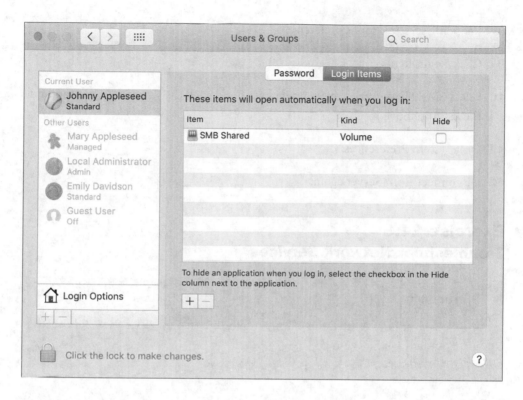

Anything in your login items list is opened every time you log in. It can include apps, documents, and folders. When you add a shared folder, you configured it to mount every time you log in. Since you also saved the server account name and password to your keychain when you connected, the connection should be fully automatic.

4 Quit System Preferences.

5 Click the Eject button next to Server in the Finder sidebar to disconnect from Server.

When you disconnect from the server, it automatically unmounts the Public and SMB Shared folders. You can also unmount them individually.

6 Log out and back in as Johnny Appleseed.

7 If a connect dialog appears, click Connect to confirm. The password is filled in from your keychain.

The SMB Shared folder is remounted and opened in the Finder.

8 Reopen Users & Groups preferences.

9 Click Login Items.

10 Select SMB Shared from the login items list and click the Remove (–) button under the list to remove it.

11 Quit System Preferences.

12 Disconnect from Server again.

Exercise 24.3
Troubleshoot Network Services

> **Prerequisite**
>
> ▶ You must have created the Johnny Appleseed account (Exercise 7.1, "Create a Standard User Account").

In this group of exercises, you learn an alternative way to connect to a share and ways to troubleshoot file sharing.

Wait for the Facilitator to Turn Off File Sharing

Tell your facilitator that you're ready for the file-sharing service to be turned off, and wait for the facilitator to tell you to proceed.

Manually Connect to an SMB Share

1 In the Finder, choose Go > Connect to Server (or press Command-K).

2 In the Server Address field, enter **smb://server.pretendco.com** to connect using the SMB protocol.

3 Before you click Connect, click the Add (+) button at the bottom of the Favorite Servers list.

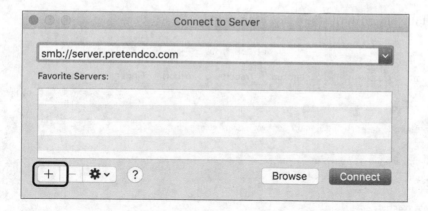

This adds the server URL to your Favorite Servers list. This is another way to allow access to a shared folder.

4   Click Connect.

After a few seconds, you receive an error message that there was a problem connecting to the server.

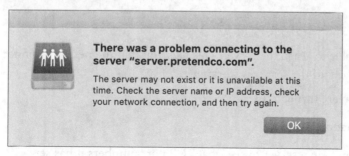

5   Click OK, and close the "Connect to Server" window.

Troubleshoot with Network Utility

1   Open Network Utility.

Since you are unable to reach the server via the SMB protocol, make sure the network connections between your Mac and the server are working.

2   Click Ping at the top of the application window if necessary.

3   In the "Enter the network address to ping" field, enter **server.pretendco.com**.

4 Click the Ping button at the right side of the window..

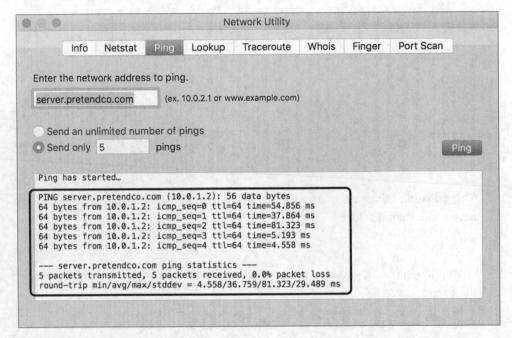

The ping probes are able to reach the server. This tells you that the network connection between your Mac and the server is working.

Go to the services you are trying to use.

5 Click the Port Scan button.

The Port Scan tool can scan a server to see what TCP port numbers it has services running on. Usually, you can tell what services are available based on the port numbers.

NOTE ▶ Many network attacks start with or employ port scans, so this type of troubleshooting might be interpreted as an attack. Before you scan ports on a target Mac, request permission from its owner or a network or server administrator, if possible. As a general rule, scan ports only on Mac computers you have responsibility for. Many environments employ automatic countermeasures. Scanning a server might get your MAC address or IP address blacklisted, preventing you from knowing whether you resolved the problem.

6   If necessary, enter the server address **server.local** in the IP address field.

7   If necessary, select the "Only test ports between" option, and set the range to **443** through **445**.

8   Click Scan.

9   Watch the scan as it identifies the open ports.

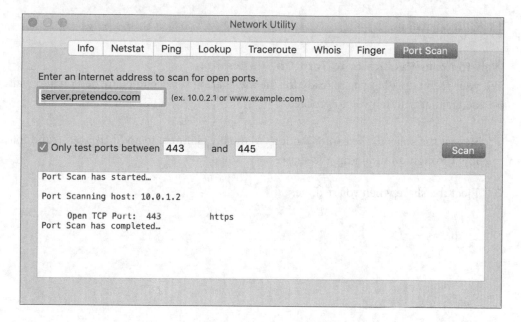

If you had scanned for a larger range, the port scan would list other open ports. In this case, the port scan lists the open ports it finds and the names of the services usually associated with them. These ports are commonly used and facilitate interoperability across different vendor implementations of the same protocols. To test whether a Mac has an HTTP (web) server, run a port scan on it to see if TCP port 80 is open. HTTPS (a TLS-secured web service) normally uses TCP port 443. If HTTPS requests aren't working, port 443 might be blocked or inactive.

For a list of many ports used by Apple devices, see Apple Support article HT202944, "TCP and UDP ports used by Apple software products."

10 Open the screenshot you took in Exercise 24.1 that shows which ports were open when the services were working and compare it with the current scan.

In this exercise, you are trying to troubleshoot the SMB file service, which normally involves TCP port 445 (microsoft-ds). This port is listed in the earlier scan but not in the current scan. This indicates that the server doesn't offer file services over SMB (which is true here since the service is turned off) or that a firewall is blocking access to the service.

11 Quit open apps.

Wait for Your Facilitator to Turn On File Sharing

Tell your facilitator that you're ready for the file-sharing service to be turned on and wait for the facilitator to tell you to proceed.

1 Repeat the steps in the earlier section "Manually Connect to an SMB Share," and follow through on mounting the share.

2 Eject the share when you're done.

Lesson 25

Manage Host Sharing and Personal Firewall

In this lesson, you focus on using macOS as both a network client and a shared resource for network and Internet services. After an introduction to shared services, you delve into remotely controlling Mac computers with screen-sharing services. Then you see how to use AirDrop—the easiest way to share files between Apple devices. You also learn how to secure access to shared resources from macOS using the built-in personal firewall. Finally, this lesson covers general troubleshooting methods to resolve issues that might arise when you attempt to share services from your Mac.

Reference 25.1
Enable Host-Sharing Services

macOS includes an assortment of shared network services. These shared services vary in implementation and purpose, but you use them all to enable users to remotely access resources on your Mac. You can enable and manage them from Sharing preferences. Standard users need to click the lock in the lower-left corner of Sharing preferences and provide administrator credentials to make changes.

GOALS

▶ Examine and enable host-sharing services built into macOS

▶ Examine and enable Content Caching services built into macOS

▶ Use screen-sharing tools to access other network hosts

▶ Use AirDrop to share files

▶ Configure a personal firewall to secure shared services

▶ Troubleshoot sharing services

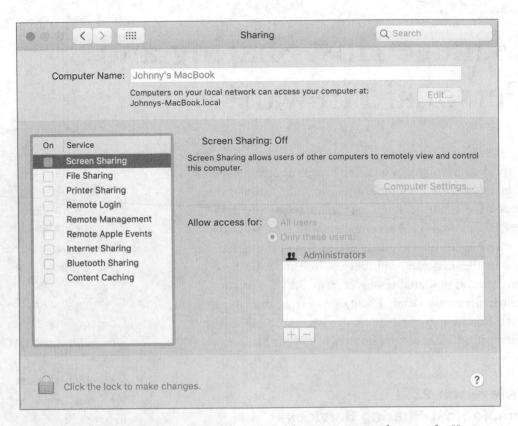

Remote users can't access services on your Mac if your Mac is in sleep mode. You can turn off your Mac computer's automatic sleep activation or enable automatic waking for network access from Energy Saver preferences. Automatic wake on wired and wireless networks works on macOS if your network hardware supports it.

NOTE ▶ To prevent your Mac from going to sleep, select "Prevent computer from sleeping automatically when the display is off" in Energy Saver preferences, as covered in Reference 28.3, "Sleep Modes, Logout, and Shutdown." If your Mac doesn't have a display, you can use the **caffeinate** command in Terminal to keep your Mac awake.

You should recognize the security risk involved in providing a service that enables other users to control processes on your Mac. If you're providing a service that allows remote control and execution of software, it's possible for an unauthorized user to cause trouble. When you enable these types of services, choose strong security settings. Use strong passwords and configure limited access to these services from Sharing preferences.

Configure Network Identification

You might be unable to control your Mac computer's IP address or DNS host name, because the network administrator usually controls these. But as long as the Mac has properly configured TCP/IP settings, as outlined in Lesson 21, "Manage Basic Network Settings," your configuration is complete for these two identifiers. If your Mac has multiple IP addresses or DNS host names properly configured, it also accepts connections from those.

For dynamic network discovery protocols, though, your Mac uses network identification that can be set locally by an administrator. By default, your Mac automatically chooses a name based either on its DNS name or on the name of the user created with Setup Assistant. However, at any time an administrator user can change the Mac computer's network identifier from the Sharing preferences. Just enter a name in the Computer Name field, and the system sets the name for each available discovery protocol.

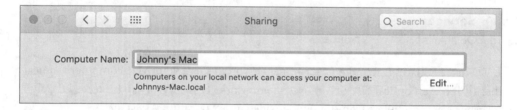

For example, if you enter the computer name Johnny's Mac, the Bonjour name is set to Johnnys-Mac.local and the NetBIOS/WINS name is set to JOHNNYS-MAC. If the name you choose is already taken by another local device, the Mac automatically appends a number to the end of the name. NetBIOS/WINS may require additional configuration if your network uses multiple domains or workgroups, as covered in Lesson 22, "Manage Advanced Network Settings."

The local Bonjour service needs no additional configuration, but if you want to set a custom Bonjour name, click the Edit button below the Computer Name field to reveal the Local Hostname field. From this interface, you can also register your Mac computer's identification for Wide-Area Bonjour. Wide-Area Bonjour uses an intermediary service to facilitate Bonjour browsing to networks outside the computer's current subnet. If this service is available on your network, select the "Use dynamic global hostname" checkbox to reveal the Wide-Area Bonjour settings.

Use this name to reach this computer from machines on your local subnet.

Local Hostname: Johnnys-Mac.local

☑ Use dynamic global hostname

Hostname: _____

User: _____

Password: _____

☐ Advertise services in this domain using Bonjour

(?)   Cancel   OK

Shared Services

The macOS sharing services include:

▸ DVD or CD Sharing (Remote Disc)—Enables you to share your Mac computer's optical disc (if it has an optical disc drive) over the network. This service can be accessed only by other Mac computers from the Finder sidebar or Migration Assistant.

▸ Screen Sharing—Enables remote control of your Mac. Using this service is detailed later in this lesson.

▸ File Sharing—Enables remote access to your Mac computer's file system with the Server Message Block (SMB) Protocol and Apple Filing Protocol (AFP) network file-sharing services. When you enable the File Sharing service, the launchd control process listens for SMB service requests on TCP port 445 and automatically starts the smbd process as necessary to handle any requests. The launchd control process listens for AFP service requests on TCP port 548 and automatically starts the AppleFileServer process as necessary to handle any requests. By default on macOS, only standard and administrator users have access to file-sharing services, but you can modify access for other users as outlined in Lesson 13, "Manage Permissions and Sharing." Connecting to file-sharing services is covered in Lesson 24, "Manage Network Services."

▸ Printer Sharing—Allows network access to printers that are directly attached to your Mac. Using this service is covered in Lesson 27, "Manage Printers and Scanners."

▶ Scanner Sharing—Allows network access to document scanners that are configured for your Mac. This service works only with other Mac computers on a local network (Bonjour) with Image Capture. This service also operates only on a per-user basis, and it is available only when the user is logged in. When this service is enabled, the launchd control process listens for scanner-sharing requests on a very high randomly selected TCP port and starts the Image Capture Extension background process as needed to handle any requests. The only additional configuration is that you can, from Sharing preferences, enable specific scanners if you have more than one attached.

▶ Remote Login—Enables remote control of your Mac computer's command line with Secure Shell (SSH). Further, SSH remote login enables you to securely transfer files using Secure File Transfer Protocol (SFTP) or the secure copy command scp. With Remote Login enabled, the launchd control process listens for remote login service requests on TCP 22 and starts the sshd background process as needed to handle any requests. By default, administrator user accounts are allowed to access the service.

▶ Remote Management—Augments the Screen Sharing service to allow remote administration of your Mac with the Apple Remote Desktop (ARD) app. Read Apple Support article HT209161, "Use the kickstart command-line utility on macOS Mojave 10.14," for more information about using scripting and a configuration profile to enable remote management for a Mac that's enrolled in your organization's MDM with User Approved MDM enrollment or through Device Enrollment with Apple Business Manager or Apple School Manager.

▶ Remote Apple Events—Allows apps and AppleScripts on another Mac to communicate with apps and services on your Mac. This service is often used to facilitate automated AppleScript workflows between apps running on separate Mac computers. When this service is enabled, the launchd control process listens for remote Apple Events requests on TCP and UDP port 3130 and starts the AEServer background process as needed to handle any requests. By default, all nonguest user accounts are allowed to access the service, but you can limit this to specific users from the Sharing preferences.

▶ Internet Sharing—Allows your Mac to reshare a single network or Internet connection with other network interfaces. For example, if your Mac had Internet access through wired Ethernet and you didn't have a Wi-Fi router, you could enable Internet Sharing for the Mac computer's Wi-Fi and turn it into a wireless access point for your other computers and devices. When you enable the Internet Sharing service, the launchd process starts several background processes. The natd process performs the Network Address Translation (NAT) service that allows multiple network clients to share a single network or Internet connection. The bootpd process provides the DHCP automatic network configuration service for the network devices connected with your Mac. When a network device connects to your Mac computer's shared network connection, it automatically obtains an IP address, usually in the 10.0.2.X range. The named process provides DNS resolution for network devices connected to the Internet with your Mac.

▶ Bluetooth Sharing—Allows access to your Mac with Bluetooth short-range wireless. Using this service is covered in Lesson 26, "Troubleshoot Peripherals."

▶ Content Caching—Helps reduce Internet bandwidth usage and speed up software installation and iCloud content sharing on Mac computers, iOS devices, and AppleTV devices. See the next section for more information.

Content Caching

You can enable and configure the content caching service in the Content Caching pane of System Preferences.

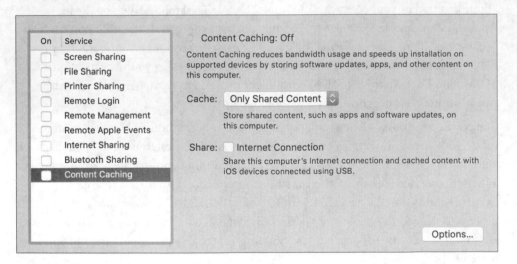

The content caching service speeds up downloading of software distributed by Apple and data that users store in iCloud by saving content that local devices have already downloaded. When you turn on content caching, you see a message that you can restart devices on your network for them to immediately start using your Mac computer's content cache.

When you turn on content caching, the option Cache Only Shared Content is enabled by default.

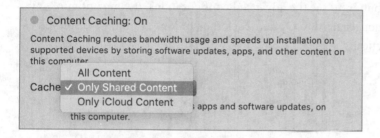

You can click the Cache menu and choose:

▶   All Content—Store shared content, such as apps and software, and iCloud content, such as photos and documents

▶   Only Shared Content—Store only shared content, such as apps and software

▶   Only iCloud Content—Store only iCloud content, such as photos and documents

The "Share Internet connection" option turns on "tethered caching" so that you can share your Mac computer's Internet connection to iOS devices that are connected using USB. This can save time, local Wi-Fi, and bandwidth when you're using a cart or USB hub and updating several devices at once, compared to updating each device individually over Wi-Fi. Use the content caching service to install large apps while preparing devices for the beginning of a larger deployment, semester, or new school year.

Click the Options button to reveal how much storage content caching is currently using on your disk. Content caching uses the startup disk by default, but if your Mac has more than one disk, you can choose a different disk for content caching to use. Use the slider to change the amount of space content caching can use before it starts removing items to make room for newer items.

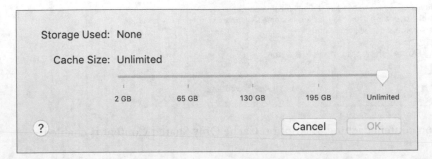

Option-click the Options button to see the advanced configurations. If you configure any advanced options, you no longer need to Option-click the Options button; it's displayed as Advanced Options automatically.

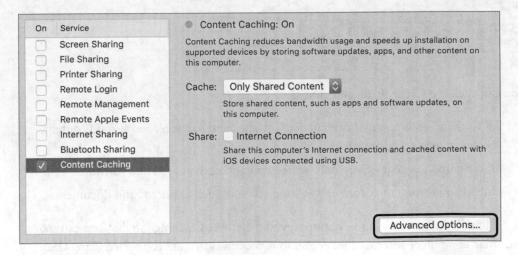

The buttons available include:

▶ Storage—Displays the configuration available when you click the Options button in Content Caching.

▶ Clients—Lets you configure which clients and networks you will provide content caching for. On larger networks with multiple Mac computers that provide content caching, it is important to ensure that a content cache receives requests only from appropriate clients. Defining clients as "appropriate" means that you can choose to cache content for clients that use the same public IP address, the same local networks,

networks that you specify, or networks that you specify in addition to clients that can't contact their preferred content cache. By default the menu for "My local networks" is set to "use one public IP address," and the public IPv4 address is discovered automatically. If you click the menu for "My local networks" and choose "use custom public IP addresses," you must define at least one range of IPv4 addresses. This requires you to perform additional DNS configuration for your network; to assist with the additional DNS configuration, click the DNS Configuration button to generate an appropriate command to run or DNS record to add, depending on what DNS service your network uses.

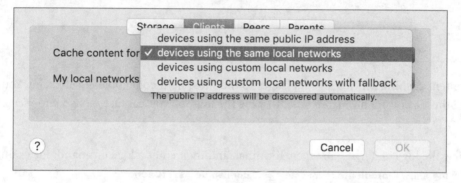

▶ Peers—Content caches on the same network are called peers, and they share content with each other. Configure which other content caches to share content with (caches with the same public IP address, the same local networks, or networks that you specify).

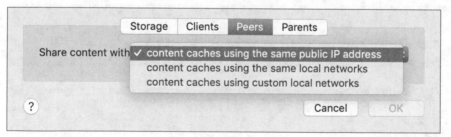

▶ Parents—You can arrange your content caches in a hierarchy. When you add the IPv4 addresses of other content caches here, they are considered parents to your Mac computer's content cache, and your Mac is a child. If you refer to a parent by its IPv4 address, you should configure the parent with a static IPv4 address. If you define multiple parents, open the menu for "Parent policy" to specify how your content cache chooses which parent to use.

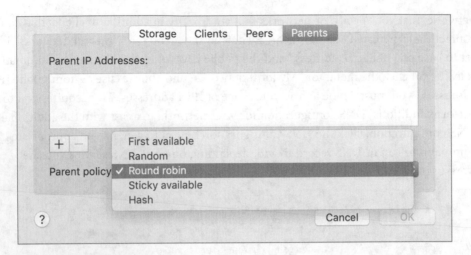

The content caching service logs messages to the subsystem com.apple.AssetCache. You can use the log command in Terminal to view the logs, or you can use Console to view the logs.

▶ View the logs in Terminal: Open Terminal, and then enter a log command; for example: **log show --predicate 'subsystem == "com.apple.AssetCache"'**.

▶ View the logs in Console: Open Console, enter **s:com.apple.AssetCache** in the search field, and then press Return. Select an entry or hover your pointer over an entry for more details.

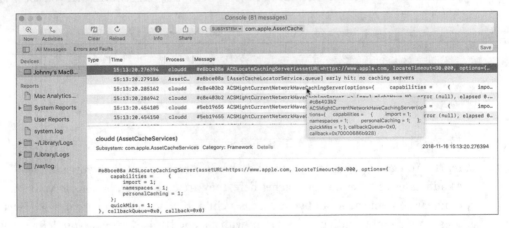

For Mac computers, use the **AssetCacheLocator** command in Terminal to view information about content caching services your Mac will use. Open Terminal, enter the command **/usr/bin/AssetCacheLocator**, then press Return.

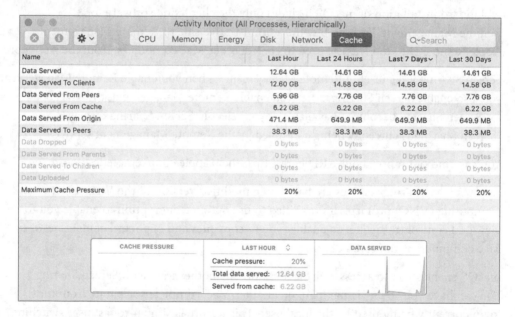

After you enable Content Caching in Sharing preferences, Activity Monitor automatically displays the Cache button in the Activity Monitor toolbar.

Name	Last Hour	Last 24 Hours	Last 7 Days ∨	Last 30 Days
Data Served	12.64 GB	14.61 GB	14.61 GB	14.61 GB
Data Served To Clients	12.60 GB	14.58 GB	14.58 GB	14.58 GB
Data Served From Peers	5.96 GB	7.76 GB	7.76 GB	7.76 GB
Data Served From Cache	6.22 GB	6.22 GB	6.22 GB	6.22 GB
Data Served From Origin	471.4 MB	649.9 MB	649.9 MB	649.9 MB
Data Served To Peers	38.3 MB	38.3 MB	38.3 MB	38.3 MB
Data Dropped	0 bytes	0 bytes	0 bytes	0 bytes
Data Served From Parents	0 bytes	0 bytes	0 bytes	0 bytes
Data Served To Children	0 bytes	0 bytes	0 bytes	0 bytes
Data Uploaded	0 bytes	0 bytes	0 bytes	0 bytes
Maximum Cache Pressure	20%	20%	20%	20%

For more information about the options for content caching, open Sharing preferences, select Content Caching, and then click the Help button. You can also read the following Apple Support articles:

▶ HT208025— "Prepare for changes to Content Caching in macOS High Sierra"

▶ HT204675— "Content types that macOS Server caching and macOS caching support"

▶ HT207523—"About macOS Sierra tethered caching"

For more information about advanced settings, read "Caching Content: Configure advanced caching content settings" at https://help.apple.com/deployment/macos/#/ior0617a3d13.

Reference 25.2
Control Remote Computers

When it comes to troubleshooting or administration of another Mac, nothing beats seeing the computer screen and controlling its mouse and keyboard. macOS includes built-in software that enables you to view and control the graphical interface through Screen Sharing, Messages screen sharing, and Remote Management.

Screen-Sharing Services

A standard installation of macOS includes only the client-side software for Remote Management. You can buy the administrative side of Remote Management, Apple Remote Desktop (ARD), used to control other Mac computers, from the App Store.

Screen Sharing is a subset of Remote Management. When you enable Remote Management, you also enable Screen Sharing. After you enable Remote Management, the checkbox for Screen Sharing becomes unavailable. If you select it, Screen Sharing displays, "Screen Sharing is currently being controlled by the Remote Management service."

You can find out more about ARD here: https://help.apple.com/remotedesktop/mac.

Apple screen-sharing services are based on a modified version of the Virtual Network Computing (VNC) protocol. It's modified to use optional encryption to enable you to view and control traffic. It also enables you to copy files and clipboard content between Mac computers with Screen Sharing.

macOS enables you to access a virtual desktop on another Mac with Screen Sharing. You can have your own virtual login on another Mac, completely separate from the login currently being used by the local user. This feature is similar to fast user switching (covered in Lesson 7, "Manage User Accounts"), except the second user is remote with Screen Sharing and potentially using the Mac at the same time as the local user.

VNC is a cross-platform standard for remote control, so if configured properly, the macOS Screen Sharing service integrates well with other third-party VNC-based systems. Your Mac can control, or be controlled by, VNC-based software regardless of operating

system or platform. For more details on VNC, refer to https://en.wikipedia.org/wiki/
Virtual_Network_Computing.

Enable Screen Sharing

Before you can access a Mac remotely with Screen Sharing, the remote Mac must have
the Screen Sharing service enabled. To enable Screen Sharing for your Mac, open Sharing
preferences, and then select the Screen Sharing checkbox.

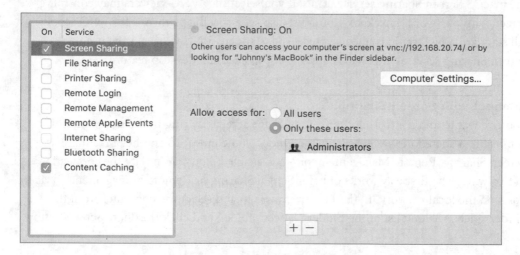

By default, only administrator user accounts are allowed to access the service. You can
adjust Screen Sharing access. Select the "All users" radio button or use the Add (+)
and Remove (–) buttons at the bottom of the users list. When you add accounts, a
dialog appears enabling you to select the users or groups to whom you want to grant
Screen Sharing access.

You can allow a range of operating systems to access your Mac computer's Screen Sharing
service by clicking the Computer Settings button. This displays a dialog where you can
enable guest and standard VNC screen-sharing access.

When you attempt to access your Mac computer's screen, the currently logged-in user must authorize the session. By default, only local authorized users and groups are enabled to use Screen Sharing. Select "Anyone may request permission to control screen" to enable anyone (from another Mac) to ask permission to share the screen. For this feature to work, you must remove any access restrictions for Screen Sharing by allowing access to all users.

Standard third-party VNC viewers can't authenticate using the secure methods used by the macOS Screen Sharing service. Thus, if you select the "VNC viewers may control screen with password" checkbox, you must also set a specific password for VNC access. All standard VNC traffic is unencrypted. And, standard VNC viewers can't use the Screen Sharing service's clipboard copy, file copy, or virtual desktop features.

Connect with Screen Sharing

You connect to and control another computer for Screen Sharing in the same way you connect to a shared file system. From the Finder, you connect to another Mac that has Screen Sharing, Remote Management, or VNC enabled. You can initiate the connection in two ways. The first way works only for Screen Sharing or Remote Management service hosts on the local network. In the Finder, browse to and select the computer from the Finder sidebar Shared list or the Finder Network folder, and click the Share Screen button.

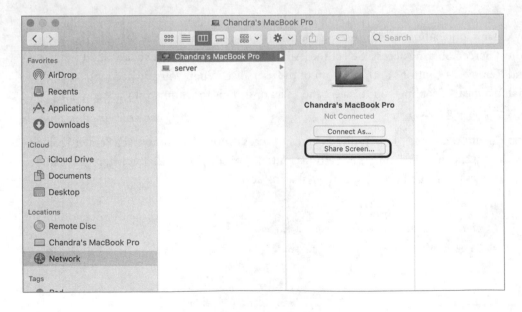

The second way enables you to connect to and control hosts that provide Screen Sharing, Remote Management, or standard VNC services. In the Finder, choose Go > Connect to Server. In the "Connect to Server" dialog, enter **vnc://** followed by the Mac IP address, DNS host name, or Bonjour name, and click Connect.

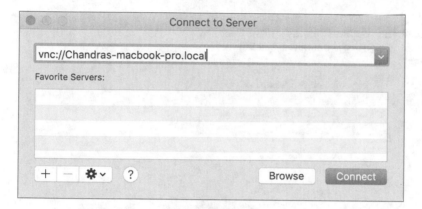

Regardless of the connection method, macOS opens the /System/Library/CoreServices/ Applications/Screen Sharing app and initiates a connection to the specified host. You see a dialog that requires you to make an authentication choice. If you use Kerberos single sign-on or saved your authentication information to a keychain, macOS authenticates for you and doesn't present the authentication dialog.

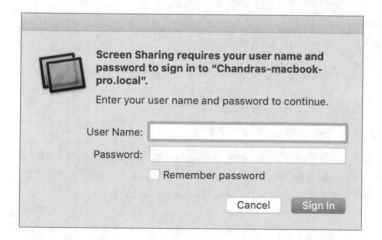

You'll see an authentication dialog with the authentication choice, "By requesting permission," only if both of the following are true:

► The remote Mac has the "Anyone may request permission to control screen" option enabled

► Someone is currently logged in on the remote Mac

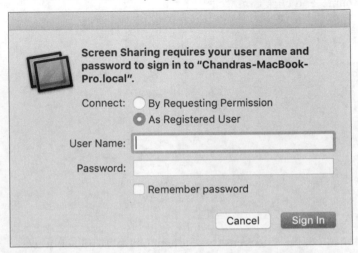

If you select By Requesting Permission and then click Sign In, a dialog that asks permission appears on the remote Mac.

The second authentication choice, As Registered User, requires you to authenticate with a user account. You can select the checkbox that saves this information to your login keychain. After you make your authentication selection, click Sign In to continue.

Depending on the remote computer's system, one of three situations occurs when Screen Sharing establishes the connection:

▶ If the remote computer isn't a Mac, you instantly connect to the current screen of the remote computer.

▶ If the remote computer is a Mac and no one is logged in, or if you authenticated as the currently logged-in user, or if the currently logged-in user isn't an administrator, you instantly connect to the current screen of the remote Mac.

▶ If the remote computer is a Mac and you authenticated as a different user from the administrator who is currently logged in to the Mac, you are presented with a dialog that enables you to choose between asking permission or logging in as yourself to a virtual desktop.

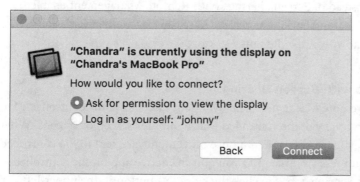

When presented with this Screen Sharing dialog, if you choose the option to ask for permission, the remote user is prompted with the Share Screen Request permission dialog.

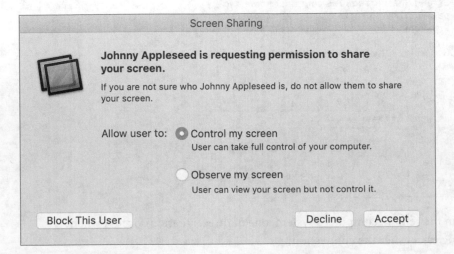

The remote user's choice dictates whether you can connect. If you choose to log in as yourself, you are instantly connected to a new virtual screen that displays the login window. In this case, the other user doesn't know that you are remotely using their Mac, but the other user might notice if they look for your account name in Activity Monitor or notice your user account is unavailable to be modified in Users & Groups preferences. Additionally, if the other user logs out and the login window displays users, the user that you connected as is displayed with a checkmark. If the other user logs in again, the user you connected as has a checkmark in the Fast User Switching menu.

If you need to control another user's session without asking permission, you should enable Remote Management instead of Screen Sharing. With Remote Management enabled, when you connect with Screen Sharing the remote user isn't asked for permission. You can use Remote Management with Apple Remote Desktop.

Control Another Mac with Screen Sharing

After you connect to a remote Mac, a new window opens and shows the controlled Mac computer name and a live view of the controlled Mac computer screen or screens. When this window is active, keyboard entries and mouse movements are sent to the controlled Mac. For example, if you press Command-Q you quit the active app on the controlled Mac. To quit the Screen Sharing app, you click the close (X) button in the upper-left corner of the window or choose Screen Sharing > Quit Screen Sharing. More options are available in the Screen Sharing toolbar.

The buttons in the toolbar show Screen Sharing features, including the option to share clipboard content between your Mac and the remote Mac. If the remote Mac is running macOS, you can drag and release files in the Finder between your Mac and the screen sharing window. Doing so opens a File Transfers dialog, enabling you to verify the transfer progress or cancel the file transfer.

Choose Screen Sharing > Preferences (or press Command-Comma) to check Screen Sharing options. Use the preferences to adjust screen size and quality settings. If you experience slow performance, adjust the settings. Some network connections, such as crowded wireless or slow Internet connections, are so slow that these settings might not help.

Messages Screen Sharing

You can use Messages to initiate a screen-sharing session and chat between the administrator Mac and the controlled Mac. Messages screen sharing also makes it easier to locate other Mac computers to control, because Messages resolves the location of remote computers based on your active chats using an iCloud account. Messages also supports reverse screen sharing—the administrator Mac can push its screen to display on another Mac for demonstration purposes.

Messages doesn't require a Mac to have Screen Sharing enabled in Sharing preferences. This is because Messages includes an authorization process for initiating a screen-sharing session with iCloud authentication and Messages. This requires that users on each Mac computer be signed in with an iCloud account both in iCloud Preferences and with Messages. Details regarding signing in to Messages and iCloud are covered in Reference 24.2, "Configure Network Service Apps."

Control Another Mac with Messages

To initiate a Messages screen-sharing session, start an iMessage chat with the other user. Select the chat history of the other user in the main Messages window. After you select the user, click the Details text button in the top right of the main Messages window. This opens a dialog where you can click the Screen Sharing button and choose "Invite to Share My Screen" or "Ask to Share Screen." Screen Sharing in Messages works in both directions.

The user on the other Mac sees an authorization dialog that offers the choice to accept or decline your request to share screens. With Messages you can't force other users to share their screens. They can allow or deny your request.

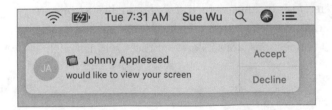

If the other user clicks the Accept button, they are prompted to verify the screen-sharing session and select whether you can control or only observe their screen.

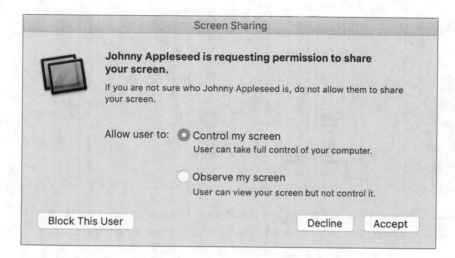

After the other user accepts the screen-sharing session, Screen Sharing initiates the connection.

If both Mac computers support voice chat, Messages starts a voice chat session. You might need to configure Audio/Video settings in Messages preferences for this feature to work.

Messages leverages the same Screen Sharing app used by the system Screen Sharing service, as covered previously in this lesson. The only exception is that, by the other user's choice, you might not have control of the remote Mac. If the remote user selects "Observe my screen" instead of "Control my screen," in the Screen Sharing toolbar, the binocular Control button is selected, indicating that you can observe but not control.

In this case, you see the pointer of the remote Mac, and your pointer turns into a magnifying glass.

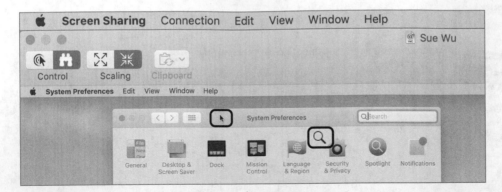

Clicking the shared screen has no effect, except that it shows a magnifying glass–style circle on the remote screen. This helps users identify something you are trying to assist them with.

Select the mouse pointer Control button to request remote control of another Mac. This issues a notification prompt to the remote user so that they can agree (or not) to enable you to control their Mac.

The other user can select the Screen Sharing menu to manage features of the Messages screen-sharing session, including ending the session.

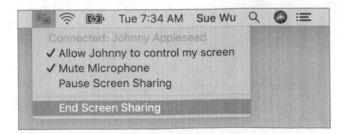

Enable Screen Sharing with Automation and an MDM Solution

If your Mac is automatically enrolled with your MDM solution from
Apple Business Manager or Apple School Manager, or has User-Approved MDM, you can
allow the Mac to be controlled with Screen Sharing by using a configuration profile with a
Privacy Preferences Policy Control payload.

For more information, read the following Apple Support articles:

▶ HT201710, "Use the kickstart command-line utility in Apple Remote Desktop"

▶ HT209161, "Use the kickstart command-line utility on macOS Mojave 10.14"

Reference 25.3
Share Files with AirDrop

macOS features a peer-to-peer Wi-Fi file-sharing service called AirDrop. It's the easiest
way to share files between Apple devices that are in close proximity.

AirDrop uses Wi-Fi networking, but you don't need to be joined to a network to use
AirDrop, because it creates a closed network between local Apple devices.

AirDrop requires no setup or configuration. It handles peer-to-peer file sharing, including discovery, easy authentication, and secure file transfer using Transport Layer Security
(TLS) encryption.

AirDrop works only between Apple devices within local Wi-Fi and Bluetooth range.
The range varies based on several factors, but it's generally limited to 30 feet. Also, with
AirDrop you share only the items you specifically offer to share with another Mac or iOS
device, as opposed to sharing one or more folders with the File Sharing service in Sharing
preferences. AirDrop is supported only on devices with the appropriate system software
and wireless hardware. You can read about AirDrop hardware requirements for iOS
devices in Apple Support article HT204144, "Use AirDrop on your iPhone, iPad, or iPod
touch," and for Mac models in Apple Support article HT203106, "Use AirDrop on your
Mac."

Send Items with AirDrop

To share files between Apple devices that support AirDrop, find other devices in the
AirDrop discovery window. Select the AirDrop icon in the Finder sidebar and choose
Go > AirDrop. Or you can press Shift-Command-R in the Finder. These methods open
the AirDrop discovery interface in a Finder window, enabling you to share any item you
can drag to the Finder window.

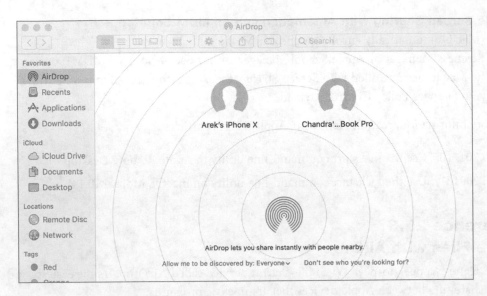

Alternatively, you can engage AirDrop to share a specific open document by clicking the Share button (the box with an up-pointing arrow) if it's available in the document window, or by choosing File > Share > AirDrop if it's available. Another option is to Control-click an item in the Finder and then choose Share from the shortcut menu. This opens the AirDrop discovery interface, but it shares the currently selected document too.

When the AirDrop discovery interface is open, macOS scans for other AirDrop devices within local wireless range. Other AirDrop devices appear as long as AirDrop is enabled and using a compatible discovery method.

After AirDrop finds the other device you want to transfer an item to, there are a couple of ways to send the item. If you are in the Finder, drag a file or folder on top of the icon representing the other device. If you are in a Share window, click the icon representing the other device. In either case, AirDrop notifies the other device that you would like to share something.

On the receiving device, a notification appears where you can accept (or decline) the incoming item. If the AirDrop window is open on the receiving Mac, you have three choices:

▶   Click the Accept button and the item is transferred to your Downloads folder.

▶   Click Accept & Open (or "Open in Photos") to save to your Downloads folder and open the item.

▶   Click Decline to cancel the transfer and notify the other user in the AirDrop interface.

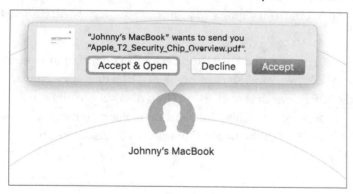

If you don't have the AirDrop window open on the receiving Mac, a notification appears in the upper-right corner. If you click Accept, you can choose Open (or "Open in Photos") or "Save to Downloads."

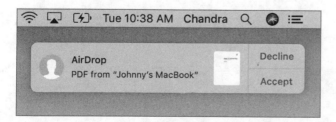

AirDrop Discovery

If your Mac can't discover another AirDrop device, AirDrop might not be enabled on that device. If so, on the other Mac, open the AirDrop window in the Finder to enable AirDrop.

You can force a newer Mac to use the previous AirDrop discovery method by clicking "Don't see who you're looking for?" at the bottom of the AirDrop screen. Clicking the "Search for an Older Mac" button will switch to the previous AirDrop discovery method.

When you open the AirDrop interface on a newer Mac, it resets to the new AirDrop discovery method.

For devices using the newer AirDrop method, AirDrop defaults to not being discoverable. This may limit your ability to discover other devices in the AirDrop discovery interface. To resolve this issue, on the other device you can set AirDrop discovery to allow everyone or to limit discovery to only users with matching information in your Contacts. To change AirDrop discoverability on macOS, click the words "Allow me to be discovered by" at the bottom of the AirDrop interface.

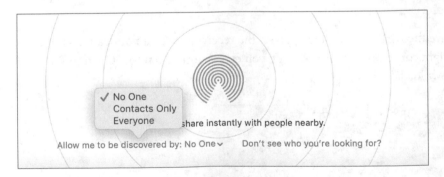

Reference 25.4
Manage the Personal Firewall

From a network services standpoint, your Mac is very secure, because, by default, no services are running that respond to external requests. Even after you provide shared services, your Mac responds only to services that are enabled.

You can configure services that could cause trouble if compromised—like File Sharing or Screen Sharing—to have limited access authorization. Still, users can open third-party apps or background services that could leave a Mac vulnerable to a network attack.

To maintain network security, leave sharing services off unless they're necessary. If you enable sharing services, limit authorization access. And after you use them, turn them off.

Personal Firewall

Most people secure network services by configuring a firewall. This blocks unauthorized network service access. Most networks have a firewall to limit inbound traffic from an Internet connection.

Most home routers, like AirPort base stations, are also network firewalls. Although network-level firewalls block unauthorized Internet traffic to your network, they don't block traffic that originated from inside your network to your Mac. Also, if your Mac is mobile and is often joining new networks, odds are that every new network you join has different firewall rules.

To prevent unauthorized network services from allowing incoming connections to your Mac, enable the built-in personal firewall. A personal firewall blocks unauthorized connections to your Mac no matter where they originated. The macOS firewall features a single-click configuration that provides network service security, which works for most users.

A standard firewall uses rules based on service port numbers. Each service defaults to a standard port or set of ports. Some network services, like Messages, use a wide range of dynamic ports. If you manually configure a firewall, you have to make dozens of rules for every potential port a user may need.

To resolve this issue, the macOS firewall uses an adaptive technology that allows connections based on apps and service needs, without you having to know the specific ports they use. For example, you can authorize Messages to accept any incoming connection without configuring all of the individual TCP and UDP ports used by Messages.

A personal firewall also leverages another built-in feature, code signing, to ensure that allowed apps and services aren't changed without your knowledge. Code signing enables Apple and third-party developers to provide a guarantee that their software wasn't tampered with. This level of verifiable trust enables you to configure the firewall in default mode with a single click, automatically allowing signed apps and services to receive incoming connections.

Because the personal firewall is fully dynamic, it opens only the necessary ports when the app or service is running. Using Messages as an example, the personal firewall allows incoming connections to the required ports only if Messages is running. If the app quits because the user logs out, the firewall closes the associated ports. Having the required ports open only when an app or service needs them provides an extra layer of security not found with traditional firewalls.

Turn On the Personal Firewall

To enable and configure the macOS personal firewall, open Security & Privacy preferences, click the lock icon in the lower-left corner, and authenticate as an administrator user to unlock Security & Privacy preferences. Select the Firewall button, and then click the Turn On Firewall button to enable the default firewall rules. Once enabled, this button changes to a Turn Off Firewall button.

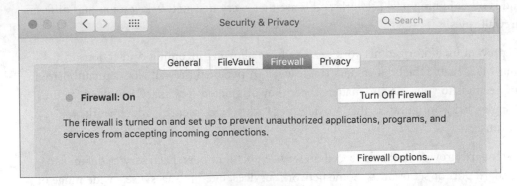

The default firewall configuration allows incoming traffic for established connections (connections that were initiated from your Mac and are expecting a return) and signed software or enabled services. This level of security is adequate for most users.

Configure the Personal Firewall

If you want to customize the firewall, you can reveal additional firewall configurations by clicking the Firewall Options button. From the firewall options window, a list of services currently allowed appears. Without any additional configuration, sharing services enabled from Sharing preferences automatically appear in the list of allowed services. Deselecting a shared service from Sharing preferences removes the service from the list of allowed services.

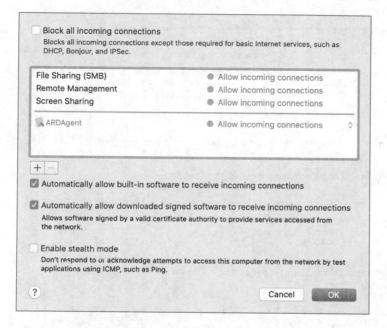

You can manually set which apps and services the firewall allows by deselecting the checkbox to automatically allow signed software. With this firewall choice, as you open new network apps for the first time or update existing network apps, you see a dialog where you can allow or deny the new network app. This dialog appears outside Security & Privacy preferences whenever a new network app requests incoming access.

If you are manually setting network app and service firewall access, you can return to the Advanced Firewall pane to review the list of items and either delete items from the list or specifically disallow certain items.

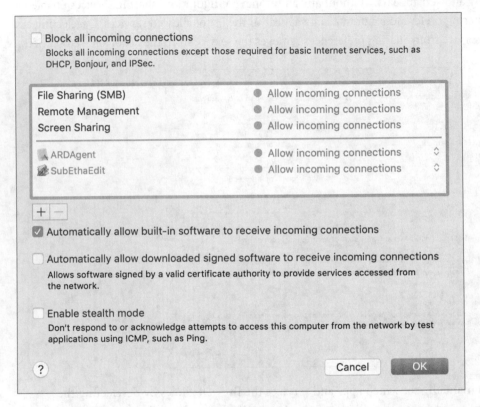

You can select the "Enable stealth mode" checkbox to prevent response or acknowledgment of a failed attempt to the requesting host. With this enabled, your Mac doesn't respond to unauthorized network connections, including network diagnostic protocols like ping, traceroute, and port scan. Your Mac still responds to other allowed services. This includes, by default, Bonjour, which announces your Mac computer's presence and prevents your Mac from being hidden on the network.

When you need more security, select the "Block all incoming connections" checkbox. Selecting this option automatically enables stealth mode.

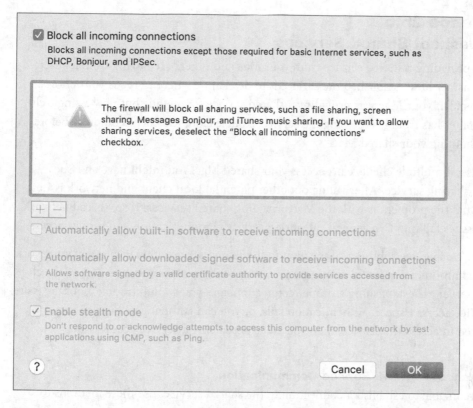

When you block all incoming connections, your Mac doesn't respond to incoming network connections except for those required for basic network services or established connections, such as those needed to browse the web or check email. This prevents shared services or apps hosted on your Mac from working remotely.

As with most System Preferences, you can click the Help button (question mark) to read more information about the preference pane you have open.

Reference 25.5
Troubleshoot Shared Services

If you're providing a shared service from your Mac and others are having trouble reaching it, consider how established the service is to determine where to focus your efforts. For example, if your Mac was providing a shared service for a while but now a single client computer has trouble accessing the service, troubleshoot the client computer before troubleshooting your shared Mac.

Otherwise, if multiple clients can't access your shared Mac, you might have an issue with the sharing service. After ruling out other potential local client and network issues, assume that the problem is with the Mac providing shared services. If so, shared network service issues fall into two general categories: service communication and service access.

If you are unable to establish a connection to the shared service, this may signal a network service communication issue. If you are presented with an authentication dialog, the client and server are establishing a proper connection, and you should troubleshoot the issue as a service access issue. If authentication fails, or you can authenticate but you're not authorized to access the service, then you are experiencing a service access issue.

Troubleshoot Network Service Communication

If you are unable to establish a connection to the shared service, use these methods to troubleshoot a network service communication issue:

▶   Double-check the shared Mac network configuration—From Network preferences, make sure the Mac computer's network interfaces are active and configured with the appropriate TCP/IP settings. You can also use Network Utility to verify the network configuration. If a DNS server is providing a host name for your shared Mac, use the lookup tool in Network Utility to verify the host name.

▶   Double-check the Mac computer's sharing service configuration—From the Sharing preferences, verify the Mac computer's sharing name and ensure that the appropriate services are enabled and configured.

▶   Double-check the Mac computer's firewall configuration—From Security & Privacy preferences, first temporarily stop the firewall to see whether turning it off makes a difference. If you are able to establish a connection, adjust the list of allowed services and apps before you start the firewall again.

▶ Check for basic network connectivity to the shared Mac—First, turn off the firewall's stealth mode, and then, from another Mac, use the Network Utility ping tool to check for basic connectivity to the shared Mac. If you can't ping the shared Mac, you're probably having a network-level issue that goes beyond service troubleshooting.

▶ Check for network service port connectivity to the shared Mac—First, turn off the firewall's stealth mode, and then, from another Mac, use the Network Utility port scan tool to verify that the expected network service ports are accessible. If the shared Mac is configured properly, the appropriate network service ports should register as open. If there are network routers between the network clients and the shared Mac, a network administrator might have decided to block access to those ports.

Troubleshoot Network Service Access

Failure to authenticate or be granted authorization to a shared service is considered a network service access issue. Use the following methods to troubleshoot these access issues:

▶ Verify the local user account settings—When using local user accounts, make sure the correct authentication information is being used. Maybe the user isn't using the right information, and you might have to reset the account password. (Troubleshooting user account issues is covered in Lesson 7, "Manage User Accounts".) Also, some services don't allow the use of guest and sharing-only user accounts. Further, the VNC service uses password information that is not directly linked to a user account.

▶ Check directory service settings—If you use a network directory service in your environment, verify that the Mac is properly communicating with the directory service by checking its status in Directory Utility. Even if you're only trying to use local accounts, any directory service issues can cause authentication problems. Some services, like Remote Management, don't by default enable you to authenticate with accounts hosted from network directories.

▶ Check shared service access settings—Several authenticated sharing services enable you to configure access lists. Use Sharing preferences to verify that the appropriate user accounts are allowed to access the shared service.

Exercise 25.1
Use Host-Sharing Services

▶ **Prerequisites**

▶ You must have created the Local Administrator (Exercise 3.1, "Configure a Mac for Exercises") and Johnny Appleseed (Exercise 7.1, "Create a Standard User Account") accounts.

▶ You must have another Mac running macOS Mojave on the same network as your primary Mac.

▶ In this exercise, you work with a partner or your facilitator depending on the number of participants in the classroom.

In this exercise, you use macOS screen sharing to control another Mac. You share the current user's session, and you use a virtual display to log in as a different user.

Turn On Screen Sharing

1   If the Local Administrator account is logged in (even as a background session), log it out.

2   If necessary, log in as Johnny Appleseed.

3   Open Sharing preferences.

4   Click the lock button, and authenticate as Local Administrator.

5   If it's not selected, select the checkbox next to Remote Management.

Although you use Screen Sharing, you configure the service using Remote Management (which is used for Apple Remote Desktop). Remote Management includes screen sharing. Notice that the checkbox for the Screen Sharing service is dimmed. This doesn't mean the service is unavailable. It means that it's being controlled by Remote Management.

6   Grant users all permissions. First, ensure that all options are selected. An easy way to do this is to Option-click a checkbox to select all checkboxes at once.

7   Ensure that "All users" is selected for "Allow access for."

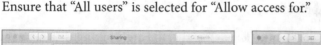

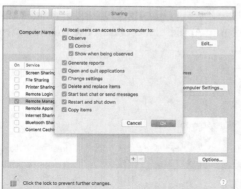

8   Click OK, and quit System Preferences.

Remotely Control Another Mac Computer Screen

In this section, you use Screen Sharing to control another Mac. Work with a partner and take turns controlling each other's Mac computers.

1   Wait for your partner to finish turning on and configuring Remote Management, and decide who will go first. If your partner goes first, wait for them to finish this section before starting.

2   In the Finder, choose Go > Network (Shift-Command-K).

The Mac you are going to control appears in the display of shared Mac computers on the local network. The display shows Mac computers that offer file sharing, screen sharing, or both.

3   Double-click the Mac you will control in the Network window.

Since the other Mac doesn't offer file-sharing service, your Mac only has the option to share its screen.

4   Click Share Screen.

5   Authenticate as Johnny Appleseed.

You can use the account short name (**johnny**), and if you are working with a partner who used a different password for the Johnny Appleseed account, use their password.

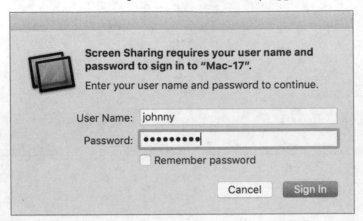

6   Click Sign In.

Screen sharing begins, and you see a window with a live, interactive view of the other Mac computer's desktop.

7   Open Desktop & Screensaver preferences on the other Mac.

8   Select a different desktop picture for the other Mac computer.

9   Press Command-Q.

This quits System Preferences on the other Mac. You can't use standard shortcuts to control screen sharing.

10   Click the Full Screen button in the title bar of the Screen Sharing window.

The window expands and takes over your entire screen. In full-screen mode, your display is a virtual mirror of the other Mac computer's display.

11 Move your mouse to the top of the screen, and leave it there for a few seconds.

The Screen Sharing menu, window controls, and toolbar appear at the top of the screen. This enables you to exit full-screen mode or access the Screen Sharing controls.

12 Choose Screen Sharing > Quit Screen Sharing.

13 If you are working with a partner, switch roles and have your partner repeat these steps.

Connect to a Virtual Display

When you connect to another Mac as a different user, you can work with a virtual display instead of sharing the local user's display. This time both you and your partner can work at once, rather than taking turns.

1 Wait for your partner to finish the previous section.

2 Reopen the Network view (Shift-Command-K), and select the Mac you'll control.

3 Click Share Screen.

4 This time authenticate as Local Administrator (you can use the short name **ladmin**), and click Connect.

Since you authenticated as a different user than is logged in to the other Mac, you are presented with the choice of sharing the current user's display or logging in as a different user with a virtual display.

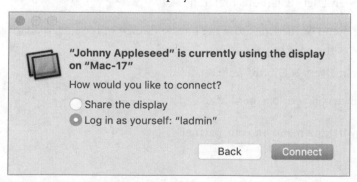

5   Select "Log in as yourself," and click Connect.

A screen-sharing window opens and displays a login screen for your partner's Mac. The orange checkmark next to Johnny Appleseed indicates that Johnny is logged in to the Mac.

6   Log in to your partner's Mac as Local Administrator.

The virtual screen makes it easy to remotely manage users' Mac computers without disturbing the users. Your partner is connecting to your Mac, but you don't notice it.

7   On the other Mac, open Users & Groups preferences.

If you use the Apple menu or the Dock, use the one contained in the screen-sharing window, not the one at the edge of your screen.

Don't make changes in Users & Groups preferences now.

8   Quit System Preferences on your partner's Mac.

9   Click the fast user switching menu on your partner's Mac.

You see that Johnny Appleseed (either your partner or the session you left logged in there) and Local Administrator (you) are logged in to the other Mac. Your virtual display is treated as a fast user switching session.

10 In the Finder on the remote Mac, choose Apple menu > Log Out Local Administrator, and then click the Log Out button.

If you disconnect screen sharing without logging out first, you leave behind a fast user switching session.

11 Choose Screen Sharing menu > Quit Screen Sharing.

12 If you are working with a partner, wait for them to finish before starting the next exercise.

13 If you are working on your own, move back to your primary exercise Mac for the first part of the next exercise.

Exercise 25.2
Configure a Personal Firewall

> **Prerequisites**
>
> ▶ You must have created the Local Administrator (Exercise 3.1, "Configure a Mac for Exercises") and Johnny Appleseed (Exercise 7.1, "Create a Standard User Account") accounts.
>
> ▶ You need another Mac running macOS Mojave on the same network as your primary Mac.
>
> ▶ In this exercise, you work with a partner or your facilitator depending on the number of participants in the classroom.

In this exercise, you turn on a firewall and start a network-aware app. You view the firewall log. You also configure the advanced stealth option and see that it blocks responses to network pings.

Enable the Firewall

1   If necessary, log in as Johnny Appleseed.

2   Open Security & Privacy preferences.

3   Click the Firewall button.

4   Click the lock button, and authenticate as Local Administrator.

5   Click Turn On Firewall.

6   Click Firewall Options.

Remote Management and Screen Sharing are on the list as "Allow incoming connections." macOS assumes that if you turn on a service in the Sharing pane, you want users to be able to connect to it, so it allows those services through the firewall.

7   Deselect "Automatically allow built-in software to receive incoming connections" and "Automatically allow downloaded signed software to receive incoming connections."

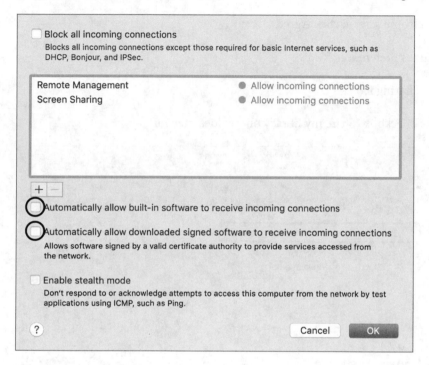

8   Click OK.

9   Quit System Preferences.

NOTE ▶ With the firewall in this mode, you might receive alerts about system components that are attempting to accept incoming connections. A common example is "ubd" (the ubiquity daemon and part of iCloud). It is generally safe to allow these connections through the firewall.

Test Firewall Settings

1   Open iTunes.

2   If you see the iTunes software license agreement, click Agree.

3 If you see a message telling you a new version of iTunes is available, click Don't Download.

4 At the Welcome screen, click Agree.

5 Open iTunes preferences.

6 Click the Sharing icon.

7 Select the checkbox "Share my library on my local network."

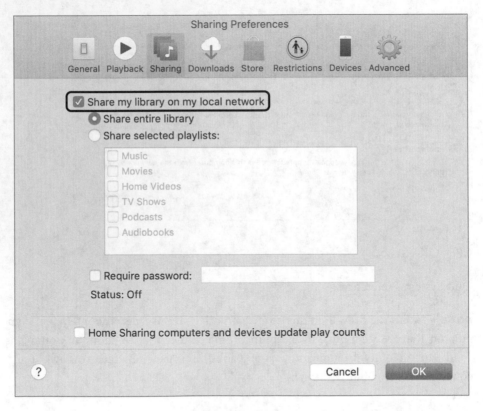

8 Click OK.

9 A dialog opens, saying "Reminder: Sharing music is for personal use only." Click OK.

10 If you see a dialog that appears asking if you want iTunes to accept incoming network connections, click Deny.

11 iTunes displays a dialog indicating that the firewall settings prevent you from using some iTunes features.

If you click Ignore, iTunes music sharing turns on, but users of other Mac computers won't be able to connect to it and listen to your songs. You will allow connections to iTunes in the Firewall rules in the following steps.

12 Click Open Firewall preferences.

13 Under the Firewall button, authenticate if necessary, and click Firewall Options.

14 Ensure "Allow incoming connections" is selected from the pop-up menu.

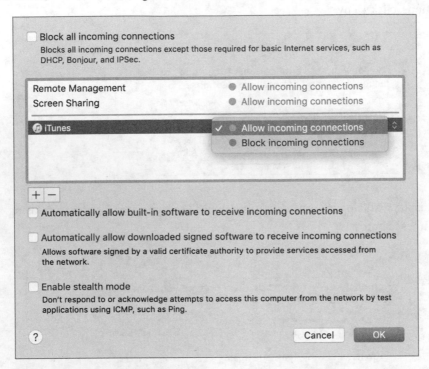

Since you have authenticated as an administrator, you can change the firewall policy for any app.

15 Click OK to dismiss the Firewall Options dialog.

16 Quit iTunes, but leave System Preferences open.

Test Stealth Mode

In this exercise, you work with a partner or your facilitator, depending on how many participants are in the class.

1 In System Preferences, switch to the Sharing pane.

Your Mac computer's Bonjour name is displayed under Computer Name.

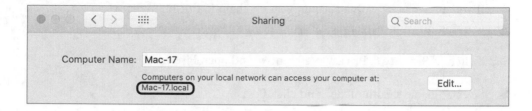

2   Open Network Utility.

3   Click the Ping tab.

4   Ask your partner for their Mac computer's Bonjour name, and enter it as the network address to ping. If you are working on your own, enter the Bonjour name of your primary exercise Mac.

5   If necessary, set Network Utility to send only five pings, and click Ping.

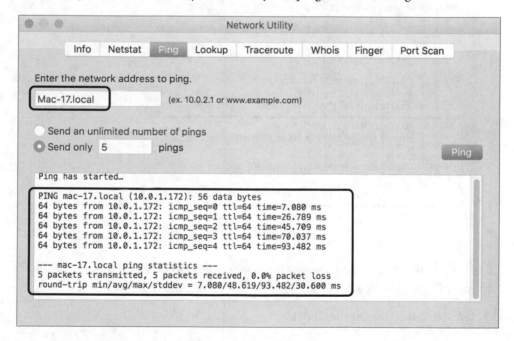

You should see successful pings.

6 If you are working with a partner, wait for them to finish pinging your Mac. If you are working on your own, switch to your primary exercise Mac.

7 Switch to Security & Privacy preferences, and open Firewall Options.

8 Select "Enable stealth mode," and click OK.

9 If you are working with a partner, wait for them to finish turning on stealth mode. If you are working on your own, switch to your other Mac.

10 Switch to Network Utility and click Ping to rerun the connectivity test.

After a few seconds, "Request timeout" messages appear in Network Utility.

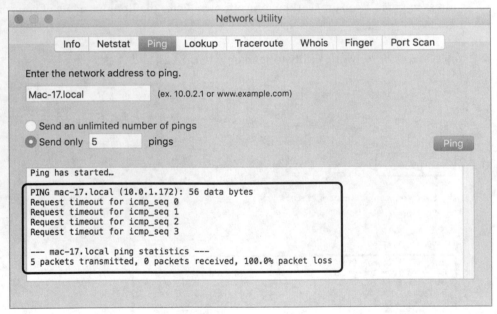

If you enable stealth mode, your Mac won't respond to ping requests, so it could be more difficult to troubleshoot.

11 On your Mac, turn off the firewall.

12 Quit running programs.

System Management

Lesson 26

Troubleshoot Peripherals

macOS is compatible with most popular peripheral standards. At the start of this lesson, you learn how macOS supports different peripheral technologies. Then you learn how to manage and troubleshoot wired and wireless (Bluetooth) peripherals connected to macOS.

Reference 26.1
Peripheral Technologies

A peripheral is any device that you can connect to your Mac and that is controlled by that computer; a network device is shared over the network. This lesson shows you how to categorize peripherals by their connectivity type and device class. This information helps you manage and troubleshoot peripherals.

Peripheral Connectivity

To communicate with macOS, most peripherals use a bus. Bus connections are the most common peripheral connection types because they allow for different peripheral devices. Bus connections also allow multiple peripherals to connect to your Mac simultaneously.

Mac supports USB, FireWire, Bluetooth, and Thunderbolt, and a few other buses that are outside the scope of this guide.

You can examine the status of each of these peripheral buses (and the items they are attached to) with System Information. In System Information, select a bus, and then select a hardware interface to view its information.

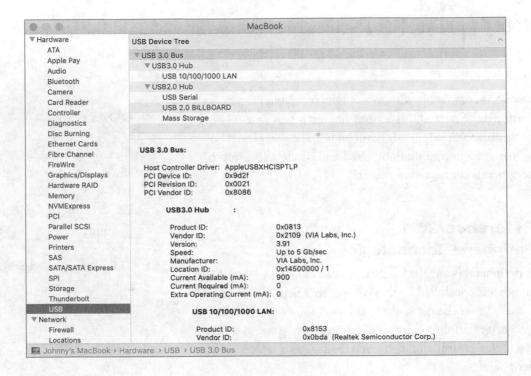

USB

USB is standard on every Mac. You can use System Information to see what type of USB ports your Mac has, how fast these ports are, and what's currently connected to them.

USB is a highly expandable connection platform that allows for daisy-chained connections. You can connect one USB device to your Mac, and then connect another USB device to the first, and so on. The USB specification allows for up to 127 simultaneous devices per host controller. Most Mac computers have at least two externally accessible USB host controllers.

USB Performance

Four USB versions are currently supported by Apple hardware: USB 1.1, USB 2.0, USB 3.0, and USB-C (USB 3.1). Despite significant upgrades in performance, USB ports on Mac computers are backward compatible with USB 1.1 devices. Find out more about USB at the official USB Implementers Forum website: www.usb.org.

USB versions offer the following performance characteristics:

► USB 1.1: 1.5-12 megabits per second (Mbit/s)

► USB 2.0: 480 Mbit/s

► USB 3.0 and USB 3.1 Gen 1: 5 gigabits per second (Gbit/s)

► USB 3.1 Gen 2: 10 Gbit/s

Mac computers provide different amounts of power to USB peripherals depending on the model. Read Apple Support article HT204377, "Powering peripherals through USB," for more information.

Some Mac computers have USB-A ports (sometimes referred to as USB 3 ports), which look like this:

USB-C describes the shape and style of a port on your computer and the connectors that you can plug into the port. USB-C ports look like this:

USB-C is a reversible connection that was developed by Intel and Apple.

You can use USB-C ports to do the following:

► Charge your portable Mac.

► Provide power.

► Transfer content between your Mac and other devices.

► Connect video output such as HDMI, VGA, and DisplayPort (requires an adapter).

► Use an adapter to connect to other technologies, such as Ethernet.

This allows for radical simplification in ports. A variety of USB-C adapters are available that allow for simultaneous connection to multiple peripherals, a display, and battery charging. USB-C is the only version of USB that supports target disk mode.

You can find out more about USB and USB-C from Apple Support article HT201163, "Using USB devices with your Mac."

Thunderbolt

Originally designed by Intel, then later in collaboration with Apple, Thunderbolt represents the latest in peripheral connectivity. This standard folds PCI Express and DisplayPort data into a single connection and cable. Thunderbolt 3 adds USB compatibility and advanced power management.

With the appropriate adapters, a single Thunderbolt connection can provide access to any other networking, storage, peripheral, video, or audio connection. For example, a Thunderbolt display can provide not only a high-definition digital display but also a built-in camera, a microphone, audio speakers, USB ports, FireWire ports, Gigabit Ethernet ports, additional Thunderbolt ports for another peripheral, and even enough power to charge portable Mac computers—all through a single Thunderbolt cable from the Mac to the display.

One Thunderbolt host computer connection supports a hub or daisy chain of up to six devices, with up to two of these devices high-resolution displays. You can use Mac computers with Thunderbolt in target disk mode without the need for a functional operating system, as covered in Lesson 11, "Manage File Systems and Storage."

Only copper Thunderbolt cabling can deliver power, but it is limited to a maximum 3-meter length. Optical Thunderbolt cabling is available in lengths of up to 100 meters.

Physically, the original Thunderbolt and Thunderbolt 2 connector is identical to the Mini DisplayPort. All of these ports have the same shape, but they use different symbols on the cable and port. Thunderbolt, Thunderbolt 2, and Mini DisplayPort ports all look like this:

Mini DisplayPort devices and cables don't support the additional PCI Express data used by Thunderbolt. So items that support only Mini DisplayPort should be the last connection in a Thunderbolt daisy chain. You can identify items compatible with Thunderbolt by an icon that looks like a lightning bolt, whereas items compatible with only Mini DisplayPort feature an icon that looks like a flat-panel display.

The latest Thunderbolt 3 standard has adopted the USB-C port.

Because Thunderbolt 3 uses the USB-C, any Mac that includes Thunderbolt 3 can also accept USB-C devices without the need for adapters. Check the specifications for your Mac model to see if it has Thunderbolt 3 (USB-C) ports. If it does, the Thunderbolt 3 (USB-C) ports support Thunderbolt 3 and USB 3.1 Gen 2. If your Mac has a USB-C port that doesn't support Thunderbolt 3, it supports USB 3.1 Gen 1.

USB-C devices and cables don't support the additional PCI Express data used by Thunderbolt. So items that support only USB-C should be the last connection in a Thunderbolt daisy chain.

Thunderbolt is the fastest external peripheral bus to date:

► Thunderbolt provides two bidirectional 10 Gbit/s channels—this means a total of 20 Gbit/s outbound and 20 Gbit/s inbound. With this first version of Thunderbolt, these channels can't be combined to provide full bandwidth to a single peripheral. Thus, a single Thunderbolt peripheral has a maximum bandwidth of 10 Gbit/s, but you can use the full bandwidth when multiple peripherals are part of a single Thunderbolt chain. Thunderbolt also features DisplayPort 1.1 signaling, which allows for high-definition display resolutions. Copper Thunderbolt cabling also supplies up to 10 watts of power to connected devices, again providing more power than any previous external peripheral bus.

► Thunderbolt 2 supports channel aggregation. A single peripheral can take advantage of the full 20 Gbit/s throughput.

► Thunderbolt 3 provides two bidirectional 20 Gbit/s (20,000 Mbit/s) channels, providing a total of 40 Gbit/s outbound and 40 Gbit/s inbound. Thunderbolt 3 also features DisplayPort 1.2 signaling, which allows for 4K and 5K display resolutions. Finally, Thunderbolt 3 is fully backward compatible with USB-C (USB 3.1) signaling and power delivery.

For more information about Thunderbolt 3, read these Apple Support articles:

▶ HT202488, "About Apple Thunderbolt cables and adapters"

▶ HT206908, "Apple Thunderbolt 3 (USB-C) to Thunderbolt 2 Adapter requires Thunderbolt 3"

▶ HT207097, "Charge your MacBook Pro with Thunderbolt 3"

▶ HT207443, "Adapters for the Thunderbolt 3 (USB-C) or USB-C port on your Mac or iPad Pro"

▶ HT208368, "About the Apple Thunderbolt 3 (USB-C) Cable"

And read "Thunderbolt 3. The most powerful and versatile port ever," at www.apple.com/thunderbolt.

FireWire

FireWire is a high-speed, general-purpose peripheral connection originally developed by Apple. FireWire was ratified by the Institute of Electrical and Electronics Engineers (IEEE) as standard IEEE-1394 and was adopted as a standard interface for many digital video devices.

If your Mac supports Thunderbolt 3 (USB-C), Thunderbolt 2, or Thunderbolt, but doesn't have a FireWire port, you can use an adapter or a combination of adapters to use a FireWire device:

▶ If your Mac has a Thunderbolt 3 (USB-C) port, use a Thunderbolt 3 (USB-C) to Thunderbolt 2 Adapter connected to a Thunderbolt to Firewire Adapter.

▶ If your Mac has a Thunderbolt 2 or Thunderbolt port, use a Thunderbolt to Firewire Adapter.

Bluetooth

Bluetooth is a wireless technology that makes short-range connections between devices (like your Mac, and a mouse or keyboard) at distances up to 10 meters (approximately 30 feet).

Current Mac computers come with Bluetooth technology built in. You can check to see if your computer supports Bluetooth:

▶ Look for the Bluetooth icon in the menu bar. If the Bluetooth icon is present, your computer has Bluetooth.

▶ Open System Preferences, and then open Bluetooth preferences. If Bluetooth preferences lists options for enabling Bluetooth and making your device discoverable, Bluetooth is installed.

▶ In System Information, select Bluetooth from the Hardware section. If the Hardware section shows information, your Mac has Bluetooth installed.

Mac computers dating from 2011 or later support Bluetooth 3.0 + High Speed (HS) with a maximum transfer speed of up to 24 Mbit/s and Bluetooth 4.0 with low-energy support. Bluetooth low-energy (BLE) mode isn't very fast, at a maximum of 200 kbit/s, but it uses much less energy, is quicker to pair with devices, and sports a larger maximum range.

Read Apple Support article HT201171, "Using a Bluetooth mouse, keyboard, or trackpad with your Mac," for more information.

Reference 26.2
Manage Bluetooth Devices

Bluetooth wireless devices are associated with your Mac through a process called pairing. After you pair a device, your Mac automatically connects to it anytime it's in range.

If your Mac came with a wireless keyboard, mouse, or trackpad, they were pre-paired at the factory. Turn on the devices and your Mac should automatically connect to them when your computer starts up. If you bought the following Apple Bluetooth devices separately, you can use a Lightning to USB Cable or a USB-C to Lightning Cable to automatically pair them with your Mac:

▶ Magic Mouse 2

▶ Magic Keyboard

▶ Magic Keyboard with Numeric Keypad

▶ Magic Trackpad 2

For more information about how to set up an Apple wireless mouse, keyboard, or trackpad, read Apple Support article HT201178, "Set up your Apple wireless mouse, keyboard, and trackpad."

One way to configure Bluetooth devices is to use Bluetooth preferences. Open System Preferences, and then click Bluetooth. The on or off status is displayed in the left side of the window. You can select the checkbox "Show Bluetooth status in menu bar" so that you can quickly see Bluetooth status and manage devices at any time.

The Bluetooth menu bar icon in the upper right of your display gives you information about the status of Bluetooth and connected devices. And at any time, to manage Bluetooth preferences, you can click the Bluetooth menu bar icon and then choose Open Bluetooth Preferences.

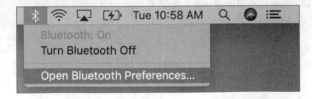

Pair a Bluetooth Device

Before you begin the pairing process, enable Discoverable Mode on the Bluetooth device you're going to pair with your Mac. Each device is different, so you might have to consult the device user guide to enable Discoverable Mode.

Continuity features use Bluetooth 4.0, but traditional Bluetooth pairing isn't required. Instead, the Continuity features automatically connect as long as all devices are signed in to the same iCloud account. Find out more about Handoff from Apple Support article HT204681, "Use Continuity to connect your Mac, iPhone, iPad, iPod touch, and Apple Watch."

When Bluetooth preferences is open, it scans for any Bluetooth devices in range that are in Discoverable Mode.

With Bluetooth preferences open, the Mac puts itself in Bluetooth Discoverable Mode. Discoverable Mode advertises your Mac as a Bluetooth resource to any device within range, which could invite unwanted attention to your Mac.

It may take several moments for the device name to appear. After it does, select it and click the Pair button. For some Bluetooth devices, you must enter a passcode to authorize pairing. Depending on the device, you will perform one of the following:

▶ Complete the pairing with little interaction by using an automatically generated passcode. This often happens with a device that has no method to verify the passcode.

▶ Enter a predefined passcode on your Mac, as specified in the device's user guide, and click Continue to authorize the pairing.

▶ Allow the Bluetooth Setup Assistant to create a random passcode, which you then enter or verify on the Bluetooth device to authorize the pairing. In this example, the passcode is generated automatically.

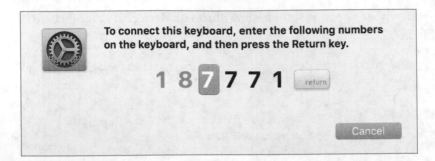

The Bluetooth Setup Assistant automatically detects the capabilities of your Bluetooth device and may present you with additional configuration screens. Continue through these screens until you complete the setup. When the pairing is complete, you can verify the pairing by reopening Bluetooth preferences. A device doesn't have to be currently connected to maintain pairing status with the Mac.

You can use the Bluetooth status menu to verify the status of Bluetooth devices. The Bluetooth status menu displays connected devices using bold letters.

macOS saves Bluetooth input device pairings, like mice and keyboards, to NVRAM so that you can use them prior to macOS fully starting up. This is necessary to support FileVault and startup keyboard shortcuts when using Bluetooth input devices.

Manage Bluetooth Settings

You can adjust settings such as the peripheral's name from Bluetooth preferences. To access all the Bluetooth management settings, open Bluetooth preferences from either the Apple menu > System Preferences or the Bluetooth status menu > Open Bluetooth Preferences.

To manage a Bluetooth peripheral, select it from the list and then Control-click to open a shortcut menu. From this menu you can connect or disconnect a device, and possibly rename a device. Some devices, such as iPhone, are named on the device and cannot be changed from Bluetooth preferences. You can also delete a device pairing from this list by clicking the small x button to the right.

Click the Advanced button at the bottom of the Bluetooth preferences to reveal a dialog where you can adjust additional Bluetooth settings. These settings are especially useful for desktop Mac computers that use only wireless keyboards and mice.

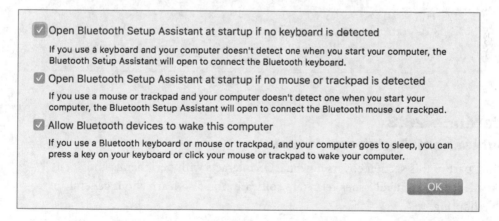

Finally, you'll find Bluetooth sharing settings in Shared preferences. Like other sharing services, Bluetooth sharing is off by default. Enable Bluetooth sharing as a last resort when traditional file-sharing methods aren't possible. Lesson 25, "Manage Host Sharing and Personal Firewall," discusses alternative file-sharing methods, including AirDrop wireless file sharing.

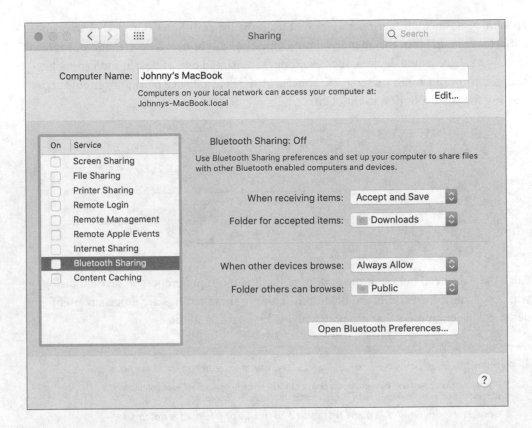

Reference 26.3
Troubleshoot Peripheral Issues

The first part of this section covers how macOS interacts with peripherals and how to identify peripheral issues related to software. You also learn about general troubleshooting.

Peripheral Device Classes

Peripherals are divided into device classes based on their primary function. macOS includes built-in software drivers that allow your Mac to interact with peripherals from all device classes. Although these built-in drivers may provide basic support, many third-party devices require device-specific drivers for full functionality.

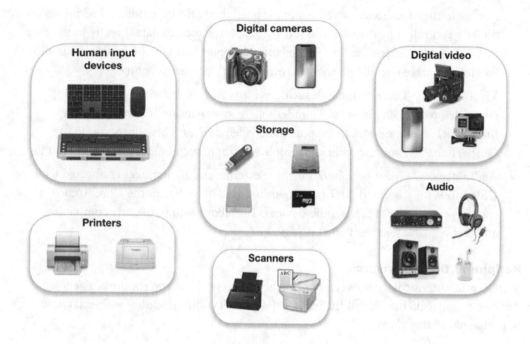

Device classes as defined in macOS include:

▶ Human input devices (HIDs)—Peripherals that allow you to directly enter information or control the Mac interface. Examples are keyboards, mice, trackpads, game controllers, tablets, and Braille interfaces.

▶ Storage devices—Internal disks, flash disks, optical discs, and iPod devices. Storage peripherals are covered in Lesson 11, "Manage File Systems and Storage."

▶ Printers—Printers of all types and fax machines. Printing is covered in Lesson 27, "Manage Printers and Scanners."

▶ Scanners—Flatbed, negative, slide, document, and drum scanners. macOS uses the Image Capture framework to support scanners. This allows you to control scanners with Image Capture or any other compatible third-party capture app, such as Photoshop. This topic is also covered in Lesson 27.

▶ Digital cameras—These peripherals include both directly connected cameras and camera storage cards. Many digital cameras, when connected to a computer, extend their internal storage to the computer. In this case, macOS accesses the camera's internal storage, or any directly attached camera storage cards, as it does any other storage device. An app like Photos then takes over to copy the picture files from the camera storage to the Mac. Some cameras support a tethered capture mode in which they are directly controlled by the Mac and send the captured picture data directly to the Mac. macOS uses the Image Capture framework to support this type of camera. This allows you to use Image Capture or another compatible third-party capture app.

▶ Video devices—These peripherals include video cameras and video converters connected with USB, FireWire, Thunderbolt, or an expansion bus. macOS uses the QuickTime framework to support these video devices. This allows you to use QuickTime Player or any other compatible video app, such as iMovie or Final Cut Pro.

▶ Audio devices—These peripherals include external audio interfaces connected with USB, FireWire, Thunderbolt, or an expansion bus. macOS uses the Core Audio framework to support these audio devices. This allows you to use any compatible audio app, such as GarageBand or Logic Pro.

Peripheral Device Drivers

macOS is an intermediary between peripherals and apps. If an app supports a general device class, macOS handles all the technical details of communicating with each model of peripheral in that class.

Here's an example: for an app to receive input, it needs to receive information from the keyboard, mouse, trackpad, and the like, but it doesn't need to handle any details about how to interpret the electrical signals from that device, because that's handled by macOS. This separation of peripherals and apps by macOS enables you to use nearly any combination of the two with few incompatibilities.

macOS uses device drivers, which are specialized pieces of software, to allow peripherals to communicate with your Mac.

For some peripherals, macOS can use a generic driver, but for other peripherals, macOS must use a device driver created specifically for the peripheral. You install most device drivers using an installer utility that places the driver software in the appropriate resource folder on your Mac. macOS implements device drivers in one of three ways: kernel extensions, framework plug-ins, or apps.

When you add support for a new third-party peripheral that requires custom drivers, check the peripheral manufacturer's website to obtain the latest version of the driver software.

Device driver implementations in macOS include:

▶ Kernel extensions (KEXTs)—macOS Mojave requires user approval to install new KEXTs, but after they are installed, macOS loads and unloads KEXTs automatically as needed. Although some KEXTs are located inside app bundles, most are located in /System/Library/Extensions/ or /Library/Extensions/. Examples of peripherals that use KEXTs are human input devices, storage devices, audio and video devices, and other expansion cards. See Reference 9.7, "Approve Kernel Extensions," for more information.

▶ Framework plug-ins—This type of device driver adds support for a specific peripheral to an existing system framework. For example, support for additional scanners and digital cameras is facilitated through plug-ins to the Image Capture framework.

▶ Apps—In some cases a peripheral is best supported by an app written just for that peripheral.

Inspect Kernel Extensions

Even though the macOS kernel manages KEXTs without user interaction, you may still need to verify that a specific KEXT is loaded. You can use System Information to view the KEXTs that are currently installed and loaded. After System Information is open, select the Extensions item in the Contents list. After the list appears, you can further inspect KEXTs by selecting them from this list. Click the Loaded column to sort the list by which KEXTs are in use by macOS and which aren't.

macOS has a 64-bit kernel. macOS ignores any KEXTs that don't support 64-bit mode or are not properly signed by Apple.

Troubleshoot General Peripheral Issues

Use the following techniques for general peripheral troubleshooting:

▶ Check System Information first. Connected peripherals appear in System Information whether or not their software driver is functioning. So if a connected peripheral does not show up in System Information, then you are almost certainly experiencing a hardware failure. If a connected peripheral appears as normal in System Information, you are probably experiencing a software driver issue. In that case, use System Information to validate whether the expected kernel extensions are loaded.

▶ Unplug and then reconnect the peripheral. Doing this reinitializes the peripheral connection and forces macOS to reload any peripheral-specific drivers.

▶ Plug the peripheral into a different port or use a different cable. This helps you rule out any bad hardware, including host ports, cables, and inoperable hubs.

▶ Unplug other devices on the same bus. Another device on the shared bus may be causing an issue.

▶ Resolve potential USB power issues. The USB interface can prove problematic if devices are trying to draw too much power. Try plugging the USB device directly into the Mac instead of a USB hub.

▶ Shut down the Mac, fully power down all peripherals, and turn everything back on. This troubleshooting technique reinitializes the peripheral connections and reloads the software drivers.

▶ Try the peripheral with another Mac. This helps you determine whether the issue is with your Mac or the peripheral. If the device doesn't work with other computers, your Mac is not the source of the issue.

▶ Use Software Update preferences to check for macOS updates.

▶ Use the App Store to check for app updates.

▶ Check for third-party app updates.

▶ Check the peripheral manufacturer's website for the latest driver updates.

▶ Check for peripheral software updates. Like software updates, firmware updates may also resolve peripheral issues.

Exercise 26.1
Examine Peripherals Using System Information

In an earlier exercise, you used System Information to view information about your hard disk. In this exercise, you use System Information to identify devices on a bus.

NOTE ▶ In a classroom environment that doesn't provide USB devices, your facilitator might demonstrate this exercise.

Examine Internal Devices

There are several ways to open System Information. In an earlier exercise, you opened it by choosing Apple menu > About This Mac and then clicking System Report. In this exercise you open System Information a different way.

1   If necessary, log in as Johnny Appleseed.

2   Click the Apple menu.

3   Press and hold the Option key.

The first item in the Apple menu changes from "About This Mac" to "System Information."

4   With the Option key pressed, choose System Information from the Apple menu.

System Information opens and shows Hardware, Network, and Software information.

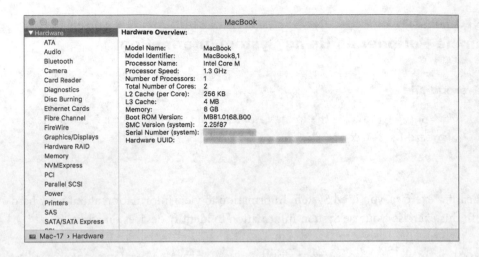

5   In the Hardware list on the left, click Graphics/Displays.

You see information about your graphics chip, the Intel Iris Pro.

6   In the Hardware list, click USB to view devices connected to the USB bus. (This is called the USB Device Tree.)

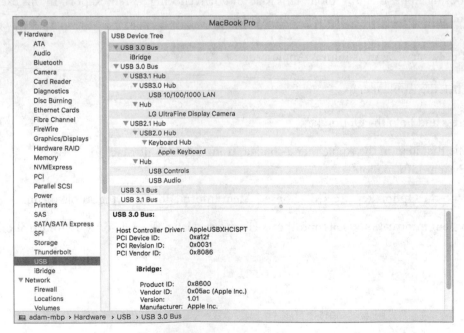

In this example, System Information indicates that there are four USB buses, two of which have devices connected to them. Several of the buses are internal to the Mac.

If a device is connected to a hub, it's listed beneath the hub and indented. This example shows a Keyboard Hub entry with an Apple Keyboard connected. Although the hub and keyboard are separate devices at the USB level, they are both parts of a single physical device: an Apple USB keyboard. Most USB keyboards contain a built-in hub so you can attach other USB devices to them.

7 Examine the USB report for your Mac and determine which devices are internal and which are external.

Examine External USB Devices

For this exercise, you need at least one external USB device connected to your Mac. If you are performing these exercises in a classroom environment, your facilitator might provide a device. If no suitable USB device is available, quit System Information and skip this exercise.

1 If it isn't already connected, plug in the external USB device, and refresh System Information. Choose File > Refresh Information (Command-R).

2 Select an external USB device in the USB report for your Mac.

Details about the device appear in the lower pane.

3 Examine the speed listed for the device.

The speed at which a USB device can run depends on its capability and the speeds of the port and intermediate hubs through which it is connected.

4 Examine the Current Available and Current Required figures.

Your Mac can supply a certain amount of electricity through each of its USB ports. If there are too many devices on the port, there might not be enough electricity. To prevent this, macOS keeps track of how much electricity is available at each point in the USB bus and disables devices if it calculates that not enough power is available for them.

5 While viewing the USB information, unplug the device from your Mac (if it is a storage device, eject it first), plug it into a different USB port, choose File > Refresh Information (Command-R).

System Information doesn't update the window unless you tell it to.

6   Locate the external device in the report to see whether it changed places or if its statistics changed.

7   If you have an external hub, try plugging the device in a port, and refresh the display in System Information again.

See if enough power is available from the hub to run the device and whether its speed decreased because it's connected through a hub.

8   Quit System Information.

Lesson 27

Manage Printers and Scanners

In this lesson, you learn how macOS works with different print and scan technologies and how to manage and trouble-shoot printers and multifunctioning devices connected to your Mac.

Reference 27.1
Printing in macOS

macOS uses a combination of AirPrint and CUPS technologies to enable you to quickly set up printers.

AirPrint

AirPrint is an Apple technology that helps you find printers and then print without downloading or installing printer drivers (software that allows computers to communicate with printers).

AirPrint is built into most popular printer models, listed in Apple Support article HT201311, "About AirPrint," which is updated monthly. If your printer was made in the last several years, it probably works with AirPrint.

If your printer isn't AirPrint-enabled, you can make sure it's compatible with macOS Mojave by checking with the printer manufacturer.

CUPS

macOS uses the open source CUPS printing system to manage local printing. CUPS uses the Internet Printing Protocol (IPP/2.1) standard to manage print tasks and PostScript Printer Description (PPD) files for printer drivers. PPD files can describe PostScript and non-PostScript printers.

> **MORE INFO ▶** For more information about PostScript, the technology from Adobe that was the first device-independent Page Description Language (PDL) and also a programming language, read www.adobe.com/products/postscript.html.

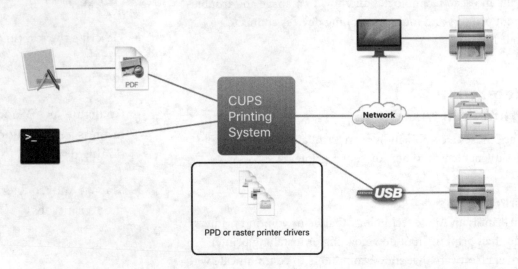

A print job starts when you print from an app or use a print command from Terminal. macOS generates a file called a spool file and places it in the /var/spool/cups folder.

The CUPS background process, cupsd, passes the spool file through filter processes known as the print chain. These processes convert the spool file to a format that is understood by the destination printer and communicate the information to the printer. To find out more about CUPS, visit the official CUPS website at www.cups.org.

CUPS Drivers

For printers that don't support AirPrint, you must associate an appropriate printer driver with the printer before you can use the printer.

Apple supplies printer drivers for most popular printer models, including Brother, Canon, Epson, Fuji-Xerox, HP, Lexmark, Ricoh, and Samsung.

New installations of macOS include only Apple and generic print drivers. macOS upgrade installations install only drivers for printers already in use by the Mac.

macOS includes support for standard PostScript and Printer Command Language (PCL) printers.

A few of the built-in Apple printer drivers are in /System/Library/Printers/Libraries, but third-party printer drivers are installed to /Library/Printers/PPDs/Contents/Resources. You might see other vendor folders that contain ancillary printer driver resources.

After you add a printer configuration, a copy of the PPD with the name of the device is placed in the /etc/cups/ppd folder and two configuration files are modified:

▶ /etc/cups/printers.conf

▶ /Library/Preferences/org.cups.printers.plist

The first time you print or access a printer queue, macOS creates a printer queue app, with the name of the device, in ~/Library/Printers in the user's home folder.

Reference 27.2
Configure Printers and Scanners

How you physically connect to a printer determines how you configure macOS to print to the printer. For example, directly attached and local network printers are automatically configured with little user interaction. Older printers or network printers might require more configuration.

For best results when you add a new printer, enable the option "Automatically keep my Mac up to date" in Software Update preferences and add printers while you are logged in as an administrator user. Software Update is covered in Lesson 6, "Update macOS."

NOTE ► If you want a user to be able to add and remove printers without providing administrator credentials, make that user a member of the lpadmin group. See the man page for **dseditgroup** for more information.

Configure a Directly Attached Printer

If your directly attached printer isn't AirPrint-enabled, contact the printer manufacturer for instructions on how to get and install printer drivers. Then connect the printer to your Mac.

If you have an older printer that doesn't support AirPrint driverless technology, your Mac might automatically install the driver software needed to use that device.

For some older printers, if you see a message prompting you to download new software, be sure to click Install to download and install it.

The previous dialog appears only if all the following are true:

► You are logged in as an administrator user.

► The "Automatically keep my Mac up to date" option is enabled in Software Update preferences.

► The printer isn't compatible with AirPrint but Apple has printer drivers available for the printer.

If "Automatically keep my Mac up to date" option is disabled in Software Update preferences, you can attach the printer to your Mac and then open Software Update to check for printer drivers. If printer drivers are available for the printer, then Software Update installs printer drivers silently. You can close Software Update preferences and continue to configure the printer.

If a non-administrator user attaches a new printer for the first time, macOS won't configure the printer if the driver is missing. Also, if a printer driver for a directly attached printer is unavailable from Apple, then nothing happens automatically when you plug it in. In this case, you must manually acquire and install the printer driver with administrator credentials.

You can verify that the printer was added by opening the Print dialog from any app (File > Print) or from Printers & Scanners preferences. In Printers & Scanners preferences, you can tell that printers are locally connected if their location has the same name as the local Mac computer's sharing name.

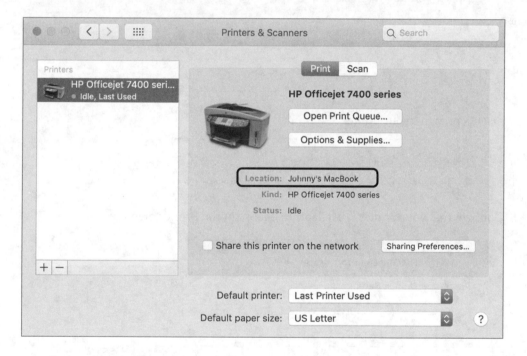

Configure a Local Network Printer

You must be logged in on your Mac with an administrator account to add a local network printer. If your Mac and printer are already connected to the same Wi-Fi network, the printer might be available to you without any setup. macOS can automatically discover standalone printers that support Bonjour (or mDNS), standalone printers that support AirPrint, and any printer shared from another Mac or AirPort wireless base station. If your network printer isn't AirPrint-enabled, use Software Update preferences to install available printer drivers.

To check whether your Mac can automatically discover your local network printer:

1   Open an app that enables you to print.

2   Choose File > Print.

3   Open the Printer menu, choose Nearby Printers or Printers & Scanners preferences, and choose your printer.

macOS prepares your printer.

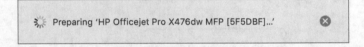

4   Confirm that your printer is available to choose in the Printer menu.

Manually Configure a Printer

If the network printer doesn't support automatic network discovery with Bonjour, you must configure it manually. Also, if a directly attached printer doesn't automatically configure, you can manually add it. Add a new printer or multifunctioning device in one of these ways:

▶   From any app, open a Print dialog by choosing File > Print. Next, from the Printer menu, choose Add Printer.

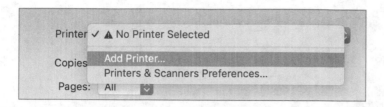

▶ Open System preferences and click the Printers & Scanners icon. Click the Add (+) button at the bottom of the Printers list. If there are nearby network printers, a menu appears enabling you to select those printers.

If the printer you need to configure doesn't appear in the menu, select the "Add Printer or Scanner" option to manually configure a new printer. This opens an Add window.

The Add window features several panes for selecting a printer or multifunctioning device. Access these panes by clicking the following buttons in the toolbar:

▶ Default—This browser enables you to select directly attached USB printers and network printers discovered using Bonjour (or mDNS), AirPrint, or network directory services.

▶ IP—This dialog enables you to manually enter the IP address or DNS host name of a Line Printer Daemon (LPD), IPP, or HP JetDirect printer. You must select the appropriate protocol from the menu and enter the printer's address. Entering a printer queue is usually optional.

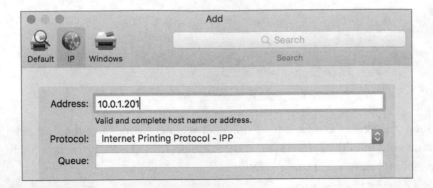

▶ Windows—This browser enables you to select printers shared with the Server Message Block (SMB) printer sharing protocol. Double-click an SMB server and authenticate to access the server's shared printers.

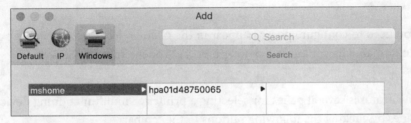

▶ Advanced—This advanced configuration choice enables you to manually enter the printer location. You need to do this only when macOS can't properly auto-locate a printer. The Advanced button is hidden by default. To see this button, Control-click in the Add window toolbar to see a menu. From this menu choose Customize Toolbar and drag the Advanced button to the toolbar. Then you can start configuring the printer by choosing the printer type.

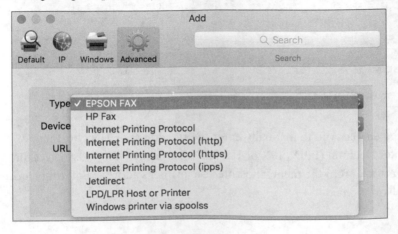

After you select a printer or multifunctioning device from the top half of the new printer configuration dialog, macOS completes the bottom half for you using information it discovered. This includes selecting the appropriate printer driver if possible. The Name and Location fields are there to help you identify the device. Set those to anything you like.

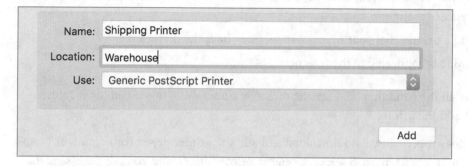

When you add a new printer, the Add window might tell you that "The selected printer software is available from Apple. Click Add to download it and add this printer."

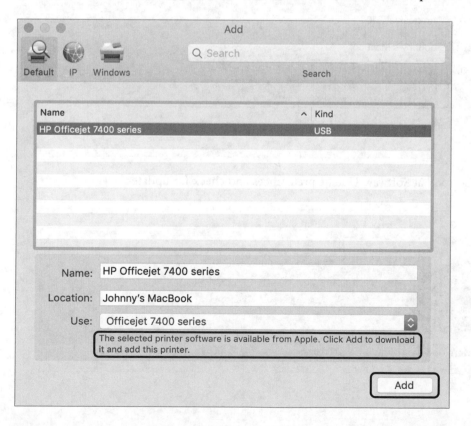

You'll see this message if the following are true:

▶ You are logged in as an administrator user (or you are logged in as a standard account user who is a member of the lpadmin group).

▶ The option "Automatically keep my Mac up to date" is deselected in Software Update preferences.

▶ You add a printer that your Mac doesn't already have the driver for.

▶ Your Mac is connected to the Internet.

If you meet all the conditions and see the message, click Add to download the printer driver and add the printer.

If macOS doesn't prompt you to download and add the printer driver (or if you aren't connected to the Internet), macOS selects a generic printer driver, and you see a message that the printer driver might not let you use all the features of the printer.

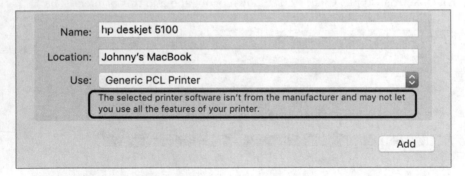

In this case, look at Software Update preferences and check for updates.

If Apple doesn't provide a suitable printer driver, you might be able to select a built-in printer driver. To select a printer driver, choose Select Software from the Use menu.

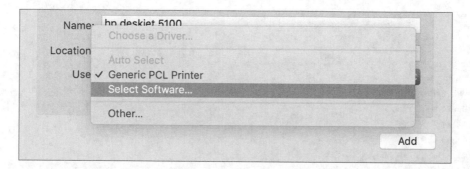

You can manually scroll through the list of installed printer drivers, but using the Search field might be quicker. After you select an appropriate printer driver, click OK to use that driver. The following figure displays most of the default printer drivers that come with macOS Mojave; there are two other Zebra printer drivers that are not displayed.

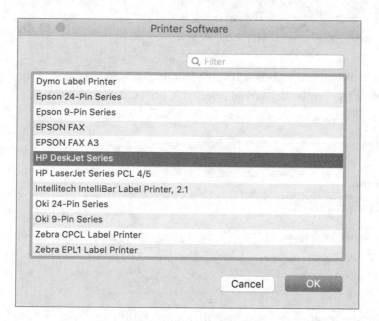

If your Mac already downloaded other printer drivers, the Printer Software window displays additional printer drivers.

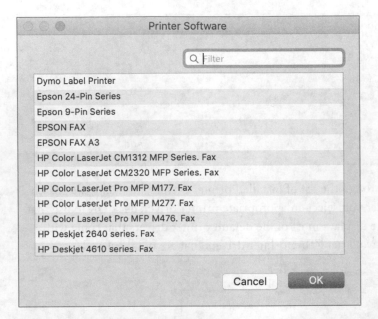

After you select the printer driver to use and click OK, the Printer Software window closes. The Use menu displays the printer driver you selected. Click Add to add the printer.

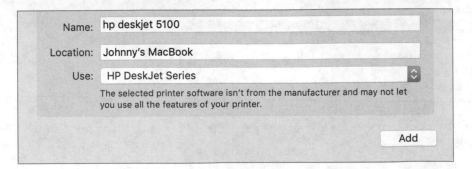

If your Mac doesn't already have an appropriate printer driver for your printer, you might be able to get a printer driver directly from the printer manufacturer. Try using Software Update to automatically install printer drivers before you try downloading printer drivers from the printer manufacturer. To select a printer driver that you downloaded directly from the printer manufacturer, choose Other from the Use menu; then in the open dialog, select the printer driver and click Open.

If there's no printer driver available for your printer, you can use a built-in generic printer driver.

If you configure an LPD printer connection, you must manually specify the appropriate printer driver. This step can occur with HP JetDirect and SMB printer connections.

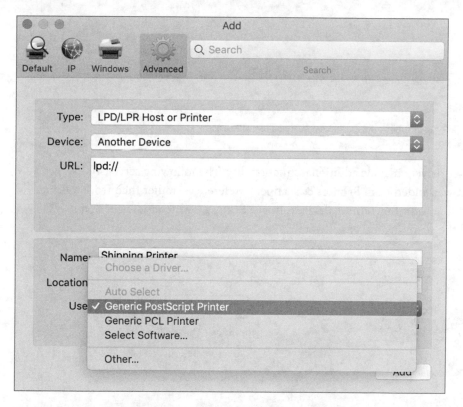

If you configure an IP printer, you see an additional dialog that enables you to select special printer options. After you complete the printer configuration, open the Print dialog from any app, or Printers & Scanners preferences, and verify that the printer is added.

In Printers & Scanners preferences, you can tell which printers are network printers if their location is shown as something different than your local Mac computer sharing name.

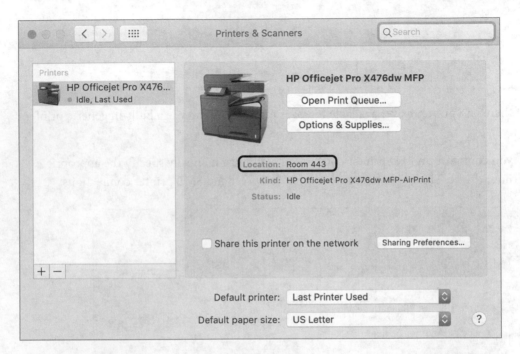

Some printer drivers include additional functionality. The following screenshot shows a printer that was added from Printers & Scanners preferences, rather than from a Print dialog, and that multifunctioning devices show a Scan tab, which indicates that macOS configured the scanning driver software.

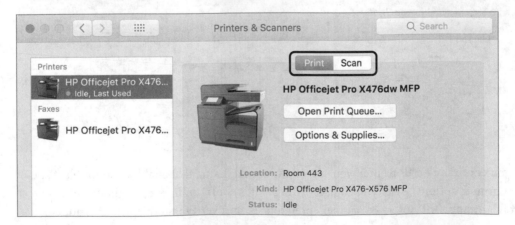

MORE INFO ▶ You can use Terminal to add printers. In Apple Remote Desktop you can go to the menu and choose Manage > Send UNIX Command to create printers on many Mac computers at the same time. See the man pages for lpadmin, cupsenable, and cupsaccept for more information.

Modify an Existing Printer

You might have to edit a printer configuration after you set it up. Depending on the printer model, you may not be allowed to modify the print driver settings from Printers & Scanners preferences. In this case, to change a printer's selected driver, you must delete the printer and add it again. From Printers & Scanners preferences, you can:

▶ Remove a printer configuration—Select the item you want to delete from the printer list, and then click the Remove (–) button at the bottom of the list.

▶ Set printing defaults—From the two menus at the bottom of Printers & Scanners preferences, choose the default printer and paper size. Be careful when you set the default printer for Last Printer Used. You will have no permanent default printer and the default destination for print jobs might constantly change.

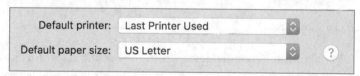

▶ Open a print queue—Select a printer from the list and click the Open Print Queue button. Details on print queues are covered later in this lesson.

▶ Edit an existing configuration and check supply levels—Select a printer from the list and then click the Options & Supplies button. In the resulting dialog, you can edit the printer configuration—including changing the printer name—and, if available, check the printer supply levels and open the printer hardware configuration utility.

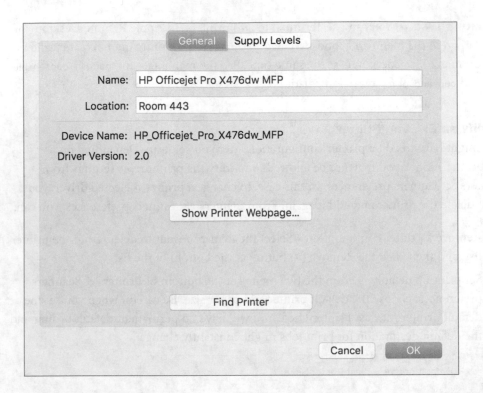

▶   Manage scanning—Select a multifunctioning device from the list and select the Scan button. From this interface, open the scanner image capture interface or enable local network scanner sharing.

Share Printers

Your Mac shared print service is made available with IPP printer sharing protocols. Although macOS and Windows are compatible with IPP, different versions of Windows might require additional drivers for IPP. IPP supports automatic printer driver configuration and installation for macOS, so when another Mac user connects to your Mac shared print service, that user's Mac automatically selects, and downloads if necessary, the appropriate printer drivers.

The CUPS-shared print service also allows other network clients to locate your shared printer configurations with Bonjour. Different versions of Windows might require additional drivers for Bonjour. Alternatively, network clients can enter your Mac computer's IP address or DNS host name to access your Mac shared print service. Configuring your Mac computer's identification for providing network services is covered in Lesson 25, "Manage Host Sharing and Personal Firewall."

Users can't access shared print services on a Mac in sleep mode. If you want to ensure that your Mac doesn't sleep, disable your Mac automatic sleep activation or enable "Wake for Wi-Fi network access" from Energy Saver preferences. Read Reference 28.3, "Sleep Modes, Logout, and Shutdown," for more information.

To share printers from your Mac, open Sharing preferences, then unlock if necessary. Select the Printer Sharing checkbox to enable printer sharing. Selecting this checkbox configures cupsd (which is always running in the background) to listen for IPP print service requests on TCP port 631.

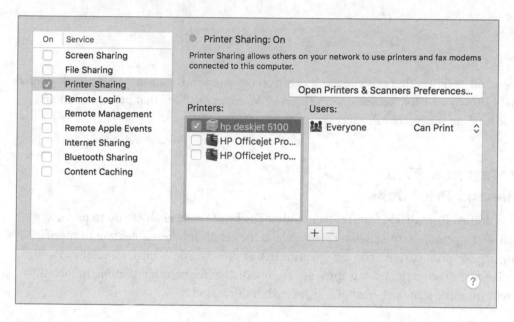

If your Mac is configured to use a document scanner, enable scanner sharing from Sharing preferences. This enables you to share the scanner with other Mac computers on a local network.

By default, no printers are shared. To enable sharing for printer configurations, select the checkboxes next to the printers you wish to share. Optionally, you can limit who is allowed to print to your shared printers. By default, all users are allowed access to your shared printing devices. To limit access, select a shared device from the Printers list and then click the Add (+) button at the bottom of the Users list.

A dialog appears where you can select user or group accounts you want to grant access to the printer. When adding accounts, you can also choose to deny access to guest users by selecting No Access for Everyone in the Users list. Also, with limited printing access enabled, users have to authenticate to print to your shared printer.

Share only printers that other Mac users can't otherwise see. If you share a network printer that's already available on your network, other Mac users will see that printer listed multiple times in the Nearby Printers list.

Reference 27.3
Manage Print Jobs

This unified Print dialog features two modes. The basic mode enables you to preview and start a print job using default settings, and the details mode enables you to specify any page or print option and manage print setting presets. Some apps, especially graphic design and desktop publishing apps, use custom dialogs for printing that might look different from the standard Print dialog covered in this lesson.

Start a Print Job

To start a print job using default print settings, from an app choose File > Print (or press Command-P). Some apps bypass the Print dialog and send the print job to your default printer when you use Command-P.

When the Print dialog appears, it sometimes slides out of the app's window title bar. Sometimes it appears as its own dialog. Most apps show a print preview, and some might show the basic print options. The default printer and print preset are selected, but you choose the number of pages, copies, and duplex (two-sided) options, if available. Customizing printer presets is covered in the next section of this lesson.

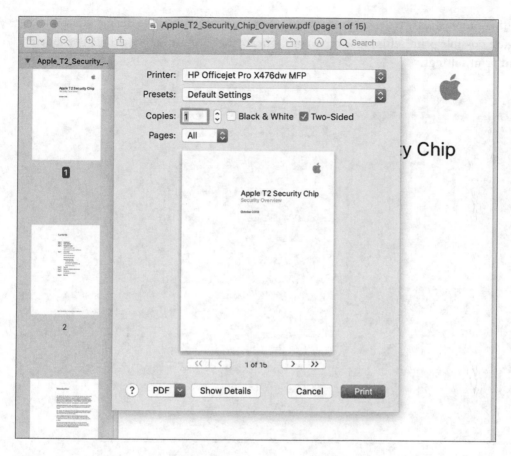

When the print job is started, macOS automatically opens the print queue app associated with the destination printer. Although no window opens if the print job is successful, you can click the print queue in the Dock.

Configure Detailed Print Settings and Presets

To start a print job that uses custom print settings, from an app open the Print dialog. When you open the Print dialog, the default printer and print presets are selected, but you can choose other configured printers or presets from the associated menu.

Clicking the Show Details button expands the Print dialog to its full details mode. In the full details mode, you can click the Hide Details button to return to the basic Print dialog mode. The Print dialog also remembers which mode you last used for each app.

On the left side of the detailed Print dialog, you can page through a preview of the print job, much like the preview in the basic Print dialog. Changes you make to the page layout settings are instantly reflected in the preview. On the right side of the dialog, you can configure possible print settings for most apps. The top half features more detailed page setup and print settings.

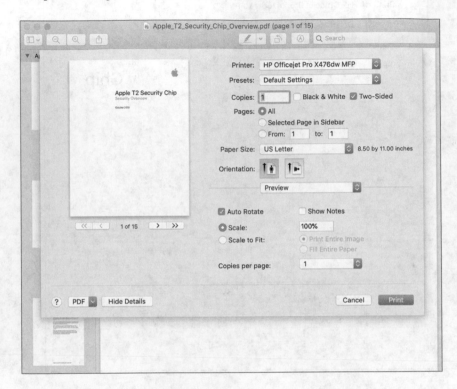

Settings on the bottom half vary depending on the app you're printing from and your printer driver. You can choose a category of print settings to modify from the menu that separates the print settings from top to bottom. The settings list and configuration options within vary for different apps, printers, and printer drivers.

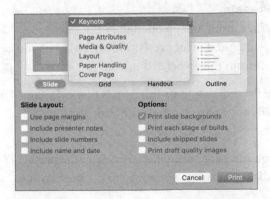

To save the current print settings as a preset, choose Save Current Settings as Preset from the Presets menu. Select whether you want this preset to apply to all printers or just the currently selected printer. By saving a preset, you make it accessible from the Presets menu in the details view of any Print dialog. The print presets are saved in ~/Library/Preferences/ in com.apple.print.custompresets.plist for presets that apply to all printers, and in com.apple.print.custompresets.plist.forprinter.*printername*.plist for presets for a specific printer, so each user has their own custom print presets. Print presets apply to all apps.

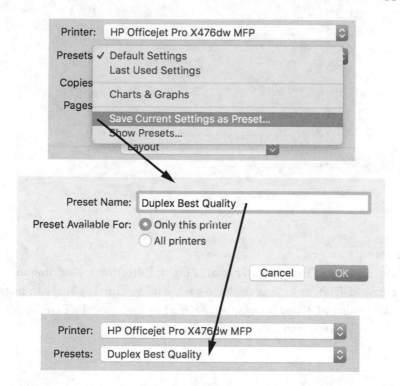

To manage existing print presets, open the print Presets dialog by choosing Show Presets from the Presets menu. In the print Presets dialog, select a preset to see its settings and values, and optionally use the Delete and Duplicate buttons at the bottom of the presets list. If you double-click a print preset you can rename the preset. When you finish managing print presets, click OK to save the changes and return to the Print dialog.

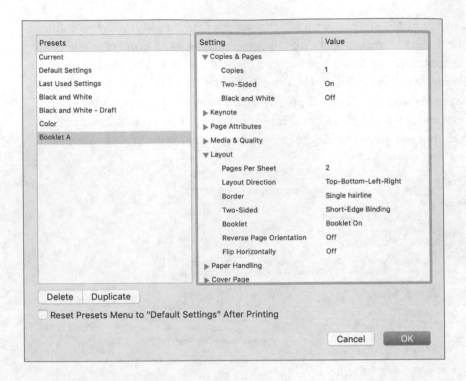

Create PDF Documents

macOS includes built-in Portable Document Format (PDF) architecture and editing tools, including tools to create PDF documents or perform basic editing. Any app that can print can also generate high-quality PDF documents. In any Print dialog, click the PDF button. A menu appears, which you can use to save a PDF to any location.

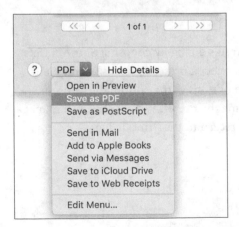

From the PDF menu, you can also choose a PDF service that accepts and processes PDF files. Some preset services are built in, but you can add your own PDF services by choosing Edit Menu from the PDF menu. Or, depending on who needs access to them, you can manually add PDF services to /Library/PDF Services or ~/Library/PDF Services. To create custom PDF services, use Automator to create a Print Plugin or use Script Editor. If your multifunctioning printer supports faxing, you can choose Fax PDF from the PDF menu.

You can also edit PDFs in Preview. Read more about this in Reference 20.2, "Manage App Extensions."

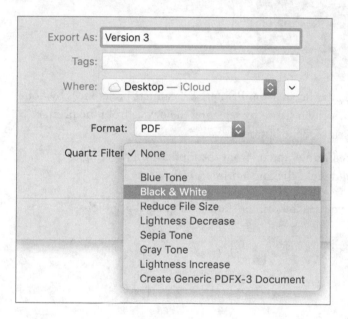

Manage Printer Queues

When a print job starts, the spool file is placed in /var/spool/cups, and CUPS takes over to process the file and send it to the printer. When you print from the graphical interface, macOS opens a print queue app to manage the print job. If a job completes quickly, the file is in the print queue only for a few moments, and the print queue app quits when the print job is done.

If macOS detects an error with a printer, it stops all print jobs that are in the printer queue. You can still start print jobs, but they just fill up in the queue.

To manage print job queues, access the printer queue app in one of the following ways:

► If a printer queue is open, click its icon in the Dock. In the following example screen-shot, the printer queue's Dock icon shows a "2" in the red badge icon, indicating that there are currently two jobs in the queue. Also, as you can see by the orange connection badge icon, this printer queue has network issues that are preventing the print jobs from completing.

► You can manually open a printer queue from Printers & Scanners preferences by double-clicking the device in the printer list or by selecting the device from the printer list and clicking the Open Print Queue button.

► You can also manually open a printer queue from the Finder by navigating to ~/Library/Printers and then double-clicking a printer.

When the printer queue opens, you see the printer status and queued print jobs.

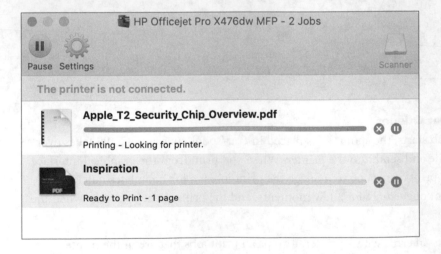

To pause or resume the jobs in the printer queue, click the Pause or Resume button (the button toggles between the two modes) in the queue app toolbar. To hold or resume a print job, select it from the job list and click the small Hold or Resume button to the right of the print job progress bar (the button toggles between the two). To delete a job, select it from the job list and click the small x button to the right of the print job progress bar.

You can select a job in the printer queue list and then press the Space bar to open a Quick Look preview window for the print job. For a held job, choose Jobs > Resume Job on Page and then specify a page number to resume printing on. You can reorder print jobs in the printer queue by dragging the job you want to reorder in the list. You can also drag jobs from one printer queue window to another.

Other features are available in the printer queue app toolbar. You can reconfigure the printer by clicking the Settings button in the toolbar. Also, for a supported multifunctioning printer, you can click the Scanner button in the toolbar to open the Scanner interface.

You might want to leave often-used printer queues in the Dock for direct access. Control-click the queue app's Dock icon and, from the shortcut menu, choose Options > Keep in Dock. A benefit to having your printers in the Dock is that you can drag a document on top of a printer icon to quickly print a single copy of the document.

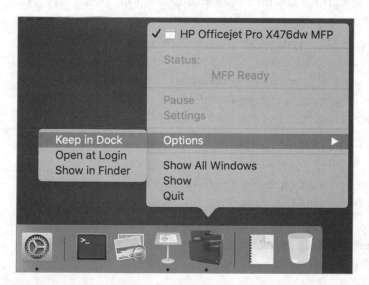

You can also provide quick access to your printer queues by dragging the ~/Library/Printers folder from the Finder to your Dock. Click this folder in your Dock to see configured devices.

Reference 27.4
Troubleshoot Print Issues

You will probably experience more printing issues that are caused by hardware rather than software. The following is a series of general print system troubleshooting techniques.

▶ Check the printer queue app first. The printer queue lets you know if there is a printer connection issue. At the same time, verify that the queue isn't paused and that no jobs are on hold. Sometimes deleting old print jobs from the queue helps clear the problem.

▶ Double-check page and print settings. If the job is printing but doesn't print correctly, double-check page and print settings using the Print dialog details mode.

▶ Review the PDF output of the app. The CUPS workflow is app > PDF > CUPS > printer. Verifying whether the PDF looks correct lets you know if the source of the problem is with the app or the printing system.

▶ Print from another app. If you suspect the app is the root of the problem, try printing from another app. You can also print a test page while in the printer queue app by choosing Printer > Print Test Page.

▶ If you have trouble adding a printer and finding an appropriate printer driver, try logging in as an administrator user before you add the printer.

▶ Check the printer hardware. Many printers have diagnostic screens or printed reports that help you identify a hardware issue. Many also have a software utility or a built-in webpage that reports errors. Click the Printer Setup button in the printer queue app toolbar to access these management interfaces. Double-check cables and connections. Lastly, contact the printer manufacturer to diagnose printer hardware issues.

▶ For directly connected printers, use the peripheral troubleshooting techniques outlined in Lesson 26, "Troubleshoot Peripherals."

▶ For network printers, use network troubleshooting techniques described in Lesson 23, "Troubleshoot Network Issues," and Lesson 24, "Manage Network Services."

▶ Delete and reconfigure printers. From Printers & Scanners preferences, delete and reconfigure a problem printer using the techniques described earlier in this lesson. Doing so resets the device drivers and queue.

▶ Reset the entire print system. From Printers & Scanners preferences, Control-click in the printers list and choose "Reset printing system" from the shortcut menu. Click OK in the verification dialog. Authenticate as an administrator user. This clears configured devices, shared settings, custom presets, and queued print jobs.

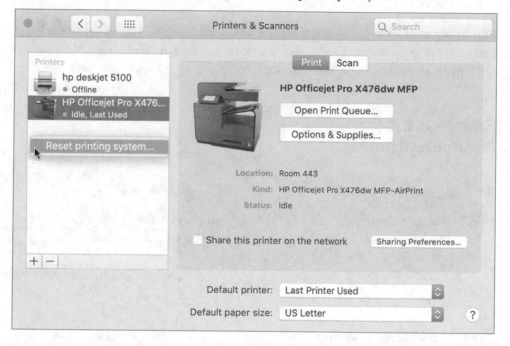

▶ For non-AirPrint printers, remove printer drivers by moving the contents of /Library/Printers to another location.

▶ Review CUPS log files. Like other system services, CUPS writes important activity to log files. You can access the logs while in any printer queue app by choosing Printer > Error Log. This opens Console to the CUPS error_log file. While in Console, you can check the CUPS access_log and page_log files in /var/log/cups. The CUPS error_log file might not exist if the CUPS service hasn't logged print errors.

▶ Reinstall or update printer drivers. You can use Software Update preferences to check for system and printer updates. You can also check the printer manufacturer's website for the latest printer driver updates. If you're using an AirPrint-enabled printer, you can check with the manufacturer to see if there's an update for your printer model (as opposed to a printer driver update).

For advanced print system management and troubleshooting, go to the Mac CUPS at **http://localhost:631**, and follow the instructions.

For more information, read Apple Support article HT203343, "If you can't print from your Mac or iOS device."

In Printing preferences, click the Help (question mark) button. One of the topics includes "Solve printing problems on Mac," at https://support.apple.com/guide/mac-help/solve-printing-problems-on-mac-mh14002.

Exercise 27.1
Configure Printing

> **Prerequisites**
>
> > You must have created the Local Administrator account (Exercise 3.1, "Configure a Mac for Exercises") and the Johnny Appleseed account (Exercise 7.1, "Create a Standard User Account").

Configure a Bonjour Printer

In this exercise, you discover and configure a network printer through the Bonjour service discovery protocol. Depending on your classroom, this printer is either a virtual print queue shared from the classroom server or a printer on the classroom network.

1   If necessary, log in as Johnny Appleseed.

2   Open Printers & Scanners preferences.

3   Click the lock button and authenticate as Local Administrator.

4   Click the Add (+) button under the printer list.

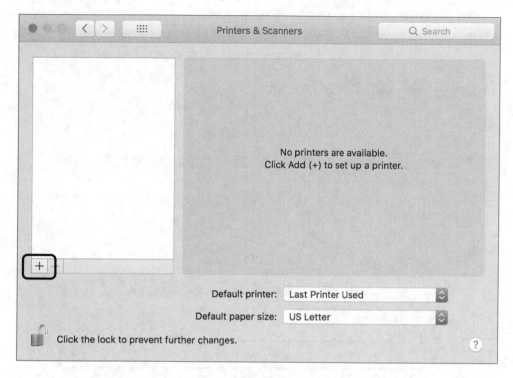

The Add Printer window opens and shows a list of nearby printers.

TIP▶ Depending on your classroom environment, what you see on your network may vary. See Reference 27.2, "Configure Printers and Scanners," for more information.

5   Select the printer you want to use in the printer list.

If you are using a print queue shared from the classroom server, it appears as "VirtualPrinter @ server."

Depending on the type of printer, one of several things might happen:

▶   If a driver for the printer is installed on your Mac, is available from the Mac sharing the printer, or is available from the printer, it's selected and shown in the Use menu.

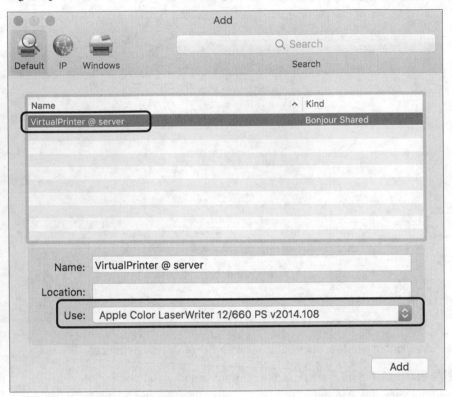

▶   If the driver isn't available locally, it might be available from the Apple software update servers.

In this case, adding the printer will automatically download and install the appropriate driver package. Depending on the package size and your Internet connection speed, this may take a while.

▶ If the driver isn't installed locally or available from Apple, a generic driver might be available to provide basic printing.

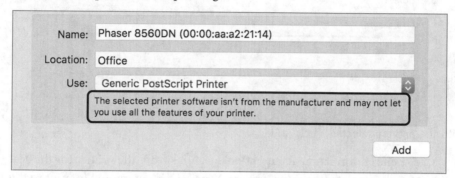

If you want full access to printer features, find and install a driver for the model before you add the printer.

▶ If the driver isn't installed locally or available from Apple, you are notified to contact the printer's manufacturer.

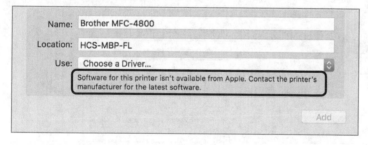

In this case, find and install a driver (probably from the printer manufacturer). Close the Add window and try again after you find and install the appropriate driver.

▶   If the printer is AirPrint compatible, you are able to add it without having a printer-specific driver.

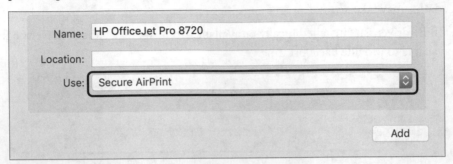

6   With the printer selected, click Add.

Your Mac fetches information about optional features from the printer (or the Mac sharing it) and completes the setup process. Your Mac is configured to print to this printer.

7   When the new print queue is set up, select it, and click the Open Print Queue button.

This lets you view and change settings for the print queue. Depending on the printer capabilities, you might see options such as a Scanner button.

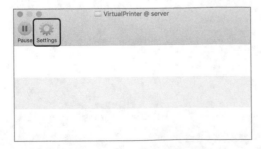

8 Click the Settings button.

A dialog opens that enables you to view and change information about the print queue configuration. These settings are also accessible from Printers & Scanners preferences when you click the Options & Supplies button.

The General pane enables you to configure the name and location displayed for the printer. It might be useful to name printers that would otherwise have their model name listed.

9 Change the name and location to something more descriptive. If you are using "VirtualPrinter @ server," use the following:

Name: **Pretendco Network Printer**

Location: **Server**

If you are not using a printer shared from the classroom server, enter a more descriptive location such as **Training Room**.

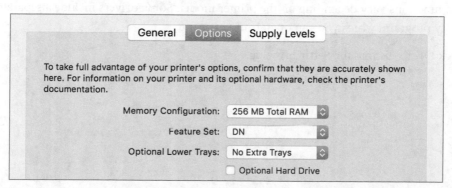

The other panes in the Settings dialogs vary considerably between different printer models. You probably won't see all the options in the following screenshots.

10 If there is an Options button, click it.

If this printer is shared from a Mac, the Mac controls what options are configured for the printer. If you are connecting to the printer directly, you can change the options.

11 If there is a Supply Levels button, click it.

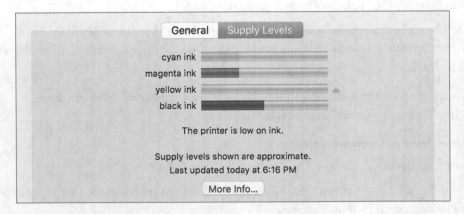

If you are connecting to the printer directly and the printer supports it, you can view the printer supply levels.

12 If there is a Utility button, click it.

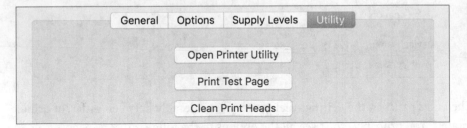

This pane of printer setup gives you access to utilities supplied by this printer driver. The functions vary depending on the printer model. Some drivers include a separate utility program, which you can open from this pane.

13 Click OK to dismiss the Settings dialog.

14 Quit the printer queue.

The printer queue isn't an app, but it acts like one, including the Quit option under the "application" menu.

Exercise 27.2
Manage Printing

> **Prerequisites**
>
> ▶ You must have created the Johnny Appleseed account (Exercise 7.1, "Create a Standard User Account").
>
> ▶ You must have at least one print queue set up on your Mac from Exercise 27.1, "Configure Printing."

In this exercise, you explore the Print dialog, including saving print options as a preset, printing to PDF, and managing PDF workflows.

Print to a Printer

In this section, you print to one of the printers you just set up. If you are printing to VirtualPrinter on Server, it doesn't connect to a physical printer, so no printed output appears.

1 If necessary, log in as Johnny Appleseed.

2 Open the Participant *nn*.rtf file from your desktop. If this file doesn't exist, open TextEdit, type text into the blank document that opens, and save it to your desktop as **Participant** *nn* (where *nn* is your participant number, or 1 if you are working on your own).

3 In the TextEdit menu bar, choose File > Print (Command-P).

4   In the Print dialog, choose a printer from the Printer menu.

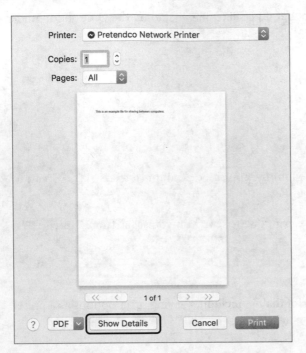

5   Click Show Details.

The Print dialog expands to show additional print settings.

6   Choose Layout from the configuration menu (initially set to TextEdit).

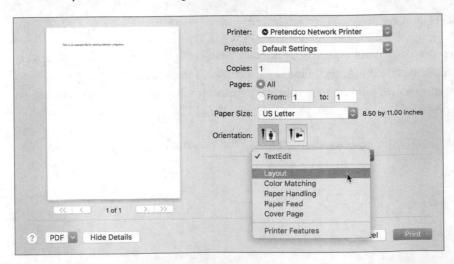

7   From the "Pages per Sheet" menu, choose 6.

8   From the Border menu, choose Single Thin Line.

As you change settings, the preview on the left shows the effects of your changes.

9   From the Presets menu, choose "Save Current Settings as Preset."

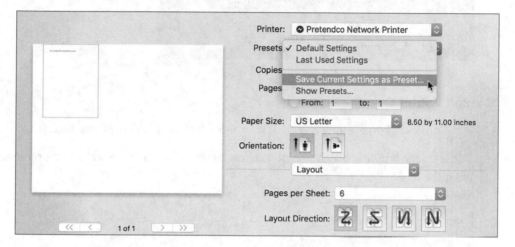

10 Name the preset **6-up with border**, make it available for all printers, and click OK.

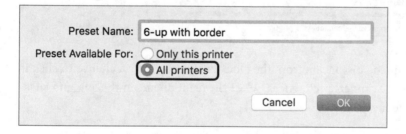

The print settings are available from the Presets menu whenever you print.

11 Use the Presets menu to switch between Default Settings and 6-up with border, and watch the effect on the print settings.

12   Click Print.

The print queue icon appears in your Dock and shows the number of jobs in the queue (1).

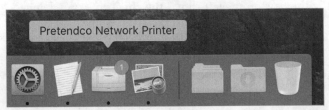

Manage a Print Queue

1   If possible, click the printer queue in your Dock before it becomes unavailable.

In the queue window, watch the job get sent to the printer (or server) and be removed from the queue.

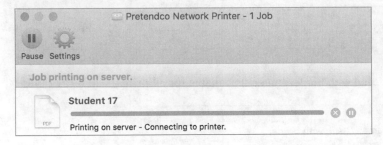

2   If the printer queue disappears from the Dock before you have a chance to click it, open Printers & Scanners preferences, select the print queue on the left, and click Open Print Queue.

3   In the print queue window, click Pause.

4   Switch to TextEdit, and print the document again.

5   When you are warned that the printer has been paused, click "Add to Printer."

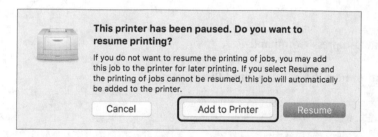

6   Switch to the print queue window. If your document isn't shown, quit the print queue, and reopen it from Printers & Scanners preferences. If the first document didn't successfully print, you might see your document listed twice.

Your document is shown as "Ready to Print."

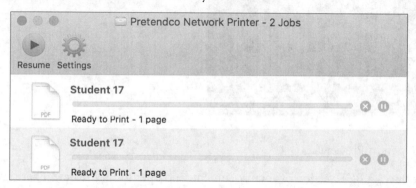

7   Double-click the document in the print queue, and then press Command-Y or the Space bar.

A Quick Look window opens, enabling you to preview the print job.

8   Close the Quick Look window, and click the Jobs menu.

This menu has options to hold, resume, or delete print jobs. Most of the options are also available in the print queue window.

9   Click the delete ("X") button to the right of the print job. If there are two documents in the queue, delete both of them.

The job is no longer displayed in the print queue.

10 Quit the print queue.

Print to PDF

1 Switch to TextEdit, and press Command-P.

2 Click the PDF button near the bottom left of the Print dialog.

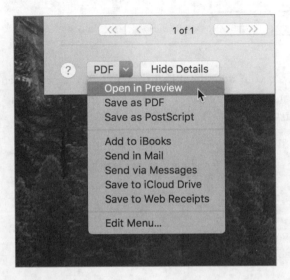

3 Choose "Open in Preview."

CUPS produces a PDF version of your document, and opens it in Preview. There are Cancel and Print buttons near the bottom right of the window.

4 Click Cancel.

This closes the document and quits Preview.

5 In TextEdit, press Command-P again.

6 From the PDF menu, choose "Save as PDF."

7 Save the PDF to your desktop.

Exercise 27.3
Troubleshoot Printing

To troubleshoot printing, you must know the print process. In this exercise, you examine print logs and reset the printing configuration.

Examine the CUPS Logs

You can view system and user event logs in Console. In this exercise, you use Console to view CUPS logs.

1 If necessary, log in as Johnny Appleseed.

2 Open Console.

3 Click the disclosure triangle next to /var/log to display the list of logs, and then select "cups."

Because the CUPS logs are in the hidden folder /var/log, they are displayed under /var/log in Console.

4   If necessary, select access_log in the second column.

If you printed, entries appear in the access log. There might also be entries in the page log for each job.

5   If there are page_log and error_log files, select them and examine their contents.

6   Quit Console.

Reset Printing

If you can't print to your printer and you've tried other solutions, you can restore the printing system to factory defaults. When you reset your printing system to the factory defaults, you delete printers from your printer list, information about completed print jobs, and printer presets.

1   Open System Preferences, and click Printers & Scanners.

2   If necessary, click the lock button, and authenticate as Local Administrator.

3   Press and hold the Control key, and click in the printer list.

4   Choose "Reset printing system" from the menu that appears.

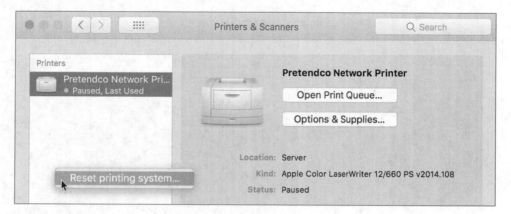

5   Click Reset when you're asked to confirm.

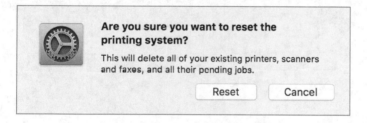

You can re-add your printers when the process is complete.

6   Quit System Preferences.

Troubleshoot Startup and System Issues

This lesson focuses on the process that your Mac goes through from the moment you turn your Mac on until you see the Finder. You identify the essential files and processes required to successfully start up macOS. You also explore macOS sleep modes, logout, and shutdown. You then learn about startup shortcuts and diagnostic modes that work with macOS. Finally, you learn how to troubleshoot system initialization and user session issues.

Reference 28.1
System Initialization

This section examines the main stages of the macOS startup procedure. The stages of system startup are initiation (the processes required to start macOS) or user session (the processes required to prepare the user environment). When you start your Mac from macOS, different screens appear to show you the startup progress, including any issues that might keep your Mac from starting up. The startup cues discussed here are what you experience during a typical startup. Deviations are covered as you learn more.

It all starts when you turn on your Mac. You can press its power button. Some Mac notebooks also turn on in other ways, like when you open the lid, connect to a power adapter, or press a key or the trackpad. Read Apple Support article HT201150, "How to turn your Mac on or off," for more details.

If your Mac has an Apple T2 Security Chip, by default Secure Boot is set to Full Security, so from the time you turn your Mac on, your Mac uses its Apple T2 Security Chip to verify every step of the boot process to ensure that the hardware and software haven't been tampered with. This way, you know your Mac is in a trustworthy state when it's started up. If there are any errors or failures in the secure startup process, then your Mac enters macOS Recovery, Apple T2 Security Chip recovery mode, or Apple T2 Security Chip Device Firmware Upgrade (DFU) mode. You can read more details in "Apple T2 Security Chip: Security Overview," available at www.apple.com/mac/docs/Apple_T2_Security_Chip_Overview.pdf. You can read more about using Startup Security Utility in macOS Recovery to control Secure Boot and External Boot settings in Lesson 9, "Manage Security and Privacy."

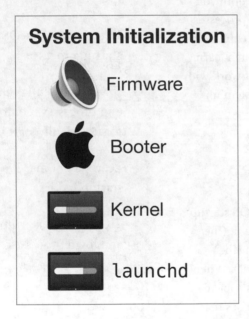

The four main system initialization stages are, in order:

▶ Firmware—At this stage, the Mac hardware is tested and initialized, and the booter is located and started.

▶ Booter—The booter loads the macOS kernel and essential hardware drivers, known as kernel extensions (KEXTs), into main memory and then allows the kernel to take over. During the booter stage, you see the Apple logo on the main display.

▶ Kernel—The kernel provides the macOS foundation and loads additional drivers and the core BSD UNIX operating system. You see a progress bar under the Apple logo on the main display when the kernel is loading.

▶ launchd—After the core operating system is loaded, it starts the first nonkernel process, launchd, which loads the rest of macOS. During this stage, you see a progress bar under the Apple logo on the main display. When this stage successfully completes, you see the login screen or the Finder, depending on whether FileVault is enabled or you are set to automatically log in.

System Initialization: Firmware

Your Mac computer firmware (BootROM) resides on flash memory chips built into the main computer board. When you start up your Mac, even before it starts macOS, the firmware acts as a mini operating system with just enough software to test and initialize the hardware and locate and start the macOS booter.

Mac computers have firmware based on Intel Extensible Firmware Interface (EFI) technology. Aside from supporting the Intel processor hardware, EFI enables your Mac to start up from macOS, Windows, or any other Intel-compatible operating system.

EFI is a flexible boot architecture and is now managed by the Unified EFI Forum. EFI will soon be known as Unified Extensible Firmware Interface (UEFI). You can find out more at www.uefi.org.

Power-On Self-Test

The first thing your Mac firmware does when it powers on is the power-on self-test (POST). The POST tests built-in hardware components such as processors, system memory, network interfaces, and peripheral interfaces. When your Mac passes the POST, the display should power on. If your Mac is from early 2016 or earlier, you may hear a startup tone. After a successful POST, the firmware locates the booter file.

Mac computers perform the POST only during a startup, not during a restart. So if you're troubleshooting hardware issues, restarting isn't enough; you should shut down and then start up.

If your Mac fails the POST, the display remains blank or off and you may get hardware error codes. Depending on the age and model of your Mac, the error codes may be audible tones, a series of flashes from the external power-on light, or internal diagnostic lights illuminating. You may even see a combination of these things. Regardless of which error code you experience, it indicates that a hardware problem exists that macOS can't control. Visit the Apple support website, at https://support.apple.com, to find your Mac error code, or take your Mac to an Apple Authorized Service Provider.

Booter Selection

By default, the firmware picks the system booter file that was last specified from Startup Disk preferences or the Boot Camp control panel in Windows. The booter file location is saved in your Mac nonvolatile RAM (NVRAM) so that it persists across Mac restarts. If the booter file is found, EFI starts the booter process and the Mac begins to start up; you see the Apple logo in the center of the main display.

If the firmware can't locate a booter file, you see a flashing folder icon with a question mark.

FileVault Unlock

If the system disk is protected with FileVault, the Mac can't access the macOS booter until you unlock the system disk. With FileVault, a special EFI booter presents you with an authentication screen much like the login window. The FileVault authentication unlock screen appears just a few seconds after POST and looks similar to the standard macOS login window.

After you authenticate and unlock the encrypted system disk, the EFI firmware is granted access to the system volume containing the macOS booter. Startup continues as usual, with one exception: because you authenticated to unlock the disk, macOS logs in without you authenticating again at the login window. This login happens only once per startup and only if you unlocked the encrypted system disk.

Startup Shortcuts

Your Mac firmware also supports keyboard shortcuts, which, when pressed and held during initial power-on, enable you to modify the startup process. Some of these shortcuts alter the booter selection, and others modify how macOS starts up.

Firmware Updates

Firmware consists of data or programs recorded onto computer chips. When your Mac is manufactured, its firmware is programmed to tell your Mac how to perform tasks. The type of firmware installed in your Mac can be updated if your Mac requires a change.

Firmware updates are usually included in macOS updates. They are also included when you use the Install macOS Mojave app, which uses your Mac model number to locate and download a firmware update specific to only that Mac. See Lesson 2, "Update, Upgrade, or Reinstall macOS," for more information.

System Initialization: Booter

The booter process is started by your Mac firmware and loads the macOS kernel and enough essential KEXTs that the kernel can take over the system and continue the startup process. Your Mac firmware also passes on special startup mode instructions for the booter to handle, such as entering startup shortcuts, as described in Reference 28.4, "Use Startup Shortcuts." The booter process is in /System/Library/CoreServices/boot.efi.

To expedite the startup process, the booter loads cached files when possible. These caches are located in /System/Library/Caches/com.apple.kext.caches. The files contain an optimized kernel and cached KEXTs that load more quickly than if the Mac had to load them from scratch. If macOS detects a problem or you start macOS in safe mode (detailed in Reference 28.4), these caches are discarded, and kernel-loading takes longer.

After the booter loads the kernel, it displays a small progress bar below the Apple icon. Some late-model Mac computers start up so fast you may not see the progress bar before the next stage is indicated.

If your Mac is set to start up from a network disk and the firmware locates the booter from a NetBoot service (deprecated for Mac computers with the T2 chip), you see the Apple icon. In this case the booter and the cached kernel information must be downloaded from the NetBoot service. This process is indicated by a small, spinning globe icon below the Apple icon. A spinning globe also appears when your Mac starts up from macOS Recovery over the Internet. The globe icon is replaced by the standard progress bar after the kernel is loaded.

If your selected startup disk isn't available or doesn't contain a Mac operating system, a flashing question mark replaces the Apple icon.

If the booter can't load the kernel, a prohibitory icon replaces the Apple icon.

System Initialization: Kernel

After the booter loads the kernel and essential KEXTs, the kernel takes over the startup process. The kernel loaded enough KEXTs to read the entire file system, allowing it then to load additional KEXTs and start the core operating system. A progress bar below the Apple icon indicates the kernel startup progress. If your Mac has FileVault enabled, the progress bar is displayed below the name of the user who unlocked the startup disk.

In most cases the kernel is loaded by the booter from cached files. The kernel is also on the system volume. This file is normally hidden from users in the graphical interface. As covered in Lesson 26, "Troubleshoot Peripherals," KEXTs reside in the /System/Library/Extensions and /Library/Extensions folders.

Finally, the kernel starts the launch daemon (launchd).

System Initialization: launchd

During system startup, the progress bar below the Apple logo is an indication that the kernel has fully loaded and the launchd process is starting other items.

launchd is located at /sbin/launchd and has the process identification number of 1. The launchd process is owned by the System Administrator (root) user, so it has read/write access to every file on the system (except those files protected by System Integrity Protection and privacy controls). launchd is the first parent process that spawns other child processes, and those processes go on to spawn other child processes.

The first task for the launchd process is to start all other system processes. Then launchd replaces the Apple logo with the login window or the user's desktop background.

If you have a Mac with multiple displays, you might notice a brief flash coming from the secondary displays as they power on. This is a result of launchd starting the WindowServer process, which is responsible for drawing the macOS user interface, but it's still a good indication that the system startup process is progressing.

The launchd process expedites system initialization by starting multiple system processes simultaneously, whenever possible, and starting only essential system processes at startup. After startup, the launchd process starts and stops additional system processes as needed. By dynamically managing system processes, launchd keeps your Mac responsive and running as efficiently as possible.

launchd Items

As covered in Lesson 15, "Manage System Resources," launchd preference files control how various processes are configured. The two locations for these launchd preference files are:

▶ /System/Library/LaunchDaemons folder for system processes

▶ /Library/LaunchDaemons folder for third-party processes

Viewing the launchd Hierarchy

Each process has a parent (except the kernel_task process). Some processes have a child process, or multiple children processes. To better understand these relationships, use Activity Monitor. Choose View > All Processes, Hierarchically. Then select any process to view its parent and any children. Detailed information about using Activity Monitor is covered in Lesson 20, "Manage and Troubleshoot Apps."

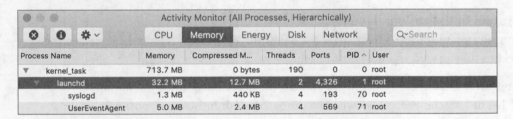

For more information about system initialization, read Apple Support article HT204156, "About the screens you see when your Mac starts up."

Reference 28.2
User Sessions

Eventually, after enough system processes start, macOS begins the processes that manage a user session.

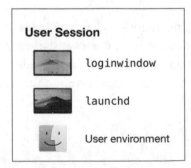

The three main user session stages are, in order:

▶ loginwindow—This is the process responsible for presenting the login screen and logging the user in. Successful completion of this stage results in initialization of the user environment, allowing user apps to run.

▶ launchd—The launchd process works in conjunction with the loginwindow process to initialize the user environment and start any user processes or apps.

▶ User environment—This is the "space" that users' processes and apps exist in when they are logged in. The user environment is maintained by the loginwindow and launchd processes.

User Session: Login Window

As soon as the system has started enough processes to present the login window, the launchd process starts the loginwindow process /System/Library/CoreServices/loginwindow.app. loginwindow runs as a background process and a graphical interface app. It coordinates the login screen and, along with the opendirectoryd process, authenticates the user. After authentication, the loginwindow process, in conjunction with the launchd process, initializes the graphical user interface (GUI) environment. The loginwindow process continues to run in the background to maintain the user session.

Some of the settings for the login window are stored in this preference file: /Library/Preferences/com.apple.loginwindow.plist. As covered in Lesson 7, "Manage User Accounts," you can configure login window settings from Users & Groups preferences.

When no user is logged in, the loginwindow process is owned by the root user. After a user authenticates to log in, the loginwindow process switches ownership from the root user to the user who successfully authenticated. Then the loginwindow process sets up the graphical user interface environment with help from the launchd process.

User Session: launchd

The moment a user is authenticated, the loginwindow and launchd processes work together to initialize the user's environment. If fast user switching is enabled, the launchd process starts additional processes to initialize and maintain each user's environment.

The loginwindow and launchd processes set up the graphical interface environment by:

▶ Retrieving the user account information from opendirectoryd and applying any account settings

▶ Configuring the mouse, keyboard, and system sound using the user's preferences

▶ Loading the user's computing environment: preferences, environment variables, devices and file permissions, and keychain access

▶ Opening the Finder, SystemUIServer (responsible for user interface elements like menu bar status icons on the right side of the menu bar), and Dock (also responsible for Launchpad and Mission Control, which gives you an overview of your open windows, thumbnails of your full-screen apps, and Dashboard, all arranged in a unified view)

▶ Automatically opening the user's login items

▶ Automatically resuming any app that was open before the last logout, by default, in macOS

Launch agents can be started at any time, as long as a user is logged in to macOS. Most launch agents are started during the initialization of the user environment, but they could also be started afterward or on a regular repeating basis. Launch agents provided by macOS are in /System/Library/LaunchAgents, whereas third-party launch agents should be located in either /Library/LaunchAgents or ~/Library/LaunchAgents.

Login items are started at the end of the initialization of the user environment. The login-window process, with help from the launchd process, starts user login items. As covered in Lesson 7, you configure a user login item list from Users & Groups preferences.

The User Environment

The loginwindow processes continue to run as long as a user is logged in to a session. The launchd process starts user processes and apps, and the user loginwindow process monitors and maintains a user session.

The user loginwindow process monitors the user session by:

▶ Managing logout, restart, and shutdown procedures

▶ Managing the Force Quit Applications window, which includes monitoring the currently active apps and responding to user requests to forcibly quit apps

While a user is logged in to the session, the launchd process restarts user apps that should remain open, such as the Finder or the Dock. If the user's loginwindow process is ended, whether intentionally or unexpectedly, the user's apps and processes immediately quit without saving changes. If this happens, the launchd process restarts the loginwindow process as if the Mac just started up.

Reference 28.3
Sleep Modes, Logout, and Shutdown

Processes are also required to pause or end a user session. Your Mac computer's sleep function doesn't quit open processes. If you log out or shut down the Mac, macOS quits open processes. You can manually issue a sleep, shutdown, or logout command from the Apple menu.

You can also quickly press and hold the power button on your Mac to put your Mac to sleep. If you press and hold the power button for more than a few seconds, you force the Mac to shut down. Shutting down your Mac might be useful if it's unresponsive. But don't shut your Mac down like this regularly because doing so might cause data loss.

Other processes and apps can also initiate sleep, logout, or shutdown commands. For instance, the Installer and App Store apps and Software Update can request a restart when installation of new or updated software requires it.

You can configure your Mac to automatically perform certain commands related to startup, sleep, wake, and shutdown:

▶ In Energy Saver preferences, use the "Computer sleep" slider to put the Mac to sleep after a period of inactivity.

▶ In Energy Saver preferences, click the Schedule button to set a schedule to start up or wake.

▶ In Energy Saver preferences, click the Schedule button to set a schedule to sleep.

▶ In Security & Privacy preferences, in the General pane, select "Require password after sleep or screen saver begins," and choose an amount of time from the menu.

▶ In Security & Privacy preferences, click Advanced, select "Log out after _ minutes of inactivity," and enter the number of minutes.

▶ In Parental Controls preferences, automatically log out managed users after a fixed amount of time per day or outside of an allowed schedule.

You can manage many of these settings remotely from Apple Remote Desktop or from an MDM solution.

The Mac sleep function doesn't quit active processes or apps. Instead, the macOS kernel pauses processes and shuts down the hardware. This reduces the power used. When you wake your Mac from sleep mode, the kernel resumes processes and apps from the point at which you left them.

Other Sleep Modes

Mac computers that are compatible with macOS Mojave support modes that use very little or no power:

▶ All Mac models that are compatible with macOS Mojave support a deep sleep mode called Safe Sleep.

▶ Newer Mac models with flash storage support Safe Sleep and also support a deep sleep mode called Standby Mode.

When Mac computers go to sleep, they copy the entire contents of system memory to an image file on the system volume. This way, if your Mac stays in sleep mode long enough to completely drain the battery, no data is lost when your Mac has to turn off.

Safe Sleep

A Mac that supports Safe Sleep enters Safe Sleep if the battery becomes completely drained, or if you leave your Mac idle for a long time. In order to restart a Mac in Safe Sleep mode you must press its power button. If you use a Mac notebook and its battery is low, connect the AC adapter first. When you restart a Mac from Safe Sleep mode, the booter process reloads the saved memory image from the system volume instead of proceeding with the normal startup process.

The booter process might indicate that the Mac is restarting from Safe Sleep mode by displaying the following:

▶ A light gray version of your Mac screen as it appeared when sleep was initiated

▶ A segmented progress indicator at the bottom of the main display

macOS displays a Safe Sleep progress bar when waking these models:

▶ MacBook (Retina, 12-inch, Early 2015) and later

▶ MacBook Pro (Mid 2012) and later

▶ MacBook Pro (Retina, Mid 2012) and later

▶ MacBook Air (Mid 2012) and later

▶ iMac (Late 2012) and later

▶ Mac mini (Late 2012) and later

It should take a few moments to reload system memory. Then the kernel resumes processes and apps. If FileVault is enabled, you see the FileVault authentication unlock screen first; then the Safe Sleep wake process starts.

Standby Mode

Newer Mac computers with flash storage enter a power-saving Standby Mode when they are asleep and completely idle for more than one hour (if manufactured before 2013) or after three hours (if manufactured in 2103 or later). Completely idle means that macOS detects zero network or peripheral activity. In order to enter Standby Mode, Mac notebook computers must be running on battery power and disconnected from Ethernet, USB, Thunderbolt, SD cards, displays, Bluetooth, or any other external connections. To enter Standby Mode, Mac desktop computers must have no external media mounted (such as SD cards, USB, or Thunderbolt storage devices). Unlike Mac computers in Safe Sleep, you don't need to restart a Mac computer in Standby Mode—you can wake it when you interact with the keyboard, trackpad, or mouse. During wake you may see a small, white, segmented progress bar at the bottom of the screen, similar to that of Safe Sleep mode, although in most cases, when a newer Mac wakes from standby it's so fast you may not notice.

You can find out more about Safe Sleep and Standby Mode, including which Mac models support these modes, from Apple Support article HT202824, "Use the Energy Saver settings on your Mac," and article HT201635, "If you see a progress bar when your Mac wakes from sleep."

Power Nap

Power Nap, available on Mac computers with flash memory, lets some Mac computers stay up to date even while they're sleeping. When the Mac goes to sleep, Power Nap activates periodically to update information. The information that's updated depends on whether your Mac is running on battery power or plugged into a power adapter. The Power Nap setting is in the Energy Saver preferences. Select Enable Power Nap to turn Power Nap on or off. The default setting varies:

▶ Desktop Mac computers that use flash storage (not including Fusion Drive)—Power Nap is enabled by default.

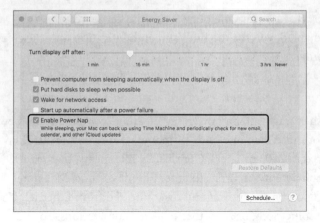

▶ Notebook Mac computers not connected to a power adapter—Power Nap is disabled by default.

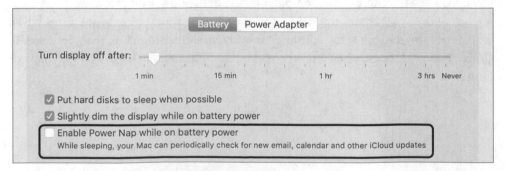

▶ Notebook Mac computers connected to a power adapter—Power Nap is enabled by default.

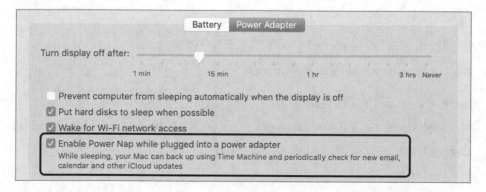

If your Mac supports Power Nap, these activities can occur while your Mac is asleep:

▶ Mail receives new messages.

▶ Contacts keep up to date with changes made on other devices.

▶ Calendar receives new invitations and calendar updates.

▶ Reminders keep up to date with changes made on other devices.

▶ Notes keep up to date with changes made on other devices.

▶ Documents stored in iCloud keep up to date with changes made on other devices.

▶ Photo Stream keeps up to date with changes made on other devices.

▶ Find My Mac updates the location of the Mac so that you can find it while it's asleep.

▶ VPN on demand continues working so that your corporate email updates securely. (Power Nap supports VPN connections that use a certificate to authenticate, not VPN connections that require entering a password.)

▶ Mobile Device Management can remotely lock and wipe your Mac.

These activities can occur while your Mac is asleep and plugged into an AC power outlet:

▶ Software updates download.

▶ Mac App Store items (including software updates) download in the background.

▶ Time Machine performs backups.

▶ Spotlight performs indexing.

▶ Help content (that appears in Help Viewer) updates.

▶ Wireless base stations can wake your Mac using Wake on Wireless.

Some Mac computers require firmware updates to support Power Nap. You can find out more about Power Nap and any required updates from Apple Support article HT204032, "How Power Nap works on your Mac."

During Power Nap, your Mac plays no system sounds.

You can use Power Nap on these Mac models:

▶ MacBook (Early 2015 and later)

▶ MacBook Air (Late 2010 and later) (Requires OS X Mountain Lion v10.8.2 and later)

▶ MacBook Pro (all models with Retina display)

▶ Mac mini (Late 2012 and later)

▶ iMac (Late 2012 and later)

▶ Mac Pro (Late 2013)

The year your Mac notebook computer was released determines how Power Nap responds to your battery power state.

Computers with 2013 or a later year in the model name use Power Nap until the battery is drained. Computers with 2012 or an earlier year in the model name suspend Power Nap if the battery has a charge of 30% or less. Power Nap resumes when you connect to AC power.

To increase battery life while using Power Nap, disconnect any USB, Thunderbolt, or FireWire devices that may draw power from the Mac.

When your Mac isn't connected to AC power, Power Nap communicates and transfers data for only a few minutes per Power Nap cycle. When your Mac is connected to AC power, communications and data transfers are continuous.

▶ Mail, Notes, Contacts, Calendar, Reminders, Photo Stream, Find My Mac, and iCloud documents are checked every hour. To receive updates during Power Nap, Mail and Notes must be open before your Mac sleeps.

▶ Time Machine backups are attempted hourly until a successful backup is completed.

▶ Software Updates are checked daily.

▶ Mac App Store downloads are checked once a week.

Logout

Users can log out whenever they want to end their user session, but they also have to log out to shut down or restart the Mac. When the currently logged-in user chooses to log out, the user's loginwindow process manages all logout functions with help from the launchd process.

After a user authorizes the logout, the loginwindow process issues a Quit Application Apple event to all apps. Apps that support Auto Save and Resume features can immediately save changes to any open documents and quit. Apps that don't support these features still respond to the Quit event, but they ask the user whether changes should be saved or processes should be terminated.

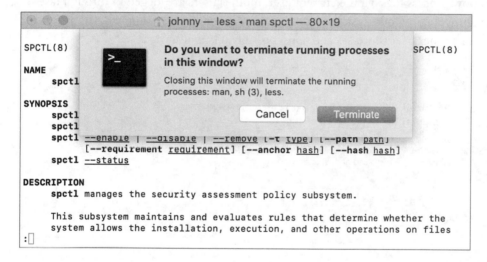

If the app fails to reply or quit, the logout process stops and loginwindow displays an error message.

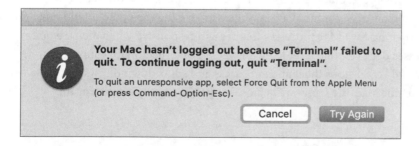

If the user's apps quit, the user's loginwindow process then forcibly quits background user processes. Finally, the user's loginwindow process closes the user's graphical interface session, runs any logout scripts, and records the logout to the main system.log file. If the user chooses only to log out, as opposed to shutting down or restarting, the user's loginwindow quits, the launchd process restarts a new loginwindow process owned by the root user, and the login screen appears.

Shutdown and Restart

When a logged-in user chooses to shut down or restart the Mac, the user's loginwindow process manages logout functions with help from the launchd process. First, the user's loginwindow process logs out the current user. If other users are logged in through fast user switching, loginwindow asks for administrator user authentication and, if it's granted, forcibly quits other user processes and apps, possibly losing user data.

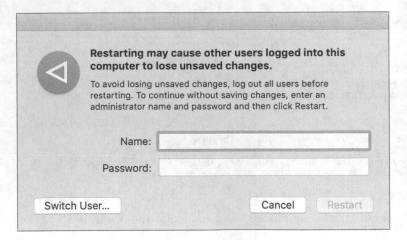

After all user sessions are logged out, the user's loginwindow process tells the kernel to issue the quit command to remaining system processes. Processes like loginwindow should quit promptly, but the kernel must wait for processes that remain responsive while they are quitting. If system processes don't respond after a few seconds, the kernel forcibly quits them. After processes quit, the kernel stops the launchd process and shuts down the system. If a user chooses to restart the Mac, the firmware begins the macOS startup process again.

Reference 28.4
Use Startup Shortcuts

Your Mac firmware supports many keyboard shortcuts, and when you use them during initial power-on, you can modify the startup process. Some of these shortcuts modify the booter selection; others modify how macOS starts up. You can use these alternative startup and diagnostic modes to troubleshoot system issues.

There are several caveats to using startup shortcuts:

▶ If the Mac has firmware password protection enabled, startup shortcuts are disabled until the user enters the Mac computer firmware password. Even after the user authenticates, the only startup shortcuts that work are shortcuts that access the Startup Manager or macOS Recovery. Using a firmware password is covered in Lesson 9, "Manage Security and Privacy."

▶ When using startup shortcuts, Mac computers with FileVault enabled must still be authenticated and unlocked to proceed with system startup.

▶ Some hardware doesn't support startup shortcuts, including some third-party keyboards and keyboards connected via certain USB hubs or a keyboard-video-mouse (KVM) switch. Also, although Bluetooth wireless keyboards should allow for startup shortcuts, they can be problematic. You should have a wired USB keyboard and mouse for troubleshooting Mac desktop computers.

▶ Startup volumes selected with a shortcut are not saved in NVRAM, so this setting doesn't persist between system restarts.

Select an Alternate System

Mac startup shortcuts that enable you to select another system include:

▶ Option—Starts up into the Startup Manager, which enables you to select volumes containing a valid system to start up from. This includes internal volumes, optical disc volumes, some external volumes, and, for Mac models that do not have the T2 chip, Wi-Fi networks and NetBoot images.

▶ Option-Shift-Command-R—This shortcut forces startup to macOS Recovery from the Internet so that you can install the version of macOS that came with your Mac, or the version closest to it that is available. Lesson 5, "Use macOS Recovery," explores this topic in more detail.

▶ Option-Command-R—This shortcut forces startup to macOS Recovery from the Internet. This option is available on Mac computers released after July 2011.

▶ Command-R—Starts up to the local macOS Recovery, if available. If no local macOS Recovery is found, Mac computers released after July 2011 start up to macOS Recovery from the Internet.

▶ D—Starts up to the local Apple Hardware Test or Apple Diagnostics (for Mac computers released after June 2013), if available. If no local resources are available, Mac computers released after July 2011 will start up to Apple Hardware Test or Apple Diagnostics via an Internet connection to Apple servers. Use of these tools is beyond the scope of this guide, but you can find out more from Apple Support article HT201257, "How to use Apple Hardware Test on your Mac," and article HT202731, "How to use Apple Diagnostics on your Mac."

▶ Option-D—This shortcut forces startup to Apple Hardware Test or Apple Diagnostics through an Internet connection to Apple servers. This option is available to Mac computers released after July 2011.

▶ Option-N—This shortcut starts up from the current default NetBoot server instead of the last-used NetBoot server. The Mac shows a flashing or spinning globe icon in the center of the main display until it locates the NetBoot server, at which point it shows the Apple logo. NetBoot isn't available for Mac computers with the T2 Chip.

▶ N—Starts up from the last-used NetBoot server, or the default NetBoot server if none was previously used. NetBoot isn't available for Mac computers with the T2 Chip.

Use Safe Mode

Safe mode (sometimes called safe boot) is a way to start up your Mac so that it performs certain checks and prevents some software from automatically loading or opening. Starting your Mac in safe mode does the following:

▶ Verifies your startup disk and attempts to repair directory issues, if needed

▶ Loads only required kernel extensions

▶ Prevents login items from opening automatically

▶ Disables user-installed fonts

▶ Deletes font caches, kernel cache, and other system cache files

A Mac in safe mode shows the words "Safe Boot" in bright red text in the upper-right corner of the login screen.

If FileVault is enabled on your Mac, the first login window is displayed without the words "Safe Boot" in the upper-right corner. After you successfully authenticate at the first login window, the startup disk is unlocked, and macOS starts in safe mode. Then you'll see a login window with the words "Safe Boot" in the upper-right corner.

You can also verify safe mode after login by opening System Information. The Software section of System Information lists Boot Mode as "Safe" instead of "Normal" when you're started in safe mode.

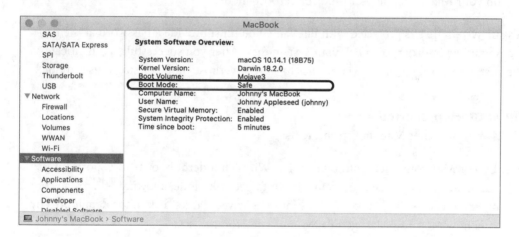

When your Mac is started in safe mode, it might take some time for your Mac to start up and for your graphics to load.

For more information about safe boot, read Apple Support article HT201262, "Use safe mode to isolate issues with your Mac."

Verbose Mode and Single-User Mode

Two other Mac startup shortcuts that modify the macOS default startup are:

▶ Command-V—Starts up macOS in verbose mode. In verbose mode, the system does not hide the startup progress from you. Instead, you see a black background with white text showing details of the startup process.

▶ Command-S—Starts up macOS in single-user mode. When starting up in single-user mode, the system starts only core kernel and BSD UNIX operating system functionality. You must be familiar with the command-line interface to use single-user mode. If your Mac has the T2 chip, pressing and holding the Command-S keys during startup results in verbose mode instead of single-user mode. If your Mac has the T2 chip, you can start from macOS Recovery then choose Utilities > Terminal instead of using single-user mode. For more information read Apple Support article HT201573, "Start up your Mac in single-user mode or verbose mode."

If your system disk is protected with FileVault, you must provide a password at the first login window in order to unlock your system disk. After you successfully authenticate at the first login window, macOS continues to start in verbose mode or single-user mode.

Other Startup Shortcuts

Here are some other Mac startup shortcuts:

▶ T—For Mac computers with built-in FireWire, Thunderbolt, or USB-C ports, press and hold this key to start up your Mac in target disk mode, allowing other Mac computers to access the Mac computer's internal drives. Target disk mode details are covered in Lesson 11, "Manage File Systems and Storage."

▶ Option-Command-P-R—This shortcut resets NVRAM settings and restarts your Mac.

▶ Eject key, F12 key, mouse, or trackpad button—These shortcuts eject any removable media.

Reference 28.5
Troubleshoot System Initialization

After you identify system initialization stages—and know which processes and files are responsible for each—you are on your way to diagnosing startup issues. The troubleshooting sections that follow are organized by each system initialization stage.

macOS diagnostic startup modes—verbose mode, safe mode, and single-user mode—help you find and resolve issues. These three modes are initiated at the firmware stage but affect the remaining system initialization process.

Troubleshoot Firmware Issues

If your Mac can't reach the point where the Apple logo appears, you probably have a firmware issue. Determine whether this issue is related to the Mac hardware or system volume.

Mac computers with hardware issues might benefit from a resetting the Mac computer's NVRAM or SMC. You can find out more about resetting these items from Apple Support article HT204063, "Reset NVRAM or PRAM on your Mac," and article HT201295, "How to reset the System Management Controller (SMC) on your Mac."

In very rare circumstances, if your Mac with the Apple T2 Security Chip becomes unresponsive, you might need to restore the firmware on the T2 chip. For more information, read "Restore Apple desktop computers that have the Apple T2 Security Chip" at help.apple.com/configurator/mac/2.8.2/index.html?#/apdebea5be51 and "Restore Apple portable computers that have the Apple T2 Security Chip" at help.apple.com/configurator/mac/2.8.2/index.html?#/apd0020c3dc2.

Hardware Issues

If you don't hear the startup sound, see a power-on light flash, or see the display powering on, the Mac hardware may not have passed the POST.

You should hear a startup tone if your Mac is from early 2016 or earlier.

You may hear audible diagnostic tones or see a series of power-on flashes. If so, your Mac has a hardware issue. For more information about the startup sounds, see Apple Support article HT202768, "About Mac startup tones."

Always check for simple things first. Is the Mac plugged into an electrical outlet? Are the keyboard and mouse working properly? A failure to pass the POST is usually indicative of a serious hardware issue. If this is the case, take your Mac to an Apple Store or Apple Authorized Service Provider.

System Volume Issues

If your Mac passes POST but you see a flashing question mark folder icon, the firmware can't locate a valid system volume or booter file. The Mac main processor and components probably work correctly, and you might have a software issue. Press and hold the Option key during startup and use Startup Manager to locate system volumes. To troubleshoot system volume issues:

▶ If the original system volume appears, select it to start up. If your Mac starts up from the system on the volume, open Startup Disk preferences to reset the volume as the startup disk. You can also try to define the startup disk when it's booted from another system volume, like macOS Recovery. Read more about system volumes in Lesson 5.

▶ If the original system volume appears but your Mac still can't find a valid system or booter, you might need to reinstall macOS on that volume. Back up important data from that volume before you make significant changes.

▶ If your original system volume doesn't appear, the issue is with that storage device. Start up from another system, like macOS Recovery, and use the storage troubleshooting techniques outlined in Lesson 11.

Troubleshoot Booter Issues

If you see a prohibitory icon, the kernel probably failed to load. To troubleshoot the booter:

▶ If you start up your Mac from a volume that contains an operating system the Mac never booted from, the prohibitory icon usually indicates that the version of macOS on the volume isn't compatible with your Mac hardware. This rare case occurs mainly when a new Mac is restored using an older system image. Reinstall macOS using macOS Recovery, which should install a version that works with your hardware.

▶ Start up the Mac, and then press and hold the Shift key to initiate safe mode. The booter tries to verify and repair the startup volume. If repairs are needed, the Mac restarts before continuing. If this happens, continue to press and hold the Shift key. The booter verifies the startup volume again, and if the volume appears to be working properly, the booter tries to load the kernel and essential KEXTs again. The booter judiciously and slowly loads the items and clears the KEXT and font caches. If successful, the booter passes the system to the kernel, which continues to safe-boot.

▶ If the booter can't find or load a valid kernel, reinstall macOS on that volume.

Troubleshoot Kernel Issues

If you see the Apple logo startup screen and the Apple icon or progress bar but can't reach the login window or log in, KEXTS, UNIX, and launchd probably failed to load. To troubleshoot the kernel:

▶ Start up the Mac, and then press and hold the Shift key to initiate safe mode. This forces the kernel to ignore third-party KEXTs. If this is successful, the kernel starts launchd, which continues to start up in safe mode. If the kernel startup stage completes through safe mode, the issue might be a third-party KEXT. Start up in verbose mode to try to find the problem.

▶ Start up the Mac, and then press and hold Command-V to initiate verbose mode. The Mac shows you startup process details as a continuous string of text. If the text stops, the startup process has probably also stopped, and you should examine the end of the text for troubleshooting clues. When you find a suspicious item, move it to a quarantine folder and restart the Mac without safe mode to see if the problem was resolved. Accessing the Mac computer disk to locate and remove the item might not be possible if the Mac is crashing during startup. This is an example in which target disk mode shines. As covered in Lesson 9, "Manage Security and Privacy," you can modify the contents of a problem Mac system volume using target disk mode and a second Mac.

▶ If your problem Mac successfully starts up in safe mode and you're still trying to find the issue, don't use safe mode and verbose mode at the same time. If startup succeeds, verbose mode is replaced by the standard startup interface, and you won't have time to find problems.

▶ If the kernel can't load during safe mode, or you are unable to locate and repair the problem, you might need to reinstall macOS on that volume.

Troubleshoot launchd Issues

If you can't get to the login screen or log in when you see the login screen, it's probably a launchd issue. If launchd isn't able to complete system initialization, the loginwindow process doesn't start. To troubleshoot launchd issues:

▶ Start up the Mac, and then press and hold the Shift key to initiate safe mode. Safe mode forces launchd to ignore third-party fonts and launch daemons. If your startup in safe mode is successful, the launchd process starts the loginwindow process. At this point the Mac fully starts up and runs in safe mode. If you can complete system initialization with safe mode, the issue might be a third-party system initialization item. Start up in verbose mode to find it.

▶ Start up the Mac, and then press and hold Command-V to initiate verbose mode. If the text stops scrolling down the screen, examine the end of the text; if you find a suspicious item, move it to another folder and then restart the Mac.

▶ You might be able to start up in safe mode into the Finder. If so, use the Finder to quarantine suspicious items.

▶ In safe mode, consider removing or renaming system cache and preference files, since they can be corrupted and cause startup issues. Remove /Library/Caches first. These files contain easily replaced information. Remove settings stored in the /Library/Preferences or /Library/Preferences/SystemConfiguration folders, but only if you can reconfigure them later. Or, rename system preference files in these folders. After you move or rename these items, restart the Mac, and macOS replaces them with new versions.

▶ If starting up in safe mode continues to fail or you locate a suspicious system item you need to remove, start up the Mac, and then press and hold Command-S to initiate single-user mode, or if your Mac has the T2 chip, start up from macOS Recovery then open Terminal. You see a minimal command-line interface that enables you to move suspicious files to a quarantine folder. If you want to modify files and folders in single-user mode, prepare the system volume. Enter **/sbin/fsck -fy** to verify and repair the startup volume. Repeat this command until you see a message stating that the disk appears to be OK. Then, enter **/sbin/mount -uw /** to mount the startup volume as a read-and-write file system. After you make your changes, exit single-user mode and enter the **exit** command to continue to start up the Mac. Shut down the Mac with the **shutdown -h now** command.

▶ If system initialization can't complete during startup in safe mode or you are unable to locate and repair the problem, reinstall macOS.

Reference 28.6
Troubleshoot User Sessions

If the loginwindow process can't initialize the user environment, the user can't control the interface. You might see the user's desktop background picture, but no apps load, including the Dock and the Finder. Or the user session starts, but the login screen reappears.

Safe Mode Login

Try safe mode login. At the login screen, press and hold the Shift key while you click the Log In button. Perform a safe mode login when you need to troubleshoot user issues, even if you didn't start up in safe mode. With safe mode enabled, the loginwindow process doesn't automatically open user-defined login items or apps that are set to resume. The launchd process doesn't start user-specific LaunchAgents. If safe mode login resolves your user session issue, adjust the user's Login Items list from Users & Groups preferences or adjust items in /Library/LaunchAgents or ~/Library/LaunchAgents.

If safe mode login doesn't resolve your issue, follow the troubleshooting steps outlined in Lesson 7, "Manage User Accounts," or refer to other troubleshooting sections in this book.

Troubleshoot Logout and Shutdown

If you can't log out or shut down, it's probably because an app or process won't quit. If you can't log out, use Force Quit from the Apple menu. See Lesson 20, "Manage and Troubleshoot Apps," for more information.

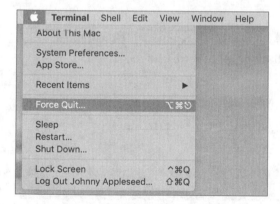

If you see a blank screen after all your apps quit, the loginwindow process closed your user session and your Mac won't shut down. Give macOS a few moments to shut down. If a few moments pass and nothing happens, a system process isn't quitting. To force your Mac to shut down, press and hold the power button until the Mac powers off.

Exercise 28.1
Examine System Startup

> **Prerequisites**
>
> ▶ You must have created the Johnny Appleseed account (Exercise 7.1, "Create a Standard User Account").
>
> ▶ You must have enabled FileVault on your Mac (Exercise 3.2, "Configure System Preferences").

In this exercise, you observe the macOS startup process—which gives audible and visible cues as it progresses. You then use the audible and visible cues to identify the steps in the startup process.

Identify Startup Steps

1 If your Mac is powered on, click the Apple menu and choose Shut Down. If you are at the login screen, use the Shut Down button near the bottom of the screen.

2 Start up your Mac.

3 As your Mac starts up, use the following table to record the startup steps where you notice an audible or visual cue.

Audible or visual cue	Startup step or process
Startup chime (Mac models from early 2016 and earlier)	
Apple logo	
FileVault authentication (if enabled)	
Progress indicator below Apple logo or FileVault user icon	
Arrow pointer appears	
Login screen (if FileVault isn't enabled)	
Desktop and Dock appear	

Certain steps might not apply because you are testing hardware issues or situations where a startup device can't be found. Refer to Reference 28.1, "System Initialization," for more information about potential issues or situations that would prevent a computer from starting up.

4 When you see the FileVault authentication screen, log in as Johnny Appleseed.

Exercise 28.2
Use Verbose Mode

▶ **Prerequisite**

▶ If your Mac has a Retina display, you might need a magnifying glass, or an iPhone with the Magnifier feature enabled, to read the text in verbose mode.

In this exercise, you start up your Mac in verbose mode. You proceed to the user interface and identify files used during startup.

Use Verbose Mode and Identify Startup Steps

1 Before restarting in verbose mode, review the sequence you observed in Exercise 28.1, "Examine System Startup."

    In verbose mode, the basic startup sequence is the same, but what you see on the screen is different.

2 Restart your Mac, and immediately press and hold Command-V. Continue pressing Command-V until the Mac restarts.

3 At the FileVault authentication screen, log in as Johnny Appleseed.

4   Fill in the following table with the cues you observe during the verbose mode startup, and compare it with what you saw during a normal startup.

Normal startup	Verbose startup
Startup chime (Mac models from early 2016 and earlier)	
Apple logo	
FileVault authentication (if enabled)	
Progress indicator below Apple logo or FileVault user icon	
Arrow pointer appears	
Login screen (if FileVault is not enabled)	
Desktop and Dock appear	

During the verbose segment of the verbose mode startup process, you see messages from the kernel and launch daemons that describe what they are doing and problems they encounter. Try to detect what is happening behind the scenes as your Mac starts up.

Because you're using FileVault, you see verbose mode showing output from the firmware phase of startup, then switching to the normal FileVault authentication screen, then switching back to verbose display of output from the kernel, launchd, and launch daemons. This is because the kernel, launchd, and the launch daemons that verbose mode displays are on the encrypted system volume and can't start until after that volume is unlocked.

5   Shut down your Mac.

As your Mac shuts down, you might see it reenter verbose mode for a few moments. This occurs after WindowServer shuts down but before the kernel shuts down.

Exercise 28.3
Use Safe Mode

▶ Prerequisite

▶   You must have created the Local Administrator (Exercise 3.1, "Configure a Mac for Exercises") account.

In this exercise, you start up your Mac in safe mode and identify visual startup cues.

Start Up in Safe Mode

When you use safe mode, macOS clears specific caches, carefully tests startup procedures, and limits automatically launched processes during each startup stage. Many nonessential system and third-party items are ignored. If your Mac fails to start up normally, safe mode is a noninvasive and effective choice to troubleshoot the startup.

1   Turn on your Mac, and then log in to your Mac as **Local Administrator**.

2   Open Activity Monitor.

3   Choose View > All Processes.

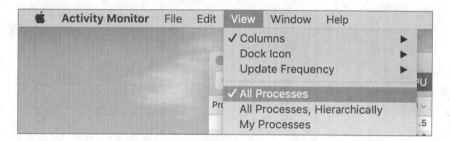

4   Sort by PID, and scroll to the bottom of the window. Record the number of processes running.

5   From the Apple menu, choose Restart. Press and hold the Shift key until you see the Apple logo on the screen. At the FileVault authentication screen, log in as **Local Administrator** to allow the Mac to start up.

After you see the FileVault authentication screen, you are past the boot process. Modifier keys you hold down are recognized, and you don't have to press and hold them.

Safe Boot appears in the menu bar.

6 Log in as **Local Administrator**.

Safe Mode disables automatic login, which is the default behavior when your Mac is protected with FileVault.

7 Open Activity Monitor and record the number of processes running.

Because safe mode starts only essential processes for system operation, fewer processes run. For example, if you try to find Activity Monitor with Spotlight, you can't. Also, your screen sometimes updates slowly.

8 Close Activity Monitor, and restart your Mac.

Index

Get Apple certified.
Stand out from the crowd.

Get recognized for your expertise by earning Apple Certified Pro status.

Why become an Apple Certified Pro?

Earn more. Studies show that certified professionals can earn more than their noncertified peers.

Demonstrate accomplishment. With each certification, you get an Apple Certification logo to display on your business cards, resume, and website. You'll distinguish yourself from others.

Reach a wider audience. When you publish your certifications on the Apple Certified Professionals Registry, you can connect with even more clients, schools, and employers.

Learn the way you like.

Learn independently with Apple Pro Training Series books from Peachpit Press.

Learn in a classroom at an Apple-authorized training location with Apple Certified Trainers.

Visit training.apple.com to learn how to get certified on these Apple products:

macOS

Final Cut Pro X

Logic Pro X

"The Apple Certification is a cornerstone of my consulting business. It guarantees to our clients the highest level of dedication and professionalism. And above all, the trusting smile of a client when you mention the Apple Certification can't be replaced."

— Andres Le Roux, Technology Consulting, alrx.net, inc.

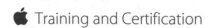 Training and Certification